Integral Impact Investments (I³)

Building and navigating a full-spectrum
systems approach to investing

by

ROBERT DELLNER

To be published in 2020 by Evolutesix Books, London, UK.
ISBN: 978-1-913629-11-3

A CIP catalogue record will be available from the British Library.

This book is published in electronic form under the standard Evolutesix Books pricing model of "Pay what it is worth to you".

Edited By Jack Reardon & Karen Holmes Cover design by Nikyta Guleria

Typeset using TEX and the LATEX 2_ε format in 6″ × 9″ paper with the Libertinus typeface at 11pt and Helvetica for headings.

This book is dedicated to my family.

Who have always been an inspiration, model and have showed me a loving way to become more fully the person I wish to be. Also, a special mention to my many significant journeymen and women, especially to Dr Ronnie Lessem and Shihan Colin Reeve who unselfishly have shown me the way.

It is my impression after seventy years on the planet that change always begins with new insights, inspirations or imaginative visions. These are rare amongst financial professionals. Robert Dellner has the capacity to develop such world-changing concepts and the experience to back up what he knows is now possible for impact investors. This book will inspire others to integrate their visions for change in ways that work for everyone. As I complete my own next book [1], I will leapfrog on this substantial piece of work with deep gratitude for a fellow traveller!

Benjamin Bingham, Founder and CEO, 3Sisters Sustainable Management, LLC, Scarab Funds, LLC and author of *Making Money Matter*

Robert Dellner adds an important advance to the necessary body of writing that will assist us towards a fair, clean, safe future civilisation.

Joel Solomon, Renewal Funds, author of *The Clean Money Revolution*

Robert Dellner's An Introduction to Integral Impact Investments offers the reader a solid onramp to considerations in both thought and practise for those exploring how best to promote investing that advancing blended value through the deployment of impact capital. By linking our understanding of self with how we then come to think about organisations and companies, Dellner provides a view into not only the future of finance, but of companies and communities as well. His weaving together of considerations regarding who we are, who we hope to be and how we might structure our capital advance are important reflections for all asset owners and impact investors.

Jed Emerson, author of *The Purpose of Capital: Elements of Impact, Financial Flows and Natural Being*

Contents

II   Changing the investment organisation

III Changing the firms in which we invest

List of Figures

About the Author

Robert comes from a multi-cultural background, blending German and Swedish descent, with a French influence in his upbringing. From an industrial and entrepreneurial family, his grandfather was the founder of Nohab Flygmotor, and later the first President of Saab after Nohab Flygmotor became part of Saab. His father founded and built several businesses, including Dellner Couplers and Bygging-Uddemann which continue to operate today. Growing up in Sweden during the 1970s and 1980s, he was deeply influenced by the "Scandinavian model" of government, culture, ethics, and society, which continues to drive much of his thinking today. He went on to study Economics in Stockholm, along with Finance and Business Administration, followed more recently by Psychology in London.

He has dedicated much of his life to fusing such disciplines to find new and more integral solutions to both organisational and human problems. He has worked within large firms such as Citigroup, as their European Head of Fixed Income Sales and Credit Officer, and with BNP Paribas Fortis as European Sales and Research Head of their High Yield Credit business. At Fortis, he became Global Head of the Client Solutions Group and a member of the corporate and public banks executive committee working on both the bank's technical structured products, and on deepening and developing its client culture. He has also worked as a psychotherapist within the NHS, specialising in addictions and relationships. Always looking to further integrate knowledge, over the past years Robert has been working on his PhD (Doctor of Philosophy) and PHD (Process of Holistic Development) which transcends and includes the PhD in Integral Development with Trans4M.

This is where I^3 took root and was developed as an extension of his doctoral thesis. Over the past few years he has been the Chief Credit Officer of Investments and involved in setting up a family office where I^3 was instigated and implemented. Fusing many realms of knowledge and disciplines, I^3 is a journey of discovery, self-reflection and an examination of values (conscience), resulting ultimately in greater consciousness (or awareness) of the multi-dimensions of impact for investments. To embody what he teaches, Robert practises martial arts at a master level; and, among his many other interests, is an avid beekeeper and gardener.

He is a member of the Worshipful Company of International Bankers, The British Association of Counsellors and Psychotherapists, The UK Council for Psychotherapy, The Chartered Institute of Credit Management, The Society for Organisational Learning and MENSA, amongst others. He is an Ambassador for the Transparency Task Force and an Advocation Partner for Reporting 3.0 (R3). He is the Managing Partner for I³ Partners Ltd, a firm charged with helping to implement I³ within organisations.

Figure 1: Ontology[a]

---

[a]Image courtesy of Kay Jackson [2]

Forewords

Mark Anielski

Dellner provides value for a new generation of impact investment practitioners, including institutional investors and investment organisations, as well as the average investor interested in how their investment may have well-being impacts on the world.

Like the sextant that constituted a new instrument for the navigation of oceans, Dellner's work provides an important new tool for investors to navigate the complex and often tricky waters that constitute investment. Like using an effective map, Dellner's I³ model helps decision makers understand and navigate their investment decisions by considering the broadest suite of possible impacts to the wellbeing of a wide variety of stakeholders affected by an investment or by an enterprise.

Most importantly, Dellner's proposed model for integral accounting, reporting and management for the investment world is a refreshing new challenge that builds on at least two decades of advances in sustainability measurement and reporting. In my mind, what has always been imperative, from the perspective of both conventional accounting and economic measurement systems, is the need for an integral form of asset accounting that goes beyond simply financial capital asset accounting. Accounting for the human, socio-cultural, natural and built capital assets, in harmony with the financial assets of any organisation, community, or nation, is critical to a wise and sustainable stewardship of the genuine wealth of nations.

Dellner presents a practical road map together with an integral 'sextant' to help a new generation of investors who are genuinely interested in measuring and accounting for the impacts of their decisions and their investment portfolios in line with the values of their clients, be they individual, institutional, or societal. Understanding how investments in companies, enterprises, and other financial instruments contribute to a well-being return on investment constitutes a new frontier in the financial world of banking and investments.

Building on a continuous evolution of new measures of progress (including triple bottom line, balanced scorecard, sustainable, and social accounting) and reporting standards such as the Global Reporting Initiative (GRI) standards, impact investment seems to be the latest fad in a financial world desperately trying to present a different model for investing financial assets with some semblance of virtue and values.

The integral approach to impact investment which Dellner presents is another value added perspective that comes from his experience in the banking and investment world. I believe it will contribute to a serious improvement in how investors and investment managers can manage investment portfolios because of its capacity to verify the positive well-being impacts of their investment choices.

My efforts as an economist, trained in accounting and forest economics, have been to shift the focus of measures of progress to well-being impact measures across all aspects of fiscal, monetary, and investment management.

'Integral' is an important word that will shape a new consciousness in the investment world; integral means comprehensive, inclusive, non-marginalizing and embracing. Integral approaches in any field attempt to be exactly that: to include as many perspectives, styles, and methodologies as possible within a coherent view of the topic. Integral is a close cousin to words like 'resilience', 'harmony' and 'flourishing'.

I believe the current system of financial capitalism has been operating without any concern for well-being impacts; it has a myopic focus on chasing financial returns, even though the degradation of human, social, natural or environmental assets may take place. There is a fundamental failure to account for losses or depreciation caused by the way we choose to live. Putting on a new set of lenses using Dellner's integral model with a four-worlds perspective involves a serious examination of both individual conscience, and the 'conscience' and virtues of the investment portfolio itself. Robert Kennedy once said that the main shortcoming of national-income accounting and measures of economic progress, namely the GDP, 'measures everything except that which is worthwhile'.

Dellner has developed a practical working model for helping impact-investment decision makers increase their consciousness of the totality of the well-being impacts of their investment portfolios and their investment choices. His I^3 model will help you, as an investor or impact-investment fund manager, help your investment choices become more virtuous and thus impact well-being and even happiness. This can be verified. To my mind, Dellner provides a tool for helping the financial world start to account for the impacts on the well-being of the communities and the environment which their actions affect.

Make no mistake, we have a long way to go before the financial and accounting worlds take seriously the importance of measuring well-being returns on their investments, and have accounting systems that can measure the well-being impacts on all five forms of capital asset classes. As with any journey, we need a map, and instruments to help us.

Consider that the double-entry bookkeeping system used by businesses around the world took more than 525 years to develop. It was originally developed by Franciscan friar and mathematician Luca Pacioli and Leonardo da Vinci in 1492. Pacioli designed the debit=credit system of accounting, together with balance sheets, as a tool for the Medici bankers of Florence, and businesses in Venice. He argued that a wise business person kept accounts of the assets, liabilities and equity of his or her enterprise because 'all wealth ultimately came from God or the Creator'. This shows increasing consciousness that all wealth (or ultimately well-being) is a gift from the Creator or God and to ensure humans flourish is to be a wise steward of all of the assets that were gifted by God.

The use of Dellner's proposed integral model for managing investments will require an ongoing reflection on the words of T.S. Eliot:

> *Where is the wisdom we have lost in knowledge?*
> *Where is the knowledge we have lost in information?*

Indeed, the beginning of wisdom within the financial sector may in fact be the realisation that wise financial asset stewardship will indeed require an integral approach and mindset, which sees everything as integral (interconnected).

The image of a circle, rather than upward sloping productivity curves and stock market indices, is the image that comes to my mind when thinking about an integral approach. Moving to this future 'promised land of integral finance' will require a fundamental examination of the nature of money itself and its creation. My critique of the debt-money system suggests that the very nature of debt-money creation, and compound interest, is the primary driver for the need for constant economic or GDP growth, as well as for a constantly rising stock market and financial performance indices.

Dellner's book is a clarion call for courageous change in a world drowning under mountains of unrepayable financial debts. The US alone has more than $70 trillion in outstanding debt, which consumes roughly 50% of the income of an American household in the form of hidden interest charges. Few economists and financial sector experts have presented alternatives to an international debt-money crisis that has no apparent solution. Stock markets must continue to grow as all of us chase unsustainable financial returns and wait for the game of musical financial chairs to stop. It is not money that is scarce but the courage and willpower to imagine a new economic system with forms of money that reflect the truth of natural laws, of abundance and of resilience as revealed in Nature.

It is clearer every day that the financial system is operating unsustainably and perpetuating — or ignoring — environmental and social problems. What few people realize is that global debt situation is essentially like an inoperable cancer. A new economic system is necessary that is built on the wisdom of the four-worlds (considering the cultural wisdom of the various cultures or nations from the North, East, North and West) that Dellner uses to construct his integral model.

Dellner's work needs to be taken very seriously by today's generation of impact investment managers and advisors, particularly those who are advising the next generation of young people who are inheriting vast sums of financial and material wealth from their parents and grandparents. Dellner's ideas and proposals provide an important map and compass for wealth-management advisors to a new generation of investors, who seem to have a different appetite for investments that contribute to a better world, rather than simply generating high financial returns. This is a new generation of investors with a higher consciousness, more sensitized to the ecological crisis the world faces. They long to invest their time and money into initiatives and companies that align with their own values for a better world.

My own proposal for a new economic system, based on well-being and measuring progress in terms of changes in the conditions of well-being of our communities and the environment as part of a new integrated five-capital asset-accounting model, is very much in harmony with Dellner's proposed integral model for impact investment. Ultimately investments are the allocation of resources, time and money into a suite of assets with an expected 'return', usually measured in financial terms (profitability, dividends and return on assets). But financial returns are only one form of well-being returns. A well-being based approach to impact investment would consider the positive and negative qualitative effects, as well as the monetary (full costs) impacts on human, social, natural and built assets of a community, nation, enterprise and even investment portfolio.

Measuring these impacts is not as daunting as some might think. Again, Dellner posits a process by which the impact investor and manager can 'journey' around the circle of the four-world views of an enterprise (in my model they can 'journey' through each of the four key asset classes) and ask the question: 'What well-being impact will my investment make on this asset class, and how can that impact be measured and verified?'

As Dellner describes it, his I³ model 'is a map-making journey through the integral lens where each of us will need to find answers that work and fit within our own context. I³ is not a thing or product, it is more of a dynamic roadmap and lens.'

Ultimately the onus will be on each of us, whether an individual investor, investment manager, banker or financial minister to put on a new set of glasses to examine our own consciences as we make investments. We will hopefully be motivated by this, and a yearning for the good of others and Nature, to determine whether our choices are likely to contribute to a better future and a well-being outcome.

This book is an important read, particularly for the younger generation of investors who want their investments and money to do good.

MARK ANIELSKI, ECONOMIST AND AUTHOR
The Economics of Happiness: Building Genuine Wealth & An Economy of Well-being:
Common-Sense Tools for Building Genuine Wealth and Happiness

Professor Dr Ronnie Lessem

Robert Dellner's formidable work follows in the footsteps of much that has come before, in the areas of social auditing, reporting, and accounting, prior to the establishment of the field he has now entered and evolved in a duly *integral* guise, namely 'Impact Investment'.

In the 1970s and 1980s, I was heavily engaged in the fields of so-called social auditing, social reporting, and social accounting. This was, at least in part, a reaction to my sterile experience of having being an articled clerk to a firm of 'Western' accountants in the City of London in the 1960s. I had become bored to tears by all the figures, all the numbers, which represented a very impoverished representation of the firms I audited around the UK.

So a decade later, now in my thirties, having joined Matrix Consultants[3] in London, whose focus was on corporate 'social affairs', perhaps anticipating what was to come over the later course of my life and work, I was given the opportunity to develop a richer form of social accounting and reporting. In my first published article, entitled Accounting for an Enterprise's Well-being[4], I wrote in the 1970s:

> Business enterprise today is being called upon to exercise significantly wider 'social responsibility' than has traditionally been the case. As a result, individuals, communities and national governments are beginning to call for statements of 'social account' which reflect a company's performance in the eyes not only of financial shareholders, but also of other stakeholders in the community at large.

As a result herein I attempt to extend fundamental accounting principles, which have traditionally embraced only monetary stocks and flows, towards physical, social and psychological exchanges. I therefore provide a foundation both for the development of the accountant's/auditor's traditional role and for a means of communication between interest groups within and without the enterprise. As such I do not attempt to develop thoroughgoing quantitative measures to the same degree of specificity as conventional financial accounts; rather I aim to develop a novel framework, to which both management practitioners and theorists may apply their own specific refinements.

Crude as this opening account may have been, to my knowledge since then there has been no other attempt to apply such 'double-entry' principles to environmental, social, psychological, and financial transactions. Yet for me such 'double-entry' (asset and liability, credit and debit) accounting involved life principles rather than exclusively financial ones. For example, for the assets acquired by a mining company in terms of, for example, coal, there is a liability incurred as far as the Earth is concerned. Such a liability at the time of writing (August, 2019) is more likely than not the cause of the continuous flooding in Great Britain, ultimately 'debiting' millions — if not billions — of pounds to the nation's financial accounts, not to mention the monumental loss of personal lives, and losses to Nature.

A year later in 1975, I[3] turned to the more broadly based field of *Corporate Social Reporting*, following up on my previous work:

> The particular field in which I requested documentation, in a letter sent out to 400 companies, was corporate social responsibility in general, social and/or human resource accounting, consumer programmes and activities, pollution control, energy conservation, recycling, community affairs, volunteer programs, race relations, corporate contributions and manpower lending

Corporate social reporting, I then ascertained, could be categorised:

- By a particular *channel*: newsletter, annual report, composite social report

- Through the particular *medium* of words, number, pictures

- Including a specific *mix* of activities, policies, results, standards, achievements

- Conveying specific information about physical and human resources, products meeting social needs, distribution of finances, internal and external stakeholders

- Employing a particular *form* of presentation: scorecard, inventory, balance sheet

- Conducted by the company itself or by an external *source*

- *Focused* on a mere account of what is, or an account of what should be, in relation to a potential standard or comparison

- *Concentrated* around the company's main product, and/or market, or on peripheral stakeholder interest

- Finally, in varying *degrees* of breadth or depth of concern.

However, by the end of the decade I had abandoned the whole social accounting/ reporting/auditing field to move onto broader and deeper managerial and intellectual pastures. In fact, for all the rich potential that I had uncovered, I discovered that most — if not all — the accounting practitioners in the field (there were very few academics engaged in it) became mesmerised by numbers: physical numbers, financial numbers, statistical numbers. I began to feel, as Nigerian social philosopher Bayo Akomolafe[5] has so recently and eloquently stated, that the whole exercise was becoming self-defeating.

Instead of getting closer to the environment, the person and the community, the 'social accountants' were putting more and more distance between such phenomena and themselves, not to mention the practising managers. The trouble was I only had a general intimation as to where to go from there, as I was not yet a social science 'researcher' in its purest sense nor had yet discovered an *integral* way. In fact it was more than three decades before I began to see that integral economic light that would pave the way for *integral* research.

Fast forward three decades. Early in the new millennium, in my article[6] written for the UK journal *Long Range Planning* (my MBA thesis at Harvard Business School was on corporate planning), I was beginning to develop an integral approach, encompassing 'North', 'East', 'South' and 'West':

> The world of economics and business has become dominated by one cultural frame of reference — 'North-Western' — to the point that the hidden strengths of other cultures, even those of China and India which are pursuing a strongly 'Westernised' economic course today, are being ignored by individuals, organisations, and societies alike. Before the demise of communism there was at least an alternative approach, albeit one in opposition. Now, the post-modern age of the information society is almost universally capitalist, and even in its latest manifestation, that of globalisation, it exploits difference (market and consumer

segmentation) rather than differentiating and integrating between and within cultures and economies. No ecology, including the modern university, can thrive for long when one element, propositional knowledge for example, is rampant.

Truth be told, for me the world of accounting, like that of business and management, is as strongly 'Westernised' today as it was in the 1970s, notwithstanding decades of social reporting, social accounting and social auditing. This is despite the fact that today social enterprise and social entrepreneurship abounds, not to mention also the advent of the 'triple' or 'quadruple' bottom-line!

In the new millennium this integral approach has been applied by Alexander Schieffer and myself at the Trans4m Centre for Integral Development to enterprise [7] and economy[8], research[9] and development[10], as well as through Trans4m Communiversity Associates[11] to *The Idea of the Community* as well as to our *Islamic to Integral Finance*.

Dellner has applied this integral approach to accounting and investment, thereby serving to uplift 'impact investment' from its somewhat — at least in terms of theory — spurious state into an emerging discipline in its own right, both in theory as well as in practise. It is now for others to take on from where he, so richly and expansively, leaves off.

PROFESSOR RONNIE LESSEM,
Trans4m Communiversity Associates, August 2019

Alejandro Cañadas

Robert Dellner's book is coming at a perfect time when there are a growing demand and supply of Impact Investment interest and implementations. It is estimated that from a total of 66.4 Trillion US$ representing all the asset managers by the top 400 ranked by worldwide and external institutional Assets under Management (AUM), 13.2 Trillion US$ of AUM is within Impact Investment initiatives. Higher interest in Impact Investment is excellent because these efforts are focused on seeing Impact Investment as an extension of socially responsible investing. Namely, they focus on companies that promote ethical and socially responsible consciousness, such as environmental sustainability, social justice, and corporate ethics. This is something positive that goes beyond traditional work in finance founded on the Efficient Market Hypotheses (EMH).[1]

---

[1]The traditional work in finance that was founded on the Efficient Market Hypotheses (EMH) that states that asset prices reflect all available information at that point in time. A

Impact investing goes a step further by aiming to reduce negative impacts and actively seeking investments that can create a significant, positive impact. Impact investing focuses on investing in companies or organizations to create measurable societal and environmental benefits while still generating a favorable financial return.

Impact investing is typically centered on addressing a social issue, such as poverty or education, or an environmental issue, such as clean water [13]. Dellner's book is an excellent complement to the growing demand and supply of Impact Investment by moving several steps forward.

Dellner developed the I³ model, which is a systemic, unified, comprehensive, holistic, and integrated system for Impact Investment that will help decision-makers understand and navigate their investment decisions for real ecological impact.

The Integral model itself is based on the Trans4M model of Integral transformation and praxis as developed over decades by Dr. Ronnie Lessem and Dr. Alexander Schieffer.

What is more, Dellner's I³ model builds on two decades of advances in sustainability measurement and reporting that uses both conventional accounting and economic measurement systems, which is the foundation of an integral form of asset accounting that goes beyond merely financial capital-asset accounting.

Dellner's I³ model assesses the accounting for the human, socio-cultural, natural/environmental, and built-capital assets, in balance and harmony with the financial assets of any organization, community, or nation, which is critical to wise and sustainable stewardship of the genuine wealth of nations.

Dellner's book brings a new paradigm in Finance because the I³ model is a unified, systemic, comprehensive, holistic, and integrated model, centered on the development of a moral core.

It is also a practical road map to help a new generation of investors who are genuinely interested in measuring and accounting for navigating the impacts of their decisions and their investment portfolios in line with the values of their clients (individual, institutional, or societal).

That is why this book is ideal for anyone who is looking for the secret key to truly integrate the whole of Finance and Economics with the world of personal and communitarian flourishing and wellbeing. Dellner' shows in his

---

direct implication is that it is impossible to "beat the market" consistently on a risk-adjusted basis since market prices should only react to new information. The EMH was developed by Eugene Fama's influential 1970 review of the theoretical and empirical research to estimate financial market returns. See the Fama's seminal paper [12].

book that exists a true harmony among Finance and Economics incarnated in real communities that create a true inherent unity between our consciousness and the world ecology.

DR ALEJANDRO CAÑADAS,
PhD, Mount St. Mary's University School of Business, USA

Author's foreword

> Few can foresee whither their road will lead them, till they come to its end.
>
> ———————————————————————————
>
> Legolas, *Lord of the Rings*, J.R.R. Tolkien.

This book is a synthesis and fusion from my decades in finance, investment and psychology. I realize they are now inseparable and I'm thankful for my journey, which has given me opportunities for constant discovery and renewal. I have encountered numerous women and men who have been instrumental in shaping my journey. As fellow travellers, I will be forever grateful for their loving guidance and thoughtful support. My objective is to share insights to help others to expand on their own 'impact' journey.

Here we can define impact broadly, as all the component parts inside an investment that we value, find important, and that make up our footprint and defined outcomes. This book is meant as an introduction; no single volume can do justice to the complexity of the subject. This book on integrative finance provides one possible way of seeing, thinking and working more deeply with impact, something that is largely missing in finance and investment literature. Today, we are witnessing an emerging consciousness enabling us to better understand the roles and responsibility that finance and investments have. And so to better understand the causes and effects of global issues, where each individual, institution, and industry is equally responsible. As the only constant in life is change, this is also a story about change, not small incremental change, but transformational change.

As we enter 'the integral age', we see deeper systems thinking. We are all looking for our own version of what is true for us and how this may be integrated into our lives. We are looking, not just for absolute truths, but also relative truths that can only be found and understood by exposing and exploring contrasting opposites within ourselves. Impact is a creative construct that has more in common with art than mathematics. That is why impact from the purely technical perspective will never be sufficient to reach the kind of impact 'which other methodologies cannot reach', because we also need to include the psychodynamic of the self, the other, the organisation and the prevailing culture of our society. This expanding lens of contrasting integration is the essence of integral impact, which this book explores to the fullest extent possible.

No system or approach per se is the solution; however, as human beings operating within the system, we are the solution. There is no envisioned outcome or objective to this book; it intends the reader to 'take what you like and leave the rest'. May our paths cross on some part of this mutual journey; until then, I wish you the very best on this important voyage of discovery that I trust will be filled with meaning and purpose.

ROBERT DELLNER, *2019*

The real voyage of discovery consists not in seeking new landscapes, but in having new eyes

Marcel Proust

Introduction

The purpose of this book is threefold,

TO PROVIDE A BASIS FOR IMPACT map making with a contrasting framework from which we can deepen and grow our own map or further help develop and an existing organisational approach.

TO HELP US TO UNDERSTAND the key imperatives of the personal impact journey, and highlight areas for further investigation and growth.

TO BUILD OUR BASIC FRAMEWORK as to how we can co-create a vision and mission for our self, our organisations, and an investee, to have real integral impact.

In reality, all investments are actually 'Impact', i.e., they all leave a footprint in human and environmental dimensions. Given the current global imperatives, they will need to be reframed as such.

So let us first make a bold prediction: over the coming years, the investment industry will change and develop to such an extent that all its activities will be framed as 'impact'.

Eventually the term 'impact' may become redundant, because we have transitioned to a full composite measurement and return spectrum, integrated into a impact investment models at ever greater stages of development. In this book we will describe models from 1.0 to 4.0.

We will investigate the key components of our impact journey, which essentially fall into three categories.

I. The need for the development of inclusive standards, protocols, and operational frameworks, ones that are less dominated by Northern and Western perspectives.

II. The need for further organisational development, integrating new forms of impact knowledge creation and culture change.

III. The need for personal leadership growth and development into deeper systems thinking, and the need to work towards integral wholeness, by developing the scope and depth of the moral core that drives impact.

As we will see, there are multiple perspectives on what represents an 'investment', and on how capital is managed.

We also must consider the self, as this cannot be excluded when working with impact.

Most of our problems stem from our incapacity to see things in systems, and to create the ability to change accordingly. As Mahatma Gandhi[14] once said

> One man [sic] cannot do right in one department of life whilst he [sic] is occupied in doing wrong in any other department. Life is one indivisible whole.

So what is 'integral'?

> The word integral means comprehensive, inclusive, non-marginalizing, and embracing. Integral approaches to any field attempt to be exactly that: to include as many perspectives, styles, and methodologies as possible within a coherent view of the topic. In a certain sense, integral approaches are 'meta-paradigms' or ways to draw together an already existing number of separate paradigms into an interrelated network of approaches that are mutually enriching[15].

So why is 'integral' needed? In large parts because of our bias toward cognitive binary fragmentation, i.e., seeing things through reduction into separate parts to assist our limitations for understanding. As Charles Eisenstein suggests[16]:

> Individually and collectively, we are on a journey from a story of Separation to a new yet ancient story of Reunion: ecology, interdependency, interbeing.

He also states that:

> Separation is not an ultimate reality, but a human projection, an ideology, a story... It is a story of the separation of the human realm from the natural, in which the former expands and the latter is turned progressively into resources, goods, property, and, ultimately, money[16].

However, in attempting to create wholeness, our understanding comes from creating, and symbolically labelling, contrasting metaphorical visualisations to simplify and construct that which can be stored cognitively. We often severely limit ourselves in this endeavour in combination with our need to be right, which keeps us stuck, preventing us seeing a need for change. As Leo Tolstoy once said:

> Everyone thinks of changing the world, but no one thinks of changing himself.

Why? Partly because it is easier to see the splinter in another person's eye than the log in one's own, but also because of our tendency towards denial. We need to better understand these dual aspects, both of which are internal, neurological processes, and are integrated into the basis of any impact process.

For most firms, the cost of inaction is becoming greater, as we are already on a trajectory of change. But we need to recognise our starting point, so I have illustrated this journey somewhat simplistically as a transition from Impact version 1.0 to Impact version 4.0.

Just as my own understanding is informed by my background and experiences, so is yours. No-one benefits if I just regurgitate information which is readily accessible elsewhere. As Noam Chomsky suggested during a 2008 interview in Boston:

> Changes and progress very rarely are gifts from above. They come out of struggles from below[17]

This book is not necessarily for those who are just seeking more specific tools to measure impact, i.e., more of the rational 'what'. Rather, it is for those who would like to understand more about their own 'how' and 'why', and the relational dimensions of their reasons for working with impact.

The role of the UN Sustainable Development Goals (SDGs)

At the United Nations summit in September 2015, most world leaders adopted a new sustainable development agenda and goals 'to end poverty, protect the planet, and ensure prosperity for all'. This was called Transforming Our World: the 2030 Agenda for Sustainable Development, or Agenda 2030 [18].

The 17 SDGs and 169 core targets is probably the most ambitious agenda in the history of humankind. Each goal has specific targets to be achieved over the next fifteen years, and these have become the main drivers behind institutional investors seeking to move into impact investments.

The SDGs are integrated and indivisible. They balance the three dimensions of sustainable development: economic, social and environmental. Given that Agenda 2030 will have to be strongly supported by equally ambitious and integrally framed holistic, transsectorial policies, the finance and investment industries are being asked to do their part. In addition, the Agenda also shifts from a North–West perspective to a shared, global responsibility.

For impact, we have a crisis of representation as good governance of water, land, air, cities and economies requires a representative government, a body politic or groupings of people to act as stewards. A quote (Keys, 1982) also attributed to Margaret Mead exhorts: 'Never doubt that a small group of thoughtful, committed, citizens can change the world. Indeed, it is the only thing that ever has.' While primarily targeting governments, the SDGs are designed to unify a wide range of industries and organisations.

Unlike their predecessor, the Millennium Development Goals (MDGs), the SDGs explicitly call on all businesses to apply their creativity and innovation to solve sustainable development challenges. Investments must contain multiple lenses and prisms that correspond and communicate across the capital spectrums; as such, they will create significant systemic complexity that models alone cannot compute or hold. As a result, for impact investments going forward, finance and economics can no longer be a disparate and disconnected part operating in a relative vacuum.

As Anne Frank once said:

> How wonderful it is that no one has to wait, but can start right now to gradually change the world!

As impact evolves and matures, the investment industry must become more open towards multiple perspectives; it must embrace forms of knowledge creation other than those found traditionally in finance and economics. This cannot be achieved without personal growth and development by the industry leadership, rooted and grounded in personal identity.

Impact and systems analysis are relevant across all spectrums of capital, from the 'finance first' returns' approach of a private equity investor to the donating philanthropist. Hopefully, legislation, regulation, and fiscal policies will provide further pro-active leadership. Impact investments per se re-connect the separate parts of finance, social, nature, and culture into a framework of wholeness that has been lost during the recent 'financialisation'.

Challenges

In our 'post-truth' world, with its spin and fake news influencing reality and dominating our discourse, it is becoming more difficult to distinguish between truth and personal honesty. The impact industry is not immune to this.

Working with impact does not give anyone a claim to a higher level of integrity; if anything, more challenges will appear as pressures mount to deliver and report on outcomes.

This is why so much 'greenwashing' occurs across all types of institutions. Our current culture is more accepting of the lack of integrity amongst our leaders, therefore it will take great courage and commitment from those who choose to take 'the road less-travelled'.

Of course, finance has thrived on smoke, mirrors, and subterfuge to build opaque linkages whilst creating enormous political power to maintain the privileged status quo. Henry Ford once suggested[19]:

> It is well enough that people of the nation do not understand our banking and monetary system, for if they did, I believe there would be a revolution before tomorrow morning.

The investment industry has always faced significant challenges, complexity, risks and requirements for its diverse needs. Investors along the risk/return spectrum of capital have differing views on asset allocation, but the universal benchmark has, to date, been rates of return. With impact investments, this paradigm is changing, and the industry players will have to re-invent themselves.

This will require the re-dialing of our multiple capital perspectives. Another relatively new phenomenon is exponential accumulation of wealth in family offices around the globe.

As we will explore later, these entities face specific challenges, for which taking an impact approach is highly relevant. Many prominent family offices have been instrumental in the development of impact investments, and no doubt will continue to do so. Whilst larger institutional investors face similar impact challenges, they tend to have more hard-coded and formulaic frameworks. This enables investments' codification to be standardized through policy and procedures inside the firm, but also leaves them potentially slower to respond to change.

The impact investment engine for any firm could be the central point through which knowledge and interactions flow, and on which the business drivers across the entire firm intersect. We may, hopefully soon, have a firm's Chief Investment Officer (CIO) becoming the Chief Impact Officer (CIO); this concept deserves further attention for each firm, which we will explore later.

Nathan Fabian, the Director of Policy and Research at the Principles for Responsible Investment (PRI), reminds us that[20]:

> The financial system is operating unsustainably, perpetuating or ignoring environmental and social problems. The continued financing of excessive greenhouse gas emissions and worsening economic inequality, for example, threaten to further divide the financial system from the interests of the users and beneficiaries it is designed to serve

Whilst the above quote succinctly sets the tone, mission, and ambition for impact investments — no easy task — in the meantime, we face many challenges at individual and organisational levels, e.g., the need for growth, and the overwhelming sense of the complexity of the road ahead.

By definition, the task of individuation implies that we personally must develop, so that we can see these previously hidden realms. Impact investment is a context that offers this deeper and more integrated developmental journey which each investor will need to consider to fully be able to become an Impact investor.

This book is intended to provide insights to this process, especially, the intentions of our investments and the important outcomes which we can measure and calibrate. It asks why impact is a personal quest, not just a financial calculus and investment modelling (which in many respects is the easiest part of the process). In a way, impact investing is the deep alignment of finance with the added expression of our values and beliefs in comporting our money with things that we care about.

This may include not just screening out the 'bad' but also allocating capital, and deciding how to influence its use, for good. Let's start with two helpful, definitions for impact investment to set the tone:

IMPACT INVESTMENTS ARE investments made into companies, organisations, and funds with the intention to generate social and environmental impact alongside a financial return.

The Global Impact Investing Network (GIIN)[21]

IMPACT INVESTING IS an investment approach intentionally seeking to create both financial return and social impact that is actively measured.

W. E. F., Mainstreaming Impact Investing Working Group

Setting the tone

These definitions clarify the base line for our position today, or what we can call 'Impact 1.0'. It is clear that we have work to do, not only in terms of our technical understanding (including developing new measurements, accounting matrixes and calibrations), but also how we define and see our social and environmental dimensions. This not only drives our understanding and intentions, but also the development of 'the self'.

This book covers several aspects of impact, but its emphasis is on the individual impact developmental journey. However, impact investments open up the potential for a new paradigm based on a natural system that seeks wholeness and personal individuation. This concept is very new in finance and economics, and will require a significant change in thinking for most people. It will require many firms to challenge how they currently do business, and to reshape to include impact.

This is an area where we can dive deep and 'get in over our heads' to truly stretch our respective envelopes in terms of what it means to be human and to walk with integrity on this incredible planet. The word integrity means much more than adherence to some code of ethics and morals; it means *the state or quality of being entire, complete, and unbroken* as in integer or integral. A little deeper, integrity refers to a living tree or a human self in its *unimpaired, unadulterated, or genuine state, corresponding to its original condition* (Webster's Revised Unabridged Dictionary 1913, p. 774).

We often need to enter a context that grows our very being, becoming, knowing, and doing, as T.S. Eliot once suggested:

If you aren't in over your head, how do you know how tall you are?

There are three main operating principles[22] that exist in all the natural systems that permeate our world:

I. The capacity to *self-organise*

II. The ability to *collaborate*

III. The ability to *operate interdependently*.

Linked and fused to these operating principles are three interdependent energies that emerged and evolved from within life forms over billions of years:

I. *Differentiation* or diversity, as each life form is distinct or different

II. *Subjectivity*, interiority, or essence that comes from seeking and getting in touch with the true core of the self and everything that exists

III. *Communion*, or community and interconnectedness, to all things as fuelled by the gravitational pull of our emergent love.

These energies offer vital lessons for the critical times in which we live, where diversity causes conflict, living is often at a superficial level, and individualism runs rampant.

The current age of gene-centrism and its linearly assumed mechanisms is now slowly passing. In its place, for example, the biological sciences increasingly recognise that life is not simply a genetically determined programme, but is a matter of information and communication systems nested in larger complex systems.

If we cannot see that we are in communion with others, we will not realize that what we do to ourselves we also do to others and to the Earth. Ecological degradation, racism, discrimination, hatred, and lack of interest in working for justice, truth, and love reflect the lack of honour of that which stands before us. In the same way, we do not realize that our lack of understanding ultimately creates fear, conflict, and violence, because we see the natural world as an object rather than a subject with its own valued interiority.

From biology we have symbiosis (cooperation between organisms for mutual benefit) and synergy (where individual elements within a system work together for the good of the whole). These are missing from most Impact 1.0 approaches so we will explore and expand on these in later chapters.

Some of these objectified thought forms reside in our individual values and beliefs and how closely these may or not be aligned with our organisation, its operational way of being and its culture. This is particularly important for investors with a short distance for capital to travel between thoughts and actions, e.g., High Net Worth Individuals (HNI) and family offices.

We can now add another helpful, broader guiding Impact definition from the Organisation for Economic Co-operation and Development (OECD)[23]:

> Impact evaluation is an assessment of how the intervention being evaluated affects outcomes, whether these effects are intended or unintended. The proper analysis of impact requires a counterfactual of what those outcomes would have been in the absence of the intervention.

This highlights an important distinction between only monitoring outcomes, which is a description of the factual, and utilizing a counterfactual equivalent to attribute observed outcomes to the impact intervention.

The International Fund for Agricultural Development (IFAD) impact evaluation guidelines define impact as the

> the attainment of development goals of the project or program, or rather the contributions to their attainment.

The Asian Development Bank (ADB) guidelines state the same point:

> Project impact evaluation establishes whether the intervention had a welfare effect on individuals, households, and communities, and whether this effect can be attributed to the concerned intervention

As such, in Impact 1.0 there are three key outcome objectives to impact: social, environmental, and financial. Each is driven by intentionality and guided by our defined measurement systems within our observable realms.

Whilst the SDG's themselves do not provide or suggest any operating approach or solutions, they act as signposts which industry must address for their impact outcomes.

Whilst we may have great intentions for our impact, some would have happened regardless of our actions. We should aim to measure the nett gain due to our actions.

The SDGs helps us to recognise and validate:

I. The gravity of the global situation

II. Increased awareness of issues behind each goal

III. Awareness of new business risks and uncertainties

IV. The necessity for a unifying framework to conceptualise and create solutions

V. The creation of significant SDG-related business opportunities.

It is possible that this book may at times seem overly critical or pessimistic but this is not the intention; rather its objective is to challenge conventional modes of thinking. Being educated and trained as an economist in Sweden before working in finance in the City of London, I can confirm that economics often conforms to the nineteenth-century Victorian historian Thomas Carlyle's definition as 'the dismal science' that tends to look at the downside of things before seeking to understand their upside.

As the athlete Dan Millman wrote,

> The secret of change is to focus all of your energy, not on fighting the old, but on building the new.
>
> ―――――――――――――――――――――――――――――――
>
> Attributed to Socrates in Millman, 1980

Integration

We will sometimes intermix environmental, social, and corporate governance (ESG)/impact to highlight the continuous integration and blurring of the lines between them.

The term 'ESG integration' was launched by the UN Principles for Responsible Investment (PRI) in 2006. The real meaning of ESG integration, although the word is used by a large number of investors and asset managers, is commonly lost in translation. A recent white paper by Stockholm (NordsIP) — Danske Bank and Invesco — questions the authenticity of many firms in ESG integration[24]. The paper suggests that asset managers easily can lose themselves between asking how investee firms integrated ESG and how they should do it themselves in their investment process. This is one reason for whetting a strong appetite for improved ESG taxonomy, and for general coordination in standards for stewardship and risk measurements.

However, the process, screening, scoring, overlaying, and filtering of impact has generated more confusion for asset managers and institutional investors. The white paper proposes, and I agree, that it is asset managers themselves who are most likely to deliver a practical answer, as they are ultimately responsible for their investments.

A recent article by John Authers in the Financial Times (FT)[25] suggests a slightly provocative and darker alternative motivation for the ESG push:

> On the side of the devil, ESG offers a rebranding for an unpopular industry, an excuse for data providers to crunch a lot of data and then charge for it, a great opportunity to bid for the huge pools of money held on behalf of public sector workers and charitable organisations that tend to be politically liberal, and most of all, an opportunity for active management to justify its existence in comparison to passive managers.

However, the ESG paradigm is here to stay. In his FT article 'The ethical investment boom' James Kynge, wrote: 'The outperformance of ESG strategies is beyond doubt.'

As we will explore in this book, we must recognise that, going forward, we can no longer be content just with ESG + Finance (F) as the driver. As each context is different, we need a more flexible and much deeper, authentic and sustainable approach, as reinforced by Allen White, Co-Founder of the Global Reporting Initiative:

> ...We want to reach beyond ESG ratings. ESG does not, by nature, carry a true sustainability gene. A company may rate very highly on an ESG score, but to say this company is an excellent sustainability performer is a very fundamentally different statement (...) Sustainability requires contextualization within thresholds. That's what sustainability is all about. Yet to this day, contextualization rarely appears in sustainability reports...We don't have decades to get serious about Context in light of the ecological and social perils that lie ahead (White, 2013.)

The other

A key point of impact investing is the capacity for each investor to build and expand their understanding and cognitive map to include 'the other' (and by extension "the others").

Of course, a hidden, silent, and oft-neglected 'other' is the environment, with its interactive biosystems, flora, and fauna. This may be part of our impact spectrum, depending on the context of our investments and our level of developed consciousness. For some, this may already be a step too far politically...i.e. *are you suggesting that I become some kind of tree hugging environmentalist?* Nothing of the sort, if we can manage to re-frame the political presupposition, for example by becoming more humanitarian. Also, many financial organisations, understandably, are built on the cult of power and 'expertise' which dominates governance proceedings. Impact, as such, can be the litmus test for our entire development.

In his 'Essays from the Nick of Time: Reflections and Refutations', Mark Slouka suggests that:

> The case for the humanities is not hard to make.... the humanities, done right, are the crucible in which our evolving notions of what it means to be human are put to the test[26].

Thus, impact includes careful consideration for 'the other' in our decision making. The question should be: 'Why, how and to what extent should our perspectives be different in this context of impact?' This does not require political persuasion, just a bit of common sense and a sufficient dose of humility to grasp alternative means of fertilizing impact so that those impacted can maximise their growth and reach their objectives.

Impact investments are facing two developmental hurdles. The first is at the individual level in terms of breadth and depth of systems thinking; the second is at the organisational level of both culture and language. Culture, given the need to shift from finance to include other dimensions of operation to the fullest possible extent; and language in that organisations speak mainly in operational languages that relate to digital bits of information, which is why organisations often struggle to understand and include culture in their conscious strategy.

If impact is going to succeed, we need to balance communication from the head and the heart, to develop alternative calibration systems, and new forms of measurement for communication. This implies that organisational communication itself needs to evolve to include processes which include organic systems, and are aligned with the contexts of the impact dimensions, such as Nature itself.

The Earth is, of course, a complex living system whose homeostatic maintenance depends on the robust interaction and communication of every living and nonliving subsystem. This is a language of perspectives, of courage and connection with what is vulnerable in us.

> Each of us, no matter what our position and occupation, must try to act in such a way as to further true humanity.
>
> ———————————————————————————
>
> Albert Schweitzer

Integral Impact Investments (I^3)

Here we discuss 'Integral Impact Investments' (or I^3 for short), based on the four-world model, recently developed by Professors Ronnie Lessem and Alexander Schieffer, founders of Trans4M in Geneva. Whilst I^3 aims to be politically agnostic, it is inevitable that it will borrow concepts, thoughts and frameworks that for many may seem 'left' or 'right'. If so, this is unintentional.

Of course, this statement of agnosticism is to some degree also contradictory. Money and capital are highly political, not intrinsically, but in how they are used and allocated in our economic system. As such, the use of capital and money also follows neurological, psychological, cultural, and political paths through the human mind, whereby our objectives are formed into expectations.

The integral framework itself is designed to be totally agnostic as we 'dial up or down' its component parts to suit our own preferences and ways of thinking.

Another key role for impact investments is to understand how closely a decision aligns with its outcomes. Essentially, a form of ongoing regression analysis with the added element of looking at the actual effect and impact; and, in addition to the intention of the thinker, to use Jungian language, we also need the feeler, judger, and perceiver.

However, as with any map making, whilst *the map is not the territory.... the word is not the thing*[27], it is equally important to filter and exclude in order to shape our cognitive map. In effect, we need full awareness (i.e., full cognition) to consider all dimensions and then re-draw the territorial map using some commonly accepted way of interpreting. Welcome to the wonderful world and down the rabbit holes of integral impact investments.

In one of his Family Wealth Reports for 2017, 21, the impact investor and author of the important book 'Making Money Matter', Benjamin Bingham, wrote:

> Investors need a map if they are going to navigate in the world of impact investing. But even before this, investors need to believe investments matter, to relate to their money in a new way; to see it as a tool for change.

Capital is not the global issue at hand, it is what capital does which is at the core of our problems, and why impact and its/our development has to permeate it.

Jed Emerson, author of another important book, 'The Purpose of Capital', says:

> Our ability to raise ever higher amounts of capital under the Impact Brand is not in question; our capacity to catalyse sustained, transformative change in our consciousness and awareness of Self and Other whereby we then may become participants in social liberation and fundamental global change, is.[28]

In addition, a challenge is that each organisation has its own evolving politics, embedded in its culture. As such, we must establish a cultural alignment between the needs between the individual and the firm to exist and develop in its geographical and cultural context. Consequently, how this is managed and operationalised becomes paramount.

Positive developments are occurring within many investment firms as they align their own impact philosophy with their propositions for attracting and retaining funds. As mentioned, all investments since time immemorial have actually been 'impact investments'; the question, as always, is through which lens and prism are we looking to understand the systemic impacts and outcomes. All investors are in effect 'impact' investors, whether they know it or not. This is the global awareness that is gathering pace.

Complex systems

> Complex systems are weakened, even killed, when deprived of stressors.
>
> Nassim Taleb

In any complex system such as economics, finance and investment, a balance must be made between the detail of the map and its territory. There is little point in making a map resemble the territory so complex that we just get lost. The map also needs to be capable to adapt to the changes in architectural design and incoming information, contain and help manage its stressors to achieve its outcomes.

As with any cognitive map we, as the 'mapmaker', can expand our experience and understanding of the map over time. In addition, for a map to be useful it is not up to the mapmaker to decide what he or she wants to include depending on personal preferences; mapping (for impact) must include the perspectives of all impacted people. The Western- orientated impact industry must refrain from imposing 'Western' paradigms onto other Impact areas which would be better served otherwise; current solutions must be much broader and deeper to reach multiple perspectives.

The French philosopher, anthropologist and sociologist Bruno Latour, suggests that:

> The West has landed on all other civilisations like an Apocalypse that has put an end to their existence. By believing oneself to be a bearer of civilisations one becomes like an apocalypse for others[29]

We ignore the invisible. The current conventional 'Western' approach tend to see and value the visible and quantifiable and ignore the more invisible and qualitative. This thinking style includes a highly systematic 'model'; whilst this is a critical component of any diagnostic process, it is also a highly detached form of observation that lacks experimental and emotional content that enables deeper understanding in a particular impact context. We will expand on this in later chapters, as it is fundamental to understanding the personal dimensions of working with impact.

The impact industry has recently made great strides in harnessing talents and resources towards the development of the necessary universally applicable frameworks and methods for assessment. The Impact Management Project (IMP) and the GIIN exemplify how the industry has responded to the need for usable tools and frameworks in order to use information clearly and concisely. These tools are crucial; using them, each firm can iterate and formulate its own methodology and ways to communicate around impact through their rounds of investment cycles.

This book will develop a deeper foundation for those interested in using and implementing impact. As the Nobel Peace prize winner, Albert Schweitzer suggested in his second ethical principle:

> He [sic] who has experienced good in his life must feel the obligation to dedicate some of his own life in order to alleviate suffering.[30]

Some context

Now fully immersed in the Anthropocene, we are entering a new period, 'the age of consequence'. We must reflect on our roles and possible contributions to solve the imbalances that we have created.

One of the many consequential drivers comes from the EU's target of reducing domestic greenhouse gas emissions by at least 40% by 2030 against a 1990 baseline[31], for which many firms are providing clearly defined solutions and seeking investment opportunities. Here we will only touch on certain specific key drivers to emphasise and validate relevant points and arguments; more specifically, our focus is on the self and the areas that we can directly or indirectly control and influence. Equally, I will not offer additional insight to the risk/reward arguments between conventional versus impact investing, as much research already exists.

Even though numbers can be understood easily and provide consistency in translation, wherever possible I will avoid using data and numbers as part of an argument or discussion. This is for several reasons.

I. They very quickly become outdated

II. They can always be contrasted with other data that either divides, unites , supports or contradicts

III. Data/numbers contain little emotional/cognitive process intelligence

IV. As abstractions, they detract from real meanings behind concepts

V. Polarisation, fragmented and digital thinking is part of the problem why we don't understand impact so data/numbers will have less value here where we seek interconnectivity and integration within systems

VI. I take the liberty to suggest that our agreement/disagreement on numbers is a bar to the insights required for integration.

Impact investment is about creating 'new' wealth, including non-extractive forms of wealth derived from our collective human, social, environmental, and cultural capital. As we enter the post-individualistic and post-modern era, we find one of the drivers towards the current, more integral and inclusive era is increased consciousness and concern for the environment. Over the past 3 decades or so, the beginnings of an 'integral age' has been suggested as the next stage on our human development and civilisation, where we become more inclusive and start to connect the links that have been lost or forgotten during previous stages of development. Impact investments therefore has to be counter- cultural; in my opinion, the very notion and beginnings of impact investments are grounded in the emergence of this integral age. It seems natural, therefore, that the next stage of development for impact investments is to become more integral in their developmental axis.

A journey of a thousand miles begins with a single step
_____
Lao Tzu

Early family lessons

Before we start examining integral impact, I would like to share briefly a little of my own journey into this area. This will not only give you a better understanding of where I am coming from and my limitations on this topic, but also provide a contrast to your own path into the investment industry.

In my family, our situation and experiences taught me first-hand some of the vicissitudes of managing capital and money. With hindsight and the good fortune of being born the youngest of four children, I realised from an early age that my family had a dysfunctional, and in some instances psycho-pathological, relationship with money. This came at the cost of many other aspects of family life, such as spending quality time together, being involved in activities and having close relationships. As a result, one of the core capacities and essential functions within any family was missing: we did not have the ability to resolve conflicts through dialogue and compromise.

Our father was highly conflict avoidant; he dealt with each of his children individually and situations were never discussed or resolved as a combined family. As a result, no one learned to fully interact, solve differences and deal with ambiguities as a family unit. In the same way that our development as human beings shapes how we handle money, experiences with money shape us.

Money can be one of the most contentious issues for a family to handle; for many family-run businesses, survival, growth and sustainability will depend on our relationship to it. We will also explore how money is held in the family's collective consciousness and how each member relates to it is of key importance not only for its creation but also for a family's total well-being and harmony.

In my family, we had a seminal event that shaped many of our relationships not only with money but, more tragically and importantly, with ourselves. I briefly share them here; my focus is on the dynamics rather than the technicalities, but I hope that my experiences resonate with some readers who may have experienced similar situations. Perhaps they will provide a basis for better management and possible reconciliation, or help prevent similar issues arising in the future.

Real pain, trials and tribulations

My grandfather was very industrious; he founded Nohab Flygmotor in Sweden which later became part of Swedish Aeroplanes AB (SAAB) where he served as their first president. He had several business relationships which my father made use of in his own activities and my grandfather's business became the foundation for many of his enterprises and businesses. My father came from a traditional background. He believed to some degree in preferential hierarchy by birth, age and sex and this created differentiated privileges which sometimes caused conflicts. He had a very trusting relationship with his own father; this was the foundation for their business agreements, so there was never a need to rely on just written or legal arrangements. I also recall a peculiar trait of my grandmother which was to gift things such as valuables whist retaining the option to take things back if things in future changed. My father continued to operate in this trusting way with his own children.

One example of the dysfunction and lack of money integrity centred around one of the main family firms, which my father had built into an important manufacturing business. The control of this business had been passed to my oldest half-brother under a mutual agreement which became disputed. Regardless of who was right or wrong and the legalities, our father felt deeply betrayed; and my half-brother told me he considered that this was his last opportunity to secure his inheritance. As a result, the legal technicalities under a loan agreement of the dispute were played out publicly in the Swedish court system and as siblings, we felt we had to take sides with our father. From the decisions made by each party, it must have been evident that this terminated the father/son relationship, a form of filicide and parricide whose only justification was money. The extended family also suffered as my half-brother's children were never able to meet and have a relationship with their grandfather.

Sadly, the relational repercussions continue today driven by possible guilt and shame creating additional barriers through which possible reconciliation and healing of wounds as yet, cannot penetrate. Just prior to my father's death, there was an attempt for them to meet for the first time following the court process. A frosty meeting which lasted ca. 1 hour where nothing of importance was discussed did not produce the much needed reconciliation. One can only hope that for the parties concerned, when they looked in the mirror they could say that it was worth it. Particularly later in life as the rationale for the decisions may be different from then and now at a stage when real legacy and relations maybe become more important than just having the money.

Being the youngest of my siblings and possibly more emotionally aware, this event had a profound effect on me. During the proceedings, my father asked me to arbitrate a solution so I became acutely aware of each person's arguments and the logic of their positions. However, this is how the proverbial cookie crumbled and, as a result, many people's lives were changed irreversibly from that point onwards.

I stayed and worked in London in the investment baking area as the remaining family firms were reorganised. This incident obliterated existing relationships and destroyed the family as a unit; the sense of divided loyalties and taking has led to an ongoing schism between some family members.

The recent sale of the firm for a ten-figure amount stirred up old emotions, no real sense of financial loss or entitlement but mainly sadness for the many relational losses incurred for the entire family but also joy for the beneficiaries to have now crystalised their future position and many generations to come. Given that the firm was originally intended to remain family-controlled, there is also an important impact for the community which will over time undoubtedly feel the effects of the firm shifting ownership from a family firm to a leveraged Private Equity model. They now have to develop new strategies whilst carrying a significantly higher return requirement to support the much larger capital structure. The present value of the purchase price, as embedded in the nature of capital, contains a forward contract on future labour and resources which has eventually to be paid.

The Swedish press recently called the whole affair 'a dark family history', highlighting the tainted effect of capital when created under such clouds. Also, it changed the traditional idea I had of the family as a mutually supportive, nurturing and sharing unit where blood bonds are meant to be "thicker than water" i.e., stronger than outside forces to provide balance, strengths and a closer sense of unity during difficult times. Also, in any family, it showed me that given its many complexities between hierarchies, culture, needs vs. wants, time-line events etc., it's virtually impossible to create a truly balanced and equal distribution, implying that everyone must reconcile such differences at some point. Also, for some families, finding equality is not necessarily a major objective and is readily dismissed. My father took no advice on such issues as he felt he would retain ultimate control to create such balance over time.

This firm was the "heart and soul" of the community where several family generations have worked and lived their entire lives. In 2012 the company moved some of its production to Poland for better cost effectiveness and access to skilled staff, albeit with a significant loss, (32%)of jobs. This was the first time large-scale redundancies had affected the local community, who deeply felt this loss and sensed a profound change. Dellner Couplers was historically also known for hiring local staff and who otherwise might not have employable elsewhere. This created a sense of unity and community spirit knowing that the firm cared about their wellbeing. And incidentally, Inga-Lill, owner of the local café, invented the "Dellner Mackan" for the company's workers and the local community. (In the local culture the firm had with affection been nick-named "Mecken" from its original name "Mekaniska Verkstaden" as the place of work.) Even the sandwich is "Integral" i.e., four segments to give a highly nourishing meal. One segment is made with "Gustavskorv", a horse meat sausage and potato salad. Another, with egg, mayonnaise and shrimp. The next has Swedish meatballs with beetroot salad, and the last, is made with cheese and mixed salad. All laid on a large half-round local bread called "siktkaka". All part of a Integral balanced diet indeed. The firm's once colourful nickname has now been replaced with a plain "Dellner". A nick-name is of course a deeply held metaphor that contains meaning and connectivity for all who use it. It's possibly also telling that the nickname has changed from their place of belonging to the label on the wall.

As such, today, I am grateful for this experience as it was a necessary struggle for me to understand myself and others. It contributed to my emancipation and individuation. It has influenced not only my being but also my becoming, knowing and doing and in having a more integrated and balanced approach to money and capital. I hope any residual dark clouds may disperse in time for future generations.

From these experiences, these beliefs and values emerged.

- A healthy and high quality dialectic contains the relational ingredients to solve disagreements; the absence of such a dialectic often creates the disputes in the first place. Money has its own significant shadow and therefore can become both a blessing and a curse.

- Ownership and entitlement must be more than the legal position in order to create integral wealth and wellbeing.

- If money becomes the key ingredient in a relationship, the relationship will soon rear its darker shadows in attitudes and behaviours, deteriorate and become negative for those involved.

- Too much money, as in any imbalance within a system, risks creating a diseased relationship with the self, others, and with money itself.

- Too much money risks robbing the holder of the kind of life experiences necessary for real growth. They may not find true meaning and purpose, which are the source ingredients for our wellbeing and real joy in life.

- At best, the law is an extremely poor substitute for morals, ethics and the capacity for solving issues in family relationships. The axiom of using the law when advantageous for oneself versus not seeking ethical or moral common ground as an operating principle may cost the family a great deal.

Many of these negative effects continue to be played out today between some family members, with the risk of latent conflicts spoiling the next generation. The sadness I feel is mainly around negative family consequences and missed opportunities. As Dag Hammarskjöld reminds us: *Forgiveness is remembering in spite of forgetting.*

Our understanding of the nature of money is paramount and foundational so that we can have a healthy primary relationship with capital and for our Impact awareness.

Of course families also follow some classic psychological dynamics; for example, we often see sibling rivalry played out in different forms. Without trying to use stereotypes, it may be more common for the oldest child to take the role as 'the achiever'. They may base their sense of self on being hard working, moral, clever, very smart or members of an elite clan, and therefore feel superior to others who do not have the same standards and qualities. Siblings may therefore feel inferior as the elder uses competitive comparisons to assert their position and significance in the hierarchy.

As a consequence of feeling superior, it is often difficult for such individuals to feel compassion and empathy, and to forgive those who fall short of the mark. It is not uncommon for positive relational attributes such as trust and honesty to become transactional as trade-offs in the positional power game; therefore, the fear arises of losing their pride in their superiority. For someone who bases his or her self-image on achievement and performance (i.e., outside objectives), a sense of insecurity can prevail leading to the need to diminish and find faults in others to prop up the self. This creates a barrier for their growth and their ability to see the other in a true light. My family story is without absolute truth, only conjecture and myriad complex assumptions and beliefs. As we often find, if there is a truth to be found, it is normally somewhere in the middle.

The good news is that, as circumstances change, everyone adapts and finds new ways to operate. I am grateful for this and my other experiences which have brought me to where I am today, more or less exactly where I want to be. Integrally speaking of course...

The 4 Worlds in Quaternity

Fundamental to integrality is the way we can dynamically expand our awareness. This can only happen inside a contrasting relationship. Even if we were one of the best meditators on the planet, a circular and recursive pattern would soon emerge that would limit the expansion of our awareness and create a boundary over which we could not pass on our own. David Hawkins in his book "Power versus Force" wrote:

> Awareness is the all-encompassing attractor field of unlimited power identical with life itself. And there is nothing the mind believes that isn't erroneous at a higher level of awareness.[32]

Working with impact therefore gives us a unique opportunity and responsibility to develop the capacity of our own mind and soul to include the relational 'other' to benefit all. This exceeds capital, which in effect now acts as the portal towards full-spectrum impact. The psychologist, C.G. Jung succinctly articulates the need for us all to make this connection:

> The Unrelated human being lacks wholeness, for he can achieve wholeness only through the soul and the soul cannot exist without its other side, which is always found in a 'You''. The 'you' in this case points both in the lateral directions towards yourself and the 'other'. 'Wholeness is a combination of I and You, and these show themselves to be parts of a transcendent unity whose nature can only be grasped symbolically[33]

Integral impact investments (I³) is a complete four-worlds approach that aims to map and be the carrying vehicle of the wholeness where we can weave together diverse parts to create archetypical unity. The integral archetype itself is, of course, an evolution from our past knowledge and wisdom. Traditions across the globe with access to historical wisdom can integrate the dislocated parts of ourselves in the search for wholeness, which is often represented in a four-worlds quaternity. C.G. Jung described the quaternity archetype as[34]

> the most useful schemata for representing the arrangement of the functions by which the conscious mind takes its bearings. It is like the crossed threads in the telescope of our understanding

A good example of a quaternity is in medicine, with the four component parts of mind/ psychology, body/physiology, heart/emotions, and soul/consciousness. Modern medicine often assumes these as separate, each with their distinct areas of expertise.

This separation, however, is changing fast with a new and deeper understanding of the mind–body connection moving from a mechanistic approach into the world of quantum physics, which reinforces many traditional ways of healing the whole person. Human beings are made up of highly complex systems and now it is the turn of finance and economics to undergo a similar process via impact investments.

The CEO of Hermes Investment Management, Saker Nusseibeh, puts this succinctly:

> Economics has developed as a science, conveniently forgetting its roots in political philosophy. Unfortunately that 'science' is severely dated, and the functioning of the global capital markets has become separated from the real world. A simple thought experiment throws light on the theoretically correct strategies for a rational saver, but leaves us with unsatisfactory answers. Neglecting the societal context of our saving activity only serves to further isolate the capital markets. Instead, a self-perpetuating system requires investors to evolve from simple allocators of capital to its steward, with far broader responsibilities. Maximising holistic returns represents practical action of the responsibility by investors, and stretches far beyond creating wealth simply for its own sake[35]

Again, we have serious work to do.

A short reminder of our global imperatives

Today, there are several core global Impact imperatives and realms that contain significant amounts of stress. We need to internalize these to make them 'ours', so that we can understand them and then define our contribution. For most, these will be framed inside the ESG acronym which explicitly means:

Environmental It is difficult to deny climate stress and environmental degradation. As one of the core foundational stones for impact investments, the landmark COP21 agreement in Paris witnessed international agreement on limiting global warming to below two degrees Celsius above pre-industrial levels by 2050. Meanwhile, the 17 SDGs established in 2015 build on the success of the Millennium Development Goals established by the UN in 2000 to fight poverty and inequality, and tackle climate change.

Social Our global economy is producing economic inequality and new levels of social deprivation, contrary to the prevailing economic theory that 'all boats float higher with a rising tide'. This has given rise to crime and migration. Hidden parts of the social and community dimension are often disregarded within a firm's mission when firms act as disconnected islands within the broader system in which they operate.

Governance We have many variations of governance and ownership structures that can provide an alternative to the current short-term shareholder. Many Western firms embody a central form of concentrated power. Sometimes this risks developing different levels of egocentric leaders with hubristic tendencies that accentuate organisational demise. Such leadership is becoming increasingly disconnected from real long-term stewardship of firms and its impact potential. We need to be aware of this.

In addition to the 17 SDGs, we also find the following key driver:

Demographics Inter-generational capital stewardship is shifting from paradigms of finance and Internal Rate of Return (IRR) into deeper thinking. This includes broader perspectives about how money is earned and who benefits from it. This includes calling more women towards working in the impact industry because they have a stronger tendency to move towards 'sustainable' investing in comparison to many men.

The good news is that, according to the Global Sustainable Investment Alliance (GSIA), $23 trillion (26%) of all assets under management in 2016 were in 'socially responsible investments' that take account of ESG issues. However, what does 'take account of' mean? And how do we significantly increase this? We will answer these questions more fully in later chapters.

> Herein lies the global knot: The seemingly irreconcilable conflict between and among the haves, they have nots, they have a little but want more, and they have a lot but are never content. There must be a better way

Beck[36]

Short overview of global trends/macro drivers

A GROWING DEBATE ABOUT HOW NEO-LIBERAL capitalism has reached its outer limits and is being replaced by 'post-capitalism'.

THE EMERGING POSSIBILITY that a global paradigm is developing towards collectivism and solidarity and away from individualism and self-centricity. This is predicted as the next stage in human development by Claire Graves (Spiral Dynamics, 2005); and Elias Dawlabani[37].

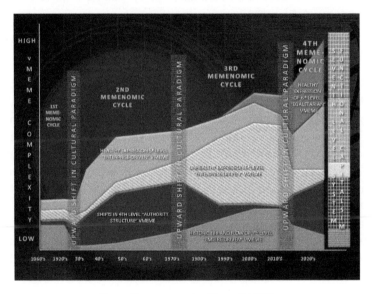

Figure 2: MEMENOMICS (Trans4M [38])

Dawlabani highlights the need for individual and organisational developmental change, suggesting;

> This is the New Frontier of leadership where political and corporate governance must have the tools and the courage to transition the world to the values that recognise the magnificence of existence and what it means to be alive on a planet in peril. (Ibidem)

INFORMATION TECHNOLOGY IS RESHAPING THE WORKPLACE, driven by several organisational micro trends:

- A restructuring around the degree and level of contractual arrangements and obligations and the overall firm/employee relationship.

- Increasing automation blurring the lines between work and free time as people become more available for alternative activities.

- The knowledge economy is morphed into the information economy as knowledge workers become less reliable and necessary as repositories of knowledge in comparison to free on-line availability.

- Alternative forms of collaborative production and services spontaneously sprouting both inside large firms (e.g., 'velcro-teams') as part of their need for innovation and to generate creative strategies, but also in new collaborative formats (e.g., self-managed spaces, the shared economy, etc.).

- Direct innovation that captures these shifts and interjects products that solve new emergent competitive gaps in finance, e.g., alternative currencies, peer-to-peer finance, not-for-profit firms, etc.

- A new market has developed for the storage and diagnostic analysis of socially-produced information as captured by firms in an attempt to create a scarcity model on which to capitalise. As a result, big technology firms attempt to privatise this information and control the data. However, as some of this data can be triangulated and made available, firms are losing their position to price correctly using only market data. As such, this model is likely to be superseded by the already growing information-abundance model, where most data is freely available. Where self-regulation can't keep up with change, restrictions will be imposed by regulators who already seek to limit the monopolisation and abuse by tech giants of such data.

COMPANY VALUATIONS AND MARKET CAPITALISATIONS have moved from tangible assets on balance sheets of circa 80% twenty years ago to circa 10%–20% today. A massive shift is occurring towards intangible valuations such as goodwill, intellectual property, customer and brand values, etc. This creates increasing market correlation risks between intangibles and therefore needs better understanding and strategic work by firms, enabled by a full-spectrum impact approach.

AS SOME INDUSTRIES AND MARKETS reach peak saturation, we see firms reaching for leverage, financial engineering, and merger and acquisitions to drive shareholder value, thus increasing risks.

OVER THE PAST 4-5 DECADES, owners of capital have been well rewarded through returns, unlike labour which, combined with increased inequality, is a core driver behind many of the social conflicts we see today.

In 1962, the economist Kenneth Arrow argued that the purpose of inventing things in a free-market economy was to create intellectual property rights. He noted: 'Precisely to the extent that it is successful there is an underutilisation of information[39]'

Most Western economies are driven by debt. The West is now so enmeshed in the debt spiral that there is no way out. Given the short-term political focus, governments will always be tempted to use debt to pay for current electoral promises and to stay in power.

In addition, debt mortgages the future for present value; it takes expected future value and brings it to the present. This has been helped largely by fixed-asset price inflation on which debt can be secured and leveraged, for example in the housing market. What we forget is that there is actually no real value being created: The house itself does not care if it is worth $100,000 or $1 million because it is still the same house; of course, the people living there care as it gives them the illusion of wealth.

This has driven GDP growth and is why governments in effect have become reliant on House Price Inflation (HPI) for economic growth. However, in many Western countries this has not only led to massive speculation on property values but also crowded out much of the next generation, who no longer can afford to buy houses at current prices. Are there any winners or have we simply playing a game of who can access finance to create HPI today, which needs to paid by the next generation?

Another related mega trend is the ubiquitous low interest rates. We need to differentiate between those who benefit from a low interest rate and those who still pay high levels of cost for capital and who are proportionally worse off than during previous rate cycles. With rate convergence, we continue to fuel the debt spiral. Some are suggesting that this may soon end; if so, given the current global economic conditions and the state of the finance industry, the last financial crisis will seem quite mild in comparison. Another outcome of rate convergence is a lowering of absolute returns and possibly reduced financial return differentiation between managers, which is where impact returns can make a difference.

The development of the I^3 methodology is underpinned by some strong developments that are currently gaining momentum within the investment management industry:

- Realisation that impact does not necessarily mean lower returns.

- Impact when connected to the bottom line makes commercial sense.

- Institutional investors are redesigning their product offerings to include impact.

- Impact is becoming an integral part of most generic risk-management models.

- Addressing new and broader impact risks such as stranded asset risk.

- Increasing fiduciary responsibilities to generate positive SDG impact outcomes.

- Legal and reputational risks are increasing in relation to, and contrast with, to ignorance of impact.

- Increased levels of resources are available, e.g., tools and systems for impact management and measurement. There is global growth of the family office where conscious capital is developing strongly.

- Impact investments are developing as the key growth area within the global investment industry.

- Open source technology is being defined and designed according to individual needs.

- Developing thematic and sectoral approaches that form part of a politically agnostic process across the industy's method, methodology and management model.

Post-modern economics

Current economic thinking (and, as a subset, finance and investment thinking and practise) is based on neoclassical economics epitomized by the Chicago School (Milton Friedman and Eugene Fama). Neoclassicism which has developed since the mid/late 19 Century is rooted in methodological individualism and has five core axioms:

   I. Individuals maximise utility and firms maximise profits.

   II. People act independently on the basis of full and relevant information.

   III. Markets provide the most efficient mechanism to allocate capital and resources.

   IV. Individualism as an agent provides a sufficient incentive for decisions – the 'rational man' [sic] theory.

   V. Equilibrium will emerge as a natural consequence of agents' instrumentally rational preferences and choices, which can be identified and associated with value.

Neoclassicism sees the financial harvest as the only driver and excludes the relationship to social and natural dimensions; it has no developmental axis that recursively helps to correct itself,

> Can we live with a forest in a way that makes it possible for the forest to evolve? To me, that's very different from asking how to harvest the forest appropriately[40]

Neoclassical economics is rooted in David Hume's Treatise of Human Nature (1739) where he famously divided decision making into three distinct modules: Passions, Reason, and Beliefs. Passions provides the core energy for the destination; Reason navigates us along a course that gets us there, drawing upon our created sets of Beliefs.

Hume also wrote that; 'Reason is, and ought only to be, the slave of the passions'. However, this is an incomplete picture for which there are only partial answers but also one which is easily and intellectually understood by cause and effect, which is the only connecting principle our limited intellect can understand in our meaning making. To activate other intelligences, we need an integral framework to dig into our deeper understanding.

Thanks to the influence of behavioural economics, neoclassical economics is evolving to add models in which economic participants are imperfectly informed, frequently irrational (or boundedly rational). As a result, Homo Economicus is slowly evolving to resemble the real human more closely. However, the basis of neoclassical theory retains its roots firmly within liberal individualism.

Another area influencing and driving the discipline of economics today is anthropology, and especially Karl Polanyi's work. Through meticulous fieldwork (often missing in today's economics) he demonstrated that other principles apart from the efficient market-exchange hypothesis and self-interest, such as reciprocity, loyalty and honour, create the glue that bonds the economy together. If society is influenced too much by market exchange, 'counter-movement' resistance develops.

Polanyi's followers today include economists such as Piketty, Varoufakis, Arnsperger, Eisenstein, Daly and Anielski who see economics through a systems lens be it rooted in political, social frameworks or from Nature-based perspectives. The risk, as always, is that any power complex that becomes over-balanced develops a neurosis and arrogance that will justify and manipulate the system to retain its position and interests. Arrogance is one of the outcomes and consequences of the power complex when it sees itself as superior in relation to perceived inferiority,

> Manipulation, like the conquest whose objectives it serves, attempts to anesthetize the people so they will not think. For if the people join to their presence in the historical process critical thinking about that process, the threat of their emergence materializes in revolution... One of the methods of manipulation is to inoculate individuals with the bourgeois appetite for personal success. This manipulation is sometimes carried out directly by the elites and sometimes indirectly, through populist leaders[41]

Mark Anielski, for example, embodies and embraces the increasing importance of the commons which is the cultural and natural resources accessible to all members of a society, including natural materials such as air, water, and our habitable earth. He has developed measurement systems for the well-being of the commons instead of just documenting economic activity, consumption and circulation of money. He has created new measures that focus us on what really matters: happiness and well-being.

Anielski also advocates alternatives to GDP which drive and dictate policies across the globe.

It is not too late

In 1968, Robert Kennedy campaigning for the US presidency, delivered a now-famous speech at the University of Kansas in which he said:

> (…) even if we act to erase material poverty, there is another greater task, it is to confront the poverty of satisfaction — purpose and dignity — that afflicts us all.

Why haven't we progressed since then? Old paradigms die hard and are difficult to shift. Investments being a prime driver and critical inflexion point of economic activity, one cannot underestimate the importance impact has as a catalyst to shift change perceptions in all areas of our society.

The banking and finance industry has been searching for some answers from its history, and is embracing the works of Peter Drucker. Drucker's thinking around moral codes and culture as the main success factors in any business has recently been resurrected as a potential key to unlocking the lack of understanding of the interlocking components of the organisation (e.g., economic, social and human, cultural, etc.) on which understanding a restitution and repair mechanisms can be built[42]. This, in my opinion, is due to the fragmented management approach we often encounter which a more integral management framework would alleviate.

Don Beck, in his audio version[43] of the book 'Spiral Dynamics' re-framed Gandhi's quote, 'Be the change you want to see in the world' into 'Do the change that others need done for them.' This suggests that if we take a deeper perspective on how we operate, our contribution will always include the self and the other. The more levels of consciousness and psychological flexibility we can generate within a specific context, the more effective and loving the contribution will be towards creating the impact we desire.

This not only refers to 'ways of knowing' but also the 'hows of knowing' that include formats of sub-conscious signalling and subliminal interconnect-edness. W. Edward Deming through his 'System of Profound Knowledge' clearly advocates that management needs to look at organisations more holistically and examine the evolutionary aspect of development and the understanding of human motivations from a psychological perspective. This is lacking in many organisations based on post-modern economic principles.

Social and environmental stresses are also redefining risk management by introducing not only new risks (such as with stranded assets) but also the risk of systemic collapse in some correlated areas, in combination with slow GDP growth, resulting in what is called the 'Seneca effect'.

Its essence is found in a line written by the ancient Roman Stoic philosopher Lucius Annaeus Seneca: 'Fortune is of sluggish growth, but ruin is rapid'. This sentence summarises the features of the phenomenon that we call 'collapse', which is typically unexpected and sudden, like the proverbial 'house of cards' effect. But why are such collapses relatively common, and what precipitates them?

Several books have been published on the subject, including The Collapse of Complex Societies by Joseph Tainter (1998), The Tipping Point, by Malcom Gladwell (2000), and Collapse by Jared Diamond (2005). Collapse is a collective phenomenon that occurs in 'complex systems,' with a special emphasis on fractures and chaos in system dynamics and the concept of 'feedback' leading to the collapse of structures such as the financial system, famines and population collapse, the fall of civilisations and, the most important of our age, the risk of collapse of our ecosystem from overexploitation and climate change.

Motivation and reward

Let us look at one of the core myths in many industries around motivation and reward, namely that higher pay inevitably produces, and is correlated to, better performance.

> In eight of the nine tasks we examined across the *three experiments, higher incentives led to worse performance* (authors highlight)[44]

The London School of Economics investigated fifty-one pay for performance plans across industries, and concluded: 'We find that financial incentives ... can result in a negative impact on overall performance'[45].

A possible psychological explanation is that if we feel guilt and shame for the rewards we receive, subconsciously we are likely to manipulate the situation/result so that we become 'worthy', even if this means lowered performance; this is also known as the 'self-sabotage mechanism'.

Based on my conversations with friends in the finance industry, many people work almost exclusively for financial rewards but would do something different and more meaningful if they were given a valid choice. This represents a major challenge over the next few years as new recruits enter the system, and this is where working with impact frameworks will make a difference.

From my experience in banking, I would argue that many firms have a poor working culture so that employees believe that they need a premium to feel motivated. Many such firms unknowingly also induce an internal fear-based culture through their operating procedures. Also, it is clear that a fear-based culture is a major contributor to the self-protective behaviour of attempting to maximise short-term personal gains (from money and prestige) without considering the overall extent and effect of one's actions (i.e., in contrast to the search for true and real impact).

Most financial firms operate without deeper understanding of their culture and, as such, do not have a compass to direct their development. However, there are many significant economic business reasons for working strategically with culture. For example, technical synergies in M&A activities are often severely depleted due to lack of mapping of the cultural fit. Given recent M&A activity in the banking industry, this is a key area where the levels of cultural integration drive ultimate shareholder value; therefore, this is a prime commercial reason for leaders to embrace and manage cultural development.

Understanding prevailing culture is key in the ongoing compensation debate. Firms need to develop new strategies for external drivers such as bonuses, titles, etc. Many firms have yet to work with their culture to fully develop both personal intrinsic and extrinsic motivational drivers. Motivation is dualistic in that it derives from either an internal (intrinsic) or an external (extrinsic) source, or both. Examples from Professor Reiss's work[46] suggest such sources of intrinsic motivations including power, order and acceptance.

Thus, it is the leader/manager who dominates the cultural integrity of the organisation. As such, it is the leader/manager that mainly represents the interface with the firm and its cultural stand. This implies that it is the leader/manager's neurological patterns and character that mainly define how employees interpret and connect with the organisation. Witness the adage: 'the relationship with one's supervisor (is) a lens through which the entire work experience is viewed'[47]. Once again this requires us to step into uncharted territory from our limited perspectives.

There are several aspects of leadership that comport with the objectives of this book.

- Leadership misalignments and conflicts of interest: Western governance structures and modes of compensation should include influences (and be open to alternatives) from, for example, Islamic and Buddhist finance.

- Incumbent leadership resists change, which creates ossified organisational structures and paradigms: Some firms have stagnated because of historical and archaic ownership structures when modernity and shifts in the organisation require change that has not been recognised (e.g., from patriarchal to collaborative, cooperative forms).

- The need for political and power relations to be uncovered: Most firms suffer from emotional abuse in various forms, including the silencing of stakeholders through dominance in equity. This is prevalent in many family firms where concentrated power exists.

- The social constructs and relationships between capital, debt and interest: For example, what are the visible social contracts such as in compensation policies, and under which economic paradigm, have they been constructed?

In this vein, to uncover and research the deactivating and development necessary for true liberation for oppressed employees to become activated each I^3 engagement is, in effect, a mini-critical-theory research project to understand the investee firm's economic and social constructs, contracts, and operational culture.

A New Era?

Libertarian action must recognise this dependence as a weak point and must attempt through reflection and action to transform it into independence. However, not even the best intentioned leadership can bestow independence as a gift. The liberation of the oppressed is a liberation of women and men, not things. Accordingly, while no one liberates himself by his own efforts alone, neither is he liberated by others. Liberation, a human phenomenon, cannot be achieved by semi humans. Any attempt to treat people as semi humans only dehumanizes them.[48]

It is therefore critical for each investment firm to become the 'libertarian' by understanding their role for transformational capital as part of a liberation of the people involved and not just of things. In this book, I will not cover the myriad psychodynamic relationships where emancipatory processes may be required (e.g., male/ female; victim/persecutor, etc.) through any I^3 process; but they exist at a deeper level if we look closer.

Andrea Jung[2], 36 the former CEO of Avon, current CEO of Grameen America and campaigner for women's rights, suggests that there is an obvious correlation between an economically empowered woman and the investments she makes.

---

[2]No relation to C.G. Jung

This helps drive her social and moral conscience and aims for bettering her community. At the organisational level, this translates into boss/subordinate and involves all the unfulfilled needs for nurturing and empowerment that we seek inside organisations and their many transient and enforced relationships.

At the deepest unconscious levels, these needs resonate with our family and social history. Consequently, it is what we have neglected to empower within ourselves that we seek in the outer world, only to become enslaved to our projects and our projections.

This key aspect validates and reinforces the way we interpret our world that includes the unconscious.

Importantly, it also establishes and reinforces the relationship between traditional emancipatory aspect of slavery and links to our variant of contemporary corporate enslavement.

Chomsky puts it this way:

> The principle that human nature, in its psychological aspects, is nothing more than a product of history and given social relations removes all barriers to coercion and manipulation by the powerful[49].

As the Western-dominated paradigm equates money with power, investment firms need to be cognisant of their position and capacity to inadvertently manipulate management into outcome objectives that have no emancipatory grounding and will, if anything, only reinforce the power structure.

A core driver for change is that the current financial system has reached its capacity to deliver genuine growth and well-being.

Impact, by definition, asks much bigger questions that require us to attend to our capacities in new dimensions; in my opinion, we also need to question our attitudes, relationship and attachment to conventional dogmas which have the money-power system at their center.

This might conflict between one's beliefs and necessities for life, so for most, the questions will never be investigated.

Some have taken a strong position, such as the American journalist and social activist Dorothy Day (1897–1980) who argued:

> We need to change the system. We need to overthrow, not the government, (...) but this rotten, decadent, putrid industrial capitalist system which breeds such suffering...[50]

If impact investments are to become a solution for the world going forward, we collectively need to include a bigger 'other'.

The foundation of political economy and, in general, of every social science, is evidently psychology. A day may come when we shall be able to deduce the laws of social science from the principles of psychology[51].

This, as we know today, is also the core driver behind many of our conflicts, inequality and system stress.

The philosopher Bernard Stiegler argues that the global economic and consumerist model is now highly toxic, and has potentially reached its outer limits of function. He suggests that those denying this want to secure the benefits as long as they can[52].

If so, at the collective level most current and traditional investment philosophy relates to a profit maximisation and continuation of the status quo.

The impetus of the emergent impact stems from the awareness that we must collectively find a new approach and better ways to invest that benefit both people and the planet.

To this discourse, we now also add the political conflict that exists in our minds between the two main hemispheres of the brain.

The left and right sides of the brain have significant differences in types and processing capacity; there is actually a political map working inside trying to reconcile these differences.

For most of our organisations, which tend to be highly left-brain dominated, this is an additional challenge because many of them have devalued, toned-down and detached right brain intelligence such as intuition and imagination.

We create conflict, become polarised and narrow-minded and close down opportunities for resolution in order to protect the ego and to prove ourselves right. However, for impact we need these sides of the brain to be more fully connected to avoid political infighting. As Albert Schweitzer said in 1959,

> Three kinds of progress are significant for culture: progress in knowledge and technology; progress in the socialisation of man; progress in spirituality. The last is the most important. Technical progress, extension of knowledge, does indeed represent progress, but not in fundamentals. The essential thing is that we become more finely and deeply human[53]

Charles Eisenstein in 'Sacred Economics'[16] (pp. 27–28, and pp. 425–426) confirms the linkages:

> Part of the healing that a sacred economy represents is the healing of the divide we have created between spirit and matter. In keeping with the sacredness of all things, I advocate an embrace, not an eschewing, of materialism. I think we will

love our things more and not less. We will treasure our material possessions, honour where they came from and where they will go (…) The cheapness of our things is part of their devaluation, casting us into a cheap world where everything is generic and expendable (…) Put succinctly, the essential need that goes unmet today, the fundamental need that takes a thousand forms, is the need for the sacred—the experience of uniqueness and connectedness (…) We are starving for a life that is personal, connected, and meaningful.

The need for further integrality

The above quote summarises the fundamental need for impact investments and the developmental axis for the integration of a deeper four-worlds journey. Lessem and Schieffer argue that to build a paradigm-shifting approach for transforming self, organisation, community, and society, we must alleviate imbalances whilst aiming to enhance a sense of calling, belonging and rootedness (local identity) with a view to catalyse a meaningful, wholesome contribution to humanity (global integrity).

Integral Worlds is modelled on natural principles and on life itself. It aspires to heal today's fragmented, conflictual and often destructive individual, organisational, communal, and societal ways of being. It holds a vital key to the necessary (and imminent) shift of global consciousness towards a more healthy, holistic, peaceful, participatory, conscious and co-creative approach to development in tune with the whole of creation.

Integral Worlds initiates processes of healing and holistic realignment by activating all complementary parts of any human system: nature and community; culture and consciousness; science, systems and technology; as well as enterprise, economics, and politics. The continuous focal point of any transformation process within an Integral Worlds' perspective is the inner core of the individual or collective entity, its deepest value base, spiritual and moral source leading to serving ourselves and our expanded others.

Real transformation has less to do with intelligence, willpower or seeking perfection, and more with finding honesty, integrity, humility, willingness, and surrender. To the extent we can evolve into servant leadership in impact, grounded and rooted in our calling, culture and the soils of our community, this will form part of our emancipation and individuation process:

> Individuation is a process informed by the archetypal ideal of wholeness, which in turn depends on a vital relationship between ego and unconscious. The aim is not to overcome one's personal psychology, to become perfect, but to become familiar with it. Thus, individuation involves an increasing awareness of one's unique psychological reality, including personal strengths and limitations, and at the same time a deeper appreciation of humanity in general[54]

The underlying circular design of the above central model acknowledges that, since time immemorial, the circular shape has been a symbol for the totality of life. It also symbolises the cycle of life that each living system undergoes.

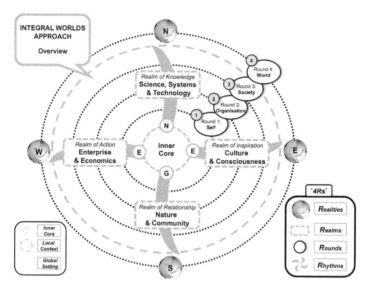

Figure 3: Integral Worlds Approach (Trans4M [38])

The Story of a Circle
A circle expands forever; it covers all who wish to hold hands.
And its size depends on each other, it is a vision of solidarity.
It turns outwards to interact with the outside and inward for self-critique.
A circle expands forever; it is a vision of accountability.
It grows as the other is moved to grow. A circle must have a centre.
But a single dot does not make a circle; one tree does not make a forest.
A circle, a vision of cooperation, mutuality and care

In Integral Worlds, the outer globe marks a worldly, holistic perspective. Embedded in the outer global circle is the local context. At the very centre of such a globally embedded context is the 'inner core'. It is here, at the core of an individual, organisation, community or society, that the impulse for transformation or development is initiated — be it through a perceived imbalance of the overall system, which becomes our objective concern, or through a particular, subjective evolutionary calling.

This inner personal core and the outer global circle are connected through the '4Rs' of Integral Worlds: Realities (world views), Realms (knowledge fields), Rounds (different levels, from self to world), and Rhythms (transformative rhythms that apply to all of them). These main themes and core values inform the integral journey.

We use the cardinal directional points of South, East, North and West as

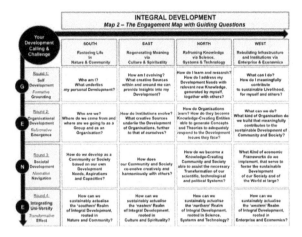

Figure 4: Integral Development: Map 2 (Trans4M [38])

holding vessels and containers for what is inside each realm of the integral approach.

SOUTHERN REALITY AND REALM OF RELATIONSHIP

Main theme: Restoring life in nature and community

Core value: Healthy and participatory co-existence

EASTERN REALITY AND REALM OF INSPIRATION

Main theme: Regenerating meaning via culture and spirituality

Core value: Balanced and peaceful co-evolution

NORTHERN REALITY AND REALM OF KNOWLEDGE

Main theme: Reframing knowledge via science, systems and technology

Core value: Open and transparent knowledge creation

WESTERN REALITY AND REALM OF ACTION

Main theme: Rebuilding infrastructure and institutions via enterprise and economics

Core value: Equitable and sustainable livelihoods

This can only be achieved if we work and engage integrally, i.e., with and inside all the four dimensions of integral development as shown in figure 4.

Below, in figure 5, we show the integral development map with its sixteen fields, presenting the major developmental task in each field. This map introduces the core challenges of the full integral development journey — challenges which can be addressed holistically with the help of integral development theory.

---

[2]Lessem and Schieffer (2014, p. 130).

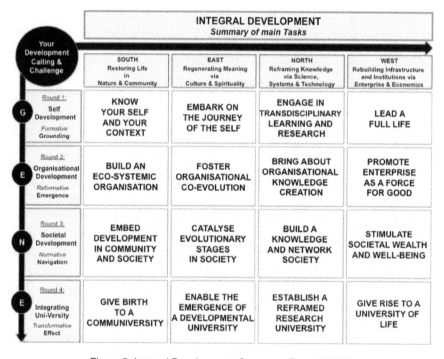

Figure 5: Integral Development: Summary (Trans4M [38])

What are Integral Impact Investments (I^3)?

Taking our cue from the above, we can see how this approach is applicable to impact investments and how I^3 originated from working through the four worlds. I^3 is not the answer to impact investments – you and your firm are. As such, I^3 is a map-making journey through the integral lens where each of us will need to find answers that work within our own context. I^3 is not a thing or product, it is more of a dynamic roadmap and lens. Like any puzzle, all the pieces eventually will fit together to make a whole, but unlike a ready-bought puzzle, the final picture has to be made, with its outer boundaries created, by you.

Only by rooting ourselves in our own being (and what we hope to become) can we develop our knowing that leads to our doing. We need to make our own impact approach using a structured approach for its development. As we will discover, a whole picture/puzzle/ map is constructed of both metaphor and philosophy grounded in how we see the world. This informs and guides our emerging methodology, which in turns creates and navigates our method.

Only then do we have the foundation building blocks that can make up our emergent model. In this way, the integral approach differs from conventional impact in that we incorporate the developmental requirements that actually drive any sustainable impact outcomes.

I^3 also integrates impact outcome objectives as part of an investee firm's strategy and culture, something that is absent in most impact approaches. Current, conventional impact approaches are heavily biased towards internal methods and models of the investor. This not only ignores many of the fundamental drivers but also excludes any possible dynamic with the investee, which I would argue is one of the most important aspects of impact investments.

I^3 is a cybernetic system four-worlds approach to investment that allows an investor to see the full-spectrum of imperatives and dimensions of an investment, whilst allowing each investor to view what is truly important in terms of impact outcomes.

Essentially, it is a map on which we can draw our own four-worlds impact intentionality and outcome objectives as we see them, centred on our purpose, driven by our values, and only limited by our own awareness. Even purpose itself is being reframed by one on the world's largest investment firms, Blackrock 'Ultimately, purpose is the engine of long- term profitability.' Larry Fink, Black Rock CEO letter to investment world.

We will look at many of these aspects in much more depth. In the depiction below, we see the four-foldness and its circular dynamic as we travel inexorably through its dimensions, whether we are consciously aware of it or not.

As we will see, the current state of affairs of our impact is exactly where we need to be. In many ways it is fine. However, much of it has been born of our current thinking and prioritisation around investments in general. Global environmental and social imperatives need to be developed further to address more fully the global changes in which impact has a major – if not pivotal – role to play. For impact to become mainstream in the future in the fullest sense of the word, in my opinion it needs to evolve further. I3 in this book highlights some of the challenges, imperatives, and the general trajectory of travel for those who understand this emergent developmental axis.

If and when we ever reach Impact 4.0, we will find the above dimensions fully integrated into all investment decisions through our methods, methodology, models, and protocols. We will have understood that our expanded investment metaphor applies to all investments as shown in figure 7.

These dynamics create four interactive and individual paths. They start with a grounding in our Southern and relational domain. This is followed by the Eastern path of renewal, in which the authentic self emerges. After that, we create the conditions to incorporate and synthesise the Northern path of our reasoning, which now directs our ongoing journey. We then have built the toolbox where we can affect, and more fully actualise ourselves, on the Western side of the path of realisation.

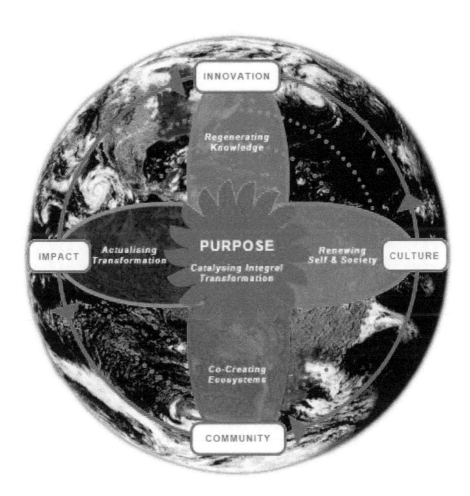

Figure 6: Culture, Community, Impact, Innovation (Trans4M [38])

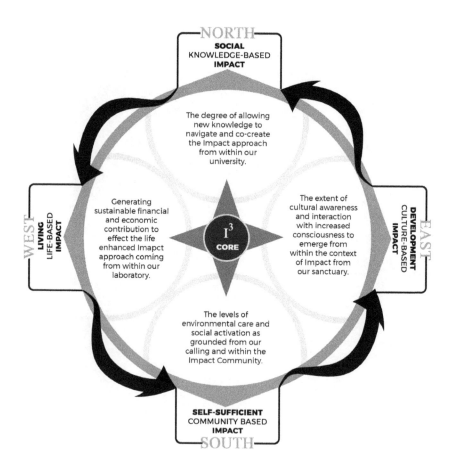

Figure 7: I³ Core

PART I

Changing
yourself

Chapter 1

Impact as a transformational journey into our calling

> God does not change people's lot until they first change what's in their own hearts.
>
> _____
>
> The Qur'ān (13:11)

Throughout my career, I have integrated learning and development (L&D). It was during 2005, whilst delivering the twenty-day flagship programme 'Deepening the relationship' at the (then) Fortis bank, that I got into a discussion with their CEO, Angus McLennan, about how banks needed to synthesise outside learning and development with inside change and alignment.

On the initiative of Angus, an enlightened and highly competent leader, to effect these changes we founded the 'client solutions group' by absorbing the structured finance area as an agent for business transformation while working closely with clients. A main reason why L&D in isolation does not necessarily deliver value is the misalignment between outside leadership messages and the inside operational culture. As Peter Drucker once said, *Culture eats strategy for breakfast*[55].

At the time I was immersing myself deeply within culture and its multiple manifestations to deliver client solutions from both a technical and relationship perspective. It became evident that there was a contradictory toxic culture within the industry in general, which could not be ignored.

During the financial crisis in 2009 and following the merger between Fortis and my former firm, BNPParibas, I decided to leave the firm to study psychology and to integrate this with my understanding of finance and economics. I was much more interested in personal human development in practise, and given my preference for a pragmatic approach to change and education, I decided to train as a psychotherapist. Importantly, this incorporates both theory and practise to affect change.

Shortly after enrolling at the Institute of Contemporary Psychotherapy, I had a discussion with Hector Sants, then the CEO of the UK industry regulator the Financial Services Authority (FSA). We discussed organisational culture and its possible role in causing the financial crisis. It was apparent that the

FSA was seeking further input on the subject, so we agreed that I would write a succinct consultation paper for him. I delivered this in May 2010 with some follow-up discussions. When Hector subsequently made his 'crossing the Rubicon' speech at the Chartered Institute of Securities and Investments Conference on 17 June 2010, he stated:

> As we have already identified, a deficient culture can play a role in, if not causing, certainly exacerbating market failures which generate inappropriate decision-making[1].

A much greater challenge following the financial crisis has been to affect positive culture change in banking. For a number of years, I had the opportunity to converse with several CEOs of some of the large global investment banks. When questioned on the subject of culture, it was apparent that much of the work done in this area lacked integrity. There were 'tick-box' exercises, with perhaps an ethics course added to the curriculum; as such, no visible change has seemingly occurred to date and much of the business continues 'as usual'.

This was a major reason for embarking on my psychotherapy program; I wanted to seek ways to heal the schism and separation in finance culture between money and consciousness through e.g., impact investments in contrast to banking as it already contains a higher level of consciousness and often has less separation e.g., in a family office between capital and consciousness. The question is whether using a deeper Impact methodology such as I^3, we can weave ethics into an investment system almost 'by stealth' within an existing working environment. As Sir Isaiah Berlin suggests[56]:

> Ethical thought consists of the systematic examination of the relations of human beings to each other, the conceptions, interests and ideals from which human ways of treating each other spring, and the systems of value on which such ends of life are based

One of the cultural axioms in finance is the emotional connectivity (or lack thereof) between 'cause and effect' and our responsibility for this.

In finance there is always a power distance between the investor and the investee, which needs to be managed. Depending on our organisation and our influence, we may feel more or less empowered and responsible for actions and impact outcomes.

As we have all experienced, particularly in large organisations, success has many owners but failures have very few. We find that in a fear-based

---

[1]Transcript available from the Financial Conduct Authority (FCA)

culture few want to understand effects because the risk of being associated with negative effects and consequences may impact their career.

This is an important axiom to understand within our own culture as impact, by definition, is about outcomes and effects. If we only operate within a conventional culture, dialectic and behaviour, we will not learn.

It takes an enlightened leader to build a culture where a full-spectrum impact approach is allowed to be created organically. Again, within governance we need to ensure that our messaging is reinforced by fully-aligned policies and procedures to create more of a virtuous circle.

Importantly, as impact contains the 'other' in as much fullness that we can muster, if our management is to provide some form of democratic representation to our usually hidden 'other', in what form and format is our governance system and culture willing to allow this 'other' to join us? How, and by whom, are 'the others' represented when we define and design our impact outcome objectives?

Do we have the level of awareness to carry and develop this responsibility in our ways of operating and conducting ourselves? We quickly see how onerous this may become; consequently, many firms will 'not even go there' unless we have an integrated framework on which we can weave our impact tapestry.

Whilst many of us swim within the myth streams of our own ego-inflated self-image, we need to find ways to integrate the shadow sides of ourselves with our true self and light. This, as in all things, is integral when we try to make whole of what previously were parts.

It is not an either/or, it is a both/and. We are both the shadow and the light; the key to integrate is to find out how we can best manage to be both at the same time.

§1.1 How we grow: renewing self and society through working with impact

> Each man had only one genuine vocation — to find the way to himself... His task was to discover his own destiny — not an arbitrary one — and live it out wholly and resolutely within himself. Everything else was only a would-be existence, an attempt at evasion, a flight back to the ideals of the masses, conformity and fear of one's own inwardness
>
> Herman Hesse[57]

As we know, personal growth and character development are irregular and non- linear functions of our capacities for creating awareness and our ability to take responsibility, all of which need to be activated within a context. Our character is a part of our directional compass in life; as such, it is an integral source of our power and guidance without which we will lose our bearings and freedom.

This is not an intellectual exercise; no one has studied the nature of life itself, only its images and consequences as they are manifested. As yet, we have not developed adequate mathematics to understand it. Linear differential equations have brought us to approximations of the nature of life but not to the essence, which can only be experienced.

This is a movement that can only come from our inside self, and it is about taking personal leadership to enable leadership of others. Remember that we can only mirror and give to any other that which we have established for ourselves. In leadership, primary greatness is character; secondary greatness is our position, whether in our organisation or in our perceived status.

We need to understand that real power is an inside-out job and comes from working on ourselves from the bottom-up, a task which cannot be skirted. This is the opposite of our prevailing culture and conflicts with how many people think.

As a result, many people will never experience the reality of true and integral leadership power, or can create a life based on a deeper awareness of self.

An emotionally immature person will tend to borrow strength from position, experience, intellect, size or negative emotions to make up for a character imbalance. Whilst awareness and responsibility are foundational, we need to understand that their ingredients come from different sources.

Awareness is sourced from both knowledge and experience, and responsibility is a function of the shape of our character, requiring both to be worked and assessed by ourselves.

The world today is full of awareness but lacking in responsibility, which is why we find the corporate world littered with examples of character failure causing corporate demise.

It reminds me of the characteristics of trust as outlined in Stephen Covey's book *The Speed of Trust*, where he delves into the two components that comprise the core components of trust: Character and Competence.

Forbes contributor Mike Myatt (2012) suggests there are fifteen common reasons for business failure, the first being 'lack of character'. If true, these reasons need to be on the risk register and part of our impact analysis. Whilst character is fundamental, our nature and the depth of our relationships also reflect our character, which is why from our integral perspective we need to start here.

From here we can move into the other realms of Being, Becoming, Knowing and Doing (South, East, North, and West). If we can develop and integrate these from within our emergent four-worlds perspective, this will lead and determine our impact contribution for society. Key to this is our humble understanding that we are born incomplete and need transformational processes for fulfilment. It is our grounded *Being* that guides our emergent *Becoming*, which in turn seeks, captures and navigates our *Knowing*, without which there cannot be any intentional effect and *Doing* that carries sustained impact value.

These are the realms and rounds of our deepening understanding which all need to be communicating with one another, find harmony and balance. Impact investment management should not be only a philosophy or a series of academic exercises. Yes, philosophy and academic exercises are important, but they are stepping stones leading into our impact architecture, which can only be synthesised in our 'doing' before we return for the next deepening circular rhythm back into our now expanded and more deeply grounded "being". These stages are context and outcome dependent.

Donald Robertson tells us:

> The ancients conceived of the ideal philosopher as a veritable warrior of the mind, a spiritual hero akin to Hercules himself, but since the demise of the Hellenistic schools, the philosopher has become something more bookish, not a warrior, but a mere librarian of the mind[58]

Theory and knowledge are part of the building block of philosophy, which we move into practise for the more advanced work of synthesis between the four-worlds, oscillating between our inner and outer worlds. This work

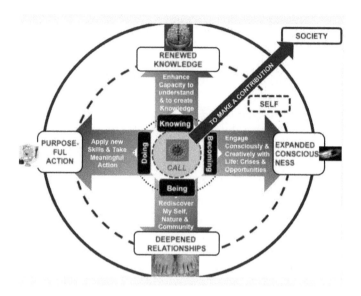

Figure 1.1: Doing, Knowing, Becoming, Being [38]

of the self includes embracing our shadow elements that have been created through culture and ego throughout our life stages.

The Jungian analyst Robert A. Johnson (1921–2018) stated this clearly:

> We are all born whole and, let us hope, will die whole. But somewhere early on our way, we eat one of the wonderful fruits of the tree of knowledge, things separate into good and evil, and we begin the shadow-making process: we divide our lives. In the cultural process we sort out our God-given characteristics into those that are acceptable to society and those that have to be put away.

> This is wonderful and necessary, and there would be no civilized behaviour without this sorting out of good and evil. But the refused and unacceptable characteristics do not go away; they only collect in the dark corners of our personality. When they have been hidden long enough, they take on a life of their own—the shadow life...The shadow is that which has not entered adequately into consciousness.

> It is the despised quarter of our being. It often has an energy potential nearly as great as that of our ego. If it accumulates more energy than our ego, it erupts as an overpowering rage or some indiscretion or an accident that seems to have its own purpose[59]

The issue is that the more comfort, lack of challenge, stuck identity, and positions we have to protect, the more likely we are to have our pride dominate opportunities for our growth, individuation, and emancipation.

Johnson provides further insight for the implication for our impact journey and life:

> Generally, the first half of life is devoted to the cultural process—gaining one's skills, raising a family, disciplining one's self in a hundred different ways; the second half of life is devoted to restoring the wholeness (making holy) of life. One might complain that this is a senseless round trip except that the wholeness at the end is conscious while it was unconscious and childlike at the beginning. (Ibidem, p.10)

In our youth we have a significant need for finding our autonomy, while valuing freedom of expression in search for our creativity. This freedom is often challenged and compromised when we enter organisational structures. Finding personal and individual freedom while remaining inside structural boxes is very difficult. Whilst inside, we are often reluctant, unable or unwilling to critique those very structures which cover our basic income needs, give us a sense of security, status and identity. Their internal culture determines what we can and cannot say, and even shapes what we can or cannot think. We may often feel our organisation is beyond any honest critique, and as a result we are unwilling to jeopardise our career path and prospects if we engage in anything that could been seen as countercultural. In entering organisations, this individual realisation causes a split in our personality with one part now compliant to conform to meet basic needs until such times when the split is too large to hold together and we feel compelled to change course.

Psychologist Stanley Milgram (1933–1984) provides a succinct summary for the effects of a misdirected culture:

> Ordinary people, simply doing their jobs, and without any particular hostility on their part, can become agents in a terrible destructive process. Moreover, even when the destructive effects of their work become patently clear, and they are asked to carry out actions incompatible with fundamental standards of morality, relatively few people have the resources needed to resist authority[60]

It is more often in the second part of life (and not just chronologically) when through our deepening maturity and consciousness we have the opportunity to work and integrate our shadows. We have to de-colonise our minds and hearts, as we all live downstream from causes created by others. We are not necessarily here just to help but if we can allow our impact work to join and become connected to others on our journey of emancipation, we cannot not grow.

Here is a shadow work practise, as taught by leadership coach Scott Jeffrey, for you to reflect on:

Remember that the shadow is elusive; it hides behind us. We each have hosts of defence mechanisms designed to keep our shadows repressed and out of view. Shining the light of consciousness on the shadow takes a little effort and regular practise. The more you pay attention to your behaviour and attitudes, the better chance you have of catching your shadow in the act. One of the best ways to identify your shadow is to pay attention to your emotional reactions toward other people. We tend to project our disowned parts onto other people. Sure, your colleagues might be aggressive, arrogant, inconsiderate, or impatient, but if you don't have those same qualities within you, you won't have a strong reaction to their behaviour or the conditions in their personality. Whatever bothers you in another is likely a disowned part within yourself. Get to know that part, accept it, make it a part of you, and next time, it may not evoke a strong emotional charge when you observe it in another.[61]

If growth at work is a main part of the journey, then impact is core — or at the very least must become a significant part of the story. As Walter Randall wrote: *No struggle, no story, no trouble, no tale, no ill, no thrill, no agony, no adventure*[62]. Our struggles in life create our essence and make life and us interesting participants in the process.

This highlights the oscillating nature of how our respective narratives are created. In most traditions, including our own, initiation rites marked the entry into adulthood, and many have now been lost. These have profound psychological and developmental benefits in how we let go of the old and embrace the new parts of ourselves as we move towards maturity and possible individuation. Jung confirms that; *The goal of the individuation process is the synthesis of the self.*

In his book *A Hero with a Thousand Faces*, Joseph Campbell outlined 'the hero's journey', which he termed 'the monomyth'. This quest has been adopted in many areas, including the film *Star Wars*, on which Campbell advised the director George Lucas. Campbell uncovered this journey whilst studying civilisations; he found that they all had a form of archetypical initiation, stemming from our psyche and deepest needs: *Each carries within himself the all (…) therefore it may be sought and discovered within.*'

The journey takes the shape seen in figure 1.2.

This is both an experiential journey and an existential journey in order to find sufficient courage for a clear calling to be tested and forged within the furnace of doubt. He said that *The cave you fear to enter holds the treasure you seek.* Only then can we move into a co-creative space where challenges, trials and tribulations shape the path ahead. If we survive this stage, we find ourselves at the depths of our idea of hell, confronting our innermost fears and shadows in preparation for our ordeal before we start the return journey

THE HERO'S JOURNEY

Figure 1.2: The hero's journey

with a new identity and place. The ultimate reward is the treasure at the journey's end: finding our true and essential nature.

Campbell asserted that:

> to realise that one is that essence; then one is free to wander as the essence in the world. Furthermore, the world too is of that essence. The essence of oneself and the essence of the world: these two are one[63].

This primordial archetype operates strongly, especially in men, which is why men find such stories highly attractive. However, whilst we cannot all be Luke Skywalker in *Star Wars*, we can use our impact context to lay a path for our own hero's journey. As the poet, Antonio Machado said: *Wanderer, there is no path. You lay a path by walking.*

Sometimes we may feel despondent and lethargic, which is why our calling has to be strong initially. Interestingly, the word 'lethargic' means a state of prolonged torpor or inactivity, inertness of body or mind; the word comes from the medieval Latin *litargia* and from the late Latin *lethargia*. The Greek word *lethargia* actually means 'forgetfulness'; its roots go back to Greek mythology where Lethe was the name of a river in the underworld, also known as 'the River of Unmindfulness' or 'the River of Forgetfulness.' Legend held that when someone died, he/she was given a drink of water from the River Lethe to forget all about his/her past life. Eventually this act of forgetting came to be associated with feelings of sluggishness, inactivity or indifference.

Drinking such waters may appear attractive at times, given our trials and tribulations, but if we do, we may forget the natural order of being on our impact journey and our collective calling, which is key to our becoming. So-called miracles are not so much violations of the natural order but a restoration of the natural order of things when being is allowed free access to becoming. So-called evil is not overcome by attack or even avoidance, but by union at a higher level. It is overcome not by fight, flight or freeze but rather by fusion or flow.

Whilst the hero's journey is universal, there are significant cultural influences which transcend into organisations. Without wishing to generalise, in many Asian cultures such as Japan, roles are identified differently. In Western culture you fight against some evil as you search for truth and love, and the hero is an all-conquering and self-made individual. In Asia, it is the person who collaborates and sacrifices him or herself for others who becomes the hero, since the individual's prime responsibility lies in taking care of the family, community, and the country.

This difference can be seen in the Japanese, Chinese and Korean form of storytelling known as *Kishōtenketsu*, which comes with four acts. In act one (*Ki*), we are introduced to the characters. In act two (*shō*), the actions follow. In act three (*ten*), a twist that is highly surprising or apparently unconnected takes place. In the final fourth act (*kets*), the audience is invited in an open-ended way to search and find harmony and answers – these narratives have no prescribed ending. Is not this approach more like real life, which has much unexpected change? Is it not more realistic as we construct our own integral approach in the search for the harmony and balance between life's conflicting parts?

This contrasts with the conventional Western approach, which often seeks to find simple, linear solutions to unexpected change, to impose static controls, and go to war with the offending parts they believe they now understand. In the East, seeking harmony in these parts is an element of the joy in finding the answer that provides the organic and most appropriate solution.

This subtle difference has profound implications in organisations in how governance is structured, how meetings are managed and how they value and reward their definitions of success. As any impact approach is formed inside an organisation through such processes, its culture will determine the width and depth of its impact lens. This is one of the reasons why there is such a challenge for large, established financial investment firms and their management hierarchies to develop anything that resembles a real impact approach. Large firms will tend to revert to the Western mode of operation, thereby missing the core aim of impact which is to alleviate imbalances and create harmony.

Often in large firms, individuals who have the greatest talent and capacity for impact will be seen superficially by management as not fitting the performance culture. The humble are seen as weak; those who challenge the status quo are seen as obstinate, and those who seek to add depth and breadth to the narrow dialectic are seen as trouble makers. As a result, and as a reaction when the modus operandi is challenged with change, the incumbent management closes ranks and seeks to re-impose and re-enforce order through control and by limiting the individuals concerned.

I have seen and experienced various aspects of this style of management throughout my career within large organisations. Sometimes it emanated from a collective management team but more often it came from a senior manager who needed to hold power through control; this culture then cascaded down to lower management levels.

I would like to end this section using Gandhi's oft-quoted seven social blunders 7 since they provide a frame and a potential personal balance sheet for where we, as individuals, need to focus our growth.

I. Wealth without work.

II. Pleasure without conscience.

III. Knowledge without character.

IV. Commerce without morality.

V. Science without humanity.

VI. Religion without sacrifice.

VII. Politics without principle.

I find it of little surprise that the first focuses on our relationship with money. These areas will be explored further in later chapters.

Chapter 2

Organic growth and development

Psychology suggests that around the age of two we develop the capacity to understand that if a ball rolls behind a chair and is unseen it is still there and has not disappeared; this phenomenon is known as object constancy or permanence (Mahler and Piaget, 1975). Depending on how such experiences are held emotionally, we become more or less comfortable in experiencing the unknown and unfamiliar.

We can all relate to specific childhood memories; when thinking about the past we often find that we have the same characteristics but less strongly. That is, the essence of our personality was present from the start and we are still discovering new aspects that form our perceptions. Many functions we performed in childhood, from building sandcastles to playing children's games, create the formative basis for understanding logical relationships; for example, we might make a stronger foundation and thicker, lower walls for our sandcastle to withstand the ravages of time and shifting sand. When we played games involving friends and foe, we formed our cognitive understanding of how to interact as either, and created our abilities to judge right from wrong. These functions in adults are, of course, more sophisticated and informed but in essence remain very similar to our early 'sandpit' experiences.

It seems we always and continuously engage in our functional preferences between sensing and intuiting, thinking and feeling to focus our attention. Having created attention our now informed decisions are then filtered through our introverted or extraverted attitude into the outside world. These experiences are not surprising since human beings are living systems, constantly evolving and maturing.

The whole process is a gradual organic development, sometimes punctuated with growth spurts but always within a whole. We can use a tree's life cycle as a metaphor, where each 'stage' reflects something unique at a specific time in its development. Using the brain scientist Dario Nardi's[64] outline *A Fresh Understanding of Function Development* as follows:

Table 2.1: A tree's life cycle as a metaphor

Stage	Tree	Tree's special qualities	Person
0	Seed	A potential tree with genetic instructions for development, heavily reliant and formed by its immediate environment	Embryo
1	Sprout	Life emerges and grown in both directions but is still connected to and nourished by the seeds ability to exploit the environment	Child
2	Sapling	Beginning to harden and take final shape but still soft and pliable and easily shaped by the development around it	Youth
3	Adult	Now taking full shape and can bear fruit/seed. Stronger and harder to withstand changes to the environment	Adult
4	Mature	Age and character showing, now with history and a clear role and position (meaning/purpose) and dependents in its environment, and to the degree possible, the self has withstood the tests of time	Senior

There are significant overlaps in these stages. For example, when a tree bears its first fruits that fruit is usually small and inedible; it is a sort of trial period for things to come. The change into the adult tree with plentiful tasty fruit can take years and is not guaranteed.

Whilst this simple example is linear, it lacks many of the feedback loops humans integrate for growth; it highlights stages of what can be called our function-attitudes, which has its own life cycle in how our behaviours and attitudes influence our experiences. Such sequences do not 'switch on' automatically at specific ages, rather, each sequence has its own functional development pattern.

For example, there is a 'concrete' (primitive, early) and 'abstract' (sophisticated, later) version of each function-attitude. Each function- attitude has a 'passive' and 'active' mode, and engaging a function-attitude can result in a 'product' in the outer world as well as a mental event.

As a person develops a function- attitude, he/she tends to engage more abstractly, but also becomes more active and sophisticated whilst experimenting, seeking integration and assimilation.

Also, each function-attitude will continually manifest itself in intriguing ways. The reason for outlining this is because, whilst we are all either in the adult or mature stages of our careers depending on where we are on our investment/impact/life journey, we still need to reflect, explore, develop, and integrate specific function-attitudes that match our life situation. As such, the whole pattern is present and operates from the beginning. An individual as a whole will only mature sequentially with experience and time, transcending and including its previous stages.

Having withstood several storms myself, I know that I'm not going to be blown over during the next one. I have developed some understanding of what to do and the resilience to withstand whatever is thrown at me. I believe that 'this too shall pass' and that all experiences are learning devices that enable me to grow and develop. We all need to recognise where our personal Impact frame sits within these attitudes, and where we think our organisation is positioned culturally.

Table 2.2: The lifecycle of a function-attitude

Stage	The experience and response to a function-attitude
0	No cognitive awareness, conscious usage or direct development
1	We experience the function in its instinctual or concrete form; we try to block out, explore, or fixate on the experience; its engagement is rough or child-like.
2	We accept and follow a social/cultural version of the function, or we passively follow the functional process; we are in its grip; its use is rigid or adolescent
3	We 'grasp' the function in its many forms; we question, alter, personalize and make it our own, as a tool with many options; its use is complex and flexible.
4	The function is highly differentiated and well-integrated; using it contributes back to the world in a unique way; its use is purposeful, creative and generative.

This approach fits with a common matrix that describes the four stages of learning or competence, from unconscious incompetence to conscious incompetence, to conscious competence and to unconscious competence that outlines the generic positions we find ourselves in our knowledge creation. These stages can often cause confusion, frustration or resistance if we misinterpret our emotional attitude towards them.

Depending on what we are trying to learn, in combination with our attitude, natural abilities and aptitude, individually we will spend different amounts of time in each stage. In his book *Outliers: The Story of Success*, Malcolm Gladwell suggests[65] it takes a human being 10,000 hours to reach mastery, or what psychologists would call unconscious competence.

Martin M. Broadwell in his 'Teaching for Learning' article from 20 February 1969 outlined these four stages of competence summarised here:

Unconscious Incompetence (stage 1) Most aspects of any process outside our awareness - we do not even know what we are missing. We may arrange our lives to avoid engaging in the process or inadvertently project negative aspects of the process on to others.

Conscious Incompetence (stage 2) We become aware of what the areas are for improvement but we use the process awkwardly, but do not understand the process from a wider perspective. We often inappropriately either over, under and mis-use the process.

Conscious Competence (stage 3) We selectively use knowledge and choose what aspects of the process will be most effective for success. Aware of how to link the process to other processes.

Unconscious Competence (stage 4) All aspects of the process are seamlessly integrated with other functions creating a sense of flow. Creativity appears spontaneously in a process as we move with effortless results.

Taking this further, we introduce the work of Richard Barrett, an important thought leader in the evolution of values, culture and leadership in business and society, whose work resonates highly with our Integral Impact development trajectory. In his book, *The Evolutionary Man* [66], he outlines an evolved developmental axis based on consciousness and their algorithms:

Table 2.3: Evolved developmental axis

Stages of Development	Age Ranges	Developmental Tasks	Positive Values	Potentially Limiting Values
7. Serving	60+ Years	Contributing to the well-being of future generations and the planet.	Compassion, Forgiveness, Humility, Contribution, Future Generations	N/A

6. Integrating	50–59 years	Connecting with others in unconditional loving relationships to make a difference.	Collaboration, Empathy, Intuition, Mentoring, Partnering, Alliances	N/A
5. Self-Actualising	40–49 years	Expressing your true nature by embracing your soul's values and purpose.	Partnering, Alliances Integrity, Authenticity, Meaning, Internal Alignment	N/A
4. Individuating	25–39 years	Discovering your true identity by letting go of your fears and your dependence on others.	Freedom, Autonomy, Accountability, Adaptability, Courage, Personal Growth	N/A
3. Differentiating	8–24 years	Feeling recognised and respected by establishing yourself in a community that values who you are.	Security, Recognition, Positive, Self-Image, Self-Esteem, Confidence	Arrogance, Pride, Conceit, Superiority, Discrimination
2. Conforming	3–7 years	Feeling safe and protected by staying close to your kin and your family.	Safety, Family, Friendship, Belonging, Harmony	Being liked, Blame, Jealousy, Revenge
1. Surviving	Conception to 2 years	Staying alive and physically healthy by getting your survival needs met.	Survival, Health, Physical Fitness, Nutrition, Financial Stability	Control, Manipulation, Greed, Caution

According to Barrett, there are three stages of the Ego-Soul dynamic: 1, 2, and 3 is about our ego-development; 4 and 5 about our ego-soul alignment; and 6 and 7 about our soul activation. The three stages of evolutionary Intelligence have the following algorithms: 1, 2 and 3 are about becoming viable and independent; 4 and 5 are about bonding to form a group structure; with 6 and 7 cooperating to form a higher order entity. Barrett's work helps understand the dynamic developmental dance we are all engaged in; and each stage needed to be integrated, transcending and including the previous. Whilst such stages should be seen as simplified outlines with many crossovers and overlaps, the question remains how we present and work within the Impact field, possibly now recognising the development required for each stage to emerge.

In addition, it is important to become familiar with some of our personal 'meta programs'[67] which are mental and neurological codified processes and repeated habitual strategies that manage, guide, and direct other mental processes including our behaviour.

Meta programs determine which of our perceptions are selected for our attention. In other words, they are processes at a higher level than the mental processes they affect and are key in uncovering individual context and how we got to where we are today. We could compare meta programs to a circuit board that controls which two phones will be connected to each other during a conversation, or a thermostat that controls whether our air conditioning system is turned on or off.

Neuro Linguistic Programming (NLP) uses a contemporary metaphor taken from computer science to describe the action of one process upon other programs. Often in computer programming, one program controls the execution of a number of other programs, selecting which ones will run at which times and sending them information they will need in order to function properly.

Many of us are fearful of, or resist reaching out into such territory because of pre- programmed boundary conditions which were created in our past such as beliefs about our limitations[68]. Some of the more important meta programs (out of ca. 50) are:

I. Toward or away (i.e. directional move from people, places and things)

II. Sameness versus difference (as preference and for comfort)

III. External or internal frame of reference (for validation/justification)

IV. Matcher or mismatcher (generate resonance/dissonance)

V. Convincer strategy (for decision making)

VI. Possibility versus necessity (as a motivating driver)

VII. Independent, cooperative and proximity (as working styles)

These programs are constructed by nurture and inbuilt by nature. Irrespective of their origins, at some stage we hermeneutically need to investigate their efficacy and relevance in our lives to understand their impact. This may at times include a regressionary journey to re-connect with our past, in particular our childhood states, and discover how this pre-programming is affecting our current status. We benefit from moving outside our created maps of our assumed realities; there are many ways of achieving these multiple perspectives to create a more independent view of our constructed activity.

The old idea of being born as a blank slate or 'tabula rasa' implies that our baseline early on gets filled with material and knowledge from early on in life. However, since a blank slate cannot learn anything, this notion cannot be the whole story. As mentioned previously, all we know is from contrast and comparison, apart from downloaded 'factual' information. This journey of discovery, and the way this knowing can be released, is in the dance of unity-in-differentiation which is also as it happens inside the language of discovering and interpreting what is true love.

Interpretation however, depends on perspective. I use the term 'power-distance' to explain how far away someone's consciousness is from understanding the outcome of their actions inside a cause and effect. This relates to how the social psychologist, Geert Hofstede views power relationships as a dynamic between superior-subordinate relationships, authority and collaborative participation[69].

During my work in investment banking, I found that some people in high office could become pathologically disconnected from their work and, as a result, sometimes became narcissistically egocentric. A large part of my inner calling was to find and re- connect disconnected parts of a business, both psychologically and technically. In my view, this power distance is a psychodynamic, connective, and spiritual developmental that includes and transcends the traditional moral development axes that psychologists such as Kohlberg, Piaget, Wilber and Gilligan have put forward, which are explained below.

Lawrence Kohlberg's cognitivist model of moral development with Habermas, Gilligan, Dreyfus and Heidegger additions:

Table 2.4: Kohlberg's cognitivist model

Stage 1[1]	Pre-conventional 1: Infantile	Satisfaction of needs and avoidance of punishment; involved ethical comportment
Stage 2	Pre-conventional 2: Egotistic	Self-interest orientation; What's in it for me? You scratch my back, and I'll scratch yours
Stage 3	Conventional 1: Tribal	Conforming to stereotypical images of majority behaviour; filling social roles

[1]Kohlberg

Stage 4	Conventional 2: Conservative	Following fixed rules, social conventions and laws; retaining the given social order
Stage 5	Post-conventional 1: Democratic	Social contract driven; conventions and laws can change; greatest good through compromise and majority decision
Stage 6	Post-conventional 2: Revolutionary	Principled; guidance by universal ethical principles; commitment to justice transcending unjust laws
Stage 7	Transcendental (speculative) Transformational	Transcendental morality or morality of cosmic orientation; integrating religion with moral reasoning
Stage 8[2]	Dialectic dialogical (last rational stage)	Rational agreement through dialectical dialogue sublimating lower levels
Stage 9[3]	Caring (first intuitive stage)	Caring, emphatic, non-cognitive, involved know-how within context of narrative of relationships that extends over time; giving up rules and maxims; contextual relativistic
Stage 10	Dreyfus 1	Expert Intuitive response to the unique situation out of a fund of experience in the culture; intuitively doing what the culture deems good
Stage 11	Dreyfus 2[4]	Authentic Visionary response to unique, concrete, existential situation, disclosed in and through resoluteness by the call of conscience

Carol Gilligan in her book *In a Different Voice*[70], discovered the stages in women's development as:

Stage 1: Selfish care (egocentric), where the woman cares only for herself

Stage 2: Co-centric, where she extends care to her own group

Stage 3: Uni-centric, being universal care, caring for all groups, and

Stage 4: Being integrated, integrating masculine and feminine modes.

---

[2]Habermas
[3]Gilligan
[4]Heidegger

> People don't care how much you know until they know how much you care

Theodore Roosevelt

We know from her work, and Ken Wilber's, that there is also a masculine/feminine dimension to moral development. We also know that it is only when a human goes beyond the egocentric and ethnocentric stages into world-centric that they can jettison their own needs. Prior to this they do not want everybody to be treated equally, which I believe is a prerequisite for working with integrity in the impact space.

Key to the grounding of the self is our capacity for humility which we will explore in a later chapter on organisational performance. In the book *The Power of Humility*[71], Charles and Barbara Whitfield categorize humility into twelve components:

I. Openness to what 'is' and our reality and the feeling of peace

II. Attitude of 'don't know': Acceptance of limited knowledge and no judgements

III. Curiosity: Awareness of the knowing that there is always more

IV. Innocence: The knowing that a pure mind is strength and peace

V. Childlike Nature: 'there is a child in you who seeks the parents' house'

VI. Spontaneity: Living as real selves in the moment of now

VII. Spirituality: Relationship with self and others and personal path of growth

VIII. Tolerance: The capacity to respect and accept ourselves and others. Overcoming resistance

IX. Patience: Overcoming the conflict of egoic attainment

X. Integrity: Wholeness and authenticity of character in alignment with true self

XI. Detachment: The ability to withdraw emotional attachment to a person, place or thing with love

XII. Letting Go: Inner process of removing the ego and surrendering the
     need to control

You may want to scale yourself from 1 to 10 in each of these components
to get a baseline reading (or, even better, ask someone else to do it for you).

Our character is also our adherence to principles. We don't want to
become what Groucho Marx is suggested to have uttered in gist as *These are
my principles. If you don't like them I have others.*

For us to find meaning and purpose in life, our work has to be grounded
in our innermost calling, then activated and expressed into a community
to which we feel connected. If not, we are always subject to our culture's
definition of success and will follow others' marching orders, i.e., the beliefs
and values, cultural codes, instructions, ideas and behaviours handed down
to us through family and society.

I fully appreciate that each of the above areas of organic growth and
development can constitute an individual chapter of this book, so apologies
for the whistle-stop tour but the aim is to outline some areas for further
exploration. When working with impact investments, we have an opportunity to catalyse our rich creative, spiritual and culturally diverse heritage.
We understand our individual selves and, when expressed in our collective
organisations, communities, and societies, we can fully release our human
potential.

This is Impact's promise. Inner growth on a highly personal level is a fundamental prerequisite for sustainable impact and its development. Without
developing this inner ability, and together with trust, strength and commitment to actively face our contemporary evolutionary, conflicting and
competing pressures, of our time, it is unlikely that we can engage meaningfully in the conscious renewal of societies and the restoration of nature.
This can only happen when we realise that we are not necessarily defending
Nature, rather, we are an integral part of Nature defending itself.

The fact that you are reading this book means that you have already had
a desire for Impact Investments, and that this may be a star to follow. The
word *desire* comes from the Latin 'De' and 'Sire' meaning 'from the stars'.
Outer growth and Impact, on a collective level, require us to understand
and create a contextual dialectic that can tap into the developmental and
cultural potential of a particular society. Culture can be understood as a
collective psychology, with shared fields of meaning and identity that act as
the creative glue within a society. When impact is such, it forms the soil for
healthy and continuous processes of renewal.

With impact, we also engage in the renewal of our values versus outside laws and marching orders. Renewal itself must be preceded by some form of loss, as emptiness makes way for new growth; every transformation requires surrendering a previous 'form', hence our need to walk with humility, acceptance and openness.

However, vigilance is also required towards the authenticity of the impact, as Hannah Arendt wrote of those who enter

> the maelstrom of an unending process of expansion, he[sic] will, as it were, cease to be what he was and obey the laws and process, identify himself with anonymous forces that he is supposed to serve in order to keep the whole person in motion, he will think of himself as mere function, and eventually consider such functionality, such an incarnation of the dynamic trend, his highest possible achievement

Culture is much more than the arts and creative expressions of a society; it is in how culture shapes the humanities and ways of being and belonging that a culture can be best experienced. Impact therefore may actively include the arts, dance, music, poetry and stories as well as the unique wisdom and spiritual expressions that bring out the inimitable 'flavour' of a place and society.

We need to be conscious that cultural differences may be viewed as a negative life-denying source of division, and an aversion to evolution. Our work life needs to bring in a radical conversation, both with ourselves and with our firm, about our gifts and requirements. The question is: what is the quality of that core conversation?

We often invest an inordinate amount of time and effort in our professional identity, which we seek to protect at great personal cost. Also, our Western culture values puts on a pedestal, our organisational identity, so we will always to some degree be pulled apart by the forces between self and our culture.

When working with impact, we have the opportunity to heal such differences by using an integral design for our impact objectives so they become a constructive and life-affirming source for unity, identity, belonging, and mutual growth. Activating the life-affirming potential of a specific culture requires continuous evolutionary processes within and between cultures, spearheaded by local agents and agencies. Any impact organisation or community can become such an agency if its development processes are sufficiently embedded within nature and culture – and if the active co-evolution with other cultures is facilitated.

Our purpose, then, is to obtain impetus and reinforcement from inside each integral realm. If we can be allowed to make what is invisible inside our organisations visible, and feel engaged, charged and activated, we are fortunate indeed and will have a strong sense of connection and belonging. The converse requires an enormous amount of energy as we will be employing our mental strategies with no inner support systems that are truly engaged.

We often spend more time inside our organisations than we do with our nearest and dearest; if we can't ask (and converse about) the great questions of life, what it means to be fully human, then these organisations inevitably become too small for us. This is one of the greatest management challenges of our time. As Marcus Aurelius[72] reminds us in his *Meditations*:

> Accept the things to which fate binds you, and love the people with whom fate brings you together, but do so with all your heart.

Few areas have more impact on our lives than our relationship and attitude towards money. In the next chapter, I will, however, share and expand on my own experiences and insights in order to stimulate further thoughts.

Chapter 3

The Integral Nature of Money

Fundamental to building our relationship with Impact is to consider some of the component parts involved in our primary relationship with money itself.

The word *nature* is derived from the Latin word natura, or "essential qualities, innate disposition", and in ancient times, literally meant "birth". The title of this chapter is therefore on one level a contradiction since money at its most basic level has no real nature, only functions. As human beings, we imbue money with meaning and purpose which creates and actualises its nature only when money is being used. Money as such acts as a transfer agent for all our psychological complexes and aspirations and we use money as a reflective mirror in which to see and form ourselves and our identities throughout our lives.

In this way we create a relationship to money which have consequences for us in all our relationships. We call this a primary relationship whose qualities affect the very nature of all others. Money also contains many paradoxes. We attach many of our positive motivations, aspirations and ambitions to money, thinking it will fulfil and satisfy. Inevitably gaps appear between these hopes and expectations and our life's unfolding reality, evoking negative feelings of fear, doubt, grief, shame, stress, disappointment, betrayal, anger and jealousy. This is one of money's many shadows.

Another is when money has been obtained or used through means which violate the integrity of the self. Our conscience knows when this happens, giving us, at some level feelings of guilt, shame, and unworthiness. Shame being a prime driver for a sense of unworthiness. As shame is a negative driver, most of which operate unconsciously particularly in relation to money, it's important to understand its depth and breadth in how shame affects our lives. In Brené Brown's book, *Dare to lead*, she defines shame as

> the intensely painful feeling or experience of believing that we are flawed and therefore unworthy of love, belonging and connection[73].

She suggests that shame drives two tapes:

Never good enough
Who do you think you are?

I would suggest as a primer on shame in its fullness to read the full chapter in Brenés' book on shame and empathy in section 4 as this succinctly outlines the foundation to its construct and how we can manage shame.

A third shadow is an imbalance of money, i.e., either too much to handle or too little to meet our needs,

> It is not the creation of wealth that is wrong, but the love of money for its own sake.

Whist money is rooted in the functions of our economy and society, we rarely seek to understand its relation to Nature, its cultural and psychological dimensions and how money shapes the realms of knowledge for ourselves and our societies. Some of these drivers of money are imbued with our values, beliefs and identity about ourselves which in turn shapes and directs our needs, wants and motivations.

To fully understand money therefore we need to look at its deeper structures, in a more holistic manner, including which dynamics and interconnected webs define it. We need to build further understandings about its true meaning, functions and uses.

A good friend of mine recently reminded me that money can be like cake. The first slice is delicious, satisfying and fulfils our immediate needs; the second slice still tastes really good, maybe less satisfying but still feels as if we deserve it; the third slice is far less satisfying and we may start to worry about the consequences of either finishing it, or perhaps we can save it for later.

The fourth slice starts to taste disgusting, giving us ill feelings and guilt for having taken too much. We now know that we will have consequences to tackle if we finish it.

With cake, our natural system and conscience seems to be able to communicate to the need for balance, often lacking in our relation to money. In my native Sweden, we have the expression and concept of "lagom" that is deeply rooted in our culture and politic.

Lagom has no direct translation to English but means according to the Lexin Swedish-English dictionary "enough, sufficient, adequate, just right", as "in moderation", "in balance", "optimal" and "suitable". As such, it is both highly personal and cultural which can only be known and felt within each context. We all as individuals need to work out what "lagom" money actually means and to find what works and delivers a full and purpose-driven life.

In my youth I was told that *money does not grow on trees*, which over time became a construct that fed into many of my values and beliefs. As a result, we develop a highly intimate relationship with money, and its importance is evident in our lifestyle and identity.

As some of us have experienced, it can take pathological proportions at the cost of other relationships.

Money is a key component in our identity, how we see and value ourselves, and how we believe others may see and value us. The Christian tradition reminds us that *For the love of money is the root of all evil*[1]. Money is not evil in itself, of course. The driver in this case is the word 'love', which for each of us has a different meaning. Money itself has no inert intentionality or objectives but it can create many false friends and genuine enemies.

Like any tool, such as a knife in the hands of a surgeon, money can, and is, mainly used for good. It is like a battery acting as a repository of static energy which, when activated and attached to something, can generate action. Money, in effect, has the ability to absorb all our nature of being, becoming, knowing and doing by stealth, often with us unaware.

So money essentially is a human construct that we have to embody to live life. As money contains the dualities of good and bad depending on how it is used, so, in William Shakespeare's Hamlet, we are reminded that *for there is nothing either good or bad, but thinking makes it so.*[2] This can also be changed to *Money is nothing either good or bad but humans makes it so.* As such the nature of the relationship that we create with money contains both our light and our shadow elements of the self and the ego. If so, our relationship to money is a human and individual journey we each must make to function in the world. How we hold money in our consciousness has been created through our experience with it, (i.e., being and becoming); how it has become infused with our values and beliefs and our identity, (i.e. knowing and doing). Money is also the facilitating agent when we create, accumulate, or spend it, on ourselves or on others, affecting how we think and feel about ourselves. Money as such acts as a psychological mirror and each time used it is like touchstone of our moral core and we are shaped in turn by its interpretative reflections. It's a double-sided mirror.

We all have to find ways to make and accumulate money on the input or income side of the equation. This side is full of ideas and myths of how we create money and our role in it. On the other side, our "output" or expenditure is a reflection of our needs and wants within our source of origin, and culture as we seek to shape our identities and positions within our communities. This side is full of thinking about how money not only creates and shapes

---

[1]Timothy 6:10
[2]Act 2, Scene 2

our wellbeing, status and persona but also what we can experience to help us grow and fulfill our dreams.

Having studied psychology and worked as a psychotherapist, I became interested in how our relationship to money actually is a catalyst and source for much of our pain and suffering but also for facilitating joy and happiness. For most people, money is intellectually and emotionally highly charged which affects values and belief systems. Money is a large part of our emancipation and individuation in our life journey; there is no escape from money as it is an integral part of who we are and whom we are becoming. We all essentially fuse our very own nature in synthesis to money and its apparent magical powers to both create and to destroy. Money carries with it the consciousness of the past as a repository so it's only in the present where we have the opportunity, not to change the past but honour it and re-balance how money is now positioned given our new level of consciousness.

Given what has just been said, it's highly likely this chapter is to a large degree somewhat autobiographical. I don't proclaim to have any special insights about money but I do, at this stage of my life, have many significant life experiences with money, both positive and negative which have shaped my own relationship with money. In my family of origin, much of our value and belief system was in relationship to money. Maybe as a result, I have worked in finance to try and make more money, later, working in a healing profession as a psychotherapist, as my calling in life changed so my relationship to money as a motivational driver changed.

§3.1 Background to functions

Money has no real intrinsic value apart from that which we and our collective cultures attach to it. Even money made from precious metals only derives its value through translation into market pricing which in itself is a cauldron of economic, financial, human and cultural streams of condensed activity, whose function is to try and find equilibrium pricing.

Another aspect we need to consider is that technically, money is also a forward contract on goods and services; it is *a claim upon society*[74]. Money contains within it the value of labour which can be eroded through cost-push or demand-pull inflation. When money is stored in the form of capital, technically we are compensated for the inflation risk through the receipt of interest which today in some countries is negative so money not only transfers economic adjustments and realities in time and space; it also contains the political policies and modes of operation which are in power.

As such, money is essentially a bearer instrument which has been created and closed based on a value exchange in the past, but as a store of wealth carries within itself a universal future right of claim or conversion into something else which has as yet to be defined. This concept becomes abundantly clear when we think about the idea behind our pensions (for those who have one) and for our savings (for those who have any). It's not without irony when we read "In God we trust" on American money, a possible double meaning occurs of blind faith and "God help this poor currency" versus a real faith and understanding in which all things are rooted and therefore from where it derives its ultimate value.

Here we must distinguish between money, capital and wealth. The word "money" itself therefore becomes an exercise in semiotics (meaning making). For Christopher Houghton Budd of the Centre for Associative Economics in Britain wrote that

> The most important thing about money…is that men consciously agree on its purpose. Something non-economic is thereby introduced. The Greek word for money means custom, consensus, convention. When men arrive at consensus, they are not involved in economic processes, but in 'rights' processes. Money belongs to the rights life, it enables the rights lore to permeate economics. The questions is: to what purpose?…Money is utterly emancipated from the economic processes that give rise to it…. The past cannot live on in money. Money by its very nature belongs to the future. The only way of knowing what can happen to money is to observe the use it is put to. Moreover, the use will reveal the intention of the user and thereby reveal the user also[75].

So in our contemporary world, money has little or no "real" value, i.e., it is "Fiat" money which is without any intrinsic value. It has been created and established as money and value is only present because a central government and body maintains its value and parties engaging in exchange agree on its transfer value.

Bernard Lietaer, one of the architects of the euro, (and proclaimed by Business Week as the world's best currency dealer) describes money as an agreement, like a marriage or a business contract or agreement within a community, to use something as a means of payment. Accordingly, money is not a living thing. Because it is an agreement with no intrinsic value, we can always make new and different agreements; that is the basis for today's social, local, digital and virtual currencies.

However, money does carry history in the form of our consciousness and how this influences our current thinking. Ben Bingham recently suggested that in this sense we need money to think backwards to the past. Loan money on the other hand, serves all stakeholders best when projects that meet the needs of the present serve as an inspiration, for example new infrastructure to serve society and the planet as a whole. Gift money and Investments are the only examples of future oriented money in practise. We use our intuition to sense what is coming and what will be most relevant down the road.

Whilst the functionality of money is well known (i.e., unit of account, store of wealth, means of exchange, etc.), wealth has a myriad of possible meanings. Conversion to and from money is one, but it also relates to our social, human, intellectual, cultural and built capital, all of which are interconnected.

The etymology of wealth is from the old English words 'weal' (well-being) and 'th' (condition), which is why we need to include well-being inside our social impact framework (i.e. to build real 'wealth'). However, since the preponderant objective for impact investments is wealth creation across numerous capitals, a big question is how this wealth may be distributed in relation to financial capital ownership, which can be highly contentious. It is only when we acknowledge the existence of other capitals such as human, social, intellectual, and environmental that we see how they have been deliberately excluded from any sort of reciprocal measurement and accounting systems.

Capital, however, is also the unit on which returns are measured and expected. Most firms today contain more intangible capital (e.g., brand, intellectual, and creative) on their balance sheets than hard assets and tangibles. The shaping and handling of the intangible impact has profound implications for the impact industry and how each firm defines its accounting. Money, as such, may function as an intermediary step, digital translator and conversion agent between all areas, acting as a flow mechanism. However, the main consideration is our relationship with value and its creation.

To see money from this perspective, we need to remember that money comes from the creation of value. Thus, the creation of value always comes first then the value is transformed by a transaction into something else, which could be:

- Money (barter, bitcoin, cash, credit)

- Innovation (in its different types)

- Competitive advantage (perhaps more valuable than money)

- Speed (in outflanking the competition)

- Collaboration (better integration, economics of trust, cohesive values, closeness to customers, etc.)

§3.2 Where money comes from

The Canadian economist, John Kenneth Galbraith, noted in his 1971 book *Money: Whence It Came, Whence it Went* that:

> The process by which banks create money is so simple the mind is repelled. Where something so important is involved, a deeper mystery seems only decent[76].

Much has been written in recent times about how governments and their respective central banks have lost control over the printing presses and the money supply. Most money today, not unsurprisingly is in electronic formats (ca. 97%) with the rest (ca. 3%) being held as notes and coins in circulation and with vast majority of the electronic money supply being created by banks in the form of loans: "Each and every time a bank makes a loan, new bank credit is created — new deposits — brand new money."(Towers, pp. 113 and 238[3])

In March 2014, the Bank of England released their report, *Money Creation in the Modern Economy*, writing,

> Commercial [i.e. high-street] banks create money, in the form of bank deposits, by making new loans. When a bank makes a loan, for example to someone taking out a mortgage to buy a house, it does not typically do so by giving them thousands of pounds worth of banknotes. Instead, it credits their bank account with a bank deposit of the size of the mortgage. At that moment, new money is created. And in the modern economy, those bank deposits are mostly created by commercial banks themselves.

Sir Mervyn King, the Governor of the Bank of England from 2003-2013, recently explained this point to a conference of businesspeople:

> When banks extend loans to their customers, they create money by crediting their customers' accounts,

Confirming (last year) that in fact it is private banks creating the majority of money. Martin Wolf, who was a member of the Independent Commission on Banking, and is Chief Economics Commentator for the Financial Times, put it bluntly:

---

[3]Graham Towers, former Governor of the Central Bank of Canada before the Canadian Government's Committee on Banking and Commerce, in 1939

the essence of the contemporary monetary system is the creation of money, out of nothing, by private banks often foolish lending[4].

Wolf explains that

Money is a social invention, indeed among the most important of all social inventions. At present the right to create money has been handed over to the private businesses we call banks. But this is not the only way we could create money and, as recent experience suggests, it may be far from the best one.

As such, every new loan that a bank makes creates new money. This may at first sight not appear to be a bad thing per se, since on one level, this is how governments have "designed" and allowed the money supply to increase to keep up with economic growth. However, this is also a political and legal abdication of economic control to private enterprise: public notes and coins in circulation carry no cost, money if originated as debt carries annual and compound interest charges which today for many debt-based economies outstrip the intrinsic natural capacities to generate sufficient economic growth to sustain the ever increasing interest and debt levels.

In addition, whilst money in circulation itself is free to use as a "facilitation agent", it's you and me that pay interest to the banks either directly as mortgage payments or indirectly through the pricing of goods and services. As a result, my colleague Mark Anielski estimates that ca. 50% of all consumer prices in the US economy and in most other debt-based economies are made up of commercial banks' interest cost of capital passed on in our goods and services. Our decisions and choices as such may seem limited in how we can avoid these costs but such choices are nevertheless highly personal. An equally important and political question is how we have allowed banks to monopolise the creation of money from thin air and at the same time get away with charging the economy at large for the privilege of its use.

As Albert Einstein said about compound interest, which he called 'the eighth wonder of the world': *He who understands it earns it... He who doesn't pays it*[77].

§3.3 Functions

The functions of money from our conventional economic lens can be viewed and defined as a unit of account, storage of wealth and as a means of exchange with the aim to facilitate economic transactions. The fundamental economic premise of money can be defined as the creative and effective movement of

---

[4]Financial Times. 9/11/2010

capital embedded in scarce resources which has alternative uses. In addition, money also represents a collectively held symbolic representation of value in the minds of its users. Over the centuries, money has taken various forms, depending on cultures, context and their anthropology, cowrie shells to carved stones, etc. This was overlaid by periods and cycles where either trust in money was broken and more universal forms of value had to be added intrinsically such as precious metals.

Such metals also facilitated trade across borders bridging trust as an acceptable means of exchange. This worked very well for long periods of time across the world but this concept was heavily reliant on the availability and cost of chosen raw materials such as gold, silver and copper, and also in trusting the issuing entity and coining government, e.g., the Mint to remain honest in terms of weights and purities to preserve value. History has shown that this is more difficult than one would think.

In the case of my native, Sweden, given its abundance of copper, the copper standard was introduced for minting in 1624. Not that long thereafter, supply began to outstrip demand so Sweden had problems in finding markets for all its copper. When the price declined domestically, currency inflation set in requiring the Mint to issue ever larger coins. This culminated in 1644 when the Mint issued the 10 Daler coin weighing in at a hefty 19.72 kg (c. 43½ lbs) which meant people having to go to market carrying their coins in wheelbarrows. As such, money had lost its practical value as an efficient means of exchange and the copper standard was thus abandoned. However, as necessity is the mother of all inventions, this gave rise to the first banknotes being issued in Europe with the Stockholms Banco issuing the first paper money.

Despite their practical attraction and success, this ended in a now predictable and classic bank failure. By 1660, the central government began minting new coins of a lower weight than the older ones to make them practical again. This meant that many depositors who had made the paper exchange now wanted their old, heavier coins back, as they had a higher metal value. This led to a run on the bank. The bank's founder, Johan Palmstruch issued deposit certificates as a security note giving the owner the right to withdraw the deposited amount in cash. The special thing about the deposit certificates, which were called credit notes, was that the bank was no longer dependent on having money deposited to be able to issue; and were not linked to any actual deposit. Instead, they were based on the public's confidence that the bank would pay the value of the note in cash upon demand.

The new certificates were handed out as loans from the bank and could be used to purchase anything and in effect were the first banknotes in Europe issued based on institutional trust. In 1663, both the Crown and the Chancellor at the time, Magnus Gabriel De la Gardie, also took out large loans and the bank duly obliged by printing more notes. This eventually led to a collapse in value, a phenomenon we now know as currency inflation.

Confidence was finally lost among the general public and many people demanded that their notes be redeemed. But as Stockholms Banco did not have enough coins they started to call in loans previously granted. This ended in a classic bank failure which the world would repeatedly witness again. The Council of the Realm – the government of the time – decided in 1664 that the loans would be repaid and that the credit notes would be withdrawn. Palmstruch was ordered to appear before the Svea Court of Appeal in 1668 and was sentenced to death for mismanagement of the bank. He was later reprieved and remained in prison until 1670 but died in the following year.

Following this experience, at the Riksdag of the Estates in 1668, the nobles pushed through a proposal to form a new institution from the ruins of Stockholms Banco, but now with the nobles, the clergy and the burghers as principals (excluding the peasants) to create common ownership and interest. What was then called The Bank of the Estates of the Realm, (Riksens Ständers Bank) is today known as Sveriges Riksbank. The world's oldest central bank was created out of necessity to reestablish trust and functionality[78].

Whilst this is a tale to be retold many times over the course of history, it is perplexing and how why such scenarios are allowed to be played to be played out.

§3.4 Integral Money

The nature of money as such, embeds all our economic hopes and fears and is highly susceptible to shifting psychology. One could even argue that money shares many of its aspects with world religions in that whilst based on trust and faith, it needs also to be grounded into a belief and value system which creates its reality. Money, like a religion, also contains the aspiration and need for future salvation, one economic and the other spiritual which like a religion, money is highly political and open to many different views and interpretations of its management, value and stewardship.

Our intrinsic relationship with money constantly evolves, but also must be aligned with its core extrinsic functions. To facilitate this, we can map and look through the lens of our Integral 4-worlds model. From our integral perspective we see all money needs to be rooted in the 4-worlds through real economic activities. In addition, trust capital will be added from the Social and Cultural realms and create resonance with the systems and intellectual capital that sustains the functionality values. This in turn will create the relevance for its user community and be held as a repository of all the symbolic representations money is referencing. If so, we have created the functional rationale for the economic realm to adopt and generate value through its use. Money, integrally speaking needs to build on, contain, and embed characteristics to flourish, (our South), flow (our East), function, (our North) and facilitate, (our West) the economic functions.

The extrinsic value now being created is the social and psychological constructs and value on which its credibility, trust capital sustainability depends.

The dearth of money explains why some parts of the economy have splintered off, enabled by technology to create new concepts of money such as Bitcoin. However, the basic security principles behind a crypto currency/block chain is nothing new. The idea has in the form of tally sticks, used as a form of debt currency since early medieval times. A tally stick was a piece of wood which had carved notches to denominate its value between a creditor and debtor which was then split so each party had an exchangeable instrument.

Each part is unique both in terms of grain pattern and the shape of the split cut so it's only when the two original pieces are reunited at redemption that the debtor and creditor can cancel the debt and destroy the stick.

On one level, there is probably no actual real need for currencies such as Bitcoin but an opportunity arose to embed certain features such as anonymity which proved highly attractive to certain parts of the shadow economy needing an unidentifiable store of wealth. As this function increased exponentially in value, but given mining constraints, Bitcoin price volatility has fuelled massive speculation and become a driver for value creation.

However, and as a direct consequence of creating money through advanced technology, the actual energy requirements to run the global digital currency market is estimated to be equivalent of the total energy consumption of Belgium. The cost implications of creating and maintaining a digital currency is highly related not only to extract value from any exchange rate but also the willingness of markets to pay for transaction costs.

These costs that can only be covered by willing participants who find compensation elsewhere in its functions and use. The value of anything as

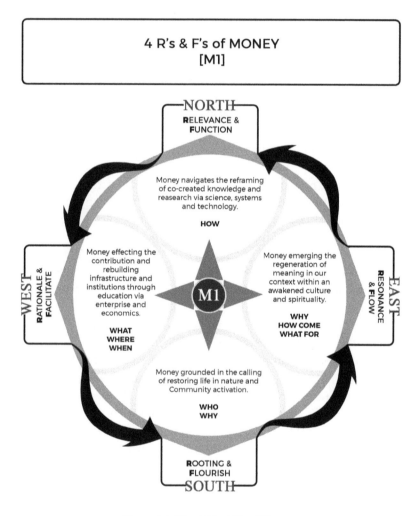

Figure 3.1: The 4 R's & F's of Money

we know is ultimately in the eye of the beholder but also in relation to any market.

It is important to distinguish that Money (and its other static and accounting forms e.g., wealth, capital, assets) only have value based on the opportunity cost of their respective abilities to generate a return or yield. If this were not so, money would depreciate with time which it does in real terms if you include inflation into its future conversion capacity and as such, money seems to have created for itself a perpetual contractual and institutionalised right to increase on itself, not necessarily per se sufficiently in value itself but as defined accounting terms. If money is a construct of our collective imagination it's also not unlike language which acts as a symbolic translation mechanism.

What is it then that gives money its functions and value? The answer lies in Nature and Natural systems itself from which all economic and financial activities ultimately derive their value namely.

Throughout our lives we create our own recipe and secret sauce for our relationship with money. The word Peara means "peppered" in Italian and is a traditional Veronese sauce made from bread crumbs, beef and hen stock, beef marrow, and black pepper.

For our own secret money sauce the beef and hen stock is a foundation for our immune system and provides all the necessary nourishment for our South; black pepper adds spice to life and some heat; for our East, beef marrow to feed knowledge to the brain in the North; and bread crumbs to provide muscles energy to get the thing done in the West.

Our personal integral broad Money Supply M^4 is made up of 4 components. From why money *Matters* in our South, searching and creating *Meaning* in our East. To the stored *Memory* of money in our North followed by our *Materialisation* phase as to what we do with our money within our West.

Wisdom tells us that one worships either heaven or hell and will eventually become the servant of one or the other through one's own decisions and their consequences.

The Gospel writer Matthew suggested that: 'For where your treasure is, there will your heart be also[5].' A danger of working with money creation through investment instruments such as debt and equity is that it may become an abstracted tool for either good or evil.

This has profound implications on how seriously we take our own development and, as a result, how we work with impact. Whatever our personal

---

[5]Matthew 6.21

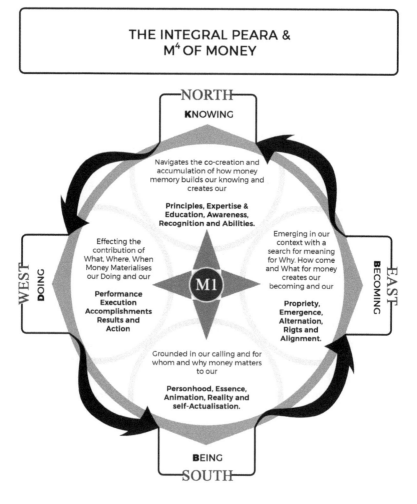

Figure 3.2: The integral Peara and M⁴ of money

understanding and what we have the capacity to include, we constantly swim in multiple myth streams of life and money.

There is, however, an underlying link and deeper meaning to the maxim 'money doesn't grow on trees' when we look at it from the lens of investment:

I. Money, as such, is part of a natural system.

II. Financial returns are rooted and need to be grounded in the nature from where yields originate.

III. Yields are a natural outcome from organic ingredients, processes and systems.

IV. Capital is re-cycling material that has an inbuilt potential and life force.

V. Too much financial money on its own, like any imbalance, can be detrimental to its host and offspring.

Stewardship of any natural resource requires balance. If the world ('our orchard') was run by accountants, we would not allow them to pull up the trees every quarter (or even yearly to prepare the annual report) to check, measure and report on the progress of the root system as the 'operating engine' and predictor of our expected 'yield'. Nevertheless, and this is hard to believe, many organisations and investment companies are unaware of the organic root system that feeds and nourishes the 'yield' of our metaphorical 'money tree'.

We must understand how we differentiate between the concepts of money, capital and wealth so we clarify its management, stewardship, and impact on our lives. In a world deluged by irrelevant and conflicting information, clarity is a prerequisite to provide the power and emphasis to act decisively. At the same time, money as a concept is being redefined and its uses/functions restructured through digitisation and the application of technology.

The integral perspective does not claim to provide solutions or simple answers to complex problems. However, looking through the integral lens, you can create a framework to develop your own contextual solutions. The integral perspective will also help you build the necessary knowledge to enable the development of an organic order that will lead to a more robust and sustainable outcome.

Let us look a little deeper at two aspects of the current state of money (and its creation) through this lens:

- The conversion from free currency to debt money creation exerts a heavy cost on society and our economy.

- Can innovation and new technology provide solutions whilst maintaining the value and functionality of money?

Money (both now and in the future), enabled by new technology such as blockchain, will take new and varied forms. From our integral perspective we see all successful and sustainable new monies as rooted in nature capital (our South) and real economic activities. In addition, trust capital will be added from the social and cultural realms to resonate (our East) with the systems and intellectual capital that sustain the functionality values. This, is turn will create relevance (our North) for its user community and held as a repository of all the symbolic representations money is referencing. By doing this, we create the rationale (our West) for the economic realm to adopt and generate value through its use. (see link to 4R's and 4F's as above).

For Impact, positive and negative effects will move outward into larger and larger systems (or inward into smaller systems). As a result, they create unintended consequences and fail to deliver the promised value. For example, when small local businesses are replaced by megastores, local money no longer absorbs into, and circulates within, the local economy. Social interactions fostered by small businesses dry up and the inner city/town may be abandoned. We therefore need to become seekers who know that it is only by venturing into the relatively unknown that we can understand the purpose of our professions and find real meaning in our work.

Impact investments open up each individual to find and hone his/her personal calling and to co-create its development with others to actualise our impact contribution for self, organisation, and beyond, fulfilling ourselves. As the German poet Rainer Maria Rilke reminds us: 'The only journey is the one within[79]'. Purpose in life is an inner and outer search for meaning. However, finding purpose is not always something we can do, engineer or muster; we sometimes have to be open and still enough to allow for purpose to find us inside relationship and experience.

However, all forms of relationships change us for better or worse; herein lies the question of discernment in choice and decision making. Developing the quality and nature of yourself in relationship with others is the real and is one of the most valuable gifts you can give to another. I have found that several contemplative practises such as meditation, mindfulness and cognitive activity (e.g., walking, martial arts etc.) can quiet the chattering mind and bring new perspectives around discernment.

We have to remember that the mind does not experience the world, it only reports from its sensory perceptions, which need an opening in order to perceive. When we sleep, during stages of dreaming we use our imaginary powers to create positions for ourselves we never could during our waking states whilst bombarded with reality. With our imaginary powers, we can also use daytime reverie and fantasised experiences to create new insights and emotional inputs that expand our horizons. In addition, when we are in a relationship with another person, we receive the gift of additional perspectives. The larger the group, the further we expand the multiplicity of such perspectives. Taking a Jungian viewpoint, it is within our psychology for individuation to seek contrasting and opposite intimate relations in order to accelerate the individuation process.

The Jungian psychoanalyst James Hollis (2009) suggests that it is only through an intimate relationship with our beloved other that we can fully expand the self-reflective mirror necessary in order to understand ourselves. I believe this statement will resonate with anyone blessed with someone who creates the capacity for us to experience this aspect of ourselves.

Every individual needs to decide whether the most important relationship we have is with our Higher Power, God, Allah, Buddha, Nature, or whoever we identify with. This aspect is also core for our impact framework; it is a central point inside our moral core that influences all parts of our four worlds and gives us an opportunity to reconnect with our source. As C.G. Jung suggested: 'Who looks outside, dreams; who looks inside, awakes.[80]'

Importantly, it's only by using and integrating the I^3 moral core as our touchstone in our integral model that we go beyond intellectual constructs of using just technique, now working dynamically inside the four worlds and moving our intentionality which fuels the core towards our real and true Impact and mastery thereof:

> Fiddling with this and that technique is of no avail…Ultimately you must forget about technique, the further you progress the fewer teaching there are[81].

Another important reason for constantly working through the moral I^3 core is humans have a tendency to forget or leave their moral compass behind when it comes to decisions made in the name of culture and what they think is organisational and economic progress.

Understanding the integral impact journey as an unfolding individuation process of self-development, growth and move towards wholeness, the Norwegian philosopher Arne Naess, first coined the concept of Deep Ecology:

The word in Norwegian is Self-realising. It is an active condition, not a place one can reach. No one ever reaches self-realisation, for complete Self-realisation would require the realisation of all. Just as no one is certain Buddhist tradition ever reaches Nirvana, as the rest of the world must be pulled along to get there. It is only a process, a way to live one's life[82].

We see reality as an extension (and reflection) of how we see ourselves. Andrew Niccol's film, *The Truman Show*, tells the story of thirty-something Truman Burbank who begins to question the reality of his life, slowly starting to believe it to be staged and controlled – which it is, in a TV show. At one point, the executive producer is asked why he thinks Truman has taken so long to realise that he is not living within a natural world; he answers, *We accept the reality of the world with which we're presented... It is as simple as that.*

Chapter 4

We are all idiots

Whilst this section title is not intended to be literal, all of us have limitations in seeing the whole picture and understanding what is happening inside our own minds. There are several psychological elements that influence how we make our choices.

- Our character, sometimes inherent, can also be developed and is malleable over time.

- We see the world through the internalised prism of the family and context of origin which needs reframing to be current and personal.

- Massive neurological filters that only let through information that is familiar and deemed acceptable which needs to be opened.

- The belief system created through our experiences. We only have two interpretative choices available when confronting experience: comply or rebel, both provide food for our beliefs which allows us to hold and justify any actions and experience within our thinking system.

- The tendency to overinflate the ego to compensate for our fears, denial, insecurity and the fantasy of the unfulfilled self. This is sometimes known as 'hubris'.

Unfortunately, for some people too much money removes or shields them from the lessons and experiences they needed to find a path for natural personal growth, development and individuation. As Jung reminds us; *Individuation does not shut one out from the world, but gathers the world to itself* [83]. Working deeply with impact may alleviate such situations. Moving our investigation of meaning making from psychology into economics, the economist, John Maynard Keynes wrote in his essay 'Economic Responsibilities for our Grandchildren',

> When the accumulation of wealth is no longer of high social importance, there will be great changes in the code of morals... We shall be able to afford to dare to assess the money-motive at its true value. The love of money as a possession

— as distinguished from the love of money as a means to the enjoyments and realities of life — will be recognised for what it is, a somewhat disgusting morbidity, one of those semi-criminal, semi-pathological propensities which one hands over with a shudder to the specialists in mental disease. All kinds of social customs and economic practises, affecting the distribution of wealth and of economic rewards and penalties, which we now maintain at all costs, however distasteful and unjust they may be in themselves, because they are tremendously useful in promoting the accumulation of capital, we shall then be free, at last, to discard[84].

So here we are in today's world and economy, wondering why many things are the same. There has been little visible change and, in some areas, such as inequality, there has been a dramatic negative shift. However, this is also where we – and our firms — have a clear role to play in alleviating imbalances.

Are we gripped by some collective mental disease, addiction to GDP, or have we been trained to be 'idiots'? The word Idiot originally is derived from the Greek word 'idiotis', meaning a 'person lacking professional skill', 'a private citizen' or 'individual'. As such, please don't be offended as "idiot" does not mean what we usually think but rather that we, as individuals, are part of a greater evolutionary whole of which we may lack some understanding.

The energetic theory of evolution postulates that there are four planes of being: the energetic, the atomic, the cellular, and the plane of creatures. Evolution suggests that each plane represents a stable energetic platform on which the next can develop; thus, integrally speaking each plane is transcended and included by the next. Each plane was created in three stages: first, individual entities learned how to become viable and independent inside the energy framework of their existence; then, these entities learned how to bond to form viable, independent group structures; and finally, they learned how to cooperate to create a higher order entity which now becomes the stable energetic plane for the emergence of the next plane of being.

The only entity able to create a sufficient stable energetic platform at the atomic plane is the carbon atom. And, at the cellular plane, the eukaryotic cell, and apparently at the plane of creatures, *Homo Sapiens*.

Human evolution, as we know it, is not a straight line, nor is it predictable, in some instances it's ever regressive and unless we work diligently to rectify all the negative and false influences, the next stage of evolution which I see as a regression may be the so called 'digital man'.

In my native Sweden, we use a word for a business or firm that encapsulates its essence, namely '*näringsliv*', meaning something that nurtures or nourishes an organism. *Näring* means nutrition and *liv* means life itself.

Figure 4.1: Human evolution, Joe Magee

If Impact Investments is to be a driver for the 'näringsliv' we are trying to create, we must develop the organisational imperative to fully understand what actual impact has in accordance with its objectives and our mission.

This is a concept far removed from conventional thinking in finance. Another imperative for Impact is to understand these critical drivers and develop alternative accounting methodologies, since many cannot be captured using conventional digital and numeric accounting standards.

Whilst we have seen enormous improvements in our economy and our well-being over the past century, we are also planting seeds for the next century in which access to capital will dominate the global agenda and drive its change, mainly in the pursuit of economic growth in isolation to generate its return.

One of the key changes is the dramatic shift towards human and intellectual capital as the engine of business, which is being challenged but also enabled by the introduction of technology and artificial intelligence, this in effect is a double edged sword. However, as we have seen countless times, advances in technology must comport with the development of our consciousness—our real challenge today as technology can only improve technique, not our intentionality. As Yuval Noah Harari writes,

> The danger is that if we invest too much in developing AI and too little in developing human consciousness, the very sophisticated artificial intelligence of computers might only serve to empower the stupidity of humans... To avoid

such outcomes, for every dollar and every minute we invest in improving artificial intelligence, we'd be wise to invest a dollar and a minute in advancing human consciousness. Unfortunately, at present we are not doing much in the way of research into human consciousness and ways to develop it. We are researching and developing human abilities mainly according to the immediate needs of the economic and political system, rather than according to our own long-term needs as conscious beings.[85] (pp. 70-71)

Whilst some of these changes may seem inevitable, the role of capital lies in designing the complementary impetus and strategic direction in alleviating some of today's imbalances. This is why any impact design has to include a deliberate dynamic for each impact realm to communicate and rebalance (by stealth or otherwise) to advance investor/ investee consciousness.

Another impulse with implications for impact is the shift in enterprise work and a much higher reliance on knowledge to drive productivity and therefore sustainability. According to Drucker,

> The most important, and indeed the truly unique, contribution of management in the 20th century was the fifty-fold increase in the productivity of the manual worker in manufacturing. The most important contribution management needs to make in the 21st century is similarly to increase the productivity of knowledge work and the knowledge worker[86]

Significant shifts in the knowledge that workers value and how they seek to make contributions, blended with technology, will create new types of winners and losers. We have heard some clarion calls about what it means to be a citizen and our collective responsibility, which have resulted in, for example, the universal basic income (UBI) movement. Whilst some of these evolved initiatives are at an early stage, they are clearly rooted in the emergent levels of consciousness alluded to earlier.

There may come a point in our own development where we recognise the harm we inflict on ourselves and others through our indiscriminate actions. Abraham Maslow wrote,

> The serious thing for each person to recognise vividly and poignantly, each for himself, is that every falling away from species-virtue, every crime against one's own nature, every evil act, every one without exception records itself in our unconscious and makes us despise ourselves. Karen Horney had a good word to describe this unconscious perceiving and remembering; she said it 'registers.' If we do something we are ashamed of, it 'registers' to our discredit, and if we do something honest or fine or good, it 'registers' to our credit. The net results ultimately are either one or the other—either we respect and accept ourselves or we despise ourselves and feel contemptible, worthless, and unlovable[87]

If true, impact investments can not only restore imbalances but also enable us to individuate and emerge as global citizens. From our investment perspective and ability to change and influence the investee, a prime objective is how we develop our Impact knowledge base and our own capacities to implement this knowledge where needed. Nowhere is this more important than for those who work on impact within other geographies and cultures. As Ziauddin Sardar writes,:

> ...throughout the Northern hemisphere, centuries-old traditions of learning and scholarship had been erased, replaced by a set of ill-fitting Western-style institutions. These institutions had little grounding in the history or culture of countries they were in...[88]

We will return to his work later when we examine ways of knowing.

Much of this disconnect, which has occurred throughout the ages, is the relationship to Nature, with creating harmony as the central idea. This has been replaced with other beliefs, including transcendence and salvation. Many primal people retain this connection with Nature and value it above all else. Huston Smith described 'primal people' as,

> oriented to a single cosmos, which sustains them like a living womb. Because they assume that it exists to nurture them, they have no disposition to challenge it, defy it, refashion it, or escape from it. It is not a place of exile or pilgrimage, though pilgrimages take place within it. Its space is not homogenous; the home has a number of rooms, we might say, some of which are normally invisible. But together they constitute a single domicile. Primal peoples are concerned with the maintenance of personal, social, and cosmic harmony. But the overriding goal of salvation that dominates the historical religions is virtually absent from them[89]

Impact processes need to include this lost element to more fully understand the contextual relationship of each investment. It is well known that people are unable to observe and recognise an event unless there is a prior experienced context and language. Peter Schwartz called this *paradigm blindness*, (Schwartz 1994)[90]. This is why our impact framework needs to be expansively systemic and dynamic and integrated with our moral core.

To a great degree, our connection with the social dimension and Nature depends on our relationship and experience with it. HRH Prince Charles suggests that:

> We need to escape the straitjacket of the Modernist world view...so that we can reconnect our collective outlook to those universal principles that underpin the health of the natural world and keep life's myriad diversity within the limits of

Nature's capacity…If people are encouraged to immerse themselves in Nature's grammar and geometry they are often led to acquire some remarkably deep philosophical insights[91].

Religion is often seen as contrary to science, which I disagree with. A key figure of the renaissance, Muhammad Abduh, wrote,

Religion therefore must be accounted a friend to science, pushing man[sic] to investigate the secrets of existence, summoning him[sic] to respect established truths, and to depend on them in his moral life and conduct(1932, p.11)

This is why we also need to include some form of spiritual practise within impact, if for no other reason than to balance an otherwise imbalanced scientific approach.

One area today requiring extreme vigilance is our reliance on technology without including the deeper self. We all know at a deep level that when we engage with, and do, the right thing we connect and draw on a spiritual energy which is otherwise unavailable. This is how important impact investments can be for you.

Chapter 5

The digitalisation of minds, hearts and worlds.

Let us set the tone by referring to the tech veteran, Marc Benioff, who said,

> The world is being re-shaped by the convergence of social, mobile, cloud, big data, community and other powerful forces. The combination of these technologies unlocks an incredible opportunity to connect everything together in a new way and is dramatically transforming the way we live and work

Our world has changed dramatically, especially with digital technology now becoming the relational driving force behind our work, how we operate our lives, and how we interact with institutions. Other issues today are an abundance of information and communication overload, which desensitise us and remove us from the locus of involvement. They create the need to retreat into more private spaces and erect defensive barriers against incoming 'stuff'. In addition, we use our basic (and misconstrued) neurological filters, which we will explore later.

Information is highly inflationary, as Herbert Simon pointed out in the mid-1970s, that when information becomes abundant, attention becomes the scarce resource. And because attention has become today's scarce resource, this is a new competition in the use of digital technology which is now a part of what we call the attention economy. This treats our attention as economic value but through which we pay for companies to have the opportunity to provide their goods and services. We can often see and experience forms of manipulation to maximise the clicks. The important difference is that whilst technology is considered and aimed to enhance the quality of life, in the attention economy the goals between parties differ so the actual relationship becomes adversarial. Our definition of attention therefore needs to be broadened, since a constant connection to technology creates immediacy and competes with our goals, e.g., when your phone pings or a news feed comes in whilst trying to read a book.

Such constant distractions change behaviour which in turn form our habits. These changes are highly addictive, as each time we satisfy intermittent variable rewards, we trigger neurochemicals such as dopamine which we then crave when not present. Technology companies, fully aware of this, structure and design interactions to make their goals your goals and by extension, to make their values and beliefs yours, thereby aiming to fuse and usurp the user with themselves and effectively substituting them for you.

Such relationships with technology undermine our fundamental abilities and mental capacities to use our own functions such as intelligence, cognition, reflection, and reason, distorting meaning and decision-making which creates dissonance and separation from the true self. What is at stake is nothing less than the coherence and operation of human consciousness, and ultimately our will and right to emancipate and individuate in accordance with our true nature. As relevant today as it was then, Aldous Huxley said on the defenders of freedom that:

> They [advocates of free press] did not foresee what in fact has happened, above all in our Western capitalist democracies — the development of a vast mass communications industry, concerned in the main neither with the true nor the false, but with the unreal, the more or less totally irrelevant. In a word, they failed to take into account man's almost infinite appetite for distractions[92] (p. 44).

We develop cynicism as a defence against both the media and political systems that have eroded public trust, and the reliability of 'fake news' and soundbites that pander to our short attention spans and to our vanity. Every vain mind confers its imprint of authenticity on the movie of life and thus engages in the classic psychological protection mechanism, namely denial, in order to maintain its 'correctness'. This only serves to reinforce the rigidity of our conventional paradigms.

This disconnected form of relating has taken over our airwaves as the mode of communication and strategy for persuasion, affecting the quality and depth of our relationships. Carl Jung writes:

> A million zeros joined together do not, unfortunately, add up to one. Ultimately everything depends on the quality of the individual, but our fatally shortsighted age thinks only in terms of large numbers and mass organisations, though one would think that the world had seen more than enough of what a well-disciplined mob can do in the hands of a single madman. Unfortunately, this realisation does not seem to have penetrated very far - and our blindness is extremely dangerous[93]

The very nature of the mind is to validate and convince us that our personal interpretation of experience is the 'correct' one. This is why we need a full-spectrum impact model that helps us not only to see systematically into the impact dimensions, but also reaches into its deepest corners. If we are to be and become the Impact light that can shine into the darkest corners, we need to find the crack to let in some of our light. Integrally speaking, we need to create soft candlelight to be able to watch our very being, i.e. in our South. We need to find the starlight, leading us towards our becoming, i.e. in our East. We can then step into the sunlight where it can shine brightly on our knowing, i.e. in our North. And we need to find a spotlight for seeing what we are really doing, i.e. in our West.

Cyberspace tends to be self-fulfilling and self-filtering where we attract and retain only those with a similar status and background. Paradoxically, this narrows perspectives, thereby deepening the social divides which Impact may alleviate. The economist Mark Anielski points out that the world's happiest countries have communities and/or rituals that foster close connections. As such, as impact map makers, we create our own boundary conditions, which is why we need to work within solid and expansive frameworks as we connect with the outer edges of our boundaries. As the poet Rainer Maria Rilke points out in his poem "Turning point"[94].

> For there is a boundary to looking *(in German, 'in-looking')*. And the world that is looked at so deeply wants to flourish in love. Work of the eyes is done, now go and do heart-work on all the images imprisoned within you; for you overpowered them: but even now you don't know them.

Whilst the internet greatly facilitated the Arab spring movement, it was actually shared values and bonds that gave rise to the movement itself; yes, it needed connectivity but pre-internet history is not short of examples where connections were made in other ways.

One could even argue that such technology may help develop some of the necessary relational shared bonds before embarking on one's mission, creating a deeper sense of commitment and resilience in the face of opposition. But whilst the benefits of mass and instant communication are clear, they often come at the cost of shallow relationships, abetted by our social media acting as an impersonal intermediary.

Against such a backdrop, it is difficult not to suppress our feelings and resist a cultural spill into our organisations and how management operates. Impact requires a different kind of operating space. As the American poet Wallace Stevens reminds us: 'Perhaps the truth depends on a walk around the lake'[1].

The digital revolution in the working environment has significant social implications for us as impact investors, something we will discuss later. However, as such, if we are to define, design and create an organisational impact

---

[1]Opening Stanza in of his poem "Notes Toward a Supreme Fiction" section VII. [95]

approach with integrity, this can only be achieved within a strong relational environment. This is of particular importance in the social dimension in which we and our investees operate. Whilst technology solves many of our personal problems and is massively convenient, the fabric of our communities suffers as we withdraw into the comfort of our homes as consumers and producers of digital pre-baked information for shopping, entertainment, work, and social interaction.

The restorative power of impact within a community is key to how a firm can embrace the historical and cultural ground in which it operates and activates a creative re-generation. A sign hanging in Albert Einstein's office at Princeton University: *Not everything that counts can be counted, and not everything that can be counted counts*, this is essential for understanding impact and how we develop our approach. Also as the historian Robert Darnton has written,

> The marvels of communication technology in the present has produced a false consciousness about the past – even a sense that communication has no history, or had nothing of importance to consider before the days of television and the internet[96]

Inferring that as we are always in 'on' mode, our filtering systems cannot compute, relate and synthesise past information easily for our meaning making in the present as there are always new demands for our attention. Who needs to understand history if a readymade account is available at the touch of a button?

As human beings, historically as a species we have had significant periods of time when our thinking and collective behaviour have fallen short of our true capacities. We call ourselves 'human beings' because it is only through 'being' that we start to form our life experience. But what does it mean precisely to experience oneself as a human being? Essentially, it means that the individual must have a sense of connection to life that transcends the immediate family and that which primarily binds him or her ethnically, culturally or nationally. 'Being' also gives a sense of playing a key part in the structural relationship that exists between the individual and others. The individual has to feel that he or she belongs to a larger environment as a part of a continuing, living existence. To be a human being, then, is to be essentially alive and connected in a living world that is bringing forth existential experience and to share a rich common ground with all other living beings.

In retrospect, we can see that often our issues arise due to the lack of systems thinking in Impact, which in turn rely on four key properties:

I. All Impact needs to be considered and understood in its wholeness. At this level, it cannot be reduced to its parts, since individually the parts will have different characteristics and patterns of behaviour which are analysed and objectified in each Impact realm, and for Impact outcomes accordingly. As with understanding wholeness in nature, this is mainly the domain of our Integral South.

II. The system is self-modifying. When there is a persistent imbalance or mismatch between inputs and its codes, the system searches for a new constellation and pattern by which it can get back to balance and function. This creates differentiation from the original system and increases complexity. It relies on our governance model and culture and how deeply we have embedded our values and belief systems as it moves through our moral core. This dynamic gets its main inputs from our Integral East.

III. The Impact system is self-regulating. It maintains a steady state by stabilising itself through feedback loops. The system adjusts to create balance between inputs, outputs and internally coded requirements so as to maintain homeostasis. This is the area of Impact mapmaking and the extent we have codified and co-created our Impact objectives and outcomes for its governance. This dynamic also defines how well we can integrate new Impact knowledge, and resides is our Integral North.

IV. The system does not stand on its own. It is part of a larger system but also contains its own sub-systems and interacts with other similar systems. This 'system of systems' adapts together. This is the level of how our Impact objectives are formulated, and then connects with our stakeholders by actualising Impact; it relies on inputs from our Integral West.

(These are related to Social quotient, SQ, our South, Emotional quotient, EQ, our East, Intellectual quotient, IQ, our North and Physical quotient, PQ, our West as discussed in Howard Gardner's book[97] which also highlights gender and global cultural differences). Clearly our difficulties are a result of differing moral and ethical levels, standards and perspectives, and how these play out in political power dynamics within a cultural context. Cultural assimilation and adaptation are key aspects in order that we feel that we belong inside a particular social construct. However, like a long-time prisoner, we may no longer recognise freedom and shy away from it on any encounter.

Our impact approach has to include, at the least, an extension of the borders of our imaginary confining walls. As Yuval Noah Harari writes,

> There is no way out of the imagined order. When we break our prison walls and run towards freedom, we are in fact running into the more spacious exercise yard of a bigger prison [but] some freedom is better than none[85] (p.133).

Another perspective is that in a band of fugitives, the one ostensibly going in the opposite direction is actually heading in the right direction.

Freedom is not just the absence of restrictive law or controls, it is about real possibility and being able to accomplish that which we value. According to Amartya Sen (1993), freedom has at least two aspects:

Process: *Ability to act on behalf of what matters.* (Agency.) Institutions, movements, democratic practise.

Opportunity: *Real opportunity* to achieve valued functionings, selected from among various good possibilities. (Capability)

There is always tension between the need for freedom and for some form of control. In areas with large amounts of freedom, without clear regulation or law enforcement and without accountability like the World Wide Web (www) we need other systems to check the truth and intention of stakeholders. Humans given free reign inside a system and following mainly commercial aims have a tendency to stretch the system and try to manipulate it for their aims. The current state of the www exemplifies how this can happen with scandals such as Cambridge Analytica and countless others making us aware of this tendency.

This does not take away the countless positives of such systems, but enables us to ask how we can create systems with the resilient dynamic for self-correction.

Technology can never be a replacement nor substitute for the development of moral and ethical codes from within the system by its users. Impact investments as a system of knowledge and practise, as currently driven by the finance & economics community is equally at risk of being reduced into a sub-set of the profession rather than what Impact has the potential for, which is to transcend and include finance & economics. Like the www, the Impact industry has the potential to solve many of the core global stresses and strains we are currently facing or become an extension from within the finance & economics field which would not only be highly limiting but also an abdication of our moral imperatives. How can this be done? Firstly, we need a framework that combines and re-connects all the actual parts involved in delivering Impact. Secondly, we need a dynamic systems approach which by design creates the necessary human increase in Impact awareness, centred on our moral core to keep our real Impact clear and on mission. It's my belief that the Integral approach provides an important touchstone and architecture for Impact on which we can build a system which has the integrity to withstand the test of time.

Freedom, as with all things, contains a shadow element. If we feel we have too much freedom (e.g. as facilitated by excess wealth), we seek our identity in new ways to manage the feelings of uncertainty and anxiety in nostalgia (i.e. searching for new homes and holding vessels), in symbolism (i.e. in things and relationships), and in new and shared experiences. As evidenced in our current politics, and in our celebrity culture, excessive freedom can easily lead to idolatry. In our impact frameworks, the need to build boundary conditions is necessary to feel safe and be able to trust our intentions throughout the investment process. The impact implication is, as Drèze and Sen suggests,

> The approach (…) is essentially a 'people-centered' approach, which puts human agency (rather than organisations such as markets or governments) at the centre of the stage. The crucial role of social opportunities is to expand the realm of human agency and freedom, both as an end in itself and as a means of further expansion of freedom. The word 'social' in the expression 'social opportunity' (…) is a useful reminder not to view individuals and their opportunities in isolated terms. The options that a person has depend greatly on relations with others and on what the state and other institutions do. We shall be particularly concerned with those opportunities that are strongly influenced by social circumstances and public policy[98] (p.6).

So what are the possible implications for the Impact space and its possible measurement?

> The primary claim is that in evaluating well-being, the value-objects are the functionings and capabilities. That claim neither entails that all types of capabilities are equally valuable, nor indicates that any capability whatsoever—even if totally remote from the person's life—must have some value in assessing that person's wellbeing. (…) The relative valuation of different functionings and capabilities has to be an integral part of the exercise (Ibidem, p.46).

Sen's *The Idea of Justice*[99] moves beyond the Capability Approach (CA) (which articulates the space in which to evaluate well-being) towards welfare economics with multiple dimensions in capability space, as well as in principles and processes.

When looking back through history, I believe we can all see when things should have been done differently; that is the 'benefit of hindsight'. 'Hindsight' means insight, i.e., now we can connect the dots that at the time we could not see. Scott Barry Kaufman, writes in his book[100],

> Neuroscientist Richard Davidson has said that the way we live today is causing a 'national attention deficit,' while researcher Linda Stone warns that modern life is increasingly lived within a state of 'continuous partial attention' (p.3)

Most of us know that state all too well — as 'tech-zombies' our attention is continuously pulled away.
Stone explains:

> In large doses, [continuous partial attention] contributes to a stressful lifestyle, to operating in crisis management mode, and to a compromised ability to reflect, to make decisions, and to think creatively. In a 24/7, always-on world, continuous partial attention used as our dominant attention mode contributes to a feeling of overwhelm, overstimulation and to a sense of being unfulfilled.

We see this epidemic in today's youth who are heavily reliant on technology for their interactions; this has, in turn, created a series of neurological deficit disorders, and reliance on medication as a solution due to a lack of other developmental resources and coping mechanisms. Also, in my experience, in certain highly specialised professions (e.g., actuaries) we may also see a tendency for dysfunction and disconnect. As Herbert Simon points out: 'A wealth of information creates a poverty of attention[101]'. Also, the integral philosopher Ken Wilber suggests in his latest book[102]:

> The entire online experience has collapsed from one of unity, open-natured expanse, and worldwide integration, into one of soiled, boxed, separatist, mean-spirited ethnic drives

As we are bombarded with media interruptions, we exercise our rejection mechanisms, thereby developing a fully-fledged capacity to automatically ignore incoming information, sometimes with feelings of disdain for its violation of our space. The seemingly overwhelming demand for our attention builds mental barriers and we must distance ourselves to feel safe. I believe that the current tendency to parry email responding is a function of this, and has now become a response culture in itself. The visual media industry, combined with its political and commercial agendas, thrives mainly on negative information, 'hot' rhetoric and gross exaggeration. It has the power to create the illusion that we have been there and experienced something. This risks us becoming numb to incessant multi-level crises; more seriously, if this is our only lens with which to see the world, we will significantly limit our capacity to step into the shoes of our elusive 'other'.

When combined with institutional materialism, short-termism, mechanisation and quantification of already-biased information, we have an excuse for not engaging. Our capacity to seek and mentally step into real issues (and experience) and their impact effects are severely diminished. Also, our impact framework stands little chance of developing into the larger connected, repairing, re-building and regenerative mechanism that our collective future demands.

As Walter Hess suggested in his Nobel Lecture[103] on December 12, 1949,

> In fact, quantitative findings of any material and energy changes preserve their full context only through their being seen and understood as parts of a natural order.

Given our own leaning towards, and reliance on, Northern and Western approaches to organisational governance and methodology, as 'Integral Impact' investors, we must vigilantly conduct our own internal assessment so as not to fall into the trap of seeking solutions from our own immediate consciousness that are driven by our own past. Rather, we must find collectively a better integral solution. This contravenes the existing paradigms within the finance industry (e.g., technical analysis and decision making in all areas of a business based on statistics) to create an intuitive creative space.

Turning again to C.G. Jung in his book *The Undiscovered Self*[104],

> The statistical method shows the facts in the light of the ideal average but does not give us a picture of their empirical reality. While reflecting an indisputable aspect of reality, it can falsify the actual truth in a most misleading way. This is particularly true of theories which are based on statistics. The distinctive thing about real facts, however, is their individuality. Not to put too fine a point on it, once could say that the real picture consists of nothing but exceptions to the rule, and that, in consequence, absolute reality has predominantly the character of irregularity (p.5).

Joseph Jaworski writes about a discussion with the physicist David Bohm,

> The attempts to suppose that measure exists prior to man and independently of him leads, as has been seen, to the 'objectification' of man's insight so that it becomes rigidified and unable to change, eventually bringing about fragmentation and general confusion[105] (p. 152)

This is the trap that impact must avoid if it is to develop; and for this we need first to develop our language as the semantics i.e. meaning making codes of the industry.

The language today of business, finance and economics is not large or expansive enough to include impact; thus, this will be challenging. As mentioned in the introduction, organisations tend to develop their internal language from their main business activities; investment management is no different and finance tends to dominate discussions. However, if we now introduce the additional three dimensions of impact, we discover that this type of language has its limits.

I have sat in many investment committee meetings and found it difficult for the group to focus on other areas. In addition, I have met with many impact investment companies and, whilst these may have good intentions when it comes to impact, some struggle to scratch the surface when they experience impact and how to communicate outcomes except from the financial reporting.

C.G. Jung in Dreams wrote,

> There are people, of course, who think it unscientific to take anything seriously; they do not want their intellectual playground disturbed by graver consider-ations. But the doctor who fails to take account of man's feelings for values commits a serious blunder, and if he tries to correct the mysterious and well-nigh inscrutable workings of nature with his so-called scientific attitude, he is merely putting his shallow sophistry in place of nature's healing processes[33] (296).

Impact investing has evolved as an extension of finance even though impact was always present. It is only now that pressures are developing and forcing our consciousness to see it. However, finance will continue to be a prime driver and, whilst there may be many benefits to this approach (e.g., the ability to attract and retain capital), it is clear that each impact dimension must include unique metrics, calibrations and outcome reporting that speak to the specific Impact dimension in the same way as ROE, IRR, ROCE. have evolved in finance.

Managers analysing each Impact area or in combination need to have the capacity to go deep and return as translators for others. In the final synthesis between impact investments and organisational management, firms seeking new financial capital will need to adjust their reporting and accounting systems to include and fully communicate its own impact credentials; this is an ongoing trend we have seen for some time.

Let us briefly reflect on the limitations of language and words to express fully what an experience is: In the Tao Te Ching, Lao Tzu reiterates that existence is beyond the power of words,

In the beginning of heaven and earth there were no words, Words came out of the womb of matter; and whether a man dispassionately sees to the core of life or passionately sees the surface, the core and the surface are essentially the same, words making them seem different only to express appearance. If name be needed, wonder names them both: from wonder into wonder existence opens[106].

As such, our collective existence is the journey. Even if we insist on our version of logic and rationality, existence is not going to start cooperating and adjust the world to fit with our logic — so who is going to have to adjust if we want less conflict and tension?

As impact investments in general are about allowing more things to exist within our map, this will create significant issues and conflicts for some because of the need to cut corners. The deeper we go, the more complex and mysterious existence becomes.

We may even reach a point where we have to let go of logic and rationality, rely on our other sources of intelligence and just listen. There is a paradox here in that the more we need to rationalise and know factually, the less we can draw on our other intelligences such as intuition, discernment and the emotional self.

It is important to understand our blind spots and familiarise ourselves with our masculine and feminine energies as we have both. Without attempting to generalise, a predominant masculine energy can tend to have a more pure, scientific approach to investments, resistant to change and can have a more mechanistic, ego-dominated way of thinking, often in its abstractions.

The predominant feminine energies can offer more cohesion, intuition, grace, a less-demanding ego, and non-resistance.

Female energy tend to be more able to synthesise, to meld into becoming one and produce a more natural and nature-based way of looking at issues. The feminine energy can also be less resistant, as opposed to being ego-orientated, which is the essence of grace. We need all of these energies in combination to see real Impact and the grace to accept our differences.

I have always enjoyed reflecting on the theologian Paul Tillich's definition of grace as: *Accept the fact that you are accepted despite the fact that you are unacceptable*[107]

Whilst we find less demarcation and more fluidity between genders, and without again attempting to be stereotypical, female energy tends to have a deeper well-spring of love from which it can drink and allow others to partake.

In a more scientific and masculine energy driven organisational culture, we often see the female energies allowed to rise when they blend their energies with the male (and less likely conversely). We consider these differences important within the context of impact management and governance.

There are several reasons for barriers to change, as discussed briefly above, that may need to be considered for an impact approach and for designing our forums for communication and governance.

   I. We have become highly fragmented and specialised as individuals and organisations.

   II. Many of our communication modes have shifted from direct and personal, i.e., dialogue to indirect and remote such as email.

   III. Much of organisational management is an abstraction and overly mechanised; it has become disconnected from the real world.

   IV. We live through our technologies, i.e., the more we operate in a digital world the more our thinking becomes digitised and we lose relational connectivity with 'the other'.

   V. Our obsession with external solutions often ignores solutions from within.

   VI. Much of our contemporary culture is about distraction which diminishes our capacities for the type of contemplation required when we seek answers from the inner self.

   VII. We no longer understand the difference between aspects inside and outside our control; as a result, we experience and justify fragmentation and conflicts.

   VIII. Many live a 'me, more, now' lifestyle, which may need rebalancing to see impact.

   IX. Most organisations don't value the inner life and journey.

   X. Leadership still focuses only on the easily measured and visible; more solutions need exploring for valuing importance and contributions from other areas.

   XI. Leadership in the investment industry tends to be dominated by left brain, logical, linear, sequential, pragmatic thinkers. Consequently transition towards impact might be slow and uncomfortable for many in senior positions and therefore resisted. Female energy drives impact in many areas and organisations.

XII. Organisational 'attention deficit disorder'. Information overload across all spectrums leads to attention deficit. We see this in the lack of response when using electronic communication, which has grown exponentially and has become an acceptable part of contemporary culture.

This is by no means a full list and each could be expanded into a book in itself. However, unless organisational leadership reflects on what is relevant and then takes counterbalancing action, its impact potential will be superficial and resistant to growth.

Impact invites us to become artists in how we synthesise and express our work. The
Russian esotericist P.D. Ouspensky says that,

> The interpretation of emotional experiences and emotional understanding is the aim of art. In the combination of words, in this meaning, in rhythm, in music, in the combination of meaning, rhythm and music ;in sounds, in colours, in lines, in forms - men create a new world and try to express in it that which they feel but cannot express and convey in simple words, i.e. in concepts[108](p.65).

Many of us, having been educated in the North/West, and having been shaped and formed by its management culture, will see any change in management style as a serious challenge to our authority and legitimacy. As such, we will resist using a myriad of tactics and rhetoric. But if we see leadership as just an evolved form of management (which we will expand on later), we miss the opportunity to develop a more authentic and transpersonal approach that includes us becoming transformational, transcultural and transdisciplinary change agents. All of these are necessary for us to reconnect with the lost self, organisation, investee and society.

Rakesh Khurana, in her 2007 book[109] highlights the often seen disconnect inside firms,

> by delegitimising the old management order and turning executives into free agents, or individual leaders, they had cut managers off from their moorings. These moorings connected them not just to the organisation they led, and the communities the organisational were embedded, but also in the end to the shareholders they were purportedly serving. The resulting corporate oligarchy had no obligation other than to self-interest (...) Lacking the religious framework invoked by the founders of the modern university based business school, such as Quaker based Joseph Wharton, or shared agreement about basic societal

values, contemporary schools have no meaningful language for civic discourse about the ultimate purpose of these secular institutions. Thus we have been left only with empty rhetoric about leadership or excellence

At the heart of any organisation is its governance function. This is the body politic that, whilst being subject to legal and regulatory frameworks, has been mandated with a fiduciary responsibility. Key to the governance function is how an investment committee and executive board have created and built ways of relating and sharing intelligence, and the type of language they use. We will investigate this other language later, specifically how to improve and deepen governance through language and make it fit for purpose when dealing with Impact.

What is this 'other' language we need to develop? Some call it the language of the heart, i.e., using words and semantics, voice and cadence relating to our whole being

(and not just our minds). The language of the heart offer our presence and attentions, not just opinions and enables courage (from the word Coeur in French which means heart) to pursue the right cause of action. As, Parker J. Palmer puts it[94]: 'My eyes were opened to new insights and my heart was opened to new life'. We often refer to the heart when we want to include our emotions and core 'gut feeling' which form part of our deeper unconscious which links the 'mind/body' connection.

Such heart language includes many additional aspects of our intelligences and areas of knowledge, such as local and non-local intuition. It is the source of love, courage, and wisdom. The heart is also the core area for our alternative ways of knowing, which include emotional, intellectual, sensory, intuitive, imaginative, experiential, relational, language, memory, faith, and physical. The ways of knowledge will be explored further in the next chapter. It is the challenge for any organisation to create the right conditions and space for these to be activated.

However, when our language is almost totally technical, strategic, tactical and mechanical, we loosen (or sever) human connections and relational links to the internal areas of our character on which our true impact actually depends (i.e., empathy, accountability, etc.). The subconscious mind is considered to be more than a million times powerful than the conscious mind in terms of processing power, with the conscious mind only able to hold five to seven units of information at any time. So, once we get beyond a certain level of digital calculation, we can no longer follow with our conscious mind how the results are determined. This aspect has profound implications as to how we communicate, govern and conduct our meetings.

What is needed to activate our hearts? Here are five interlocking habits of the heart confirming the work we need to do; these are deeply ingrained patterns of receiving, interpreting and responding to experience that involve our intellect, emotions, self-image, and concepts of meaning and purpose. These five habits, according to Parker J. Palmer are crucial to sustaining a democracy (Ibidem p. 46) I believe they are equally applicable for our impact context. We must understand that we are all in this together — ecologists, economists, ethicists, investors, philosophers of science and other diverse leaders who have all given voice to this theme.

Here are some of the key ingredients and habits suggested by Palmer:

- We must develop an appreciation of the value of 'otherness'. This can remind us of the ancient tradition of hospitality to the stranger.

- We must cultivate the ability to hold tension in life-giving ways...When we allow these tensions to expand our hearts, they can open new understandings of ourselves and our world, enhancing our lives, and allowing us to enhance the lives of others...

- We must generate a sense of personal voice and agency. Insight and energy give rise to new life as we speak and act, expressing

- our version of truth while checking and correcting it against the truths of others.

- We must strengthen our capacity to create community.

- The steady companionship of two or three kindred spirits can kindle the courage we need to speak and act as citizens.

Sadly, much of our contemporary society has over time become fear-based and, as we distance ourselves from our communities and families, our sense of abandonment can become acute. We often try and fill the void with distractions and consumerism, while much of the commercial world is designed and structured, to sell more goods and services, to fill the emptiness by tapping into fear. This often operates by fuelling existing fears and offering a product that will solve a particular problem miraculously. As any advertising executive knows, this is the magic formula that sells, and it is something that we frequently witness and absorb unconsciously in our media consumption.

The antidote to fear is always having a map of reality, which today may seem even more difficult. However, and again as everything stems from inside, let us first understand our own reality, our life situations, our identities and our relationships, etc.

One of the roots of fear is lack of self-knowledge and awareness; this can translate into low self-esteem into which we pour outside-in, fix-it solutions. When you see an advertisement by a well-known brand that desperately tries to create a negative psychological mirror, and then adds the famous advertising slogan *because you're worth it*, think to yourself, *Why would I not be otherwise?* If we have closed our hearts due to a low self-image which we are trying to fill and boost outside of ourselves, it's difficult to be aware of the weak, silenced, hidden or oppressed who are actually inside our impact sphere.

Paulo Freire writes,

> Our advanced technological society is rapidly making objects of us and subtly programming us into conformity to the logic of its system to the degree that this happens, we are also becoming submerged in a new *Culture of Silence*[48](p.15)

After the financial crisis, many financial institutions realised that there was a correlation between losses incurred and the power complex which is still unresolved. As Milton Friedman once said. 'Concentrated power is not rendered harmless by the good intentions of those who create it'[110].

One aspect of the power complex is the power distance, where derivatives create a palpable separation between cause and effect. Another is a function of the psychology of the traders themselves in that the more ego-centred they are, and disconnected the greater the likelihood of them taking inordinate risks.

Likewise, as is known in criminology, technology allows a perpetrator to distance him/herself from their actions, for example in the military when drone strikes are made thousands of miles away. We know that soldiers, having made enemy kills, suffer more severe forms of PTSD when they return from battle if such kills have been in close combat. In some of the merger & acquisition activity that I have experienced, I have witnessed PTSD in some staff who were either victims or perpetrators of perceived violence. We now see technology driving this within our global social context; for many, this has reached epidemic proportions as our world becomes technology operationalised.

We need to be acutely aware of these phenomena in our impact practise and governance, and vigilantly re-balance. I am not suggesting that technology is either good or bad, since it is intrinsically neutral. As with guns and the gun lobby, the argument is that it is not guns that kill people, it is people with guns; consequently, the issue lies with the people.

As we become major technology consumers, we must individually manage our use of it and find quiet and contemplative spaces to re-balance. This is the aspect that relates to governance and how we manage our investment processes and meetings in order for impact to be heard properly. Albert Einstein is attributed to have said:

> The intuitive mind is a sacred gift and the rational mind is a faithful servant. We have created a society that honours the servant and has forgotten the gift (Samples 1976, p. 26).

Technology and internet addiction is now considered to be one of our most urgent and profound issues as it touches and changes people and organisations. Many believe that the epidemic increase in ADD, depression, and other issues affecting today's youth is the price of young people having externalised their identities, with few real developmental and working relationships.

What is the antidote, apart from having external therapy? Our answer is to rebalance from within and create the spaces which allow truth to emerge. The key space is our own contemplation, which can only be achieved within some form of solitude. William Deresiewicz's[111] suggests that people are afraid to be alone because our post-modernist society emphasises the need to be recognised, whether through idolising celebrities or being constantly connected with the great 'contemporary terror'.

He validates this claim by exploring the evolution from our relative seclusion to today's alternatives for having our social needs met, and how solitude is now considered by many to be a failure or an inadequacy. However, he also said in his book 'Solitude and Leadership' (2010) that: *Without solitude—the solitude of Adams and Jefferson and Hamilton and Madison and Thomas Paine—there would be no America.*

I believe the same could be said for many others, including Nelson Mandela, Vaclav Havel and Mahatma Gandhi, who endured often enforced solitude from which a strong and clear sense of truth emerged.

Deresiewicz also addresses the contemporary habit of dealing mainly with bite-sized bits of information.

> Multitasking, in short, is not only not thinking, it impairs your ability to think. Thinking means concentrating on one thing long enough to develop an idea about it. Not learning other people's ideas, or memorizing a body of information, however much those may sometimes be useful. Developing your own ideas. In short, thinking for yourself. You simply cannot do that in bursts of 20 seconds at a time, constantly interrupted by Facebook messages or Twitter tweets, or fiddling with your iPod, or watching something on YouTube. (Ibidem)

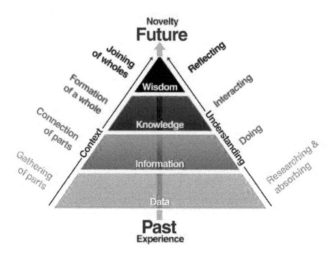

Figure 5.1: Connectivity towards wholeness

The Canadian spiritualist, writer and animal rights activist Anthony Douglas Williams puts it this way: 'Knowledge comes from learning. Wisdom comes from living'. To this I would add 'and knowing ourselves' to bring in the part of us that needs to develop our reflective selves.

A long time ago I heard an expression that I love: 'sometimes data becomes information, sometimes information becomes knowledge, and sometimes knowledge becomes wisdom' also known as DIKW. Here again we see the need for connectivity towards wholeness that can be illustrated as in figure5.1.

We can now also relate this to integral maps and across time lines (Figure 5.2).

In other words, wisdom is an inside-out job. It comes from within and is connected to intuition for which mind power is not sufficient; this is where the power of the heart enters.

The true power of the heart, and how it can interact with others, is shown in research by the Californian Heart Math Institute.

This research suggests that while the brain has electromagnetic impulses that can be read and measured by an MRI at a couple of centimetres distance, the heart is about sixty times greater in amplitude, more than 100 times stronger and can be detected up to three feet away from the body in all directions, using SQUID-based magnetometers.

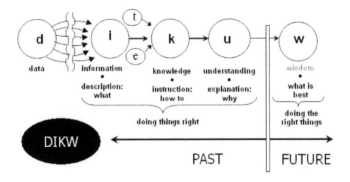

Figure 5.2: Integral maps and time lines

Impressive difference, keeping in mind of course that the heart does not think per se.

This challenges many who have over-invested in the mind and possibly neglected the heart. Again, this highlights the need to re-balance aspects that are exaggerated to regain coherence and connectivity to our environment. We can learn from other sciences, such as medicine, biology, etc., as Aaron Antonovksy wrote,

> We are coming to understand health not as the absence of disease, but rather as the process by which individuals maintain their sense of coherence (i.e. sense that life is comprehensible, manageable, and meaningful) and ability to function in the face of changes in themselves and their relationships with their environment.[112] (p.27)

This statement has profound implications for our social impact dimension, in particular how an organisation embeds itself and develops positive support for its community.

In my martial-arts practise, our practise is based within the traditional forms of the whole person as emotions, spirit, mind and body (our integral South, East, North and West).

In this context, we know that true mastery of the art cannot be achieved through technique alone. If anything, focusing on technique is a barrier; it gets in the way of working deeper with Qi (life energy), which manifests as the invisible inside-out force field.

All true art, as we know it, only manifests once we have been able to go beyond its visible techniques.

This was put succinctly by Yukio Mishima in his book The Way of the Samurai.

> A man who is completely absorbed in his technical skill degenerates into a 'function', a cog in a machine. One who devotes one's life whole-heartedly to the Way of the Samurai does not become a devotee of a particular skill and does not allow oneself to be treated as a simple function….When a Samurai prepares himself mentally to bear single-handedly the burden of the whole (han), when he applies himself to his work with great self-confidence, he ceases to be a mere function. He is a samurai. He is the Way of the Samurai… A total person does not need a skill. He represents spirit, he represents action, he represents the ideal principles on which his realm is founded[113] (p. 72).

As all relationships begin with our own projections and fantasised expectations, let us briefly cover two primordial aspects of this inner psychology which operate interdependently, namely overwhelment and abandonment. They are a source of many of our power complexes that can lead to conflicts and issues within relationships. Simply put, some complexes are contained inside two related existential threats, namely being overwhelmed and being abandoned by others. When these are triggered and evoked, we tend to invoke our preferred coping strategies.

I want to take the opportunity to dig a little deeper into the realm of consciousness that is a key element in the development of any I^3 approach. There is much symmetry between consciousness and other words such as awareness, knowing and perception; however, we need to clarify that, whilst the full-spectrum of consciousness includes multiple states inside waking, dreaming and sleeping etc., we are referring to the waking state and its closest realms, e.g., reverie. When we fragment, separate and create duality, we split consciousness into an inward focus and an outward objectification. As consciousness creates our experiences, if we can reconnect any fragmentation of who we really are, we become liberated not just by negation (i.e., knowing what we are not) but also by what we have or can become, including the essence of our true nature.

I like Rupert Spira's[114] definition of consciousness, suggesting that consciousness is made up of essentially three elements or processes:

I. One in which all experiences appear

II. One with which all experiences are known, and

III. One that out of which all experiences are made.

The two first are inward focusing, establishing the presence, primacy and nature of consciousness, whilst the last enables the collapse between consciousness and experience, or consciousness and objects, which is essential to create a true relationship and understanding with the outside world. Experience and understanding are, of course, very closely related and overlap on several neurological levels. We can now see how this confirms and validates the I³ approach as part of our overall inside-out dynamic.

Spira suggests that there are three stages of understanding, each necessary to create and take on board an experience (Ibidem, Ch. 8)

  I. Awareness: whilst the core witnessing self is innately empty of any object. This is how we through our sensation become aware of any object that creates a screen in the mind's eye.

 II. Contemplation: the neurological filters and processes which create and build upon the initial interpretation and that seek to find the reality behind the screen.

III. Knowing: all the mind now thinks it knows through our senses and perceptions.

Spira summarises his thinking on these relationships as follows:

First, we discover that all experience appears in and is known by the open, empty space of Awareness. Then, we discover that Awareness is not just the container and knower but the very substance or reality of all experience. As the distinction between Awareness and the apparent objects of the body, mind and world collapses or, more accurately, is seen to be utterly non-existent, it is realised that all we ever know or come in contact with is the knowing of experience. In fact, it is not the knowing 'of experience', because experience, independent of Knowing, is never found. We just know Knowing. However, the 'we' or the 'I' that knows Knowing is not separate or distinct from it. Knowing is not known by something other than itself. All that is ever known is Knowing, and it is Knowing that knows itself. There is only the light of pure Knowing[115].

Thinking, as such, is just a modulation of the mind's attempt at thoughts, feelings and sensations to build a believable screen on which to create our experience. As we have previously said, all experience is created through the subjection of contrast, which is one of the main aims of working within the four dimensions of I³. Later we will investigate how the world is constructed through our neurological filters and how this theory of knowledge relates in practise to our impact context.

Let us discuss the two previously mentioned existential threats that most of us can relate to; these are prima facie the main elements in the 'game-dynamic' as part of any relationship.

Fear of being Overwhelmed; the wound of being faced with too much and relative powerlessness to resist what comes from life and the other. This feeling obliges distancing. Coping strategies include:

- Avoidance in its many forms, e.g., forgetting, suppression and repression, projection, distraction and disassociation, each of which can develop into a personality disorder.

- Power complexes to try and regain power over the environment. This includes the sociopath who continuously seeks power over others.

- Compliance, where we deny the self and hand our power to another, often for the assumed exchange of acceptance, recognition and our need to belong. Co-dependencies have their root system in this complex.

Power is not negative in itself, but, when triggered inside a complex, has a tendency to play out in one form or other in our relationships; it can form a shadow governance system inside ourselves and, by extension, our organisational culture.

Fear of Abandonment: The wound of receiving too little and the distancing and neglect by the 'other'. This feeling obliges re-connection. Coping strategies include:

- Most forms of co-dependencies, e.g., seeking approval and praise from others whilst abandoning the self

- Strategies to re-gain any of the five As: attention, acceptance, appreciation, affection, and allowing in a relationship

- Seeking substitute connections with alternatives, e.g., addiction and compulsive disorders.

We see these played out in virtually all organisational settings, including family life and in our meetings. Organisations and their leaders are another holding area for our lives, and a venue where we project and transfer family dynamics onto work dynamics. Michael Gelb writes that,

One of the simplest ways to practice the art of connection is to look for opportunities to perform acts of intentional, deliberate connection and kindness in daily life. Smile and make eye contact with the teller at the bank and the clerk at the pharmacy. Hold a door open, slow down to allow another driver to enter your lane, offer your seat on a crowded subway, and help someone get carryon luggage down from the overhead bin. Notice how you feel when you do these simple acts. You'll delight others, but you'll also find that you feel better, more energized and connected. [116]

This is, in essence, what is needed in our impact practices on a daily basis to help expand connective capacities and consciousness. This, as we know, is also part of the question: which journey are we passing through at this point? The Jungian psychologist, James Hollis puts this succinctly:

The transit of middle passage occurs in the fearsome clash between the acquired personality and the demands of the self… The first must die. Such death and rebirth is not an end in itself; it is a passage. [117]

The challenge, therefore, is to let go of some of our unhelpful historical marching orders of being told what and how to do things from the past to rebuild and reconnect with Impact in a regenerative way. However, to do this we have several challenges to overcome and work through. So, for our context of impact and investments, where do we go from here?

In Saker Nusseibeh's paper 'The Why Question' for the 300 Club, he suggested that we stop looking at economics and financial theory purely through the lens of science and return to its roots within political philosophy:

Arrested development: Scientists, of course, would find the idea of a science that relies on the concept of 'externalities' and an attempted aggregation of 'individuals' often disparate behaviours and mood shifts to explain why the laws postulated by this science do not seem to work dynamically or universally, somewhat baffling. In his book The Origin of Wealth, Eric Beinhocker relates a meeting between economists and scientists in the mid 1990's in Santa Fe.

What the scientists found most fascinating was how economists took a snapshot of science in the late nineteenth century, applied it to their discipline, then evolved this discipline with scant regards to the huge advances made in science thereafter. Economics as a discipline has therefore developed within the confines of how science saw the world at that point in time, while science moved on.

Thus, economists still talk of 'equilibrium' — in 1880 all the rage in physics — while scientists today talk of entropy, for example. Perhaps there is also still a misreading of Adam Smith where many students of economics read The Wealth of Nations, but pay less attention to his The Theory of Moral Sentiments which contextualises it, and so fails to place Smith within the context of the moral philosophy of the eighteenth century that believed in the rationality of humans. [35]

Here we see a call from within the depths of the investment management industry for more wholeness and interconnectivity between systems. This demands nothing less than a fearless and thorough moral inventory of ourselves through our impact and finance work to reconnect with the separated parts of ourselves and others.

Finance, perhaps more than any other industry, is highly susceptible to normalising its own operational behaviour through self-reinforcing and self-validating practises. Frederick Bastiat poignantly writes in his book "The Law",

> When plunder becomes a way of life for a group of men living together in society, they create for themselves in the course of time a legal system that authorises it and a moral code that glorifies it[118].

Our awakening conscience and everything we know has been seen through the contrasting lenses of perceived difference and formed by experienced perspectives.

Integrality carries with it a psychodynamic and consciousness-based healing perspective that can contribute to any change dynamic. The multiple lenses of impact investing that we work with need to contain such dynamic drivers to create and expand on our contrasting lenses and spheres of impact knowledge.

This is a challenge. If we need to repress our true selves and normalise a culture and type of operation, we can then more easily join some other like-minded work community, e.g., a Goldman Sachs, for our validation and recognition. They will also have developed and run their own cultural contribution and validation system, based on how they want to operate to generate and maximise profits.

The power-complex dynamic has been studied for centuries. As Michel de Montaigne noted in the fourteenth century:

> The corruption of the age is made up by the particular contribution of every individual man; some contribute treachery, others injustice, irreligion, tyranny, avarice, cruelty, according to their power[119, p. 192].

Organisations, in this sense, have a 'pastoral' responsibility as one of the core holding vessels of a human being during his/her lifetime. This invites us into a broader conversation as to how, and why, we extend ourselves into the world and our multiple dimensions of interaction. These can be seen as the

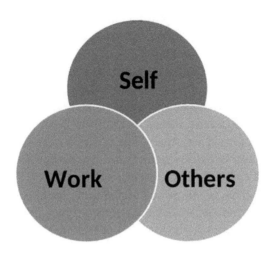

Figure 5.3: Multiple relationships

overlapping and interconnecting areas of work, self-relation and relations with others.

As previously highlighted, these cannot be seen in isolation as they feed each other and overlap in multiple dimensions. As with the Venn diagram (Figure 5.3), multiple relationships are created from the initial ones. Each overlaps, and can be seen as equivalent to the touchstone of our integral moral core.

At the heart of building community activation in our social dimension are our conversations with ourselves pertaining to what the world needs of us and what we need of the world. Other functions and dimensions will also include the level and capacities of tact, patience and maturity we can bring into these conversations.

As such, similar needs for connection and expectations interplay within these realms and we cannot separate these requirements in our lives. Also, with inner conversations, we find similarities, common themes and our own specific and approach.

This includes understanding the boundaries of what 'me' is and what is not me, i.e., where I and my influences and responsibilities begin and end.

It is sometimes more important to know what we don't want rather than knowing what we do want. If so, when encountering what we don't want this is equally a gift.

The loss of experience is not putting ourselves into the position of investigating how so, or being indifferent in a situation. This may take time and psychological maturity to understand.

William Wordsworth's poem 'Intimations of Immortality from Recollections of Early Childhood' reflects mainly on the loss of intuitive powers of perception and joyful existence that we have in childhood, and on growing up and developing the poetic, moral, and philosophical faculties as we lose the primal powers of the child. Again, this suggests stage development as he meditates on the loss of the divine original vision that the child was born with and how this shapes his own experience.

This is followed by an attempt to explain the nature and causes of this loss and, following this, deals with the compensating gain of another type of vision, namely the philosophical vision of the adult poet. This life vision includes the intimation of finding a form of a star (desire is French for 'from the stars') to follow, knowing that we are constantly compromising our true self. This is of particular importance in our fast changing, constantly moving world which tries to manipulate us into following in their direction.

The reason for including work in this context is that there are few other areas in our lives where we are asked to contribute more, build and maintain relationships with others, develop our relational field with money, property and prestige and develop a relational identity based on self-worth and appreciation. In short, whether we like it or not, we are likely to spend most of our time making work a priority.

Of course, work is not only about providing for ourselves but also about providing for others. In the Venn diagram above, we centre our core beliefs, values and spiritual dimension inside our relational fields. This core relational field is beyond our conscious calling in life and must find a home in our work to be fulfilled. Such relational environments, like the family of origin or work, profoundly influences the outlook and values system that develop.

As we move into a more integral age, firms (an example is highlighted in Frederic Laloux's book) gain competitive advantages by moving into integral perspectives and 'going to teal'[120](pp. 60, 245 – 265). A teal organisation is an emerging organisational paradigm that advocates a level of consciousness including all previous world view stages within the operations of an organisation. This aspect needs to be translated and remodelled into an investment methodology that spans the schisms and heals the divides between financial drivers and the additional impacts they inevitably have across the four worlds.

It is key that we constantly reinterpret our past history, not only within the current context but also how we re-create and renew the underlying issues which have arisen. We all have a need, and capacity to be relationship-driven human beings who seek meaning in and for our lives. The way I³ works is that each person will have some reframing occurring from previously held thoughts whether from finance & economics or from other areas in life.

I³ can be a catalyst to re-shape and change the interpretation of positions and events. In addition to being influenced by our past and our current relationships, we are also shaped by, and have a need to conform to, our culture and our available relationships. Truth, therefore, as we will explore later, is often a subjective, interpretative and socially constructed world view. These views contain the seeds to explore multiple perspectives, but only if we are open, willing and able to do so. As Parker J. Palmer wrote,

> I want my inner truth to be the plumb line for the choices I make about my life — about the work that I do and how I do it, about the relationships I enter into and how I conduct them[121].

This journey requires us to develop our experiential and interpretative capacities for discovering new knowledge from and outside of the more clinical settings of data-driven finance in what is called 'hermeneutics'. This is the study of how we interpret and reflect on what makes insights sound or unsound, right or wrong. Thus, it is a meta-critical activity, a deliberate and thoughtful criticism of criticism, which explains why people arrive at particular answers to particular questions. As such, it never fully concludes because there will always be more to learn about learning and knowing.

When we step beyond self into other collective relationships, e.g., multi-culturalism, we find that our own perspectives are never sufficient and we may need frameworks to extend our psychology. This is one of the main limitations in most impact methodology today and why many find it difficult to develop their own interpretation and approach. This is why, in my opinion, the family office is such a unique and important venue, whereby any family can responsibly develop it as a vehicle for real meaning and growth for its members.

An example of these expansionary frameworks is the Johari Widow. Luft & Ingram developed the Johari model as a window into the 4 parts of our perceptions.

Table 5.1: Johari model

	Known to Self	Unknown to Self
Known to Others	OPEN (Public knowledge; what I show to you)	BLIND (Feedback – your gift to me)
Unknown to Others	HIDDEN (Private; mine to share if I trust you)	UNCONSCIOUS (Unknown; new awareness can emerge)

Looking at a situation and context through a Johari window creates and expands our understanding between conscious and unconscious material coming from the self, and how others may help us to gain new insights. Incorporating this into an organisational perspective, a Johari window may be further developed as follows:

Table 5.2: Johari model in a organisational perspective

	Known to Management	Unknown to Management
Known to Staff	PUBLIC IMAGE Reputation & Culture Antidote: Marketing, Branding, Internal information, HR reviews	BLIND SPOT Underdeveloped possibilities & latency. Antidote: 360 degree reviews etc. anonymous feedback, Consulting etc.
Unknown to Staff	HIDDEN ASPECT OF THE ORGANISATION Insider/confidential information, strategy etc. Secrets and organisational angles. Antidote: Open & trusting communication	UNKNOWN ASPECT OF THE ORGANISATION Untapped potential, Blue space & Competitors Antidote: Organisational development & Transformation. External consultancy and roles of Non-exec Directors etc.

Another framework that generates a forward-looking expansion of our awareness through questioning is the Cartesian Coordinates (Figure 5.4)[122], which connects our context with our calling and clarifies from the subconscious to the conscious how to move forward with both.

We uncover the hidden internal answers which otherwise would have

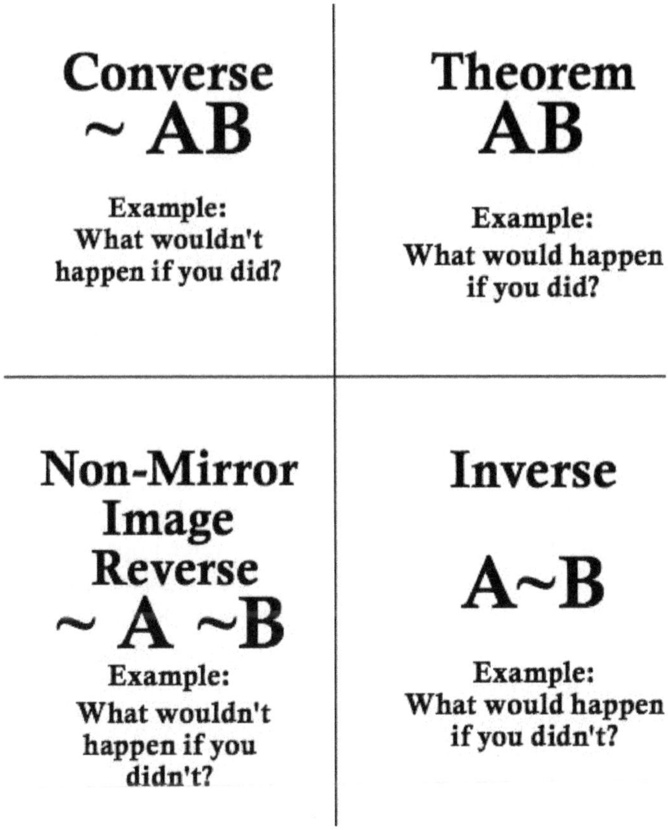

Converse
~ AB

Example:
What wouldn't
happen if you did?

Theorem
AB

Example:
What would happen
if you did?

Non-Mirror
Image
Reverse
~ A ~B

Example:
What wouldn't
happen if you
didn't?

Inverse

A~B

Example:
What would happen
if you didn't?

Figure 5.4: Cartesian Coordinates

been obfuscated by mental filters and barriers.

As an example, take a current problem, distil its essence and insert it into each 'X' above. It is better if someone else asks us the question so it comes across independently, so be aware that whoever is involved will also hear our answers (unless we perform this by silently saying the answers, which is also possible).

As we build our impact approach, we need to consider fully our neurological programs and our interpretative constructs and capacities (e.g., through the governance of organisations). One can argue that the hermeneutic construct of such programs and their interpretation from another's perspective is a key component of our impact context, and an organisation harmonises common programs to enable the catalysation of effects and outcomes. My own context is made up of, and driven by, many such thought programs that come both from my history and upbringing and also from my capacity to re-program those programs that have become conscious and no longer serve me, or have become outdated. As we know from personality and psychometric indicator tests such as the Myers Briggs[123], we have a certain highly personal behavioural preference and ways to perceive and process information which is helpful for us to understand e.g., communication styles & strategies and our selection bias in relationships. Such preferences are often understood in the following ways of mental processing.

How do we see the world: Do we focus, generate feedback from the outer world (Extroversion, E) which is where our energy comes from active involvement and different activities or our inner world (Introversion, I) is where our energy comes from internally processing ideas, pictures, stories, etc. as self-talk?

How do we process information: Do we pay attention to basic information and their physical reality (Sensing, S) or do we prefer impressions, symbols, meaning and abstractions (Intuition, N) of the information received?

How do we make decisions: Do we first look at the objective logic and truth in principles (Thinking, T) with a preference for impersonal facts and consistency or do we prefer to consider people and our relationships, (Feeling, F) including our values and how a decision will affect others?

How is our orientation to the outside world: Do we like to get things decided (Judging, J) in an orderly, organised, controlled way or do we stay open (Perceiving, P), flexible and adaptable to new information, experiences and options?

> Perception involves all the ways of becoming aware of things, people, happenings, or ideas. judgement involves all the ways of coming to conclusions about what has been perceived. If people differ systematically in what they perceive and in how they reach conclusions, then it is only reasonable for them to differ correspondingly in their interests, reactions, values, motivations, and skills (Ibidem).

Very generally, we tend to like and bias relationships with people who are similar to ourselves, as this creates more harmony in our interactions and communication. Organisationally, we tend to hire or promote people we seem to like subconsciously so there was no great surprise when one organisation I worked for learned that ca. 70% of their management structure had the same psychometric profile which may be wonderful for harmony but disastrous for diversity of thought. This tendency not only can become a

EXTERNAL BEHAVIOR

INTROVERT (I)
territoriality, concentration, internal, depth, intensive, limited, relationship, energy conservation, internal reactions, reflective

EXTROVERT (E)
sociability, interaction, external, breadth, extensive, multiple relationship, energy expenditure, external events, gregarious

INTERNAL PROCESS

SENSOR (S)
sequential, present, realistic, actual perspiration, fact, down-to-earth, specific, practicality

INTUITOR (N)
random, future conceptual, inspiration, theoretical, head-in-clouds, fantasy, ingenuity, general

INTERNAL STATE

THINKING (T)
objective, firm-minded, laws, firmness, just, clarity, critique, policy, detached

FEELING (F)
subjective, fairminded, hearted, circumstance, persuasion, humane, harmony, appreciate, social values, involved

ADAPTATION OPERATOR

JUDGER (J)
resolved, decided, fixed, control, closure, planned structure, definite, scheduled, deadline

PERCEIVER (P)
pending, wait and see, flexible, adapt, flow, openness, open-ended, tentative, spontaneous, what deadline?

Figure 5.5: Personality type

shadow of the hidden organisational self, it also stifles benefits that comes from diversity such as creativity, tolerance and humility.

In the organisational shadow lies its opposite, the bias and tendency to look past or even dislike people who express the other side of our own preferences as we don't "get them" or understand easily how they communicate, their thinking and actions. Confirmation bias is one if not the most common errors we make in decisions. All these preferences have their place and value to us as no one is better or worse, just different. In organisations, diversity is a key asset and unless we are aware and work through our biases, this aspect may one day find its way onto the risk management heat map.

As human beings in relationship to others, we are all a part representation of any whole, but we need the whole map to understand our part and what is missing. However, we also have the psychological flexibility to move into other dimensions and areas outside our preferences. This dynamic dance is what develops our understanding and reconnects us with the sources of our calling and being in the world.

Understanding the world to reconnect with your source[9]

I. Understand how the world is constructed: From a qualitative and interpretative perspective, it is to develop the understanding as to how my world is constructed with the notion of its multi-layered complexity.

II. Give 'the other' a voice: Hermeneutics as 'tradition-informed understanding' relies on the connectivity to others to inform and ground the development of our self-understanding.

III. Interpret reality indirectly: Our knowledge comes from taking independent and multiple perspectives as constructed activity.

IV. Reconstruct self and society: Create within our context dialogical and interpretative units that can reframe your interface to become constructor of meaning.

V. Move from spectator to active agent: Moving from responder to communicator and creative innovator of the future.

VI. Evolve from interpretive to transformative: Reviewing the narratives to reconstruct, re-invent, and re-position the creations.

VII. Reconnect with the source: Interpret the multitudinous and conflicting ways which various worlds are constructed and human meanings developed beyond our social constructs and frameworks.

Again, we need to recognise that awareness around these territories of the self not only creates confidence and self-esteem (both of which are foundational for any of our relationships), but how we hold 'the other' also creates a mirror of ourselves which is a gift. This enables us to understand relationships in order to build capacities for a more integral governance system and approach for our firms and investments.

§5.1 Understand how the world is constructed

> Life is not a problem to be solved, but a reality to be experienced.
>
> Soren Kierkegaard

Each personal world-view is constructed individually and can be better understood by a careful exploration of our tradition-informed and cultural-historical position within the social structures in which our map was created. This is an area of countless misunderstandings, strife and destruction of value and capital, which is why it is so important in Impact investments where we merge many world views and imbue them with the additional fuel of capital.

Our governance structures must include integral designs that not only take such into account but build perceived weaknesses into strengths. In my training and development as a psychotherapist I have been able to devote some time over this very necessary epistemological sequence in my journey. This started by looking into how my world is constructed and my path, from the perspectives of both nurture and nature. Neurolinguistic Programming (NLP) suggests that our world map is constructed from passing through massive individual and personalised filters. These filters are bombarded with data from our five senses which needs filtering for perceptions to create generalisations, deletions and distortions and to enable comprehension. Some of these filters are cultural, created via nurture (e.g., distorting by selection patterns and cognitive biases), and some are created by nature, (e.g., deletions due to sensory and cognitive overloading).

From this comes one of the key NLP presuppositions: The map is not the territory, the word is not the thing. As a founding principle of NLP, the

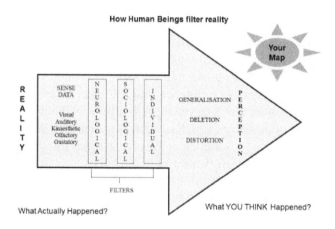

Figure 5.6: How humans filter reality

distinction between a map and a territory originated in Alfred Korzybski's seminal work[27]. The idea seems simple enough but contains significant levels of complexity. For starters, we cannot always be in the territory to observe the terrain, so we need simplifications. These are by definition reductions of reality to become understandable and practical for later use when we have left the territory. Secondly, in my view, there is nothing wrong with having interpretations differ. A map adds to the diversity of perspectives and expands our knowledge base and consciousness whilst helping us to arrive at the same end destination.

In my own practise, from a psychotherapeutic and recovery perspective, we always aim for a healthy and balanced perspective of reality. As the Greek Stoic philosopher Epictetus suggested:

> It is not what happens to you, but how you react to it that matters. When something happens, the only thing in your power is your attitude toward it; you can either accept it or resent it.

Understanding one's relationship to reality is, of course, something we must work at constantly. It is a never-ending task, as the filters above suggest, but gives increased levels of meaning when we explore previously lost territory. For any firm, the very act of implementing I³ creates vehicles for understanding how the world is constructed as we work through the integral model. Each of the four Impact worlds being and becoming self and co-created through our mutual involvement and interaction in the process.

I³ becomes the mechanism of not only cleaning the filters but also making them larger so we can get a better picture of the reality in our territory.

I have previously suggested that all investments are integrally impactful, and if so, to what degree are we aware of our limited filters, and how are we working to improve our map making for the real Impact territory we encounter?

What has been enlightening is that whenever I have engaged with colleagues from the impact world, I³ truly resonates and contrasts with their existing work, with the additional benefit of integrating culture.

Whilst impact is by definition trans-cultural (at the very least between investor and investee), by using a cultural method (e.g., Competing Values Framework (cvf) or Spiral Dynamics or another interpretative map) we create the conditions for transformation through depth analysis thereby increasing trans-disciplinary understanding of how imbalances are uncovered within cultures.

This can inform how a potential investment can precipitate alleviating imbalances and allow changes to evolve naturally. The spiral model is not the only cultural model the final I³ is based on, and we sometimes 'cross-train' the cultural diagnostic maps with others for a more complete perspective.

In particular, we develop a trans-personal lens which gives 'the other' a voice using leadership diagnostics that uncover biases for the dominant 'self' and organisational imbalances for, and within, the economic realms. Impact provides the perfect context and opportunity within our map-making to move deeper into the understanding of self and others.

As Robert Goldman and Stephen Papson state,

> Unless one is looking for it, one rarely sees in maps these transactions of political-economic and cultural power. This is because maps offer us cooked representations of raw data. In their cooked form maps seem to objectively chart territories.
>
> Mapping offers a way of seeking that appears fractal, realistic and proportional. However, mapping is a representational process that distorts through selectivity and omission, emphasis and combination, exaggeration and simplification. While conventionally we think about mapping from a geographer's perspective, we might also speak of mapping from a cultural studies perspective.
>
> Capital not only produces flows of goods and monies but also flows of signs. Capital has been pressing into new spaces for about three centuries. At each stage of expansion, there is a cultural dimension as well – and this is the matter of the representation of Capital in its landscapes [124](p. xx).

This highlights the severe limitations of any map, but also that capital investment as such, creates and leaves behind a cultural 'echo', which needs to be included inside our impact frame.

§5.2 Give 'the other' a voice

It is a blessing that anyone working with Impact has the possibility of choice and multiple others with whom to interact. Many individuals who seek personal isolation for enlightenment find that, after a number of years on the metaphorical and sometimes physical mountain top, they need 'the other' again for their next stage of development.

From this perspective, there is no 'me' without a 'you'. As in the African perspective of 'Ubuntu', *I am* because *you are*. As such, by giving the other a voice, we gift ourselves with a resonance and participative contribution that otherwise would not have been created.

My 2010 paper constructed a transformational and trans-disciplinary bridge within the FSA by giving my own perspective on culture to introduce a trans-personal voice and depth of the missing 'other' in banking and finance.

Also, as I depicted earlier, when two interact, a third relationship develops from the interfacing perspectives and creative interactions.

Some would argue that the cost implications for Impact 1.0 are a barrier for implementation, so why add more through adding culture.

Let us therefore have a short discussion on one of the often heard key economic issues for Impact, namely the general cost burden associated with implementing an impact approach in whatever form we may choose.

It is evident that any impact approach will add costs to an investment firm that would not have been incurred under the old paradigm. This requires significant consideration and creates a dilemma, for which we will borrow some thinking from Ronald Coase and his 'Theory of the Firm.'

The dilemma for investors in working within Impact 1.0 (and possibly moving to 2.0 and beyond) is the relative difficulty in developing the necessary resonance for investment into the prerequisite systems, people and control functions to operate within the impact sphere.

We will now look at some of the possible reasons for this within the context of economics.

- Accounting protocols to date have not been able to fully or reliably connect ESG+C Impact with finance and stronger links to a firm's bottom line.

- As such, for many digital thinkers Impact sits outside the value chain and drivers of equity value.

- Goodhardt's law, expressed simply as: 'When a measure becomes a target, it ceases to be a good measure.' In other words, when we set a specific goal, people tend to optimize for that objective, regardless of the consequences. This also operationally simplifies any processes.

- For many firms, impact measurement and management falls into the 'compliance' area. It is not, as yet, part of a 'hearts and minds' strategy; it is directly allocated as an 'operational cost' that needs to be minimised wherever possible.

- As Coase inferred, firms' internal allocations of talents and resources are not necessarily driven or priced according to market forces but by internal policy and politics. Without direct economic benefits that flow to return on equity, seemingly there is only an agency transaction cost with no visible benefit.

- Many impact outcomes are longer-term than reporting cycles, and what shareholder growth demands from dividend increases, so there is a strong risk of impact greenwashing and Impact minimisation to reduce costs and show Impact falling within reporting cycles.

- Shareholder and stakeholder messaging and signalling for impact requires careful positioning, both with regards to risks (i.e., negative associations) and core corporate prioritisation (e.g., reliance on additional capital requirements). This requires strong non-diluted messaging about returns and growth prospects so Impact objectives are aligned.

However, as impact overlaps with risk mitigation, we have a traditional finance ally in how the downside is assessed. According to Jim Collins in his book[125] from our impact investment perspective, the upside and success principles of most companies are quite similar but they differ dramatically in how they decline. As his extensive research suggests, company decline is far more nuanced, specific and complex depending on what happens mainly inside a firm. He makes the analogy to family dynamics as Tolstoy posited in Anna Karenina that: *Happy families are all alike; every unhappy family is unhappy in its own way.*

On a more personal level, ignorance may be bliss but authentic investment 'happiness' requires the addition of something opposite. Looking for happiness is not like digging for gold; gold is defined independently of who we are, but the 'new gold' of who we are becoming is created by digging for it. As such, impact investments could become one of the core activities that lead us and which define our contribution, meaning and purpose in life by creating 'good spirit' wherever we create a footprint.

The Greeks had a word, eudaimonia, ([eu dai monía]) for this process, which is commonly translated as happiness or welfare; however, 'human flourishing' has been proposed as a more accurate translation. Etymologically, it consists of the words *eu* (good) and *daimon* (spirit). In this sense, the new gold we uncover can be more closely aligned with real wealth.

If we combine this with the word 'economic', which comes from the Greek *oikonomia* meaning 'the management of the household', we have retraced the original meaning back to economic wealth in our activity. If we look closely, we find that our language is crucially important. The meanings of original words have changed over time to align with today's reality. Take the word 'mortgage' which means in French 'a pledge unto death'. Another important word is 'value', which comes from the Latin *valorum*, 'to be worthy.' Here we see that much of the etymology in finance and economics was rooted in ethical and moral codes that have been lost along the way.

Word are just signposts and never actually the 'thing' and every so often our culture changes the direction of these signposts. However, words contain an emotional 'charge' and an accompanying cognitive construct; that is why words and language are paramount for our impact constructs. They are so important in The Bible that we find the statement: 'In the beginning was the Word'.

Whatever we experience influences our thinking and feelings about who we are and what we do. In particular, those experiences have the capacity to dislodge our values and belief systems, which very often happens during conflict, not only when we have conflicting views with others but also conflict within ourselves that demand we change. Let us therefore try and make impact the correct process by first building a 'good spirit' within ourselves and being animated by it, which means being governed also by our feelings and the desire to grow with power of self-construction and continuity. John Stuart Mill puts it:

> It is better to be a human being dissatisfied than a pig satisfied; better to be Socrates dissatisfied than a fool satisfied. And if the fool, or the pig, are of a different opinion, it is only because they only know their own side of the story[126] (p.93).

It is important to recognise that, whilst we may include the environment in 'the other' as part of our mapping, we must recognise that Nature itself is not 'the other' but is the essence and primacy of life, without which there is no life. The structure of Nature is the blueprint and architecture on which all living organisms depend for their success, and on which all our materials in the physical realm rely for its successful creation. This leads us to one of our prime drivers in life: namely how we define, create and value our so-called success and what, if any, implications this may have in how we work with impact if we are be to some degree aligned with Nature.

Chapter 6

Re-defining success

> Success, like happiness, cannot be pursued; it must ensue, and it only does so as the unintended side-effect of one's personal dedication to a cause greater than oneself

Viktor Frankl

Our views on 'success' and what we are willing to do to achieve it, are highly dependent on what stage of our life we are at. Personally, I can relate to the early years of being very goal-orientated in achieving results, whether in school or sports; later in life, with a young family to house and feed, 'success' related to what my family considered it to be. Then there was how I needed to perform to become 'successful' in my chosen career, where recognition came with appraisals, advancement and remuneration. Whilst this created a comparative hierarchy, it was difficult to define real 'success' since much depended on the nature of our clientele.

At this stage of my life, I started to recognise conflicting messages between family and work. As my career and family has matured, I can now afford to re-define my own formula for success in accordance with my situation in life and my needs. I now find that an increasing amount of 'success' includes internally defined parameters based on external 'doings'. Let us look at this through a lens with which you are probably already familiar (figure 6.1)

Depending on our individual circumstances, we will have fulfilled all of these to various degrees. We will also have identified our levels of needs versus shortfalls. Chronological human development suggests that, in general, we achieve these levels in stages during our lives. This implies that we will have different views and objectives to fulfil depending on these stages, and these may need to be taken into account when designing an impact objective.

Most obvious is that in the first half of life we need to cover more of our basic needs by earning money, and if possible, generating capital and savings. Whereas, in the second assuming things have gone reasonably well (which may be a big assumption for some), we realise this does not necessarily fulfil us. We can then afford to make more informed and aligned choices and we

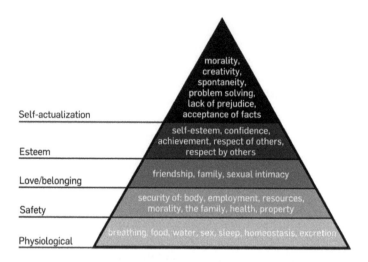

Figure 6.1: Psychologist Abraham Maslow's hierarchy of needs

opt for greater self-realisation. We can find this when we work creatively with impact. Maslow[87] (p.145) suggests that:

> To summarise, SA [self-actualising] creativeness stresses first the personality rather than its achievements, considering these achievements to be epiphenomena emitted by the personality and therefore secondary to it. It stresses the characterological qualities like boldness, courage, freedom, spontaneity, perspicuity, integration, self-acceptance, all of which make possible the kind of generalised SA creativeness, which expresses itself in creative life, or the creative attitude, or the creative person.

The word 'epiphenomena' means: 'a secondary phenomenon accompanying another and caused by it; specifically: a secondary mental phenomenon that is caused by and accompanies a physical phenomenon but has no causal influence itself' (Merriam- Webster)[127]. It is a by-product of something else. In this case, Maslow tells us that creativity is simply the second stage of being a virtuous individual; this is what our organisations need to espouse and nurture. As Warren Bennis suggested 'There are two ways of being creative. One can sing and dance. Or one can create an environment in which singers and dancers flourish'(Whitaker & Lumpa 2014, p. 148).

If through their processes firms can help a person to develop the character traits of boldness, courage, freedom, integration and self-acceptance, such a person will contribute positive creativity and heart into any impact process. As Eleanor Roosevelt (2012) wrote, 'Success must include two things: the development of an individual to his utmost potentiality and a contribution of some kind to one's world.' Creating impact success is, therefore, the key ingredient in nurturing ourselves and helping us to build our legacy of success. The Bauhaus architect Walter Gropius, in a letter to his students in 1964 put it as follows, 'If your contribution has been vital there will always be somebody to pick up where you left off, and that will be your claim to immortality'[128](p. 68).

We must learn to embrace change, ambiguity and learning from whatever source. As has been discussed, this is an inside-out process, much like a diamond cutter must polish away the imperfections of the rough stone to uncover its inner splendour and beauty. Idowu Koyenikan[129] says: 'Success comes from the inside out. In order to change what is on the outside, you must first change what is on the inside'.

Maslow suggests that,

> The muscular person likes to use his muscles, indeed, has to use them in order to self-actualise, and to achieve the subjective feeling of harmonious, uninhibited, satisfying functioning which is so important an aspect of psychological health. People with intelligence must use their intelligence, people with eyes must use their eyes, and people with the capacity to love have the impulse to love and the need to love in order to feel healthy. Capacities clamour to be used, and cease their clamour only when they are used sufficiently [130] (p.41).

Maslow said this in another way as well: 'What one can be, one must be.' Here we have clear instruction on what we need to do with our Impact desires and ambitions.

How can we move towards affluence. When we think of affluence, we tend to think of cars and houses and baubles of all kinds. But Eric Butterworth[131] writes,

> Its literal meaning is 'an abundant flow,' and not things at all. When we are consciously centred in the universal flow, we experience inner direction and the unfoldment of creative activity. Things come too, but prosperity is not just having things. It is the consciousness that attracts things. The goal should not be to make money or acquire things, but to achieve the consciousness through which the substance will flow forth when and as you need it.

If we ask people what they want in life, many would answer 'happiness'. But is our happiness coming from internal or external experience? And to what extent do we engage in activities we would rather avoid versus things we enjoy and would want more of? When we adjust our goals towards making a contribution, the quality and enjoyment of our lives improves.

With impact we have the opportunity to improve the lives of others; when we do this, our own lives automatically improve. Money is both related and unrelated to our happiness. On the one hand it is inert, similar to static energy; it has no real intrinsic value and is useless on its own. On the other hand, it can be activated through an outside force and become embedded with the capacity to generate and catalyse energy beyond itself.

As such, money is another clear example of 'cause and effect'. It also has a complexity that we have inherited along the way. For many people, a significant disconnect occurs between the desire for money and the need to make it. For example, some people dislike their job but it pays for a level of need and lifestyle; essentially there is a 'package' between the things they need to do to make money versus the 'happiness' they get from spending it. We don't need to make judgements about this choice but individually we need to understand our own 'happiness' strategy and take responsibility for evolving and develop it in healthy and conscious way. However, as Tom Brokaw reminds us: 'It is easy to make a buck. It is a lot tougher to make a difference[132].'

Here's the rub: if we expect happiness to come from a precondition being satisfied, we are often disappointed and disillusioned, particularly if these conditions come mainly from external sources. It may seem like a paradox but the relatively poor country of Bhutan scores more highly than the US and the UK in term of happiness. Over the past decades, they have developed a 'Gross National Happiness Index' (GNH) that includes nine domains:

- Psychological well-being

- Health

- Education

- Time use

- Cultural diversity and resilience

- Good governance

- Community vitality

- Ecological diversity and resilience

- Living standards

Whilst each of these contains many separate ingredients and combinations, each are considered important as a contributor to what we call 'happiness'. Whilst money touches all of these in some form, the core drivers and outcomes are beyond what money can buy; at best, money is the catalyst and facilitator for something we may value.

From a psychological perspective, one can assert that happiness is more of a surface objective that seems like an attractive goal but we often lack real personal understanding of its depth to create any needed change. Importantly, if we reflect on our own experiences we might find that the happiness we found was ephemeral; more often than not, its residual values had less energy the next time we experienced them. So what is going on here? If happiness is not a goal in itself, then what is? To find out more we have to delve deeper.

Whilst this is a highly personal journey and will be different for each of us, each journey has some common ingredients. But sometimes we need to remove something or at least experience the threat of losing something to appreciate what we have. As the lyric of a famous song by Kelly Clarkson goes, 'what doesn't kill you makes you stronger'. Hang on we might say, 'Do I have to have near death experiences to be happy? And if so, I'm out of here...'

Some of us may go through physical near-death experiences; most of us will go through metaphorical 'small deaths' of our beliefs, pre-conceived expectations and the small death of our false self and ego. Underneath lies the real self and our connection to something bigger than ourselves. Here we find the true soil of the soul in which we can grow our understanding of our identity and our purposes in life. As impact investors, this is where the connection to real impact lies; this is where the lens and prism are formed into what we see and do.

Throughout my career, I have had to re-frame my understanding of my work purpose many times, not only to meet my own needs but also because of how this related to others. Our capacities to see the 'other' is a product of seeing ourselves 'less' in all our affairs. In my view, impact investing provides an ideal platform and venue to work on this aspect. One could even argue that this is the purpose of Impact investing, i.e., to include more than just our own needs and wants. When we do, we connect with something bigger that nourishes the very soil on which we stand. As Rick Warren[133] writes, 'True humility is not thinking less of yourself; it is thinking of yourself less.'

So how does this relate to 'success'? I have contemplated many variations of what constitutes success in life. If we can consider ourselves to be 'successful', we may find that elusive 'happiness' in our lives. If so, success must be important and highly relevant to what we do and how we do it. But do we have a clear understanding of what success means for us? Is it really ours, or has it been superimposed on us by others?

Our culture, and our family of origin, aim to tell us what 'success' is. The 'marching orders' which might include other's antiquated belief systems set in historical contexts and cultures that come in many forms, overt and covert, are often persuasive, subliminal and attractive as we seek answers to our questions about who we are and what 'tribe' we want to belong to. It often takes time to experience the dissonance necessary to challenge, and have the courage to challenge these so called 'marching orders' if we are to find our own life within life itself.

Let us look more deeply through 'The Stockdale Paradox' which suggests: 'Confront the brutal reality of the situation you're in... while never losing faith that you will prevail in the end'[134].

'The Stockdale Paradox' relates to the journey that Walter Stockdale made whilst a prisoner during the Vietnam War. In Jim Collins' book[135], he asks Stockdale

> "Who didn't make it out?'.
> 'Oh, that's easy,' Stockdale said. 'The optimists.'
> 'The optimists? I don't understand,' Collins said.
> 'The optimists. Oh, they were the ones who said, "We're going to be out by Christmas." And Christmas would come, and Christmas would go. Then: they'd say, "We're going to be out by Easter." And Easter would come, and Easter would go. And then Thanksgiving, then it would be Christmas again. And they died of a broken heart.'
> Then he turned to Collins and said, 'This is a very important lesson. You must never confuse faith that you will prevail in the end — which you can never afford to lose — with the discipline to confront the most brutal facts of your current reality, whatever they might be'

Impact investments allow us the opportunity to confront and examine not only our own reality as stewards of capital but also our responsibility for our impact outcomes. As Socrates reputedly said: 'The unexamined life is not worth living[136].' To create a real and worthy life journey one must create a mirror in which we can thoroughly examine one's own life; out of this examination comes an awareness of the true nature and direction of one's soul that, in turn, needs to be satisfied by the exterior manifestation of our outcomes. Our psychological foundation is comprised of many things, including core complexes that we wish we could eliminate but cannot easily be dealt with. Indeed, a good dose of long-term therapy can't eliminate them either. According to James Hollis, therapy can help us better observe our core complexes and their impacts.

This, in turn, will help the individual become a more conscious person with a more mature vision of life: 'Therapy will not heal you, make your problems go away or make your life work out. It will, quite simply, make your life more interesting.' Thus, the examined life is more interesting, with the resulting corollary, that:

> Consciousness is the gift and that is the best it gets....The theologian Paul Tillich once observed that the chief curse of our time is not that we are evil, though often we are, but that we are banal, superficial. The recovery of depth will never come through an act of intellect, unless that intellect is in service to wonder. We can recover depth, however, by opening ourselves to the numinous which nods at us and invites us. We can also use our imaginative power to seize such moments of beckoning and the images which rise spontaneously from them[137](p.30)

If the results of our choices, or un-reflected actions, are akin to Greek tragedy or drama, then we might also ask what is the myth that best represents our life journey and best explains our existence to us?

Hollis writes that myth: 'as it is used here, refers to those affectively charged images ('imagos') which serve to activate the psyche and to channel libido in service to some value'[138].

Are we living second-hand lives, the unresolved cast-offs of our parents' experience? Are we living reflectively or reactively?

This is also where stage development is important, as I need to understand the differing facets between the activities of the first half of life versus the second. For me, there is now a very clear distinction between these two (and possibly many more) stages.

On one level, the first half seems now more like a preparation and experimentation period akin to a dress rehearsal; in contrast, during the second half I can correct so-called 'mistakes' and align myself more towards my interior needs rather than being driven by external forces and expectations.

I have, in effect, regained sovereignty over myself to shape my kingdom as I see fit. For Hollis: 'The larger life is the soul's agenda, not that of our parents or our culture, or even of our conscious will.' This takes time, effort and courage to disentangle and break free.

C.G Jung in his concept of how we all move into individuation states that it: 'has to do with becoming, as nearly as one can manage, the being that was set in motion by the gods.' This, then, at a practical level is a process of psychological and spiritual maturity as we enter the world and express ourselves in the exterior dimension.

A test for this maturity lies in one's capacity to deal with anxiety, ambiguity and ambivalence. Hollis writes: 'The more mature psyche is able to sustain the tension of opposites and contain conflict longer, thereby allowing the developmental and revelatory potential of the issue to emerge.'

I can recall many times when anxiety about money directed me to change jobs, only to find out that later that this did not fix the problem and the underlying anxiety persisted. Following this, we also examine and re-shape our attitudes and practises for the second half of life. These include: 'amor fati', the necessity to accept and love one's fate; that the examined life is essentially one of healing the wounds from the past; that the examined life is also healing for our ancestors.

In Bert Hellinger's work and therapeutic methods best known as Family Constellations we can experience such intergenerational links, identify our own role in our history and re-shape its impact on our future. Our unconscious is the primary authority in our lives. Individuation lies, in part, in reflecting upon the processes of the unconscious mind and regaining sovereignty over how this control function exerts power, influences, and affects our outer world and its relationships.

We can also refer to the myth of Oedipus as reflective of our human condition and journey. How did Oedipus live out the second half of his life? We may each have our own personal myth to discover, a myth with which we identify and which gives our life substance, meaning, and depth. Oedipus, however, is an archetype that represents every person in his/ her flight from the darkness at his/her core to the discovery of soul and meaning in his/her inner and outer worlds. After Thebes, and after the stunning humiliation of midlife, Oedipus spends his final years in humble wandering, contemplating what the gods wished him to know. He un-learns, learns and absorbs during his difficult exile to Colonus, where he is finally blessed by the gods for the sincerity of his journey. It was not so much that he had created his life than that he finally allowed life to create him, as the gods had actually intended. The price to pay for this gift, both precious and perilous, was exile and suffering; however, the price of not finding his calling was ignorance, lack of meaning and annihilation of the soul. Suffering, therefore, is also a function of lack of ability to find our true purpose and meaning and, in the process, individuate. Impact stewardship should aim to alleviate this.

Worth mentioning is the difference between inner versus outer control and power:

On September 9, 1965, I flew at 500 knots right into a flak trap, at tree-top level, in a little A-4 airplane—the cockpit walls not even three feet apart—which I couldn't steer after it was on fire, its control system shot out. After ejection I had about thirty seconds to make my last statement in freedom before I landed in the main street of a little village right ahead. And so help me, I whispered to myself: 'Five years down there, at least. I'm leaving the world of technology and entering the world of Epictetus[139](p.7)

It is hard for us to imagine getting shot down while flying a combat mission, knowing that we will be beaten and tortured and imprisoned and then, in the remaining seconds of our freedom, to remember the wisdom of Epictetus: "As I ejected from that airplane was the understanding that a Stoic always kept separate files in his mind for (A) those things that are 'up to him' and (B) those things that are 'not up to him.' Another way of saying it is (A) those things that are 'within' his power' and (B) those things that are 'beyond his power"(ibid) It is difficult to imagine Stockdale, floating down into impending doom, reminding himself that NOTHING outside of his mind can determine how he will respond.

Here's a passage from Enchiridion that captures this perspective:

'Of things some are in our power, and others are not... examine it by the rules which you possess, and by this first and chiefly, whether it relates to the things which are in our power or to the things which are not in our power: and if it relates to anything which is not in our power, be ready to say, that it does not concern you (2016, Section 1).

This reminds me of Viktor Frankl who endured the horrors of a World War II concentration camp. In his book[140], he states:

Everything can be taken from a man but one thing; the last of the human freedoms, to choose one's attitude in any given set of circumstances, to choose one's own way (p. 86).

This attitude comports with the realm of the second part of life. As Frederic Laloux writes,

All wisdom traditions posit the profound truth that there are two fundamental ways to live life: from fear and scarcity or from trust and abundance[120] (p.15).

Finding such answers means asking meaningful questions, which we will address later.

Chapter 7

The basis and dynamics of relationship

> The truth about intimate relationships is that they can never be any better than our relationship with ourselves. How we are related to ourselves determines not only the choice of the Other but the quality of the relationship. In fact, every intimate relationship tacitly reveals who we were when we commenced it. All relationships, therefore, are symptomatic of the state of our inner life, and no relationship can be any better than our relationship to our own consciousness...

> Hollis[117], p.47

Highlighting again the need for creating a reflective mirror which creates a bigger self. We are going beyond Newtonian physics, with its limitations in predicting or modelling the behaviour of large and moving objects. At the micro level, quantum physics has confirmed that we are constantly in relationships which go deeper but has yet to discover an adequate theory that explains phenomena such as black holes. Scientists are still searching for a unified theory of the universe. Relationally, perhaps the term 'quantum entanglement' suggests something that we have long intuited but science has only recently been able to observe:

> in the world of quantum physics, it appears that one particle of any entangled pair 'knows' what is happening to another paired particle—even though there is no known means for such information to be communicated between the particles, which are separated by sometimes very large distances.[141, adapted from Rohr R.]

Arguably, the most important aspects in anyone's life (and for our well-being) are the level and quality of such relationships. And the most important relationship is, of course, the one we have with ourselves from which all other relationships are viewed and grounded. We can only see or hear another person as a mirror of our own maturation, awareness and consciousness, all which are ingredients for our judgements.

As an important teacher reminded us several thousand years ago: 'first take the plank out of your own eye, and then you will see clearly to take the

splinter out of your brother's eye.' If our judgements are forms of simplification to fit someone else's round peg into our limited square hole they are
also a form of deflection; essentially the ego trying to make right for itself
that which is, in reality, different. Our insistence and reliance on judgement,
therefore, is a major barrier for us to open up the impact lens.

A fundamental question is: who do we actually think we are in a relationship with? The always elusive 'other'? Who do we include and exclude, and
for what reasons? As impact is all about defining and designing the outcome
contributions of our four realms, we need to look deeply into how we not
only build but execute our relationships for agreed impact outcomes.

As the spiritual teacher Jiddu Krishnamurti said:

> Action has meaning only in relationship…and without understanding rela-
> tionship, action on any level will only breed conflict. The understanding of
> relationship is infinitely more important than the search for any plan of action
> [142](p.207)

Many might disagree with this statement, as it may contravene everything we have worked for. However, if you delve deeper you will find its
absolute truth. As such, it is also one of the biggest challenges for us and
for the impact industry to understand and build into our respective impact
workings and approaches.

Whilst working on Integral Impact perspectives, I thought it would be
useful to understand our relationships within the integral framework. Our
aspect, attitude, depth and our relationships are probably our most important
work, since we are in constant relationship with virtually all things around
us, including money.

As we walk through the four worlds, we can briefly introduce the first
integral dynamic which we call the 'GENE'. GENE stands for Grounding,
Emergence, Navigation and Effect. Each drives one of our realms, e.g., the
Grounding of our very being happens in the southern realm of nature and
relationships. The GENE dynamic is also the function that we work through
to deepen our self-understanding within each realm.

From our informed Integral Impact map, we need to explore and delve
deeper into relational dynamics and how we can use the GENE to make
these come alive as part of our development process. We can do this through
a simplified integral four-worlds representation for these relational fields,
which I call the 4Rs of Rooting, Resonance, Relevance and Rationale.

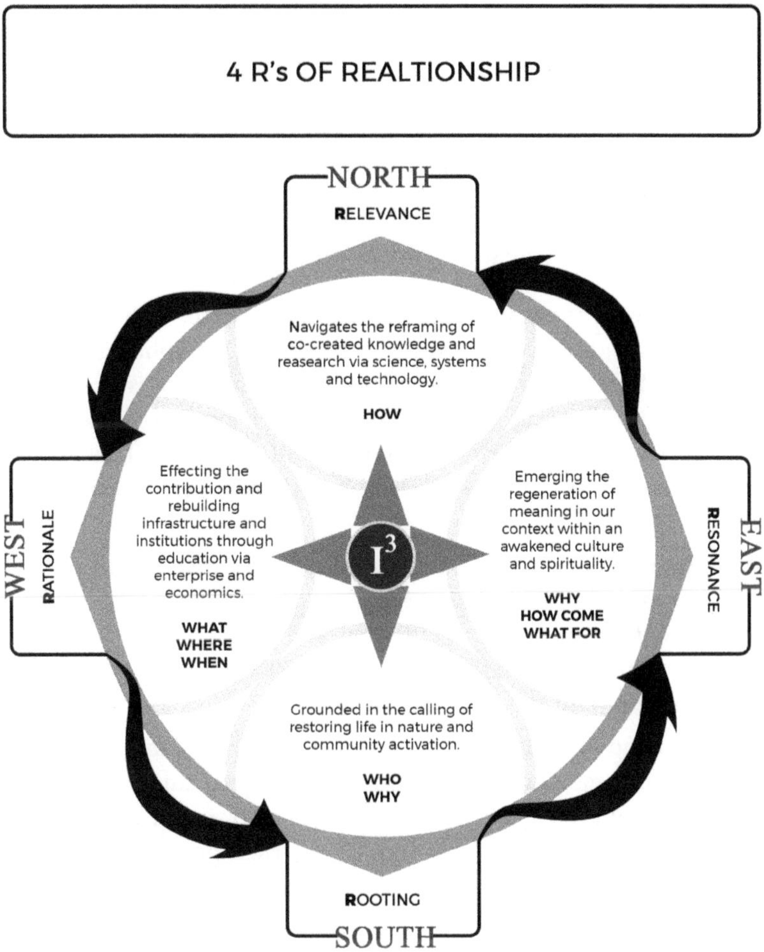

Figure 7.1: 4R's of Relationship

§7.0.1 Integral South: Rooting

Inside-out: From our firm's perspective, starting from the grounding within our Southern dimension, we need to understand the soil in which our relationships to people, places and things have evolved, and how it has created our calling. Within our community, we have shaped our cognitive map through those with whom we are in close relationships, who have given us the vast majority of our values and beliefs. It is here where we are given our 'marching orders' and learn what is right and wrong, and what is socially acceptable. These frameworks and ideas sometimes only emerge in the second half of life as we realise that they belong to others and to our past, and have little relevance today. They manifest as autonomous complexes, which are then projected and can create negative consequences for us.

Outside-in: If we want to work on Impact investments with some integrity, we need to root ourselves not only in the 4Ms (Metaphor, Methodology, Method and Model) but also expand our capacities to re-root ourselves in the soil of a particular investment. This is why we need to develop and work through the 4Ms and, in particular, our first M: Metaphor. This will ground the investment philosophy at organisational level before we impose our model onto others.

If we assume, for example, a corporate equity investment in Pakistan, we can ascertain the firm's stakeholder relationships and the nature of its relationship with, and reliance on, the community in which they operate. This in turn feeds into our 'social' bucket within ESG. This aspect is restorative and developmental for the firm and its people.

In the second half of life, we also have the opportunity to reflect and withdraw from some of our long-held relational and cultural ties that hold back our emergent needs of the soul. We can re-frame or discard old ideas about how we see the world through a historical perspective, whilst still grounding ourselves in valuable lessons from our ancestral history. These lessons play out in how our firm frames its reasons for being, adding value to what the firm may say is important. Who is inside-outside any 'clubs' such as career 'fast tracking', social events, etc.? How does the company manage and work with its employees? How are remuneration, career progression and corporate power structured and managed, and what are the key drivers?

In essence, such questions and their answers give us part of a culture, and the extent people feel the organisation is one to which they want to belong.

§7.0.2 Integral East: Resonance

Inside-out: Within our context, here we seek the emergence of our meaning making and what nurtures our soul. When we do this, we awaken our true relationship with our investment context and we go deeper into understanding why we are pursuing this route. We seek to engage with our core feelings for what we are engaged with, and we also look for different perspectives to include the possible 'other' and what influence this may have on our emotional self.

Each Impact investment opportunity must resonate within the firm and find the necessary connectivity to progress. Our Impact approach will also need to resonate with our investee to guide our discussions towards the design of the component parts of our Integral Impact Investments Outcome Objectives (I^3OO). The I^3OO is our context, the formal agreements in which we can negotiate our key priorities for Impact. How we have achieved this will keep the I^3OO alive and well within the firm, and keep it on track.

Outside-in: Having grounded ourselves in our specific relationship, we look at how we emerge into multiple levels and why we are suited to create this specific type of relationship. This includes looking at the nature of the investment from the investees' cultural and spiritual perspectives, which are operationalised through its behaviours, rites, and codes of conduct...Here we may need to reach beyond the immediate management with whom we may have most of the relational contact into its stakeholders to find cultural resonance and validation.

To that extent does our own culture and Impact investment philosophy resonate and align with the investee? Is conventional equity the right instrument that helps or hinders any current power complex? What is the alignment between strategy, time-lines, exit, policies, procedures and other aspects of its operations that one will have to work with? If misaligned, might this result in future conflict? Once this is understood, we can begin to structure the investment accordingly and design our involvement in its management/governance.

What are the levels and resonance of relationships between the firm and its community? How does this investment impact on the community and does it comport with our impact outcome objectives? Does this aspect need re-design or re-rooting to embed and align the community into the well-being and success of the firm? All of the above will inform and shape the governance aspect of ESG.

§7.0.3 Integral North: Relevance

Inside-out: Becoming integrally informed through understanding the initial grounding in our roots and the emergence of our resonance, we see the connected relevance as related to our calling, in our context and how this begins to inform and navigate our capacity for Impact co-creation. Now we activate and build the necessary intellectual resources and creativity on which we will rely for strengthening our resolve and resilience in the face of challenges. We start to communicate and garner interest and relational strength from others for collaboration and co-creation in line with our Impact objectives. This creates and speaks to how we build 'buy-in' for Impact credibility with all stakeholders, intentionality and sustainability.

Outside-in: In many respects, this is the realm in which we start making sense to our outside stakeholders and our investee about the Impact approach. We start connecting Impact with their priorities. Again, resilience and sustainability are rooted in the process of embedding Impact changes into the fabric of the firm.

§7.0.4 Integral West: Rationale

Inside-out: Having travelled through the previous three realms, we now enter the area where we need to create our contribution and effect. This emerges from the rational conclusions within meaning making to make decisions for our actions and behaviours. The sense making based on knowledge from our Integral North can now close the circle as it creates the deeper narrative for what our Impact contribution and effect will look like.

We now enter our 'doing' phase with enthusiasm and conviction for our mission and the benefits it will bring. We align our strategic intentions with mission and purpose to fully engage in implementing and executing our master plan. Having completed the I^3 process, and with our I^3OO now completed with our investee, we implement and execute the agreed plan.

Outside-in: Our Integral Impact map can now be completed and readied to be travelled by stakeholders, who can now fully engage and implement it. From their unique perspective, they can justify what, where and when they are doing what they are doing. We see alignment and 'walking the talk' as stakeholders understand their role and their meaning.

To make a contrast, in romantic relationships we are also beginning to understand what works well or not. In John Gottman's research which is

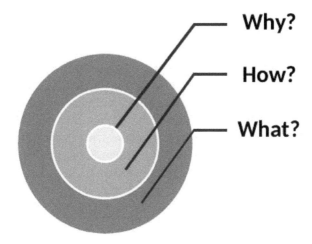

Figure 7.2: Psychologist Abraham Maslow's hierarchy of needs

based on 40 years of studying intimate relationships and marriages, and based on a series of questions he was able to predict with an astonishing 90% accuracy, the probability of divorce rates of married couples. Gottman called these drivers "the four horsemen of the apocalypse[143]: criticism (a shadow North in the form of attack of the others personality or character); defensiveness (a shadow West by victimising ourselves through blaming the other); stonewalling (a shadow East through withdrawal, creating separation through disapproval of the other);and contempt (a shadow South by attacking the others sense of self with the intent to insult or abuse), with contempt being the larger driver in a romantic partnership.

Let us now look through this lens from a more pragmatic business perspective. As the author of the book Start with Why, Simon Sinek writes: 'People don't buy what you do, they buy why you do it[144].'

If you want to get more insights into this aspect, watch Sinek's TED Talk 'How great leaders inspire action[145]', where he explains 'the golden circle' of an organisations what? how? and why? I think when most people seek to understand a firm from the 'outside-in' through an conventional investment process; the vast majority will be quite clear about the What? of the firm; fewer would know the How?; and even less the Why? of the company which we need to asses and align with our Impact capacity diagnosis.

Sinek asserts that 'great leaders' communicate, and I would add 'manage' the company, starting with the Why? then moving to the How? and finally covering the What? He relates this to the biological evolution of the human brain from the neo-cortex (relating to the first circle of What?) and corresponds it to our analytical and rational capacities including our language. The other inner two questions relate to the limbic brain, which can generate feelings and corresponds to trust, loyalty, decision making, and behaviour. These two are related to our capacity for language which also corresponds to our psychology so it's only when we come to the What? where we usually see communication, now incorporating the previous. As Will Durant suggests, quoting Plato: 'Human behaviour flows from three main sources: desire, emotion, and knowledge'.

We may have by now noticed that this comports with the integral model, albeit with the difference that we need to start with the Who? which then fully takes into account 'the golden rule' that exists with all cultures and faiths: 'Do unto others what you want them to do unto you'. There we have it: an inside-out in combination with an outside-in perspective, or now fully integrally informed. The golden rule to my mind suggests we stay firmly focused on ourselves and our task. It does not suggest crossing the line of co-dependency where we can overextend our need to rescue, care-take etc., and thereby lose ourselves in one another.

Rather than two individuals, one seeking to better him/herself at the expense of the other or extending charity to the other, they are simply two cells of the one great Life, each equally precious and necessary. And as these two people merge, as in a marriage, experiencing that one Life of unity, they discover that 'doing unto the other' is not a loss of one's self but a vast expansion of it, because the indivisible wholeness of reality of finding an expanded love is the core need and requirement of the True Self.

I can't think of a better reason for working with integrity towards wholeness and for seeking real impact.

'Wholeness does not mean perfection; it means embracing brokenness as an integral part of life'[146] (p. 5). When we talk about Integrity we also mean how we have created an integral wholeness meaning that you have unified your life so that regardless of any drawer that you open you can see who that person really is.

Nothing is at last sacred but the integrity of your own mind

Ralph Waldo Emerson

Authentic love is one piece; how you love anything is how you love everything. Until we love and until we suffer, we all try to figure out life and death. If you have never experienced human love, it will be very hard for you to access love as an inner revelation. If you have never let someone else really love you, you will not know how to love humanly in the deepest way.

We must understand that the nature of relationship needs to include the qualities that are needed when they are put into tension, stress or shock. What we saw in the financial crisis was another example of how our conventional economic system has built purely transactional relationships mainly on the principles of expediency and efficiency, while minimising the nature and grounding necessary to have real relationships based on trust and integrity. Politically and culturally, the message was that the banks were too big to fail, and thus people were too small to matter, which is the root of many social issues today.

These types of relationship will break apart when put under pressure and are unlikely to reconnect. Without the $2 trillion bailout, the chains would have broken and would only have been able to re-establish themselves at a completely new and much lower level.

All natural systems have a key inbuilt ingredient, namely resilience. They have latent capacities to absorb unexpected change, which can hold the structural chains together. In finance this is equivalent to collateral, but I would also include other assets such as creativity.

When we design and build Impact systems, we need to consider carefully the relational foundations for each impact dimension, their potential weak areas in the chain and the implications if a break should occur including our fallback position for repair and remedy.

Turning to Carl Jung for clarity: 'The creation of something new is not accomplished by the intellect but by the play instinct acting from inner necessity. The creative mind plays with the objects it loves[147]'(p.48).

All firms live and die by their relationship with stakeholders and particularly of course, their clients as their only source of cash from operations. The dynamics around client need are highly context dependent and, for some, culture will have less importance than quality of production.

However, when we design our cultural client dimension, empirical research from over one billion client interviews by Gallup suggests that across industries there are four needs-based client drivers.

- At the lowest level, clients expect accuracy. Without product accuracy and delivery, no amount of additional service will retain a client.

- The next level is availability. The banking industry's move to ATM, and internet banking, increased the availability of existing products and services.

- At this level a client expects partnership. They expect to be listened to, the firm to be responsive to their needs with a sense of being on the same side.

- The most advanced level is advice. Clients build the closest bond to firms that have helped them learn and develop.

The first two levels of client expectations are quite easy to meet but, as such, they are also quite easy for competitors to replicate.

Chapter 8

The five A's of relationship

If you are here unfaithfully with us / you're causing terrible damage.

Rumi[148] (p.56).

As the old saying goes, do you want to be right or do you want to be in a relationship? Looking through the four Rs, we see that this is a function of levels i.e., we are in relationship with everything but it is a question of quality. Another driver for a person's inner calling into relationship is what the psychologist and Buddhist teacher, David Richo refers to as the necessary 5As of healthy adult relationships: ATTENTION, ACCEPTANCE, APPRECIATION, AFFECTION and ALLOWING[149, p. 55]. These can be seen metaphorically as five fuel tanks that are full at birth but over time can get depleted as we experience situations that use up and modify them. We can probably all think of examples and areas where we need to replenish our levels. Richo suggests that during our lives these components make up our internal love which we have for ourselves and others.

ATTENTION refers to our capacity to be aware of others and ourselves, whilst being the focus of someone's loving attention. This aspect is fundamental to our impact as it is the same as being present in seeking real Impact in the dialectic for governance.

So in our interactions, how much of ourselves do we bring into the room? And our capacity to give attention to ourselves, which is a function of the level of self-identity we have acquired.

ACCEPTANCE means being seen with mercy, love, respect and understanding by those whom we believe are important to us. In order to create intimacy and real relationships, we have to feel safe, accepted, relaxed and worthy. In our context, this aspect is fundamental to our capacity to understand perspectives and to remain open to new learning. Creating a non-judgemental space is important to generate creativity and clear decision making.

APPRECIATION for self and others is essential to our feeling loved and accepted and to maintaining good relations. This includes contentment, gratitude and being humble enough to see the gifts that come our way. Benjamin Franklin stated succinctly: 'Content makes poor men rich; discontent makes rich men poor[150].'

Situations of relative and unearned wealth may need work in order for us to value our contribution and see the results that Impact adds to capital. Here our ego is the trickster, as we often judge others as lesser or greater than ourselves; in each case, this will dramatically narrow our capacity to appreciate others and their contribution. C.G. Jung says it clearly: 'Thinking is difficult, that's why most people judge[151].' This resonates with Tal Ben-Shahar's wisdom,

> The word appreciate has two meanings. The first is to be thankful—the opposite of taking something for granted—and the second is to increase in value, the way we say that assets appreciate when their value rises. When it comes to the role that appreciation plays in our life, both these meanings are relevant. Psychological research has repeatedly shown that when we are thankful for the good in our life, the good grows and we have more of it. The opposite, sadly, is also true: When we fail to appreciate the good, when we take it for granted, the good depreciates. [152, p. 144]

AFFECTION is derived from the word 'affect', meaning impact or change in physicality, emotions and feelings. As humans, we need emotional, spiritual and physical affection; infants who do not receive these may die as a result. Affection includes the three keys of attention, acceptance and appreciation, but it also requires direct behaviours that demonstrate proof. This aspect can be quite confusing, particularly when we are confronted by relational challenges.

ALLOWING means letting ourselves and others be fully who we are meant to be. As directed by our upbringing, norms and culture provide a framework for our rules, requirements and expectations which direct our behaviours. Allowing also determines our capacity to let in and receive the four previous As. To what extent do we, and others, deserve the good things that come our way? This aspect also contains the understanding and need for control, and it is through such filters that we shape our environment and relationships. If we don't allow much to enter for ourselves, it is unlikely that we will feel allowing towards others. In our governance structures this is an important aspect for allowing others to be heard, which we will address later. However, collective culture again trumps individual needs and requirements, with the need for conformity being a main driver.

As Herbert Marcuse mentions, 'The way in which a society organises the life of its members involves an initial choice between historical alternatives which are determined by the inherited level of the material and intellectual culture' [153]. That is: I am aware that my personal history colours and fragments the way the industry has developed, and my role will be to understand and map the historical choices and pathways of development.

Claire Graves, who developed Spiral Dynamics, saw clearly that our development is neither assured nor self-evident. This step often requires individuals to venture from conformity to find solutions that actually work, and then attempt to re-admit themselves into some form of influence. Said Dawlabani in his book MEMEnomics, much based on Graves work,

> Our problems today can no longer be solved from a first-tier subsistence toolbox that has been exhausted and corrupted. That system is in decay and the final stages of entropy are at hand. Will humanity decide to take the momentous leap forward and begin to design from a systemic perspective that is informed by the lessons learned from the subsistence value systems and past human behaviour or would we continue to squander our human potential by providing Band-Aid solutions and hope for the best? If we choose the former, we will evolve to the 'being' level of existence on our upward journey of human emergence. If we choose the latter, we will condemn ourselves to becoming a footnote in the universe's cosmic reality' (p. 172).[37]

Having now looked at the background, and some of the needs for taking a more Integral Impact approach, we will now delve deeper into how we can use questions to gain further insight for our Impact approach.

Chapter 9

The value of questions

> I find intelligence is better spotted when analysing the questions asked rather than the answers given.

Sir Isaac Newton[154]

When working with high levels of information, such as in investment analysis, we must be attuned to the value of questions with stakeholders. Questions perform a function that cannot be made visible by working through information alone. Appropriate questions have the ability to draw out deeper, previously hidden insights.

As a psychotherapist, I know a client cannot be helped or cured by anything I may say. Questions elicit the contextual answers that are right for each individual from the subconscious levels of our mind. This has been known for centuries within religious traditions; Judaism, for example, uses the term 'midrash' which is to question, to keep spiritual meanings open, often reflecting on a text or returning questions with more questions.

In dialogue, limited by our own level of maturity and consciousness, we cannot find solutions or outcomes that go deeper than our own perspectives unless we include "the other". This is what Thomas Aquinas hinted at: 'Whatever is received is received according to the manner of the recipient' (Aquinas 1a, 1, 9)

It is by allowing and posing open questions that we can surmount these barriers and limitations. Modernism is often dominated by answering 'How?'. We need to find balance and meaning from deeper questions, such as 'Why?'. The Czech economist, Tomas Sedlacek suggests that this is how one can define modernism,

> The era of scientific thought set a goal of pushing through a method of examining the world that would not allow doubt and would be free of any subjective, disputable dimension. Perhaps the most important character of the modern era has been the change in emphasis from the question 'why?' to the question 'How?'. This shift is from essence to method. The scientific era has tried to demystify the world around us, to present it in mechanical, mathematical, deterministic and rational garments and to get rid of axioms that cannot be empirically confirmed, such as faith and religion [155] (p.171).

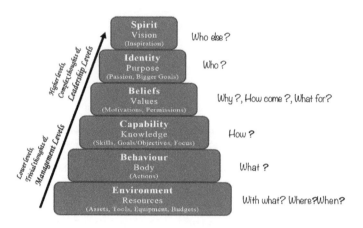

Figure 9.1: The Neurological Levels

These questions, however, have a structure and hierarchy to help us understand what levels of our neurology are being activated and analyse thought. The anthropologist Gregory Bateson initially conceived 'The Neurological Levels[156]' to which I have added ingredients to highlight some of the areas inside each system.

We know that organisations need to operate at all levels but we also know that, depending on the type and nature of each firm, specific levels have to be fully engaged and activated. For example, consider the different requirements between a generic equipment manufacturing business versus a creative and innovative business which only has intellectual property. Looking at the value chain with its drivers and stakeholder analysis through the integral impact lens uncovers pivotal balancing items.

The neurological levels concept was further developed by Dilts (1990, Ibid), inspired by the work of Gregory Bateson (a leading anthropologist, philosopher and seminal figure in the early development of NLP) and particularly by his logical levels of learning construct (1972)[157]. For this model of abstracted levels of what we learn and how it affects us, Bateson drew on the logic of mathematician and philosopher Bertrand Russell. Taking his cue from Bateson, Dilts conceived a hierarchy of levels used by the mind to order its relationship with the world. Dilts linked these 'logical levels' to neurological functions and the structure of the brain — thus, 'neurological levels'!

While the supposed 'logicality' of the model has been attacked, and Dilts' use of neurology is sometimes open to question, almost everyone who has worked with the model testifies to its power to describe what we might call 'nominal level adaptation'. In other words, the match of Identity - towards the Values and Beliefs which flow from Identity - into the base layer of our Environment in which we find ourselves and can identify with.

According to Dilts, the key to a healthy psyche is to align the levels from top to bottom so that the identity has the values and beliefs to acquire the necessary skills and knowledge in order to demonstrate behaviour appropriate to the environment. For example, someone who is a teacher (identity) would almost certainly behave differently in the classroom (environment) than when they are being a worshipper (identity) in a church (environment).

Where neuroscientists have found Dilts' insight creates further understanding of functioning is at the levels of attribution in brain structures and our capacity to be phenomenally perceptive. This generates the relationship between values and beliefs, and skills and knowledge. Skills and knowledge (also known as capability) involve higher-level processing primarily in the cerebral cortex of the brain. Here mental maps are formed from sensory information, other mental representations, where imagination can form, and from which our plans are made. However, values and beliefs, which relate to the question, 'why?' are also associated with the limbic system and, in particular, the amygdala's stimulation of the hypothalamus.

The limbic system's integration of information from the cortex and regulation of the autonomic nervous system means that physiological changes such as tingling of the skin and increase in heart rate often occur when we are operating at this level. However, the amygdala can react to certain sensory information faster than the cortex can evaluate it and plan, resulting in what Daniel Goleman calls 'emotional hijacking'. People can act before thinking (and without any sense of the consequences) when their values and beliefs are challenged.

Categorizing information according to different levels is a way of making important distinctions in our experience. The influence is generally affected from top to bottom; in other words, changes made at one level affect all underlying levels. How? and Why? are therefore integrally connected – but how does this apply to us when we are working in finance?

Hermes' CEO Saker Nusseibeh in his paper[35] suggests:

In a lecture I heard some years ago, a philosopher asserted that science tries to answer the question 'how', while philosophy tries to answer the question 'why'. In looking at the corpus of work produced by academics and practitioners on finance, it seems to me that most, if not all, are trying to answer the 'how' question, but almost none attempt to answer the 'why' question. I think this is because finance as a discipline sees itself as an extension of economics; and economics, since the nineteenth century work of French economists such as Walras and later of Marshall, has been seen in essence as a science, and therefore this preoccupation with the 'how' question is a result of a spillover of that assumption.

Impact investments suggest that we do more than cover the usual finance and commercial business areas; as 'scientific' investors, we must develop the capacities that transcend the 'How?' and move to the heart for further and deeper questions that inform our language. As Terry Tempest Williams says[158],: 'The human heart is the first home of democracy. It is where we embrace our questions. Can we be equitable? Can we be generous? Can we listen with our whole beings, not just our minds, and offer our attention rather than our opinions?'

In Man's Search for Meaning[140], Victor Frankl explores the deepest areas of the human differences between 'Why?' and 'How?' within the context of a German concentration camp. Within such a unique – and hopefully never to be experienced again – environment, the ego is stripped down to its bare bones as our perceived identity collapses in on itself. Frankl found that, regardless of physical health, strength, age and other factors that would usually be related to longevity, how we give meaning in our lives was the preponderant factor. Frankl's credo became Nietzsche's famous phrase, his noble end peroration: 'Those who have a 'why' to live, can bear with almost any 'how'' (Ibid. p. 95).

With impact, we have the potential to build our own 'Why?' into something truly beautiful and beneficial for ourselves and our bigger 'other'. If we do this, we become balanced and fully aligned with our 'How?'. As such, there is a deeper layer to this 'how' question as Richard Rohr suggests:

> If we did not enter deeply the learning process of 'how', we will use our actions to defend ourselves, protect ourselves from our shadow, and build a leaden manhole over our unconscious. We will settle for being right instead of being holy and whole, for saying prayers instead of being one [159]

Much of this development of perspectives comes only with maturity. As a natural progression of changing priorities and requirements, as we age, we must ask different questions than in our youth and mid-life, since the earlier questions no longer serve us.

We can turn again to Parker J. Palmer writing,

> I won't know the answer until I get there. But on my way to that day, I've found a question that's already brought me a new sense of meaning. I no longer ask,

what do I want to let go of, and what do I want to hang on to? Instead I ask, what do I want to let go of, and what do I want to give myself to?' The desire to hang on comes from a sense of scarcity and fear. The desire to give myself comes from a sense of abundance and generosity. That's the kind of truth I want to wither into [160](pp. 26-27).

This more mature and generous state of mind is fundamental to seeing and hearing what is inside the Integral Impact dimensions. Starting from the bottom, let's now walk through Bateson's neurological levels.

Environment: WHERE? & WHEN?

The level of environment includes obvious things like our surroundings, the external context, the Where? and the When? But it also embraces more nebulous elements like our social environment.

There is also our internal environment, which we create through our thoughts, feelings and sense of well-being.

Behaviour: WHAT?

Behaviour is what we do — or don't do. It involves both deliberate and 'accidental' actions, occurring at both conscious and unconscious levels.

Issues on these levels relate to what is happening or being done, for example, actions necessary to carry out tasks like complete a project, write a report, start a new task, etc.

Capability: HOW?

Capability is about the how and the how-to of life: the knowledge, skills, processes and talents that we may have both physically and mentally.

These abilities may be inherent or learned. New skills can be learned and, with a positive attitude and desire, our capabilities can expand.

Beliefs and values: WHY?

Beliefs and values provide the criteria for judgement and action – the Why? – for individuals and organisations. Our beliefs and our values shape our understanding of why things are possible or impossible. They provide us with a rationale and drive our actions.

As such, they also relate to a deeper, personal level which is linked to what we believe to be true and reinforces our motivation. For example: Do we believe the project will give us value? What factors are important to us? What value do we perceive in learning a new skill?

Identity: WHO?

Identity is the sense of self: who we are and how we describe and express ourselves. This could be our personal identity or a relationship identity.

Psychologically, this area is felt to be most significant and will be the most well-defended. If someone feels criticized at this level, they will tend to react very strongly!

Spirit: FOR WHOM/FOR WHAT?

This level relates to a bigger picture where questions about some larger purpose come into play, such as our personal mission in life or our degree of 'passion', e.g., what we want to achieve, what contribution we want to make. For us as individuals, this often means the spiritual. It takes us into questions about our mission and vision.

The dimension of mission and vision can also apply to groups. Because these give deep meaning to our life by answering questions about for whom and or for what, they can be emotionally supercharged and heavily defended or aggressively promoted, as in certain religious groups.

The Neurological levels can help:

- Clarify how we perceive a situation, e.g., our thoughts and ideas, what the real issues are

- Highlight at what level work needs to be done to achieve change, or how we may need to intervene or interact

- Identify the genesis of a problem within an organisation or relationship to help find a solution and move forward

Whilst learning and change can occur at different levels, change is usually easier in the context of the first level 'environment'. Change at a higher, logical level usually impacts on the lower levels. However, change at a lower level will not always affect change at a higher level. Therefore, to solve a problem at one level, a change may be required at a different level first. We may want to change our behaviour but we struggle because the change may be linked to another logical level which we need to address first.

As an example, let's look at the simple sentence: '*I can't do that here*'.

I can't do that here. The emphasis is on the IDENTITY level: who could do the task, or what could you do?

I *can't* do that here. The emphasis is on the BELIEF level: why, what factors are important to help you continue?

I can't *do* that here. The emphasis is on the CAPABILITY level: how, do you need additional skills or knowledge to proceed?

I can't do *that* here. The emphasis is at the BEHAVIOURAL level: what actions can the person do? Does the task have a positive intention and link with your personal development?

I can't do that *here*. The emphasis is on the ENVIRONMENT E.g.: where, when or with whom could you take action? Where do you need to work? What time of the day will be best? Where do you need to be to do the task?

Moving these types of questions from the self to the organisation, Peter Drucker with Jim Collins (2008) suggest starting with a 'self-assessment' as a process and method for what you are doing, why you are doing it, and what you must do to improve the organisations performance.'

They suggest asking five essential questions:

    i. What is our mission?

    ii. Who is our customer?

    iii. What does the customer value?

    iv. What are our results?

    v. What is our plan?

This self-assessment method is designed to bring real meaning to a firm whilst meeting the growing needs for solutions for the environment and social-sector organisations, all of which need to focus on a clarified mission, demonstrate accountability, and achieve measurable and reportable Impact results to stakeholders.

As you may already have realised, whilst these questions are ostensibly simple, you and your organisation might spend a lifetime ascertaining their meaning and implications. Needless to say, these are equally important for any investee company and can form an integral part of our due-diligence process.

A short summary follows:

Mission: As a construct of our mutual core desires, this needs to be constructed from our deep values and beliefs in combination with the firm's fundamental purpose. For some firms, their clarified mission is only skin deep (e.g., around profit maximisation for shareholders in extractive industries) as such missions create no unity, and contradicts deeply held personal values. Mission must, however, be combined with how the firm operates in its practises, structures, processes and cultural norms. These, in turn, need to be aligned with its tactics and strategy, which must also be flexible enough to change with market conditions. In this way, we have a constant core of principles that act as an anchor, plus a changing set of operational and implemented drivers which are integrally informed by the mission.

Customer: Here we look at our primary customers and our secondary customers who are the broader decision makers, influencers, and initiators of a purchase. As any parent knows from experience when their child implores them to purchase a toy (without which life would be miserable!), influence can be the key trigger. In addition, we have supporting customers from whom we may take advice on our purchases. The rule is that there is always someone other than the prime customer who may say No.

In addition, we must know our customers inside-out, including their deeper motivation and their value proposition. Theodore Levitt's famous suggestion that someone who buys a drill does not actually want a drill but is trying to make a hole in the wall is pertinent here.

Customer value: This question is strongly linked to organisational knowledge creation as customer value can reside deep inside motivation, about which most firms will make significant assumptions. A starting insight might be whether a value activates neurology which creates and reinforces energy and value to flow across the types of customers. What is the firm's process to ascertain the value proposition, and how is this linked to the impact proposition?

Results: These must be created and clarified through the lens of how we define a firm's success as outcome objectives, targets and goals. This includes quantitative and qualitative forms of measurement both now and in the future. These outcomes and outputs also ask constantly what needs to change to fully align any business model to its market place. Separately, but intrinsically linked, are how leadership and management defines what constitutes development and results in accordance with the firm's strategy. Importantly, this requires a firm to understand the difference between a person's individual contribution i.e., anything within a person's control and sphere of performance versus riding along on extrinsic waves of performance due to external market drivers and factors. For the impact investor, this is key in directing the management and leadership of the investee to become more 'integral' rather than simply linking performance to a share price or exit.

Plan: We are back to 'begin with the end in mind' regarding a cross-section of goals, which flow from our identified mission. Here we need to look at the overall alignment between the 'plan' and our finances and operations, organisational areas that are often full of contradictions and mixed messages. Ownership and economic performance participation are also intrinsic cultural and operational drivers toward which management and staff will align with its vision and mission. Ownership implies executional responsibility and accountability for any goal and plan of action. None of the above can be fulfilled (or even held static) without transformational management on which we will expand on later.

Whilst neoclassical economists argue that nothing can have value without being an object of expected 'marginal utility[161]', the classical economists, including Adam Smith, David Ricardo and Karl Marx, argue that value is determined by intrinsic labour. In Lady Windemere's Fan (1892) Oscar Wilde's Lord Darlington in Act 3 suggested that a cynic was 'a man who knows the price of everything and the value of nothing[162].' Let us try to move away from such cynical suggestions. David Graeber suggests schools of thought on value that can converge in the present[163].

I. Sociological: conceptions of what is ultimately good, proper, or desirable in human life.

II. Economic: the degree to which objects are desired, particularly as measured by how much others are willing to give up to get them.

III. Linguistic: dating to the structural linguistics of de Saussure (1966), and might be most simply glossed as 'meaningful difference'.

In today's market economy, social constructs have been eroded by a more transactional and distanced approach to value creation. This has implications for our Impact approach if we have an Impact outcome that includes restoring the lost cohesion and fabric within a community and local landscape for a grounded business.

Karl Polanyi[164] (p. 43), states that there are three different forms of value in a market economy,

I. Commodity value: The intrinsic value of a good or service under market conditions.

II. Exchange value: The representative value (not price) when traded and exchanged against other goods and services.

III. Experiential value: The altruistic and experienced social value derived from providing a good or service outside of price and monetary compensation, e.g. blood donations, which decline in numbers if monetarily compensated.

If we are to become fully integrated Impact investors, we need to expand our capacity to feel and experience value. Even firms transitioning from finance-only impact returns into Impact 1.0 may do so badly, and without any real conviction. This will require their management to dig into possibly untapped capacities, given that any additional impact at any level has cost implications for firms.

However, as discussed, even if the prime driver is for firms to follow the market and clients into Impact, the experiential value stems from clients willing to contribute to the bottom line. A distinguishing characteristic of the market society is that humanity's economic mentality has been changed as a result of commoditisation and financialisation, where we see transactional parts as separate events. Prior to 'the great transformation', people based their economic needs and requirements on human values such as reciprocity and redistribution which connected across personal and communal relationships. Competitive markets were created that undermined these earlier social needs, replacing them with formal institutions and corporations that promoted a self-regulating, market economy.

The expansion of capitalist institutions with an economic liberalist mind-set not only changed the operating legal frameworks but fundamentally altered mankind's economic and social relations. Prior to the great transformation, markets played a very minor role in human affairs and often were not capable of setting prices because of their small size, the distance between parties and lack of information. It was only later that the myth of our propensity toward rational free trade became widespread. However, Polanyi asserts instead that 'man's economy, as a rule, is submerged in his social relationships (Iid, p.48). He therefore proposes an alternative ethnographic economic approach which he labelled 'substantivism', as opposed to 'formalism'.

For Polanyi, these changes destroyed the basic social order that had previously reigned. Central to the change was that factors of production, like land and labour, could now be capitalised and sold on the market instead of allocated according to tradition, redistribution or reciprocity, or used in the commons. He emphasises the scope of the transformation because it was both a change of human institutions and human nature (Ibid. p. 35-36). And more recently, through globalisation and the attendant financialisation of our economic resources to generate more returns than just from production. Many aspects of finance have become completely separated and disconnected from human nature with several forms of finance being highly extractive and costly to human life.

Polanyi is important for Impact investments since his thesis looks at the potential schisms in social impact and aims to highlight the lost social structures within a particular culture. This aspect is key when we operate and invest in cultures with stronger ties to social bonds, including reciprocity and redistribution. Investments for them need to be designed to at least maintain the local social fabric and at best be a catalyst for regeneration and growth:

> Reciprocity is a matter of keeping the gift in motion through self-perpetuating cycles of giving and receiving...Through reciprocity the gift is replenished. All of our flourishing is mutual[1]

Without entering the political debate on the validity of redistribution and finance as both an enabling and extractive industry, it is clear that for some investments there is a trade-off between financial returns and making contributions to impact areas which support the system but where there is less clear linkage to a firm's economic performance (e.g., community building and activation).

At the core are the words suggested by Rabbi Hillel the Elder in his Ethics of the Fathers, 1:14, more than two millennia ago[165]:

- If I am not for myself, who is for me? This is the story of the unique self, how I need to learn, respect, honour and teach myself before others can, and the golden rule.

- If I am only for myself, what am I? This is the story of the collective us and how we weave our shared values into a togetherness with our lives and the 'other'.

- If not now, when? This is the story of the present which is always a constant. The rest is a construct by our ego, minds and emotions.

The stories that we tell ourselves about our world are our perceptions, which become our projections. That perception is projection is a well-established psychological axiom, but we forget that this acts as double-sided mirror that reverberates back and forth to create justification and our take on truth. This is why our narrative for our Impact philosophy is critical for our success.

This leads us into how the dynamic of such stories shape our views on how we work within Impact. One of our key attributes as humans is our developmental level of curiosity; this is one of our key drivers for growth,

---

[1]Robin Wall Kimmerer. Braiding Sweetgrass

given that it emanates from our capacity for both love and courage. Curiosity is one of the greatest gifts we possess as humans; it is curiosity that drives most of our endeavours, innovation and risk taking. Filling the gap that our curiosity has created, is one of the most satisfying feelings we can experience. When our curiosity is left unsatisfied or incomplete, we often go to some lengths to close the loop.

Scientists have known this phenomena for decades and it has influenced our story telling for millennia. Building an investment thesis is equally about creating a story that not only convinces and can be validated, but also persuades and can close the various loops and narratives that make up our creative story. In this context, curiosity is an important ingredient not only to evoke but also to expand narrative accounting, measurement and reporting.

In his paper 'The Psychology of Curiosity' (1994), Professor George Loewenstein highlights four ways to involuntarily induce curiosity in humans:

I. the 'posing of a question or presentation of a puzzle'

II. 'exposure to a sequence of events with an anticipated but unknown resolution'

III. 'the violation of expectations that trigger a search for an explanation'

IV. knowledge of 'possession of information by someone else'.

This reads as the perfect structure for any integral investment thesis and beautifully fits into our four-worlds model.

I. South: The question is really whether this is Grounded (GENE) and Rooted (4Rs) in our Calling (4Cs). If it is not, it will not create the energy for us to care in the first place.

II. East: This is about whether this exposure of events Resonates (4Rs) within our Context (4Cs) which creates the Emergence (GENE) of the anticipated gap which we think needs to be resolved.

III. North: The grasping, searching and Navigating (GENE) of the Relevant (4Rs) knowledge and understanding that violates its expected closure and that can co-creatively (4Cs) fill the gap for our explanation and find any possible solutions.

iv. West: The gap is filled by the co-created Contribution (4Cs), which now closes the gap in our Rationale (4Rs) so we can fully Effect (GENE) our investment story/thesis.

We know from our own experience that information gaps gnaw at our need to find the answers. That is why I³ is designed and structured in this iterative and dynamic way so that the required impact thesis that leaves no unconscious or deliberate gaps that later need filling.

The dualistic mind presumes that if you criticize something, you don't love it. Wise prophets would say the opposite but institutions prefer loyalists and sycophants 'company men/women' to prophets. We're uncomfortable with people who point out our imperfections.

> One does not become enlightened by imagining figures of light, but by making the darkness conscious. The latter procedure, however, is disagreeable and therefore not popular.
>
> Carl Jung (1967, p265-266)

Human consciousness does not emerge at any depth except through struggling with its shadow. It is in facing our own contradictions that we grow. It is in the struggle with our shadow self, with failure or with being wounded that we break into higher levels of consciousness. People who learn to expose, name and still thrive inside contradictions are what I would call prophets; they have transcended knowledge into wisdom.

Let us now explore the creation of knowledge and how this may relate to our Impact approach.

Chapter 10

Ways of knowing

I wash my hands of those who imagine chattering to be knowledge, silence to be ignorance, and affection to be art.

Khalil Gibran

This is the realm of epistemology, defined as the theory of knowledge, especially regarding its methods, validity and scope, and the distinction between justified belief and opinion.

The key understanding for impact is that, in our search for reality in each dimension, we develop additional knowledge beyond finance. We need to understand the component parts of knowledge acquisition and retention that exist in different formats from those we traditionally find in finance and economics. It's where we move and create knowledge throughout the integral realms since knowledge only gets embedded if it moves through the heart to the head and into our hands i.e., through action.

In its identification with the ego, the mind cannot, by definition, fully comprehend reality; if it could, it would immediately dissolve upon recognising its own illusory nature.

The neurobiologist Candice Pert (1986) argues that whilst the brain resides inside the cranium, the mind resides throughout the body. If true, we need to develop new neuropathways that help inform the whole system of knowledge and understanding away from our predominant mode of scientifically using the brain. This is important, not only to understand our maps (and dogma) around finance but also in opening the heart for information, whose capacity is infinitely greater in holding ambiguity and difference without entering brain dominated areas of conflict, right/wrong arguments and thereby shutting down primary intelligence from the other.

The severe limitations of our knowledge-creating institutions, such as conventional colleges and universities, are well understood. Such institutions create and train epistemically-obedient, highly-select members. They act as gate keepers to control what types of knowledge making are allowed, celebrated, disavowed, and devalued. They often preserve the past, while only valuing the quick easy and measurable. Institutions that look at modernity as the only solution are removed from natural principles and are unlikely to develop the types of knowledge need for real impact, so we must look elsewhere.

Kant (1988) proposed four fundamental questions:

- What is the human being? (our relational 'South')

- What can I hope? (our inspirational 'East')

- What can I know? (our knowledge creating 'North')

- What ought I to do? (our action oriented 'West')

However, much debate exists around the knowledge of subject and object and the space of presence we travel between the two. For example, what can we actually know about an object through only improving our own presence? Our presence is only known by some influence, interaction, and presence from the other side. As such, it becomes mainly a subject-to-subject, knowing and creating the knowledge of an object, and never just a straight line from subject to object.

Here we begin to see increased dimensional diversity, which for us is a personal journey and formed within our own context and culture. Whilst the Western world draws almost exclusively on the intellectual 'North', Impact requires a more complimentary, balanced and deeper approach, with the integral approach and GENE starting in the 'South'.

This impact practise may then become both our vehicle and fuel for the journey in which we can deepen our knowledge and soften the hard edges that have built up through our life experiences.

Kant reminds us that: 'He who is cruel to animals becomes hard also in his dealings with men. We can judge the heart of a man by his treatment of animals' and Kant also suggests that we need to mature our knowledge through practise 'Science is organised knowledge. Wisdom is organised life' (1997, p. 37). Ultimately impact can only be created by knowledge leading to wisdom. We are mindful of T.S. Eliot, who asked: 'Where is the wisdom we have lost in knowledge? Where is the knowledge we have lost in information?'

Let us now go a little deeper. Richard van de Lagemaat[166], says:

The main question in the theory of knowledge (TOK) is 'how do you know'? The course encourages you to think critically… involving such things as good questions, using language with care and precision, supporting your ideas with evidence.' The theory of knowledge includes exploring the emotional, intellectual, sensory, intuitive, imaginative, experiential, relational, language, memory,

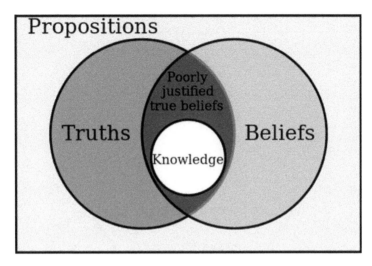

Figure 10.1: Propositions

faith, and physical aspects of how we, as humans, develop our capacities in each of these areas.

These knowledge areas are the component parts of the propositions that we hold and justify as ingredients for our impact TOK and decision-making processes. Consequently, we need to be cognisant about how they are constructed inside the Impact approach.

This is true both for ourselves and also our investees in that: 'In an economy where the only certainty is uncertainty, the only sure source of lasting competitive advantage is knowledge[167]'.

If we expand the diagram above, we enter the realms of the possibility of knowing, which extend out from the knower into ways of knowing and areas of knowledge into how we link concepts, which gives us our neurological constructs. Given our differing neurology and perceptional filters, there is little wonder that we all end up in different places – but this is also our strength as contributors within the organisational system.

As David Bohm suggests: 'The ability to perceive or think differently is more important than the knowledge gained.' This leads us into further possibilities of knowing which is a dynamic to expand, and can be included on, the map we are creating for our Impact.

To create the integral socio-economic Impact weave, we need to tie these strands of knowledge together into the organisational form of a socio-economic laboratory that combines learning, experimentation, and innovation.

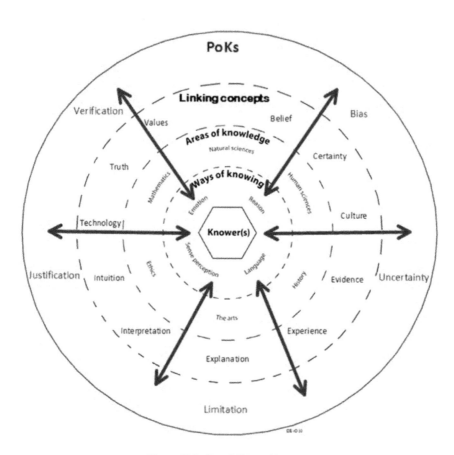

Figure 10.2: Possibilities of knowing

Drawing from Wolverton and McNeely in their book[168], these forms can be linked together as:

- Integral Research/Action Research: In action research, scientific research is inseparable from democratic social action. Scientific knowing, like all other forms of knowledge for individuals and enterprise, is a product of continuous cycles of action and reflection.

- Integral Development/Cultural Topography: There is a rupture between the institutional design of a private enterprise and the cultural philosophy within most societies. This needs to be brought to the surface, making us conscious of the rupture prior to re-constructing enterprises.

- Integral Enterprise/Sustainable Development: Differing capitals are made up of natural and human as well as manufactured and financial capital. The resulting multifaceted flow forms enable companies and communities to engage in sustainable development.

- Integral Economy/A Genuine Well-Being Assessment: is analogous to a corporate annual report to shareholders. It reveals the economic, social and environmental conditions of well-being, using indicators that actually matter to people.

With our integral design, everyone can participate in experimental knowledge creation. Scientific knowing for individuals and enterprises, like all other forms of knowledge, is a product of continuous cycles of action and reflection.

As a form of action research, we must acknowledge power relations and the politics behind them. If we want to listen to people, we need to hear them and empower them. Before we can expect to hear anything worth hearing, we have to examine (and possibly challenge) the power dynamics of the context and its social factors.

For the management philosopher Reg Revans, considered the originator of action learning (2011), the end goals of individual countries and their enterprises will not be found by looking for some miracle in 'globalisation' or outside themselves; rather, their salvation will be found within their own shores and within the will of their own people.

Revans argues that, at the level of the individual enterprise, it is not unreasonable to suggest an essential part of any R&D policy is the study of the human effort, out of which the saleable products of the enterprise

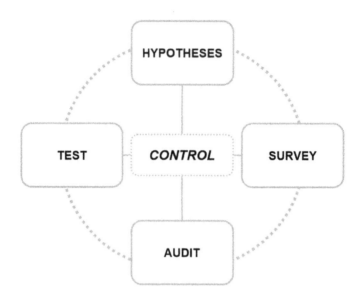

Figure 10.3: Action Learning Cycle

are largely created. Such a study involves the 'scientific method' (survey, hypothesis, test, audit and control — the core elements of the action learning cycle).

Knowledge creation and learning therefore must demand not only research and analysis, but power in order to get the knowledge needed to see one's part in the big picture. In particular, one needs to know the effect of one's behaviour upon those with whom one works. For Revans, this is best achieved within small 'action learning' groups. In the Japanese context, he referred particularly to the establishment of such work groups; not only do they have a high degree of autonomy but are organised to enable people a continuing opportunity to develop.

You learn with and from each other, in small groups or 'learning sets', by supportive attacks upon real and menacing problems, through[9]:

- an exchange of information – ideas, advice, contacts, hunches, concepts

- interaction between set members, offering each other support/challenge

- behavioural change resulting more often from the re-interpretation of past experience than the acquisition of fresh knowledge

Importantly for Revans, through the action learning process 'you learn more from comrades in adversity than from teacher on high'. These three group dynamics are, in my experience, one of the success factors (if not the preponderant one) behind the Client Solutions Group I ran at Fortis Bank, which allowed people to feel empowered and gain real ownership of their outcomes. Having in brief looked at some of the dynamics behind knowledge, let's also investigate some of its ingredients.

Chapter 11

Areas of knowledge

Mathematics, natural sciences, human sciences, history, the
arts, ethics, and to which I add religious knowledge and
indigenous knowledge

Author, Areas of knowledge

Factors that transcend individual ways of knowing and areas of knowledge:

- Nature of knowing: what are the differences between information, data, belief, faith, opinion, knowledge, and wisdom?

- Knowledge communities: what is taken for granted in a community? How can we decide which beliefs should be checked further?

- Knower's perspective and applications of knowledge: how do age, education, culture, and experience influence selection of sources and formation of knowledge claims? If we know something, do we have a responsibility to use our knowledge?

- Justification of knowledge claims: why should claims be assessed critically? Are logic, sensory perception, revelation, faith, memory, consensus, intuition and self-awareness equally reliable justifications?

- Use of coherence, correspondence, pragmatism, and consensus as criteria of truth.

No form of knowledge can be purely intellectual; it always passes through our psyche, our emotions and our spiritual self. One supporting definition of religion that I recently heard was "Giving the best that you have to the best that you know". The direction of knowledge creation in most philosophies and religions can be defined as either Ascenders (pointing us upwards toward the One, the Eternal, and the Absolute) or Descenders (pointing us downwards toward the sacred within the many, the momentary, the mystery and the earth); it is seldom simultaneously both.

For the renowned authority on Islamic Studies, Seyyed Hussein Nasr, in the Orient, of which the Near East is a constituent part, knowledge has always been related to the sacred and to spiritual perfection. To know has meant ultimately to be transformed by the very process of knowing. [169]

This last sentence is key for any impact approach and we will return to it frequently.

The political scientist Adam Webb has developed four separate ethos — four self-understandings, four images of the ideal character — as opposed to the more narrowly defined, ubiquitous and atomistic 'Western' one (Webb, 2006, pp.36-45).

Each of these four is universal, cropping up repeatedly in different civilisations and eras. As permanent focal points of human culture, they have existed in creative tension with each other. But in modern times, the first of the four and the simplest — atomisism — has gone on the offensive and wrought havoc across the globe.

The second ethos is *demoticism*. The Greek word demos means the common people as a whole (the integral 'North'), and *demot*, the member of an ancient township.

The third ethos is the 'Eastern' perfectionism (the integral 'East'). Perfectionists reject the demotic ideas of sameness across all human beings. This perfectionist ethos has two major flavours: aristocratic and mystical. Whilst aristocratic perfectionists seek self-cultivation within the world, mystical perfectionists seek this beyond the world. Both focus on refining the best elements within themselves, elements that set them apart from humanity's common denominator.

The fourth ethos (the integral 'North') Webb calls *virtuocracy*. The word combines the Latin *virtus* (virtue) and the Greek *kratia* (ruling). Historically, virtuocrats have included the Catholic clergy, the Islamic *ulama*, the Indian *brahmins*, the Confucian *mandarins*, literati, and other public-minded intellectuals. For perfectionists, the idea of transcendence of special qualities and insights distinguishes a minority. With demots, they are embedded in a social world where one can realize oneself by affecting others.

In Chinese Taoism, the perfect person is seen as one who knows the Tao and lives according to this knowledge, implying that he/she lives according to the 'how' in 'nature'. The originator of Taoism, Chuang-Tzu, wrote: The man of virtue can see where all is dark. He can hear when all is still. In the darkness he alone sees light. In the stillness he alone can detect harmony' (Giles, 1961, p. 119).

In Judaism, according to Nasr (1997), the significance of *hokhmah* (wisdom) is critical. In the books of Job, Proverbs, and Ecclesiastes, the term *hokhmah* (later translated as *sophia*) appears nearly one hundred times. The Jews also believe that the Torah is the embodiment of wisdom.

In Islam, the traditional names used by the sacred scripture are all related to knowledge: *al-qu'ran* 'recitation'; *al-furqan* 'discernment', and *umm-al-kitab* 'the mother of books'. The Qu'ran refers to the importance of intellect and knowledge in almost every chapter; the first verses pertain to 'recitation' which implies knowledge (*ilm*) and science (*ta'lim*). The Arabic word for intellect, *al'aql*, is in fact related to the word 'to bind', for it is that which binds man to his origin. Etymologically it could be compared to religion itself, for in this case *religio* also means what binds and relates man to God. Even the Arabic world for poetry (*al-shi'r*) is related to the root meaning of consciousness and knowledge rather than 'making' in the Latin root *poesis*.

Turning to Christianity, in modern times its sapiential dimension has been forsaken but Nasr maintains it cannot be totally divorced from it. Thus, in John's Gospel: 'In the beginning was the Word' was interpreted for centuries as an affirmation of the primacy that logos was the prime source of both revelation and knowledge. Thereafter, our secularized reason created the separation of the sapiential gospel from the pursuit of science.

Perhaps the most universal way to identify the two spiritual traditions of knowing and not-knowing is through light and darkness. The formal theological terms are *kataphatic* or the 'affirmative' way (employing words, concepts, and images) and *apophatic* or 'negative' way (moving beyond words and ideas into silence and beyond-rational knowing). I believe both are good and necessary; they affirm the need to understand our respective mirrors and shadows and only together do they create a form of higher consciousness. This is why our impact approach must be based on working with and exploring defined polar opposites in each of the coordinates.

However too much of a good thing (e.g., light) can damage, so we must find a balance. In addition, we can only make visible much of our darkness by shining light on it, in the same way as we see the moon by the light from the sun. However, lunar light is more subtle, filtered and indirect, so we can observe and find nuances that sharp, direct light cannot see and which often creates its own shadows. Equally, we need to have courage to face our shadows as if and when we numb out the dark we also numb out the light. All things are a mix of shadow and light, and as such we need to embrace and include these in our map making. The Islamist futurist Ziauddin Sardar (2006) offers a relevant point: namely that research and teaching at universities today have almost no relevance to the problems of poverty and underdevelopment; much of our open-ended enquiry for context-specific impact should incorporate a plurality of views but free thinking is either absent or strongly discouraged. Yes, this is context dependent but we should be aware of such imbalances from our predominantly 'Western' perspective.

At least five Islamic concepts, according to Sardar, have direct bearing on knowledge: justice – *adl*; knowledge – *ilm*; worship in its broadest sense – *ibadah*; human trusteeship of the Earth's resources – *khilafa*, and philanthropic endowments – *waqf*. Of these, *ilm* is distributive knowledge: it is not a monopoly of individuals, a specific class, group or sex; it is not an obligation of only a few, absolving most of society; it is not to a particular field of enquiry or discipline, but covers all dimensions of human awareness and the entire spectrum of natural phenomena.

Our impact interactions must reflect such distributions. Epistemology and societal structures feed on, and navigate, each other: when we construct our images of society, and develop social, economic, political, scientific, and technological structures, we use our conception of knowledge and its epistemology. So why in our 'Northern' perspective do we have such a strong focus on knowledge and its epistemology?

Epistemology is so important because it is the major operator that transforms a world view into a reality. Any organisation will have to navigate this terrain and create unique and distinct skills, capabilities, and competitive advantages. For such knowledge to become integrally informed, we need the dynamic built into the integral model as we move deeper into each realm.

We can now build our integral topography to see how these are connected developmentally, distinguishing between four layers (images, ideologies, institutions and inclinations) which Lessem and Schieffer call the '4Is' (2014, p. 413). All are required for the eastern socioeconomic laboratory that builds integrally on what has come before. For thoroughgoing integral impact development to occur, all four levels need to become dynamically interconnected.

We begin with the images at the deepest level of the enterprise. They form the source of individual or institutional creativity and imagination.

Table 11.1: Development Topography

Topography	Developmental Layers	Expressions	Integral Realities
Top-Soil	Inclinations	Visible attitudes and behaviours / outer practise	West

Sub-Soil	Institutions	The institutional frameworks that organise and direct our attitudes and behaviours, as well as the scientific disciplines underlying them	West & North
Bedrock	Ideologies	The philosophies and worldviews that inform our way of thinking / this layer includes ontology and epistemology, defining what counts as valid knowledge and how new knowledge is to be created	North & East
Core	Images	The deep-rooted images, beliefs and archetypal structures that inform, often unconsciously, our lives and that are directly related to our physical, psychological and spiritual existence ('human infrastructure') / these root images provide in turn the foundation for philosophies and worldviews, as well as for institutional and conceptual frameworks	East & South

Images: Touching the Core

The deepest source of individual and organisational — and indeed societal — development is archetypal images drawn from ancient stories (such as

---

[0]Source: [170] (p.401)

creation myths), and the humanities (from the cultural depths of religion and spirituality) inclusive of language in its original context. They inform and fuel our imagination, from which we can begin to create our vision. Examples and manifestations are what the PR and advertising companies use to build images in consumers' minds.

Ideologies: The bedrock on which we stand

At the bedrock level, we are dealing with philosophies and ideologies that lie well below the surface of everyday life and which we take for granted as dogma. Often this bedrock is imported from elsewhere as part of our historical marching orders. An example is Russian and Chinese socialism, where the countries were forced to change without being aligned with the local cultural and societal core, causing immeasurable pain and suffering.

All M&A activity will expose clashes of ideology between companies, resulting in many conflicts. As such, ideologies always risk distorting whatever processes of renewal may be taking place unless we, as part of our impact approach, address such disintegration consciously, and from the start, as part of the process.

We also see this phenomenon when outer ideological imprints fall upon stony ground because they are not embedded or creatively assimilated in the individual, organisational, and societal consciousness.

Institutions: constructed from our collective intelligence

Institutional and conceptual frameworks create the holding vehicles in which we can understand and formalise our relationships and interactions. They include legal systems, political and economic structures, and predominating forms of public, private or civic enterprise. We must distinguish carefully whether we relate with a Spanish cooperative, a Zimbabwean *integral kumusha*, an American corporation or a Japanese '*keiretsu*' (business group).

Included in this subsoil of de-personalised systems, we also find the management models, usually restricted to Western ones, which inform the design of much of our conventional business institutions. Whereas it is individuals who characteristically initiate with their personal, formative and idiosyncratic inclinations, institutions keep things going over the long haul with their standardising rules, policies, and procedures. Anyone who deals with institutional change and culture would recognise immediately the power complexes of any system.

Inclinations: the visible surface

Now we come to the practise of our individual and organisational inclinations, including attitudes and behaviours. Engaging with diverse development contexts, here we may discover how cultural differences operate, from exchanging business cards in Japan, whether or not to shake hands with Arab women, how formal or informal we should be with the French, and our attitude to time whether in Harare or Hamburg. Many everyday nteractions with different people and cultures tend to be conducted in almost instinctive 'topsoil' terms, and are thus focused on individual traits and identities.

What is therefore crucial for our socio-economic impact laboratory is that it taps into, and stays connected with, all layers. In many individuals, organisations, and societies, in particular in the developing world and its impact methodologies, we will discover significant ruptures between the four layers. We will notice that ideologies (bedrock) are often imported and not sufficiently home-grown or assimilated at the core level. Equally, in particular in the business world, we see a lack of connectedness between the institutional design of a private enterprise in the Anglo-Saxon style (institutional layer) with the guiding cultural philosophy (bedrock) within many societies, and so on.

The development topography as part of our impact assessment can help us reveal these ruptures, make them conscious and subsequently engage in re-constructing our enterprises, enabling them to become more authentic and sustainable. We can now turn to the implications for sustainable development and Impact.

§11.1 Integrating capital stocks

Paul Hawken, together with his compatriots Amory and L. Hunter Lovins, has reconceptualised business in an ecological light to promote sustainable development (2010).

What is required, Hawken suggests, is the diligence to understand when and where Western-style markets are dysfunctional and misapplied, and to choose the correct targeted actions to help them operate more holistically while retaining their pragmatic vigour and efficiency.

If true, it is the fulcrum on which impact pivots and on which much of its future rests.

At an enterprise level, Hawken and his colleagues seek to ensure four distinct capital holdings or stock (in line with Anielski): financial, manufactured, natural, and human. These should be as prudently stewarded as money is by the corporate finance director.

This leads to our I³ suggestion: not a purely financially-oriented enterprise investment model but ultimately a more holistically-based market integration of all capital stockholdings, as I³ and much of impact seeks to achieve.

What we can foresee as a result is that the next revolution (after the current digital revolution) will possess a particular structural and developed process. Within it, four kinds of 'capital stock' (structural) would be recognised, each one manifesting itself in four types of interconnected 'capital flows' (process). These capital stocks are natural, human, manufactured, and financial. The flow forms enable companies and communities to engage in sustainable development, leading to technically productive, biologically integrative, economically facilitative, and ecologically restorative development. This is what is meant by transformative sustainability.

If we do not transform our historical pain in our psychology, we will most assuredly transmit it – usually to those closest to us: our family; our neighbours; our co-workers; and, invariably, the most vulnerable, our children and all those impacted by our presence. Consider the analogy of energy circuits: most of us are relay stations and only a minority are transformers – people who actually change the electrical charge that passes through them. Impact has to become a transformative part of the process but is often kept static at the level of an old and limited belief system.

§11.2 More on beliefs

Our beliefs are formed when we take on board something that for us has become true. A core belief may contain hundreds of smaller beliefs that support it; consequently, it may be difficult to change.

Our values are also supported by many such affirming beliefs and they tend to reinforce each other. We may have had the experience that a previously deeply held view is shaken by new information; whilst it shudders as it finds new ground, when it lands it must comport with the rest of our system. Most people hold untested beliefs as private certainties, since our analytical model of the world cannot easily accept contingent states. These are reinforced by our language, semantics, and behaviour to claim universal validity for our take on 'reality'. In Jarowski's book[105], he discusses with David Bohm the relationship between language and 'reality',:

The implicate order is in the first instance a language. It is not a description of reality but a language, an inner language, where you cannot associate each word to a thing. It is more like music. You cannot say one note means anything. It is like a painting. There are various spots of paint in an impressionist painting, but when you step back to see the picture, there is no correspondence between the spots of paint and what you see in the picture. Similarly, the implicate order and its mathematics does not directly come to describe a sort of correspondence with reality. It is simply a language. This language is referring to something that cannot be stated. The reality which is most immediate to us cannot be stated (p. 174)

This will have implications for us as we move impact into its next stages of development.

As John Beckett wrote in Under the Ancient Oaks: 'Hold your beliefs lightly, but while you hold them, treat them as though they were true and explore them as deeply as you can.'

As we have seen when looking at neurological filters, we don't necessarily have the capacity to process incoming information and data to assess their true meaning. Essentially, we sift reality through several filters to create our simplified version, i.e., our perceptions.

The Danish existentialist philosopher Soren Kierkegaard once wrote that: 'Life is not a problem to be solved, but a reality to be experienced.' From this, we also see that it is through our internal representation, including our language, that we create our world. Our world has no shape or meaning until we describe it, and it is only when we describe it that it activates possible distinctions that help govern our behaviour and actions. However, we do not really describe the world that we see but rather we see the world as we describe it.

Understanding one's relationship to reality is a constant challenge and a never ending task. If we can see behind these filters, we get increased levels of meaning. Organisations are no different because they are organised and run by people who are challenged and limited by their own filters. We often see this discourse played out in our internal politics in the form of tensions and disagreements.

Much of a firm's culture is hidden even to senior management, particularly if there is no conscious attempt to understand it, as I have discovered from my experience in most financial firms. Much of what is contained inside its shadow elements comes out occasionally for all to see and experience during stressful moments. The shadows also contain the hidden agendas and conflicts of interest which remain unspoken, which the firm prefers that the world does not know[171] (p. 27).

As in life, and in our investment thesis, the question is how we find

Figure 11.1: Map of the organisational psyche

reality and then return to it. Denial and other deflections are the mind's protection mechanisms to avoid that which cannot be reconciled or accepted coming through the filters. This is why hindsight provides such a convenient solution to discourse. As the well-known quote from John Maynard Keynes states: 'When the facts change, I change my mind. What do you do, sir?'

It is only when we get to the end of a particular journey that we can look back over the territory and join the dots. As meaningless as an event may have seemed at the time, we are meaning-seeking and relationship-driven creatures, and as such, it is by synthesising the very constructs of experiences that we can reframe their internal drivers which connect how we see potential and future possibilities.

As these mental constructs multiply, and we realize the enormity of our project at hand, we may be touched by what C.G. Jung defined as 'synchronicity' as our own, private, 'acausal connecting principle' of meaning. He suggested that synchronicity is 'a meaningful coincidence of two or more vents, where something other than the probability of chance is involved' (Rowe et al.,1997), i.e., cannot be explained just by cause and effect.

This can be trained into deeper awareness and eventually become part of our everyday belief system. Depending on how this system was established and how we now hold it in terms of negative versus positive, our potential is diminished or enhanced. We can be ready, and even look forward to, any 'drama' if we can see the connectedness and synchronicity with how it will eventually turn into something positive.

From my own beginnings only I, and no one else, can (or is qualified) to see this unfolding. Others may have opinions on what could have been done, i.e., if ABC was done differently, then XYZ would have been different, but this is at best wishful thinking. It is an illusion, since it is the individual who is connected to their past and must take responsibility.

This is also a question of ownership. If you don't feel you were in control and responsible of your beginnings (and to a degree I hold this view) to the same degree are we able to see and tie together our future potentials with possibilities, own and hold them to empower us into the next chapter of our journey.

Elisabeth Kübler-Ross said:

The most beautiful people we have known are those who have known defeat, known suffering, known struggle, known loss, and have found their way out of those depths. These persons have an appreciation, a sensitivity, and an understanding of life that fills them with compassion, gentleness, and a deep loving concern. Beautiful people do not just happen.

If true – and clearly one can't sit on the fence about this – then, as Frederick Douglass said: 'Without a struggle, there can be no progress.

Since progress is a fundamental driver in the universe, we have to embrace our struggles since without them there is no story from which to grow. Liking this with the need to grow inside our Impact journey, C.G. Jung suggested that, 'The greatest and most important problems of life are all in a certain sense insoluble... They can never be solved, but only outgrown...This 'outgrowing', as I formerly called it, on further experience was seen to consist in a new level of consciousness. Some higher or wider interest arose on the person's horizon, and through this widening of view, the insoluble problem lost its urgency. It was not solved logically in its own terms, but faded out when confronted with a new and stronger life-tendency' (Jung in Wilhelm 1931, 1962, pp. 91f).

Without our troubles, we would have no lessons in life and no tale to tell from which others can gain insights. Neither would we have the input from which to shape our personalities for the better, gain acceptance and grace on the journey, and compassion for all things which can positively transform ourselves.

The ancients have known this for millennia. Marcus Aurelius in Meditations instructs us to: 'Accept the things to which fate binds you, and love the people with whom fate brings you together, but do so with all your heart[172].'

My own interpretive narrative is formed by the conscience, and constructs of the self which are immediately reshaped and reframed as new aspects, angles and inputs are added to the puzzle. I know from my own experience that, regardless of how I interpret something today, rethinking it immediately changes the way I will view. If I 'sleep on it', meditate, and let it rest within myself, it transforms into a different form and new intelligence.

Whilst we swim in the force fields of our perceived reality, everything we know is through the lens and prism of difference, and experienced perspectives.

Given a core issue of our time is increasing inequality in how capital is created, measured, and allocated, much-needed insight is required to address these imbalances. We must find organisational approaches, since it is within our organisations that we spend much of our time, and encounter our psychological mirrors.

I collaborate with Mark Anielski, the economic strategist who developed the Genuine Wealth model[173] (p.65–78) as a pragmatic tool for governments and business to measure trust, relational capital, and well-being; in the book's foreword, Herman Daly referred to Mark as 'God's auditor.' In his book, Anielski elaborates on key areas which directly relate and complement our integral work, namely:

- How to rediscover the original meaning of the language of economics.

- How to measure genuine wealth, which consists of five capital assets: human, social, natural, built and financial.

- How nations, governments, communities, and businesses are using the genuine wealth model to build the new economy of well-being.

- How at the family level, applying the genuine wealth model creates happiness.

I fully endorse Mark's search to create new knowledge to build happiness, which in turn helps inform and navigate the construct and direction of I^3. All such co-created knowledge is constructed activity in which knowers are active contributors and shapeshifters. All knowledge comes in multiple forms (explicit, implicit, and tacit) and all inputs are interpreted by the individual receiver based on their perceptual filters and background.

This means that from our impact perspectives we need to pay particular attention in cultures with deep roots different from our own.

David Peat offers a challenge,

> The knower and the known moreover are indissolubly linked and changed in a fundamental way. Indigenous science can never be reduced to a catalogue of facts or a database on a computer, for it is a dynamic and living process, an aspect of the ever-changing, ever-renewing processes of nature [174](p.6)

This is often missed completely by the Western paradigm impact-driven organisations that professes to do investments where indigenous social structures prevail but whose structures are in actuality negatively impacted. How we engage with reality is critical, as is how we interact with the narrative that evolves as part of our meaning-making activity. As our map forms clarify and crystallise, we activate our new narrative stories with the world so we can develop new meanings and social impacts. As a continuous interpreter of such stories, we look to how we can become catalysts, social innovators and transformers of society, communities and people.

Chaos theory suggests that nothing is lost in the universe. The world's top physicists used to believe that anything that entered a black hole was obliterated, but no longer do. Current research shows that black holes transform objects rather than destroying them[175]. For us humans, such transformation comes from developing our new levels of consciousness, our character, and our creative capacities.

According to the quantum physicist, Amit Goswami[176] (p. 1) the stages of creativity are: apparition; incubation; insight; transformation; and manifestation. Whilst our creativity is rooted in our notional spaces of ideas, images, and ideals, many years ago researcher Graham Wallis described what happens as people approach problems with the objective of constructing creative solutions. His four-stage process is (1926, p.10) :

I. Preparation: we define the problem, need, or desire, and gather needed information; we establish the criteria for verifying the solution's acceptability.

II. Incubation: we step back from the problem and let our minds contemplate and work it through. Like preparation, incubation can last minutes, weeks, even years.

III. Illumination: ideas arise from the mind to provide the basis of a creative response. These ideas can be pieces of the whole or the whole itself. This stage is often very brief, involving a tremendous rush of insights within a few minutes or hours.

IV. Verification: one carries out activities to demonstrate whether or not what emerged in illumination satisfies the need and the criteria defined in the preparation stage.

How the above is implemented is predicated on the level and format of governance and procedures that we have constructed, in combination with the level of open spaces that our culture has created. These are questions about our inner capacity for respect, trust, open listening, courage to speak, humility and resolve in finding answers and solutions. As all questions and answers require frequent self-examination and self-correction, if we can achieve this, we can build the space within our protocols to allow a possible Impact 2.0 and beyond to emerge.

C.G. Jung said: 'Only the mystics bring creativity into religion' [177] (p. 477). He was referring to the need to create positive referential discourses in our otherwise static environment.

Paulo Freire's offers clear instruction on how to relate to knowledge,

For apart from inquiry, apart from the praxis, individuals cannot be truly human. Knowledge emerges only through invention and re-invention, through the

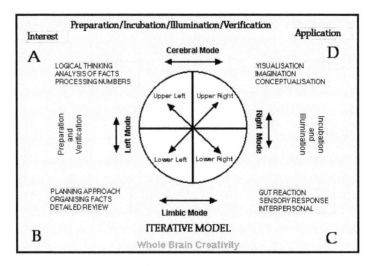

Figure 11.2: Iterative Model

restless, impatient, continuing, hopeful inquiry human beings pursue in the world, with the world, and with each other (p.72) [48]

Our understanding comes from our capacity to create and label contrast. The colour green would not be 'green' unless we could picture it and position it within a colour spectrum in relation to our own context. The French label this 'vert' and its representation differs according to how we have cognitively created the multitude of pictures that subconsciously emerge whenever the word is mentioned or retrieved from memory. In English '*vert*' may also conjure up areas such as 'intro/extrovert' and 'invert' which stems from the Latin verb '*vertere*,' meaning 'to turn or overturn', so different pictures emerge.

The same applies to words such as 'money', 'capital', and 'investments'. An investment firm generates specific meanings for each according to our culture and myth streams. All investment firms will have gained a form of relational stewardship of capital based on a combination of capabilities, market position, track record, expertise, and espoused brand values, including trust and integrity.

In addition, people individually represent their own cultural brand in conjunction with (and contrast to) their firm, particularly with clients and other stakeholders. This need for compliance and alignment may create a challenge with the firm which manifests as personal stress. This dimension is critical since to a large extent it dictates how the firm and its employees interact with the outside world, and the type and strength of its culture.

In my experience working within large financial organisations such as Citigroup and BNPParibas, understanding culture was highly surface orientated. Working with a deeper cultural awareness was often actively discouraged. Given the dominant dimensions of technical expertise, a highly technology-driven business, and a linear, hierarchical mode of organisational management, there was little room for much else.

I love Herbert Spencer's quote in the Alcoholics Anonymous Big Book, which reminds us of one of our main barriers to knowledge, namely contempt: 'There is a principle which is a bar against all information, which is proof against all arguments, and which cannot fail to keep a man in everlasting ignorance—that principle is *contempt prior to investigation*'[178] (568, author's emphasis.)

Whilst technical problems can often be solved by higher levels of thinking, all other problems are 'adaptive problems', i.e., they cannot be solved technically and require a shift in thinking and behaviour. One can argue that understanding culture and organisational relationships is often diametrically opposed to the prevailing knowledge base of most financial institutions. This may seem paradoxical, given that most firms and their management would claim the very opposite.

- Technical expertise requires significant investment in time and effort but, once mastered, is relatively simple to implement and use because it comprises logical, digital, linear left-brain thinking patterns based on prevailing logic and learned paradigms.

- Culture and relationships are ostensibly easy to acquire. For many organisational leaders, psychology is considered inert knowledge; thus many believe it is easy to acquire and they can easily become an 'expert'. However, unlike technical knowledge, this dimension is difficult to implement. Many organisations have failed, leaving behind costly and painful corrective cultural development and behavioural change programs.

- Senior management often stays within less risky technical 'comfort zones', giving rise to an incoherent strategy built on existing operational culture minus a progressive approach.

As E. F. Schumacher suggested: 'Any intelligent fool can make things bigger and more complex...It takes a touch of genius — and a lot of courage to move in the opposite direction[179].'

Quantum physics has shown the interconnectedness and oneness of the operating principles of the universe and its relationship to our consciousness. Joseph Jaworski ([105] pp. 99 -100) outlines a discussion with the physicist David Bohm about Bell's Theorem (later confirmed by Alain Aspect) on pairing and time-travel in particle physics, where Bohm confirms that: 'The oneness implicit in Bell's Theorem envelops human beings and atoms alike'. The physicist Henry Stapp of University of California at Berkeley said that Bell's Theorem is 'the most profound discovery in the history of science' (Ibid).

It proves that the elements of the world are fundamentally inseparable. This is one of the key premises for our integral four worlds and our understanding of true impact. In Jaworski's discussion, Bohm explains that,

> Yourself is actually the whole of mankind. That's the idea of implicate order-that everything is enfolded in everything. The entire past is enfolded in each one of us in a very subtle way. If you reach deeply into yourself, you are reaching into the very essence of mankind. When you do this, you will be led into the generating depth of consciousness that is common to the whole of mankind and that has the whole of mankind enfolded in it. The individual's ability to be sensitive to that becomes the key to the change of mankind. We are all connected. If this could be taught, and if people could understand it, we would have a different consciousness (Ibid, p. 80-81)

This statement has profound implications for our understanding of impact. There is an implicit order in impact that only our consciousness can uncover and enfold, and which our map making will have to include. Consciousness is the key here, not knowledge.

Bohm goes on to tell Jaworski. 'You've got to give a lot of attention to consciousness. This is one of the things of which our society is ignorant. It assumes consciousness requires no attention. But consciousness is what gives attention. Consciousness itself requires very alert attention or else it will simply destroy itself. It is a very delicate mechanism.' (Ibid, p. 82).

When we work with impact, we emphasise the states of consciousness and how we can generate more, not less consciousness. Much of our workplace is paradoxical: the more we assimilate to our place of work, the less able we are to find ourselves and new avenues for growth. Deeper insights often seem to come from other insights, activities and venues.

Another paradox is that most firms state how they embrace diversity and difference whilst this is not valued at operational levels. Management often finds it easier to manage compliant staff, while supporting employees who 'toe the line'. We will investigate these dynamics in greater detail later, but we know that to accomplish things we must not only dream (our South), but also believe (our East); not only plan (our North) but also act (our West), iteratively in that order.

> All men dream; but not equally. Those who dream by night in the dusty recesses of their minds wake in the day to find that it was vanity; but the dreamers of the day are dangerous men, for they may act their dream with open eyes, to make it possible.
>
> T.E. Lawrence

Chapter 12

Ontology is everything

Ontology, introduced in 1606, is the philosophical study of the nature of being. Traditionally listed as part of a branch of philosophy known as metaphysics, ontology examines what entities exist (or may be said to exist) and how such entities may be grouped and subdivided. A simple definition of ontology is the examination of the meaning of 'being' (Wikipedia); as such, it is foundational in our Integral South.

For our context of impact, the ability and capacity to see and hear the other's ontology through our own is critical. This is important in cultures where they may differ significantly. As such, we need to draw on the integral theory of knowledge to expand our lens and prism. This can be mapped into the four worlds as follows:

In our relational South, we are co-creating knowledge by grounding ourselves in community activation. On the Southern relational path, we activate the *G-E-N-E* as follows:

- G-Grounding: Focusing attention on opening and embedding our impact approach into our soil and that of the investee.

- G-Emergence: Accepting and incorporating new insights and real impacts.

- G-Navigation: Allowing our investment thesis to be shaped and directed by what has emerged.

- G-Effect: Focusing attention on areas of greatest investee impact.

Moving into the emergent East, we explore ways of knowing through their processes, and seek to awaken our integral consciousness. On the Eastern path, we look for renewal of the soil on which our impact stands.

- E–Grounding: Understanding the ways of knowledge as a grounding for any development.

- E–Emergence: Allowing our impact to generate new knowledge for resilience and cohesion.

- E–Navigation: Re-navigating the impact process and path with our new consciousness

- E–Effect: Generating impact additionality in the renewal of the investee.

Heading into our North of reason, we institutionalise the impact attributes as a new area of knowledge creation. During our emancipation on the Northern path, we seek to rationalise our impact objectives and, using reason, build strategies for their outcomes.

- N–Grounding: Generating new areas of knowledge from the grounds of the investee.

- N–Emergence: Letting the emergent new knowledge area become embedded into the firm.

- N–Navigation: Allowing areas of knowledge to influence change and development

- N–Effect: Creating research, strategies and tactics around new knowledge.

In our coordinate West, we seek to transform and create value out of our knowledge and embody its development and deployment. In the Western path, we design and realise the creative process:

- E–Grounding: Aligning and implementing our impact thesis, as grounded in our investee.

- E-Emergence: Building feedback loops and bottom-up information flows that allows impact to generate transformation.

- E-Navigation: Re-navigating and strengthening the impact objectives using new knowledge from doing.

- E-Effect: Re-generating and re-energising the impact objectives through the value-creating process.

PART II

Changing the investment organisation

Chapter 13

Introduction

Our economic system is reaching its limits to perform the basic functions of creating wealth, stability, and well-being. Much has been written from ecological, socio-economic, and post-financial crises perspectives, strongly suggesting that the current paradigms need radical reconstruction.

As discussed previously, our impact map must include our own perspectives, and to every extent possible those of our investees. The latter being a function of the nature of ourselves and our investment objectives and our capacity to create an investee relationship in which our impact approach can be implemented.

Here we focus on a full engagement and influence model which we may find in private equity or private debt, in order to focus on our now expanded perspectives without limitations. Whilst we can have the best impact intentions on the planet, they will be impotent unless we can create behavioural and strategic change within the firm(s) in which we invest. This means looking at our investee through our own lens and within a broader economic system. There is a saying that 'a truth that's told with bad intent is worse than any lie you can invent.' Likewise, a well-intended Impact objective based on false intentionality can create worse outcomes than what initially would appear.

There have been many innovations in post-neoclassical economics, such as evolutionary game theory, complexity economics, behavioural economics, neuroeconomics, and experimental economics. However, these cannot provide the integrality of a full-spectrum approach. In addition, behavioural economics is probably the only genre that includes the psychological dimension in any meaningful way, but current research and writings mainly explain market movements and their decisions, with relatively limited value for our Impact approach.

The integral four-world theory and praxis has four main research paths: relational (Southern); renewal (Eastern); reason (Northern), and realisation (Western); and on our four-world transformative trajectory: from grounding (origination) and emergence (foundation) to navigation (emancipation) and effect (transformation) (our GENE). So our approach is local–global, not just global–local.

Figure 13.1: Care

For the development of I³, the implications are profound. As discussed in Part 1, for the impact industry in general, we can no longer look at these component parts in isolation. We need to create frameworks with a deliberate connection and integrally informed outcomes. In essence, we need to take what we call Integral CARE: another dynamic that ties together the tasks in each world to build our virtuous circle of deepening understanding:

C: Community and Collective Calling and Activation;

A: Activating Awakening and Awareness / Consciousness;

R: Research driven Innovation and Realised institutionalization;

E: Embodied and Transformative Education and Evolving Enterprise.

The banking and finance industry not only represents the core mechanism for the transfer, accumulation, and accretion of capital, which corresponds with the relation between stakeholders, but they are also the specific objects of cultural critique serving as society's custodians for the role of capital in society and business inside our whole historical and social context—a key issue for critical theory. Chomsky said,

> Before the 1970s, banks were banks. They did what banks were supposed to do in a state capitalist economy: they took unused funds from your bank account, for example, and transferred them to some potentially useful purpose like helping

a family buy a home or send a kid to college (p.38). [180]

In the information age, with increased pluralism, flexibility, risk, and uncertainty, positions taken by traditional authorities within the finance industry are being challenged by diverse voices and disruptive technologies. Just like in other areas for example, people living together in the same home are increasingly challenging and negotiating their relationships, rather than accepting traditionally mandated roles.

In my own experience, finance was dominated by money and power dictating the entire organisation. Money (and attributable value) was tracked and measured as the life blood of the firm. Other economic systems, (for example, Islamic finance which sees interest as usury, as did Christians, along with the periodic forgiveness of debt through the concept of the jubilee), see the firm's quintessence in the exchange of value and the commercial transaction rather than its lifeless derivative, money.

I^3 re-establishes the lost connections for a firm between its integrative parts, making them visible and manageable as part of the firm's re-created self. Unlike banking, the investment industry has a unique educational opportunity to reconnect role in work with the work of soul, and find ways to shorten the power distance between money and impact. In addition, much wealth today is accumulated and held by individuals who have varying degrees of consciousness about the nature of money.

In Pedagogy of the Oppressed[48], Freire introduced a radical distinction that has since become an enduring feature of progressive educational thought: the difference between 'banking' and 'problem-posing' education:

> [Banking education] attempts, by mythicizing reality, to conceal certain facts which explain the way men [sic] exist in the world...Banking education resists dialogue; problem-posing education regards dialogue as indispensable to the act of cognition which unveils reality. Banking education treats students as objects of assistance; problem-posing education makes them critical thinkers...Problem-posing education bases itself on creativity and stimulates true reflection and action upon reality, thereby responding to the vocation of men as beings who are authentic only when engaged in inquiry and creative transformation.

In this sense, I^3 is the dialectic teacher guiding the 'student' (i.e., the firm) through questioning and creating new levels of cognition about their role in life and society. This opens the possibility of the firm becoming the 'teacher' towards its environment and relationships.

> Teachers and students (leadership and people), co-intent on reality, are both Subjects, not only in the task of unveiling that reality, and thereby coming to

know it critically, but in the task of re-creating that knowledge. As they attain this knowledge of reality through common reflection and action, they discover themselves as its permanent re-creators.(Ibidem)

Traditionally, finance education is a relationship of domination in which the teacher has knowledge that s/he deposits in the heads of passive objects –her/his students. Such education maintains students' immersion in a culture of silence and positions them as objects outside of history, control and agency,

> It is not surprising that the banking concept of education regards men as adaptable, manageable beings. The more students work at storing the deposits entrusted to them, the less they develop the critical consciousness which would result from their intervention in the world as transformers of that world. The more completely they accept the passive role imposed on them, the more they tend simply to adapt to the world as it is and to the fragmented view of reality deposited in them.

> The capability of banking education to minimise or annul the student's creative power and to stimulate their credulity serves the interests of the oppressors, who care neither to have the world revealed nor to see it transformed. The oppressors use their "humanitarianism" to preserve a profitable situation. Thus they react almost instinctively against any experiment in education which stimulates the critical faculties and is not content with a partial view of reality always seeks out the ties which link one point to another and one problem to another. (Ibidem)

One of my objectives in writing this book is to provide, an I^3 blueprint for each investment institution for their own 'problem-posing' questions, namely:

- What kind of firm are we?

- How do we want to invest our capital? and

- What sort and level of impact are we looking to achieve?

These questions are mission critical for each investment firm. Asking (and by extension answering) these questions will provide the basis of their identity, and will determine their target market for attracting funding. In my own experience, it became palpably abundantly clear whilst I was working in large financial firms that I was, in effect, prostituting myself into a social system that was existentially toxic, based on manipulative and false premises. These were led by egocentric and narcissistic 'leaders'. As such, there were no real emancipatory processes in place; rather, most forms of insight into possible positive change were often discarded or disparaged.

> The most potent weapon of the oppressor is the mind of the oppressed
>
> Steven Biko, (1978)

The recipe for success, as defined by the culture, requires surface-orientated measuring sticks to be obtainable so that success can easily be transferred to another institution, since longevity and trust does not exist between the parties. With I[3], the reconstruction can start with alternative definitions of success.

As Parker J. Palmer writes:

In the face of resistance, an ungrounded leader will revert to bureaucratic mode: the teacher will revert to lecturing rather than inviting inquiry, the manager will revert to rule-making rather than inviting creativity. In the face of resistance, leaders will do what they are taught to do: not create space for others, but fill the space themselves—fill it with their own words, their own skills, their own deeds, their own egos. This, of course, is precisely what followers expect from leaders, and that expectation prolongs the period during which leaders of community must hold the space—hold it in trust until people trust the leader, and themselves, enough to enter in.[1]

As an example, some of the changes in our social impact thinking must include the following:

Table 13.1: Changes in our social impact thinking

Old Thinking	New Thinking
Community is a goal.	Community is a gift.
We achieve community through desire, design and determination.	We receive community by cultivating a capacity for connectedness.
Community requires a feeling of Intimacy.	Community does not depend on intimacy and must expand to embrace strangers, even enemies, as well as friends.
Community is a romantic Garden of Eden.	Community that can withstand hard times and conflict can help us become not just happy but 'at home.'
Leadership is not needed in Communities.	Leadership and the authority to lead toward community can emerge from anyone in an organisation.

---

[1]Palmer, P.J. (1998). *Thirteen Ways of Looking at Community.* The Inner Edge. p.6

| Suffering is bad and should be avoided. | Suffering lets our 'hearts break open' enough to hold both vision of hope and the reality of resistance without tightening like a fist. |

As we know, our own leadership and courage are the only shift changers. I agree with the U.S. Marine Corps Definition of Leadership as 'The qualities of moral character that enable a person to inspire and influence a group of people successfully'

However, leading in Impact is much more than that; Impact leadership involves at its core the ability to transform self and others. It means being an awakener, a liberator, bringing new awareness and discoveries through study and experience with a passion for seeing people grow. Impact leadership cannot just be defined by position or authority; it's a gift granted to you by others as a way of being, becoming, knowing, and doing by its very practise.

To lead is to learn, to awaken, to grow and to liberate: to honour the past, to dream of the future, to live in the present.

Colin Reeve

Having set the scene for our own organisational impact change, let's investigate what this means specifically for our 'family office' and creating the impact frame.

Chapter 14

The family office as a custodian and steward of capital

As discussed in our introduction, the recent emergence of the family office (FO) is a unique force with a privileged role to play in today's world. This chapter will investigate more deeply the specific opportunities and dynamics that may create challenges specific to this type of organisation.

Family offices fuse economics and finance with family psychology inside a turbo-charged environment that has the risk of not being grounded in reality. The best and worse in each family member can surface inside a mix of family dynamics and misconstrued ideas around entitlement. It will take a highly cognisant owner and steward of capital to understand and to build mechanisms to prevent tension.

Making a thorough and searching moral diagnostic and inventory is essential for any owner in order to minimise and avoid future disharmony and dysfunction. Here I speak with some experience and practise. However, this is where I believe Impact can help transform a family into a positive force whilst delivering meaningful objectives and member. Contexts, cultures, and family-espoused values and beliefs will vary enormously and form a greater (or lesser) part in how a particular family considers its structure and philosophy and conceptualises money and capital.

Advantages include:

- The short power distance between capital and decision making.

- More flexibility in aligning mission with values.

- A more direct linear relationship between consciousness and capital deployment.

- Intergenerational shifts in the perception of capital.

- Save future generations from the risk of too much money and lack of purpose.

As such, FOs have more potential to shift the needle quickly pertaining to impact investments vis-à-vis larger institutions, particularly if starting through the more open portal of philanthropy where a higher level of consciousness already exists. Make no mistake, large institutions also have unique opportunities to align their product with new market demands (and just by sheer volume are large investors); however, the essence of impact management is often lost inside larger institutions. Family firms can visualize values and beliefs with a more dynamic operating level of integrity in executing Impact with their now-clarified intentions binding intentions and outcomes.

Another area of consideration for any family is inter-generational wealth transfer and its effects on family members. I once worked with a Danish family that guaranteed for life that their children would receive the equivalent average salary of a national police officer. In effect, the children received a 'living wage' on which they could build their own self-concept and value. No one would be destitute but if they wanted a lifestyle above this level they would have to work for it. Conversely, I have been involved with families where abundant wealth was literary 'sprayed' across generations, no doubt with good intentions but with little regard for the consequences.

The danger is that once the need to generate one's own wealth is removed, something within the soul is lost and cannot be replaced. In my experience, a family's biggest challenge is taking the time to carefully design the architecture of this wealth transfer process to fit its members. I have seen many situations with early signals that everything is fine, only to see family members struggle to find their meaning and life's purpose.

As the German poet Rainer Maria Rilke reminds us: 'Our task is to be defeated by ever larger things'. If, however, being is an 'ever larger thing', then this is a pathway to self-fulfilment. As this is a psychodynamic process, given sufficient funding, the inside lack of fulfilment can very easily spill into outside life.

Excessive consumption exists across the entire spectrum; just witness the race to create bigger identities and 'who has the best and biggest' within the guise of 'I deserve it'. What is the point in giving a five-year-old a $25,000 gold Rolex for his/her birthday; it is of little use except to show off conspicuous wealth to friends. (A related area to consumerism is the prevalence of behavioural, emotional and chemical addictions.)

The French philosopher, Blaise Pascal, spoke of three discourses on the conditions of the highest in the societal hierarchy which sought to provide three lessons of understanding for the ruling elite at the time. Superficial physical greatness such as wealth and birth from a base discourse, including beauty, strength, and inheritance as legitimised through law. Above this is a discourse of natural abilities and greatness of genius and science, e.g., Albert Einstein and mastery of the arts such as the music of Mozart and achieving institutional greatness in temporal power e.g., being CEO, and positions based on noble birth stand above superficial physical greatness.

Pascal implies that it is mathematically easy to determine who is higher placed in the social echelon since it is often based on the culture. According to Pascal there is a third kind of discourse – the order of divine connection. The fact that a divine (or highly conscious or enlightened person) is rich or poor, strong or weak, highly intelligent or illiterate does not add or subtract anything because that person's greatness is on a different level and infinitely superior. This is the only level where true joy and happiness can be found[1].

Whilst Pascal's outline is helpful, more useful is asking key questions about how a family office is being managed. Here I provide some to help frame answers around family mission and vision:

- What are the differences in values between the original makers and custodians of capital?

- How have we created unified vision?

- How have we clarified the mission?

- Building a stable core: What are our ethics and morals? What is the real power distance of money?

- How do we manage intergenerational transfer? Are there adhering principles?

- Is there a difference in treatment between the first and second half of life?

- How do we account for shifting needs/requirements of family members?

- How do we see and manage inevitable agency issues e.g., professional fund managers?

- When do we allow ethics and morals to enter our economic calculus?

- How have we become disconnected, and how can we re-focus what is important?

---

[1][181] Part 3. Ch. 4, p. 1-3.

- Are some family members more advantaged than others?

- Are there members who do not espouse Impact values and are driven mainly by a need for more capital at whatever cost?

Impact investment can enable the intergenerational shifts of capital to have real purpose. If we embody an integral approach in how our family manages capital and builds a broader definition of wealth, there are no limitations to the benefits. This will build the next generation of capital with real purpose.

If we are in the fortunate position to have this luxury 'problem', we need to question deeply about how our family can and will transition in the healthiest way possible. This is a case of both responsibility and stewardship as I don't believe we have a choice in today's world where money can buy almost anything and risk our happiness, peace of mind and joy in the process.

There is an inverse correlation between money and happiness, as the former can build a false, rampant ego which is enforced by more money. This can give an individual 'God-like sensations'. As Anne Lamott suggests: 'You can safely assume that you have created God in our own image when it turns out that God hates all the same people you do[182].'

Our capital transcends our death so it is important to consider our legacy. How will the capital benefit those left behind? Money and capital may be inert and neutral, but family money is not; it is accompanied by marching orders from our past, codes and aspirations. How do we make it a real legacy, and not a curse that separates, divides and destroys relationships and our planet?

Do we believe in Maya Angelou's statement: 'Your legacy is every life you've touched' Many suggest that the key to fulfilment in life is joy, so what is 'joy'. A good description occurred in April 2015, when Archbishop Desmond Tutu visited His Holiness the Dalai Lama at his residence in exile in India. Their interaction, facilitated by Douglas Abrams, became The Book of Joy[183].

They suggested that suffering in life is inevitable but how we respond to that suffering in earnest is our choice. More important is how we feel about ourselves after the experience. Whilst money can buy a solution from somewhere else, we may remove form ourselves valuable lessons and experiences. Also, not even oppression or occupation can take away this freedom to choose our response. 'As our dialogue progressed, we converged on eight pillars of joy. Four were qualities of the mind: perspective, humility, humour, and acceptance. Four were qualities of the heart: forgiveness, gratitude, compassion, and generosity'. Archbishop Tutu said: 'Our human nature has been distorted,(…) I mean, we are actually quite remarkable creatures. In our religions I am created in the image of God. I am a God carrier. It is fantastic. I have to be growing in godlikeness, in caring for the other. I know that each time I have acted compassionately, I have experienced a joy in me that I find in nothing else.'

The interlinked areas of succession, legacy, and the meaning of joy enable us to now move closer into Part 2 of our journey.

§14.1 A very short discussion on addictions.

The addiction and overdose crisis…does not so much reflect moral failings of individuals as it does reveal a sickness that has infected the country and our collective consciousness.'

The question for each of us is not whether we are addicted but how we are addicted, and to what. Denial of the existence of addiction in your life is not a mark of moral accomplishment but a sign of blindness.

Timothy McMahan King[184]

You may ask what a discussion on addictions has to do with a book on impact investments. Given the prevalence of and risks associated with addictive behaviour, for anyone with addictive tendencies (and that's all of us), the capacity for seeing and hearing real impact will be severely impaired. This is because we can only be truly free and emancipated if we can face our mirror of truth. Also, all addictions (and sometimes related issues which are more difficult to see, such as ADHD and ADD without the hyperactivity trait) often lead to a need to de-stress and zone-out of the real self.

In addition, the ego dominates in addictive people; that is, 'the other' is not quite there and if it is, it is just to facilitate and strengthen the ego. At the base of all addictions lies a lack of wholeness and oneness. Whilst for some, impact can provide an entry point (and even a full-recovery process) money often obtrudes as we seek easily accessible alternatives. Many addictive tendencies are maintained and afforded by an excess of money, with all its attractions and possibilities. As such, if we experience this existential vacuum, I believe in using real depth in Impact investments, if managed in accordance with integral principles, as a potential solution to alleviate such problems. One fact made eminently clear by contemporary psychology is that wholeness can only occur if we embrace the whole of ourselves—not only what is the highest in us, but the shadow elements of ourselves, many of which we are unaware. For our purposes, we will ignore the myriad theories hypothesizing why individuals become addicted, and mainly focus on the relevance within our context of capital and Impact.

So what are addictions and why are they so pervasive, as they all lead to pain? Why are they 'Hungry Ghosts' as per the title of Gabor Maté's recent book on the subject? Addictions can include the desires of the mind and soul that we think and feel; it is what we seek and do when anxious or having negative feelings to perk us up. With unfulfilled desires, this inevitably leads to pain. Money in this sense can superficially alleviate and disguise. Capital and money can also self-select and deter deeper relationships, since the tendency with increasing wealth is to become more selective about who we socialise with, which can lead to social isolation and a lack of diversity.

It becomes very easy — and sometimes necessary — to separate where we live from where we go. Witness the increased isolation of very wealthy people who separate themselves from others by either perceived or real security needs to find like-minded and like-experienced people with whom to socialise on similar terms and conditions. The adage that 'birds of a feather flock together' describes a natural tendency and quite often a limiting self-selecting bias.

This is an important aspect of how people with addictions socialise, as the opposite creates an uncomfortable window into the truth of their inner self. Alcohol, being socially accepted in many cultures, provides an ideal façade and subterfuge to hide behind being. I once met a rampant but functioning alcoholic who was in complete denial when she exclaimed 'Moi, an alcoholic, never, I only drink Champagne,' even though this amounted to several bottles a day. Draw your own conclusions…There is of course no mystery that some types of alcohol are called by the name 'spirit', as it has for millennia been the replacement or drug of choice for the infinite and what in recovery programs is the need to fill 'the hole in the heart', "Addictions represent finite answers to infinite longings. But adding up the finite over and over will never equal the infinite.(Ibid)"

What is this 'hole in the heart'? For me it is the need for connection, proximity, and the search for union with a higher power or our own deeper consciousness. The union is about finding and rediscovering the unconditional love in which we were born and also includes higher levels of justice, truths, and peace. This hole needs to find substitutes which may include addictions. There is a risk that if we don't find healthy ways to manage the emptiness, we may think of becoming a higher power ourselves, when the darker side of the ego takes over and can develop overextended views about the self, leading to narcissism and grandiosity. The grandiose person is often preoccupied with gaining acceptance from others, needing to excel at everything, over-function and overachieve. They are supposed to always be "up" but when their grandiose intentions don't materialize, they can easily fall into a downward depression which can lead to addictions, in essence a form of bi-polarity between grandiosity and depression.

Developing our real and healthy spiritual self over time is a fundamental need for any human being but which can also develop many false and more easily accessible substitutes such as addictions. If we can find a path where our conscience or higher power draw us into a deeper relationship with justice, truth and love, this obviously has important implications for our impact journey and for using an approach such as I³, which seeks to enhance our relationships and is a portal for reaching them. We therefore need to create and facilitate organisational governance and management Impact processes for openness and vulnerability as natural pathways to find truth, justice and love.

The question is not whether we have addictions, but which ones? To the degree we fear the silence of existence we often seek distractions to find ways of distancing or removing ourselves from the self. As Blaise Pascal wrote: 'All of humanity's problems stem from man's [sic] inability to sit quietly in a room alone' (Pensés)[185] From excessive TV watching, to exercise, to the use of technology, in essence these impoverish our relationships.

In some industries, technology addiction is not only a risk, it can be a prerequisite for apparent success. Tracy Kidder in his Pultizer prize winning book "The Soul of a New Machine"[2] quotes Joseph Weizenbaum the risk for industry computer programmers to suffer from "the compulsion to program". The signs were of "bright young men [sic] of disheveled appearance, often with sunken eyes who play at megalomaniacal fantasies of omnipotence at computer controls".

Gaming addicts, engaged in online games, experience connection, earn status, and are given a joint goal to pursue. We all search for missions to accomplish to fulfil our core mutual desires. Players can change their more mundane, but also real, identity to become an archetypical hero in a quest in a narrative of crisis, struggle, and resolution. That is something that is hard to beat compared to what might be going on in their real world.

Gaming disorder is now classified as a disease by the World Health

---

[2][186] Ch. 5 quoted from [187].

Organisation (WHO). When I was working as a psychotherapist one of my clients, a man in his mid-thirties, suffered from this condition. He could spend an extraordinary amount of time gaming to the detriment of all else. He had lost several jobs, mainly from lack of sleep, had no real social life and a disorganised home life. He was understandably anxious and depressed, but initially was in denial. His on-line virtual identity, and hero persona, had become more powerful than his own real self. The goal-oriented narratives in the story lines were becoming so strong that there was room for little else.

This is why, in our impact narratives, we need to build in dynamics that create, shape, nurture, and strengthen our real identities. This is also why, for certain family firms, working deeply with impact is an antidote and possibly a solution for family members who risk getting lost in building their real selves, as excess capital may have taken away the need for any real pursuit or journey of identity. As money can buy many distractions and diversions, and solve many development needs, I would argue that a wealthy family actually has a fiduciary obligation to its descendants to create a management structure whose governance ensures that their individuation is not jeopardised or stolen by access to, and the availability of, capital.

Neuroscientists tell us that the brain's rewards systems fire up more when we solve issues along our journey rather that when we reach our goals. As we struggle, we feel joy as we resolve problems in pursuit of our goal. If we fail at one hurdle, we cry out as our emotions remind us what is of real value.

§14.2 Poverty of the self

At the core of every addiction lies an emptiness and fear that the addicton is trying to fill or mask. Put simply, addictions come from autonomous complexes that are acting as an alleviating anxiety-management system. Addictions manifest as compulsive and autonomous repetitive behaviours, patterns and actions that we cannot stop with our free will. As long as we have poverty inside our deeper selves, which includes a lack of real loving connections and meaning, surface alternatives can become addictive to alleviate anxiety. Real meaning can only be found in pursuits and connections that transcend the self. The teacher Eckhart Tolle writes[188],

> Basically, all emotions are modifications of one primordial, undifferentiated emotion that has its origins in the loss of awareness of who you are beyond name and form. Because of this undifferentiated nature, it is hard to find a name that precisely describes this emotion. 'Fear' comes close, but apart from a

continuous sense of threat, it also includes a deep sense of abandonment and incompleteness. It may be best to use a term that is as undifferentiated as the basic emotion and simply call it 'pain'.

As we know, by implication free will requires a certain level of conscious awareness and freedom from such 'pain' so that our choices can include many options and solutions. Hence the need to work through an integral map to develop and understand the alternatives.

Another view is that all addictions are patterns and habitual behaviours with negative consequence for ourselves and others; they also include activities where the costs become greater than the perceived benefits. The addict struggles to live in the present moment as it is too painful, so the thinking will often project on the past or towards the future.

The ego will always tell us that we don't have a problem, especially with money. An addiction has to be affordable before any signs of unmanageability appear. On many occasions, an excess of money creates affordability and a practical level of 'manageability', in combination with several expensive cross-addictions, to mask the real underlying issues.

The basic need of the ego is for more of whatever gives us temporary relief, so it is not coincidental that people with money have deep-seated addictions that form a core part of their selves. However, as with all addictions, there is a heavy cost to the self that becomes buried by distractions. This is why it is essential for families with capital to include integrality in how capital is managed, since we are not born with addictions but they are learned as adaptive behaviours and strategies.

In Gabor Maté's very readable book[142], he tells the interesting story of the Canadian business tycoon Conrad Black. His rise and decline was related to his addiction: with sufficient capital, it was very easy for him to slip into the spiral of seeking higher highs after the inevitable lower lows,

> The addict is never satisfied. His spiritual and emotional condition is one of impoverishment, no matter how much he achieves, acquires or possesses'... Scruples vanish in the face of the addictive 'need' — hence, the ruthlessness. Loyalty, integrity and honour lose meaning

One could therefore argue that incipient addictions are attendant on having excess capital which takes incredible vigilance not to succumb. In addition to the more classical physical and chemical addictions (such as tobacco, alcohol, drugs, shopping, etc.), there are emotional addictions such as sex and love. These are particularly difficult when you have wealth, as love and sex are so easily confused with physical intimacy, which is just the poor substitute for real love – what psychologists call historical 'attunement', which we all need and addicts crave.

Attunement is when a person feels 'in tune' with someone else's emotional state; it is considered the real language of love. If we were deprived in our historical past, or our parents were emotionally and physically absent or dysfunctional, we will seek substitutes in others for the lack of connection. These will often be based on the same faulty paradigm and love strategy that we learned within our family. This is also key in sex and love addiction: seeking love but mistakenly assuming that affordable sex will fix the hunger. How can we know whether we are in a 'real' relationship or with someone for convenience, which money facilitates? To what degree is any attraction based on a transaction around our wealth, fame, position, power, etc.? The answer, as always, lies in the reality of our own understanding and our relationship with ourselves as a function of our own emotional and spiritual development.

Addictions can also be embedded in the incessant search for what is always 'the best', e.g., cars, food, vacations, accommodation, etc. This may not be a problem per se, and can in some ways be positive, but when this search becomes a prime driver that characterises many of our decisions, we limit our possibilities and can overinflate our ego. And whilst sometimes the good is in the way of the better, it often takes a better and bigger person to know the difference. As C.G. Jung reminds us to grow, 'We all walk in shoes too small for us'.

If addictions are antithetical to the wealth family package, we need to construct our capital management functions to encourage alleviation. If we only look through the lens of finance, and distribute without much discernment, we are brewing up problems. If you adopt a counterbalancing practise, such as the integral approach, such risks are alleviated. The integral approach means that no family member needs to be excluded since each one has a role to play within the full-spectrum, and there are outlets for their respective talents, creativity, and ambitions.

This way forward requires not only insight but sufficient humility and grace. It is no coincidence that part of the solution for addictions in recovery programs such as AA is being of service and contributing to something greater than ourselves, that is becoming stronger embedded in Impact. Another part of the solution is a belief in a 'higher power' (of our own understanding), believing in something greater than ourselves that attenuates our ego, which in turn may allow greater understanding, meaning and purpose. Timothy McMahan King said: "Grace points to the possibility of a redemption that is not just recovery but the opportunity to grow deeper and become stronger than we were before [184]."

This is combined with solid principles such as 'detachments with love' to create space for the real self to re-emerge and jettison the ties to another relational and emotional addiction, namely co-dependency. When we talk about detachment we do not mean cutting off or running away, we mean the ability to separate two different things and handling them within the contexts in which they each belong. It also means being able to understand and see as separate our inside worlds e.g., consciousness; and emotions with our outside worlds e.g., job, finances, relationships etc., of ourselves. This is an art to enable us to understand and distinguish that which truly belongs to us and is our responsibility, and that which belongs to others. This aspect is often confused in addictions, causing countless areas of conflict, chaos and stress, resulting in resentment and anger as solutions cannot be easily found. We may all have met people who seem to attract and even enjoy the ensuing drama in life which comes from chaos. For many, this drama is not only a good reason to alleviate the stress, but also to identify as the helpless and powerless victim on which their addictive tendencies rely.

The first step (of twelve) in e.g. AA's addiction recovery program: 'We admitted we were powerless over X (e.g., money/alcohol, etc.) and that our lives had become unmanageable'. To admit is tricky enough, given our inflated egos, so many can't even get past the first step, which requires humility and grace. You must judge yourself using self-reflection whether these are out of kilter preventing you from discovering your real self, and whether you have incipient addictive tendencies. This is extremely difficult and requires a clear mirror.

Most of us know that tinkering with acquisitions and distractions is not sufficient to create real meaning; however, making an authentic contribution to another's well-being, completing a labour of love, or contributing to the social good, is. Much of the need for distractions through distant experiences is because we are not happy nor content so we seek "greener grass". The reality of course is that if we invested more locally, we would not need not feel the want of having such experiences.

As mentioned before, limiting biases in our relationships affects our social capacity to hear and see the 'other', which causes existential loneliness. This should be an area of concern if we are to take Impact seriously. The reality is that we can sit in a sports stadium with 100,000 like-minded people and still feel very lonely. C.G. Jung suggests that:

Loneliness does not come from having no people about one, but from being unable to communicate the things that seem important to oneself, or from holding certain views which others find inadmissible[189].

As we know, excess in anything can be destructive even if it begins positively, so we need to be ultra-careful, especially when the family has the means to disguise, distort, or deny a problem and can support an individual financially to prevent a person hitting their 'rock bottom', which may be the gateway to recovery. This requires careful listening skills, both of the self in silence and the ability to hear "the other".

When people really listen, when they are fully present with one another, it is, as pioneering psychotherapist Carl Rogers describes, 'astonishing how elements which seem insoluble become soluble.' Rogers adds that when genuine connection occurs, 'confusions which seem irremediable turn into relatively clear flowing streams[190].'

When we reach a stage of maturity in our life where we have diminished or tamed the false ego, we will have developed our real capacity to listen to the self and others. At this stage, we have may have also generated the humility and capacity of holding ambiguity without needing to be right or needing to force solutions. This aspect has important implications for us in our governance systems and Impact approach, which seeks to develop real connective relationships which requires taking personal risks. Let's hear the wisdom of the American dancer Agnes deMille:

> Living is a form of not being sure, not knowing what next or how. The moment you know how; you begin to die a little. The artist never entirely knows. We guess. We may be wrong, but we take leap after leap in the dark[191].

The artist's way introduces the creative spirit and our imagination as core assets, which also keeps much of our work and family life alive. Without this at the forefront we can easily lose the connective tissue between our experiences and what makes us come alive. When we walk into our office with a sense of 'knowing it all' and lacking new stimuli, we feel that life is passing us by; we need to re-engage with our imaginative acts of creativity.

Twyla Tharp writes, 'Art is the only way to run away without leaving home [192].' We all need to escape and run off sometimes but let us run towards areas that nurture, are positive, and enable us to grow and develop.

However, many organisations and their leaders prefer conformity and are uncomfortable with someone who is more of a creative artist, who is more concerned with freedom from precedents and constraints. This is an important aspect that needs to be challenged if we are to work with real Impact. Firstly, as mentioned, Integral Impact can and should include input from diverse talents and traits, which would enable family members to reconnect meaning and purpose with capital. Secondly, I believe that approximately 50% of real Impacts are sufficiently tangible to be measurable and quantifiable; thus much of the real Impact dimension needs to seek alternative forms of transmitting information as a bridge between our reality and ourselves.

This is where I believe art has an important role to play since it contains much more information e.g., Feelings rather than just numbers. Thinking itself is also an art form. Just as art flourishes against a backdrop of a certain culture, aesthetic resonance with the self, knowledge and atmosphere, can only flourish within an equally diverse set of practises, as influenced and co-created with our relationships.

§14.3 Traits and thinking patterns

A personality trait shared by addictions and ADHD is self-medicating to distract from distressing states. These can be internal, such as tuning out, and external, such as stimulation by substances, food, activities, and other people.

Both addictions and ADHD are disorders based on an historical lack of secure relational attachments, which are played out as poor emotional self-regulation and differentiation with a deficient control of one's impulses, '... because he sic]does not want to be disturbed, to be made uncertain, he establishes a pattern of conduct, of thought, of relationship. He then becomes a slave to the pattern and takes the pattern to be the real thing... [81].'

There are also several thought patterns attendant with addictive behaviours, such as being self-centred, 'black-and-white' thinking, polarised opinions that must be strongly argued and defended, sometimes at any cost.

Another thought pattern is that the world is against sufferers and, when the proverbial 's***t' hits their fan, they blame everyone else. As such, they often cannot contain and manage responsibility for their actions.

Other recognizable thought patterns include magnifying or minimising catastrophizing of events, over-generalising, labelling or mis-labelling.

We also may see self-pity — 'I'm a good person' and 'I'm a unique person in special ways'; a lack-of-time perspective; engaging in selective efforts based on own needs; use of deceit and manipulation to control; seeking pleasure first, etc.

We often hear words such as 'should', 'shouldn't', 'ought to', 'must', 'must not', 'have to', 'need to', 'it is necessary', 'supposed to', etc., which are neuro-linguistically referred to as generalised 'modal operators of necessity' (see Appendix 2). In everyday language, they suggest thinking typical of addictions.

Common to all addictions is a psychological self-protection system, namely denial.

Denial can be held onto for many reasons until the person hits his/her 'rock bottom'. However, sufficient funding of addictions will distance denial until other signs and triggers appear.

Many families cannot see that the very thing that made them successful and contributed to their happiness can detrimentally affect family members, who cannot healthily adjust. They cannot admit their powerlessness and may fear social stigma in relation to the family's elevated status and to their inner circle of friends. As such, denial becomes part of the modus operandi, with those holding the purse strings now needing to stay in denial, otherwise their entire edifice on which their wealth has been built may be questioned. What we deny at home, we most likely will deny at work, so hence the need to understand its impact in other areas. Most people also have 'cross-addictions', so that no single addiction becomes visible or 'unmanageable', for example, easily justified workaholism to generate even more wealth, power, status, sex and love; excess consumerism; various forms of gambling (otherwise known as process addiction); exercise; adrenaline sports, etc.

Walk around London's fashionable Mayfair in the evening and you will get a flavour for what's on offer. We do not necessarily say that there is anything wrong with such activity; if you collect fine wines, watches, clothes, antiques and cars, this can be perfectly reasonable and manageable. However, money, power, property, and prestige can be highly addictive in their own right as part of the acquisition addictive strategy. It's worth reinforcing that a real risk for families with sufficient accumulated wealth is to enable members not to engage with real work to generate a living and learning how to stand on their own feet, limiting their emancipation and individuation. As such, they may have removed the incentive for the real self to fully develop and individuate in order to create a self-generated contribution. Such a contribution is the final step in our integral West, fundamental for our self-esteem and is a core component of our ultimate identity.

Another key area is friendships and relationships which wealth can superficially buy and possibly maintain. But if these are based mainly on transactions, they will have no visceral meaning or value for the individual. If these are not installed and nurtured, the individual may substitute these with addictions. This is why impact is so important for family offices: it provides the requisite four worlds' ingredients for members to work with and individuate, using and reconnecting with their family capital.

Tradition 6 Alcoholics Anonymous (AA) is: "An (recovery) group ought never endorse, finance or lend the (group) name to any related facility or outside enterprise, lest problems of money, property and prestige divert us from our primary purpose. The recovery movement recognised that money, property and prestige are three culprits that divert and risk the development of the individual from fulfilling his/her primary purpose. There are several such culprits that we may need to understand a little deeper:

§14.3.1 The 4 Ps Power (out Integral South)

Here I include money as a form of latent power and in whose creation we ground ourselves through our own thinking, actions and being. As such, money also is shaped and used in accordance with our calling and our consciousness, and is an Integral part of our relational development journey.

§14.3.2 Prestige (our Integral East)

We use our accumulated power to create a synthesised image and identity of ourselves which reflects the emergent nature of what we believe we are and want to become. Our self-image of how and where we fit into our culture and context shapes how we use prestige to reinforce our becoming.

§14.3.3 Position (our Integral North)

Having begun to integrate our identity, we now co-create our position of our self-image knowingly within our context and world. We seek to navigate ourselves into a position aligned with the nature of how we understand our inner self-image.

§14.3.4 Property (our Integral West)

We can now use our understanding to affect and create the types of property our inner self-image seeks by doing. Our contribution will be a function of the quality of our journey and become verified and justified by the previous stages of our journey.

As you may have gathered, these four stages and levels, as with others, are containers and expressions for how we shape our inner and outer worlds so that we have elements from both our higher selves and shadow selves. We need these balanced elements to individuate, emancipate, and find peace and reconciliation with ourselves and others.

> There are no contests in the art of peace. A true warrior in invincible because he or she contests with nothing. Defat means to defeat the mind of contention that we harbour within(p.92).[81]

§14.4 Moving ahead

Economies can also become addicted to core ideas, for example the constant rise in GNP (and cheap oil to facilitate it); our consumer culture based on empty acquisition; and negative marketing to make us feel bad about ourselves for which their product is the solution, which in turn requires and facilitates addictions. As such, one could argue that addictions are inescapable.

But how can we prevent their appearance and limit their impact? In our postmodern culture, we have rampant narcissism that can also be translated as an addiction to the ego. Ostensibly, this might contravene our thinking: what's wrong with everyone pursuing his/her 'American dream' or its many global cultural equivalents. The late American writer Hubert Selby Jr.[193] puts it beautifully:

> I believe that to pursue the American dream is not only futile but self-destructive because ultimately it destroys everything and everyone involved with it. By definition it must, because it nurtures everything except those things that are important: integrity, ethics, truth, our very heart and soul. Why? The reason is simple: because Life/life is about giving, not getting.

Here we have it laid out in black and white. If we are to justify receiving anything inside a relationship, (e.g., capital returns), we must counterbalance it by giving in at least equal measure from those areas where we have capacity and resources — integrally informed, of course.

Chapter 15

Ownership and governance as the keystone to culture

For the purposes of this book, the concept of ownership may extend from equity into other structural forms of capital participation that afford similar privileges. Here we will explore some of the more philosophical aspects of what constitutes ownership, stewardship and governance, and their relation with culture.

Ownership, like money, can be completely neutral, e.g., a percentage in a share register which may require no involvement by the investor. However, there comes a point where it is more than just a number and therefore some form of relationship is formed.

No other aspect of an investment relates more to the concept of the power complex than ownership. Ownership is the foundation of the nature of our participation and relationship with an investee, as this is where not only our formal and legal agreements are constructed but also informal ones, such as the shape and form of how we see and position 'the other' in our affairs.

Whilst it is easy to grant upfront voting rights and other forms of board participation to gain influence and control, it is only through forming a relationship with our stakeholders that any of our differences can surface. It is in the grounding of the relationship and the quality of our dialectic that any such differences will be resolved without creating conflict and without either participant activating a power complex.

Any board or organisational executive committee is bound by mores, rules and requirements for its effective functioning; it is also a social body that needs to develop its own modes of operation. In my experience, boards tend to gravitate in language and thinking towards whoever has power or can dominate the discourse. This is usually how we get listened to. Providing contrast, valuable as this may be, creates dissonance and thus minimised in importance (or rejected outright) to maintain a false sense of group harmony.

Eckhart Tolle tells us that: 'Power over others is weakness disguised as strength[188].' Throughout my own career, ownership and participation have been a source of attempts of manipulation by smart people who control the levers of equity. Their rationalization, after events unfold, as to why they cannot deliver on previous discussions or commitments fascinate.

As if by magic, as soon as something has value, history gets reinterpreted; attributable values are re-assigned to those who control the power complex.

I have personally been involved in several business where much was promised and little delivered by the owners, to the long-term detriment of the firm. In my view, any start-up or early-growth firm needs to have an initial, binding contractual commitment from the initial owners to deliver on shared ownership promises.

As someone who firmly believes in the ethics and commercial rationale for equity participation across a broad spectrum of a firm's employee pool, it pains me when this aspect is not considered or delivered reluctantly by incumbent owners.

Whilst governance is often an extension of ownership, the closer the power distance or reliance on conventional hierarchical structures, the more likely that its governance methods become a result (and reflection) of the same ownership, power and influence structures.

This leads to the need to consider the governance of a firm as a separate requirement dependent on life-cycle business needs and the necessary stake-holder participation in its governance and social design. Whilst governance has considerable legal and compliance requirements and responsibilities, its effective co-creative function is driven by the level of relationship its members can develop.

Few boards operate as democracies; whilst there are some extremely important and valid reasons why this may not be appropriate (e.g., in relation to equity capital at risk), firms become more vulnerable through the concentration of power within their control functions. Also, there is a dynamic between the collective and individual intellect that we need to be aware of:

> A group experience takes place on a lower level of consciousness than the experience of an individual. This is due to the fact that, when many people gather together to share one common emotion, the total psyche emerging from the group is below the level of the individual psyche.
>
> If it is a very large group, the collective psyche will be more like the psyche of an animal, which is the reason why the ethical attitude of large organisations is always doubtful. The psychology of a large crowd inevitably sinks to the level of mob psychology.
>
> If, therefore, I have a so-called collective experience as a member of a group, it takes place on a lower level of consciousness than if I had the experience by myself alone.

Many private firms are well-run under strong and concentrated leadership. However, vulnerability comes via group-think, lack of broader and inclusive perspectives, and vital intelligence from others.

This is always a compromise so should be part of a firm's design, not just from the accidental outcome from how ownership was created. In the areas of functionality and a firm's culture, this design is mission critical.

We have investigated the Four Rs of Relationships in detail, and we explore them from the governance perspective:

I. *Rooting (South):* How are we connected and in what ways do we belong together? What are our common values for respect, commitment etc.? Are there ways in which we establish our common callings, grounding and world views?

II. *Resonance (East):* In our communication and ways of being, how do we compliment, expand and enhance each other to make any weaknesses less relevant? Can we openly share, and do we understand each other's values and belief systems? Why are we together within this context?

III. *Relevance (North):* How do we operate as a group? Are we co-creating the future and, if so, is this balanced? Are roles clear and lines of authority respected? How are opinions heard and made relevant?

IV. *Rationale (West):* What are the key contributing factors that make our Impact approach work, and are they all present and correct? Are the executive capabilities operational and fully aligned with vision and mission?

These are just some examples of questions one can ask in trying to understand the governance culture and Impact dialectic in which all things come together. Can we bring the language of the heart, and impact, into these conversations or will they be ignored, rejected or ridiculed? Can we live by what Emily Dickinson elegantly offers about having our words living on through Impact: 'A word is dead when it is said, some say. I say it just begins to live that day[1].'

As we weave impact outcomes into the fabric of our investments, can we have conversations that expand the impact lens and its objectives? We have built the loom on which this fabric will be woven within our governance functions. Will this loom hold under tension? Is it robust enough to hold ambiguity, competing claims and conflicts? Such tensions are the natural

---

[1][194]. A word is dead when it is said.

consequences of a healthy environment. It is when things become straight-forward and lack a vibrant dialectic that we should worry because this may indicate conformity, fear, and the power complex rearing its head.

Here we again need to look differently at the political dynamics between larger and smaller organisations and how these affect the possibility of integral impact design. In my own experience when working for large finan-cial institutions, politics was often the modus operandi. Unless we actively participated in these politics and were good at managing the management hierarchy, we were destined to limit our career prospects.

In his 2009 West Point Academy Leadership address, William Dere-siewicz said

> I'm sorry to say this, but like so many people you will meet as you negotiate the bureaucracy of the Army or for that matter of whatever institution you end up giving your talents to after the Army, whether it is Microsoft or the World Bank or whatever—the head of my department had no genius for organising or initiative or even order, no particular learning or intelligence, no distinguishing characteristics at all. Just the ability to keep the routine going, and beyond that, as Marlow says, her position had come to her—why? That's really the great mystery about bureaucracies. Why is it so often that the best people are stuck in the middle and the people who are running things—the leaders—are the mediocrities? Because excellence isn't usually what gets you up the greasy pole. What gets you up is a talent for maneuvering. Kissing up to the people above you, kicking down to the people below you.

This is another reason why real impact investment is more likely to emanate from smaller firms and family offices where politics do not prevail so extensively. Larger firms often suffer from inertia as their strong processes, capacities and resources have been firmly embedded into their culture and leadership so it will take a greater effort and understanding for any change to be actualised. Deresiewicz makes another important point when he links the cognitive thinking capacities of leaders to the lack of creative vision in many areas of organisational life. In essence, connecting the gap between the Why? and How?:

> We have a crisis of leadership in America because our overwhelming power and wealth, earned under earlier generations of leaders, made us complacent, and for too long we have been training leaders who only know how to keep the routine going. Who can answer questions, but don't know how to ask them. Who can fulfil goals, but don't know how to set them. Who think about how to get things done, but not whether they're worth doing in the first place. What we have now are the greatest technocrats the world has ever seen, people who have been trained to be incredibly good at one specific thing, but who have no

interest in anything beyond their area of expertise. What we don't have are leaders. What we don't have, in other words, are thinkers. People who can think for themselves. People who can formulate a new direction: for the country, for a corporation or a college, for the Army—a new way of doing things, a new way of looking at things. People, in other words, with vision. [195]

Surely when we design impact-orientated organisations, we aim higher. We seek to improve ownership structures and governance so they are not just a conventional iven, but an outcome, fully informed and synthesised with the culture, stakeholders, and impact outcome objectives.

Let us look briefly at some innovative ways of reinventing ownership. One model at the forefront is the concept of 'FairShares' which incorporates six different definitions of 'wealth'[196].

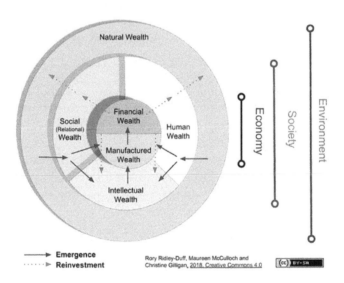

Figure 15.1: FairShares

Similar to I³, the firm needs to travel through six stages of navigation to understand the best fit in terms of outcomes. The FairShares Model is implemented through:

I. Five values and principles.

II. Six key questions.

III. Five learning and development methods.

iv. Four legal identities.

v. Seven ICT support platforms.

vi. Six forms of wealth contribution.[2]

The main point here is that to build resilience and sustainability, the firm needs to become more adaptive and align with its real impact stakeholders. These initiatives, if adopted, should contain the full suite of impact objectives in which ownership and wealth recognition/distribution are key components in building an impactful businesses.

Another important concept is 'Equity for Good' (EFG), which originates from the social-enterprise sphere and is based on recent, positive developments in how businesses treat their employees (e.g., 'Investor in People'); how businesses manage their transparent supply-chain with suppliers (e.g., 'fair trade' or 'anti-slavery'), or what a business chooses to do with its profits (e.g., '1% for the planet').

The EFG approach gives businesses and investors the chance to clarify their mission and publicly demarcate how created shareholder value will improve practises in the economy. The aim is to provide transparency for social-enterprise stakeholders, reassurance for customers, and brand value for mission-driven companies and investors.

The EFG investment model is rooted in a legally binding pledge made by impact investors. The pledger agrees to reinvest (or donate) a set percentage of the value of any net capital gain in a social-impact investment through any combination of the following:

- Reinvesting into another social enterprise or social impact investment fund.

- Gifting to a registered charity of our choice.

- Gifting to a not-for-profit that is not registered as a charity.

The EFG concept defines 'net capital gain' as the money made in addition to the initial sum invested, net of tax and a nominal inflationary return on the original investment (set at UK GBP annual LIBOR rate + 2% per annum). In this way, the EFG approach does not cap a return per se, but ensures that a clear proportion of any 'excess' return is ploughed back into defined areas of 'doing good' as one sees fit.

---

[2]For a full description of each, see [196]

In addition, alternative initiatives such as 'B Corp' provides a holistic certification that a business has met minimum standards in its relationship with workers, customers, suppliers, the community and the environment.

This concept of reciprocity also applies to our personal finances. Many people may not have a retirement fund so their family and community becomes a de facto relational insurance. With wealth, we often distance and separate ourselves from such reliance. If our very lives depend on it, we are more likely to honour and cherish our nearest and dearest, treating them with care and respect, since we not only need these relationships, we have also have built up reciprocal stores of relational capital in combination with our other possible forms of capital.

In her book[197], Lynne Twist points out that modern science is discovering a similar truth in nature,

> Contrary to those models of Nature as innately, intensely, and almost exclusively competitive, more recent scientific study has illuminated the powerful role of mutuality, synergy, coexistence, and cooperation in the natural world...The idea that scarcity and competition are just the way it is is no longer even viable science. Respected evolutionary biologist Elisabet Sahtouris notes that Nature fosters collaboration and reciprocity. Competition in Nature exists, she says, but it has limits, and the true law of survival is ultimately cooperation...Sahtouris and others note that contrary to the competitive theme that "survival of the fittest" connotes, a more accurate description would be "survival of the cooperative and collaborative."

§15.1 Some early personal experiences

After a somewhat 'classical' background of having studied Economics in Stockholm, followed by Business at the London School of Foreign Trade, I joined the investment banking profession with Paribas Capital Markets. My own style of learning was by 'doing'; more specifically, I knew that by integrating doing with learning, I accelerated the doing and better embedded the learning. This often confused prospective employers, who seldom look beyond specified degrees and prerequisite knowledge that they believe are key components for a particular job.

After a few years in the industry, I realised that I lacked the technical insights of my investment management clients so I enrolled in the London Business School's three-year Corporate Finance and Investment Management evening programme, which had the same curriculum as their MSc in Finance. Whilst this course gave me a deeper appreciation and a technical background to finance, I became aware of its limitations, and that its paradigms resided within the neoclassical 'Chicago' style of thinking and doing. This paradigm was mechanistic and disconnected, ignoring my belief that every human and their creations must function within a living and interconnected system, whether it is a cottage garden powered by soil and sun or a company powered by employees.

Living systems (sometimes called complex adaptive systems) are ubiquitous: hospitals, the human body, the stock market, estuaries, neighbourhoods. Although subject to the law of entropy, living systems are also governed by the countervailing processes of evolution. They don't just run down, they also somehow grow up.

For this reason, one of the basic premises of regenerative development is that every living system has the inherent possibility to move to new levels of order, differentiation, and organisation. This capacity to create increased order is the opposite of entropy and, in my view, is one of the core components of integral impact investing.

Ben Okri encourages us to see impact as a major part of our legacy and our gifts to our families and mankind: And just as astonishing is the knowledge That we are, more or less, The makers of the future.

> *And just as astonishing is the*
> *knowledge That we are, more or less,*
> *The makers of the future.*
> *We create what time will frame.*
> *And a beautiful dream, shaped*
> *And realised by a beautiful mind,*
> *Is one of the greatest gifts*
> *We can make to our fellow beings. [198]*

When working in banking and needing to conform to its culture in order to remain employed and also advance, it became obvious that there was some personal dissonance and differing views around the core operating principles of the industry. I would even argue that a person with strong ethics and morals was incompatible with building a successful banking career. All too often the least trustworthy people, who were personally connected and knew how to manage the firm's politics, rose in the firm's hierarchy.

With my own values and beliefs about how business could be better conducted now being challenged, I became someone who could help to repair such differences. One such driver, as discussed previously, was the universal need to conform to the 'success principles' for recognition and advancement. At the organisational level, this becomes a self-selective, iterative, and recursive process.

Core operating principles, in my experience, were based mainly on transactional quantitative measures relating to money, power, and prestige. This was something we had to live with; given the prevailing culture, there was little alternative but to conform fully, since this was all management could see and value. This experience led me to explore what I call the 'power distance' between cause and effect. This contrasts what the social psychologist Geert Hofstede terms 'power distance', which is a function of how people belonging to a specific culture view a power relationship, e.g., superior-subordinate relationships, authority, and collaborative participation.

In my work for the Client Solution Group at Fortis, my quest to connect disconnected parts of a business became a key area for my own growth. In my view, moving from our previous Power Distance 1.0, centred on overt power such as position, status and other hierarchies (and including physical distance). A possible shift to Power Distance 2.0 will include a psychodynamic, connective, and spiritual developmental aspect that both includes and transcends the traditional moral development axis. In the banking industry, I witnessed our ability to disconnect from outcomes and not take responsibility for them.

Similar phenomena have been researched in other areas, such as the military, where following orders freed individuals from guilt and shame, and liberty of consciousness. This confirms the link between our levels of consciousness and how a prevailing culture can influence human behaviour at the cost of awareness and responsibility.

This link was recognised as an element of the banking crises; I am very interested to see how these power distances can be shortened in the integral economy and, if possible, made whole again. In impact investing, we must be acutely of this power disconnect and work to eliminate it. When designing outcome objectives with organisations, we need to embed and connect fully the individual deliverables with responsibilities. At the same time, we need to take into account the serendipity of life and what C.G. Jung called 'synchronicity of life', which at times creates opportunity and adversity often in unequal measures, providing us with our 'fork in the road' choices.

As Alain de Botton reminds us: 'We should not feel embarrassed by our difficulties, only by our failure to grow anything beautiful from them[199].'

Let us now turn return to the integral approach to see how it should be influenced by natural designs and solutions.

Chapter 16

Integral design

There is no evolution without revolution, and designing for evolution doesn't mean designing evolution. Natural design is a key component of the integral approach; as such, we need to look briefly at some of its key components.

Since Charles Darwin published The Origin of Species, generations of evolutionary biologists have been refining, correcting and adding new layers of insight, drawing on a growing body of scientific knowledge. While evolution is generally understood as a movement from simple to more complex, understanding the process through which it occurs is the subject of theory, research and debate.

A particularly relevant school of thought views cooperation (deriving from the mutuality of interest among organisms and ecosystems) rather than competition as evolution's primary driver. For more than a century, natural selection has been conceptualised as the result of competition over scarce resources. This view dogmatically dominates much of finance. The idea of organisms battling one another for survival still holds sway in popular culture, but science tells us that this isn't the whole story.

According to Martin Nowak, Director of the Program for Evolutionary Dynamics at Harvard University:

> Cooperation is needed for evolution to construct new levels of organisation. The emergence of genomes, cells, multi-cellular organisms, social insects and human society are all based on cooperation.[200]

And Darwin himself wrote:

> The most important of all causes of organic change is . . . the mutual relation of organism to organism—the improvement of one being entailing the improvement or the extermination of others(p.68)[201]

Many interpretations of Darwin's work have misleading emphasised extermination rather than improvement of species. Evolutionary biologist Elisabet Sahtouris has asserted that competition is a dominant phase of the juvenile stage in evolution, since a species needs to spread itself over enough territory to get enough resources to multiply. However, at some point as species start to bump into one another, cooperation takes over. She argues that a tendency toward competition marks an immature level of biological development, occurring when a relatively new species strives to establish itself before it learns to form much more efficient cooperative alliances.3

> Young immature species are the ones that grab as much territory and resources as they can, multiplying as fast as they can. But the process of negotiations with other species matures them, thus maturing entire ecosystems. Rainforests that have evolved over millions of years are a good example. No species is in charge—the system's leadership is distributed among all species, all knowing their part in the dance, all cooperating in mutual consistency. [202]

Sahtouris also observes that:

> Multi-celled creatures are relatively huge cooperative enterprises that could never have evolved if individual cells had been doomed to struggle in scarcity. [203]

For her:

> The best life insurance for any species in an ecosystem is to contribute usefully to sustaining the lives of other species, a lesson we are only beginning to learn as humans.(Ibid)

Herein lies the rub: the interdependency is absolute and it is only our lack of consciousness that tricks us into thinking otherwise. We have the false belief that knowledge is intelligence, and that intelligence is sufficient. This is why in the integral four worlds we need each touchstone to inform and navigate the next. Without these, knowledge and intelligence on their own (as we humans have experienced on many occasions) become the disease that kill the host.

As the German spiritual teacher, Eckhart Tolle, tells us:

> In fact, if mental development and increased knowledge are not counterbalanced by a corresponding growth in consciousness, the potential for unhappiness and disaster is very great. (…) The crowning glory of human development rests not in our ability to reason and think, though this is what distinguishes us from animals. Intellect, like instinct, is merely a point along the way. Our ultimate destiny is to re-connect with our essential Being and express from our extraordinary, divine reality in the ordinary physical world, moment-bymoment. Easy to say, yet rare are those who have attained the further reaches of human development. [188]

Hence our rooting and grounding in the integral South, the home of Being. Evolution, as such, is not guaranteed nor a given. Again, in Sahtouris's words:

The evolutionary process is an awesome improvisational dance that weaves individual, communal, ecosystemic and planetary interests into a harmonious whole.[202]

At our stage of human development, we have managed to move this notion of evolution into creative competition in sport, art, design, talent, cooking and other areas. Our competitive roots have evolved into drivers for excellence, e.g., the best behaviour or best product. 'Best' is seen as a function of our culture.

The implication for impact investing is profound. As we begin to epistemically weave the integral four worlds together, an evolutionary process is being activated by design which cannot be ignored nor pushed aside. This is why the integral design for any organisation is paramount if the pieces are to hold together, and for the sum of the parts to become greater and more transformational than the independent pieces. This is also why we need to travel through the 4Ms and ask (and answer) the 'Why question' before we quest to model and create the structures to hold and develop each component.

One of the practical applications is to look at conventional value chains as virtuous circles. In a process flow format, the familiar corporate value chain highlights where value is added to a set of activities beginning with basic raw material coming from suppliers, moving on to a series of value-added activities involved in producing and marketing a product or service, and ending with distributors getting the final goods into the hands of the ultimate customer. This chain tends to have a beginning and an end, thereby disconnecting and fragmenting any possible integral leverage, unlike a flywheel where momentum requires less energy to accelerate as each part assists and supports the next.

§16.1 Causal models build virtuous circles

It is necessary to establish a causal model, or fly-wheel, of the plan for any system that highlights the drivers of strategic success. In a financial services company, such a model might take the following circular shape, which highlights the learning and self-leveraging effects of the system.

Table 16.1: Cycle

Selection & Staffing	New Hires, Education, Work Experience
Employee Satisfaction	Supervision, Support & Fairness, Compensation
Employee Added Value	Empowerment, Accountability, Investor Credibility
Customer Satisfaction	Advice & Ideas, Execution, Price/Value
Investor Transaction Behaviour	Transaction Frequency, % of Wallet, Margin vs. Risk
Profitability & Sustained Revenue	Wallet Migration, Margin Retention, Client Survey

Here we see that each component feeds the next; thus, becoming necessary to reinforce the prior area so that momentum and harmony can be built up. This, as we know, is rarely seen in organisations where fragmentation and operational silos often prevail due to politics and the ubiquitous power complexes. Our impact design must be based on causal models with no loose ends where things just stop and energy dies. We now have sufficient basis to look into the integral four-worlds more fully.

Figure 16.1: Virtuous circles

Chapter 17

An introduction to the integral four worlds

Recently popularised by Ken Wilber and his All Quadrants, All Lines (AQAL) integral theory, integral is a four-quadrant grid which suggests the synthesis of all human knowledge and experience. It fuses the four worlds with the evolutionary and developmental dynamics necessary for progress. In addition, the organisational psychologist Don Beck, together with Lessem and Schieffer, has become a catalyst for creating natural and resilient change, developing new perspectives to help create public awareness for how integral understanding can be beneficial. It is the only way to comprehend complexity in today's world.

Furthermore, we have recently witnessed an increased global interest in higher levels of consciousness and integration, resulting in an awareness that we are now witnessing an emergent and interconnected 'integral age' from which generic versions of impact investments have emerged that could not have happened otherwise. What most of these integral thinkers share is their attempt to combine into an integral perspective diverse cultural value and belief orientations The key feature across these approaches is the propagation and advancement of new evolutionary levels of human consciousness, enabling humanity to transcend fragmented, isolated perspectives into integrative ones. Integrally speaking, we call this 'transcend and include' as we cannot skip developmental stages, and if so, significant dysfunction will emerge at the new levels. This is why impact investments have to become a staged process for both the individual and organisation, as I^3 is designed to be.

Whilst this may sound somewhat esoteric, impact investment philosophy will only become a reality based on each individual's developmental levels of awareness and consciousness. Otherwise, it will be at best a 'tick-box' exercise that quickly regresses into creating suitable numbers and statistics for a detached, remote audience whose responsibility fades correspondingly.

§17.1 Re-Connection

For millennia, economic activity was a localised community affair with developed systems of capital and currencies performing specific roles and functions, reflecting specific needs and cultures. Core to such systems is the close communal sharing of knowledge of values, trust and reciprocity which enabled relational flows to occur and disputes to be settled by members. Such aspects were lost as distances between people and transactions increased which was replaced with the law and rule -based systems.

With such distancing comes a psychological lessening of responsibility towards outcomes and effects. Impact investing reconnects some of this awareness and responsibility. Complexity increased during the neo-classical period by increasing the political economy, based on more anthropological ideas than the previously self-interested and behaviourally-driven now termed homo economicus.

The early ideology was established 250 years ago by the classical economist Adam Smith who wrote[204]: 'It is not from the benevolence of the butcher, the brewer, or the baker that we expect our dinner, but from their regard to their own self-interest'. This is still the basic operating economic principle today. But Smith also wrote that[205]:

> Man naturally desires, not only to be loved, but to be lovely; or to be that thing which is the natural and proper object of love. He naturally dreads, not only to be hated, but to be hateful; or to be that thing which is the natural and proper object of hatred. He desires, not only praise, but praiseworthiness; or to be that thing which, though it should be praised by nobody, is, however, the natural and proper object of praise. He dreads, not only blame, but blame-worthiness; or to be that thing which, though it should be blamed by nobody, is, however, the natural and proper object of blame

Love of 'praise' and of 'praiseworthiness', and dread of 'blame' and of 'blameworthiness'. What could be a more apt philosophy for the development of our evolved impact investment methodology? The mistaken 'imperative' in current investment philosophy is that the only option is to compete aggressively in business and pursue the largest possible amount of personal financial gain.

We see, particularly from the recent financial crisis, that such behaviour is highly egotistical and damaging, stemming from the misplaced and paradoxical hope that the good of all results from the behaviour of the individual's ego. Today, we realize that this is a fatal flaw. Whilst Smith also attributed 'sympathy' and 'fellow-feeling' in his vision of both people and society, this has largely been ignored in policy making, with only the pursuit of increased wealth as a measure of success. Impact re-addresses the balance and understanding of the systemic nature between the component parts that constitute and drive wealth, creating new definitions of capital and wealth in the pro-

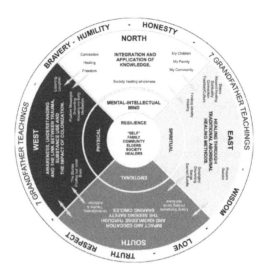

Figure 17.1: Participant Medicine Wheel. Adapted from Vickers (1992-1993).

cess. As mentioned earlier, such healing is driven by increased awareness, deeper levels of consciousness, our sense of mutual connectedness and our responsibility towards not only our fellow human beings also to our planet and other living systems.

This knowledge has existed with our traditions of wisdom for millennia but has largely been forgotten since the Industrial Revolution. The indigenous people of Turtle Island (North America) still have this ancient sense of the human being and all creation as the sacred hoop or medicine wheel. This was misinterpreted by Abraham Maslow when he came to Alberta to learn about the four directions of the medicine wheel from the Blackfoot tribes.

We again see the four-fold aspects of our nature and wisdom[206], each of which must be balanced in a healthy individual through the development of volition, i.e., will.

As Edgar Cayce writes:

> By awakening the Native American teachings, you come to the realisation that the earth is not something simply that you build upon and walk upon and drive upon and take for granted. It is a living entity. It has consciousness.[207]

The anthroposophist Rudolf Steiner (1861-1925) developed the idea of a threefold social organism where he recognised three domains of human social activity: economic, legal, and cultural. Steiner maintained that the health of human society depends on an adult population that understands the characteristics of each domain and could thereby organise society so that each domain enjoyed independence and autonomy.

In his economic lectures he speaks about price setting by bringing together all stakeholders involved. Steiner maintained that economic life at this time was encompassed by what he called the Law of True Price:

> A true price is forthcoming when a man [sic] receives, as counter-value for the product he has made, an amount sufficient to enable him to satisfy the whole of his needs, including of course the needs of his dependents, until he will again have completed a like product. [208, p. 111.]

Impact investing should re-establish a healthy dialectic between the constituent parts of the 'law of true price'. The impact community developed awareness for and about impact, with accompanying methodology that now widely suggests moving from Version 1.0 to Version 2.0. The main difference between the two versions is the shift from a 'finance first' impact towards 'mission' as anchored in each firm's values, beliefs and vision.

Thus, it becomes apparent that for firms there is a need for an emancipatory, organisational, hermeneutic impact process. The traditional Internal Rate of Return (IRR) is firmly embedded and can only be reconstructed through the validation of an alternative approach, such as I^3, which can highlight the impact dimensions as rooted in reality. This will require some change in investment leadership along the lines of cognitive and consciousness-based development, as outlined previously.

As discussed, levels of awareness depend on the current level consciousness and are driven by changing life conditions. Jeffrey Sachs put our challenge as follows:

> The truth of good economic doctoring is to know the general principles, and to really know the specifics. To understand the context, and also, to understand that an economy may need some tender loving care, not just the so-called hard truths, if it is going to get by[209].

Whilst we swim in the force fields of our perceived reality, everything we know is through the lens and prism of contrasting experienced perspectives. The psychoanalyst James Hollis expands on interaction between the force fields of fate, choice and destiny, and uses Greek drama to describe experiences that seem to be common to many people[137]. He suggests that our lives are circumscribed by:

Fate, or Moira, which embodies the world of givens, the world of limitations, the world of cause and effect. Our genetics, our family of origin, our Zeitgeist, the interplay of intergenerational influence each is part of our fate.

Again, as with impact, 'integral' is nothing new. In many cultures the number four is an ancient symbol for wholeness within diversity. Anthropology confirms that the human race has been seeking connection and unity with something larger than itself for eons.

The integral approach, which is a form of structured and organised system thinking, has been mapped and developed from theory to practise, and popularised by Ken Wilber. Briefly, Wilber's four worlds consists of four quadrants:

I. The interior of the individual – the 'I' space which is accessed by introspection and meditation, and contains thoughts, images, emotions, insights.

II. The exterior of the individual – the 'it' space, the 'scientific' view of the organism, including atoms, molecules, organ systems.

III. The interior of the collective – the 'we' space including shared values, worldviews, ethics.

IV. The exterior of the collective - the 'its' space of systems, social institutions, techno-economic modes of production. These quadrants are key to Wilber's AQAL Framework – All Quadrants, All Lines

Virtually every discipline focuses almost entirely on just one quadrant and builds all its theories around it, while denying others. Wilber calls this 'quadrant absolutism'. We can also have 'level absolutism', for example identifying all of spirituality with just the mythicliteral level and dismissing all other levels. We can have 'line absolutism', focusing on a single line or intelligence; 'state absolutism', whereby the exclusive focus is on scientific materialism at a gross-physical level. All create pathologies and shadow elements within each quadrant that can only be made conscious if we can see this in the mirror from a different quadrant.

With regard to overall development, Wilber discusses general levels (structure-rungs) and states (with their realms).

But a crucial point is that specific lines of development are growing and moving through the various levels (see table below).

In order to develop within our impact perspective, we must travel through each line as part of grounding ourselves in our key questions.

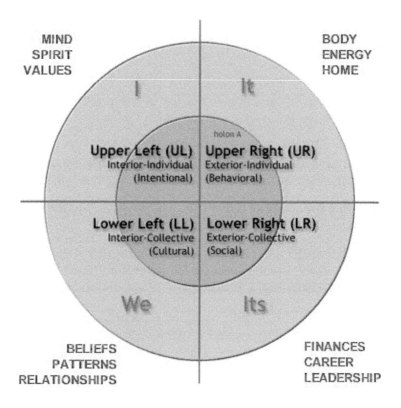

MIND
SPIRIT
VALUES

BODY
ENERGY
HOME

I

It

holon A

Upper Left (UL)
Interior-Individual
(Intentional)

Upper Right (UR)
Exterior-Individual
(Behavioral)

Lower Left (LL)
Interior-Collective
(Cultural)

Lower Right (LR)
Exterior-Collective
(Social)

We

Its

BELIEFS
PATTERNS
RELATIONSHIPS

FINANCES
CAREER
LEADERSHIP

Figure 17.2: Mind, Body, Beliefs, Finances

Table 17.1: Lines-Formats of multiple intelligences

Line	Life Questions	Typical Researcher
Cognitive	What am I aware of?	Piaget
Self	Who am I?	Loevinger
Values	What is significant to me?	Graves, Beck
Morals	What should I do?	Kohlberg, Gilligan
Spiritual	What is of ultimate concern?	Fowler
Needs	What do I need?	Maslow
Kinaesthetic	How do I physically do this?	Gardner
Emotional	How do I feel about this?	Goleman
Aesthetic	What is attractive to me?	Housen
Linguistic	How best to word this?	Vygotsky

Integral seeks to create and incorporate ontology (theory of reality), epistemology (theory of knowledge), and methodology into a structured holistic lens through which we can see the whole world in which we operate. Importantly, it helps us to see ourselves in relation to our world, a necessary view to understand our relationship to impact investments.

Some investment management firms, such as Hermes Investment Management in the UK, already incorporate holistic approaches. They seek 'outcomes beyond performance' writing on their website[210],

> We are an asset manager with a difference. We believe that, while our primary purpose is helping beneficiaries retire better by providing world class active investment management and stewardship services, our role goes further. We believe we have a duty to deliver holistic returns – outcomes for our clients that go far beyond the financial and consider the impact our decisions have on society, the environment and the wider world. Our goal is to help people invest better, retire better and create a better society for all.

In addition, part of the drive towards the next predicted age of 'integrality' is the continuous globalisation and enmeshments between cultures; because of this, differences need to be better understood in order to better succeed when interacting.

Dr. Ronnie Lessem and Dr Alexander Schieffer, both previously at the Harvard Business School, argue that the current education system has a very static and limiting understanding of knowledge, and lacks a developmental axis or dynamic for any real transformation. As a result, they collaborated on a four-worlds model that incorporated a strong psychological and developmental dynamic. From this basis in 2006 they formed their organisation, Trans4M in Geneva,[211]

> Trans4m is a local-global movement driving integral transformation processes to address today's burning issues by actualising positive impact via new integral thinking and action.

The Trans4m's Integral Worlds approach is an interconnected, holistic approach to understand consciously evolving, living human systems. It addresses visible imbalances within an individual, organisation, community, and/or society;, and within specific fields such as economics, enterprise or human development. This, in turn, is our foundation for the I^3 approach. It is designed to effectively address digitised and fragmented imbalances, which are familiar within the context of quantitative investments research, analysis, and modelling.

In 2014 I enrolled in the Trans4M PhD programme on Integral Development at the Da Vinci Institute in South Africa. After initially working on the topic of integral accounting for my thesis, I quickly became aware that investments were the ideal context in which to deploy this approach, examining how the vital psychological axis I had studied previously could be included and integrated more fully.

Lessem and Schieffer have written more than thirty books on integral transformation, all grounded in extensive research into the most practical and relevant theories that have successfully been applied across business contexts. Many such businesses have become integral role models, and operate mainly in Europe, Africa, the Middle East and Asia.

The integral four-worlds approach is simultaneously:

- Transcultural, encompassing the combined wisdom of South, East, North, and West;

- Transdisciplinary, spanning the natural and social sciences and the humanities;

- Transpersonal, straddling individual and community, organisation and society; and

- Transformational, evolving from particular local grounds towards an integral global effect.

To me, it quickly became apparent that the integral four worlds is a full-spectrum approach for the holistic development of individuals, organisations, communities, and societies. When applied to a particular context, in our case impact investments, it becomes a powerful lens through which to see the world. Life is not mechanical and neutral; life is value that has taken physical form.

It is deeply marked by the experience of value because for an organism to exist does not mean that it is merely 'there', as matter is; rather, it is the striving to exist that is always building itself up in order to be there. Researchers such as Kull, Hoffmeyer, Marguilis and Francisco Varela, as such, replace the blind 'struggle for life' of biological Darwinism, with deeper meanings.

As a revolutionary paradigm, integral four worlds draws on the particularity of each person, organisation, community, and/or society, aiming to build and enhance a sense of core calling, belonging and rootedness (local identity) to catalyse a meaningful, wholesome contribution to humanity (global integrity).

The integral four-worlds' system is modelled on the dynamics and movements of life itself. Where applied, it contributes to healing today's fragmented, conflictual and, sadly, often destructive individual, organisational, communal, and societal ways of being. It holds a vital key to the necessary and imminent shift of an integral global consciousness towards a more healthy, holistic, peaceful, and participatory approach to development, in tune with the whole of creation.

Integral four worlds initiates processes of healing and holistic realignment by activating all the complementary parts of any human system, such as nature and community, culture and consciousness, science, systems and technology, as well as enterprise, economics and politics. The starting (and continual) focal point of any transformation process within an integral worlds' perspective is the inner core of the individual or collective entity – its deepest value base, spiritual and moral source. This is the foundation stone on which we construct impact investments to represent and create an ever-deepening systems-based impact within our respective organisation.

As Scholastic theologian and thirteenth-century philosopher, St Bonaventure of Bagnoregio said very clearly[1]:

Unless we are able to view things in terms of how they originate, how they are to return to their end, and how God shines forth in them, we will not be able to understand.[212]

The underlying circular design of the central model acknowledges that the circular shape has been a symbol for wholeness and totality since time immemorial. It also symbolises the cycle of life that each living system undergoes. In integral worlds, the outer circle marks a worldly, holistic perspective. Embedded in the outer circle is the local context. At the very centre is the inner core. Here, at the core of an individual, organisation, community, or society, the impulse for transformation or development is initiated — be it through a perceived imbalance of the overall system, which becomes our objective concern, or through a particular, subjective evolutionary calling.

This inner personal core and the outer, global circle are then connected through the '4Rs' of integral worlds:

- Realities (world views spanning South and East, North, West, and Centre)

- Realms (knowledge Fields straddling nature and culture, technology, and enterprise within an all-round polity)

- Rounds (different levels, from self and community, organisation, and society to world)

- Rhythms (transformative rhythms, applied to all from origination to transformation, including integration).

Unlike most of dominating organisational and operating models from our Western and Northern perspectives, an integral methodology importantly connects the often missing or imbalanced realms, which contain the life energy, that connects and acts as drivers for all.

The rhythms represent the dynamic self-reinforcing, anti-clockwise movements in between these realms as we develop through. In Ken Wilber's book[213] he maintains that human beings have two major types of available development: Growing Up and Waking Up. He argues that the states of awareness that constitute meditative states, or enlightenment states, or awakening states or other types of 'peak experience' states, have been understood by humans for millennia. However, the 'hidden maps' and governing processes that drive our Growing Up (GU) are not so obvious, and were not really 'discovered' until a century ago, with the birth of modern psychology.

Parts of GU have long been understood and made part of the initiation processes into adult life within all wisdom traditions. How we experience our life, for Wilber, is directly related to the stages of GU that we have reached. In addition, Western culture has completely lost track of its own sources of Waking Up. It has no ultimate or unifying truth to act as a North Star, i.e., it

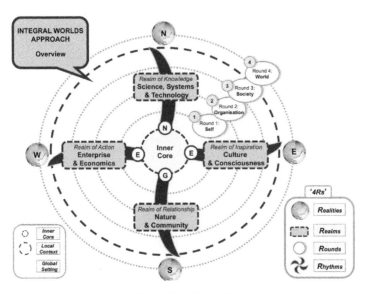

Figure 17.3: Trans4M

has no idea where it is heading. Generally speaking, Western culture throws up its hands and awaits technological advances to address our headaches. Such technical solutions can only reflect relative truths, and therefore relative solutions; with no ultimate unifying truth there is no Waking Up. We are diving, he says, headfirst into the shallow end of the pool, and encouraging our fellow citizens to do the same. Yet ultimate truth cannot be rationally demonstrated.

> Sharpen the eye that observes and the eye that sees.
>
> Miyamoto Musashi

According to many indigenous traditions, humans have at least three modes of knowing: the eye of the flesh; the eye of the mind, and the eye of contemplation.

The eye of the flesh is what grounds conventional science (for many of us this would be quantum mechanics); the eye of the mind gives us rationality and logic, whilst contemplative experiences create the basis for our awareness and consciousness to grow, with the possibility of our eventual enlightenment. As we will explore later, contemplation is the practise that binds these together and brings impact alive.

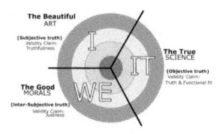

Figure 4: The Value Spheres of Humanity, the Big Three. Derived from Wilber's (2000a, p.64) Integral Theory.

Figure 17.4: The value spheres of humanity.[214]

From our integral perspective, this begins with our own grounding in the South where our calling as our life-engine is rooted and built. A large part of this book is about how we build this engine from our calling and within our context of impact investments. As an example, the Munich-based AQAL Capital GMBH has taken the Wilber model and developed an impact investment approach. Their co-founder Mariana Bozesan outlined their core steps in journeying into Integral[1],

> We are part of the post-post-modern generation that seeks to integrate financial sustainability with the ideals of the so called 'cultural creatives,' which in the year 2000 represented between 25 and 30 percent of the Western population (Ray and Anderson, 2000). That means the integration of sound financial, economic, environmental, governance criteria with geo-political sustainability for the benefit of all...Unfortunately, neither the traditional philanthropic, economics, finance, investing models in general nor the Venture Capital models in particular gave us the necessary framework to invest with both our values as well as with our money.

> As discussed in Bozesan (2013a, 2013b), traditional investment systems are outdated and missing important aspects of life just as much as existing philanthropic models do. Having been part of the human potential movement for decades, we knew that trust toward others begins by trusting oneself. [...]

> We knew that they could only come from our heart and soul, and from what we were willing to give to the world rather than want to receive from it.Hence, we looked for an integration vehicle for all our value systems, which Plato (1961/1938) called the True, the Good, and the Beautiful—or Science, Morals, and Arts. We felt the need to self-actualise (Maslow, 1999) through an integration of all our activities, not just the financial, the business ones, or the philanthropic ones...

---

[1]Extracted from [214]. Vol. 4, Issue 1, February 2015, p. 49-71

Our investment motto became the six Ps: the Parity of People, Planet, Profit, all of which we wanted to integrate with our own Passion for life and in line with our ultimate life's Purpose. In the late 1990s, we discovered the ideal framework for our six Ps, namely, Ken Wilber's (2000) integral theory that is based on Plato's (1961/1938) work (Figure 17.4).

Lessons Learned

We feel deeply responsible for the integral impact of our portfolio companies due to our intention to create integrally sustainable companies from the very beginning. (…) As a result, our portfolio companies (1) solve real customer problems; (2) implement innovative business ideas; (2) have a specific sector focus (transformative technology, climate change, lifestyle, cultural innovation, megatrends); (3) have the ability to massively scale into a worldwide marketplace; (4) are led by dedicated, resilient, and integrally acting management teams; (5) are committed to integral sustainability criteria including, financial, environmental, social, and governance measurements; (6) display ethical behaviour; (7) create a corporate culture based on higher values and levels of consciousness; and (8) support transparent reporting.

When an Investment Failed

When the investment failed, the reasons were mostly related to factors including the following (1) we failed to identify early enough the lack of team alignment and missing common values of the original team or the team changed and became misaligned over time; (2) the organisations were geographically and culturally located too far away from our immediate circle of influence; (3) the technology was too early and ahead of its time; (4) we neglected the importance of a regulated market; (5) the main founder(s) did not want to exit and thus, we could never retrieve our investment; (6) we were too hands-off; (7) we were diluted; (8) we invested against our intuition and gut feeling; (9) we trusted the entrepreneurs at face value, did not have proper scientific tools to assess moral and ethics, underestimated the importance of proper legal advice and paperwork thus leading to major losses; (10) alternative solutions caught up faster and came to market before ours did; (11) global times of crisis.

This confirms, and validates, the integral investment approach, and that it must be developed inside organisations. With I³, provide an open-source platform that includes the additional integral transformative dynamics (GENE, CARE, 4Cs, etc.) that form part of the Lessem and Schieffer integral four worlds.

Let us now investigate these dynamics.

§17.2 How we can release Gene-ius with 'C+A+R+E'

Embedded in the integral worlds' approach are several powerful dynamic processes of change that activate and guide the integral development of individuals, organisations, communities, and societies. Two of these processes are central: the GENE-process (geared to release the GENE-ius of a human system), and the CARE-process (assisting to fully embody, embed and sustain the form of I³ that we may have developed).

For some, this may already be a step too far but I will assume that by now we understand that impact is a part of our self-discovery and should not be seen as a threat.

Remembering C.G. Jung's words: 'An encounter with the self is felt as a defeat for the ego[215].'

§17.3 The GENE-PROCESS: releasing individual and collective GENE-ius

No system is static. With every human system in continuous evolution, the integral worlds incorporate an inbuilt transformational rhythm, which makes the entire approach reflexively dynamic. We call this rhythm the GENE (Grounding, Emerging, Navigating, Effecting), representing the four-fold spiralling force and movement, which activates the entire integral worlds model and I³. We could trace this rhythm back to natural and cultural systems and their respective evolution.

The GENE rhythm is embedded in diverse reality views and knowledge realms that we need to understand within the integral worlds if we want to coalesce them into a transformative interaction whilst working with I³. While we see the GENE as a spiralling, iterative and ever-unfolding force, we nevertheless start most of our transformational processes in the South, thereby beginning with a conscious grounding in a given impact investment context before we engage in its understanding, and in mapping the impact objectives and change directives.

The fourfold GENE rhythm flows as follows:

- *'Southern'* grounding: The issue at hand and the people involved, are grounded in a particular nature and community which must be fully understood. For any living system, the Southern grounds represent a rooting in 'local identity' and its connection to a common source of life and sustainability. Southern grounding is about 'being' in, as well as feeling and 'experiencing', a particular life world. It is seeking to activate the relational 'feeling' or 'heart'-level of a human system, as well as participation and engagement. This is the foundational and formative part of any impact process that forms the basis for our calling, in the same way that when our way of 'being' shifts our sense of identity also shifts. It is also the soil in which we grow our social and community dimension. Taking 'being' a step deeper, we enter the various realms of consciousness and areas of non-duality where 'being' is the ubiquitous knowing prior to identification with physical form, which becomes an important area of our development for later stages in how we evolve our impact approach.

- *'Eastern'* emergence: 'Eastern' emergence lifts the issue and the people involved to deeper insights. Here the people and the issue engage in dialectic process with others, thereby co-evolving towards new insights. Such a process always includes stepping into the unknown and letting go of some previous assumptions. It therefore requires us to consciously transcend our prior life world. New insights – often in forms or images and visions – emerge that provide clues for the impact process ahead. 'Eastern' emergence is therefore about 'becoming'; it deals with 'intuiting' and 'imagining' the new form that is emerging. Here the 'local' perspective of the Northern grounds evolves to 'local-global' viewpoints. This is the 'reformative' part of the impact process. Here, we create the conditions, and seek to activate 'inspiration' or the 'spirit'-level, of a human system that allows the true imperatives within a context to emerge. This is also the consciousness on which we build our impact approach and embed our impact culture.

- *'Northern'* navigation: The move to 'Northern' navigation requires new insights (images, visions) to be translated structured and system-aticality into new concepts and new knowledge. 'Northern' navigation is about 'knowing' and 'making explicit' what hitherto had been im-plicit. Now, the local global viewpoint is turned into a more general, abstract global viewpoint. New norms, related to the issue at hand, are developed. Northern 'navigation' is about activating the 'mind'-level, the conceptualising prowess of the human system at hand. This is the 'normative' part of the impact process, where the design of our co-creation is formalised and agreed. Here we seek intellectual and technical insights and developments to our impact approach.

- *'Western'* Effect: Moving to the 'Western' effect requires integrating the prior three levels into action. It is about pragmatically applying the new insights and knowledge that have been developed, thereby actualising what they contain. The 'Western' effect is about 'doing' and 'making it happen'. Now the 'global' viewpoint is turned into a 'global local' standpoint, whereby what has been globally developed is locally implemented. We call it 'global local', as the local application is taking place with the larger 'global' impact perspective in mind. This is the ultimate 'transformative' level of the GENE-process: metaphorically activating and joining the 'body' or 'hand' with the other component parts.

However, the process does not stop here; rather, it continuously circles another round and moves on. Any active impact effect has to be continuously revisited and reviewed, exploring whether it resonates with the 'Southern' grounds it seeks to serve. Any impact solution is considered a temporary stepping stone where the contribution, and hence its impulse continues along its ever-strengthening path.

By continuously engaging and working within the GENE rhythm, we reflexively and reflectly address imbalances within the larger system. As such, we can consciously contribute to the ongoing evolution of ourselves within the impact context and any of the other human systems (from organisations to society, from economics to development) that we may bring forth. We thereby release the 'GENE-i-us' of a system: individual gene-i-us ('i') and collective gene-i-us ('us'). This was expressed in the Coptic Gospel of Thomas which says that:' If you bring forth what is within you, what you bring forth will save you. If you do not bring forth what is within you, what you do not bring forth will destroy you.'

§17.4 The 4Cs and the CARE-PROCESS: Fully embodying integral innovation

With the GENE-process as the overarching developmental rhythm, we now bring in two further parallel trajectories that assist each transformation agent to successfully undertake the journey, and to transcend the individual contribution towards a collective embodiment of the integral impact. The ultimate objective is to transcend a singular and individual impulse of renewal to arrive at a collective, and, ideally, institutionalised action to sustain this impulse on a long-term basis.

The initial internal trajectory, with a focus on outcome contribution, follows the 4Cs:

- Call: Discover our Call which, as discussed, is the cornerstone of our being, identity, and working within impact.

- Context: Understand ourselves and/or our organisation in the right-sized operational Context and realms of impact.

- Co-Creation: Define, design and build a newly Co-Created impact reality that is fully connected to the investee and the broader societal impact.

- Contribution: Implement, measure, intelligently re-shape, and refine the impact Contribution in line with agreed outcome objectives for maximum leverage and sustainability.

In conjunction, and in parallel, we will be working towards 'full CARE' – an external process and acronym representing:

- C = Community Activation, where we need to look deeply at the organisation and the people around us to understand their own calling and relationship to impact to build alignment and an Impact root system with a common grounding.

- A = Awakening of Awareness collectively seeks to develop the co-created alignment towards the strong 'Why?' question for Impact.

- R = Research-to-Innovation is how the co-created dialectic and diagnostic progresses build into the formulation of the overall Impact approach, with its Integral dynamic end in mind.

- E = Embodied Action creates the aligned and mutually agreed Impact contribution of what, where, and when the outcome objectives have been filled before we take the next turn.

Here we illustrate how both the integral rhythms run in parallel, working towards a singular contribution on the one hand and a full-fledged collective and embodied action on the other.

Both parallel trajectories (4Cs and CARE) mutually reinforce and navigate each other. Both also follow the GENE logic which demonstrates that the integral fourfold rhythm, when applied, will continuously and holographically reinforce our own unique take, development, and creation of the I^3 approach. When completed, each of the processes supports the full activation, re-balancing, and development of a living system.

We can now turn to the practical component dimensions of building our own I^3 and how we may think metaphorically about the design structure

Figure 17.5: CARE Process aligned with the 4C's (Trans4M [38])

and align its functional parts. Each firm must work this out through their culture and investment offering, since this defines their now more developed investment thesis and values chains therein. Below we look at the integral organisational forms and functions; we also need to work with some of the ingredients that make up the whole.

I have, over time, developed this 'cheat-sheet' to aid my thinking (table 17.2).

We can see the direct relationship between the integral matrix above with the one below developed by Max Neef, a Nobel Laureate in Economics. Neef does not prioritise, nor judge or differentiate between different value statements as all are equally necessary and important; they vary depending on context and individualisation. As such, dialing up or down contextual requirements happens later within the I^3 model.

Table 17.3: Matrix of Needs and Satisfiers[216]

Fundamen-tal Human Needs	Being (qualities)	Having (things)	Doing (actions)	Interacting (settings)
Subsis-tence	physical and mental health	food, shelter work	feed, clothe, rest, work	living environment, social setting

Protection	care, adapt-ability, autonomy	social security, health systems, work	cooperate, plan, take care of, help	social en-vironment, dwelling
Affection	respect, sense of humour, generosity sensuality	firendships, family, re-lationships with nature	share, take care of, make love, express emotions	privacy, intimate spaces of together-ness
Under-standing	critical capacity, curiosity, intuition	literature, teachers, policies educational	analyse, study, meditate, investigate	schools, families, universities, communi-ties
Partic-ipation	recep-tiveness, dedication, sense of humour	responsibili-ties, duties, work, rights	cooperate, dissent, express opinions	associa-tions, par-ties, POW, neighbor-hoods
Leisure	imagi-nation, tranquility, spontaneity	games, parties, peace of mind	day dream, remember, relax, have fun	landscapes, intimate places, places to be alone
Creation	imagi-nation, boldness, inven-tiveness, curiosity	abilities, skills, works, techniques	invent, build, design, work, compose, interpret	spaces of expression, workshops, audiences
Identity	sense of belong-ing, self esteem, oonoio tency	language, religion, work, customs, values, norms	get to know one self, commit one self, grow	places one belongs to, everyday settings
Freedom	autonomy, passion, self es-teem, open minded-ness	equal rights	dissent, choose, run risks, develop awareness	anywhere

Each firm (and investment) is calibrated across each dimension. Once we understand the mapping, nature, and relative importance of each ingredient, we can integrate what the functional drivers of our I^3 may look like for each area.

The model is driven by answers to specific questions from each Integral ingredient, which consolidate at each level into a calibrated measurement

4 Worlds, Integral Realms, Dimensions and GENE	Core Methodology & Key Themes	Possible Organisational Problems and Adizes PAEI	Organisational motivational theory	The basic human needs & Core Value	Intellects and Energy needs	Highest human manifestations	Result of growth and prime human driver	Key Terms	Main Focus
South - Being and Community / Heart, Environmental, Nature & Relational Capital and cultivation of vitality / *Community/ Grounding/ Body & Feel* / Self Sufficient Economy	Nature capital usage/deployed and Environmental impact. Human and community capital, Organisational "goodwill", Development and co-creation of eco-systems. *Restoring life in Nature and Community*	Misaligned Systems that create confusion. One fit all approach to motivation. Solution: Aligning; create top priorities that drive systems, structures and processes. Also, Psychometric awareness that build relations. *Adizes: Entrepreneur*	Good human relations, good treatment and support systems	Love; *Healthy & Participatory co-existence*; *Be*	EQ; Security	Connection &; Love &; Passion	Guidance/; Relations; *Treat me kindly and build with me secure connections*	Relationships & Content; Community; Care	Community based; Learning and; Development
East - Becoming and Sanctuary / Spirit, Social, Inspirational and Cultural Capital and awaken creative potentials / *Culture/ Emerging/ Left Hand* / Developmental Economy	Equally a capital component of "goodwill" of an organisation and accounted for as EV over tangible assets. Cultural levels as strategic & tactical capital to be managed. *Regenerating meaning via culture and spirituality*	Lack of unified vision. Underutilised talent and potential that limit motivation. Solution: *Stake holder values based approach. E.g. Spiral Dynamics. Empowering. The unleashing of voices, talents and creativity* / *Adizes: Integrator*	Finding purpose and meaning. Need for contribution and integrity	Leave a legacy; *Balanced and peaceful co-evolution*; *Becoming*	SQ; Significance	Awakened; Conscience &; *Self Realisation*	Power/; Consciousness; *Doing meaningful and significant work in principled ways*	Inspiration & Catalysation; Consciousness; Conscientisation	Societal Learning; and; Consciousness Raising
North - Knowing and University / Product: Science, Systems & Technology; Intellectual Capital and reframing knowledge towards innovation / *Innovation/ Navigating/ Mind & Head* / Social Economy	Conceptual Strengths. Institution Building; Structural, organisational and technological assessments. IC build. Intellectual Property, Patents, Technology and other operational competitive advantages etc. *Reframing Knowledge via science, systems and technology*	No purpose or vision that undermine objectives. Traditional Hierarchy & Structures. Solution: *Pathfinding, i.e. on the same page for your top priorities. Cybernetics and natural systems for knowledge creation* / *Adizes: Administrator*	Identify, develop, use, recognise, and grow talent	Learn; *All sustainable Open and Transparent Knowledge Creation*; *Knowing*	IQ; *Self expression*	Education &; Discipline &; Development	Wisdom/; Understanding; *Use me creatively and enable my-self expression*	Knowledge & Content; Concepts; Complexity	Scholarship; Research and; Knowledge Creation
West - Doing and Laboratory / Enterprise & Economics; Body Corporate, Financial Capital and engagement co-creatively / Living Economy / *Impact/ Effecting/ Right Hand*	Traditional corporate finance analysis & financial diagnostic and risk assessment from both a quantitative and qualitative perspective. All physical, financial resources, methodologies and policies *Rebuilding infrastructure and institutions via enterprise and economics*	Low Trust that tax the organisation/team. Archaic motivational & compensation systems. Solution: *Modeling, setting the example and building trust. Integral approach to motivation* / *Adizes: Producer*	Survival, Security, Physical and Economic	Live; *Equitable & Sustainable Livelihoods*; *Doing*	PQ; Sustainability	Collective &; Action &; Vision	Security/; Capacity; *Pay me fairly and give me purpose*	Action & Capacity; Co-Creation; Contribution	Capacity Building; Practical Orientation; Individual Realisation

Table 17.2: cheat-sheet

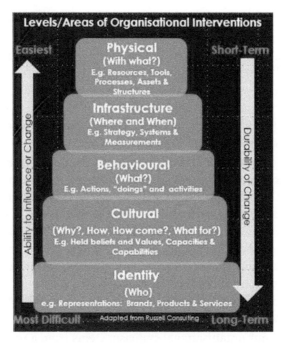

Figure 17.6: Levels/Areas of Organisational Interventions

that at the end helps decide whether to invest. Each investee will grapple with each level; an investor can intervene or provide expert advice and experience as an incoming stakeholder.

Closely related to standard employee and management/leadership engagement models, we address our firm's capacities at each level. We see that each level is also subject to two additional dimensions: the time-line, and the difficulty of creating possible change. Their weighting will be context dependent and also mission critical if any investment by itself shifts the balance. The resistant barriers for flow (and their dynamics) tend to be related to different levels within each organisation. When we address change and work with dynamic shifts in culture, each level must be addressed and create its own answers that feed and navigate the next. As the Hermetic mystics suggest: 'As above, so below' in all things.

Based on Gregory Bateson's neurological level, which we looked at in Part 1, we can now see how this typology of hierarchical levels is illustrated:

Each firm needs to answer questions pertaining to its situation and context at each level. Each level informs, defines, designs and either reinforces or contradicts the others.

In my experience, most organisations have difficulties with this, as mixed messages can contradict at other levels. A classic problem in my work as an investment banker was the incessant messaging around the need for better teamwork, collaboration, and cooperation whilst the entire compensation and progression system was based mainly, if not entirely, on individual performance. We all know who won that battle but management often ignored the cultural damage and the incipient cynicism which most of us have experienced when receiving conflicting messages.

Cynicism comes from an overly romanticised, idealised or optimistic outlook and imagined expected outcome of others' motives and behaviours. When eventually the situation crystallises, our sometimes fantasised expectation is forced to retreat back to the current reality. We then must reconcile this reality with new meaning which challenges our need to be right and letting go for any new learning to enter. It's when we are unable to do this adequately that cynicism enters as the bridge, explanation and justification between the tensions of holding the two differing positions; and unless we can move towards reality, risks marooning us in our thinking until the next experience where our cynicism can get reinforced again.

So much of our organisational cynicism stems from a romanticised idea of expected outcomes, and how we interpret our relationship to them. Many are also constructed from 'presumptive contracts', i.e., agreements we believe exist — or should exist — between parties. These are mainly unspoken and based on our moral codes of conduct. This is an oft-ignored consequence in management which can corrode culture and undermine the entire organisational journey and its values.

If we now transpose the above questioning and move into our context of impact, we must seek answers that correspond, align, and communicate when develop our organisational Impact framework. From an integral perspective, we need to travel counterclockwise, grounding ourselves first in the South, doing each round inside what I now call the 4Ms. This is in effect the loom on which we can weave our impact approach and culture.

It may not have gone unnoticed that this aspect is closely related to any designed governance of the investee. If we want to create a governance structure that can creatively hold the tensions which will inevitably occur, without breaking the thread that holds our impact together, we need to transition through each area using a democratic format and without invoking a power complex.

Looking at other governance structures that espouse democratic virtues, we find them intrinsically designed to hold opposites in tension until the co-creative spark moves the issues at hand into a decision-making forum. We will have more on this later, when we look inside the core of our governance structures and procedures.

Looking through the integral lens, we need to construct and develop four realms (4 Ms) that can integrally inform and reinforce each other so we don't just create what otherwise would be a disconnected Western model.

The conventional 'Western' approach includes using a highly systematic model; whilst this is a critical component of the diagnostic process, assessment and analysis, it also is a detached form of observation which lacks the experimental and emotional content that enables deeper understanding.

A key difference with I^3 is that these four worlds are not viewed or managed in isolation. Starting in the integral 'South' we ask 'core' questions inside each realm to fully develop, engage, and activate each of our realities, which informs and navigates our eventual model.

At this point we have created our integral evaluation process and index in order to value the investment itself.

Jung writes that: 'The goal is important only as an idea; the essential thing is the opus which leads to the goal: that is the goal of a lifetime.'

In the 4 Ms, we seek to understand the soil and natural homes for each of the component parts in our toolset, and ask core questions to build an impact approach and framework.

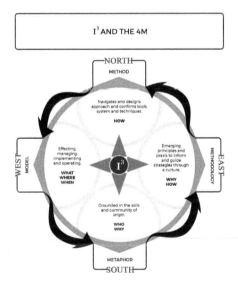

Figure 17.7: I^3 and the M4

Metaphor: In martial arts and in most religions, metaphors (story) has been used for centuries to transmit vital instruction and information as the process of understanding creates meaning making that goes deeper into memory than just words. For Impact, we need to understand the power and benefit of using metaphors, since Impact itself, of course, is a metaphor. This is our philosophical home, where we have grounded our calling and where the relationships to the self, others, and nature can be established and restored. It is where the interdependent fabric of our community is continuously expanded. When forming any relationship, a metaphorical archetype is created (to its very nature, to ourselves and others) which acts as our images of the relational fields therein. We ask ourselves the extent of the Who? and their involvement, and also root our basic understanding of our Why? in the context of community and nature.

Key questions: What are my autonomous core beliefs and emotion-laden ideas that I hold as truths but change as I turn the prism toward the 'other'? By what fiction or construct am I currently engaging with Impact? By what authority do I live and direct my work? What is my vocation (from the Latin, vocadus, 'to be called') for this stage in my career?

James Cameron, director of the movie Titanic, stated in a 2010 interview that the Titanic acts as a metaphor for life and what it can teach about love, loss, hubris, and ourselves. The movie depicts a person's true nature in showing how they react in distress to their fellow human beings by running away or disguising themselves. Everyone can ask themselves: Who am I? How would I react? It also illustrates the hubris of engineers and ship-owners who trusted the ship's infallible technology. It highlights the social differences between the first-class and steerage passengers. Also, the ship was recklessly driven too fast just to appease the management. The movie depicts the full social impact once the initial structural hierarchy was stripped away. It shows the emotional hurt, anger, betrayal and fear of loss across relationships, wealth and status. There is death itself, but also the smaller deaths of hopes and dreams.

How we interpret a loss partly defines how we feel love. Here again we find ourselves looking through a double-sided mirror. As the Titanic set sail in 1912, it was declared 'unsinkable' because it was constructed using a new technology. The ship's hull was divided into sixteen sealed and watertight compartments. The engineers confidently stated that up to four of these compartments could be damaged, or even flooded, without the ship sinking. But, as we know, the Titanic tragically sank on 15 April 1912 at 2.20 AM, and 1,513 people lost their lives.

We are all living on a metaphorical Titanic, which is why this film speaks to so many people. Many people and organisations make the Titanic's mistake, erroneously assuming they can divide their lives into different, isolated compartments.

So for each impact investment project, we must consider and build our metaphor before we test it and the gain the knowledge required across the other three dimensions, returning back to re-grounding the investment in the South.

Methodology: From the soil of our grounding, we now can focus on our impact context to build and justify our map of the world and our praxis. This emerges out of our impact philosophy as the shared 'Why?', while understanding our culture as the driver for our methodology. This is also our impact sanctuary, where a person's soul feels nourished and can be refreshed, and where the cultures of our impact worlds are equally represented.

Key questions: By what cultural and coordinate points of reference do I make my key decisions? Are these mine or an historical inheritance which serves the past? What are the transcendent values that we try to gain and strengthen through working with impact?

Method: Moving co-creatively from impact philosophy into the 'How?' of diagnostics, and calibrations will help navigate the impact architecture where reflection, knowledge creation and action learning occurs, and where new ideas are developed into concepts and processes that form our toolbox.

The Western word 'measure' and the Eastern, Sanskrit word 'maya' have the same root. In Sanskrit maya means 'illusion' given the Eastern philosophy of the immeasurable as primary reality. It suggests that our ordinary perceptions, logic and reason shroud us from our primary reality which cannot be perceived, articulated or thought through our senses. Our methods create the architecture on which our model will be based and continuously renewed. This approach effectively forms what we call our Innovation and Knowledge Impact Academy that will, over time, continue to build and develop the impact approach. Werner Heisenberg once said that: 'What we observe is not nature itself, but nature exposed to our method of questioning[217].'

Key Questions: What are the operational paradigms and knowledge thereof that influences my decisions? What is the nature and background of my co-creation partners? (to e.g. generate diversity). How are we governing the creative and analytical processes?

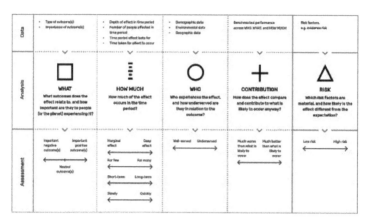

Figure 17.8: The Impact Management Project (GIIN [21])

Model: Integrally informed from our previous three realms, we now have a framework to build our detailed impact map into our generic I³ model, which will comport with how we evaluate our contribution and its intended effect. This forms our ongoing laboratory, where we create and adjust the model, and where our new integral practise can be piloted and strengthened.

This approach reduces the risk of model blindness that can occur when it is constructed in an isolated Western dimension. Model blindness occurs when a digital, mechanistic, financial model becomes the central point and repository of gathered intelligence; and it is difficult to see and include the other Integral influences necessary for real Impact. Modelling creates its own semantics and culture which circulates within a small group of experts from whom this 'map of the world' becomes the truth and reality. As Richard Buckminster Fuller famously said, 'You never change things by fighting the existing reality. To change something, build a new model that makes the existing model obsolete[218]'.

Of course, in contrasting this more tailored and self-developed impact approach we must understand industry needs for standardisation and building common highways to assess impact. If we superimpose this I³ framework onto what the Global Impact Investing Network (GIIN) is doing inside the Impact Management Project, we see how these parts drive each other, especially within our 'West' and 'South' areas, given their respective roles and mandates.

We see now that the 4Ms are not static but dynamic and self-reinforcing. Looking at this from the bottom up, it circles around itself, constantly transforming and developing into a full-impact approach.

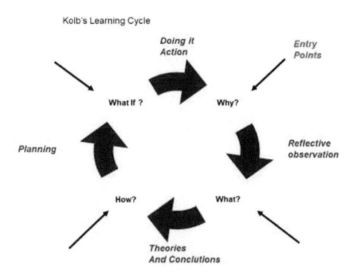

Figure 17.9: Kolb's Learning cycle

This ties in with Kolb's learning cycle. In 1983, David Kolb published his learning styles model from which he developed his learning styles inventory.

His model works on two levels: a four-stage cycle of learning, and four separate learning styles. Much of Kolb's theory relates to internal cognitive processes and how awareness is created. He suggests that learning first involves the acquisition of abstract concepts that can be applied flexibly into any context, with the impetus for developing new concepts provided by new experiences.

This is done by answering core questions, 'Learning is the process whereby knowledge is created through the transformation of experience[219].'

§17.5 Impacting the integral Self: Becoming an Agent of Transformation

> God doesn't call the Qualified. He qualifies the Called.
>
> Corinthians 1:27-29, KJV

To become an effective, integral and impactful agent of transformation, each individual must fully engage with his or her 'inner calling', and embark

Figure 17.10: Expansion of self

on purposefully developing his/her full potential to actualise it.

Next time you consider your reasons for working with impact, explore the deeper questions about what activates your calling because therein lies the embers from which the fire burns to fully develop and actualise yourself. Consider what, and who, keeps the fire going, and what may dampen it. Fully articulate this by journalling or speaking to someone trustworthy. It is through the process of clarifying your call that you will find direction for the inner–outer journey; you will also tap into the inner, transformative energy required to make significant impact in your organisation and the world.

This is part of your journey of self-actualisation and individuation, of which the predominant goal is to reach higher levels of fulfilment and meaning. If you do this, you will find you are on the road to transcend an initial, possibly narrow view of yourself towards a more inclusive, self-and-other oriented perspective. Like a stone (you) hitting water (our context), how far do the ripples extend and what do they contain before dissipating?

It is whilst we work with integrity within the process of impact investments that we discover ourselves and the sometimes elusive 'others'; we learn that life is about interdependency, relationships and love. We gradually grow from a self or 'me' orientation to include the 'other' and move from 'I' to 'we'. As we do so, we become more fully engaged as participating citizens, serving not only our own development but also that of others, society, and nature, which we are all part of.

If we have the ability to embrace life to the fullest, our inner growth becomes the greatest gift we can make to anyone or any organisation we touch. History is full of examples of how the personal development axis was a prime driver for values that are today considered self-evident. As Ken Wilber suggests,

> The main reason slavery was present, say, 2000 years ago, was not because there was an oppressive force preventing world-centric freedom, but that a world-centric notion of freedom had not yet emerged anywhere on the planet. [102]

Our thinking about our fellow human beings did not change until the 'Age of Reason' (a mere 300 years ago) introduced the idea that all men [sic] are created equal. This led to Britain's slavery Abolition Act in 1833. The French colonies re-abolished it in 1848 and the U.S. finally abolished slavery in 1865. However, let us not forget that it is how we evolve, and reframe epistemically the semantics and our syntax that allows aberrations such as slavery to become the 'new normal'.

During the Renaissance, the idea developed for the exploitation and commoditisation labour and trade in African slaves, which allowed a quantum leap in the use of 'capital'; this then accumulated and was used by financial institutions in Europe. It was only by framing the lives of slaves as an expendable cost of trade and production that humanity could be separated as distinct parts. It took another 300 years for humanity to reconnect with their splintered disciplines, which still operate today, e.g., 'Human Resources'.

If designed on integral principles, impact investments offer continuous interaction and interweaving between self and other, community and enterprise, society and world. This, in turn, seeks to create alignment of the inner calling of a person with the central developmental issues confronted by our communities, institutions, and societies.

The following figure serves as a 'guiding image', expressing this combination of inner alignment (all the aspects of the personality) and outer alignment (the person in relation to the impact investment context):

It is important to recognise that there is additional complexity in our respective inner and outer calling in the form of 'Realms and Rounds'[8]

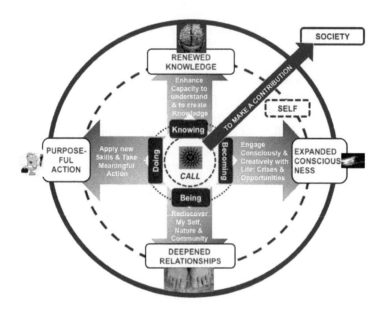

Figure 17.11: Following the Call: Becoming an Integral Impact Agent of Transformation (Trans4M [38])

or 'Levels and Lines'[220]. More specifically, the origin, connectivity, and grounding of each of our call with others and how they synthesise these within the organisational context.

Simply put, taking Bateson's neurological levels (Bateson 2000 [221]) as discussed in Part 1, we can see how a particular calling needs to be mutually reinforcing in order to gain depth and breadth. As such there is an origination story and starting point in each calling that develops and intertwines with other adjacent callings as they grapple with the neurological constructs at each level.

The psychologist John McLeod[222] believes that the complex layers of the world implies that it can be viewed from different perspectives. In the process of qualitative research, a new understanding of our worlds can emerge in knowledge phenomenon, knowledge of others, and reflective knowing[8].

An important element of making any such choices is missed opportunities and future outcomes. The reality is that whenever we make a particular decision and focus our attention on fulfilling it, we forego the alternative choice. In the film Sliding Doors, the main character alternates between two parallel universes, based on the two paths her life could take depending on whether or not she catches a train. This gives viewers a glimpse of the multiple perspectives our lives can take.

The internal context and the collective calling must be aligned with the greater realm and the larger collective to find connections with their generic calling. As such, the 4 Cs, the GENE and CARE within an impact approach, must be aligned and eventually mirrored with the greater – and hopefully ever-increasing – circles of influence as it develops, builds and creates the convergence of a greater calling. Like ripples in a pond, and tantamount to the converging waves of quantum physics, this is referred to as 'converging waves'[223].

Here again, we must be cognisant of our organisational impact language, modes of communication, and the nature of our forums for dissemination and decision making so that we don't remain stuck in conventional thinking.

His Holiness, Tenzin Gyatso, the fourteenth Dalai Lama puts the deeper perspective this way[224]:

> As soon as we name an aspect of reality, we mentally eliminate all other aspects and we designate the chosen object by a word that applies only to that object and this enables us to recognise it. Then, according to how that object is used, we establish distinctions: this is good, this is bad and so forth, when in fact it is impossible to attribute intrinsic properties to anything. The result is a vision of reality which is at best partial and at worst plain wrong. However rich language may be, its power is therefore very limited. Only non-conceptual experience enables us to apprehend the true nature of things.

For me, my martial arts practise comes close to synthesising the full-spectrum of human experience: Mind, body, heart, and spirit work together and express their combined essence within a single moment. As an undisciplined human being, I need the social cohesion and community activation to practise the art. Within our washindo (the way of the peaceful mind/heart) community, we constantly seek to deepen our practise to regenerate and re-new the collective reasons for being there. Peace itself is not just the absence of conflict; rather peace has to be felt as a connection which also balances with its surroundings. So within, so without. First, create your own way of peacefulness as only then can you offer the gift of peace to another. Peace and grace have more value and do more good than knowledge in almost any situation. The question is, how do you see and value such people yourself or in your organisation?

The purpose of our impact practise, and the core of I³, is to alleviate such imbalances and find much sought-after peace. The sensation of peace can then open up the mind to include and transcend previous understanding.

The essence and presence of practising peace in real art or mastery can be transferred into any context or arena. What may be missing is specific technique or knowledge related to the context.Every artist knows the essential and transferable qualities which they carry within them, without which they would be mainly craft performing.

The practise you may choose for yourself is, of course, just a metaphor for life, and how you may wish to conduct yourself given surrounding negative energies. Also, this physical practise builds capacities to separate the thinking mind from the deeper subconscious mind which is associated with flow states. Physical fitness itself is considered

To be a balance between strength (our South), aerobic (our East), flexibility (our North), and anaerobic (our West) practises. Martial arts mastery can only come from a deeper practise of mind, emotion and spirit. Our thinking mind is its own barrier, since it is almost exclusively connected to the repetition of previous patterns and opposes new models and modes of being and becoming.

I can make the connection with this form of artistry and technical embodiment and impact, which is summarised in the Washindo College credo:

If you're tired – practise
When life is heavy – practise
When you're happy – practise
When it is cold and wet – practise
When it would be easier not to – practise
The way of Washindo is to practise
To explore the very edges of human experience
To discover what's possible
To enjoy the art of living
To honour the past
To dream of the future
To love in the present

Figure 17.12: Washindo College

COMMUNITY THROUGH ARTISTRY AND GRACE

> I argue that art is part of man's quest for grace. For the attainment of grace, the reasons of the heart must be aligned with the reason of the reasons

Gregory Bateson[81, p.81]

In many cultures, seeing something in its wholeness is a preponderant contemporary issue. Not surprisingly, we often need help in its understanding and practise. Japanese culture has a four-quadrant concept called ikigai that we all need to understand and develop; it indicates the value that we find in our life. It refers collectively to our mental, emotional, physical and spiritual circumstances that make us feel that our lives have purpose. It is what is inside our 'moral core', which is the center in which we synthesise and create purpose out of each of the four worlds.

Having covered some of the territory of integral impact and the four-worlds approach, we can now address challenges or barriers to our work. As Maslow writes,

> Man demonstrates in his own nature a pressure toward fuller and fuller Being, more and more perfect actualization of his humanness in exactly the same naturalistic, scientific sense that an acorn may be said to be 'pressing toward' being an oak tree, or that a tiger can be observed to 'push toward' being tigerish, or a horse toward being equine. [87]

And Rollo May,

> The acorn becomes an oak by means of automatic growth; no commitment is necessary. The kitten similarly becomes a cat on the basis of instinct. Nature and being are identical in creatures like them. But a man or woman becomes fully human only by his or her choices and his or her commitment to them.

Figure 17.13

People attain worth and dignity by the multitude of decisions they make from day by day. These decisions require courage. [225]

In this way, our future work within impact is already within us, bursting to emerge. However, we need to watch out for nay-sayers while delicately balancing organisational and political requirements with our own, by constantly asking: 'How aligned is my calling with my firm's? What is my becoming creating within my firm's context? Can I co-create the future I see for myself and others within the firm's impact sphere and approach? Am I proud of my impact contribution and how I enable this firm to grow and develop? If I was not here tomorrow, what would be my legacy?'

Maslow suggests:

So far as motivational status is concerned, healthy people have sufficiently gratified their basic needs for safety, belongingness, love, respect and self-esteem so that they are motivated primarily by trends to self-actualization (defined as ongoing actualization of potentials, capacities and talents, as fulfilment of mission [or call, fate, destiny, or vocation], as a fuller knowledge of, and acceptance of, the person's own intrinsic nature, as an unceasing trend toward unity, integration or synergy within the person). [130]

Working with impact investments is the perfect arena and context for us to work through our individuation and self-actualisa tion. If we do, everyone we contact with will benefit from our gifts. This means possibly venturing into the relative unknown and stretching our 'normal.' Eckhart Tolle summaries our challenge ahead: 'The insanity of the collective egoic mind, amplified by science and technology, is rapidly taking our species to the brink of disaster. Evolve or die: that is our only choice now[226]'.

Given our place in the world, it is clear that on several levels we are dysfunctional, and the new normal is looking more like hallucinated insanity on a large scale. Maslow succinctly states 'Certainly it seems more and more clear that what we call 'normal' in psychology is really a psychopathology of the average, so undramatic and so widely spread that we don't even notice it ordinarily.[87]'

Tolle adds that:

By far the greater part of violence that humans inflict on each other is not the work of criminals or mentally deranged, but of normal, respectable citizens service to the collective ego. One can go so far as to say the on this planet 'normal' equals insane. What lies at the root of this insanity? Complete identification with thought and emotion, that is to say, ego [227]

Being and becoming impact investors and stewards of capital will require everyone to clarify their unique gift that can be added to the fabric of the industry. Each contribution is mission critical for us, our firms and, most importantly, our impact sphere. If this is the journey we have chosen, make it one to remember.

> Man is not born perfect. He is born incomplete, he is born as a process. He is born on the way, as a pilgrim. That is his agony and his ecstasy, too; agony because he cannot rest, he has to go ahead, he has always to go ahead. He has to seek and search and explore. He has to become, because his being arises only through becoming. Becoming is his being. He can only be if he is on the move. Evolution is intrinsic to man's nature, evolution is his very soul. And those who take themselves for granted remain unfulfilled. Those who think they are born complete remain unevolved. Then the seed remains the seed. It never becomes a tree and never knows the joys of spring and the sunshine and the rain, and the ecstasy of bursting into millions of flowers. That explosion is the fulfilment, that explosion is what existence is all about—exploding into millions of flowers. When the potential becomes the actual, only then is man fulfilled. [228]

As meaning-seeking, relationship-driven human beings, we look for vehicles that enable deeper understanding of who we are and why we are here. These vehicles can be found in our eco-system, organisations, books, mediation, and contemplation or any other format, including knowledge in morphogenetic fields as suggested by Rupert Sheldrake.

However, our personal capacities are constrained by our ability to handle ambiguity, ambivalence, uncertainty, change and pain, as confirmed by Jung: 'Psychological or spiritual development always requires a greater capacity for anxiety and ambiguity[229].' There can be no becoming without coming into being, as Jung reminds us that: 'Every human life contains a potential. It that potential is not fulfilled, that life was wasted[230].'

Chapter 18

Integral enterprise theory

> We need to ask, what would a way of thinking, a way of living, and ultimately an economic system look like that worked based on the principles of the larger natural world and how do we create such a way of living in out organisations and societies, step by step.

> Peter Senge (2008), The Necessary Revolution

For the following section I have used extracts from Lessem and Schieffer's book[7], with some of my own additions and modifications.

§18.1 Transforming the enterprise into a core development agent in society.

The role of business in society over the past two decades continues to evolve from promoting general philanthropy, corporate social responsibility, and corporate social investment towards more holistic ways of their relationships including well-being. We have seen a gradual expansion of the traditional notion of private enterprise, whereby an increasing number of organisations are emphasising greater societal engagement. Corporations are reaching out towards culture, education, environment and areas. Cross-sector partnerships are encouraged, and 'public-private-civic partnership is part of the business vocabulary.

Businesses are reaching out to society, acknowledging that such engagement is vital to ensure their own survival. It is in this context that I^3 resides in the integral enterprise – a theory that is increasingly being applied globally.

§18.2 The development of the integral impact enterprise embedded in, co-evolving with, and serving society.

Integral impact work on organisational development and transformation seeks to understand how an organisation can be designed to align with its impact outcome and purpose, become sustainable and, in the process, become more embedded with investees and in society. Thus, the firm would not only respond more directly to the real needs of its investees and society, it would also help to evolve them, and to co-evolve with them. In other words, it would strengthen its own sustainable organisational functioning and seek to influence that of others. Such a shift would take the firm out of its narrow, artificial institutional borders and would place it as a living, interacting and continuously adapting entity within its equally living, interacting and ever-changing societal environment.

§18.3 Barriers for an integral impact enterprise.

With awakened consciousness at the core of any interaction, we cannot metaphorically put the genie back in the bottle, and only through forced amnesia can we regress to previous levels of understanding. For many firms, a full impact approach might too difficult: 'not necessary as we're doing quite well already, thank you!' There are myriad reasons why it can't be done, including the dominance of the status quo, along with the fear of facing the realities of oneself, vulnerabilities and all. Who can argue with the existing levels of success which justify and validate the no-change policy?

The barriers of denial, rejection and deflection are strong and pervasive across the industry; on one level, this is fine. We can design for evolution but we cannot dictate its progress. We can, however, say that all development has to transcend and include the preceding stages, so the question becomes: what conditions will enable our firm to take the next evolutionary leap? C.G. Jung outlines the challenge:

> There is no coming to consciousness without pain. People will do anything, no matter how absurd, in order to avoid facing their own Soul. One does not become enlightened by imagining figures of light, but by making the darkness conscious. [231]

According to the inner logic of the Lessem and Schieffer integral approach, whereby the four-worlds/vectors and the centre represent the core functions of any social organism, the major functions of an enterprise can be depicted in a more relational or flow-orientated integral manner. This is illustrated by the figure below. The integral representation removes the organisation visually out of the conventional hierarchical or matrix format.

We envision the organisation more as a natural and living organism, with the coordinating force (CEO, managing director, president) not on top of the organisation but at its very centre. Organised around this centre are the four core functions of the enterprise: Sales and Marketing; Human Resource

Management and Organisational Development; Operations Management and IT, and Financial Management and Accounting.

Conventional Business Functions – Integrally Visualised[38]

Disconnected functions: The functions of the organisation are often disconnected and departmentalised from each other, or at least do not sufficiently build on the dynamics of each other. The I^3 process requires that the organisational functions have stronger, mutual reconnections. North-Western dominance: An overemphasis is often given to the 'Northern' and 'Western' functions of the enterprise: operations and finance. As in conventional development theory, one clearly sees a privileging of the technological and financial dimension over the human and ecological dimension. I^3 uncovers such imbalances and provides restorative measures. In many private organisations we encounter a singular dominance of the financial function over other functions, e.g., GE and GM where the finance division took over manufacturing.

We often find that the genesis of organisations (like Unilever, Bodyshop, or Avon to name a few) contain a profound societal vision – an urge to respond to a societal predicament. Such organisations were deeply grounded in their societies. However, many organisations as they operationalise, lose this initial impulse and grounding, instead focusing on more efficient processes ('Northern' function), and/or cash flow and return on investment ('Western' function). As a result, the enterprise is always in danger of becoming static as the functions stop playing an equal role – interaction and continuous evolution of each organisational function becomes solidified, and thus the organisation itself is inhibited.

One can witness similar disturbing patterns in many development organisations (DFIs) that now compete with commercial firms for market share. They have lifted anchor from their original mandate and purpose and, by doing this, have lost the very parts which defined them. Their previous societal links have been severed as they now serve the political mandate to generate value/income for their respective governments. Though mandated to 'serve the poor', many such organisations spend significant resources on fundraising and project evaluation ('West'), as well as on gathering and preparing relevant statistics ('North'). They lose touch with the communities they are supposed to serve ('South'), and fail to understand and activate the cultural and spiritual context of their activity field ('East'). Their impact, in effect, becomes aligned with conventional market standards rather helping evolve and crowd in other forms of capital.

Limited functional definition: The understanding of many organisational functions is often very narrow. In such cases, the functions do not reach out and connect to human and societal functioning. An example: the 'Southern' sales and marketing function of an enterprise is often primarily focused on the communication and distribution of products providing for individual wants, rather than comporting with the nature and community of a society and responding consequently — through products and services — to its developmental needs. Another example: in such organisations, the individual becomes a mere 'human resource' (what a disrespecting term for the working human being!), and consequently feels alienated from the organisation — a situation which many organisations face today. The I^3 process uncovers and restores such disconnects, and strengthens the understanding of their specific integral contributions.

Overall closeness of the organisation: The above shortcomings result in an internal and external closeness of the organisation, which constricts the flow of new perspectives; this, in turn, diminishes the organisation's innovation potential. An example: if we consider only the ideas and practises already introduced through our financial and economics practise, we lose enormous transdisciplinary stimulation for the organisation. Many organisations don't deal proactively with new insights provided by other disciplines. Integral enterprise seeks to overcome these shortcomings. The three levels of self, organisation, and society are interconnected, as are the organisational functions. Each original function transforms and broadens its scope.

Functional Transformation: Building the integral enterprise: The transformational process that each organisational function undergoes is complex. For example, the current evolution of the marketing function towards embedding 'relationship management', 'social marketing' and 'eco-marketing', is a clear sign that firms are reorienting the marketing function towards nature and community building. Equally, concepts like 'knowledge management', 'intellectual capital', the 'networked operation' and the 'virtual organisation' signal a fundamental change of the Northern function and the concept of the 'knowledge worker'. Furthermore, new enterprise forms (such as the social enterprise and the social business) illustrate a strong orientation towards community building and sustainable development.

What we find emerging out of needs and macro-drivers are promising 'pockets' and 'cases', but not a fundamental rethink of the conventional enterprise. What has not happened, as yet, is a redefinition and reintegration of the core organisational functions as highlighted above in the virtuous circle. Also, business curricula have not changed towards a more integral organisational theory and practise despite 'add-ons', such as 'corporate social responsibility', 'business ethics' and 'social business', which mainly act as PR tick-box exercises to satisfy compliance requirements.

Real change only occurs through experiential actualisation. As Paulo Freire reminds us: 'People educate each other through the mediation of the world[48]'.

The Lessem and Schieffer base theory on integral enterprise promotes a transformational renewal of the enterprise functions. True to their 'North-East-North-West' rhythm, 'integral' transforms the very functions of the enterprise in the following ways:

- South: our relational path. To re-ground the enterprise and its products in nature and community, as well as in societal developmental needs, thereby promoting 'community building'.

- East: our path of renewal. To re-link the enterprise's evolution, given its own cultural and spiritual foundations and those of its surrounding society, thereby tapping into its creative resources and initiating a process of 'conscious evolution'.

- North: the path of reason. To rebuild and design organisational structures and processes based on developmental needs and co-evolutionary processes, thereby transforming the Northern function from technocratic operations to 'knowledge creation'. West: our path of realisation. To redefine the role of finance within the organisation as supporting all other functions, and redesign it so that it supports the overall 'sustainable development' of the organisation and society.

- Centre: The role of the centre is inspiring, coordinating, and overall transformational. Strategy ceases to be implemented top-down by a governance unit but rather is a central process of 'strategic renewal', that links and stimulates interaction between the different functions of the enterprise. Leadership is understood in a lateral sense and contains a strong ethical component: the 'leader' serves others to make a transformational difference in the organisation.

Each of the five functions is a transformational process, based on the GENE. The following graphic depicts an overview on the integral enterprise, its transformed functions and the transformational GENE spiral in its centre.

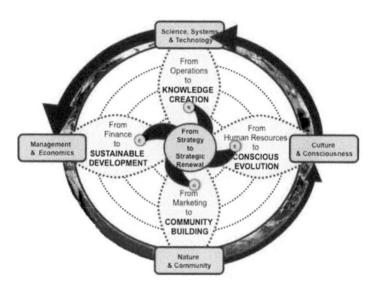

Figure 18.1: The Integral Enterprise – An Overview (Trans4M [38])

Integral theory and practise maintains that any reconfiguration of the enterprise requires an inbuilt transformation process, enabling each enterprise to continuously evolve its own theoretical base and organisational practise. Integral Impact 3.0 is based on this design and blueprint.

§18.4 Different cultural characteristics (morphologies) build on each other

The following table illustrates the cultural strengths and gifts within each of the four worlds. While each has developed a particular set of cultural strengths, each needs to embody the other three worlds; in fact, each world needs to continuously reach out to the other worlds in order to be in an integrated state of dynamic balance.

The four morphologies are a geographic representation, while constituting an archetypal representation of the inner fourfold of living organisations, such as individual people, organisations, and societies. As such, integral associates the 'inner' South with humanism and nature, the East with holism and culture, the North with rationalism and science, and the West with pragmatism and enterprise.

It is, however, important to see how this pattern still resonates to some degree on a global level, while acknowledging that migration and modern

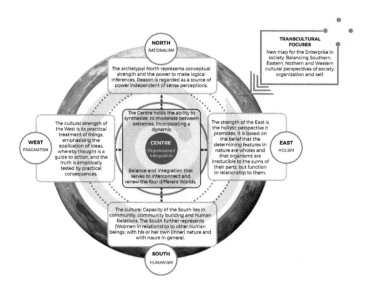

Figure 18.2: Activating Transcultural Forces (Trans4M [38])

communications lead to many hybrid combinations. The four-worlds are rooted in an ancient archetype of wholeness and integration, which can be found in endless variations in all cultures, from the mandala to the medicine wheel. In this archetypal image, the North, which is most closely related to physical nature and to his or her fellow (wo)man, is represented by humanism.

The archetypal East is home to the evolutionary dimension of the person (holism), while the archetypal North represents a person's rational dimension. The archetypal West holds the pragmatic dimension which, as in the other cases, is only of full value if it embodies, and thereby stays connected to, the other three dimensions.

Integral is not saying that, for example, humanism is only rooted in the North (e.g., in Scandinavia or the US), or holism is only rooted in the East (e.g., in India, Japan or China); rather, over time each world region has evolved one inner dimension that seems to be more strongly developed than the others. The East has arguably the longest and deepest tradition in holism, spirituality and non-materialism; while the West, has developed an enormous capacity for pragmatic and material expression. Moreover, each world, when isolated and conflict ridden, has its downside: tribalism and nepotism in the North; fundamentalism in the East; totalitarianism in the

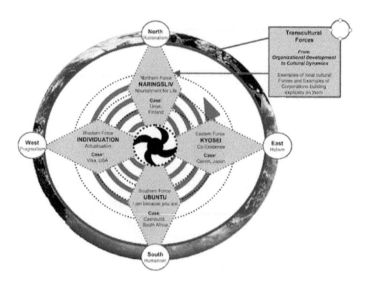

Figure 18.3: Examples of Transcultural Forces (Trans4M [38])

North; materialism in the West.

Of course, we can find each aspect in every society, organisation and individual. The integral impact perspective argues that it is ultimately about integrating these four positive dimensions within the fields of the self, the organisation, and the society, albeit retaining our particular, for example 'Western', emphasis. The pragmatic West needs not only the rational Northern dimension, but also the holistic Eastern dimension and the humanistic (people, community and nature-orientated dimension) of the South. Each needs the other in order to be meaningful and effective. When one dimension is effectively isolated, it becomes distorted and risks stagnation.

Based on the four morphologies, different cultures have developed particular commercial and organisational orientations. Drawing on the innermost forces within a particular self, organisation, or society, provides the context for any possible transformational journey.

Examples for expressions of such local cultural forces are African, '*Ubuntu*' (South); Japanese, '*Kyosei*' (East); the Nordic '*Naringsliv*' (North); and the Anglo-Saxon '*Individuation*' (West). As such, each society, organisation, and individual resonates mostly with one cultural force, with others less present.

The illustration above provides some examples of cultural forces in the four-world regions, including some corporate examples that have been consciously built on such cultural forces. It may by now seem obvious how these cultural forces are — as a dominant cultural expression — an integral part of the identity of a person, organisation, or society. Consequently, transformational processes such as building an impact framework will always have strong cultural forces lodged in a particular local identity. From such a strong 'home base', an organism can productively contribute and coherently engage with it. Thus, Lessem and Schieffer calls the core rhythms of a healthy transformation process 'From Local Identity to Global Integrity'.

Ultimately, the four-world model provides a new map for the enterprise. With this approach, Lessem and Schieffer illustrate how each world region has developed its particular cultural strengths and capacities; if successfully activated, these form the basis for local transformation and social innovation. This particular strength can then contribute to global impact solutions if in balanced interaction with other cultural capacities.

The four worlds form a framework for such creative interaction, allowing each society, organisation and individual to identify particular strengths and the strengths of 'the others'. It is remarkable to see, how the four worlds, as an 'archetypal' representation, equally resonates on the level of the global cultural level as well as societal, organisational, and individual levels.

§18.5 Creatively engaging with diversity on all levels

The four-world approach focuses on the 'creative activation' of the diverse elements of each social system while working towards more integrated perspectives.

Creative interaction between the parts of a whole is only possible with a rich understanding and appreciation of cultural, sectoral, societal, organisational, and individual diversity.

Reactivating these cultural forces is a core aspect of this approach, ensconced in the insight that, in order to fully activate and harness the specific strengths of an organisation, it must be firmly lodged in its societal and cultural grounds.

Transformation starts with the development of a local identity (of self, organisation, and society), whether this is rooted, for example, in the Ubuntu philosophy of interdependence in Southern Africa or in Japan's concept of Kaizen, promoting continuous improvement.

If we do not understand who we are and where we come from, we cannot possibly know where we wish to go and how to get there.

As individuals, we know that we cannot transform consciously by ourselves and achieve our full individual or organisational potential unless we are able and willing to transform towards the local identity of our culture.

Only with an understanding of our local identity can we contribute to the global integrity of the system we live and work in.

Only then can we meaningfully and productively link the local and the global, and one culture with another.

Such transformation processes will also overcome fragmentation on an individual, organisational, communal, and societal level.

We now turn from transcultural forces to the transdisciplinary fields that underlie transformation management.

§18.6 Transdisciplinary impact fields: science and technology

§18.6.1 Beyond enterprise, management and leadership

The origins of our thinking and our present-day situation lie in the foundational disciplines that conventional business schools and programmes deliver, such as business administration, management, and leadership.

In general these are centred in the social sciences, in economics, statistics, behavioural and social psychology, as well as a sprinkling of systems theory and sociology. While anthropology, ecology, psychology, and political theory are virtually ignored.

In addition, this narrow base is effectively drawn from the perspectives of the 'West', essentially from America, with the other three worlds having little or no presence. Particularly limiting for our purposes with impact management is the omission of the humanities. Given that transformation management draws upon local identity in order to develop global integrity, enterprise, management and leadership from our impact perspectives are fundamentally flawed.

As has been discussed, local identity draws pre-eminently on nature and culture, meaning that anthropology, ecology, philosophy, theology, geography, art, architecture, music, dance, literature and theatre are all important.

This is rarely seen in any impact approach; it is not even on the map.

§18.6.2 From monodisciplinary to transdisciplinary impact perspectives

Approaches to business enterprise and entrepreneurship developed out of economics predominantly from the 'North-West', (i.e., Britain, America, France, and Austria). Interestingly, even Germany, the birthplace of Karl Marx and the centre of European philosophy, hardly gets a mention – never mind

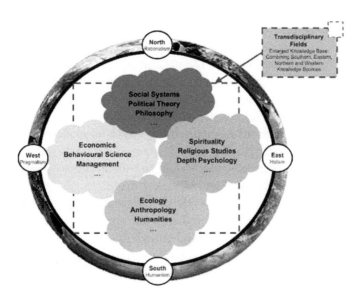

Figure 18.4: Transdisciplinary Fields: Overview (Trans4M [38])

Italy, Spain or Russia. Only very recently have sociologists, psychologists, and philosophers engaged with various forms of 'social' entrepreneurship.

Interestingly, the field of organisational management, and the leadership studies and disciplines closely linked are totally Western (American) in their origins, with a significant exception of discrete elements of Japanese management. In fact, with the global consolidation of the American-style business school, the underlying economic, monodisciplinary orientation has become even more pervasive.

As a counter, since the new millennium we have witnessed several significant trends towards transdisciplinary orientation:

- the diversification from business to social and even eco-enterprise, which draws upon psychology, sociology, political science, and ecology.

- the comparatively recent advent of 'cross-cultural management' and 'corporate culture', which has something of an anthropological tone to it, extending its reach into literature and theatre via storytelling.

Yet today these are like drops in the economic and behavioural ocean, which is why overall social, as opposed to technological, innovation is inhibited.

§18.6.3 Technological to social innovation

Interdisciplinary development in the natural sciences, and in biochemistry, neurobiology, and medical electronics, have led to the proliferation of innovation, facilitated by the application of the scientific method. In the social sciences and humanities, however, such innovation has been inhibited for two major reasons: different social disciplines, such as economics, anthropology, political science, and psychology, have remained largely segregated from each other. And the 'scientific method' in the social sciences has remained academically esoteric rather than practically useful.

As we previously considered, a transdisciplinary perspective enables the organisation to build an enlarged and relevant knowledge base. Further, by applying research to such an enlarged knowledge base in a transformative way, the enterprise can become a social innovator, which in turn is a key objective for any impact approach. We can now turn to business functions.

§18.6.4 Transpersonal impact functions: economics and management

In order to fully 'function', individuals, organisations, and society need to differentiate and integrate their life-sustaining activities. However, the functions of the three levels are often disconnected. A main reason is society's pervasive specialisation that occludes the big picture. Secondly, are the hierarchical governance systems that can silofy a firm. Using an integral approach, we overcome that 'disconnection' (fragmentation) and we move from a narrow understanding of business administration to a transpersonal and trans-sectoral perspective for ourselves and our investee.

§18.6.5 Understanding the shared functioning of self, organisation and society

Each human organism (self, organisation, and society) needs to integrate various functions in order to stay alive. Today these functions are merely outer expressions of the deeper original meaning they once had. Engaging in transformation, we need to understand more deeply the four oriented functions to enable them to build (and mutually reinforce) each other.

Each level's four functions resonate deeply with the cultural morphologies, as depicted in the following table.

Table 18.1: Functions of living systems

	Functions of Living Systems			Shared Functions
	Self	*Organisa-tion*	*Society*	
South Humanism	Communi-cation	Marketing	Markets	Community Building
East Holism	Conscious-ness	Human Resources	Labour Force	Conscious Evolution
North Rationalism	Compe-tence	Operations	Science and Tech-nology	Knowledge Creation
West Prag-matism	Capacity	Finance	Capital	Sustainable Develop-ment

> Specialised knowledge by itself produces nothing. It can become productive only when it is integrated with task...Intellectuals see organisations as a tool; it enables them to practise their techne, their specialised knowledge. Leaders need to see knowledge as a means to the end of organisational performance. Both are right.
>
> Peter Drucker[232]

§18.7 Functional grounding to effect

Whilst we know that living system functions in management need to be integrally connected, in leadership and entrepreneurship this no longer applies. In fact, when Lessem and Schieffer reviewed the emerging literature on leadership and entrepreneurship, they found that the conventional functions — marketing, human resources, operations, and finance – were totally omitted, as if considering the body, spirit and the soul of enterprise, but not the mind.

Let us now consider how the core functions can be further evolved in order to release their GENE-ius. We build here on existing trends that can be found in each function, although there is no consistent framework and curriculum to provide a learning and development context for an integral evolution of all functions across all fields.

The Southern function: from marketing to community building

The Northern 'functional transformation' is the evolution of marketing into community building. The fulfilment of individual and communal needs, inherent within a 'Northern' humanistic approach has been overtaken by the 'Western' exploitation of the consumer, thereby aggressively satisfying wants. Such an evolution is a process which entails the fulfilment of authentic communal needs through mutual exchange as a substitute for the exploitation of inauthentic individual wants. This is a core evolution in our social impact dimension, which now becomes embedded in the investee.

The Eastern function: from human resources to conscious evolution

The Eastern 'functional transformation' is the move from human resources into conscious evolution. As Personnel Management evolved from the management of people to Human Resource Management (HRM), so people became an economic resource like any other. From a holistic perspective, the 're-sourcing' of the human involves a developmental approach to enhance the levels of consciousness of individuals, organisations, and societies. This is now the realm which provides resources to the cultural drivers and their development.

The Northern function: from operations to knowledge creation

The Northern 'functional transformation' is the evolution of operations into knowledge creation. With the advent of the Japanese manufacturing revolution, the development of the knowledge worker and the knowledge-creating enterprise has transcended land, labour, and capital; and the management of ideas has overtaken the management of employees. From such an evolved perspective, management and workers are replaced by knowledge workers. This is where we, as a firm, can help impact and evolve the investee into a knowledge-creation enterprise, aligned with their commercial purpose.

The Western function: from finance to sustainable development

The Western 'functional transformation' is the evolution of finance into sustainable organisational development. The notion of reciprocity and exchange, inherent within economic relationships and double-entry book-keeping, can connect to inclusive natural life principles rather than purely exclusive contractual financial relationships. The role of money in society thereby evolves from transactional to nurturing, ultimately giving rise to community-sourced impact solutions and other means of sustainable development that are aligned with the firm's mission.

However, pragmatically, if impact is to become fully integrated and validated into an investment process, it must be designed to inform and enhance the core investment decision that drives the expected return.

Impact parameters, credentials and principles built into any system need to act like principles. As human beings, we know that there are principles

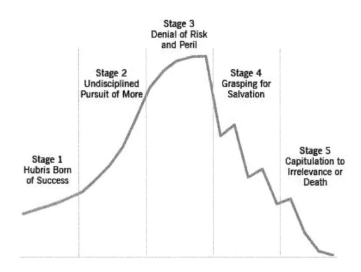

Figure 18.5: Chronological stages of organisational decline

for us to enjoy a healthy and fulfilling life, e.g., good diet, sleeping well, exercise, relationships, etc. As we expand and rebalance our map of good principles to include full impact, we have a much better understanding of what potentiality a firm needs to change for its success and sustainability.

Whilst this is common sense, again, as in our lives, it is often difficult to actualise. Regardless, in our investment diagnostic and final analysis would we prefer to understand these principles or be blind to them? Given that potential future investment losses are today unpredictable, on what level, and degree of principles, should our investment thesis include the full-spectrum of probabilities? For many failed (or declined) firms, this could not have been predicted from the accounts. We often hear that for many firms, a 'bad' culture becomes the key ingredient for its decline and is an area of risk.

Clearly this becomes critical for firms, with not only direct exposure into impact-sensitive areas but also for firms whose future cash flow depends on impact areas such as culture and community. Jim Collins writes that a declining institution is not unlike a human with cancer. As the firm declines in its early stages, it is difficult to detect and diagnose but easier to cure, but in later stages it is much harder to cure but much easier to detect. Here we have the analogy for the visible strength of the firm on the outside versus it already being sick in the inside.

Here are Collin's[125] five chronological stages of organisational decline.

I. *Hubris born of success.* 'Outrageous arrogance that inflicts suffering on the innocent.' Outrageous arrogance to neglect our original calling, to believe that our success was derived entirely of our own doing. Believing that just because our intentions are good and our purpose noble, our decisions must be good. Bad decisions taken with good decisions are still bad decisions. They lose the grounding from which their initial success. When the rhetoric of success replaces understanding, insight and connection, decline follows. It dismisses the role of outside chance in success, while magnifying inside skill and intelligence.

II. *Undisciplined pursuit of more.* Overreaching, going too far, too much growth, expansion, etc. How would we know if we're overreaching? Breaking 'Packard's Law': if we allow growth to exceed our ability to have enough of the right 'fantastic' people in the key seats to execute it, we will fail. Regulate growth and regulate reach by asking 'Do we have all the seats filled with fantastic people? If not, then we do not move until we have them.' This is born out of the hubris that became part of culture in stage 1, and how management now has redefined success to suit the new narrative.

III. *Denial of risk and peril.* Critical here is 'denial'. Myriad excuses why this is a temporary 'blip' or singular event, combined with lack of responsibility and accountability. When a culture of denial takes hold, we are fully in stage 3. Again, from the outside we may look great, which makes it easy to deny. Look at the following table. Are we a team on the way up or on the way down? In this stage, management will discount negative data and amplify positive data, putting a positive spin on ambiguous data, taking outsized risks whilst denying the consequences. As such, the culture shifts again.

Table 18.2: Leadership Team Dynamics

Teams on the way up	Teams on the way down
Employees can bring their realities to the table for discussion. Leaders don't criticize those who speak truth.	People shield the team and the leaders from the realties of a situation for fear of retribution, criticism exclusion.
It is easy to discuss an issue, and people are comfortable to bring solid facts into the dialogue.	Strong opinions are often asserted through power without providing evidence and solid logic.

The leadership uses strong and open questioning to positively challenge and learn more through insight.	The leadership uses more statements than questions to avoid critical input. The leadership may also allow poor reasoning and unsupported opinions if it strengthens their views.
Once made, the team can easily unify behind a decision and create the clarity to work together, even when initially opposed.	The team cannot easily unify behind a decision, and will continue to reiterate the old views, even undermining the decision afterwards.
Members credit each other for any successes and enjoy the confidence and support of the team without having to 'blow their own trumpet'.	Individuals seek to gain as much credit as possible for any successes and are not confident in team members.
Team operates a no blame culture within open forums to gain valuable wisdom and insights from any experiences.	Team members find blame in others and circumstances and ignore the realities of the situation.

IV. *Grasping for salvation.* No one can deny that we are falling. A search begins, looking for a silver bullet. Greatness is never a single event – it is a cumulative process, what is called the 'flywheel' effect. It does not happen any other way. Here we will see re-engineering, radical transformation, bold strategies by new, charismatic leaders, cultural change, blockbuster products, game-changing acquisitions, and other silver bullet solutions. The danger is that management believes the possible initial upsurge in numbers from short-term benefits as indication of strategic success.

V. *Capitulation to irrelevance or death.* Hopes and financial strength have eroded and good management abandons the ship; it is over[233]. One of the core aspects that ties these stages together is the growth in hubris which, in turn, often leads to arrogant neglect because of the need to maintain power, position and the ego's need to be right.

So, what is a possible antithesis of entering stage 5?

All eighteen 'Built to Last' companies are still standing today, with an average of over 100 years of endurance. Why are they still standing? A great question, and it is because they had a reason to endure the struggle.

If it is just success, if it is just money, it is not enough. They have to answer the question: 'What would be lost if we disappeared? Would we leave behind a gaping hole if we went away?[125]'

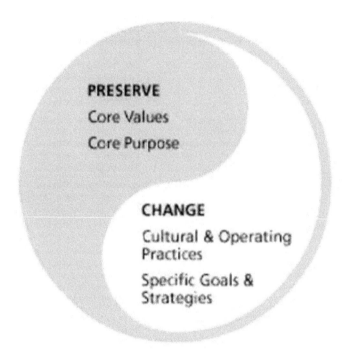

PRESERVE

Core Values

Core Purpose

CHANGE

Cultural & Operating
Practices

Specific Goals &
Strategies

Figure 18.6: Cultural complimentary dynamic forces

In their research, Collins and his team found that companies that who survived and thrived were driven by a purpose beyond money and success which is rooted in core values.

Imagine the power of values and purpose in work. They found a paradox:. Core values are not open to question.

For change... they separate what we stand for... but on the other hand, they recognise the signature of mediocrity was not the unwillingness to change, but chronic inconsistency.

Successful companies have to be willing to change and move from their positions of 'either/or' towards expansive and ambiguous thinking, such as 'both/and', which signals the ability to hold opposing thoughts and still have the ability to function.

So how do we preserve the core and stimulate progress? It is the 'both and and' that holds it together.

The opening wedge of the expanded mind is 'willingness', which many traditions teach as the fundamental principle for new awareness and growth. We all know this to be a fundamental truth which requires no defence; we

Figure 18.7: Stages of grieving, By Bertrand Grondin[a]

have all experienced the sensation of creating an opening for new information and learning to enter. It's the learning of today that challenges the learning of yesterday.

As a psychologist, it is of course of some interest to me – but no real surprise — how organisational decline correlates with psychodynamic phenomena such as grief and addictions, which depend on the willingness to admit a problem and make amends. In the 12 steps recovery programs, it's no coincidence that only at step 8 is ready to become "willing to make amends". The previous steps involve admitting our powerlessness and changing our belief system away from self-centredness, while asking us to become truthful about ourselves and our actions. It is the truth that will set us free, our ticket to emancipation. The problem for most of us is that we stop at the first hurdle since we don't want to hear the truth about ourselves so it remains in denial and part of our shadow self. The gift of grace, forgiveness and clarity of purpose only emerges after facing our real truths, which only happens to the degree we have developed humility in ourselves and for others.

The addictive pattern follows a similar path, so the psychological dimension on organisational decline should not be ignored. A key outcome

Figure 18.8: Collins 5 Levels of Leadership

of Collins' research was that a company could fall into the grim depths of stage 4 and still recover, i.e., companies, like addicts sometimes need to hit 'rock bottom' before they recover.

As in his previous book From Good to Great, Collins cites the common linkage between high-performing companies,i.e., those that reach Level 5: their 'leaders display a powerful mixture of personal humility and indomitable will[235].' In contrast, in How the Mighty Fall the common linkage is e denial, hubris, and arrogance. Again, we don't have to be a psychologist to see the performance correlation.

What is key for impact, of course, is to incorporate the dimensions of leadership and culture as required depending on the timeline and needs of the investee. Each level affects and navigates the other for how the organisation might perform going forward and also how the co-created Impact via the I³ Outcome Objectives (I³OO) will be implemented and managed.

As discussed earlier, we learn about investments not just by looking at the positives but by looking deeply into the negatives, by comparing and contrasting within our quantitative and qualitative diagnostic framework; i.e., we learn from mistakes. This is why we need to build an iterative, reflective, and self-reinforcing process into any system, i.e., a circle which strengthens and renews the I³OO and the commitment for sustainability.

The seemingly paradoxical need for continuity and stability versus an actual requirement for change cannot be solved just at the level of thought

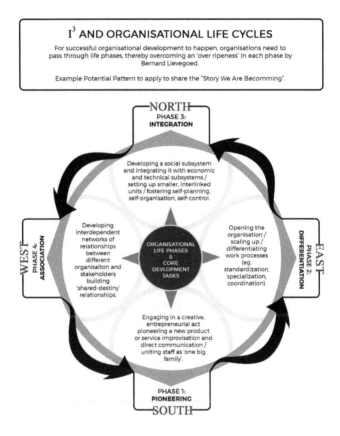

Figure 18.9: Organisational life cycles

and through will-power. This reverts to our language and narratives as we enable them to meet their contrasting opposites within our governance systems.

This forms part of the organisational life cycle, and where on the Impact time-line we find ourselves and our investee. Simply put, within the four-worlds this may look like figure 18.9.

At this point, we can discuss Ichak Adize's seminal work[236], which studies the typical path of corporate growth and development. This adds another dimension to the timeline assessment of our I³oo and how this impacts management—change requirements.

As any investor realizes, companies go through several stages towards possible growth or decline; management must be reformulated and rebalanced accordingly to bring the focus area to the forefront of management capacity, and if possible by rotating the senior management team.

I have worked very successfully with several firms that have used this dynamic as part of their strategy. For example, I was part of the financing for a cable operator in Spain that essentially segmented their management focus and emphasis in three phases as they operationally managed themselves towards their profitability breakeven point.

    I. Build phase as driven by engineering and IT (the CEO at the time was an engineer and former COO).

    II. Content, product packaging and sales and marketing. (CEO was previous Sales Manager)

    III. Reduce churn and finance (CEO was the former Finance Director) which meant the firm actually had three CEOs but were rotated from the same management team over this 5–7 year period.

Life cycles are highly relevant for impact as we need to build impact resilience across the time line and the management bench. The framework and discussion below is a combination between extracts taken from Adizes' public website[237] and the book "Managing Corporate Lifecycles"[236] with a summary of the Life Cycles by Ramakrishnan (Ramki)[238] and with my own additions.

Adizes based his work on more than thirty years experience in more than thirty-five countries. Using a traditional bell curve, he charts corporate development through stages of growth and decline.

A key concept here is PRIME—a healthy organisation operating effectively and efficiently. Like the work on spiral dynamics by Claire Graves[239], Adizes has unearthed fundamental principles of change, leadership, and management styles that are useful for understanding and affecting organisational growth. Whilst Spiral Dynamics challenges the individual and the organisation to progress along an upward and outward continuum that reflects internal and external integration with new cultural settings, Adizes adds the evolutionary dynamic that completes the firm's more operational side.

§18.7.1 Key questions around how businesses evolve as they grow

- We seek to understand the prerequisite stages of growth, the applicable structure and people's roles; this is key to successfully transitioning the organisation.

- Understanding the entrepreneur/CEO/business-driver role and their positioning, as aligned with capacities and capabilities, drives the defined success.

- Creating a management team with processes and procedures that are 'fit for purpose' and can speak truth to power.

§18.7.2 Every business environment has its unique dynamic drivers

- Market cycles – seasonal, demographic

- Technological, legal, compliance developments

- Market scope expansion – local to global

- Product mix, target markets and propositions

- Personnel shifts – changes in capability/education of people

- Ownership – changes in goals and risk tolerance

- Business structure transitions – as the company moves through its definable stages.

The smooth management of the lifecycle is mission critical to reach the next stage. We need to allow some dispensation for young companies who often are:

- Highly flexible and entrepreneurial, limited resources and hard to control (or predict)

- Resource strapped

- Key risks may lie elsewhere e.g. revenue concentration risks

§18.8 What is needed to create a successful management team?

The answer is complex and varied. However, it is certain that the most effective management team functions as cohesive, cooperative units. Each person completes certain tasks or fills a specific role, and supports and complements the others within the group, although defining these roles can be challenging.

Here, we introduce the PAEI Model, which outlines four distinct roles that our management team needs in order to be successful, and in addition, will become part of our qualitative corporate investment evaluation model within I^3. The PAEI Model is particularly useful for constructing a new management team. It is an easy checklist for ensuring that we have a well-rounded group of people who can work together effectively and achieve the team's goals.

§18.9 The PAEI (Producer, Administrator, Entrepreneur, Integrator) Framework.

Each mode is necessary. Adizes suggests the four together are sufficient for good management but if any one mode is not adequately performed, mismanagement can evolve.

These modes are allegorical. The Adizes methodology holds that, under normal circumstances, all people are able to operate in all four management modes; however, we are naturally strongest almost from birth in only one. A secondary mode develops as we mature, and by adulthood we are usually very capable in our second mode. A third mode can be learned with more effort, and in our weakest mode we can function but will almost always benefit from some help. Management teams whose style profiles are complementary are the only way to address all four areas of concern with equal importance and competence[240].

Neil LaChapelle highlights a relationship between PAEI and our perceptions as mapped into presuppositions of "is" (Our West), "should" (our North), "want" (our East), and "ours" (our South), these can be personal presuppositions but can also be communal and collective.

However, there is often a source of confusion in perceptions — in life in general and very often on management teams. People believe they are discussing the "we" case, but in reality they argue the "me" case, failing to understand that their perceptions are based on their personal understanding of "is", "should", and "want", and what it means for them and then generalise, assuming others will have the same thinking. In our governance systems, this is often an issue, so here PAEI can help in understanding the basis for such individual perceptions.

Integrator (our Integral South)[236]

Team-builders: Integrators are the 'heart' of a team or organisation with a high degree of emotional intelligence and empathy. They manage the

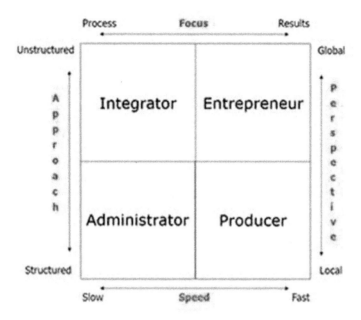

Figure 18.10: The PAEI model

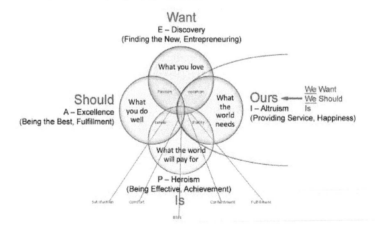

Figure 18.11: By Neil LaChapelle, adapted from the Google Plus stream of Dorothy Shapland

interpersonal, interdepartmental, supplier, and client relationships that allow the organisation to function as an organic whole. Attend to people's needs, views, motivations complaints and conflicts to foster a constructive working environment and help people focus on shared goals. Less concerned about formal roles and titles, and more concerned that people pull together, each doing whatever it takes to achieve harmony and their collective mission. They can take a creative approach when solving problems, and tend to work more slowly and methodically, since they focus on the process and not the end result. They often lead with kindness and know how to build trust and respect within a team, and will take time to help a colleague. Integrators play a key role in building an organisation's culture, especially in its early stages.

The shadow (more extreme and darker side) character: the super follower who will do what he/she is told.

Entrepreneur (our Integral East)

Self-starters and visionaries who are energised by ideas, novel challenges, exciting opportunities, and future achievements; and enjoy aligning with new developments. May have difficulties seeing the integral impact approach as necessarily relevant as they scan the environment constantly for changes, in a search for novelty. Manage at a high level of abstraction, looking mainly for trends and anomalies. They are good at building shared visions and taking calculated risks.

Organisations depend on entrepreneurs at an early stage of development to create big ideas that allow them to maintain strategic advantage and enter new markets. They rely on people to spot opportunities and threats, and help others respond to change. Entrepreneurs can often have an unstructured approach to solving problems and decision making, and their focus is more global. Entrepreneurs are more often in extroverted roles such as in senior leadership, sales & marketing, or research and development teams.

Shadow character: the arsonist who will set on fire what has been built.

Administrator (our Integral North)

Often quiet, cautious people who are more concerned with how we should complete tasks, rather than what we should do. They understand the integral impact approach as a sequential roadmap to be followed analytically and diligently. Quite uncomfortable with ambiguity or uncertainty, they can become stressed by unplanned activities, unstructured environments, which feels chaotic so they prefer a system of routines for smooth operations.

As such, they prefer clear rules and policies that help a team/organization function and follow its procedures correctly. Can be slow and careful in decision-making because a concern for details and to ensure things are handled properly so may lead to rejecting new proposals reflexively, to slow things down so they can have more time to think for problem solving and decision making. Organisations depend on administrators to develop systems and processes, and often work in accounting, finance or in other process-oriented departments.

Shadow character: the bureaucrat who thinks it's all in the detail.

Producer (our Integral West)

High-energy/octane, active people often with knowledge of the chosen field. May tend to view integral impact with caution, and possibly as a diversion from delivering the main objectives in the business plan. Likes to be incessantly busy with multiple tangible interests as they love achieving many results. Have little patience with distant tasks, and brainstorming as they are mainly interested in getting the job done rather than how it gets done. Producers excels in meeting goals and objectives and are often the driver responsible for many organisational achievements as they embody the primary goal of any organisation. The producer role is often responsible and in charge for the product offered and will typically achieve this by meeting the needs of internal and external clients and ensuring that the end product delivers the expected results. Producers often work fast.

Shadow character: the lone ranger who goes off to do what needs to be done.

A typical diagnostic output from a management team may be like figure 18.12

§18.10 The Corporate Lifecycle

Of course, there are significant overlaps and combinations, as with any personality-type map, so we have to be cautiously whilst recognising its benefits and uses. We can see that whilst all are necessary to manage a firm successfully through its lifecycle, sometimes an imbalance will develop that will require diagnosis and adjustment. If laid out as part of a sustainable impact plan, this becomes predictable, and it will be much easier to smoothly transition through stages. In the example above, there is a need to develop

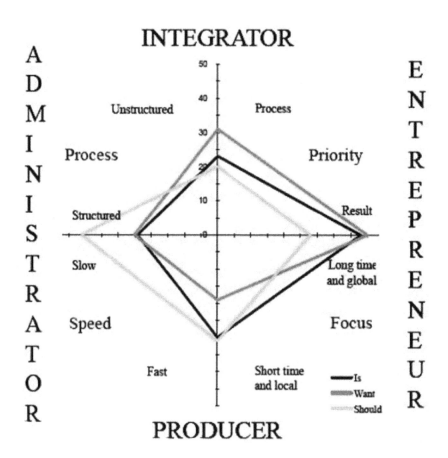

Figure 18.12: Integrator Producer

the left side as the firm may now move into a more structured phase with a need to consolidate information and to standardise more processes.

All change involves events that can be both opportunities and challenges. For every opportunity introduced by change, we must generate a solution that will lead to more change, so that we face new realities leading to new set of challenges. This is where our creative governance enters. Darwin said, 'it is not the most intellectual of the species that survives; it is not the strongest that survives but the species that survives is the one that is able best to adapt and adjust to the changing environment in which it finds itself.[241].'

The fundamental truth about all organisations is that they are living organisms that need to be understood accordingly. As such, they have a lifecycle and undergo predictable and repetitive patterns of behaviours. At each new stage of development, an organisation is faced with a unique set of challenges; the question is how well management addresses these inside the hierarchy in order to successfully transition from one stage to the next.

For management, this is not easy (or even obvious), so this is a key inflection point appears where an impact investor can provide an additional valuable contribution through the I³OO process to provide the investee valuable input. However, the same methods that produce success at one stage can create failure in the next, so each transition is critical. During each transition, fundamental changes in leadership and management may be required, combined with an approach that delicately balances the amount of control and flexibility needed for each stage, 'When the rate of change inside an institution becomes slower that the rate of change outside, the end is in sight. The only question is when.' Jack Welch As confirmed by Jim Collins, leaders who fail to understand what is needed (and not needed) can inhibit the development of their companies or plunge them into premature aging, decline and death.

The challenges that every organisation must overcome at each developmental stage first manifest themselves as tensions and problems that arise from the growth and success of the company, as well as from external changes. This simple, unavoidable reality leads to the following five insights about the nature of problems in organisations:

- Problems are the normal result of growth and are desirable as catalysts for productive change. Like people, companies that get stuck atrophy and decline. When we conduct due diligence on investee firms where management assumes no problems, we will have a problem. Problems detected and dealt with early will prevent future problems. If a company faces a high level of external change, the challenge is magnified and the faster the rate of change, the faster problems appear; the firm needs to be structured accordingly.

- The role of leadership is not to prevent problems or slow the pace of change, it is to accelerate the organisation's ability to recognise and resolve problems. The ability to work quickly together as a team is to gaining competitive advantage. The question is: what is the team map and order of combat?

- Some problems are normal and others abnormal. Normal problems are expected for a given lifecycle stage and even desirable as in-flight corrections; abnormal problems are unexpected and mostly undesirable as they drain time and resources. Since no one has enough time or resources to address all problems, focus is better placed on their abnormal problems as many normal problems can be deprioritised to see if they resolve themselves during the natural course of growth and development.

- Addressing and mapping through the I^{3}OO can drive our organisation faster when the road ahead is known and predictable. Most of the issues we will face are common to all organisations, so let's not reinvent the wheel. By understanding thoroughly the nature and requirements of all ten stages in the lifecycle, we can adroitly manage the transition from one stage to the next.

- The prime stage is the 'fountain of youth' for organisations. One key difference between the lifecycle for human beings versus organisations is that living things mature and inevitably die, while organisations may not. A company's age in terms of its lifecycle is unrelated to its chronological age, the number of employees, its assets, etc. Instead, a firm's lifecycle age is defined by the interrelationship between flexibility and control. An organisation that is in prime has achieved a balance between control and flexibility. A prime organisation knows what it is doing, where it is going and how to get there. It also enjoys both high growth and high profitability. Once an organisation reaches prime, leadership must work to maintain that position.

What follows is a short synopsis and introduction to the Adize's lifecycle[236, 237].

The Business Life Cycle
Source: "Corporate Lifecycles" - Ichak Adizes 1988

P=Production, A=Administration, E=Entrepreneurism, I =Integration

Cultures: PAEI

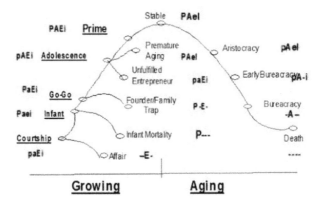

Figure 18.13: Business Life Cycle

Courtship: Just like the beginning of a relationship, courtship occurs when an individual or several people begin to throw around ideas. The focus here is to develop and test the possibilities on which the firm may be founded. Many potential businesses never make it beyond this first stage, as the ideas or relationships fall apart or are not worth pursuing. Adizes named it courtship because the dynamic is similar to a pre-marriage relationship.

The primary goal at this stage is to develop the founder(s)'s enthusiasm and commitment to his/her dream. The higher the risk, the deeper the required commitment. As in a marriage, testing the commitment must happen beforehand. As in a divorce, the relationship does not end when a judge signs the papers, but much earlier when it ran out of commitment.

The emphasis in this stage is building commitment around our "why." 'He [sic] who has a why to live can bear almost any how.' (Nietzsche). In courtship, it is normal to experience fear, uncertainty and doubt. Here we return to some core questions:

- What exactly are we going to do?

- How is it going to be done?

- When should it be done?

- Who is going to buy this, and why etc.?

Now is the time to test the vision as we link it back to our core calling and context. Challenges in courtship include the realisation that once we test the harsh realities, our 'love' may evaporate as commitment wanes. Perhaps, looking back, it was essentially an affair. What is an affair with lots of enthusiasm, some romance but with no real commitment? Only time can tell, unless we constantly polish our reality goggles during our governance meetings to return to our true situation[242].

Infancy: Here the founder(s) marry commitment and courage to provide their time, core or sweat equity, and seed capital for the journey ahead. As William Murray reminds us:

> Until one is committed, there is hesitancy, the chance to draw back, always ineffectiveness. Concerning all acts of initiative (and creation), there is one elementary truth, the ignorance of which kills countless ideas and splendid plans. That the moment one definitely commits oneself, then providence moves, too. [1]

Synchronicity may appear in the form of help and coincidences. Often the basics of administrative paperwork and organisation take a back seat at this point, as the company is focused on production and cash generation by closing sales so long hours and high-stress, are common.

Unexpected crises may appear with little notice as the system is stretched to its limits as the infant organisations lack developed systems, so moving from one crisis to the next is quite normal. New employees are often attracted to infant companies for reasons that go far beyond money, such as mission and vision which creates strong feelings of loyalty to the cause and team. This stage is high risk with many possible reasons for failure as the firm may eat through its cash and working capital before sufficient sales are generated. Investor relations, seeking and having alternative sources of capital, may become mission critical. The infant needs autocratic, centralized decision-making, which might inhibit the realisation of the next stage[243].

The Wild Years: Go-Go: Usually the founders of the business will still be making all decisions at this point, which is both a positive and a negative. Mistakes are common during the Go-Go stage, as the company may start to feel overconfident and stretches everything possible to bring in more revenue.

---

[1]https://www.forbes.com/quotes/9915/

A Go-Go organisation has a successful product with growing sales and cash flow. The company is beginning to survive, and starting to flourish. Key stakeholders, clients and investors are all engaged and benefitting from the early successes.

With this success everyone quickly forgets about the trials and tribulations of infancy. Continued success can rear its shadow and transform confidence into arrogance with an 'I told you so' attitude. If overconfidence gets established, so can overstretching and overextension i.e., if one dream can be realised, why not others? This arrogance can be a major asset of the Go-Go but, when taken to extremes, it also can get them into trouble with rapid diversification and spreading themselves too thin.

A high sales orientation may have addictive qualities: as sales become all important, other issues are brushed aside or denied. The company still has to build much infrastructure, including data and risk management systems, internal controls etc., to successfully stabilize.

A premature focus on profitability can also inhibit the company's long-term potential with everything prioritised to pursue the latest hot project. Communication suffers as previous maps of success are pursued and assumed to be understood by all.

Those who can interpret and read the tea leaves of the founder's ideas become their critically important insiders and trusted confidants and are promoted quickly. Go-Go leaders often have little time to actually manage and take stock of issues.

Work is hastily assigned, with scant attention to detail. When pressed for clearer assignments, the response might be, 'You figure it out; I don't need to be involved in the details.' As a result, well-meaning, hard-working employees often make mistakes, further evidence to a stressed founder that, 'if I want something done right, I have to do it myself.'

If perpetuated, this inability to delegate effectively will plunge the Go-Go into a premature aging syndrome known as the 'founder's trap'. Information and accounting systems remain weak and need attention, only supporting the basic needs of production/ operations, customer service and accounting; any need for impact accounting and reporting can be seen as an added frustration and problem. Accounting typically has its hands full trying to properly account for revenue, expenses and cash flow with additional cost accounting, and accurate reporting of individual product profitability, remains a hopeful expectation; while important information is often gained by hovering around the coffee machine or in after-work social activities.

The company is organised around its key people and projects, with assignments on a project-by-project basis with new tasks often conflicting with previous arrangements. Organisation charts are fluid and do not reflect the way the actual work gets done, primarily intended for the benefit of outside investors and the board.

Employees can become frustrated with the workload, unclear responsibilities and fuzzy goals; as a result, they may find it increasingly difficult to be productive. Later, in the adolescent stage, it often turns out that people promoted into management positions during Go-Go did not in fact have the requisite skills and experience, so some good people now may leave for new opportunities.

As the company continues to grow, development of its infrastructure occurs in response to emerging opportunities or unexpected problems. As things become more complex, it takes longer to fix mistakes, with some solutions creating new problems. Still on a high growth trajectory, the company cannot (or will not) slow down or take time to properly design and implement replacement systems. Instead they make do by enhancing or patching what is already in place. Despite this, things still work, but just barely.

As the load increases, people rely on more patches and quick fixes. At some point, the systems breaks, which may threaten the operations, loyalty of major clients, or the business itself.

If disaster strikes, no one is willing to take responsibility (except possibly the founder) because with weak controls, accountability is unclear and people blame inadequate information and lack of authority which can create a stress and blame culture. If averted, the typical reaction by the founder might implement further controls and accountability, although the founder may be the first to ignore them, as he/she struggles with establishing workable delegation and decentralization.

The relationship between founders and their Go-Go management can be stretched and they can become removed as the founder feels the need to escape day-to-day details to stay focused on the big picture, delegate authority, and focus on outside issues. Whilst he/she may want to delegate, he/she feels they can't since no one has demonstrated adequate replacement ability. Sometimes, without much notice or consultation, the founder re-centralizes power, only to later detach, creating anxiety among management. With repeated detachments and returns, the peripatetic leader creates more frustrations with management now unwilling/unable to act decisively, leading to paralysis. Whilst employees often have deep feelings of affection and respect for the founder, at the same time he/she is driving them crazy and they wish he/she would change. Founders often think they are irreplaceable and at this juncture may often feel betrayed and unfulfilled

Adolescence The transition from Go-Go to adolescence is difficult with the adolescent company verging on success or disaster. This can be a period of difficult growth for a business as it begins to assume aspects of a mature business. As the culture is changing, conflict is common among the team, especially between old and new employees, and there may be inconsistency in organisational goals and compensation and incentive systems. During this stage the company is effectively reborn, which is emotional; the company must find a life apart from that created by its founder.

The founder may still be regarded as a genius with a golden touch. However, if the company starts to fail, the founder, accustomed to adulation, is transformed into 'one of us', no longer capable of leadership.

Adolescence can be especially stormy, characterised by internal conflicts and turf wars to gain position and adulation. Politics plays an important role and can become part of a toxic culture as the hierarchy hardens. This can lead to presumed injustices creating high and volatile emotions with ecstasy in one quarter for those who have temporary success, and dejection in another. As with all point scoring and politicking, this can easily lead to resentment, particularly if the founder is seen to have favourites.

Unless these conflicts are resolved, adolescent companies can find themselves in premature aging, which can lead to early departure of its leadership and management, leading to the pathologies of divorce.

The shift from management by intuition to a more professional orientation occurs as new leaders create systems, designs compensation packages, redefine roles and responsibilities, and institutionalise rules and policies. This creates another shift in culture as the new leader puts on the breaks and says no no no when people are used to go go go. Organisation now can achieve a balance between self-control and flexibility — they know more of what they're doing, where they're going and how to get there. There is more clarity in the delegation of authority. Part of the reason the organisation survived the Go-Go phase is because they were cognisant of the requirements for cash, and the limitations on time and capacity. Consequently, management may decide it is time to delegate only, instead of delegating properly, so they inappropriately decentralize decision making without assigning clear tasks with the appropriate authority and accountability to complete those tasks.

If management is not able to establish and maintain accountability they risk 'upward delegation', which refers to subordinates' resistance to accept the responsibilities assigned to them. Rather than assuming a project and doing the proper research, they present their dilemma to their manager and wait for him/her to report back.

The founder is still the president, salesperson, financier, and innovator but as yet does not recognise the need to change to enable the organisation to grow and mature organically.

Whist a transition occurs from sales to profit, the president still ignores many of the new policies put in place. This is normal; to the extent the founder can mature with the needs of the organisation, they will survive this phase and proceed to the next.

This is where a new governance culture may be required to create the necessary diversity to deal with new goals, objectives, and their complexities.

This significant switch in goals and objectives must be implemented through a complete overhaul of the structures, management information, resource allocation, and reward systems of the adolescent organisation. This transition looks easy on paper, but is very difficult as the culture which is seen to have delivered the current success now has to change.

Some solutions may enable this transition to be more effective. First, the founder must be aware of what strengths he/she brings to the table and the weaknesses.

A more creative and inclusive mode of decision-making is also required that seeks the best overall solution rather than one based on the founders' agreement.

The founder must let go of the fear of losing control, and allow the management team to find their own synthesis between complimentary capabilities. After full gap assessment and needs requirement analysis, new recruits now get properly and positively inducted into the organisation to add previous systems experience and inputs.

The main driver of success here is the how the governance systems and management can deliver requisite controls, the implementation of which requires the organisation to spend time away from the daily operation of the business which will require highly effective leadership.

As control and planning now delivers better activity, the focus can now shifts to exploring the change in having achieved a stronger position with both customers and the marketplace[244].

Prime: This is the ideal spot for a business, where the organisation finally balances control and flexibility. Prime is actually not a single point on the lifecycle curve. Companies successfully occupying this stage will fight to remain.

It is best represented by a segment of the curve that includes both growing and aging conditions. Prime has learned how to balance both flexibility and self-control which inherently are incompatible, with no stable equilibrium. Sometimes the prime organisation is more flexible than controllable, and sometimes it is not flexible enough.

Now that it has an organised structure in place, the company is operating efficiently but is still young enough to keep a watchful eye on innovation and development. At this stage, there may even be new businesses that develop from within the organisation, adding to the potential for future growth.

Early prime characteristics: Vision and values: they 'Walk their talk' and have institutionalised their governance processes with mature functional systems and structure delivering better integration and cohesion. Controlled and nurtured creativity with conscious focus and priorities with predictable excellence and growth in sales and profit margins. Simply having vision and values does not make for a prime organisation; a challenging culture is needed that shapes its operations for the better.

They now operate in a more focused, energised and predictable manner where stretch goals are set, aligned, and consistently achieved. There is an enterprise-wide focus on earning customers' long-term satisfaction and building loyalty. At the same time, the organisation knows when and how to say a high quality 'no'. It is disciplined enough to protect itself with clear priorities so they know what to do and what not to do. It is composed, with a peace of mind when making tough decisions as the entrepreneurial spirit is now fully institutionalised. There is strong evidence of organisational fertility with creativity repeatedly producing controlled, profitable innovation. Organisational structures work well with balanced opposing forces. There is clear alignment between vision, strategy, structure, information, resource allocation, and rewards.

A company in prime is continuously and smoothly realigning their subsystems. The infrastructure provides reliable support through an institutionalised governance process with people understanding where and how decisions are made. The culture has changed again with governance systems now more collaborative and cooperative with decision-making done in an environment of healthy, constructive conflict where differing points of view are considered constructively and pro-actively. There is intra- and inter-organisational integration and cohesion with clients, suppliers, investors, and the community. This internal cohesion enables the prime organisation to devote much more of its energy externally.

People embrace change and enjoy working at the company, creating low staff turnover with a backlog of position applicants. Prime companies work hard to adapt to market changes so that they can gain share from weaker competitors, and as a result they enjoy consistent, above average growth in both sales and profits.

Challenges of prime: This is a temporary condition, not a permanent destination so there is a real risk for complacency and atrophy. Senior management needs to manage and maintain the delicate balance between flexibility and control as it takes little to shift a company in either direction. If administrators lead the change, the company's balance may swing in the direction of excessive control, losing flexibility, while with entrepreneurs the company may grow more flexible but can lose control. Prime companies often have a shortage of management and competent people. There may be less entrepreneurial activity with increasing time spent in the office as we rely heavily on what has worked in the past, all of which are signs of aging. Prime needs to learn to live how as Jascha Heifetz, one of the world's best-known violinists, once said:

> If I don't practise one day, I know it; two days, the critics know it; three days, the public knows it.

On the lifecycle curve, Prime is not at the top. This is because the curve depicts the vitality of an organisation. When a company starts to age, it is still producing the desired results as measured by short-term sales and profitability. Aging is negatively affecting the company but not yet reflected in sales or profitability. Therefore, the lifecycle curve is still rising but the rate of change is slowing, so the rising curve is leveling off.

If prime organisations don't refuel their momentum, if they keep harvesting rather than nourishing it, the curve will reverse direction and the company moves into aging. Here the leadership needs to be vigilant and assess and diagnose the organisation and its culture tactically and strategically to look for negative shifts and misalignments with the core mission[245].

The Signs of Aging & The Fall: Whilst the fall is positioned at the pinnacle of the lifecycle curve, companies are ageing and have lost some of their vitality which brought them there. Clear indications of decline or symptoms are not found in its reports, normally it's the opposite as companies coming out of Prime usually are financially strong.

At this point, many companies become complacent as memories fade and become disconnected from original success. The risk here is that the company is seen as a cash cow which atrophies the culture and regresses it back to a more controlled and static way of doing business. The company may see indications of peak margin, market share, customer growth, etc., signalling the need for a "steady as she goes" attitude so the company loses further flexibility and creativity, and sticks to what worked in the past. If the firm rewards those who toe the line, some highly creative people will leave the firm. The culture may shift towards interpersonal relationships as the company looks inward for solutions rather than staying focused on driving external opportunities and managing risk[2].

Aristocracy: Companies become ossified and may fall behind the times. Things other than running a successful business become more important such as image. They might become a take-over target or seek to acquire other businesses, rather than trying to innovate, with little interest in conquering new markets, technologies, and frontiers.

The company emphasises how things are done rather than what/why it is done. Red tape abounds and the company may find itself on the decline if their culture and decision-making process do not change.

The company now is cash-rich with strong financial statements, but having lost many of its growth drivers, they seek to protect cash generation by reducing risk. The company invests more in control systems, benefits, and facilities than R & D or L & D. The culture has now taken on a more ridged hierarchical structure and tone, with any promotions and advances based more on tenure or forms of status e.g., education than performance. The leadership is suspicious of change as form now dominates function and they increasingly value and reward uniformity, consistency, and formality in dress, decorum, and behaviour.

The effects of the steady decline in flexibility, which began in prime, start to become more palpable. The company's focus becomes increasingly short-term and with less of a long-term view, the culture is static and stale[246].

Recrimination: When an aristocracy is unable to reverse its downward spiral, and artificial repairs finally stop working, management's mutual admiration society abruptly ends. With results suffering, the blame game begins. A once friendly culture becomes the opposite. as problems and conflicts gets personalised.

As the organisational culture becomes more toxic, employees fight for position and take credit for revenue or anything positive. Much of the previous positive energy is wasted in turf wars, disagreements and arguments sapping key areas. The talented people who have remained and have other opportunities are now considering abandoning the sinking ship which can lead to an exodus as more blame is heaped across the organisation, exacer-

---

[2]https://adizes.com/the-fall/

bating the problems. The culture is shaped by innuendo and rumour, with relative silence in real information, and fear and anxiety now dominating communication. Even strategic business decisions e.g., a change in a product price is difficult to get through management since no one wants to be tainted if the strategy goes wrong. As fear and a paranoid fight for survival dominate, management now plays survival politics. As operational performance continues to decline, these stresses worsen, and if not corrected, the firm either enters terminal decline and bankruptcy or becomes a fully-fledged bureaucracy[247].

Bureaucracy: It is quite possible that a company may die before reaching this stage as revenues and margins decline. However, if the organisation has survived to this point, the bureaucratic nature of its operations may continue to compound. The company is kept alive by artificial life support, or the company because it has a unique market product or position, operates in a virtual monopoly or has little or no contractual obligations such as debt. It struggles to generate and allocate resources where needed, and justifies its existence in that it serves a purpose of interest to another entity willing to subsidise and support it.

The culture of control has by now built lengthy manuals in place for what is only remnants of its former flexible systems with employees busily following rules and worrying about who is after their role, so much time is spent on rituals and reading the tea leaves. As creativity and the capacity to innovate has died and little of real value is being produced, its survival is at stake. With reporting overload combined with fear of the future, leaders feel disempowered and disassociated, with much time helping clients circumnavigate bureaucratic obstacles. With no inclination to change, everyone's day is filled with following rules, policies and procedures.

The culture now has regressed to an almost childlike state of parent/child control, and if asked the question "why?" the answer is, "because the policy/rules say so". Bureaucratic managers are among the nicest people because to effectuate any change across organisational lines, they need to cooperate and collaborate, which is a near impossibility in a bureaucracy. When meetings take place, ritual is a substitute for action. There is plenty of debate and democratic process, but with little, visible real action.

Bureaucratic companies are internally disintegrated as there is individual responsibility for a particular task, but no collective responsibility. Employees don't know the inner workings of other departments and the customer service area often consists of telephone reps whose job it is to listen, record complaints and answer them with a standard, routine. Bureaucracies do not ask in advance for everything they will require as they resent outside disruptions and new information that challenges what they are doing. As such, they will keep the outside world at bay. Like some elderly people, they can become highly agitated and resentful if change is required or suggested, while only allowing very limited and narrow channels to enter.

In a bureaucracy, the left hand does not know what the right hand is doing; as a result, customers are puzzled, frustrated, and lost, and may start building their own systems to deal with ineffectiveness. We see this when businesses that work with bureaucracies have to establish dedicated departments, systems and people that are experts on the inner workings

of a particular government agency. Because such bureaucracies rely on laws and regulation that provide them with a virtual monopoly on services and allocation of funds generated by taxation, heads of bureaucracies spend most of their time in halls of government and with politicians, safeguarding their sources of revenue, so heads of bureaucracies carefully need to manage risks of any negative press as it is a main risk to their career. If you ask people in a bureaucratic organisation, 'Who is your client?' The answers generally include a long list of state or federal agencies that either supervise its performance or its budget, other bureaucracies, along with unions, newspapers, and the media. Last, of course, are the customers whom the bureaucracy is supposed to serve. 397

Death: Some businesses will die quickly, while others will drift away slowly until they are no longer sustainable. Either way, extinction is the natural and obvious end as the company can no longer bring in the needed cash to stay alive. Any residual value of the business or what remains of its products will be acquired, liquidated or stripped to cover liabilities. Monopolies, some duopolies and government agencies that are quarantined from competitive pressure and provide a large employment base often live long and have expensive artificially prolonged lives.

Summary: We all can relate to f these stages and living through the transitions inside an organisation. In my own experience, I can certainly recall times when some of these characteristics were prevalent and part of the culture. It's important to remember again that whilst we are using stages to more clearly illustrate and explain differing levels of characteristics, there are often cross overs and overlaps. As with humans, organisations are much more complex, and our purpose here is to understand that organisations going through different cultural shifts will introduce new risks and need to work with Impact in different ways, as aligned with their culture at the time.

A main task of the Impact Investor is to understand the implications for the investment and Impact thesis and work with the investee through these changes as a natural process of maturing, enhancing the outcome for all. These changes, are required because the capabilities and methods of working that produce success in one stage can be the source of failure in subsequent stages. As such, corporate lifecycles and culture change form an important part and strategic overlay of our Impact theory of change not only to arrive safely at our Impact outcome objectives but also to help manage and provide insight to the investee, thereby reducing negative impacts within their organisation and stakeholders.

A predominant theme here is leadership quality with the capability to respond to organic change; and since people don't just follow systems and procedures, they follow people, we need to take pre-emptive action is cases where we see the leadership stuck or failing to change inside a stage transition. However, if they have respect for their leaders, they will be more inclined to follow the policies and procedures helping to balance flexibility and control[248].

The reason we have taken some time on this topic is that again, Adizes has provided us with a generic time-line map of what organisations experience during their life cycle which we can use, which is often lacking in our conventional due diligence processes. Also, importantly, this life-cycle change dynamic is often hidden or denied by management since they are often too close and embedded in day- to-day operations or have conflicting vested interests. As investors, we can contribute significant insights, help achieve recognition and acceptance to inform the I³OO process to pro-actively include any such time-line cycle predictive changes and requirements.

This aspect links back into I³ through our culture lens but essentially is an overlay that feeds into the overall investment diagnostic and assessment. It is never easy to sustain success but understanding how the lifecycle works can help us integrally manage our organisation as it moves from one stage to the next.

Key life-cycle questions:

- What stage, or stages can we see operating in the organisation?

- How does the management need to change as it grows?

- What particular challenges occur as the founder seeks to build a long-term management team?

- Is the corporate strategy simply the addition of individual business unit strategies?

- When should business units be integrated and when should they remain distinct?

- What level of strategic alignment among business units is desirable?

- How should boards allocate resources across business units when they have different risk profiles and time horizons?

This returns us to the work of Jim Collins[135]. From empirical data, Collins draws important insights which can help us understand the need for, and I³ design for our area of culture. In From Good to Great, we find key ingredients for a firm's performance needed to link into both I³ and our time-line cycle. Collins uses strict benchmarks to identify a group of eleven elite companies that made the leap from good to great and sustained that greatness for at least fifteen years.

As part of cultural change, good-to-great transformations often look like dramatic, revolutionary events to those on the outside, but they feel like organic, cumulative processes to people on the inside. The confusion of end outcomes (dramatic results) with process (organic and cumulative) skews our perception of what really works over the long haul. Collins' companies had no name for their transformations; there was no starting line, launch event, no tag line, and no seismic event.

There was, in other words, no miracle moment when each company transformed from good to great. Each went through a quiet, deliberate process of ascertaining the steps to be taken to create the best future results, then took those steps individualy, until they hit their breakthrough moments.

§18.11 Great firms espouse several key tenets and embedded cultures

Disciplined People: Level 5 leaders are people orientated and focus on other stakeholders and how to make them perform better. They combine a blend of both humility and strong willpower which might seem paradoxical. They know the individual requirements for key roles and ensures that the right person is in the right seat so they always think first about 'who' and then about 'what'.

Disciplined Thought Confronts the Brutal Facts: Strong faith in the cause, and regardless of trials and tribulations, they face the brutal facts of reality and in the end, prevail. Follows a simple idea Collins calls "The Hedgehog Concept": Greatness comes about by a series of good decisions consistent with a simple, coherent concept. This is an operating model that reflects understanding of three intersecting circles: a) what we can be best in the world at; b) what we are deeply passionate about; c) what best drives our economic or resource engine.

Disciplined Culture of Action: People who engage with and work in a structure of disciplined thought and action – operating in balance of freedom and control within a framework of aligned responsibilities which delivers accountability and a sense of autonomy. This is the cornerstone of a culture that creates and builds great results. They build effective operational flywheels based on small, incremental shifts, all aligned to reinforce one another. Grounded in reality, the culture understands there is no grand master plan with defining actions, no one killer innovation or application.

Clock Building, Not Time Telling: Organisations become great when the culture allows and encourages multigenerational leaders, which is the opposite of many organisational boards and cultures today who falsely pin their hopes on a charismatic and personality- based leader as their saviour or maverick, often catered around a new vision, product, idea or program of change. The culture of great organisations has in effect matured, developed and emancipated to such an extent that it recognises that all attributes required lies in its people.

The culture embodies the set of timeless core values which represent their core reason for being. However, this consistency has to be married with a relentless drive for change and progress – a creative compulsion that often manifests in what Collins has called BHAGs (Big Hairy Audacious Goals). Great organisations clearly distinguish their steadfast core values and beliefs and the operating strategies and cultural practises (which endlessly adapt to a changing world) which are constantly revised and improved to better align within the organisational flywheel[249].

§18.12 The Hedgehog Concept

In his famous essay 'The Hedgehog and the Fox,' Isaiah Berlin [250] divided the world into two groups, based on an ancient Greek proverb which pitted these two natural enemies against each other. Foxes dart for one thing to another, scattered and pursuing many ends simultaneously, seeing the world separately in all its complexity; never integrating their thinking into one

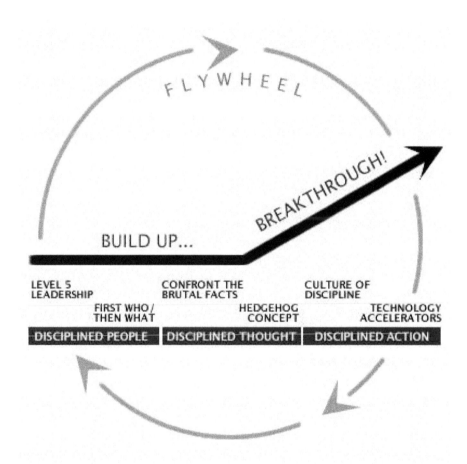

Figure 18.14: Good to Great framework

overall concept or unifying vision. Hedgehogs, on the other hand, simplify a complex world into a single idea or principle that unifies and guides everything. Regardless of the world's complexity, the hedgehog reduces all challenges and dilemmas to simple ideas — anything that does not somehow relate to the hedgehog idea holds no relevance.

This reminds us of the 'fig' quote by Wendell Holmes which is one of my favourites: 'I would not give a fig for the simplicity this side of complexity, but I would give my life for the simplicity on the other side of complexity.' He added that: 'Insanity is the logic of an accurate mind overtaxed' so when someone provides us with the gift of simplicity this also serves the dual role of keeping us 'sane'.

When foxes and hedgehogs are pitted against each another, the hedgehog usually wins. Collins' research shows that those who built the good-to-great companies were hedgehogs, to one degree or another, using their hedgehog nature to drive toward a Hedgehog Concept, a simple, crystalline concept that flows from deep understanding about the intersection of the three key dimensions: What can we be best at? This standard goes far beyond core competence; just because we possess a core competence doesn't necessarily mean we are best at it. Conversely, what we can be best at might not even be something in which we are currently engaged.

What drives our economic engine? To get insight, search for the one denominator or driver that has the single greatest impact. If we could pick one (and only one) ratio or matrix to systematically increase over time to make a greater impact, what is it? This denominator can be subtle, and not obvious. The key is to use the denominator to gain understanding and insight into our economic model.

What are we deeply passionate about? Good-to-great companies did not pick a course of action, then encourage their people to become passionate about that direction. Rather, they decided to do only those things that they were passionate about. They recognised that passion cannot be manufactured, nor can it be the end result of a motivation effort. We can only discover what ignites our passion and the passions of those around us.

If you were to summarise the difference between the fox and the hedgehog it would probably be that it's the hedgehog who knows itself the best, understand its strengths and weaknesses and has developed the wisdom necessary to use them in alignment with its environment. It's important to understand that the Hedgehog Concept is not to be pursued as a goal, strategy or intention in itself to be the best. It is part of a cultural understanding of one's capabilities and how this can be aligned with what one is best at.

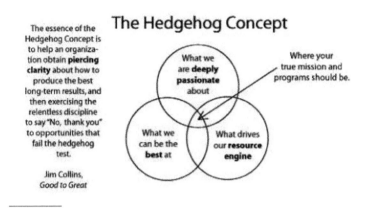

The essence of the Hedgehog Concept is to help an organization obtain **piercing clarity** about how to produce the best long-term results, and then exercising the relentless discipline to say "No, thank you" to opportunities that fail the hedgehog test.

Jim Collins,
Good to Great

Figure 18.15: The Hedgehog Concept

This distinction is absolutely crucial and has foundational implications for our I³ Impact framework.

What Collins confirms and verifies is the Integral notion and dynamic between the questions, all which are included and expanded upon when we work within the I³ framework, which is the architecture for our own flywheel for Impact.

Collins confirms that a culture that has developed the necessary resilience despite facing setbacks and mistakes has characteristics which enable, 'visionary companies [to] display a remarkable resiliency, an ability to bounce back from adversity. As a result, visionary companies attain extraordinary long-term performance.'

Resilience is key. Nassim Taleb expands, introducing 'anti-fragile: 'beyond resilience or robustness. The resilient resists shocks and stays the same; the antifragile gets better.' If we are to make both our own organisations and that of our Investees anti-fragile, we now have the prerequisite map and dynamic between what the four worlds of realms, rhythms, rounds ,and realities can provide in terms of insight; and we have the culture and governance systems to revisit them as and when required.

Collins says that:

> Core ideology provides the bonding glue that holds an organisation together as it grows, decentralizes, diversifies, expands globally, and attains diversity within.

This ideology is part of our culture; however, don't confuse tenets with culture. Tenets are the defined, clarified and codified principles on which the firm operates. Culture, as the collective psychology, gives us the codes as to 'how' things are done.

One of the primary tasks in taking a company from good to great is to create a culture wherein people have an open opportunity to be heard. To accomplish this, we must engage in four basic practises:

- Lead with questions, not answers. Leading from good to great does not mean developing answers and motivating everyone to follow a messianic vision; rather it means having the humility which we find rooted in our Integral South to understand that we do not yet have all the answers; and then ask questions leading to the best possible insights.

- Create a culture to engage in dialogue and debate which we find in our Integral East, not coercion. All good-to-great companies have a penchant for constructive debates, discussions and healthy conflict. Dialogue is used to engage people in the search for the best answers.

- Face reality and conduct autopsies without blame. Good-to-great leaders must take an honest look at the decisions made and their outcomes. These autopsies go a long way toward establishing understanding and learning which we find in our integral North, creating a climate where the truth is heard.

- Build red-flag mechanisms that enables information not to be ignored, so it must be acted upon which we now do in our Integral West. Good-to-great companies have no special access to information or formula than any other company; they simply give their stakeholders ample opportunities to provide unfiltered information and insights that can act as an early warning for potentially deeper problems.

Every institution, regardless how great it is, is vulnerable and at risk of decline. The law of nature, and research from credit ratings confirms that anyone can fall and statistically, most eventually do. But, as Collins' research emphasises, some companies can recover, and in some cases, if they are antifragile, become even stronger.

Decline, it turns out, is largely self-inflicted, often caused by hiring a charismatic leader from the outside who has not created the necessary internal relational capital for driving a successful company. The old adage that "prevention is better than cure" is apropos, as it seems that at the earlier stages, a disease is harder to detect but easier to cure versus easier to detect but harder to cure in later stages.

The right path to our recovery, as always, lies largely within finding reality in the situation. There are overlaps with Adizes' life cycle in terms of cultures and behaviours, which helps us to better frame the Impact investment and our outcomes.

Amidst the landscape of fallen great companies, Collins asks: How do the mighty fall? Can decline be detected early and avoided? How far can a company fall before the path toward doom becomes inevitable and unshakeable? How can companies reverse course? Collins' research suggests that not every marker shows up in every decline, and the presence of a marker does not necessarily mean that we have a disease, but it indicates an increased possibility of being in decline. Collins uncovered five stages of decline which we can use as a self-diagnostic checklist:

STAGE 1: HUBRIS BORN OF SUCCESS

As success feeds arrogance and a sense of being special, discipline begins to falter and poor decision-making enters. The role of luck is ignored and replaced with skill, expertise etc., to bolster the egos. The rhetoric of success and the formula is culturally static. "What" has now replaced our "why" with the knowledge around what drives the primary flywheel now preplaced with operational optimisation/maximisation.

STAGE 2: UNDISCIPLINED PURSUIT OF MORE

Hubris from stage 1 ('We're so great, we can do anything!') leads into stage 2, the undisciplined pursuit of more of whatever those in power see as 'success', confusing "Big" with "Great", setting up a vicious cycle of stress and strain. This leads to undisciplined leaps into areas with limited capacities and resources, misaligned with values, overreaching into spaces they don't belong, lacking consistent tactical excellence. Easy cash erodes cost discipline, while maintaining margins by increasing prices and drive revenue attendant with a more bureaucratic system and culture.

STAGE 3: DENIAL OF RISK AND PERIL

As the evidence of declining performance mounts, the culture dismisses, discounts or ignores the facts in an attempt to explain away the incoming reality whilst highlighting only the positive. The familiar "he, she, it" caused the problem, i.e., they externalise the problems and blame any likely suspect. The healthy characteristics which held everything together beccomes unstuck and the leadership takes more uncalculated risks without empirical validation. With increased tensions, communication suffers with a marked decline in the quality of dialogue and debate, flipping between consensus and dictatorship in an attempt to make decisions. Here the leadership often kneejerks and announces a new strategy and multiple reorganisations leading to a preoccupation with internal politics and survival. With leaders detaching themselves further their power and status becomes amplified as the organisation begins to become static.

STAGE 4: GRASPING FOR SALVATION

Instead of seeking ways to come out of denial, the leadership reaches for hope-driven expectations of what could save the company, which include a charismatic and visionary leader, a bold but untested strategy, a radical transformation, a dramatic cultural revolution, a hoped-for-blockbuster product, a game changing acquisition, or any number of other silver-bullet solutions. Given the leadership's investment in these silver bullets, their credibility is at stake so they will do anything to "sell the future", hype and paint these changes in a positive light. People inside the culture however, may at this point have already realised the truth and who was wearing the emperor's new clothing. The risk is that they feel anxious and now exhibit hasty, reactive behaviour, bordering on panic.

Panic as it happens is often a form of hubris. It comes from the false belief and sense of knowing exactly where the organisation is now heading: down. The culture now exhibits much confusion and cynicism about the leadership and their strategy. Cynicism is also often a result and reaction to over-romanticised expectations of the future which now faces the incoming reality.

STAGE 5: CAPITULATION TO IRRELEVANCE OR DEATH

Here leaders may sell, leave or disband but in many cases the organisation just runs into the sand, atrophying into insignificance, or just dies and disappears.

One of the reasons we have spent time on declining organisations is that one can learn more about how an organisation can succeed from decline than from success. Exploring and knowing the downside of things gives us information about what we don't want; we need to position our so-called failures as stepping stones for increased knowledge and direction.

Having added the life-cycle framework, let us examine more deeply our personal integral impact journey, like Socrates who said that 'The unexamined life is not worth living.'

Chapter 19

From CIO to CIO, the new role and meaning of the Chief Impact Officer

> A radical inner transformation and rise to a new level of consciousness might be the only real hope we have in the current global crisis brought on by the dominance of the Western mechanistic paradigm.

Stanislav Grof[251]

Leadership development is psychologically similar to parenting. The neurological set-up and construct of a leader contain the same seeds from our primordial relationships as in other areas of life. Depending on how these primordial relationships were installed and now held, we will have some surplus and deficiencies in the 5 As, (attention, acceptance, appreciation, affection and allowing) which we explored earlier.

It is quite possible that the cultural leadership norm in finance is based on an egocentric approach to ensuring one's perceived needs are met first (through money, property and prestige) while the firm's long-term needs are relegated to a secondary position. It is possible that many senior managers within finance would, from a psychological perspective, be diagnosed with varying degrees of several pathologies and neuroses, such as delusional and extreme self-centeredness, impostor syndrome, heightened entitlement expectancy, lack of empathy, and lack of understanding of cause and effects. For example, Kets de Vries writes[252],

> My experience has shown that feelings of neurotic imposture profligate in contemporary organisations: I encounter this type of dysfunctional perception and behaviour all the time, particularly when working with executives in high-powered consulting firms and investment banking... Power is so intoxicating, so addictive, that only the hardiest individuals can survive it without psychopathology.

This is why we need to carefully consider the governance design and the management of power complexes within the I^3 framework. Paul Babiak and Robert Hare suggest that many boardrooms are riddled with individuals who otherwise would be diagnosed as psychopaths[253]:

Only a fraction of psychopaths are in prison. The rest thrive in the many target-rich environments that make up society, including business, religious, political, and social organisations, and the Internet.

Importantly, egocentric people struggle to see (and value) those who exhibit grace, peace, gentleness and care, as these are often mistaken as weaknesses. Not surprisingly, the latter are often left behind in the climb up the corporate greasy pole and are rarely in positions where the power complex dominates. During my own career it was evident that to progress in the upper echelons of management one needed to assimilate whatever culture was prevalent. In a particular firm, which professed to run a 'meritocracy', the reality was opposite, with a highly politicised culture and favouring of conformity. Part of the same firm's culture was that they only hired PhDs; however, PhD stood for 'Poor, Hungry and a Desire to become seriously rich'. Ego, money, prestige and power dominated the hierarchical drivers and left the culture undernourished in terms of its additional human needs.

> The economic stream, on the other hand, flies in the face of empirical reality: persons' actions are shaped, redirected, constrained by the social context; norms, interpersonal trust, social networks, and social organisation are important in the functioning not only of the society but also of the economy.

Our relationships are based on our ability to conceptualise others; we label and add content to another person's identity upon first meeting. Our own conceptual identity is a source of many dysfunctions as it is always in a state of un-fulfilled identity and, as such, may use others to feel superior. It is always looking to enhance itself if in deficit; if we can't do it by being better than others, then we can become different, e.g., become a victim.

Most religions say that parts of our ego must die us to find our true self, as explained by the psychotherapist Kathleen Dowling Singh:

> The ordinary mind and its delusions die in the Nearing Death Experience. As death carries us off, it is impossible to any longer pretend that who we are is our ego. The ego is transformed in the very carrying off. [254]

Although character and virtue have been discussed since Aristotle, organisational scholarship is only just beginning to assess the contribution of character strengths and virtuous behaviours within the realm of leadership as a subset of organisational development. In essence, character strengths represent the way we have operationalised the neurological constructs of virtue.

A 'character' was initially an imprinted symbol used by bricklayers to indicate the source of a brick[255], which indicated the character of the creator and thus the product's quality and integrity. When the distance and complexity between maker/producer and user/ consumer is short and personal, character can be of paramount importance. We know that traditionally in Japan, if a swordsmith's sword broke during battle, the client could die or be wounded. This was a direct reflection of the quality of the sword itself and its maker, often resulting in the maker taking hara-kiri to create restitution. It is no coincidence that in such traditions quality and attention to detail prevails to this day.

Character is pervasive and influences a person's 'vision, goals, self-concept, strategies, work ethic, attitude, perception, code of ethics, behaviour, and the search for excellence[256, p.36]' There is an adage that states that the measure of a person's character is what he or she does when no one is looking; furthermore, 'character may not even be relevant unless someone is called on to use it[257]'. As such, development of character strengths such as humility are fundamental for leadership positions as evidenced by Adizes and Collins.

Norman Schwarzkopf suggested:'99% of leadership failures are failure of character, leadership is a potent combination between strategy and character, and if you have to lose one, lose the strategy.'

As teachers of ancient wisdom have suggested, we are shaped by our challenges and experiences; if overcome, we embrace new insights as gifts. The late Steve Jobs said that: 'The only way to do great work, is to love what you do

Impact investment enables us to embark on a new path of individuation. As mentioned, part of our problem in understanding full-spectrum impact lies in our capacity to integrate and find balance in our many intelligences. For most of us, this is the need for the head to descend into the heart or 'combine soul with role'. The heart is our core, in which all aspects of our 'how' wrestle with the questions on which our impact intentionality hinges. Can we explore and listen to the views and opinions of 'the other'? Can we hold ambiguity and difference within our dialectic so that our deeper intelligence can find solutions rather than our ego create conflicts? Do we have enough courage (heart) not to be afraid of things we don't want to hear? Do we avoid dialogue with those we disagree with ??

Another personality area is one of deserving and being worthy of creating, giving, and receiving good things. This function is embedded in our sense of self-worth, self-esteem, and identity. Do we see ourselves as the true and honoured recipient, or do we generate negative feelings (including guilt and shame) once we have overreached in our capacity levels to hold these gifts? This often subconsciously invokes self-sabotaging strategies once we have reached a level we consider to be sufficient for our self-worth. We want to remain within our comfort zone. Many 'achievers' are not necessarily more proficient or capable but they have not been loaded with as much negative self-talk.

This is important for impact, since we can only give to another that which we have ourselves. This is why impact is a form of 'soul work', for which I³ can provide the dynamic dance and framework in order to expand the capacities of the soul.

Aristotle writes in his Nicomachean Ethics:

> Greatness of soul, as the very name suggests, is concerned with things that are great, and we must first grasp of what sort these are... Well, a person is considered to be magnanimous if he thinks that he is worthy of great things, provided he is worthy of them; because anyone who esteems his own worth unduly is foolish, and nobody who acts virtuously is foolish or stupid[258].

The first step to becoming a great soul is to think that one is worthy of great things. The point is to be committed and to serve something bigger than ourselves i.e., Impact.

For those whose ways of creating reality come from the predominantly tangible (and only from the head) the above will be almost incomprehensible. The soul and heart with their invisible dynamics are more at work here; if not, we risk our core being like an alienated species which belongs to a different world. However, inner and outer realities constantly interact as the source of our creativity, and in co-creating the realities in which we live.

Head domination may have worked brilliantly with the 'finance and economics only' Western dimension and the intellectual North, so we may have not realised that this distorted view does not work when we have to rely on, or integrate other areas. As such, we often see that traditional CIOs require significant back-up from other people who may better represent these other dimensions, hence the need in many firms for a 'Head of Impact.'

It is not a coincidence that such positions today are filled by evolved females who may carry more capacity than men within the heart area and, more often, can view the world from the inside out. They often have a greater ability to think with the mind descended into the heart, integrating cognition and emotion to create a different type of courage necessary to create new knowledge and intuitive insights. However, let us also carefully consider the 'Head of Impact' role within the power complex, as quite often this is the more conventional CIO role.

What tensions are created between the finance dimension and others, and how are they resolved? What levels of influence does the CIO have? Do co-creative solutions solve issues, or does a pragmatic CIO trump the final decisions as the 'senior' committee member by diminishing the relevance of other ideas?

A CIO's role includes creating spaces where we can go deeper, so that the intellect and a new dialectic can emerge, where the inner and outer realities converge with the core where our capacities and faculties lie. In our meetings, this will undoubtedly create both inner and outer tensions within ourselves and between others. However, if we hold these tensions in a co-creative space where we can leverage our collective intelligences, solutions and outcomes will be better. How we create our forum is an integral part of our governance, and therefore its impact effectiveness.

In C.G Jung's 'Definitions' he reminds us yet again of the imperative that:

> As the individual is not just a single, separate being, but by his[sic] very existence presupposes a collective relationship, it follows that the process of individuation must lead to more intense and broader collective relationships and not to isolation [93]

These tensions enable the heart, like any muscle, to exercise and grow; thus, people are less likely to explode in fury and anger. When managed healthily, conflict is an opportunity for a group to expand, build further resilience and share an open heart. Absence of conflict is not necessarily a sign of a healthy group but rather that the power complex is alive and active.

Our awakening conscience is through the lens of difference and experienced perspectives. Integrality carries a psychodynamic and consciousness-based healing perspective that can contribute to any change dynamic. Organisations, in this sense, have a 'pastoral' responsibility as a person's core-holding vessel.

What people see is far more important than what they hear. People do what they see. As John Maxwell writes[259]:

> Eighty-nine percent of what people learn comes through visual stimulation; ten percent through audible stimulation and one per cent through other senses... What they hear they understand. What they see they believe!' Such environments, like the family of origin, profoundly influence the developing outlook and values system.

As we move into a more Integral age, firms gain new competitive advantages by moving into deeper and broader integral perspectives. This needs to be translated into an investment methodology that spans the schisms, and heals the divides between financial drivers and their inevitable impacts across the four worlds. The new leadership models now include intuition and foresight as part of the central ethic of the CIO whose role, in essence, is to predict the future by knowing the unknowable and seeing the unforeseeable. This requires additional and deeper capacities, many of which will transcend space and time.

The American parapsychologist and Noetic researcher Dean Radin suggests that the window of consciousness has perceptional capacities on which we can draw[260],

> When you step back from all the research and studies, what you find is a spectacular body of converging evidence indicating on our understanding of time is seriously incomplete. Those studies mean that some aspect of our mind can perceive the future. Not infer the future, or anticipate the future, or figure out the future. But actually perceive it.' So this is all good news.

It is part of our nature to explore and investigate. Depending on the outcome of such experiences, we become more (or less) comfortable in experiencing the unknown and unfamiliar. These are just some examples of the territories?? we may need to explore to understand the limitations and barriers we experience as a leader and as part of our own individuation using impact.

As mentioned, unless we find a way to integrate impact as part of our individuation process, we will not only short-change ourselves and those around us but also not fully reach our potential. C.G. Jung reminds us that,

> Individuation has two principle aspects: in the first place it is an internal and subjective process of integration, and in the second it is an equally indispensable process of objective relationship. Neither can exist without the other, although sometimes the one and sometimes the other predominates.

Life, as we know it, is an extraordinary experience. Whilst pondering its component parts, I constructed the following humouristic representation which attempts to depict how the summary of life is made up from several characteristics and drivers inside and outside of our control.

COMPONENT PARTS OF LIFE

$$\sum \infty = \frac{\Delta(q \times \beta)}{\Omega} + \alpha^3(\epsilon + r)$$

$\sum \infty$ = Sum of Life; Δ = Decisions

q = Choices; β = Impact

α = Attitude; ϵ = Experience

r = Response; Ω = Luck

The integral CIO now has to embrace systemic complexity and ambiguity to form a broad spectrum of precedents and areas that report into him or her. So what does this mean in terms of requirements and the work ahead?

Joseph Jaworski puts it succinctly[105],

The capacity to discover and participate in our unfolding future has more to do with our being – our total orientation of character and consciousness – that with what we do. Leadership is about creating, day by day, a domain in which we and others continuously deepen our understanding of reality and are able to participate in shaping the future. This, then, is the deeper territory of leadership – collective 'listening' to what is wanting to emerge in the world, and then having the courage to do what is required.

Whilst this applies to all leadership, the integral CIO needs to create an investment environment where this can occur but which may include new roles and areas as integrally outlined. Several organisations such as AP Fonden of Sweden, and Robeco of the Netherlands have created the new role of Chief Active Ownership Officer in line with PRI guidelines which indicate a shift in thinking and actions.

Eric Butterworth writes:

You may say, 'But I am only human.' This is the understatement of your life. You are not only human—you are also divine in potential. The fulfilment of all your goals and aspirations in life depends upon stirring up and releasing more of that divine potential. And there is really nothing difficult about letting this inner light shine. All we must do is correct the tendency to turn off our light when we face darkness.

§19.1 From transformation to contribution

> Individuation does not shut one out from the world, but gathers the world to itself
>
> ——————————————————————
>
> C.G. Jung. On the Nature of the Psyche

This becomes the question of how we, through the medium of impact investments, build ourselves into a person of character and humility in the face of complexity, ambiguity, and contrast, formed through questioning and challenging the conventional wisdom within our firms.

Paulo Freire writes that our task ahead is crystal clear:

> If I am not in the world simply to adapt to it, but rather transform it, and if it is not possible to change the world without a certain dream or vision for it, I must make use of every possibility there is not only to speak about my utopia, but also to engage in practises consistent with it. [261]

As has been highlighted, our lives are a journey of becoming more fully, so the question is: what are we becoming and do we like what we see? Do we have a mirror, and if not, why not? How do we clean our mirror when it becomes dirty or foggy? The creation of capital by itself is useless, unless it fuels us towards our destination. What level of participation and vulnerability have we managed to create for ourselves? Have we extended the frontier of what defines our reward in work to include defined areas of Impact?

John Ruskin reminds us that: 'The highest reward for a person's toil is not what they get for it, but what they become by it[262].' As we step into the realities of impact, we realise that there are multiple truths and perspectives. Like with any muscle, we have developed the capacity to hold tensions and ambiguities that come with the territory.

Within our organisational settings and hierarchy, do we have the courage and imagination to hold this reality as truth, in order to empower all of us? Paulo Freire highlights the challenge but also calls for courage on our impact journey[48]:

> The radical, committed to human liberation, does not become the prisoner of a 'circle of certainty' within which reality is also imprisoned. On the contrary, the more radical the person is, the more fully he or she enters into reality so that, knowing it better, he or she can better transform it. This individual is not afraid to confront, to listen, to see the world unveiled. This person is not afraid to meet the people or to enter into dialogue with them. This person does not

consider himself or herself the proprietor of history or of all people, or the liberator of the oppressed; but he or she does commit himself or herself, within history, to fight at their side.

To what extent have we transcended, and included, a bigger self and understood the limitations of our ego with its made-up beliefs? Can I move into that space where I'm being challenged and feel the life-blood pumping in? There is no other way of being alive than being in that conversation. Ken Wilber sets the scene:

> For authentic transformation is not a matter of belief but of the death of the believer; not a matter of translating the world but of transforming the world; not a matter of finding solace but of finding infinity on the other side of death. The self is not made content; the self is made toast. [263]

Finding the forum, community, and safe space for the dialectic to emerge was key to my understanding that everything we know is through difference, comparing and contrasting our internal dialogue with others. Are we asking the right questions? Back to Paulo Freire[48]:

> How can I dialogue if I always project ignorance onto others and never perceive my own? How can I dialogue if I am closed to – and even offended by – the contribution of others? At the point of encounter there are neither yet ignoramuses nor perfect sages; there are only people who are attempting, together, to learn more than they now know.

This can be viewed as per the Swedish social researchers, Alvesson and Skoldberg, in three theoretical hermeneutical strands that each individual needs to develop for their own understanding and interpretative practise[264]:

- a hermeneutic understanding of history, language and meaning

- a social theory of society as a totality, and

- a theory of the unconscious.

Impact therefore asks us to become our own social researcher and dig into our hermeneutic background and culture to explore how these may differ from others when we look towards our impact sphere. It has been said that it is our eyes that are the windows to our soul; it is also only through our own eyes that we can see ourselves in the mirror. If we don't look for transformational development for our own internal Impact, we will only be able to perform the impact tasks intellectually as ordered by our organisation. Such a state would be incongruous if we are to live as authentic impact investors; we have to find the light from within that can shine into our world of impact.

The Swiss-American psychiatrist Elisabeth Kubler-Ross put this aspect most beautifully[265], 'People are like stained-glass windows. They sparkle and shine when the sun is out, but when the darkness sets in, their true beauty is revealed only if there is a light from within.' There it is, made categorically clear, the inside-out and outside-in, double-sided mirror in which we can reflect our Impact consciousness back out into the world.

Within our firms, when we look at the ingredients for good organisational culture, we find that these are human characteristics from which we need to draw our understanding of our organisational impact culture. Here's an exercise: please rank each principle below on a scale of 1(worst)–10(best) for your organisation. Then honestly ask yourself: where are the gaps?

Table 19.1: Fr. Byron's Principles of Good Corporate Culture

Integrity. Wholeness, solidarity of character, honesty, trustworthiness and responsibility

Veracity. Telling the truth in all circumstances; accountability and transparency

Fairness. Treating equals equally, giving to everyone his or her

Human dignity. Acknowledging a person's inherent worth; respectful recognition of another's value simply for being human

Participation. Respecting another's right or not to be ignored on the job or shut down from decision making within the organisation

Commitment. Dependability, reliability, fidelity, loyalty and consistency

Social Responsibility. An obligation to loon to the interest of the broader community and to treat the community as a stakeholder in what the enterprise does

Common Good. Alignment of one's personal interests with the community's well-being

Subsidiarity. No decision should be taken at a higher level that can be made as effectively and efficiently at a lower lever in the organisation... never do for others what thet can do for themselves... respect for proper autonomy

Love. An internalized conviction that prompts a willingness to sacrifice one's time, convenience, and a share of one's ideas and material goods for the good of others.

Developing the new CIO role is not easy, and none of this can be accomplished unless we are willing and able to work with the inner self and not rely on our organisational position to make things happen. The temptation is always to take a seemingly easier route, a short-cut that we think no-one will notice.

We need balance to our endeavours that does not compromise the end objective of becoming. This means going beyond conventional thinking, as the former four-star general Colin Powell states: 'Leadership is the art of accomplishing more than the science of management says is possible[266].'

As an emerging CIO in integral guise, a key question to be asked is: What new life and life-forms seek to enter the world through me? This meditative question may take a lifetime to answer, and in many ways I hope it does; our work is never done. If our sole purpose is working towards retirement where we can finally relax, sit back and enjoy the good things in life, we will have missed the point.

§19.2 Impact contemplation

We are in a constant process of creation. Each transaction is an opportunity for the best of our inner selves to emerge. With the integral approach that means the whole of us, every single component part, and to the very depth of our soul. This means taking time for contemplation.

Joseph Campbell instructs us:

> You must have a room, or a certain hour or so a day, where you don't know what was in the newspapers that morning, you don't know who your friends are, you don't know what you owe anybody, you don't know what anybody owes to you. This is a place where you can simply experience and bring forth what you are and what you might be. This is the place of creative incubation. At first you may find that nothing happens there. But if you have a sacred place and use it, something eventually will happen. [267]

Indeed, something always happens; there is always something around the metaphorical corner. The theologian and teacher, Beverly Lanzetta writes:

> Contemplation is beyond the normal consciousness of the mind, granting access to the mystery, known only by love. Here, the normal activities of the human personality come to rest, in order to hear what has remained unheard and to see what has been hidden or veiled. The mystics call this kind of knowing 'unknowing' insofar as it approaches reality from the spiritual core of the person and not from the mind alone.

> Far more than a meditative practise or a temporary respite from worldly concerns, contemplation revolutionizes conventional attitudes and roles in order to transform the foundation upon which life is lived. And to illuminate the hidden teaching of love inscribed in our souls. [268]

In 2012, Pope Benedict XVI invited Rowan Williams, then Archbishop of Canterbury and leader of the Anglican Church in England, to address the

Synod of Catholic bishops. Williams emphasised the broader, foundational and radical importance of contemplation and building further on the 'why', which we can clearly see its importance and for impact[269]:

> Contemplation is very far from being just one kind of thing that Christians do: it is the key to prayer, liturgy, art and ethics, the key to the essence of a renewed humanity that is capable of seeing the world and other subjects in the world with freedom— freedom from self-oriented, acquisitive habits and the distorted understanding that come from them. To put it boldly, contemplation is the only ultimate answer to the unreal and insane world that our financial systems and our advertising culture and our chaotic and unexamined emotions encourage us to inhabit. To learn contemplative prayer is to learn what we need so as to live truthfully and honestly and lovingly. It is a deeply revolutionary matter.

We also must understand that there are cultural differences in how any such practises are actualised. For example, in many African and African American cultures contemplation is a communal outward experience, in contrast to the West, where it is more individual and private.

I hope that by taking some time to travel through some of the background and key tenets of the integral four worlds, we have gained an appetite for more understanding and for knowing how to implement this approach in ourselves and our organisation.

Impact investments is a blend of art and science. We have been looking mostly at the artist in us, complemented by a scientific framework. I make no excuses for the integral approach; yes, it is complex, but that is because it is complete. Like all things, progress comes with practise. Our journey will be straight, it will always have corners, behind which we find new experiences and insights.

When we travel, the unexpected fills the journey with new and expanded meaning but, if we don't have the wherewithal to see it, it will pass us by and be lost forever. Our task is to be open and contemplative to what the impact dimension can bring into our lives using both mind and heart. As C.G. Jung said, 'Your vision will become clear only when you can look into your own heart. Who looks outside, dreams; who looks inside, awakes[270].' We cannot sleepwalk into impact as if it is just another technical subject we need to conquer.

A last word on the importance of impact on contemplation:

> All forms of contemplation share the same goal: to help us see through the deceptions of self and world in order to get in touch with what Howard Thurman called 'the sound of the genuine' within us and around us. Contemplation does not need to be defined in terms of particular practises, such as meditation, yoga,

tai chi, or lectio divina. Instead, it can be defined by its function: contemplation is any way one has of penetrating illusion and touching reality.[160]

Our individuation depends on how we interact with the function and practise of impact in its entirety; as in marriage, we ignore or leave important pieces out at our peril. Trust our instincts, and when we move into the realms of possibility we will find that faith meets us. It is our homecoming into the house of belonging.

THE HOUSE OF BELONGING

I awoke this morning in the gold light turning this way and that thinking for a moment it was one day like any other. But the veil had gone from my darkened heart and I thought it must have been the quiet candlelight that filled my room, it must have been the first easy rhythm with which I breathed myself to sleep, it must have been the prayer I said speaking to the otherness of the night.

And I thought this is the good day you could meet your love, this is the black day someone close to you could die. This is the day you realize how easily the thread is broken between this world and the next and I found myself sitting up in the quiet pathway of light, the tawny close grained cedar burning round me like fire and all the angels of this housely heaven ascending through the first roof of light the sun has made. This is the bright home in which I live, this is where I ask my friends to come, this is where I want to love all the things it has taken me so long to learn to love.

This is the temple of my adult aloneness and I belong to that aloneness as I belong to my life.

There is no house like the house of belonging.

David Whyte, 1996

PART III

Changing the firms in which we **invest**

Image courtesy of Kay Jackson [2]

Chapter 20

Impact 1.0

> Long-term commitment to new learning and new philosophy
> is required of any management that seeks transformation.
> The timid and the fainthearted, and the people that expect
> quick results, are doomed to disappointment

William Edwards Deming[271]

Let us clarify: when we simplify by denominating things into a hierarchy (e.g., a 1.0 to gain structure, simplification and order), the risk is always to assume that one thing is better or worse than another rather than digging deeper into our understanding. Hierarchies based on natural order, however, 'transcend and include.' One serves as a foundation for the next, without which it could not exist or come into being.

Calling anything 'Impact 1.0, 2.0 and 3.0', as in this book on impact, grossly oversimplifies the rich field of the impact industry with its nuanced variations and overlaps, so my apologies as we illustrate what is required for moving towards a transformative development at each stage. Today we see a continued distinction between a world dominated by conventional investments on the one hand and philanthropy and gifting on the other. Impact currently aims to fit inside this paradigm, and each of us must find our home. This depends on context, culture, and possibly religion, for example with the use of Islamic finance. However, Impact 1.0 has evolved historically out of corporate social responsibility (CSR), social auditing and reporting, and well-being economics. It is now embedding ESG as its next evolutionary stage.

We have now evolved from the mindset and culture of 'doing less bad is not good enough' into trying to do more good. The history of CSR can be traced back to Ancient Mesopotamia (1700 BC) when King Hammurabi introduced a code in which builders and innkeepers were put to death if their negligence caused the deaths of others, or major inconvenience to local citizens. In Ancient Rome senators grumbled about the failure of businesses to contribute sufficient taxes to fund their military campaigns, while in 1622 disgruntled shareholders in the Dutch East India Company issued pamphlets complaining about management secrecy and 'self-enrichment'.

With industrialisation, the impacts of business on society and the environment assumed an entirely new dimension. The 'corporate paternalists' of the late 19th and early 20th centuries used some of their wealth to support philanthropic ventures. By the 1920s, discussions about the social responsibilities of business had evolved into the beginnings of the 'modern' CSR movement. As the current format of CSR emerged out of the social consciousness soup of the 1950s, the primary focus was to add business responsibilities prevalent at the time. 'The phrase Corporate Social Responsibility was coined in 1953 with the publication of Bowen's Social Responsibility of Businessmen' (Corporate Watch Report, 2006).

In the 1960s and 1970s managers began implementing CSR alongside traditional management functions. However, in the 1980s business and social interest grew closer and firms became more responsive to their stakeholders. New inclusions into annual reports evidenced that CSR added value to a firm. In 1990 CSR became standard in the industry with companies like Price Waterhouse Cooper and KPMG becoming consultants. CSR has now evolved beyond just code of conduct and reporting, creating initiatives in NGOs, multi- stakeholder, and ethical trading. (Corporate Watch Report, 2006)[1]

By the late 1990s, CSR became a part of boardroom discussions, with Shell Oil, the first company to implement CSR, in 1998. (Corporate Watch Report, 2006)[272]. With more generally well-informed citizens, social awareness was increasing. With tensions resulting in social unrest, CSR potentially threatened firms if not managed properly. During the 1990s, CSR became almost universally approved, and coupled with strategy literature. During the 2000s, CSR became an important strategic issue, but today the CSR has taken more of a backseat vis-à-vis ESG.

It is also important to note that, whilst CSR was in essence the first introduction within firms of a structured social dimension impacting the firm, it has for many firms become more of a box-ticking exercise. This caused Unilever to introduce their 'beyond CSR' program. This arrested development in social responsibility has many reasons, one being that CSR has been driven mainly by commercial interests, and thus has never exited the narrow Western and Northern dimensions. As such, as the early social drivers diminished, CSR eventually detached itself from its roots never to be renewed in its originating social grounds.

As history risks repeating, particularly when the paradigm that created the initial problem has not changed, implications for impact are important.

---

[1]Essays, UK. (November 2018). Corporate Social Responsibility: History, Benefits and Types. Retrieved from

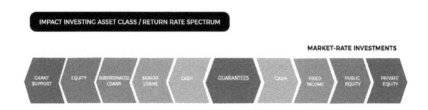

Figure 20.1: Impact Investment Spectrum[a]

---

[a]The Global Impact Investing Network (GIIN)[273]

As CSR did not have a GENE to continuously ground itself back into the roots of the social dimension, it died, which impact will repeat during the coming decades unless we work integrally and with the GENE.

Another reason for its demise is that, like impact, CSR straddles the often-perceived conflict between financial return and social responsibility. The spectrum of capital is mainly a construct by financiers to segregate and understand different buckets or risk/return. Most firms don't necessarily care about what we call our 'capital' or product, as long as it fits with their needs and serves the purpose of financing the firm. However, if we are to influence the firms in which we invest for impact, this spectrum is mission critical for reasons previously discussed. Our impact approach must be framed accordingly, as this positions the nature and scope of our entry, and sets the tone for any ongoing relationship with a firm. Such a spectrum can take the following shape of figure 20.1

Following the drive over the past fifty years to develop full-cost accounting, out of which the recycling movement emerged, some key concepts were further developed which have also been historically foundational for Impact. First the triple-bottom-line (TBL/3BL), introduced by John Elkington[274] in the mid-1990s, accounting for:

- People, the social equity bottom line
- Planet, the environmental bottom line
- Profit, the economic bottom line

The TBL has been widely explored and adopted. The Anglo-Dutch oil company Shell's first incorporated it in their 1997 sustainability report. These pillars have been further developed:

- People can be viewed in three dimensions — organisational needs, individual needs, and community issues.

- Profit is a function of both the sales stream, with a focus on customer service, and the adoption of a retention and new client strategy to reduce and replace churn and leavers.

- The planet can be divided into a multitude of subdivisions, although reduce, reuse, and recycle is a start.

We then evolved into the Integrated Bottom Line (IBL) which takes the accounting methodology further by suggesting that firms integrate their financial, economic, and social performance reporting into one integrated balance sheet, thereby providing a more holistic and 'integral' lens into the firm's performance, enabling strategies for long-term value creation. A weakness is the assumed adoption of consensual accounting principles which has limited its methodology. As we will discover, accounting principles and standards are the Achilles heel of any Impact end process.

Here we need also to mention the important work of Jed Emerson who coined the term 'blended value' in which he makes it clear that:

> In truth, the core nature of investment and return is not a trade-off between social and financial interest but rather the pursuit of an embedded value proposition composed of both[275, Page 37]

His proposal comports with the integral approach, since blended value assumes that the nature of value is whole and indivisible; yet is fundamental natural drivers of financial, social, and environmental value.

The value itself is then pursued, mined, and expressed through the different types of organisational forms, capital structures and investment instruments in which we seek to embed them. It is from this basis and foundation that we see the emergence of the SDGs and today's 'impact' investment frameworks.

If we return to our basic premise that all investments are (and actually have) 'impact', and should therefore be viewed through the same basic lens, clearly impact needs to develop further to become the new global market convention that many now predict. This may be done by blending returns from multiple capital perspectives and sources, each investment firm creating their own formula seeking to attract outside capital, positioning themselves deliberately, with clarity and communication, by dialing up and down each dimension, which accounting methodology speaks to both the impact and return that comports with their vision and mission.

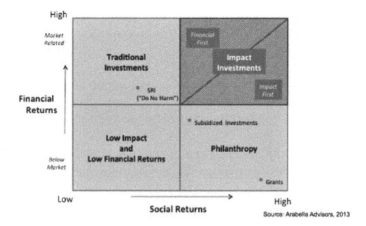

Figure 20.2: Capital Intentions

Also, creating social and environmental impact through more traditional investment vehicles has the potential to migrate and crowd-in significant amounts of capital to work towards creating positive impact, and thus increase the appeal to mainly philanthropically motivated investors. These aspirations and expectations are depicted in the following matrix, along the spectrum and dimensions of financial return and social impact.

Whilst traditional investments are typically made without regarding social impact, and philanthropic contributions are made without any real consideration of financial returns, impact investing incorporates both. This sometimes creates a schism equivalent to a psychosis; and as C.G. Jung once defined insanity as a 'separation from self' we need to integrate the splinter parts of ourselves.

Don't get me wrong, philanthropy has a significant role to play within the capital spectrum but should not substitute for alleviating a guilty conscience for those with 'excess' capital, made from the conventional economic and financial model of organisational management. As Aristotle understood:

> To give away money is an easy matter, and in any man's power. But to decide to whom to give it, and how large and when, and for what purpose, and how, is neither in every man's power, nor an easy matter. Hence it is that such excellence is rare, praiseworthy, and noble.[276]

This reverts to the notion that if all investments are impact investments, and when looking through a lens such as I³, we also need to include industries that are considered 'bad' (e.g., oil and gas, mining, etc.), and how responsible investors can influence them to improve and develop more positively. Whilst sometimes the good obstruct the better, as investors we possess stakeholder influence to work effectively with companies across the good/bad spectrum. In addition, many financially motivated investors now see impact as a smart 'lens' through which to view their investments. Here are a few reasons:

I. Investors are connecting their financial portfolio and their philanthropic giving more as a system. For example, if we make a pure investment in fossil fuels, while simultaneously donating to environmental causes, it means that the capital in the financial portfolio may contravene the capital in the philanthropic allocation.

II. More investors understand that it is 'good business' for companies to incorporate positive social and environmental practises into their operations, and that they are more likely to reduce associated risks and create more value for investors over time.

III. Undoubtedly there are also some big financial opportunities connected to impact (e.g., in renewables). PWC's megatrend analysis points to several areas, suggesting that health care, education, urbanization, the rise of emerging economies, and climate change will be amongst the biggest challenges and opportunities.

IV. Last, but not least, as discussed, we are moving into an 'integral age' as more investors are aligning their financial portfolios with their clarified personal values.

As these trends accelerate, the aim is for impact to continue to develop accounting systems that measure financial capital returns, and for other capitals such as social, natural, and cultural to become imperative. Unless achieved, at the collective level most of the current and traditional investment philosophy will continue to relate to pure and simple operational profit maximisation and continuation of the status quo, trying to maintain the industrial and investment landscape without attempting to change its models, structures or axioms.

If financial capital is to assume its rightful, equal position in any organisational capital hierarchy, owners of such capital will need to value capital in other forms and understand that the purely rent-seeking approach must be complemented or the rent will be adjusted downwards over time.

It seems that the core of the emergent impact investment philosophy stems from the awareness that we must collectively find a better approach that benefits both people and the planet. Our economy is to a large degree intrinsically destructive of everything non-financial and of investment in the future due to short-termism, which means that a large amount of global capital is diverted into speculation.

At the individual level Impact investment, even in its current infancy, could become the catalyst to re-introduce a portion of the human spirit back into capitalism, thereby reestablishing a developmental and personal individuation process which is currently lacking in most organisations. If anything, the current operating model requires dis-individuation, a disconnection between task and true meaning and the individual. Also, individual investment thinking processes need to shift from conventional linear digitisation and abstract rationalisation toward systems-based thinking. Only thus can we re-build the lost linkages and connectivity which lie deep inside our consciousness and operational thinking.

As former US President, Bill Clinton suggested:

> If ordinary people don't perceive that our grand ideas are working in their lives then they can't develop the higher level of consciousness, to use a term that American philosopher Ken Wilber wrote a whole book about… He said, 'You know, the problem is the world needs to be more integrated, but it requires a consciousness that's way up here, and an ability to see beyond the differences amongst us'[277]

Firms with an impact methodology need to address and re-balance this aspect as part of the investment process, otherwise results will be devoid of the all-important ethic of the moral code and risk being executed without any real integrity for the ultimate outcomes. Impact can potentially turn the traditional transactional and resource-competitive relationship with an investee into more of a partnership. Therefore, firms seeking impact investment frameworks must recognise the psychological processes that are evoked, and the need for these processes to become sustainable in themselves.

Whilst individual members of the investment community contemplate and deliberate this 'new' approach and how to position themselves on 'the spectrum of capital', it is also imperative to recognise that, from a historical and cultural perspective, impact investing is nothing new; rather, we are rediscovering some of the core elements of finance that were lost during the industrial revolution and over the past decades of asset monetisation and globalisation.

In essence, impact investing will heal the wounded planet and its people. But as we know, healing requires the patient to come out of denial and into awareness and truth, which is extraordinarily difficult. As Naguib Mahfouz points out in his book Palace of Desire:

> The problem is not that the truth is harsh but that liberation from ignorance is as painful as being born. Run after truth until you're breathless. Accept the pain involved in re-creating yourself afresh. These ideas will take a lifetime to comprehend, a hard one interspersed with drunken moments. [278]

The question therefore, is through what lens are we looking and what map are we using to diagnose, understand and address the issues at hand? Another integral question is how we define and value 'success' in our organisations.

Chapter 21

Impact 2.0

> Sometimes the good can be the enemy of the better
>
> C.G. Jung

As the drivers behind the Impact 1.0 movement accelerate, Impact 2.0 is evolving and becoming the modus operandi within the industry. This second level is categorised by several meta characteristics:

- Funds specialising in already clearly defined and understood positive impact themes (e.g., renewables, low-cost housing, health, micro-credit, etc.) As the second generation of Impact 1.0, many funds remain small in comparison to finance-first and market-based equivalents. However, these funds have developed a concise message to investors with advances in communication and impact reporting methodology.

- Finance-first and market-return investors experimenting with impact as an offshoot from their existing business. This is characterised by clearly defined thematic approaches in, for example, healthcare and agriculture, and possible synergy within existing fund management expertise and experience.

- Funds looking for commercial Impact perspectives are growing exponentially.

- The spectrums and prisms of capital are merging and overlapping (see the map below), where blocks of capital are migrating towards areas of commercial opportunity and high impact areas. On the one hand, going from Finance only looking for mainly financial returns to Philanthropic where returns are either not required on capital or of capital.

- Multiple providers and standard bearers of impact methods and methodology that are in creative tension and compete with each other as supported and financed by interest groups and/or are sponsored by multinational governments.

- Large institutional investors moving decisively towards impact, realising the shift in trends and commercial opportunity.

- Investment consciousness building, gaining momentum given current rates of diminishing financial returns combined with climate and social change.

An important prism inside the capital spectrum is investee influence and control, which evokes the power complex and relates directly to ESG governance. With power complex we mean all the psychological and relational dynamics invoked in an investment, including levels of ownership, dominance, and advantages that occur during the investment journey, at which point these are activated. Whilst influence and control are separate, they are a function of the type and structure of the investment, in combination with the importance within the capital structure of a firm.

At one obvious extreme, most derivatives do not qualify for involvement, so holding a small stake in a public company would require mobilising with others; this occurs across the globe though shareholder activism. Impact potential between investor and investee, however, is about the collaborative and co-creative dialectic that occurs from the initial encounter, and during the capital negotiations and due diligence. Here the firm can add significant value from an industry impact perspective, and can help the business find solutions to develop.

It is during these interactions that impact potential turns into impact objective outcomes and the investee gets aligned with its implementation. This is the fulcrum on which our actual impact acts as the double-sided mirror between ourselves and the investee. As we move into Impact 2.0 and 3.0 this is a key developmental axis. We must go beyond tick-box exercises of pure data numeric, such as job creation and GHG. Whilst these are of prime impact and highly important, they provide little qualitative information or insights from which we can build real and deeper impacts.

Since Impact 2.0 may, for many, be a perfectly fine place to evolve to, we will outline its key differences to Impact 1.0. Whilst Impact 1.0 has evolved out of the sustainability movement to include ESG as the major stepping stone, it still operates from a simplified 'cause and effect' matrix, while focused on digital measurements' systems and reporting. These are foundational, of course, so we need to 'transcend and include' them as we develop a deeper and broader framework.

The missing link from 1.0 (moving towards 2.0) is the introduction of organisational culture, as Warren Buffett writes: 'Culture, more than rule

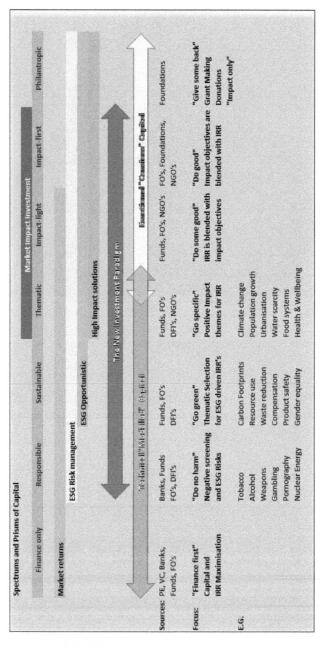

Spectrums and Prisms of Capital

	Finance only	Responsible	Sustainable	Thematic	Impact-light	Impact-first	Philantropic
	Market returns				Market Impact investment		
		ESG Risk management					
			ESG Opportunistic				
				High Impact solutions			
			The New Investment Paradigm				
	Traditional "Market" Capital				Functional "Conscious" Capital		
Sources:	PE, VC, Banks, Funds, FO's	Banks, Funds FO's, DFI's	Funds, FO's DFI's	Funds, FO's DFI's, NGO's	Funds, FO's, NGO's	FO's, Foundations, NGO's	Foundations
Focus:	"Finance first" Capital and IRR Maximisation	"Do no harm" Negative screening and ESG Risks	"Go green" Thematic Selection for ESG driven IRR's	"Go specific" Positive Impact themes for IRR	"Do some good" IRR is blended with impact objectives	"Do good" Impact objectives are blended with IRR	"Give some back" Grant Making Donations "Impact only"
E.G.		Tobacco Alcohol Weapons Gambling Pornography Nuclear Energy	Carbon Footprints Resource use Waste reduction Compensation Product safety Gender equality	Climate change Population growth Urbanisation Water scarcity Food systems Health & Wellbeing			

Table 21.1: Spectrums and prism of capital

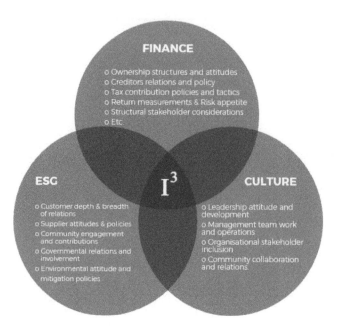

Figure 21.1: I³

books, determines how an organisation behaves[279].' Culture, not only in isolation but also how it dynamically influences and drives ESG through our 'outside-in/ inside-out' mirror.

I³ therefore now evolves into the following format:

Here we need to integrate finance and economics ('F&E') with environmental, social, governance ('ESG') and enterprise culture ('EC') throughout the investment process to drive desired outcomes, create sustainable value and, as a result, build enterprise value.

This impact approach considers leadership and organisational culture as the core imperatives for business success. These non-financial factors are typically underappreciated within the investor investment industry; they need to be fostered to become (or remain) assets, so they don't become significant liabilities.

I believe that when organisational culture is grounded and aligned with key internal and external stakeholders, financial returns are enhanced, impact is maximised and risks are reduced.

$$I^3 = F\&E + (E + S + G) + EC$$

I^3 enables a user to clearly identify and assess broader stakeholder impacts to enhance expected returns, minimise risk and build brand value. In an early due diligence stage, this validates the company's business plan and its ability to absorb any capital investment, in line with building an enterprise culture that empowers employees, and enhances performance and sustainability.

In practical terms, to the degree the investment commands influence, I^3 is intended to be implemented via mutual agreement with the firm's management. This process documents what I call the integral Impact Investment Outcome Objectives ('I^3OO'). Here we move beyond the desired investment outcomes of a typical investment agreement to include elements which have evolved critical to the implementation of the value enhancing drivers. This necessitates a deeper impact engagement with the business during the due-diligence process.

The outcomes must be company specific, and may include actions related to HR management, change management, environment and societal objectives, while comporting with commercial considerations in order to be sustainable. Following the formulation of the I^3OO by management, an implementation plan would formulate critical success areas, including key performance indicators within the I^3OO to monitor progress. A selection of these could be documented inside any legal contractual agreement and be aligned with other preceding and subsequent covenants.

We will now explore I^3 from its three perspectives: finance and economics; ESG; and enterprise culture.

F&E At this level, the entire I^3 process starts and ends with the finance thesis. No investment or impact is sustainable unless the economics of the enterprise can be validated and substantiated, (i.e. it must be capable of delivering attractive risk-adjusted returns). The financial return, therefore, is a natural outcome from the ingredients that constitute I^3 and interdependent components of 'doing the right things' as well as 'doing the things right'. Within a financial context, I^3 informs and enriches the overall framework by further identifying systemic risk and deepening understanding. It highlights how well the company is activating its broader commercial stakeholders, e.g., customers, suppliers, the community, and regulators. These relationships testify whether or not the company is performing to its true potential.

ESG Each ESG dimension has a menu of key material imperatives and requirements according to a chosen protocol. Some are more 'soft-coded' in the ESG DNA, which we may include wherever possible as this aligns with the firm's mission and values.

Apart from adhering to the existing guidelines, ESG also needs to be embedded into the corporate mission and values, policy re-formulation and implementation. To become embedded into the organisational DNA, ESG must be understood and lived, as part of a firm's governance and investment philosophy.

At this level, successful implementation of ESG outcomes depends mainly on three key factors:

- Mutual agreement (I^3OO) between the investor firm and the investees.

- Pragmatic implementation policies that can be easily understood and implemented.

- Alignment and buy-in within the organisation as a whole.

Following a staged due diligence process, and post-investment, ESG and I^3 now inform and guide decisions across the risk and management spectrum. The magnitude of impact, combined with risk management, will inform the I^3 Outcome Objectives (I^3OO); these will then inform the KPIs and covenants within any agreed package. By focusing on business imperative factors, this should increase the buy-in and the pragmatic implementation which will help increase the probability of meaningful and sustainable impact.

EC One helpful, though general, definition of organisational culture offered by Edgar Schein of MIT's Sloan School of Management:

> a pattern of shared basic assumptions that the group learned as it solved its problems of external adaptation and internal integration, that has worked well enough to be considered valid and, therefore, to be taught to new members as the correct way to perceive, think, and feel in relation to those problems [280]

Whilst there is significant international momentum in impact investment, along with the development of universal and generally agreed tools, there is also disagreement among key global protagonists over how such tools can be unified and standardised to provide an all-important comparative and statistically referenced agreed system. Current thinking ignores culture, both at organisational levels and relating to sustainability, and the developmental axis beyond.

As any business person knows, culture not only matters but is the key driver for how the organisation changes, develops and manages to operationalise its functionalities toward its stated outcome objectives. Simply put, how can we simplify the term 'organisational culture'? Culture aims to understand the emotional, psychological, and physical manifestations that work inside firms. In addition, any change implies inner growth, without which there is a reversion to previously held levels.

On a personal level, such growth is a prerequisite for sustainable development to be contained and not reverted. The latter has been my experience on several occasions – although not always; for example, at Fortis Bank we successfully managed this change by applying a whole-systems change approach.

Culture must be included in Impact 2.0 to create an integral approach, which is the only way to create change that can deliver sustainable results. From this vantage point, we see further development into the important work of Laloux on 'Reinventing organisations'[120].

All of this provides the background to the emergent foreground of the four worlds integral perspective. I^3 2.0 should enable us to clearly identify and target our investees' broader stakeholder impacts to enhance expected returns, minimise risk, and build brand value. I^3 should not only validate the company's business plan and its ability to service debt, but also support it in building an enterprise culture that empowers employees, enhances performance, and builds broader stakeholder value. By applying a deeper stakeholder view to investees, I^3 ensures that risks and opportunities are properly identified, planned and actively managed to enhance downside protection and increase execution.

As culture represents how an organisation drives its operations, creates its reward systems and manages all its stakeholder relationships, it is imperative to understand how culture levels and background affect investment outcomes. As Peter Drucker once said: 'Culture eats strategy for breakfast, operational excellence for lunch and everything else for dinner'[281]. For most firms, leadership and organisational culture is a core driver for business success and needs to be managed tactically and strategically. When organisational culture is aligned with key internal and external stakeholders, financial returns are enhanced, impact is maximised, and risks are reduced. As we should recognise in our management approach: values determine culture, culture determines behaviour, and behaviour determines outcomes.

Culture in organisations can be found in several areas such as:

i. The espoused values championed by the company's leadership.

ii. The observable artefacts, such as mission statements, guidelines, procedures, and policies.

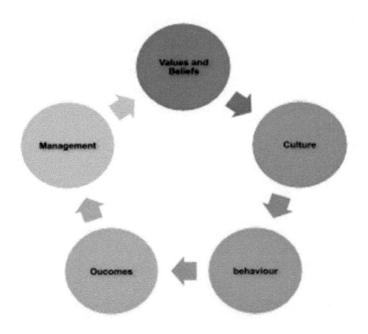

Figure 21.2: Alignment Chain

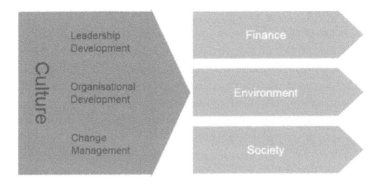

Figure 21.3: Conventional Culture Drivers

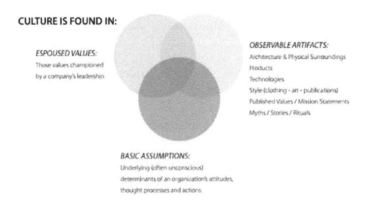

CULTURE IS FOUND IN:

ESPOUSED VALUES:
Those values championed
by a company's leadership

OBSERVABLE ARTIFACTS:
Architecture & Physical Surroundings
Products
Technologies
Style (clothing - art - publications)
Published Values / Mission Statements
Myths / Stories / Rituals

BASIC ASSUMPTIONS:
Underlying (often unconscious)
determinants of an organization's attitudes,
thought processes and actions.

Figure 21.4: Culture Areas

III. Finally, and most importantly, attitudes and behaviour towards employees, customers, and suppliers.

The collective psychology of the enterprise culture can be summarised as 'The way we do things around here'. If implemented and worked through, I³ aims to facilitate more effective organisational leadership, environmental, and social accountability by working with management to align these elements across an organisation. By addressing the leadership capability and to change management requirements, one aims to build a positive enterprise culture that can sustain these values throughout the timeline of any investment and beyond.

The investor may seek to influence enterprise culture in the following three areas:

I. Leadership development: Diagnosis can raise the awareness of the company's leadership strengths and weaknesses. The investor now has the opportunity to advise directly (or indirectly) to support management and equip them with the necessary tools for implementation.

II. Organisational development: By assessing the corporate life cycle (e.g, via Adizes' corporate-life cycles and against the organisational change required within the business plan), the investor can identify gaps and recommend specific action in building the necessary capacity. A firm would provide cultural diagnosis e.g., through the Competing

Values Framework (CVF) by Cameron and Quinn, or Spiral Dynamics Integral (SDI), so the business could improve its management style and effectiveness.

III. Change management: With a better understanding of leadership dynamics, management style and potential organisational challenges, there is now more clarity in identifying gaps in the organisation change-state indicators and whether or not specific change management processes and programs need to be implemented.

A generic investments process for a private equity/private debt firm may look like figure 21.5. We may also find a generic road map useful in figure 21.6.

As all investment creates impact, we must make this impact positive. Through the integral lens, we can dig deeper in each of the four realms and also include culture as the key driver behind the other three.

The aim is to "shift the needle" in each to create sustainable improvements in stakeholder value. Finance, like other disciplines such as art, medicine, and politics, crosses borders both physically and metaphorically in terms of legal frameworks, modus operandi, and cultural differences. However, it is mainly through the transcultural exportation, ideology, and the imposition of a Western approach to finance that imbalances have occurred. This suggests we see:

- Overemphasis on entrepreneurial personal success: each person rationally calculating what is to their personal advantage.

- Motivation is largely economic; people are responsive to perks, bonuses and money rather than loyalty, belonging to a group, or long-term employment.

- Rational capacities allow people to test many options.

- Competition improves productivity and fosters growth. This is probably the dominant meme in America today (a meme is a unit of cultural information, a concept/idea, belief, behaviour, style or practise that spreads from person to person, often with the aim of conveying a particular phenomenon, theme or meaning).

- Main concerns are autonomy and manipulation of the environment. Usually results in free market economy and multi-party democracy as influenced by e.g., Ayn Rand, Wall Street, Rodeo Drive, etc. When

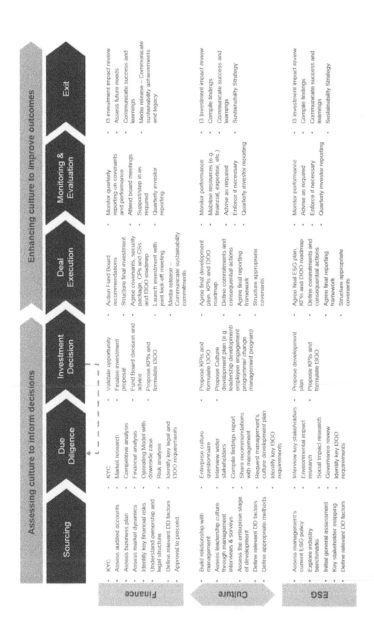

Figure 21.5: A generic investments process

	Sourcing	Due Diligence	Investment Decision	Deal Execution
	I3 Orientation	I3 Orientation	I3 Orientation	I3 Orientation
Objective:	– Build relationship with management – Induction to the I3 framework – Capture company's stated ESG & Culture activity (if any) – Capture company's stated ESG&C strategic purpose – Capture company's stated ESG&C measured performance (if any)	– Deepen the understanding from initial assessment – 2nd iteration of I3 model to inform and help navigate with management – Diagnose gaps, explore and begin mapping possible mitigating / expansion strategies – Prepare value creation investment thesis for 1st submission to IMC for decision in principle	– Agree final component parts of I3OO and its implementation plan with management – Evolve corresponding thesis and I3OO for submission to IMC for their final decision – Mitigate and minimise all forms of risk	– Initiate launch, implementation and execution of agreed I3OO plan – Assign agreed stakeholder reporting requirements
Engagement	– Desktop research – Initial interview with senior management	– Management interviews/discussions/questionnaires – Building consensus and working with deal team/IMC – Survey broader stakeholders e.g. staff, suppliers etc.	– Complete desktop research – Instruct 3'rd party service providers – Finalise I3OO with Management – Interview Stakeholders & questionnaires	– Legal council – Agree Management communication / delivery of I3OO – Engage and contract with 3'rd party service providers e.g. management consultants / coaches
Tools	– I3 orientation questionnaire (internal)	– SDI – Spectral Integrator – Integral Leadership Survey – Organisational Culture Assessment Instrument (OCAI) Competing Values Framework (CFV) – Adizes Corporate Life Cycles assessment – Governance questionnaire – Wellbeing survey (Arielski) – Selection of the above to be used	– Interviews – Desktop – Consultants	– Legal and contractual loan agreements (may contain I3OO components) – Sign off I3OO by all parties – Communication, activity and rituals for activating culture direction
Outputs	– Documented ESG&C activity – Initial assessment of managements ESG&C: • consciousness • strategic intent/alignment • implementation • measurement – Identify early leadership culture indicators – Identify organisations stage of development – Identify ESG&C DD factors – Select appropriate DD toolkit	– Integrate company ESG&C current orientation – Populate first level I3OO from initial discussions – Evolve the strategic mapping of the ESG&C elements that will drive change and growth – Identify "quick wins" and key imperatives – Agree first level KPI's and measurements	– Full I3OO: • Final agreement on all specific areas of implementation • Agreed budgets and cost of implementation • Fully mapped implementation plan • KPI's and all measurement systems and milestones for monitoring progress • Responsible parties, stewards and key stakeholders	– Comprehensive implementation plan with sign-off from all parties and stakeholders – Use of proceeds allocations made – Monitoring & Maintenance plan initiated – New board /management appointees or observer rights initiated

Figure 21.6: Generic road map

this mode becomes institutionalised, imbalances occur from previous, traditional modes e.g., differing views on the charging of interest in Islamic finance. The reason for using this example is that many believe that the Western-based return on capital model is the core issue, as we are slowly but surely running out of capacities to finance development. Such capacity limits come in many forms, mainly environmental, resource-based, and monetary.

- Lack of frameworks to validate other forms of capital contributions e.g., nature and human.

- Key is how interest is charged and distributed within the current, predominant so-called Orange Meme.

- The financial capital ideology is mainly a function of markets and this results in returns that redistribute wealth from borrowers to holders of capital. If left imbalanced, these could be considered the largest social issue of our time.

A main aim for I³ is a better understanding of the component parts of capital, how interest is constructed, and how excess returns are generated and accumulated. Here is a current stack/situation on a typical (and hypothetical) 10% loan:

Excess return	3%
Liquidity Risk	0.5%
Migration Risk	0.5%
Return on Capital Employed	3%
Costs	1%
Expected Loss	1%
Risk Free Rate	1%

I³ develops a true understanding of the IRR which dislodges the conventional IRR paradigm. Only through valuing the component parts of impact can this change the need for excessive returns which extract a social and environmental toll. By now we can see that I³ 2.0 formulates the deeper dimensions of Impact. These can be mapped back into the SDGs as in figure 21.7

However, each SDG relates back to several of the four-worlds as we now have established their relational interconnectivity. This is a highly simplified I³ model, since each SDG is driven by multiple realms. As each investment represents a specific context, the SDGs should be mapped accordingly.

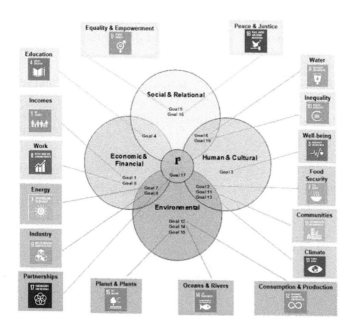

Figure 21.7: I³ & SDGS

§21.1 Going transformational: missing depths

In this book we see quite clearly that all transformational change comes from within and is a function of a person's capacities to work through their interior domains to understand the hermeneutic constructs and their ability to withstand mental pain.

Carl Jung is attributed to have said:

> There is no coming to consciousness without pain. People will do anything, no matter how absurd, in order to avoid facing their own Soul. One does not become enlightened by imagining figures of light, but by making the darkness conscious.

Regardless of the supposed source, it's correct as the search for personal depth requires new levels of discovery combined with an open mental attitude for development. This is the leadership challenge of our times. In my opinion, the depth of our commercial impact follows other similar psychological or moral development stages, in that as we expand our horizon to include broader and deeper aspects of the 'other', we morph with the 'other' so that we transcend and include previous versions of ourselves. When this realisation happens, we cannot continue previous wrongs since 'me' now includes a 'we and us'.

As discussed in previous chapters, this refers to the 'power distance' that separates actions from their effect on the environment.

Hermes CEO Saker Nusseibeh writes:

> Let us now leave our thought experiment and turn to examining the 'why' question. I would like to suggest that the reason we 'invest' our savings goes beyond the simple quest for the accumulation of wealth. The reason for such an assertion has to do with the fact that we, as citizens, shape the society we live in through our work, our taxes, which finance public policy and through the daily pursuit of our businesses and the way we live our lives. I would contend, therefore that our savings form part of this open adaptive system. In other words, the $75 trillion is not separate from the economic-social fabric we live in, but rather an intrinsic part of it. Moreover, it is a tool we should use to control it, in the same way that the taxes we pay to finance government initiatives that help shape the direction and structure of our social economy are equally part of it. If we accept this assertion then we arrive at two main reasons as to 'why' we invest. The first is the straightforward accumulation of wealth, by trying to plug into economic growth. But the second, and I would suggest equally important reason, has to do with the shaping of our social economy...[35]

Here is the reconnection and the potential to re-balance the rationale between capital and social awareness. Nusseibeh asserts that such thinking has to go beyond ourselves and take on an intergenerational intent to be truly transformational.

> Equally importantly, is an inter-generational concord so that we leave the next generation a viable economic landscape in the same way those who came before us left us with an economic base we could build on. This is in fact an ancient concept described in a Hebrew (and Arabic) parable of Caesar and the old man planting fig trees in the parable. Why do you bother to plant trees you would never benefit from, asks Caesar? Because those who came before us planted trees for us to harvest and I plant trees for the next generation to harvest, answers the old man.(Ibid)

This is where we see the organisational shaping and the specific impact context merging and fusing with questions around the higher purpose for our impact objectives. Unless we make this connection, we are not only doing ourselves and others a disfavor, but reneging on the contracts with our soul.

A main challenge for many investment firms is changing the culture sufficiently from a predominant finance and economics operational paradigm based on digital short-term thinking, to one more efficient and expedient. If a limited or incomplete paradigm is used to build their impact processes, this would not allow members to re-connect and nurture those parts within their impact calling that speak to them. I believe,however, this is a fundamental cornerstone for real impact and its organisational development to occur.

If we succumb to the much easier 'box-ticking' exercise to only satisfy reporting requirements we do impact integrity a disservice, contravening our identity which can only damage us. Thomas Merton noted

> If you want to identify me, ask me not where I live, or what I like to eat, or how I comb my hair, but ask me what I think I am living for, in detail, and ask me what I think is keeping me from living fully for the thing I want to live for. [282, p.40]

So we must ask the questions of ourselves before attempting to ask the other. These questions include being honest about how we as impact investors can alleviate suffering as stewards of capital.

The American Declaration of Independence writes that, 'All experience has shown that mankind is more disposed to suffer – while evils are sufferable – then to right themselves by abolishing the forms to which they are accustomed.' Impact investments, therefore, can become whatever we want them to become; the question is, how far are we prepared to go 'down the rabbit hole' in our search for the truths inside each investment?

Our accumulated contributions, which at some point will provide the narrative for the story of who we are, will also become our legacy. In our media there are many dramatizations of dysfunctional family life + wealth, e.g., Dallas, Dynasty, Titans, Blood and Oil; the films Wall Street, and The Big Short.

J.B. Priestley's An Inspector Calls prisms the wealthy and highly dysfunctional Birling family through a suicide. Their intergenerational pride and status is the bedrock for a lack of social responsibility, which creates a web of lies and deceit. The inspector acts as a catalyst for the family's conscience, which subsequently evaporates. However in Act 3 the inspector instructs the family in no uncertain terms:

> One Eva Smith has gone – but there are millions and millions of Eva Smiths and John Smiths still left with us, with their lives, their hopes and fears, their suffering and chance of happiness, all intertwined with our lives with what we think and say and do. We don't live alone. We are members of one body. We are responsible for each other. And I tell you that the time will soon come if men will not learn that lesson, then they will be taught it in fire and blood and anguish. We don't live alone, Good night.[283]

Set in 1912, Priestley's fictional family illustrates a time of increased social tension and questioning of the economic system, with parallels to the present day.

Depending on where we are in our careers, we have more or less freedom to make decisions and how we perform and conduct impact. Early in our careers, we often feel that compliance to our family marching orders is the safer route, since we have not developed our own compass to negotiate alternatives. Also, given our reliance on uninterrupted income, we subscribe to 'he who pays he piper', which dissent may jeopardise.

At some point the childhood messages and family marching orders will collide with the true natural, more spontaneous, and instinctually grounded self. This conflict expresses itself as 'symptoms' and or addictions. Our psychology solicits our true aims and aligns with the natural self, bringing meaning to our lives.

Many of us, entering the impact investment industry with high hopes of having our souls nurtured, may at times feel limited and confined. As perception is projection, and if we hold and suppress the real self, we create neurosis in various forms. As Sigmund Freud suggested: 'The price of our civilisation is neurosis'.

Our current civilisation and culture values freedom almost above all things but freedom without cultural limitations and boundaries leads to idolatry. Some social scientists and anthropologists suggest that a tell-tale sign of a civilisation in its latter stages of decline is the emergence of the need for idols such as messianic leaders, politicians, and celebrities, on which we can project our lack of self. To satisfy our need to position ourselves within 'people, places and things' we can use excess capital to purchase our target identity.

One such apparent classic phenomenon in civilisations prior to a collapse is the celebrity chef culture in search of the best, most expensive, sophisticated, and exclusive. The need arises to seek ever greater heights of culinary pleasure, sensations and uniqueness of experience which can be shared and discussed within our peer community to fill the need within our perceived status.

If capital is to be healing and developmental, our impact awareness must include a movement from the false self towards the real self, which includes our individuation; however, and most importantly: 'Neurosis is suffering that has not yet found its meaning[284]' so let us go find it in impact. Yuval Noah Harari writes:

> The most important thing I realised was that the deepest source of my suffering was the patterns of my own mind. When I want something and it doesn't happen, my mind reacts by generating suffering. Suffering is not an objective condition in the outside world. It is a mental reaction generated by my own mind. Learning this is the first step toward ceasing to generate more suffering. [285]

Here again we find that the task is to create and find meaning in all our impact endeavours, meaning that has been there all along, undiscovered and unattended, until we find the impetus to resuscitate it.

Love is part of every human being, sometimes buried due to trauma, or dormant due to experiences, but always there. Sometimes it is sparked via a resonant movie or music snippet. Love pushes through our outer shell and shines light on our inner places and shadows. Love, as such, is the engine of being and gives us the power and courage to become who we truly are meant to be. Love seeks what is ultimately real and true, and goes beyond personality and behaviour.

Truth, of course, is about unity as no real truths can be held in for long, separate from reality. Truth has to resonate with its own realities and is validated by love. As we can only give away that which we have created for ourselves, including love, I encourage you to build your own love story with impact as love seeks what is real for you to actualise your essence.

The poet Rumi puts this relationship beautifully:

Figure 21.8: Porter's 5 Forces

The moment I heard my first love story I started looking for you, and knowing how blind that was. Lovers don't finally meet somewhere, they're in each other all along. [286]

We need to move from the head to the heart. We will here and now explore some similarities and overlaps with the familiar models such as Michael Porter's 5-forces, and the format of the balanced scorecard.

Now that we are familiar with the generic four worlds and I³ approach, we can see some parallels in conventional models such as the classic Porter's 5 Forces[287] in figure 21.8.

Here we encounter the same counter-clockwise movement as in the integral compass, with the centre now representing competitive rivalry. This is of course correct, as this model explains the core drivers behind the value chain that leads into strategy, which drives corporate performance and ultimately market valuations.

We see here that each of Porter's 'four worlds' combine a number of components from a developed I³, informing and clarifying a company's strategy. Porter's bargaining powers are about relationship (our South) and product differentiation (our North). His threats are about finance and economics (our West) and product brand (our East).

There are overlaps and cross-overs as this model has a different aim, e.g. price sensitivity versus brand value proposition, but we can see the logic of the four-worlds' approach embedded in other core business principles and models.

The balanced scorecard originated from the need to include multiple stakeholders, but was developed purely from Western and Northern perspectives with a strong dose of 'performance management' as its driver.

The BS is a strategic system that is used globally in business, government, and nonprofit organisations to align business activities with an organisation's vision/strategy, improve internal and external communications, and monitor the organisation's performance against strategic goals. The BS was developed by Kaplan and Norton in the early 1990s to add strategic, non-financial performance measures to traditional financial metrics to afford a more 'balanced' view of organisational performance. Whilst it has reached its limits, it has served its purpose for management in understanding the additional needs and dimensions. Hence for Impact we have an understandable template as its base.

§21.2 The multidimensional scorecard

Taking the evolutionary leap from Kaplan and Norton's balanced scorecard (BS) methodology, we can construct our own impact scorecard. First let us remind ourselves of some of the (non-exhaustive) reasons why firms implement a BS:

- Increase focus on strategic objectives and clear, specific results

- Improve organisational performance by measuring what is important

- Align organisation strategy and priorities with daily work

- Focus on agreed drivers of future performance

- Improve communication of the company's vision and strategy

- prioritise projects/initiatives

- Clarify management goals and objectives and what actually matters

- Staff satisfaction and empowerment

Its roots can be traced to General Electric's pioneering work on performance measurement in the 1950s, and the French process engineers who created the Tableau de Bord (literally a 'dashboard' of performance measures) in the early twentieth century. The BS has evolved from a simple performance measurement framework to a full strategic planning and management system.

Today's BS transforms an organisation's strategic plan from a passive document into daily 'marching orders.' It provides a framework for planners to identify what should be done and measured, and enables executives to execute their strategies. recognising some of the weaknesses of previous approaches, the BS offers a clear prescription what companies should measure in order to balance the financial perspective.

The BS is a management system (not just a measurement system) that enables organisations to clarify their vision/strategy and translate it into action. It provides feedback about internal business processes and external outcomes in order to continuously improve strategic performance and results. When fully deployed, the BS transforms strategic planning from an academic exercise into an organisation's nerve centre.

Kaplan and Norton state:

> The balanced scorecard retains traditional financial measures. But financial measures tell the story of past events, an adequate story for industrial age companies for which investments in long-term capabilities and customer relationships were not critical for success. These financial measures are inadequate, however, for guiding and evaluating the journey that information age companies must make to create future value through investment in customers, suppliers, employees, processes, technology, and innovation. [288]

We see here again, a variation of our Integral four worlds approach.

§21.3 Perspectives

The BS suggests that we view the organisation from four main perspectives, and then develop metrics, collect data and analyse it relative to each of these perspectives:

§21.3.1 Learning and growth

This includes employee training and corporate cultural attitudes for individual and corporate self-improvement. In a knowledge-worker organisation, people — the only repository of knowledge — are the main resource.

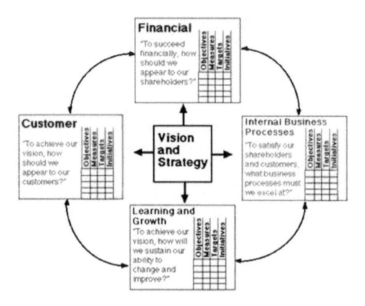

Figure 21.9: Kaplan and Norton

Learning and growth constitute the essential foundation for the success of any knowledge-worker organisation. Kaplan and Norton emphasise that 'learning' is more than 'training'; it includes mentors and tutors within the organisation, and ease of communication among workers that allows them to get help with a problem when needed. It also includes technological tools; what the Baldrige criteria[289] calls 'high performance work systems.'

§21.3.2 The business process

This refers to internal business processes. Metrics based on this perspective allow managers to know how well their business is performing, and whether its products and services conform to customer requirements (the mission). These metrics must be carefully designed by those who know these processes most intimately, and not by outside consultants.

§21.3.3 The customer

Recent management philosophy has increasingly emphasised the importance of customer focus and customer satisfaction. These are leading indicators: if customers are not satisfied, they will eventually find other suppliers. Poor performance from this perspective is a leading indicator of future decline, even though the current financial picture may look good. In developing metrics for satisfaction, customers should be analysed by needs/requirements etc. (e.g., price sensitivity versus service level) and the processes required for each product.

§21.3.4 The financial

Kaplan and Norton do not disregard the traditional need for financial data. Timely and accurate data will always be a priority, and managers will do whatever necessary to provide it. In fact, there is often too much handling, processing and volume of financial data. With the implementation of a corporate database, hopefully more of the processing can be centralized and automated. But the point is that the current emphasis on financials leads to the 'unbalanced' situation regarding other perspectives. Here, we should include additional financial-related data, such as risk assessment and cost-benefit data.

§21.3.5 Strategy mapping

Strategy maps are communication tools used to tell a story of how value is created for the organisation. They show a logical, linear, cause-and-effect nexus between strategic objectives. Generally speaking, improving performance in learning and growth enables the organisation to improve its internal process perspective objectives, which hopefully leads to desirable customer and financial results.

Once an organisation has analysed the above results, they are ready to utilise the BS to improve deficiencies. The metrics must be SMART (Specific, Measurable, Achievable, Realistic and Timely) – we can only improve what we can measure! Metrics must also be aligned with the company's strategic plan. So here we have an initial integral blueprint to evolve into our Impact approach.

In 2016, Thomas and McElroy took the BS concept and methodology further, confirming its ongoing evolution, and published The MultiCapital Scorecard® [290], which builds the framework into the additional and previously missing social, environmental dimensions, creating triple bottom line performance (3BL) reporting from which we can seek input for our I³ four-worlds scorecard. In addition, the integrated reporting framework provides a generic blueprint for investigating the process between reporting

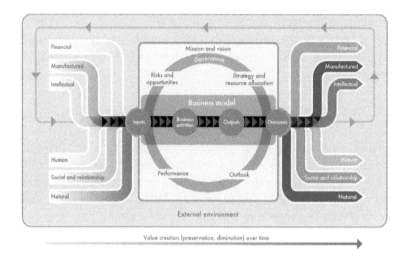

IRC's value creation process with six capitals. The IIRC's 'octopus' diagram represents an iterative process with a generic business model in its centre. Six capitals feed in from the left and emerge, transformed to the right. The business model can generate, maintain or destroy value in any of the capitals, such value can be tangible or intangible, or both.

Figure 21.10: Process between reporting inputs and outputs

inputs and outputs as in figure 21.10[1].

Any model and scorecard must be iterative, and designed to reinforce, validate, or negate cross-referenced information. Each item is either from a standard convention, or must be developed and emerge out of deep discussions with the investment team.

At the macro level, the scorecard amalgamates each line item into the ESG+C framework to be assessed in conjunction with the F for Finance, which can aligned with other metrics, e.g., 1–5 with hurdle rates or targets from both quantitative and qualitative sources.

In this case, the objective is that all data collection points across all dimensions are similarly scaled to ensure comparative analysis, consistency and cross-referencing for any ensuing narrative and decision making.

Each macro-line item is weighted according to its importance, then reweighted at the top level to arrive at the overall transaction score.

We now have a map that quantifies and qualifies a framework of answers to ever deeper questions. Below is a hypothetical, generic example for a typical private investment firm.

---

[1]Image courtesy of The International <IR> Framework,[291]

The summary page is driven by each dimension and is rebalanced at each level of inquiry, resulting in a final weighted score as the reference point, which can be risk measured and targeted if required.

The main objective is the same for any diagnostic: to understand the interrelationships and imbalances so that the correct dialogue can ensue for possible mitigation.

I³ Analysis

Project XYZ

Opportunity name: PROJECT XYZ
Opportunity sector: AGRICULTURE, FORESTRY & FISHING
Opportunity sub-sector: CROP PRODUCTION

Summary Scorecard	Weighting	Score	Weighted Score
Environment	30%	2.7	0.89
Social	35%	3.05	1.07
Corporate Governance	20%	2.57	0.51
Culture	15%	2.34	0.35
Transaction Score	100%		2.74
Environment			
Legislation, policy review, and standards	10.0%	2.33	0.23
Risk identification and opportunities	10.0%	3.17	0.32
Processes, responsibilities, and capacity	5.0%	2.00	0.10
Monitoring, review, and reporting	5.0%	3.00	0.15
Waste and pollution	5.0%	3.00	0.15
Energy and water use	5.0%	3.00	0.15
Greenhouse Gas (GHG) emissions and climate change	5.0%	3.00	0.15
Pesticides and other agrochemicals	10.0%	3.00	0.30
Contaminated land or land with liabilities	10.0%	3.00	0.30
Biodiversity and ecosystems	10.0%	3.00	0.30
Other questions	15.0%	3.00	0.45
Sector specific environmental questions	10.0%	1.00	0.10
Summary	100%		2.7
Social			
Legislation, policy review, and standards	10.0%	2.33	0.23
Risk identification and opportunities	15.0%	3.17	0.48
Processes, responsibilities, and capacity	20.0%	2.00	0.40
Monitoring, review, reporting	5.0%	3.00	0.15

Employment	10.0%	4.00	0.40
Occupational health and safety (OHS)	5.0%	3.00	0.15
Productivity and skills development	5.0%	3.00	0.15
Community health, safety, and security	5.0%	4.00	0.20
Resettlement or economic displacement	5.0%	3.00	0.15
Indigenous peoples	5.0%	4.00	0.20
Other questions	6.0%	3.00	0.18
Sector specific social questions	9.0%	4.00	0.36
Summary	100%		3.05

Governance			
Legislation, policy review, and standards	20.0%	2.33	0.47
Written policies & procedures (p&p)	15.0%	3.00	0.45
Risk identification and opportunities	10.0%	3.17	0.32
Processes, responsibilities, and capacity	10.0%	2.00	0.20
Monitoring, review, reporting	10.0%	3.00	0.30
Stakeholder Engagement Program (SEP) and grievance mechanism	5.0%	3.00	0.15
Shareholders / board structure	5.0%	5.00	0.25
Internal & external audit	5.0%	3.00	0.15
Communication & training	10.0%	2.83	0.28
Sector specific governance questions	10.0%		
Summary	100%		2.57

Culture			
Artefacts	16.7%	2.44	0.41
Values & beliefs -	16.7%	2.00	0.33
Vision	16.7%	2.67	0.44
Mission	16.7%	2.38	0.40
Employee engagement	16.7%	2.07	0.35
Management capacity and capability	16.7%	2.47	0.41
Summary	100%		2.57

Moving into the design of the underlying model, we may be familiar with some of the questions from the GIIN. As discussed in previous chapters, the model's design exemplifies a much deeper strategic process from the investment management team as they have worked through their own impact methodology and what they want their firm to represent.

Each detailed item is a depository for underlying data, much of which is based on conventional and readily available sources, including the SASB Materiality Maps, GIIN/IRIS, B-Corp, etc. Each item is also assessed for identified gaps/missing components.

The consideration of any standards on ESG-related issues are founded on three pragmatic principles:

I. Transparency: Are the company's ESG-related impacts transparent to interested parties (internal and external)? If public disclosures are made (annual reports), do they include ESG-related considerations? (Please note: the level of transparency depends on the audience, which needs to be appropriately considered.)

II. Accountability: Are the costs/benefits from ESG-related impacts adequately accounted? Does management reasonably monitor and mitigate costs, as well as monitoring and fostering benefits? Are these documented in policies and procedures, and discussed regularly within the executive committee or board of directors? Are there clear alignments for impact responsibilities?

III. Sustainability: Are the ESG-related impacts (especially costs) sustainable over a predictable time horizon? Are these impacts integrated into financial forecasts and budgets?

These principles can be assessed in relation to the relevant risk level. In assessing a potential investee's ESG considerations, any analyst could confirm (or propose) sufficient documentation around these principles, and also assess management's intentions and levels of consciousness pertaining to these principles.

Environment

LEGISLATION, POLICY REVIEW, AND STANDARDS Environmental legal framework applicable to the company
International environmental standards applicable to the company
Environmental policy
Environmental objectives

RISK IDENTIFICATION AND OPPORTUNITIES
Company assessment of its own environmental risks
Company assessment of environmental opportunities for mitigation
Company assessment of environmental risks from 3rd parties (vendors, suppliers, external stakeholders)
Company assessment of environmental opportunities from 3rd parties (vendors, suppliers, external stakeholders)
Company assessment of environmental threats (emergencies, failures, acts of god)
Responsiveness and preparedness to environmental threats
Responsiveness and preparedness of 3rd parties (governments, NGOs) to related environmental threats

PROCESSES, RESPONSIBILITIES, AND CAPACITY
Company processes that ensure the effective
implementation of environmental objectives
Roles and responsibilities assigned to update and monitor environmental processes and objectives
Appropriate capacity, authority, and skills for those assigned roles and responsibilities
Management involvement in environmental processes, policies, and objectives

MONITORING, REVIEW, AND REPORTING
Company monitoring of environmental policies, processes, and objectives
External oversight or involvement in environmental monitoring
Independent auditors or consultants for assessment of environmental impact
Feedback from results into company's processes

WASTE AND POLLUTION
Environmental impact of company's existing processes
Environmental impact of any waste produced or other by-products (note: consider phase-outs or bans)
Arrangements for storage, handling, management, and disposal of by-products and waste (training, control of spills, chemical containers, etc.)
Company assessment of alternatives to existing processes, wastes, or arrangements
Company assessment and monitoring of 3rd parties involved in waste (contractors, disposals, transportation)
Company assessment of existing and potential contingent liabilities
Company assessment of other forms of pollution (e.g. noise, electromagnetic fields, odours, pathogens, visual impacts)?

ENERGY AND WATER USE
Environmental impact of company's energy consumption
Environmental impact of company's water consumption
Assessment of alternatives to existing sources and consumption patterns

GREENHOUSE GAS (GHG) EMISSIONS AND CLIMATE CHANGE
Company monitoring of GHG emissions
Actions undertaken or plans to undertake to minimise GHG emissions

Resiliency of company's operations or assets to risks from climate change

PESTICIDES AND OTHER AGROCHEMICALS
Environmental and regulatory assessment of pesticides and agrochemicals used
Company assessment of alternatives to current pesticides and agrochemicals used
Storage and disposal of pesticides and agrochemicals
Monitoring of pesticide and agrochemical usage

CONTAMINATED LAND OR LAND WITH LIABILITIES
Company assessment of its existing and potential liabilities from contamination

BIODIVERSITY AND ECOSYSTEMS
Company assessment of its risks and impacts on biodiversity (i.e. conversion of habitats to other uses, introduction of non-native species, etc.)
Company assessment of impacts on wider ecosystem relied upon by local communities
Company assessment of its indirect risks from biodiversity via 3rd parties
Where relevant, company's Biodiversity Management Plan (BMP)
Company's assessment of its impact on endangered or critically endangered species
Company's assessment of its reliance directly or indirectly (via supply chains) on particular ecosystems
Introduction of non-native species of flora and fauna
Engagement with NGOS / government agencies around biodiversity

OTHER QUESTIONS
Company assessment of and response to:
Land required for company vs. quantum of local supply of productive land
Reputational concerns
Impact on critical habitats
Assessment of concerns / impact of genetically modified organisms

Social

LEGISLATION, POLICY REVIEW, AND STANDARDS
Social legal framework applicable to the company
International social standards applicable to the company
Social policy
Social objectives and outcomes

RISK IDENTIFICATION AND OPPORTUNITIES
Company assessment of its own social risks
Company assessment of social opportunities for mitigation
Company assessment of social risks from 3rd parties (vendors, suppliers, external stakeholders)
Company assessment of social opportunities from 3rd parties (vendors, suppliers, external stakeholders)
Company assessment of threats to social stakeholders (infrastructure failure, chemical release, other emergencies)
Responsiveness and preparedness of company to social threats

Responsiveness and preparedness of 3rd parties (governments, NGOs) to related social threats

PROCESSES, RESPONSIBILITIES, AND CAPACITY
Company processes that ensure the effective implementation of social objectives
Roles and responsibilities assigned to update and monitor social processes and objectives
Appropriate capacity, authority, and skills for those assigned roles and responsibilities
Management involvement in social processes, policies, and objectives

MONITORING, REVIEW, REPORTING
Company monitoring of social policies, processes, and objectives
External oversight or involvement in social monitoring
Independent auditors or consultants for assessment of social impact
Feedback from results into company's processes
Reporting on social activities

EMPLOYMENT
Company's employment policy
Local / national employment standards
International employment standards applicable to company
Company's compliance with relevant standards
Consideration of employees as key stakeholder
Non-discrimination practises
Labor and working conditions
Compensation
Additional benefits
Company stance towards collective bargaining
Diversity of workforce at all levels of organisation (in company's context)
Company's use of 3rd party contractors and temporary workers (Scaling note: Very high = no reliance)
Company's policy towards 3rd party contractors and temporary workers
Terms of employment for 3rd party contractors and temporary workers (compared to full-time staff)

OCCUPATIONAL HEALTH AND SAFETY (OHS)
Company's OHS performance
Company's assessment of OHS risks
Company's assessment of alternatives to existing work arrangements vis-à-vis OHS
Company resources (human and financial) dedicated to OHS issues
Company training related to OHS issues

PRODUCTIVITY AND SKILLS DEVELOPMENT
Company's assessment of worker productivity
Company's performance of worker productivity
Company resources allocated to training and skills development

COMMUNITY HEALTH, SAFETY, AND SECURITY

Company's impact on:
-> Emissions or wastewater discharges
-> Transport, storage, disposal or use of hazardous goods
-> Changes in availability or quality of water
-> Fire and explosion risks
-> Emissions or wastewater discharges
-> Risk of diseases (including STDs and water-borne)
-> Burden on or expansion of local infrastructure
-> Emissions or wastewater discharges
Company assessment of its impacts on community health, safety and security
Company emergency response management system in response to local community risks

RESETTLEMENT OR ECONOMIC DISPLACEMENT
Company's assessment of its impact on surrounding peoples and economic displacement
Company's response to identified impacts

INDIGENOUS PEOPLES
Impact of company on indigenous peoples
Company's assessment of risks to indigenous peoples
Company's response to identified risks
Extent to which Free, Prior and Informed Consent has been obtained

OTHER QUESTIONS
Company's use of armed security guards and track record (low = reliance and incidents; high = no reliance)
Other investments in social / societal sectors by company

SECTOR SPECIFIC SOCIAL QUESTIONS
Company assessment of and response to:
-> Land required for company vs. quantum of local supply of productive land
-> Reputational concerns
-> Existing informal land users concerns
-> Existing traditional rights to access land
Competition over limited or remote water resources
Exposure to harsh elements for workers (sun, heat, cold, insects, etc.)
Company's assessment of impact of migrant workers on local communities

Corporate Governance

LEGISLATION, POLICY REVIEW, AND STANDARDS
Standards of legal and regulatory framework applicable to the company
International regulatory standards applicable to the company
International accounting standards applicable to the company
Corporate governance policy standards
Corporate governance objectives standards

WRITTEN POLICIES & PROCEDURES (P&P)
Level of detail and scope of employments rights & obligations / handbook

Level of detail and scope of anti-corruption, anti-bribery and AML p&p, incl. for dealings with 3rd parties

Level of detail and scope of whistleblowing p&p including no discrimination of whistleblowers

Level of detail and scope of compensation p&p

Level of detail and scope of legal & regulatory compliance p&p

Level of detail and scope of ethics/non-discrimination p&p

Level of detail and scope of code of conduct p&p towards internal stakeholders, incl conflicts of interest, confidentiality, privileged info, gifts

Level of detail and scope of code of conduct p&p towards external stakeholders, incl conflicts of interest, confidentiality, privileged info, gifts

Level of detail and scope of effective record keeping p&p

Level of accessibility to employees/stakeholders across company

Ability to challenge/revise p&p across company

Applicability of p&p to group associates

RISK IDENTIFICATION AND OPPORTUNITIES

Company assessment of its internal governance policies and procedures

Company assessment of opportunities for internal policy & procedures review

Company assessment of effectiveness of risk management controls (operational and/or financial)

Company assessment of legal and regulatory risks from 3rd parties (government, courts, regulatory bodies)

Company assessment of legal and regulatory opportunities from 3rd parties (government, courts, regulatory bodies)

Company assessment of country/sector exposed to corruption, bribery

Responsiveness and preparedness of company to business integrity (AML, corruption, sanctions, criminal activities)

Responsiveness and preparedness of 3rd parties to assist/audit company in business integrity

PROCESSES, RESPONSIBILITIES, AND CAPACITY

Company processes that ensure the effective implementation of governance objectives

Roles and responsibilities assigned to update and monitor governance processes and objectives

Appropriate capacity, authority, and skills for those assigned roles and responsibilities

Management involvement in governance processes, policies, and objectives

Monitoring, review, reporting

Company monitoring/review of governance policies, processes, and objectives

Degree external oversight or involvement in governance monitoring

Independent auditors or consultants for assessment of governance impact

Feedback from results into company's processes

STAKEHOLDER ENGAGEMENT PROGRAM (SEP) AND GRIEVANCE MECHANISM

Company SEP
Company grievance mechanism
Feedback from internal stakeholders
Feedback from external stakeholders
External oversight or involvement in SEP and grievance mechanism

SHAREHOLDERS / BOARD STRUCTURE
Ownership structure conducive to company purpose
Owner involvement over company day-to-day business
Rights of minority shareholders
Internal stakeholder involvement (ESOP, bonus shares)
Succession planning
Composition and independence of Board of Directors
BoD involvement over company day-to-day business
BoD committee meetings

INTERNAL & EXTERNAL AUDIT
Internal audit mandate (access, frequency, competence)
Escalation process for internal audit
External auditor standards (local, IFRS)
Qualifications escalated by external auditors
Rotation requirements for auditors
Audit committee meetings

COMMUNICATION & TRAINING
Communication of strategy / mission
Training on policies & procedures

Having covered the three ESG parts, we need to treat and analyse culture differently. Organisational culture is a set of shared values, the unwritten rules and codes of which are often taken for granted. It guides employees towards acceptable and rewarding behaviour and affects all stakeholders. Organisational culture exists at two distinct levels: visible and hidden. The former exists in artefacts, symbols and the visible behaviour of employees. The latter is the underlying values, beliefs, codes and assumptions for acceptable and unacceptable behaviour.

Here our interpretative look differs from ESG's tenets and levels of transparency, accountability, and sustainability to capture what we may consider the following three principles for a healthy organisational culture:

1. Alignment: The degree at the current operational state, this aspect or

area is appropriately sized, applied and developed to fit with organisational requirements.

II. Clarity: The level and ease of related information being forthcoming and their willingness to collaborate to gain clarity.

III. Commitment: Evidence of actual delivery in the relevant areas and the organisation 'walking the talk' in their culture.

During the diagnostic assessment, the investor collaboratively with the investee seeks to co-create impact outcome objectives which create the contract with a specific investee as to how implementation, assessment, monitoring and reporting will occur, never losing sight of the main objective: to create positive impacts.

Culture

ARTEFACTS: visible components of culture; they are easy to formulate, have some physical shape, yet its perception varies from one individual to another.
Rituals & Ceremonies
Symbols & Slogans
Stories & Myths

VALUES & BELIEFS: The shared conscious and unconscious affective desires, convictions and assumptions what is good or bad for the organisation. Describes the "How" and the kind of conduct and behaviour it wants to promote and reward.
Degree of visibility:
Integrity (Morals, Ethics, Honesty)
Respect (Ability, Expertise, Admiration)
Trust (Character, Competence, Reliability)
Excellence (Quality, Performance, Service)
Accountability (Responsibility, Commitment, Transparency)
Teamwork (Collaboration, Cooperation, Tolerance)
Innovation (Creativity, Ingenuity, Mastery)
Achievement (Entrepreneurship, Contribution, Delivery)
Fairness (Justice, Inclusive, Equality)
Care (Stewardship, Compassion, Empathy)
Passion (Enthusiasm, Perseverance, Ambition)
Leadership (Influence, Competitive Attitude, Modelling)
Learning (Continuous Improvement, Knowledge, Effectiveness)
Customers (Satisfaction, Retention, Value proposition)
People (Engagement, Belonging, Diversity)
Safety (Health, Wellbeing, Challenge)
Community (Citizenship, Involvement, Benefits)
Environment (Sustainability, Awareness, Eco-Attitude)

VISION: The projection and intent of its direction and sense of purpose of a future state in order to fulfil its aspirations. A Vision describes the "What", sets its objectives, motivates its actions and generates a sense of pride and shared meaning amongst the organisation members.
Clear vision lived inside the organisation.
Vision for stakeholders.

MISSION: An ongoing and time-independent guide. Describes the "Why" actions and importance to achieve the Vision and defines the purpose and broader goals for being in existence.
Well articulated, stated and lived mission and purpose.
Top priorities
Unique and distinct differentiators and competitive advantages/disadvantages
Creative spaces and the freedom to generate innovative solutions.
Collaboration and cooperation across stakeholders.
Clear and sustainable market value proposition.
Degree of Financial Inclusion
Systemic understanding of competitive advantages.
Inclusive priorities for communities.
Impacts on cultural heritage which may require special assessments. (e.g. ESIA)

EMPLOYEE ENGAGEMENT
Meaningful work
Relationships with management
Relationships with co-workers
Teamwork
Open, honest, trusting relationships.
Opportunities to grow.
Ideas are taken seriously.
Sense of belonging
Positive workplace focus
Work satisfaction
Balances financial stress
Income sufficiency for household needs
Salaries are reflective of contributions
Health & fitness orientation
Talent optimization
Values alignment
Work-life balance
Trust in firm & management
Positive performance management

MANAGEMENT CAPACITY & CAPABILITY:
"Mission aligned" management remuneration policy.
Smooth-functioning, cohesive and high performing teams. E.g. through consensus
Good working inter-personal relationships e.g. listening well and providing sup-

portive and constructive feedback.

Helping others improve their performance and obtain personal development opportunities

Manages Innovation by encoraging others to generate new ideas

Manages future expectations by communicating clearly and facilitating its accomplishment.

Fostering an orientation towards continuous improvement among employees in everything they do

Created culture with a healthy level of competiveness towards its performance targets.

Inspirational and motivational and energises the firm by "going the extra mile" toward its key objectives. Prides itself on exemplary "best in class" customer service, brand and relationships.

Facilitates acculturation by helping others to understand what is expected of them, the firms' culture and its standards.

Optimises measurement & control functions towards aligned operational objectives e.g. performance and product delivery.

Foster the coordination & facilitation of information sharing across functional boundaries.

Clearly focused on key imperatives and not easliy diverted / distracted.

Healthy status creation

Lives and breathes the "code-of-conduct" policy.

Prerequisite skills present

Skills gaps identified

Current L&D / OD positioning

Solid track record in change management through the cycles

(All materials can be downloaded from the resource centre at www.robertdellner. com)

Once the Impact diagnosis is virtually complete and we have gained the necessary Impact understanding, the following principles can then be added at the next stage in preparation for the I^3 Outcome Objectives (I^3OO), namely:

I. Importance: To what degree is this aspect or area key, critical or relevant for the firm to succeed?

II. Feasibility: The likelihood of this aspect or area being aligned and implemented by the firm.

III. Impact: The expected materiality of this aspect once aligned and implemented.

As Investor, we have our limitations on how to influence Impact; the I³OO is therefore co-created with the investee to optimise and make the business and organisation sustainable, viable, profitable, and successful in partnership with how the management of the investee sees Impact being aligned and beneficial for their future.

This can take several iterations between the diagnosis and the principles to mutually agree and document. These principles are then assessed in relation to the relevant risk associated with the industry, sector, and jurisdiction.

Within the cultural diagnostic, assessment of employee engagement is taken from the well-being surveys by Mark Anielski. Many of the line items in 'Management Capacity and Capability' are derived from the Competing Values Framework (CVF)[292] by Cameron and Quinn.

Given CVF's alignment with the four worlds, CFV provides a transparent and easily accessible toolset e.g. the Organisational Culture Assessment Instrument and the Management Skill Assessment Instrument (OCAI and MSAI) which provide the underlying sources of information.

This links into the I³OO, since we also need to use a culture model which we can easily work in collaboration with the investee organisation.

§21.4 Clan culture

A relational organisation (our Integral South) where people share many things in common, resembling a family, based on loyalty and tradition. Leaders are seen as mentors or even as father/mother figures. Values are centred on openness, teamwork, cooperation, and finding consensus. As a result, engagement and morale are high and success is based on the needs of the customer and other stakeholders with an emphasis on the long-term benefits of human resource development.

§21.5 Hierarchy culture

A structured and formal environment with strong operational policy & procedure frameworks (our Integral North). Success is defined as effective and efficient with emphasis on coordination and organisation and a long-term focus on stability and results. This translates into a context of reliable delivery, smooth planning and low costs where the human resource department ensures certainty, clarity, and predictability.

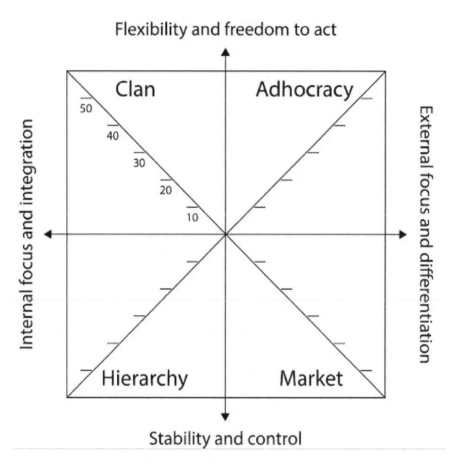

Figure 21.11: Clan, Hierarchy, Market

§21.6 Market culture

A result-oriented organisation where people are competitive, goal-focused, and action orientated (our Integral West). Success is defined in measurable market share and by customer revenue targets. Leadership is driven to complete tasks, work hard and increase competitive advantages.

§21.7 Adhocracy culture

A creative, innovative and dynamic organisation where people can take initiative and have a sense of freedom (our Integral East). Success is defined by creating and pioneering new products, services, and markets; and being entrepreneurial. The long-term emphasis is on growth and the need to take risks to set new trends and develop customers.

The I^3OO is an iterative process with the investee to develop an impact mission and strengthen the bonds of commitment and delivery. Most logically, this would follow parallel iterations and rounds of other DD processes, pre and post any Investment Management Committee (IMC) decision. The I^3OO can then become a living document and a part of developing clear and concise legal or committed contract. Such a contract and its conditionality can either as precedent and or subsequent in any formal legal financing agreements. The generic I^3OO as outlined below could be a hypothetical example for a debt investment into e.g., an emerging markets telecommunications company. Impact elements are split into those that can enter the actual legal loan agreement, either as conditions precedent or subsequent, or as covenants with the remainder falling into e.g., a letter of intent.

Table 21.4: I³OO Agreement Road Map (LA.: Loan Agreement, Cov. Covenant, GS: Green Steward)

Underlying Issue	Agreement[2]	In L.A.	Bud-get/Debit[3]	Impact/Credit[4]	KPI's[5]	Respon-sible Party	Initiation /start date[6]	Implemen-tation	SDG's
Environmental									
GHG / carbon foot-print could be im-proved in multiple areas at both at or-ganisational and stakeholder levels. (1-6)	From "diesel to elec-tric" green program	Cov	$700.000	$200.000	% of OPEX 50/50	COO	1-year	10 years	7, 12, 13, 14
	Travel less / use conf. facilities		$100.000	$200.000	Miles / per-son	GS	3-months	5-years	12, 13
	Equipment recycling Audit	Cov.	$10.000	$10.000	Audit report on off-take programs	CFO	12-months	1-year	9, 12, 13
	Offtake partners col-laboration/integration		$5.000	$50.000	Tonnes/recy-cled	COO	12-months	1-year	12, 13

[2]Key high level agreements
[3]Cost of implementation
[4]Benefit from implementation
[5]Key Performance Indicators
[6]Denotes time for initial implementation

Underlying Issue	Agreement	In L.A.	Bud-get/Debit	Impact/Credit	KPI's	Respon-sible Party	Initiation /start date	Implemen-tation	SDG's
	Tower partner diesel to solar program		$50.000	$100.000	No. towers converted	COO	24-months	10-year	12, 13, 14
	Handset recycling facilities		$50.000	$200.000	Carbon neutral handset goals	COO	2-years	10-years	1, 9, 12,
Insufficient funding towards environmental projects (level to be understood/agreed).	Plant carbon sink plantations	Cov	$100.000	$200.000	No. Trees / acre	TBA	2-years	20-years	13, 14
Lack of training / awareness of environmental issues.	Training program on environmental issues for industry/company	Cov.	$20.000	$400.000	No. attended program / year.	OPEX savings TBA	1-year	5-years	9, 12, 13
Not high on the management agenda / strategy.	EXCO member responsible for area (Green Steward, GS)	Cov.	$2.000	$0	No. agenda items. Deliverables	CEO	3-months	1-year	12, 13, 17

Human & Cultural

Underlying Issue	Agreement	In L.A.	Bud-get/Debit	Impact/Credit	KPI's	Respon-sible Party	Initiation /start date	Implemen-tation	SDG's
Lack of diversity in senior management team based on growth projections.	Hire 2 members, 1 for BD and Operations	Cov.	$300.000	$0		CEO	12-months	5-years	8,
Little or no employee involvement in management.	Employee management representation	Cov.	$0	$500.000	Election by members	Board	3-months	20-years	5, 8, 10, 16

Underlying Issue	Agreement	In L.A.	Budget/Debit	Impact/Credit	KPI's	Responsible Party	Initiation /start date	Implementation	SDG's
Adversarial relationship policy towards suppliers.	CEO / COO No. 2's appointments		$20.000	$100.000	Board to agree selection process	Board	6-months	1-year	
Local management allocate for "pet projects" which lacks commercial cohesion or local empowerment.	Thematic brand aligned project plan		$200.000	$0	No. / program	HR / L&D	12-months	10-years	1, 11,
Succession planning and talent development required	L&D plan + appointment		$700.000	$1,400.000	Dev. Key program	Board	6-months	5-years	16
No L&D strategy/budget	Management team leadership development		$70.000	$100.000	Appointment + no attended	HR	12-months	5-years	16
Base/core culture as yet not identified, articulated or communicated.	Culture survey (management & staff)		$10.000	$50.000	results	HR	6-months	1-year	

Underlying Issue	Agreement	In L.A.	Budget/Debit	Impact/Credit	KPI's	Responsible Party	Initiation /start date	Implementation	SDG's
Culture is driven locally with no purpose/mission for group. No consistent "bottom-up" intelligence to shape company.	Define Corporate Mission/Purpose statement		$2.000	$0	Communication + feedback	Board	3-months	5-years	16
Key cross cultural company value to be funded / implemented e.g. Arts development.	Arts Academy		$100.000	$100.000	Enrolment	Local MD's	12-months	10-years	10, 11,
Develop Local ICT Talent	University Maintenance Engineering Program		$1.000.000	$5.000.000	No. enrolled & recruits	Local MD's	18-months	3-years	1, 3, 4, 5, 8, 11
Social & Relational									
Adversarial relationship policy towards suppliers.	Supplier collaboration plan		$5.000	$25.000	Feedback survey	COO	6-months	1-year	12, 16, 17
Lack of commitment / coordination towards community development.	Coordinated community development plan aligned with brand & commercial drivers		$500.000	$100.000	No. projects	Board	12-months	10-year	3, 11,

Underlying Issue	Agreement	In L.A.	Bud-get/Debit	Impact/ Credit	KPI's	Respon-sible Party	Initiation /start date	Implemen-tation	SDG's
Imbalanced approach towards employee development.	Support program for employees		$25.000	$100.000	Bottom up needs identification survey	Board	6-months	5-years	3, 4, 10,
Commitments spread across too many areas/themes and not connected to corporate brand or culture.	Branding agent to position company around key themes		$25.000	$100.000	Ap-point/instruct agent	Board	6-months	3-years	
No strategic provision for family support.	Family programs		$100.000	$200.000	Bottom up needs identification survey	Board	6-months	3-years	1, 3, 5,
Economic & Finan-cial									
Investment to gener-ate 1,000 increase in employment based on current business plan.	Employment increase	Cov.	$10.000 000	$40.000 000	No. employ-ees etc.	HR	12-months	3-years	1,

Underlying Issue	Agreement	In L.A.	Bud-get/Debit	Impact/Credit	KPI's	Respon-sible Party	Initiation /start date	Implemen-tation	SDG's
Overly concentrated economic model which is not in line with values around sharing success and employee / community development.	Employee bonus pool	Cov.	$800.000	$0	2% of EBIT	Board	6-months	1-year	1, 2, 8,
Lack of CAPEX for "Green" strategies (link to Environmental).	Green Innovation Scheme		$100.000	$500.000	% / $ reduction in Energy usage	GS	6-months	10-years	9,
Mainly "lip service" i.e. no funding for community development (link to Social & Relational).	See. No. 2 Social & Relational								
ESG commitments has none or at best, little alignment with commercial goals/KPIs.	Overlay to No. 4 Social & Relational		$200.000	0$	1% of EBIT + Direct KPI links	CFO	12-months	3-years	
Corporate objectives/KPIs entirely financially driven.	Suite of new KPI's across ESG & Culture		$0	$0	Proposal by YE	Board	6-months	1-year	10, 16

Underlying Issue	Agreement	In L.A.	Bud-get/Debit	Impact/Credit	KPI's	Respon-sible Party	Initiation/start date	Implemen-tation	SDG's
Develop new suite of operational/customer focused KPIs that im-pact client behaviour	"Customer first" Delivery		$50.000	$500.000	Defined KPI's	Board	6-months	1-year	
	Totals		$15,524,000	$50,135,000					

A key follow-up question is how this approach can be sustained and developed inside any organisation, strengthening our Integral North, which requires us to look deeper into organisational research.

§21.8 Organisational Research

> If we knew what it was we were doing, it would not be called research, would it?
>
> ---
>
> Albert Einstein

Organisational research is creative work undertaken on a systematic basis in order to increase the stock of a firm's knowledge, including knowledge of its connection to its people, clients, culture and to society. It is used to establish (or confirm) facts, reaffirm the results of previous work, solve new or existing problems, support theories, or develop new theories.

A research project may also expand on past experiences and developments. To test the validity of instruments, procedures, or experiments, research may replicate elements of prior projects, or the project as a whole. The primary purposes of basic research (as opposed to applied) are documentation, discovery, interpretation, and research and development (R&D) to advance human knowledge. Approaches to research depend on epistemologies, which vary considerably both within and between humanities and sciences.

To this we can add the process methodology used and how research is approached in what is called a 'Mode 1' and a 'Mode 2' university as our supposed paragons of knowledge creation. The term 'Mode 2' was coined in 1994 by Gibbons et al[293]. They argued that a new form of knowledge production emerged in the mid-twentieth century that was context-driven, problem-focused, and interdisciplinary. They distinguished this from traditional research, labelled 'Mode 1', which is academic, investigator-initiated, and discipline-based (our Integral North).

This evolutionary step in knowledge from mode 1 to mode 2 acknowledges how knowledge creation needs to be integrated into the 'doing' realm (our Integral West) which has led some organisations to acknowledge that they must structure, organise, facilitate and create new knowledge. Mode 2 originates from the sociology of science, and refers to the way (scientific) knowledge is produced.

In Mode 2, multidisciplinary teams work for short periods of time on real world problems. This Mode also defines how research funds are distributed among scientists, and how scientists focus on obtaining them. In contrast, Mode 1's knowledge production is motivated by scientific knowledge alone (fundamental research) unconcerned with applicability. It is also founded on a conceptualization of science as separated into discrete disciplines (e.g., a biologist does not do chemistry).

Limoges[294] writes that: 'We now speak of 'context-driven' research, meaning 'research carried out in a context of application, arising from the very work of problem solving and not governed by the paradigms of traditional disciplines of knowledge.'

Similar distinctions were drawn between academic science and post-academic science by John Ziman[295].

Gibbons et al[293]. built on the Mode 2 knowledge by extending their analysis on implications for production for society. This has become more important as the economy has moved from industrial production into creative intellectual and technological production.

My own experience when working recently with a so-called Mode 2 university was quite mixed. In the middle of my studies, their culture reverted and regressed back to mode 1 causing much of the practical work by implication to become irrelevant in their assessment.

Being solely focused on intellectual knowledge and using highly simplified and digital ways of measuring progress, universities have significant limitation in knowledge creation... This has been an issue for Trans4M as the universities they worked with, this means that for Trans4M, they have had to seek alternatives for their "big PHD" which also seeks to transcend and include its smaller relative, the PhD. In my own PhD/PHD journey, this conflict became so acute at one stage I decided to walk away from the smaller PhD as it became obvious that I needed to reach beyond its confines.

Throughout history, in martial arts, teaching methods and learning have been passed down from master to pupil through the mind, emotions, spirit, and finally into the body as embodied learnings. As Japan industrialised and the Universities began to teach e.g. Karate-Do as a form of mass exercise, the art lost its spirit and became a series of step techniques that could easily be taught by one master to many students. This enabled many to be taught in easy 1-2-3 steps of highly structured physical movements with the only objective being the end result and outcome of the technique.

This facilitated easy grading as now the master no longer needed to be a master of any art, but merely a teacher of technique in which the focus was the finer details of the final posture and position. All such techniques being visible and quantifiable, typical of most Martial arts today. It may look good on screen in a film but has lost all its practical potency in any real context of combat and as a martial art which is based on the holistic knowledge and essence of any human. The parallels to today's universities are obvious and has created a disconnection with real learning where head, hearth and hand become integrated as one and learn from experiencing each other.

The book by Takuan Sōhō (1643-1745), The Unfettered Mind, is based on letters from a Zen master to a master swordsman on creating a mind of no mind, also known as Mushin. In one section he instructs:

> The right mind is the mind that does not remain in one place. It is the mind that stretches throughout the entire body and self. The confused mind is the mind that, thinking something over, congeals in one place…. If the mind congeals in one place and remains with one thing, it is like frozen water and is unable to flow freely: ice can wash neither hands nor feet. When the mind is melted and is used like water, extended throughout the body, it can be sent wherever one want to send it. This is the Right mind. [296]

In our four worlds practise for Impact, the mind must be able to flow freely.

I know that my own mode of creating knowledge is a combonation of 'knowing and doing' which for me creates more experiences and insights that are retained. But this is not how most universities tend to teach, operate or validate knowledge. I have been very lucky to realise that for me, organisational and academic modes of knowledge creation are limited; I have also been fortunate to create necessary knowledge mainly outside such organisations through many courses and programs in combination with much reading.

Professor Ikujiro Nonaka, dubbed 'Mr Knowledge' by the Economist magazine (May 31, 1997), is one of the most influential thinkers in the knowledge management movement. He states:

> In the act of creating, people argue. They have heated dialogue. They get upset! Without real exchange, you can't create knowledge. Knowledge creation is a human activity. [297]

This must be the basis for the governance and investment management culture in which we forge our impact approach. Also, and only possible by extension from our own culture, we now have the formula for working with our investees to enable change.

§21.9 Innovation driven research and realised institutionalization

> Tacit knowledge is personal, context-specific, and therefore hard to formalize and communicate. Explicit or 'codified' knowledge, on the other hand, refers to knowledge that is transmittable in formal, systematic language
>
> Ikujiro Nonaka

Much of our impact knowledge will lie inside the tacit knowledge domain and, unless this is reflected in organisational design, our impact will be only superficial. Many organisations grapple with the additional complexities that go beyond the more traditional and commoditised forms of a Human Resource (HR) function of providing a learning and development (L&D) environment. Many such corporate approaches comport with a Mode 1 University, with explicit knowledge transmitted in formal environments and 'brain-dumped'; knowledge becomes abstract, mechanistic theoretical and disconnected. Nonaka suggests that:

> Companies and leaders who treat knowledge management as just another branch of IT don't understand how human beings learn and create.' Unlike land, capital, energy, labour, and technology — the conventional 'inputs' into business practise — knowledge is innately self-renewing: It is produced and consumed simultaneously. Its value increases with use, rather than being depleted as with industrial goods or commodities. Above all, it is a resource created by humans acting in relationship with one another. [298]

One of my key developmental learning points when running the Client Solutions Group (CSG) at Fortis Bank was reformatting their linear approach and creating a learning environment from the tacit knowledge already at hand. This was synthesised with the existing client and organisational or financial problem/issue seeking a solution. At the time, even though I knew relatively little about knowledge creation, within CSG we created the diagnostic framework and collective space from which creativity and solutions could emerge.

I benefited from similar work in fixed-income sales at Citibank, which gave me the confidence to trust my own instincts despite nay-sayers. As results started to speak for themselves, with a near doubling of non-lending revenue (termed 'cross-sales'), this was a major break with what had previously occurred and became a major catalyst for personal and organisational development. As Confucius said: 'Real knowledge is to know the extent of one's ignorance.'

Nonaka's concept of a knowledge-creating company resembles a community in which generosity is prevalent, people feel recognised as distinct individuals, and informal, honest communication is commonplace. Many organisations fail to understand this when they (consciously or not) treat humans as interchangeable parts, receiving and processing data. This is why so many investments in knowledge management systems fail to deliver innovative results. As Benjamin Franklin quipped[299]: 'We are all born ignorant, but one must work hard to remain stupid'.

When Ikujiro Nonaka attended the Japan-America Institute of Management Science (JAIMS) facility in Oahu, Hawaii, in August 2008, he took time to expand on his work. He told his interviewer that they were creating 'ba', a Japanese term that describes a field or space where people can freely share what they know in the service of creating something new.

'Ba' resembles the concept of 'flow' discussed by the psychologist Mihaly Csikszentmihalyi in his eponymous book[300]. It is a mental state achieved when a person is fully immersed in the now but, unlike flow, 'ba' is never individual or solitary; it emerges and is a co-created interaction between at least two people. As Nonaka says: 'In ba, there is no you or me, there is only us, sharing a here-and-now relationship.'[301]

Ba can occur in a work group, a project team, an ad hoc meeting, a virtual email list or in frontline relationships. It serves as a test-tube in which shared insights can be cultivated. Organisations can foster 'ba' by designing processes that encourage people to think together.

For example, at the Toyota Motor Corporation, an exercise called the 'five whys' enabled employees to diagnose problems, as depicted in Managing Flow[167]:

I. Why is there a problem with overstock? Because we overproduced parts.

II. Why did we do that?

III. Because we were instructed to produce them.

IV. Why was this order given?

V. Because we attend [only] the front end of the production cycle.

VI. Why do we do so?

VII. Because our production line is based on a push-down system, where the front end defines and directs our needs and sets goals.

VIII. Why doesn't the back end have input?

IX. Because it has no functionality or incentives to communicate its needs.

After this methodical approach reached the fifth why, division leaders got the perspective they needed and subsequently redesigned the production line to more effectively pull stock from the front line.

Many organisations would have attempted to solve the overstock problem by controlling and 'managing' the frontline individuals who produced excess parts, but Toyota, by understanding the tacit knowledge involved, was able to identify the more fundamental and less visible issues.

Nonaka points out (and we also acknowledge from a psychological and spiritual perspective):

Why is ultimately a question of purpose

e.g., Why do we exist? In most organisations, people are not encouraged to explore such questions. As a result, he says, people become frozen and resign themselves to a situation or issue they could actually resolve if they had 'a way to frame their knowledge within a larger solution.'

§21.10 A model that incorporates subjectivity

In Managing Flow, Nonaka and his colleagues trace the developmental path to knowledge creation in robust detail. Interestingly, the companies in their book also follow a spiralling course, comprised of four stages:

socialisation: The need to mobilise people for face-to-face communication creating shared experiences that help them develop empathy for customers.

Externalization: Translating tacit experience into words and images that can be shared with a larger group.

Combination: Extending tacit knowledge into explicit forms to be disseminated throughout the organisation.

Internalization: Reabsorbing explicit knowledge back into daily practise. This means returning to the realm of the tacit, but with an awareness of larger and more complex issues.

Nonaka also quotes Katsuaki Watanabe, president of Toyota:

it is the continual dynamic synthesis of actual experience and abstract expertise [meaning tacit and explicit knowledge, respectively] that enables an organisation to sustain innovation.[302]

Similar to the workings of spiral dynamics on organisational culture, these stages reinforce and oscillate with one another. Also, as intimated above, knowledge creation is part of consciousness; we can draw on many traditions and disciplines to understand the hierarchy of how knowledge transcends the information stages.

As John Locke suggests[303]: 'Reading furnishes the mind only with materials of knowledge; it is thinking that makes what we read ours'. This means that there is also a distinct cultural dimension to knowledge creation, e.g., the nature and purpose of maintaining structural hierarchies based on position, race, contribution, qualification, family etc., and, of course, knowledge.

Ba can be seen as shared contexts and interactions that build and create knowledge. We can also look at ba through the four worlds:

South: Originating ba is defined by individuals and face-to-face interactions; it includes all the shared experiences and sensations that such interactions evoke. Referring to socialisation, as above, we emerge with a greater sense of connectedness and relational fields.

East: Dialoguing ba is defined by collective and face-to-face meetings and through shared mental models and skills converted into common terms and articulated as concepts involving the conscious use of metaphor and analogy, as well as negation and affirmation, to make the tacit explicit.

North: Systematised ba is defined by de-personalised and virtual interactions through on-line networks, groupware, documentation and databanks, etc. as the system for collaboration.

West: Exercising ba is defined as personalised, individual (as well as virtual) interactions. Individuals embody explicit facts and concepts, which are then communicated through virtual media such as written manuals or simulation programmes, making the explicit tacit.

Whilst finance is dominated by neoclassical economics, at the same time current economic conditions crave innovative ways of repairing the system and to better understand the prevailing risks.

We now use the theory of Nonaka and Nowotny[302] in order to provide an initial framework design, and to elaborate the nature of the research format envisaged. The main aspects of the organisation design are:

- An initial three-layered organisation design in which knowledge is created.

- Each area is adapted to support knowledge creation activities, containing a project team, business-system, and knowledge-based layer.

- The hypertext organisation has a bottom layer (the knowledge-based layer) where tacit and explicit knowledge are embedded.

- This tacit knowledge is based on organisational culture and procedures, while the explicit knowledge is from documents, filing systems, and digital databases.

- The top layer is the project and business system, comprising multiple knowledge-creating self-organising project teams where most routine operations and procedures are carried out in traditional, hierarchical, bureaucratic organisations.

The teams are loosely linked to facilitate an interconnectedness that improves the knowledge creation process. If the same ethos, mission and vision underlies the knowledge creation efforts, there is alignment of purpose that drives the process. Knowledge creation is therefore conceptualised as an ongoing dynamic cycle of knowledge and information flowing through the three layers.

The project teams in the top layer of traditional organisations are comprised of members from diverse functions and departments from the business-system layer. Traditional teams cooperate towards the knowledge goals established by company management. When a team successfully completes its task, it is dis-assembled and reintegrated into the centre, to be re-engaged with the next project.

The project team members then move to the knowledge-based layer to create an inventory in which the outcomes of their knowledge creation activities are stored. They then move back to the business-system layer and re-assemble until called upon for another project.

These layers of knowledge creation cross over management matrix layers of organisational hierarchy, and is based on Nonaka's view on sequential development[304].

An additional aim of the model is that knowledge creation can occur in these modes, and that knowledge assets oscillate from tacit to explicit.

When these modes can be managed in each quadrant to form a spiral, the collective knowledge assets will grow, passing through every mode,

THE HYPERTEXT ORGANIZATION (SOURCE: NONAKA & KONNO, 1993)

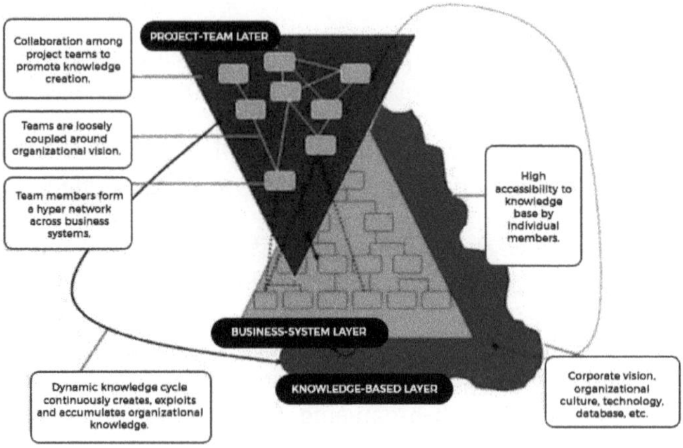

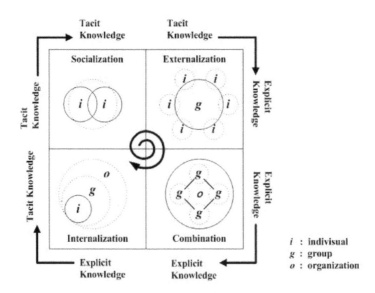

Collaboration among project teams to promote knowledge creation.

Teams are loosely coupled around organizational vision.

Team members form a hyper network across business systems.

High accessibility to knowledge base by individual members.

PROJECT-TEAM LATER

BUSINESS-SYSTEM LAYER

KNOWLEDGE-BASED LAYER

Dynamic knowledge cycle continuously creates, exploits and accumulates organizational knowledge.

Corporate vision, organizational culture, technology, database, etc.

Figure 21.12: The Hypertext Organisation

Tacit Knowledge   Tacit Knowledge

Socialization   Externalization

Tacit Knowledge   Explicit Knowledge

Tacit Knowledge   Explicit Knowledge

Internalization   Combination

Explicit Knowledge   Explicit Knowledge

i : indivisual
g : group
o : organization

Figure 1. Knowledge Creation as the Self-Transcending Process

Source : Nonaka and Konno (1998) , p.43

Figure 21.13: Knowledge Creation

in the same dynamic as for I³. These conversion modes have influenced considerably how knowledge management theory approaches the actual process of knowledge creation.

The second contribution to knowledge management theory which we can utilize originates from Nonaka in which the knowledge management effects of top-down and bottom-up management are combined into the hybrid form of middle-up-down management. This enables managers to use more self-organising teams within their quadrant, which creates its own spiralling momentum and direction, allowing their collective chaos to become less path dependent and more innovative within the field of shared expertise and experience.

The third contribution that we draw upon includes creative chaos, redundancy of information, requisite variety, and love, trust, care, and commitment. These have strong, self-enhancing psychological bonds (and boundaries) that can be managed, enhanced and facilitated within each quadrant. A department then creates its collective form at a higher level of identity, mission and purpose.

The fourth contribution suggested by Nonaka is the providing solution when converting tacit into explicit knowledge. Through the use of narrative storytelling, delicate metaphors and analogies, knowledge that otherwise could not be transferred can now be passed on, often subliminally and unconsciously. However, this principle has its sceptics, e.g., Ambrosini and Bowman[305] and Gourlay[306].

Ambosini et al. propose structured storytelling and cognitive mapping as alternative methods of transferring tacit knowledge but which ultimately also relies on respect, intention, and trust in the integrity of another's knowledge transfer.

The Law of Requisite Variety is of particular importance and also a presupposition of Neuro-Linguistic Programming (NLP): the system/person with the most flexible behaviour will control the system; this is also the first law of cybernetics. This law is constructed from building blocks that separately create a good structure and framework, whilst also recognising that this law also evidences a limitation in the Hypertext organisation model. A key challenge for any firm is to what degree they can/would follow such a format. Key is how the knowledge-based layer can accumulate and provide a custodial function to its collective organisational knowledge memory. This requires a framework of holding spheres that can be passed on such, as is intended for organisations adopting the I³ approach.

We now move into Nowotny and others in order to ascertain if their suggested modes of knowledge can further elucidate. Their main argument is to propose the recontexualisation of science through four distinct interrelated processes[307].

> Firstly, it is contended that the emergence of more open systems of knowledge production – Mode 2 science – and the growth and complexity in society – Mode 2 society, are linked in a co-evolutionary process. The implication is that not only does science speak to society but society speaks to science – a needed oscillation for impact. Second, the process of reverse communication is transforming science, and this, in its simplest terms is what is meant by contextualisation. Thirdly, the process of contextualisation moves science beyond merely reliable knowledge to what she terms socially robust (for us relational) knowledge. Fourthly, this implies a more complex role for scientific and technical expertise in the production of socially robust knowledge[308]

Key tenets toward a more reflexive self, which we now address, start with the contribution of feminism as an ingredient in our pre-requisite variety:

Table 21.5: Feminism

Feminism, Giving the marginalised a voice: Co-Creation between science (research methodology) and Society (enterprise and economy)
Feminist research complements the androcentric (masculine) perspective.
We strive to represent, and accommodate, human diversity.
We aim for self-creation and social innovation through a reflexive social science.
We see knowledge as a tool for communal liberation not individual domination

Much of finance is dominated by masculine drivers and thinking. In order to rebalance, we require feminine involvement and contributions. Unless this changes in the short term, individually men need to be aware and build capacities to draw on their own feminine sides. We need to include not only the social reality of both but also the female perspectives that extend into experience and behaviours.

Other aspects will include the power relations that often dominate male thinking and behaviour. These may include scarcity and competitive thinking that underpin the power struggles that form our structures and systems. As feminism is seen containing less rigid boundaries that separate the subject of knowledge (the knower) and the natural object of the knowledge, we can build into our system a more reflexive approach, e.g., the social, communal and even experiential, maternalistic modes of thinking. This will be important looking at I^3 in the Southern relational and Nature-based quadrant to ensure the inclusion of the female consciousness.

Decision-making processes must become more diverse to include the feminine side of consensus building and the relational needs of harmony, friendship, and closeness that can inspire trust and our sense of belonging, akin to how feminine energy creates and sustains a family. This implies that some firms need to become more conscious of how they cooperate and collaborate and create the spaces to flourish.

We need to include changing the organisational roles and conditions of women. Finance has many roles required for the industry to function. These include many roles which benefit from feminine energy input and insights, such as now being developed for Impact and if we can develop our Impact map, the need for such roles can only grow. Each four worlds' quadrant therefore needs to balance the male/female influence and redress the balance when the female voice is not allowed to be heard.

Chapter 22

Digging deeper into the integral worlds

> We humans, through old habits... have a tendency to make static, definite, and, in a way, absolutistic one-valued statements. But when we fight absolutism, we quite often establish, instead, some other dogma equally silly and harmful. For instance, an active atheist is psycho-logically as unsound as a rabid theist

A. Korzybski[27]

> Korzybski is saying that as soon as we are trying to describe reality in any kind of language, we are creating a map; the universe of discourse is the universe of maps; reality, the 'territory', is forever beyond it

Sabbadini[309]

A core issue for impact is how capital is created, measured and allocated; insight is needed to address any possible gaps emerging imbalances between the 4 worlds and capital.

Unless sufficiently Grounded (First G in the integral GENE) in critical theory or research, change cannot withstand the influences of the predominant culture; as such, there is a risk of reverting back to previous norms.

In my view, the G component is part of a spiral to which we need to return, travelling up and down to ensure that the foundational criteria and baselines are refreshed, renewed and reinvigorated.

This will enable the subsequent Emergence, Navigation and Effect to benefit from concurrent interdependent developments.

As such, it is equally the case with the E, N and E as they similarly evolve, 'transcend and include' as spiral dynamics suggest, through their previous levels.

Understanding these principles are important if we contemplate moving from Impact 2.0 to 3.0, as it takes the cultural dimension into new and further depths.

We now call it Spiral Dynamics for simplicity but the fuller explanation was The Emergent, Cyclical, and Double Helix Model of the Adult Human

Biopsychosocial Systems'[1]. The GENE, in that sense, shares the developmental double helix and its dynamics with the spiral, and our biological gene, from which the spiral metaphor is drawn.

Clare Graves, delivering a lecture at the University of North Texas in 1978, quoted Radoslav Tsanoff,:

> The twilight in which we seem to be moving today is the twilight not before dark, but before dawn. That we are reaching the end of the dark days of materialism and that the modern mind without surrendering the tools by which it has achieved mastery of nature will now more fully vindicate its own self recognition and a more human life, individual and social [43]

As with Graves, this implies an optimistic developmental axis on which the Trans4M GENE can re-Navigate and replicate itself in GENE-stacks that develop as previous GENEs reaches their limitations within the Activated consciousness, and evolve to break into new Realisations and Awareness into a Co-created new version of themselves.

This rarely happens in isolation; it is more likely a co-evolved and co-created development allowing other voices to co-mingle with one's own, including voices that cannot be heard or have been silenced.

As within the Trans4M framework, Freire's work, Education for Critical Consciousness[41], is a major reference for engaging in critical thinking, dialogical pedagogy, and critical literacy.

Freire's work has been frequently appropriated by academics, adult educators and others who inhabit 'politically charged' and 'problem-posing' Westernised ideology in ways that often reduce it to a pedagogical technique or method.

However, using the four worlds within the Trans4M integral framework, requisite descriptions invoke terms like 'education for critical consciousness', as framed within the A in CARE of Awakened consciousness.

Whilst there are maps, like the spiral dynamics integral, which can show the way beyond our own, our current map becomes our level of 'arrested development' and the organisation may atrophy. However, these cultural dynamics, as diagnosed through, for example, a CVF tool in I^3, must link into economic and financial thinking, integrally speaking.

---

[1]Claire Graves speech. (1981).[310]

§22.1 Our integral power and ideology

> With the development of industrial capitalism, a new and
> unanticipated system of injustice, it is libertarian socialism
> that has preserved and extended the radical humanist mes-
> sage of the Enlightenment and the classical liberal ideals
> that were perverted into an ideology to sustain the emerging
> social order

Noam Chomsky[311]

Whilst I'm not expecting anyone to agree with the above quote, at the
very least it challenges us to consider how we balance our economic needs
with the social order.

The integral economy is composed of clear and distinct component parts
that blend together. In our impact approach, our economic touchstone must
be similarly defined. As we approach Impact 3.0, we will see a greater diversity whereby investment firms position themselves with predominance in
areas which speak to their calling, consciousness, cocreation, and contribution (their 4Cs).

Fundamental for us is the re-integration of the economic perspective
which constitutes our finance paradigm.

I. From our **G**rounded South, we build and co-create economic principles
that are rooted inside the communities and the collective common
areas in which we operate. A grassroots and recursive economy is
envisioned and developed. This is shaped into economic subsistence
strategies, a circularity that drives and reinforces the grassroots, nurturing the soils of the social structures.

II. From our **E**mergent East we form the cohesive and binding energies
that build our economic life. The levels of our consciousness and cultural development dictate how co-evolved the economy has become
for mutual benefit and survival. Reciprocity value exchange is created,
and we may create not-for-profits, charities and other forms of associative structures that link economic development without the need
for a financial return.

III. In our North we **N**avigate our knowledge and collaboration for the
formation of social structures, such as cooperatives and networked
solutions, that reinforce our social economic bonds. We seek open

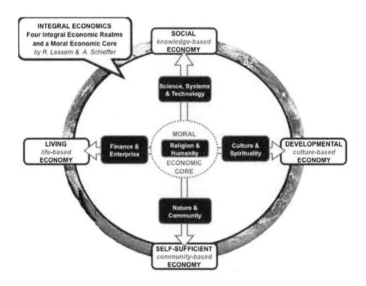

Figure 22.1: Integral Economics (Trans4M [38])

markets for the common good in proportion to our own needs, and we evolve ownership and governance systems accordingly.

IV. From our Western perspective, we put into Effect the component parts for a sustainable enterprise, now based on life-enhancing and ecologically sound principles that can generate real wellbeing. Wealth generation is more broadly defined and appreciated.

As we move each into its integral dynamic, we see the integration of each component within the overall Integral map which includes the 4Rs of realities, realms, rhythms and rounds. When we draw Impact outcome objectives from our own perspective and for our investee, a new I^3 is created from the core center where our fundamental belief and values system reside. This is the dynamic economic dance which depends on our respective backgrounds; the rhythm which we have either taken for granted, or was previously invisible to us.

Inside the Integral map, we have an organisational developmental and transformational journey defined 'from what' into 'to what' to navigate a potentially deeper I^3 process and approach. If we can achieve this, we can move towards the kind of Impact 3.0 this process is intended to facilitate. Such processes can now become part of our impact intention by integrating

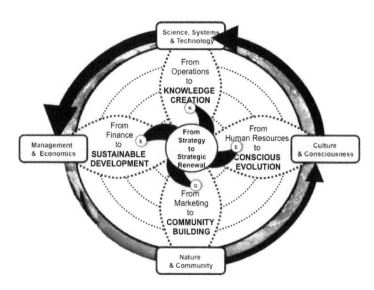

Figure 22.2: Linkages between I³ and the SDG's (Trans4M [38])

this strategically into our current organisational structures and moving our governance dynamic into a format of impact renewal.

In developmental terms, we see this through another set of developmental 4Rs of how we integrate a renewal process more deeply into the fabric of a firm and its now expanded view of how culture drives impact.

> Our approach to culture is entirely different on two counts: one, we see culture in the larger movement of humankind's journey through the Four-worlds, and two, we perceive culture as a natural extension of nature. [7]

The '4Rs', Realities, Realms, Rounds and Rhythms, are four constituents which are dynamically and interactively interwoven as follows:

Transcultural realities: Integral development acknowledges diverse reality viewpoints within each context and across the world. It captures this diversity by differentiating and integrating four archetypal realities:

- Southern relationship-based viewpoint

- Eastern inspiration-based viewpoint

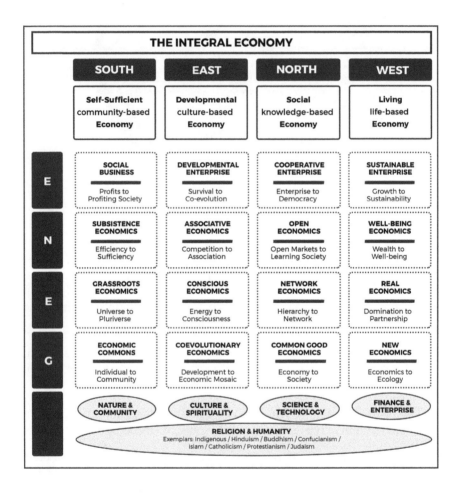

Figure 22.3: Integral Economics (Trans4M [38])

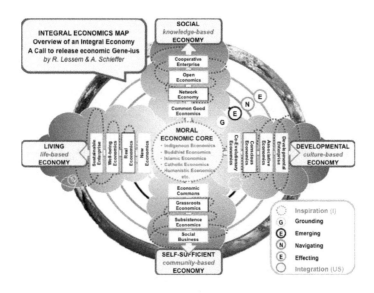

Figure 22.4: Integral Economics Map (Trans4M [38])

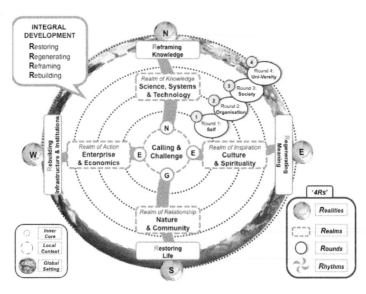

Figure 22.5: The four paths (Trans4M [38])

- Northern knowledge-based viewpoint

- Western action-based viewpoint

Each reality relates to a rich cultural variety of typological and structural patterns across civilisations.

Transdisciplinary realms: Each reality viewpoint has a different emphasis, leading to four different knowledge fields, each providing a particular perspective. Any given development challenge requires transdisciplinary engagement with all realms:

- Southern realm of relationship: nature and community

- Eastern realm of inspiration: culture and spirituality

- Northern realm of knowledge: science, systems and technology

- Western realm of action: enterprise and economics

Transpersonal rounds: Each development challenge is to be followed through (or rounded out), traversing each realm via four interconnected rounds:

- first round of self-development

- second round of organisational development

- third round of societal development

- fourth round of universal development

Transformational rhythms: Realities, realms and rounds are aligned with, and are hence subject to, four transformational rhythms:

- Southern formative and grounding (G)

- Eastern reformative and emerging (E)

- Northern normative and navigational (N)

- Western transformative and effecting (E)

These rhythms stimulate and enable dynamic and interactive processes towards authentically addressing the Integral Impact Development challenge. They are designed to release the GENE-ius of a particular self, organisation, community, and society.

This will take forms (within our respective capacities and structures for knowledge creation) which we identify as: phenomenological (existential); interpretive (hermeneutic); rational (semiotic), and empirical (pragmatic).

Integral accounting, protocols, and impact measurement systems require a re-definition of how the methodology in each dimension is formulated, which is grounded in a particular philosophical soil. This means that no impact approach can ever become a full-spectrum methodology without travelling through the lens of the specific investor.

The current Western approach of numerical measurements can never adequately capture impact. This will require a new ontology (theory of reality) across each area. As a reminder, conventional double accounting (developed by the Venetian merchant, Luca Pacioli to keep track on financial flows) creates a mutually understandable and common language through figures to interpret the symbolic representation of the numbers. As maybe only 20–30% of actual impact can be re-represented through numbers, by definition we need to explore and expand on this methodology and ontology.

Here we return to our main challenge as Plato understood when he mentions in Sophistes that:

> The materialists pull everything down from the sky and out of the invisible world onto the earth as if they wanted to clench rocks and oak trees in their fists. They grasp them, and stubbornly maintain that the only objects that exist

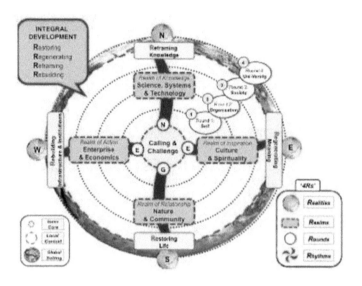

Figure 22.6: Integral Development (Trans4M [38])

are those that are tangible and comprehensible. They believe that the physical existence of an object is existence itself, and look down smugly on other people — those who acknowledge another area of existence separate from the physical. But they are totally unwilling to listen to another point of view. [312]

Principal questions of ontology include:

- 'What can be said to exist?'

- 'What is a thing?'

- 'Into what categories, if any, can we sort existing things?'

- 'What are the meanings of being?'

- 'What are the various modes of being for entities?'

And categories, how someone is assessed:

- What it is (its 'whatness', or essence)

- How it is (its 'howness' or qualitativeness)

- How much it is (quantitativeness)

- Where it is (its relation to other beings)

Following on the theme of interpretative language and semantics, we now cross into the ontology and epistemology within the areas of phenomenology, hermeneutics, critical rationalism and empiricism, from whose rich soils we can formulate our language of impact.

We need to understand that our language combines the four dimensions on which we have created our meaning. However, if English is our native (and only) language, and regardless of our proficiency, we visit a foreign country, we will struggle to make ourselves understood despite our readily available on-line English dictionary. This leads us into semiotics, i.e., meaning-making.

From an integral perspective, and as map-makers, we need to interpret our territory from multiple perspectives: from the self (i.e., inside-out), and including 'the other' (i.e., outside-in). Whilst following Occam's razor, (Entities should not be multiplied without necessity), I^3 can therefore never be the total, all-encompassing 'dictionary' or medium.

We the investor, with our Investee, is the medium and translation mechanism of Impact. This is how Marshall McLuhan's seminal work, Understanding Media (1964), begins. Marshall introduced the phrase, 'The medium is the message' which has since become a significant subject of research,

> In a culture like ours, long accustomed to splitting and dividing all things as a means of control, it is sometimes a bit of a shock to be reminded that, in operational and practical fact, the medium is the message. This is merely to say that the personal and social consequences of any medium – that is, of any extension of ourselves – result from the new scale that is introduced into our affairs by each extension of ourselves, or by any new technology. [313]

McLuhan argues that the impact of the medium is more significant than its content; that each medium, from light bulbs to computers, conveys a message to its users. The internet, for example, isn't important because of its endless supply of content but because it has created a world where we expect immediate and endless content; as a result, we have been influenced and changed by it. McLuhan explains the 'Message' via railroads:

> The message of any medium or technology is the change of scale or pace or pattern that it introduces into human affairs. The railway did not introduce movement or transportation or wheel or road into human society, but it accelerated and enlarged the scale of previous human functions, creating totally new kinds of cities and new kinds of work and leisure. This happened whether

the railway functioned in a tropical or Northern environment, and is quite independent of the freight or content of the railway medium. [314]

I^3 should never become our 'medium'; we are the medium. I^3 is the framework on which we structure our impact approach, which in turn transforms the medium i.e., ourselves. All impact analytics and diagnostics, with their measurements and calibrations, will have limitations in terms of 'messaging' as they enter our feedback loops, only reaching the depth to which our consciousness can stretch.

Here we move from grounding our methodology and method, which we saw in the 4Ms in the East and North, to allowing them to be integrally informed inside each realm. As mentioned earlier, as long we look through our Western lens where rational empiricism prevails, much of the current impact world will remain focused on statistics. This is clearly insufficient if we are to find the real soil in which to grow and create impact. One can argue that if the reflection of accounting in our world is reduced only to numbers, the inevitable outcome is our current natural and social crisis.

As an example of our need to delve deeper, let us investigate two areas which are often missing: our integral South and East.

§22.2 SOUTH: Relational Path

In the relational Southern research path, we find phenomenology (the philosophical study of the structures of experience and consciousness) as our main methodology to uncover truths and realities; this is different to what we find (and is accepted) in conventional organisations. Here we seek to uncover Nature and the character and identity of communities whose needs we serve through our impact. We encounter phenomenology as the main influence on our research methodology, which returns us to the realms of interpretative language.

The founder of phenomenology, Edmund Husserl, suggested that the market-based economy is so pervasive in the 'Western' perspective that it has lost touch with 'real' phenomena. The American accounting academics Robert Kaplan and David Johnson, wrote their renowned Relevance Lost: The Rise and Fall of Management Accounting in the 1980s, arguing that accounting had become a servant of number crunching, with no clear picture of how to serve management's fundamental responsibility to build a healthy business.

Kaplan and Johnson then parted ways: Kaplan took tenure as a professor at Harvard Business School where he became famous for his work on the Balanced Scorecard, which retained the number-crunching credentials of measurement; and Johnson continued to develop his thinking on phenomenology in measurement systems, and wrote Profit Beyond Measure (2008) with Anders Broms[315]. This book deals with companies that manage their cost base by means instead of managing it by results. To actualise this, organisations need to create an environment where the profit of individual businesses, as well as the health and long-term survival of all ecosystems are inextricably linked.

Managing by Means (MBM) suggests that instead of an organisation (which of course is a living system) being driven to meet preconceived accounting targets, they must be governed and guided by the three precepts that guide all living systems: self-organisation, interdependence, and diversity.

We can infer that how we experience phenomena is culturally biased, which is why for impact we need to distinguish how we conduct impact research. We need to conduct our research within overlapping worlds whilst we interrogate the supposedly objective view of the sciences, what has been termed the 'view from nowhere'. Here we need to understand that the essence of language is not to use it to create universal abstract conceptions but to blend our existence into our level of lived experience. A key tenet is to understand that words are only signposts pointing toward an arbitrary meaning and a disclosure whose meaning can only be grasped symbolically. As such[316], 'all signs arise from a showing within whose realm and for whose purposes they can be as signs'.

If we are to become 'the vehicle of truth', our signs need to create a linguistic, iterative dance between navigating a signpost through our historical mental map and the current context, which depends on our neurological meaning making. If so, our language as the vehicle and instrument of measurable designation need to equally evolve so that we can attach precise significance to fixed signs. This is a challenge in developing our phenomenologically-based impact measurement tools. The impact tenets for our analysis will have the following trajectory:

Table 22.1: Methods of Theorising (Origination)

Seek to reveal more fully the essence and origin of human experience within the Impact sphere.

Uncover objective/subjective and qualitative/quantitative factors and drivers.

Engage total self as Impact participant, in a state of passionate involvement with the investee and its community.

Do not seek to predict or to determine casual Impact relationships.

Illuminate them through careful, comprehensive descriptions, vivid and accurate renderings of experience, rather than measurements or ratings.

Table 22.2: Phenomenology (Foundation)

Engage in a process of radical inquiry with Impact stakeholders.

Immerse yourself in a life world of immediately lived experiences from the investees' perspective.

Concentrate on illuminating the nature of the Impact purpose with the 'inner self'.

Focus on the subjective view of the Impact experience.

Locate every unique cultural history as an episode in the larger Impact story.

Go beyond reductive positivism and naïve empiricism.

Table 22.3: Feminism (Emancipation)

Aim to go beyond just Impact by creating social change.

Use gained Impact knowledge as a tool for liberation not domination.

Strive to represent human diversity across Impact stakeholders.

Complement the often more dominant androcentric (masculine) perspective.

Include the researcher… and also Mother Nature as 'the Other'.

Table 22.4: Participatory action research (Transformation)

The issues and impacts are defined, analysed and solved co-creatively with the community.

As scientific methodology, PAR facilitates an authentic analysis of social reality by stakeholders within the Impact sphere.

Build active and full impact participation with the community.

Aim to build bridges towards any of the exploited, poor, oppressed and marginalised.

Create awareness of individual's resources, mobilising for self-reliant development.

Transform the held social reality towards alleviating Impact imbalances.

> Become a committed participant, facilitator, and learner in this
> Impact process.

Key tenets for phenomenology include:

- Uncover the unique origins/origination of your self/enterprise/society

- Reveal the natural and communal essences of your enterprise

- Go beyond surface traits and empirical 'facts'

- underlying moral values

- Locate what is particular to the place that makes you authentically who you are?

A well know case is the Cashbuild business of Alfred Koopman in South Africa, which he describes in Transcultural Management [317] and outlined in Lessem's book "Management Development Through Cultural Diversity" [318] :

> Cashbuild was started as a wholesaler in 1978 and became a very successful business in a short space of time. Situated predominantly in the rural areas of South Africa and focusing on the black housing market, our staff consisted of 84% black, 13% white and 3% Indian. However by mid-1982, with 12 outlets, profits started sliding. Everything 'Northern' was in place – systems, procedures, technology, combined with a booming market – but something was going wrong and I did not know enough about the North, at that point, to recognise where to start looking.
>
> Key questions went through my mind. Why do the workers actually work? What is their social or Divine Will? What went wrong in Cashbuild with respect to capital and labour? What were we actually trying to achieve as a business organism? How do we bring together the rights of people, their spiritually based humanity and the economic process as represented in the workplace?

Koopman realised that Western-style capitalism and its business practises demand quotas, productivity, and quality without understanding their human capital origins. Workers are seen as part of the production-distribution-consumption process, without recognising their spiritual, work and social ethic.

The protagonists of class-consciousness and its power complexes became a rallying point in the name of social justice, without actually giving expression to the human case. Koopman decided to change tack by pursuing a course grounded in human capital, requiring a social strategy that could accommodate the freedom to be enterprising, and harnessing the spiritual consciousness of all stakeholders:

> I could now see that if I recognised and restored the dignity and pride of the workforce I could achieve a new human spirit that would drive the enterprise for the betterment of all. I would therefore be able to change, not by losing my individual competitive value system but by finding 'Northern' solidarity as Managing Director with all the people in the organisation. To do this I had to go 'North'!

This entailed at a technical level:

- taking Cashbuild employees on a journey, strengthening their relationships with management

- turning all employees into stakeholders of the organisation

- aggressively addressing the distributive aspect of the business, through profit sharing, in the ultimate interest of the business, its workers and their families

- promoting excellence of quality and productivity, within the organisation, and fostering a communal climate for its achievement.

Here we have the basis of a phenomenologically orientated strategy shift – the quintessential grounding for our impact research strategy.

Let us briefly turn to the integral East, North, and West to uncover some of its research tenets.

§22.3 EAST (Path of Renewal)

The term 'hermeneutics' is related etymologically to the Greek God Hermes, who in the Iliad and the Odyssey, was the messenger of the gods, carriing messages from the divine realm to the human. In doing so, he had to bridge the gap between the thinking of the gods and that of humans. According to legend, he had a mysterious helmet, which could make him invisible, magical wings on his sandals to carry him swiftly over long distances, and a magical wand that could put humans to sleep or wake them up. He not only bridged physical distances and the ontological gap between divine and human, but also the visible and the invisible, and the unconscious and conscious.

He is the quicksilver god ('Mercury' in Latin) of sudden insights, ideas and inspiration. He is also the trickster god of thefts, highway robbery and good-luck windfalls; and is the god of trade, merchants and commerce.

We can see possible similarities to finance and its dualistic culture. Norman Brown wrote a book, Hermes the Thief[319]. Hermes is also the god of crossroads and boundaries, where piles of rocks (herms) were placed to honour him. As such, Hermes led the dead into the underworld, so he crossed the line between the human world and Hades. Hermes is truly the 'god of the gaps', of margins, boundaries, and the limits of many things. Equally, I[3] bridges gaps in consciousness between different worldly realms, seeking balance by the interpreter so in that context we all walk through 'Herms' in our search for integrality.

Although Aristotle's treatise Peri Hermêneias defined hermeneutics very narrowly in terms of determining the truth and falsity of assertions, the words hermêneuein, hermêneia, and their cognates were widely used in ancient Greek to mean interpretation on several levels: the oral interpretation of Homer and other classic texts (Homer's interpreters were called hermeneuts); translation from one language into another; and the exegesis of text[320].

The exegesis brought out the meaning, sometimes a hidden meaning. In antiquity hermeneutics, as the exegesis of texts, related to rhetoric, which had a much broader scope than it does today. It also applied to explaining dreams, oracles, legal texts and precedents, and literary and religious texts.

Hermeneutics also reconnects a people with their own natural source of being, which is why it needs to be included for Impact. Such a 'return' is not a return to tradition or stasis, an antiquarian quest for an already existing authentic past tradition; rather, we are engaged in the past affirmation, present and future role, of our historicity. This involves a process of careful inquiry into the present world, which is why Hermeneutics is so important and relevant for Impact. The analytical tenets will have the following trajectory:

Table 22.5: Narrative Methods (Origination)
Individual and communal impact stories are still unfolding.
Each one, personally and collectively, is considered impactful and legendary.
Every event in the lives we touch is therefore novel.
The narrative mode leads to gripping drama and creative Impact origination.
Tie Impact potentials and possibilities to their respective beginnings.
No struggle, no story; no trouble, no tale; no ill, no thrill.

An Impact plot which is shaped by many of the larger strategy-stories in which it is set.

Table 22.6: Hermeneutics (Foundation)

Understand how the Impact world is constructed.

Give 'the others' a real Impact voice.

Interpret the Impact reality indirectly.

Reconstruct self and society in the light of Impact objectives.

Move from spectator to active Impact agent.

Evolve from interpretive to Impact transformative.

Reconnect with the source.

Table 22.7: Critical Theory (Emancipation)

As a critical theorist, make research rooted in concrete Impact experience.

Make it arise out of problems of everyday stakeholder life.

Make it strongly emancipatory in orientation. Uncover power relations within the stakeholder community.

Analyse specifically any undue suffering.

Impact reality is regarded as socially constructed and multiple interconnections

Table 22.8: Co-operative Inquiry (Transformation)

Engage in a politically oriented process, in a participative form of inquiry.

Get involved in a knowledge-orientated process - epistemic in nature and scope.

Engage in an alternating current of informative and transformative inquiry.

Undertake the research in successive action-reflection cycles.

The validity sought is goodness, trustworthiness and authenticity.

§22.4 NORTH, (Path of Reason)

The analytical tenets will have the following trajectory:

Table 22.9: Method of Theorising (Origination)

Nature and social life consists of essential uniformities – patterns of Impact events.

It is the aim of science to discover these uniformities to uncover a universal Impact statement, which are true because they correspond to the forces of nature.

Sensory experience is rejected as a secure foundation for scientific theories.

Observations do not make much sense until they have been organised by some 'conception' an organising idea; hypotheses formulated to bring order to data.

As a process of conjecture and refutation, we can never hope to actually establish a truth; we can only eliminate those Impact theories which are false.

Table 22.10: Critical Rationalism (Foundation)

Empirical Impact science is never absolute.

Derive Impact theories from tentative conjectures.

Falsify rather than verify.

Strong Impact theory drives out the weak.

Natural and social science are values neutral.

Ultimately formulate an overall deductive Impact and stakeholder strategy.

Table 22.11: Postmodernism (Emancipation)

Pursue multiple Impact discourses.

Focus on Impact meanings as multiple and shifting.

Socially construct Impact meaning.

Engage in the art of thematic decomposition.

Use language as cultural representation.

Table 22.12: Socio-technical Design (Transformation)

Adopt a problem-solving orientation.

The Impact research is inevitably linked to action.

The Impact research is geared towards social betterment.

Use co-generative approaches to organise Impact development.

Act as friendly outsider.

---

§22.5 WEST, (Path of Realisation)

The analytical tenets will have the following trajectory.

Table 22.13: Experimental and Survey Methods (Origination)

Formulate and ask good, impactful questions, and interpret the answers.

Become an open listener, not being trapped by your own ideologies and preconceptions about what constitutes Impact.

Seek to adapt so to capture new situations as new Impact opportunities.

Create a solid grasp of the Impact issues studied.

Remain unbiased by preconceived notions, and be responsive to contradictory evidence.

Table 22.14: Empiricism (Foundation)

Search for Impact truth across stakeholders.

Seek positive facts that can drive real Impact.

Separate facts and values.

Collect observational data and build theories around Impact themes.

Control the Impact research through closed systems.

Table 22.15: Critical Realism (Emancipation)

Critical realism around Impact is critical of the status quo.

Become involved with a stratified or layered Impact reality.

View such a layered perspective on Impact reality as fallible.

Conceive Impact reality as both transitive (subjective) and intransitive (objective).

There is a hermeneutic as well as an empirical side to critical Impact realism.

Table 22.16: Action Research (Transformation)
Start out with appreciative Impact inquiry.
Challenge power relations and complexes.
Converge and diverge Impact perspectives.
Undertake social research beyond Impact into social change.
Knowing how is more important than knowing what.
Action Impact research incorporates action learning.

In summary, impact research and its measurement systems are highly dependent not only on how the 4Ms are developed but on each investment firm's scope of investing. This, in turn, is a function of influence and commitment; influence meaning the ability to enter into a meaningful dialogue with any investee, and commitment meaning the extent to which an investment firm has the requisite resources to pursue a specific impact strategy.

As an interpretative systems-based approach, any impact model can develop in line with the consciousness of the organisation doing the interpreting. Gleeson-White, whilst recognising that accountants face a tough task, outlines the way forward:

> The revolution demands that we go beyond merely accounting for traditional financial and industrial capital and take account of the benefits and detriments to the natural world and society. It urges us to include four new categories of wealth: Intellectual (such as Intellectual property), human, (skills, productivity and health), social and relationship (shared norms and values), and natural (environment). [321]

The future demands that business enterprises consider their social and environmental responsibilities equally important as profits and shareholder value. 'The revolution is here, but will we embrace its potential or deny its urgency? Can accountants save the planet- or will we destroy it for future generations?'(Ibidem) As such, we cannot underestimate the need to develop the integral impact research methodology to generate depth; each organisation will need to consider carefully how this can be best achieved without losing itself in the process.

Pertaining to the four worlds, all firms are in in some form of transformation; 'from what to what' is the question. If we seek a more fundamental transformation in building our integral I³ design, we need to travel through the 4Fs to manage each component.

We start with our capacity for transformational flows, the influence of transcultural forces, the balance of transdisciplinary fields, and the depths

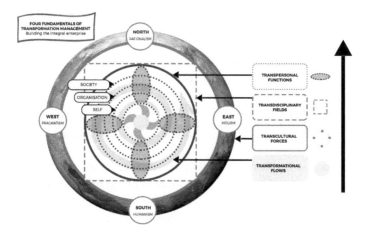

Figure 22.7: Fundamentals Transformational Management (Trans4M [38])

of transpersonal functions. The four interlinking forces that drive such transformation are as in figure 22.7.

§22.6 The Four Fundamentals of Integral Transformation through I³

(1)

Transforming Competitive Strategy into Strategic Renewal *via Transformational Flows*:

- Throughout your working life, root your transformational flows in natural systems and community to endeavour for their continuous renewal, and as a catalyst for change.

- The natural transformational flows of I³ in its design transcend the previous mechanical transactional of investing and transforming the 'being' of the enterprise.

- Engage in a circular fourfold process of Grounding, Emergence, Navigation, and as we begin to implement I³, the transformative Effect.

- I³ is simultaneously applied to the four main levels of oneself, the investee, the investment management community, and the broader society.

- The transformational flows generated by the I³ from the investment firm and the investee, continuously stimulate each to ground itself in its particular social and cultural Context. Thereby, they not only connect with their respective Contexts, but this flow connects the cultural Grounds and Capacities, generating new alternative strategies.

- Within investment firms that adopt I³ these transformational flows, I³ help institutionalise a strategic renewal of purpose, which substitutes for the conventional competitive and extractive strategies.

(II)

Transforming Organisational Development into Cultural Dynamics *via Transcultural Forces*:

- I³, as catalyst, enables us to build on our particular set of cultural capacities, and by working with and through I³, builds a unifying integral technology, both re-ground and renewed in our collective transcultural perspectives.

- Through the I³ work, the previously simplistic singular culture perspective is lessened and we learn to manage and navigate inside new diverse worlds and systems.

- By creatively working with and thereby activating the particular respective strengths of the Northern, Eastern, Northern, and Western perspectives, the transcultural forces further stimulate Innovation in I³, and the organisational designs and strategies of those affected.

- If so, within the I³ sphere of involvement, the transcultural forces are embodied in renewed fields of cultural dynamics that transcend conventional OD and theories of the firm.

(III)

Transforming R&D into Social Innovation *via Transdisciplinary Fields*:

- By establishing I³ as a unifying principle and methodology for investing, we need to connect the transdisciplinary fields and gain access to the Impact industry, but build a bridge from conventional investing methodologies, linking them to more global knowledge grounds. By doing so, we combine the social sciences with the humanities, linking them with levels of consciousness development.

- When working with I^3, we activate an integral pool of knowledge which is relevant for the development and alignment of the firm, which will surmount the heretofore dominance of neoclassical economics.

- With the expansion of the firm's knowledge base and the creative Interaction of different disciplines, the capacity to engage in aligned social Innovation is strengthened.

- Within our firm, the transdisciplinary fields are embodied in revised R&D, focusing on generating social Innovation through the implementation of I^3.

(IV)

Transforming the Functions of Investment Management *via Transpersonal Functions*:

- Based on transformational flows whilst working through I^3, transcultural forces and transdisciplinary fields, the firm is now ready to evolve and align its own design and functions towards a higher level of integration and sustainability.

- Within the firm, the four core functions of Marketing, Human Resources, Operations, and Finance, are gradually transformed into community building, conscious evolution, knowledge creation, and sustainable development as they re-connect with their grounds of being, becoming, knowing and doing.

- Through the same I^3 process, the firm can now align and resonate with the self, stakeholders, community, and society.

For too long the debilitating effects of material poverty have been divorced from the spiritual causes of poverty that begin with what we value, with the way we think, and with the resulting economic systems and practises. In this book, we have revealed that the greatest poverty is that of our economic thought, encapsulated today in 'Western' neo-liberal economics. [8]

In our own valuation and validation. As when Cassius says in Shakespeare's Julius Cesar: 'The problem dear Brutus, is not in the stars, but in ourselves, that we are underlings'[2] so let it begin with me.

---

[2][322], Act I, Scene III, L. 140-141

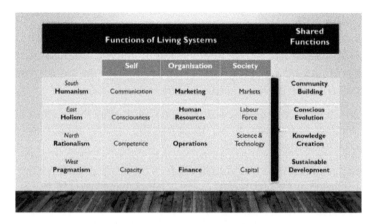

Functions of Living Systems				Shared Functions
	Self	Organisation	Society	
South Humanism	Communication	Marketing	Markets	Community Building
East Holism	Consciousness	Human Resources	Labour Force	Conscious Evolution
North Rationalism	Competence	Operations	Science & Technology	Knowledge Creation
West Pragmatism	Capacity	Finance	Capital	Sustainable Development

Figure 22.8: Functions of Living Systems

For us, then, the ultimate resolution of the financial crisis, if not also the energy crisis, and indeed the crisis of our civilisation, lies neither in government ownership, nor in financial regulation, nor indeed in the media indulgence in 'the blame game', but rather in a much more fundamental transformation and re-integration of enterprise and society. Building such an Integral Enterprise is indeed the core objective of Transformation Management. [7]

Finance has significant interdependencies within organisational culture. Taking a four worlds perspective on how investments can be reconceptualised within the integral perspective would significantly awaken a socio-economic consciousness and community activation.

I³ creates the opportunity at the trans-personal level to move into a third-person position in a highly structured way. A firm's key challenge is to extend the integral composite of I³ into new rounds of the collective.

The trans-cultural dimension is a key portal which is opened via looking through the lens of the spiral and uncovering the hidden depths of our own cultural sphere and the unhidden spheres of and for others. This re-balances trans-disciplinary and trans-personal aspects.

It is palpable that, having experienced to some degree the multiple political and moral contexts of business/finance and its psychology, I believe I have created within my own interpretative dialectic significant reframing of my interface to become constructor of meaning not only from within myself but also from my relation with others.

Of note is that the etymology for psychotherapy is derived from the Ancient Greek *psyche* (meaning 'breath; spirit; soul') and *therapeia* ('healing; medical treatment')[323]. that has been converted to 'adhering/listening to the soul' within the psychological profession.

Also, all therapy is differing forms of re-framing, suggesting that we are all psychotherapists, active and waiting to emerge and become transformative agents for others. However, if we are to become healthy, reflective mirrors, we all have reconstructive recovery work to do.

> The creation of something new is not accomplished by the intellect but by the play instinct acting from inner necessity. The creative mind plays with the objects it loves. [147]

Reconstruction of the individual self does not happen by force or coercion. To understand I^3, we have to reframe and reconstruct parts of the self which were previously either stuck or imbalanced. This usually starts with a transpersonal inventory of a required change. The prime driver may have come from either a trans-cultural, transformation or trans-disciplinary realisation, or a combination of all four; however, once a possible reconstruction is realised, the soul cannot rewind and erase the new input. Like a spiritual awakening, the effect cannot be reversed.

The aim of I^3 is to be the catalytic vehicle that synthesises pre-conceived ideas and beliefs to re-align with the messaging of the soul. This is where we move from passive responder to active communicator, and creative innovator of our new future as social innovators. This difficult task requires not only a break from the past's family marching orders but also courage and a conviction relating to our process of becoming. Our map and architectural blueprints are becoming visibly manifest. We engage with our innermost motivation and connect deeply with the 4Cs, especially co-creation and contribution, both prerequisites to become an active agent.

We qualitatively review the prevailing narratives in order to re-construct the creations into transformative agents within the levels of change capacities. Taking a spiral-dynamic perspective (i.e., Korzybski's 'change variations scale' – see Appendix 1), we see that the transformative approach needs to be semantically re-framed to comport with the cultural and consciousness levels to which it is being applied.

I^3 seeks to become the interpretative bridge between investor and investee where capital can be a source for transformational effects. Key to I^3 is creating responsibility, ownership and bringing transformational change to the heart of the methodology for all concerned.

As in the first line of this book, 'The real voyage of discovery consists not in seeking new landscapes, but in having new eyes'[324]. The unlocking therefore begins with 'finding new eyes,' and in our case, the four worlds through new eyes e.g., I^3. Again, the key driver is trans-personal.

In psychotherapy, a key learning point is to understand how the level of intended intervention creates what kind of outcome. This has two dimensions: time and level. Many patients have been damaged by well-intended therapists who, because of lack of time, pursued a particular approach that overwhelmed the patient, resulting in regression and negative outcomes. Hermeneutically, therefore, we need to re-search, re-connect and re-interpret the historical narrative and constructs from our past in order to create the necessary perspectives from which we can address the current issues inter-socially and cross-culturally.

As a psychotherapist, I know I cannot change anyone. I can only impart aspects of myself that may create sufficient dissonance and reflective change to enable their re-framing of a particular phenomenon and their own historical context. With this transformation, they become their own psychotherapists.

As human beings we are not complete, so we operate within a social and cultural matrix to which we seek to belong for our own completion. Our research task, as such, is to 'interpret the multitudinous and conflicting ways in which various worlds are constructed and human meanings developed.'[9]

> If only a world-wide consciousness could arise that all division and fission are due to the splitting of opposites in the psyche, then we should know where to begin.[104]

Finance is one of our main operating contexts, so we need to interpret the finance and investment industry from our historical perspective both cross-culturally and regionally. Much has been written about the present financial crisis and how it has re-shaped the world, but not much investigating how the banking culture has changed as a result of its impact on the world.

From a psycho-therapeutic perspective, the need sometimes for regression (reconnection) can illuminate neurological pathways so that reprogramming and re-framing can enable new meaning to emerge. The theta brain activity via dreams and the hypnogogic trance states, are often powerful ways that the brain and its psyche re-orientates neurological material to create new meanings for the individual.

We can also read this reconnection of meaning with a 'source' as one's inner dwelling, soul and all-knowing self, and my higher power or the God of my understanding.

Returning to 'synchronicity' from previous chapters, we find that it contains a hermeneutical systems' approach that is historical, reinterpretative, and meaning-seeking. C.G. Jung's favourite saying on synchronicity was from Through the Looking Glass by Lewis Carroll[3], in which the White Queen says to Alice:

> 'It is a poor sort of memory that only works backwards.' 'The rule is, jam to-morrow and jam yesterday—but never jam to-day.'
>
> 'It MUST come sometimes to 'jam to-day,'' Alice objected.
>
> 'No, it can't,' said the Queen. 'It is jam every OTHER day: to-day isn't any OTHER day, you know.'
>
> 'I don't understand you,' said Alice. 'It is dreadfully confusing!'
>
> 'That's the effect of living backwards,' the Queen said kindly: 'it always makes one a little giddy at first—'
>
> 'Living backwards!' Alice repeated in great astonishment. 'I never heard of such a thing!'
>
> '—but there's one great advantage in it, that one's memory works both ways.'
>
> 'I'm sure MINE only works one way,' Alice remarked. 'I can't remember things before they happen.'
>
> 'It is a poor sort of memory that only works backwards,' the Queen remarked.

Here we find Alice within her vortex of hermeneutically constructed contexts, which is swirling backward trying to find meaning before the event happened. This may be what some people feel when encountering I^3 for the first time; thus, it requires careful positioning. The risk, as always, is a sense of being overwhelmed coupled with denial and resistance. I^3 needs to connect serendipitously to 'the source'.

At individual and organisational levels, we connect our 'soul with role' in our work, broadening our definition of stakeholders, the meaning of 'success' and how the firm connects to manage its relationships and responsibilities. As discussed previously, we each have limited perspectives, often based on object distance along with highly distorted, deleted and generalised filters of understanding the different varieties within the cultural dimension.

Living and working purely in a city with little interaction with Mother Nature, we risk developing a limited connectivity, not accessing the environmental dimension within ourselves. We may begin to see Nature as removed and as an abstraction. If we lack such natural exposure, we may need to dig deeper into ourselves to seek rebalance and find a more experiential relationship to natural systems that deeper impact calls on us to recognise.

---

[3]Carroll, L. (1871). Through the Looking Glass. Ch. 5 Wool & Water.[325]

Chapter 23

Introduction to working with deeper culture

At the next level of impact, we need to understand some of the deeper systems to uncover and develop additional knowledge about culture. Any change excluding cultural dynamics is either doomed to fail or to significantly underperform.

An organisation's culture is a highly complex construct of policies and procedures, politics, psychology, attitudes, experiences, beliefs and values. This expresses itself through behaviour and interaction with all stakeholders. Abstract as this may sound, make no mistake that culture is part of any progressive, pragmatic and conventional business approach; it is through the firm's culture that the level of motivation is formed and its performance subsequently derived. As such, it can be argued that levels of intellectual property and human capital are developed through the filters of culture and thus expressed economically in the firm's value.

Culture forms the direction and default outcome of the firm. To use the analogy of a car, culture can be viewed as the driver; irrespective of the quality of component parts and the level of fuel in the engine, the driver (culture) determines the quality of the ride, the path, and if the car reaches its destination. Culture permeates the firm's core direction and must be managed strategically by senior management like any other asset of the firm. At this crossroad, for many firms, if denial prevails this will prevent change. Alas, old habits die hard.

This understanding is key in e.g. mergers where cultural differences can easily outweigh expected operational synergies and erode any 'value' on paper. My own experience from the Citibank/Salomon Brothers, BNP/Paribas and subsequent Fortis mergers is that, in the longer term, cultural differences and politics dominate, causing mistrust and even misallocation of resources.

In the case of Fortis, given the bank had been formed from banks in 3 different countries it could be argued that national cultural differences in operational procedures were a root cause of subsequent distress as the organisational infrastructure had evolved mainly through political decisions with duplication within several jurisdictions, for example in credit and risk functions. These functions became diluted across the firm to the point where no true or final responsibility could be allocated.

For any organisational change to be effective, it must be driven through the filter of culture and tuned accordingly. Market technology can quantify cultural organisational DNA-like codes, e.g., spiral dynamics. The good news is that these aspects of culture can be understood if they are properly identified, and can become a real asset driver that management can then shape over time. However, it is unlikely that management from within their own perspectives will achieve the requisite clarity and cognition; it may therefore be necessary to introduce a specific role that can focus on cultural development.

Banking leadership must address the underlying issues within the cultural dimension, alongside barriers to change, and find solutions to develop themselves organisationally. As a possible example, other industries have begun appointing chief culture officers (CCO) to understand the cultural drivers strategically. In finance, this notion may face resistance; the regulator may need to nudge the industry towards a deeper understanding and strategic intent for their culture. The CCO role must be understood and endorsed by senior management; if not, it is tantamount to asking an electrician to rewire a house with the power on.

Part of the solution will require a new approach to the moral and ethical development of leadership, and the development of an understanding of the developmental layers of cultural value 'codes', otherwise known as VMEMES. Don Beck introduced the term meme's[326] to describe the different value systems after reading the evolutionary biologist Richard Dawkin's book The Selfish Gene. Dawkins proposed a model of cultural information transfer in which ideas (memes), such as patterns of behaviour, habits and beliefs, proliferate in a way similar to biological genes, as humans connect with one another socially. Rupert Sheldrake, in The Presence of the Past[327], draws the comparison between Dawkins' meme and the idea of the morphic field, where ideas that have been generated propagate and appear simultaneously at different, apparently unlinked, locations.

A meme as such refers to a set of values or an organising principle. The technology and tools exist today to understand fully the psychology and underlying value systems operating at different points within the banking system, 'The greatest danger in times of turbulence is not the turbulence—it is to act with yesterday's logic' Peter Drucker.[328].

The acceptance of mobile phones across cultural and geographic boundaries, in a short space of time, is a contemporary manifestation of a meme. A VMEME acts as a value 'attractor' that becomes expressed within a culture. The assembly of our VMEMES becomes a values system.

Now we come to the core area of strategy and execution. Whilst a strategy may be the most brilliant and intellectual plan ever devised, it is the leadership that delivers it through its culture. Anyone witnessing a misalignment in this can attest to the waste of human and financial resources and increased stress, along with poor outcomes.

In an 2015 article Sull et al. surveyed 8000 managers in 262 companies across thirty industries to better understand the issues and linkages between strategy and execution[329],

> 400 global CEOs found that executional excellence was the number one challenge facing corporate leaders in Asia, Europe, and the United States, heading a list of some 80 issues, including innovation, geopolitical instability, and top-line growth. We also know that execution is difficult. Studies have found that two-thirds to three-quarters of large organisations struggle to implement their strategies.

Quite clearly, here we find that many organisations have not made the vital link to culture. This also plays out in areas where a larger part of the strategy, by definition, is about change, e.g., turnaround, venture capital, private equity, etc. In their article, Sull et al. discuss a few key myths:

Myth 1: Execution equals alignment.

When they asked firms to describe how strategy was executed, the picture was remarkably consistent:

> The steps typically consist of translating strategy into objectives, cascading those objectives down the hierarchy, measuring progress, and rewarding performance. When asked how they would improve execution, the executives cite tools, such as management by objectives and the balanced scorecard, that are designed to increase alignment between activities and strategy up and down the chain of command. In the managers' minds, execution equals alignment, so a failure to execute implies a breakdown in the processes to link strategy to action at every level in the organisation. (Ibid)

Managers create an operational and mechanistically observable link between cause and effect, which is hard-wired into policies and procedures. Most of these will be extensive, and based on sound process principles, so outcomes appear predictable. The authors confirm that 'more than 80% of managers say that their goals are limited in number, specific, and measurable and that they have the funds needed to achieve them. If most companies are doing everything right in terms of alignment, why are they struggling to execute their strategies?[1]'

Once again, the answer must lie elsewhere. To find out, they asked survey respondents how frequently they can rely on others to deliver on promises, which is a reliable measure of whether things in an organisation get done. The results confirmed that whilst 84% of managers say they can rely on their boss all or most of the time, when asked about commitments across functions and business units, the answer was,

> Only 9% of managers say they can rely on colleagues in other functions and units all the time, and just half say they can rely on them most of the time. Commitments from these colleagues are typically not much more reliable than promises made by external partners, such as distributors and suppliers. (Ibid)

When managers cannot rely on colleagues, they tend to compensate with dysfunctional behaviours that undermine execution, leading to conflicts between functions and units: 'these are handled badly two times out of three—resolved after a significant delay (38% of the time), resolved quickly but poorly (14%), or simply left to fester (12%).[2]'

Whilst managers typically equate execution with alignment and coordination, when asked the single greatest challenge in executing their company's strategy: '30% cite failure to coordinate across units, making that a close second to failure to align (40%). Managers also say they are three times more likely to miss performance commitments because of insufficient support from other units than because of their own teams' failure to deliver.[3]'

Most companies have established effective processes for cascading goals and objectives downward in the organisation, but not so for managing horizontal performance,

> More than 80% of the companies we have studied have at least one formal system for managing commitments across silos, including cross-functional committees, service-level agreements, and centralized project-management offices—but only 20% of managers believe that these systems work well all or most of the time. More than half want more structure in the processes to coordinate activities across units—twice the number who want more structure in the management-by-objectives system. (Ibid)

Whilst commitment is the operative word, the kind of commitment we are seeking cannot emerge from our willpower but from our power which

---

[1]Ibid
[2]Ibid
[3]Ibid

lies beyond will. We find again that deeper insight into culture is completely absent, with the solution sought in more structure and systems.

Myth 2: Execution means sticking to the plan

Strategy commonly means creating a detailed road map specifying who should do what, by when, and with what resources. It remains the core blueprint of execution for most organisations; it is no surprise that we find the strategy department in many consultancies still heads the list of top areas to work. However, the authors found that

> After investing enormous amounts of time and energy formulating a plan and its associated budget, executives view deviations as a lack of discipline that undercuts execution.

This is also part of the psychological phenomenon of locked-in perceptions.

As the execution map meets organisational reality the need for change increases, with politics and culture determining the extent of open and transparent dialogue. The authors suggest that:

> Strategy execution, as we define the term, consists of seizing opportunities that support the strategy while coordinating with other parts of the organisation on an ongoing basis. When managers come up with creative solutions to unforeseen problems or run with unexpected opportunities, they are not undermining systematic implementation; they are demonstrating execution at its best.'…'When asked to name the greatest challenge their companies will face in executing strategy over the next few years, nearly one-third of managers cite difficulties adapting to changing market circumstances.

> It is not that companies fail to adapt at all: Only one manager in 10 saw that as the problem. But most organisations either react so slowly that they can't seize fleeting opportunities or mitigate emerging threats (29%), or react quickly but lose sight of company strategy (24%). Just as managers want more structure in the processes to support coordination, they crave more structure in the processes used to adapt to changing circumstances (Ibid)

Here again we find that in general, management tends to seek more of the same, for example mechanistic solutions rather than looking at what actually creates and drives agility via deeper insights into culture.

Their solution to a large extent lies in resource allocation. However, in their survey they found that:

Only 11% of the managers we have surveyed believe that all their company's strategic priorities have the financial and human resources needed for success. (Ibid)

If this is true, this does not really address the problem.

Myth 3: Communication equals understanding

Most managers believe that the more we communicate, the better the staff will understand strategy and the firm's top priorities. Having witnessed this on many occasions, I have experienced the effects of information inflation, which is akin to passengers 'switching off' despite being told to pay attention when flight attendants offer safety procedures.

Only 55% of the middle managers we have surveyed can name even one of their company's top five priorities. In other words, when the leaders charged with explaining strategy to the troops are given five chances to list their company's strategic objectives, nearly half fail to get even one right. (Ibid)

We find here that, unless we make numbers a living experience that we can relate to, they become an abstraction and disconnected from our time-line and theory of change.

Not only are strategic objectives poorly understood, but they often seem unrelated to one another and disconnected from the overall strategy. Just over half of all top team members say they have a clear sense of how major priorities and initiatives fit together. It is pretty dire when half the C-suite cannot connect the dots between strategic priorities, but matters are even worse elsewhere. Fewer than one-third of senior executives' direct reports clearly understand the connections between corporate priorities, and the share plummets to 16% for frontline supervisors and team leaders. (Ibid)

These are quite shocking results and have severe implications for our Impact projects. Many firms measure communication in terms of the frequency of meetings, number of emails, etc., which in our over-inflated information world will make it difficult to find a way for Impact information to take root.

In addition, much confusion ensues from tweaking objectives whilst under way without clear reconnections; companies often identify large numbers of 'top' priorities when designing objectives which creates confusion and lack of ownership.

When asked about obstacles to understanding the strategy, middle managers are four times more likely to cite a large number of corporate priorities and strategic initiatives than to mention a lack of clarity in communication. Top executives add to the confusion when they change their messages frequently—a problem flagged by nearly one-quarter of middle managers. (Ibid)

As such, most firms believe that the solution lies in increasing layers of complexity through more prioritisation and initiatives, rather than re-focusing on what drives the mission/vision of their culture as the glue to find simplicity beyond the complexity.

Myth 4: A performance culture drives execution

Many of us may have worked with a firm for whom a performance culture is top priority. An example is a well-known investment bank which strategically dismisses the bottom 10% of 'performers' each year to squeeze performance out of the other 90% and keep them on their toes. No wonder culture suffers under such conditions. When firms fail to translate management strategy into results, many executives point to a weak performance culture as the root cause. The authors' data, however, tells a different story,

> It is true that in most companies, the official culture—the core values posted on the company website, say—does not support execution. However, a company's true values reveal themselves when managers make hard choices—and here we have found that a focus on performance does shape behaviour on a day-to-day basis... Past performance is by far the most frequently named factor in promotion decisions, cited by two-thirds of all managers... Overall, though, the companies in our sample have robust performance cultures—and yet they struggle to execute strategy.

> 'Why? 'The answer is that a culture that supports execution must recognise and reward other things as well, such as agility, teamwork, and ambition... When making hiring or promotion decisions, for example, they place much less value on a manager's ability to adapt to changing circumstances—an indication of the agility needed to execute strategy— than on whether she has hit her numbers in the past. Agility requires a willingness to experiment, and many managers avoid experimentation because they fear the consequences of failure. Half the managers we have surveyed believe that their careers would suffer if they pursued but failed at novel opportunities or innovations.

> The most pressing problem with many corporate cultures, however, is that they fail to foster the coordination that, as we've discussed, is essential to execution... When it comes to hires, promotions, and nonfinancial recognition, past performance is two or three times more likely than a track record of collaboration to be rewarded. Performance is critical, of course, but if it comes at the expense of coordination, it can undermine execution.

Here we find a deepening recognition that some of the drivers of execution lie inside the relationships of the persons doing the executing. The authors also recognise the massive gap that exists in most hiring processes, which are overly reliant on surface indicators rather than understanding or valuing the expertise and capacities for collaboration and being a 'trim-tab' (Stephen Covey's term for someone who can influence and re-direct team efforts where they are needed most).

Myth 5: Execution should be driven from the top

Much has been written about the mythical heroic leader who rallies the troops with a strong personality and charisma. In his book Execution[330], Larry Bossidy, the former CEO of AlliedSignal, describes how he negotiated performance objectives with managers several levels below him and personally monitored their progress. For many, accounts like this reinforce the myth of the hero CEO who drives execution; for others, it indicates excessive micromanagement.

It seems that when a firm uses a 'strong' leader to hold the culture together, on his/ her departure, if his/her culture was overly individualised and not adopted, it dissipates and creates a vacuum. I have experienced this quite often. At Citibank, management rotated their roles every eighteen to twenty-four months. For me, who lived or died on my long term performance in one particular area, having a new boss so often needed careful management to avoid the new boss suggesting quick fixes and knee-jerk strategies, and the reality that they could never take real ownership of outcomes. The concentration of power and lack of delegated authority within a culture is the root cause of the problem.

> if top executives insist on making the important calls themselves, they diminish middle managers' decision-making skills, initiative, and ownership of results. In large, complex organisations, execution lives and dies with a group we call 'distributed leaders,' which includes not only middle managers who run critical businesses and functions but also technical and domain experts who occupy key spots in the informal networks that get things done... Distributed leaders, not senior executives, represent 'management' to most employees, partners, and customers. Their day-to-day actions, particularly how they handle difficult decisions and what behaviours they tolerate, go a long way toward supporting or undermining the corporate culture... They do an especially good job of reinforcing performance, with nearly nine in 10 consistently holding team members accountable for results. [331]

As we discussed earlier, most of the time we interpret a firm's culture from within our own department. This is our relational sphere; whilst senior management may communicate codes of culture, it is within our context where and how this communication is interpreted that we build our picture of the organisation's politics, power complexes, and power games. The authors write:

> Conflicts inevitably arise in any organisation where different units pursue their own objectives. Distributed leaders are asked to shoulder much of the burden of working across silos, and many appear to be buckling under the load... Top executives could help by adding structured processes to facilitate coordination. In many cases they could also do a better job of modelling teamwork. One-third of distributed leaders believe that factions exist within the C-suite and that executives there focus on their own agendas rather than on what is best for the company.(Ibid)

In my experience, this is a preponderant cultural fault line in large financial institutions where politics and hidden agendas easily can overtake strategic imperatives.

I have witnessed organisational breakdown and failure as a result, together with painful journeys for everyone involved. This disconnect between culture and operations exists in most financial firms, as they have few measurement tools at their disposal apart from straightforward quantifiable performance indicators. This often results in individuals gaining promotion way beyond their capabilities for the simple reason that they generate a strong profit – but this is not relevant to the skills required to succeed at the next level. This is also known as the Peter Principle, the observation that in many hierarchies, people rise through promotion until they reach a level of incompetence.

In addition, profit attracts many owners when it comes time to take credit for performance contributions; this is an area where culture again prevails. Despite many firms' well-meaning rhetoric about collaborating and building teamwork, the reality is that if the culture does not reward these behaviours, these will be downplayed, faked and ignored. Again, most management will seek simple solutions that will not rock the boat. The authors frame this as follows:

> Many executives try to solve the problem of execution by reducing it to a single dimension. They focus on tightening alignment up and down the chain of command—by improving existing processes, such as strategic planning and performance management, or adopting new tools, such as the balanced scorecard. These are useful measures, to be sure, but relying on them as the sole means of driving execution ignores the need for coordination and agility in volatile

markets. If managers focus too narrowly on improving alignment, they risk developing ever more refined answers to the wrong question.

In the worst cases, companies slip into a dynamic we call the alignment trap. When execution stalls, managers respond by tightening the screws on alignment—tracking more performance metrics, for example, or demanding more-frequent meetings to monitor progress and recommend what to do. (Ibid)

This can lead to cultural micromanagement, which throttles creativity and raises risk perceptions resulting in a static institution that lacks the dynamic agility to respond to market and client demands. It is no coincidence that the word 'institution' means something that stands still rather than can move.

Whilst execution is critical, over-alignment can create a downward spiral as management turns to the tool they know best. In the same way, our shoe laces need to be aligned to work properly and allow for some movement so blood can flow and create comfort; overtightening will lead to pain, blisters and a possible misdiagnosis that our shoes are too small.

Organisational culture contains multiple complexities, both at personal and leadership levels and as an organisation's collective psychology, we need to find ways to operate through the firm's politic, policies and procedures. For many firms, execution needs to be re-framed to include our integral perspective which includes the expanded Impact strategy and outcome objectives that translate Impact into full spectrum results.

To what extent is there an empirical link between organisational culture and performance? Below, we summarise available research, from the book The Handbook of Organisational Culture and Climate (2011)[332].

- A strong link exists between corporate culture and performance but the 'cause and effect' is complex.

- Companies with 'culture first' perform better in customer satisfaction and sales. Companies without culture improvements become less profitable.

- Culture is today at the heart of winning because it is the only true sustainable competitive advantage that can't easily be replicated.

- Perceptual measures and objective measures are equally important.

- In Collins' book From Good to Great[135] (as measured by equity returns), level 5 leadership is based on characteristics rather than competence or capacities. In addition, all five levels are cultural components.

- Customer orientation explained 46% of earnings before interest and tax; 41% of corporate citizenship; 38% of performance and behaviour standards, and 22% of identification of the company.

- The four culture orientations of innovation, team, humanistic, and task orientation were significantly related to return on assets (ROA), net operating profit, and sales turnover. In addition, achievement and adaptive-culture orientations were directly related to performance measures.

- Culture aspects such as identification, team orientation, professional development, partnership and adaptability of the organisation could explain up to 31% of the variance of financial performance measures.

- The relationship between organisational culture and leadership effectiveness explains 40% of variances.

- Bureaucratic and hierarchical cultures have a significant negative effect on innovation success, explaining 30% of the profitability of new products.

- In their sample, firms find that ROA is significantly correlated with culture strength.

- During change the culture may benefit from a more authoritarian management style.

- Culture plays different roles in change: influencing, being influenced, and providing a context for action.

- Culture is systemically complex and therefore difficult to correlate and measure direct linkages.

In addition, in Fredrik Laloux[120] provides convincing evidence that companies that have adopted strong 'teal' (highest level and 'turquoise 'in the spiral) cultures include:

Corporate culture has long been linked to company performance, but how exactly are the two related? A recent study 'Which comes first, organisational culture or performance? A longitudinal study of causal priority with automobile dealerships'[333, 334] suggests the relationship is strong but nuanced.

For instance, a positive corporate culture—one that engages and motivates employees—helps a company's bottom line. But the reverse apparently isn't true: A company's success isn't enough to ensure a positive culture, and companies that succeed without a positive culture are likely to see their performance decline[335].

> Prior research supports a link between organisational culture and performance but generally falls short of establishing causality or determining the direction of a culture– performance (C-P) relationship. Using data collected from 95 franchise automobile dealerships over 6 years, we studied longitudinal culture–performance relationships to determine whether culture or performance has causal priority, or alternatively, whether a reciprocal relationship exists. Results from cross-lagged panel analyses indicate that culture 'comes first,' consistently predicting subsequent ratings of customer satisfaction and vehicle sales. Furthermore, the positive effect of culture on vehicle sales is fully mediated by customer satisfaction ratings. [333]

To better understand the effects of workplace culture, the longitudinal study investigated the relationship between culture and sales in ninety-five auto dealerships over a period of six years. To evaluate culture, the researchers asked employees to answer questions about their sense of involvement and their mission at work.

'We found that culture causes performance, not vice versa,' says Michael Gillespie, one of the researchers. Companies that got good culture grades from employees early in the study generally had higher profits later. Gillespie writes:

> 'The culture of a sales department right now is going to influence the customer satisfaction from that department two years from now, and that customer satisfaction is going to drive vehicle sales two years from that point. [335]

On the other hand, many companies that performed well financially scored low on employee surveys early in the study. The researchers found that companies that didn't show any improvement in culture generally became less profitable. David Grossman, a Chicago-based leadership consultant who wasn't involved in the study, says a good reason to strive for a better company culture is that it can provide a unique competitive advantage.

'Culture change today is at the heart of winning because it is so difficult for [other] employers to copy,' he says (Ibid).

When a company faces operational challenges, a good culture is much more resilient in adhering to the positive principles that created the success.

Yes, this is context dependent, but the principle of applying a deeper approach to client relationships, e.g., the 4Rs, leads to better understanding, real and improved Impact outcomes.

Let us briefly look at the Hawthorne effect[336] as an example of the power of relational attention. It is named after a series of industrial experiments in the late 1920s and early 1930s at a Western Electric Company plant in Hawthorne, a suburb of Chicago. These experiments marked an important change in management thinking about work and productivity. Previous studies, like Taylorism, mainly focused on performance improvements by the individual, while the Hawthorne experiments hypothesized that the social context influences employee performance equally to personal capabilities.

Hawthorne was mainly supervised by Elton Mayo, a sociologist who eventually became a professor of industrial research at Harvard[337]. The original purpose of Hawthorne was to study the link between employee productivity and physical conditions. Two groups of workers were selected: For one group, randomly, the lighting in the work area was improved significantly while the other group's lighting remained unchanged. The researchers were surprised to discover that productivity of the former increased dramatically compared to the control group.

Some conditions of the employees' working hours, rest brakes etc., were changed, with productivity improving in all cases and surprisingly, productivity even improved when the lights reverted back again with productivity now at its highest level including significantly lower absenteeism.

Mayo concluded that rather than the physical conditions per se affecting workers' productivity, a motivational effect had been created in that someone seemed to genuinely care about the workers' wellbeing and workplace conditions. An interesting finding was the positive effect of working in groups on the individual:

> The desire to stand well with one's fellows, the so-called human instinct of association, easily outweighs the merely individual interest and the logic of reasoning upon which so many spurious principles of management are based.

Later in life Mayo added,

> The working group as a whole actually determined the output of individual workers by reference to a standard that represented the group conception (rather than management's) of a fair day's work. This standard was rarely, if ever, in accord with the standards of the efficiency engineers.

Fritz Roethlisberger, a leading member of the research team, wrote:

The Hawthorne researchers became more and more interested in the informal employee groups, which tend to form within the formal organisation of the company, and which are not likely to be represented in the organisation chart. They became interested in the beliefs and creeds which have the effect of making each individual feel an integral part of the group. [338]

Here, we see the power of culture at play, and how it can influence production, with implications for us as Impact investors to work with culture as an integrated part and driver of our Impact objectives.[4]

Organisational culture, of course, occurs at our collective organisational levels. In his book "First, Break all the Rules"[340], Marcus Buckingham suggests that at the individual level, performance is a function of interactions, skills, knowledge, and talent. The distinction between these last three is that skills and knowledge are thought processes whereas talent, whilst inert to an individual, needs to be honed to develop. Skills are the transferable how-to-do of any role whereas knowledge is what we are aware of. There are two kinds of knowledge: factual knowledge, and things we know through experience.

Talents, however, are the interactive highways in our mind that carve out and reinforce our recurring patterns of thought, feeling and behaviour which cannot be taught or transferred. Talents for some people is feeling strong empathy, interpersonal relations, and to dedicate themselves to the success of a team (our South); whilst some exhibit a great soul, can build direction and have courage in overcoming resistance (our East). Others may care deeply about precision and accuracy, keeping discipline, and have responsibility (our North), whilst others have a drive to compete, be competent, and strive to achieve a mission, or to dedicate themselves to a certain belief (our West).

These three talents are distinguished in that thought is related to effectiveness, quality and clarity developed over time. Feelings such as empathy and relationship are psychologically developed from preferences. Talents can be further delineated:

- Striving: explains the why of a person. Comes from our internal values and is a prime driver of motivation, e.g., achieving, stamina, service and ethics (our East and West)/

- Thinking: explains the how of a person. How we construct our mental processes determines the outcome and the quality of what is done, e.g., focus, responsibility, problem solving, and creativity, (our North)

---

[4]For further reading: [339]

- Relating: explains the who of a person. How they build and maintain relationships and how they function cognitively, e.g., empathy, team spirit, persuasion, and courage, (our South and East)

The resulting individual behaviour on display is the sum total of our processes and the externalisation towards others of our personality. Understanding talent at this deeper level assists the selecting process within the organisation. Empirical research suggests that the most successful organisations manage talent to enhance individual strengths rather than 'fix' the person's weakness. This aspect is paramount when connected to psychometric and behavioural energy models such as Myers Briggs etc.

§23.1 A reflection on human capacities in a dynamic environment and introducing the Graves' model of spiral dynamics

Here we will look at what a full-spectrum impact I³ culture assessment may look like, our own levels of thinking and the trajectory of development in what is called 'spiral dynamics'.

In the words of Sri Aurobindo:

Our first decisive step out of... our normal mentality is an ascent into a higher Mind...capable of the formation of a multitude of aspects of knowledge, ways of action, forms and significances of becoming... [Its] most characteristic movement is a mass ideation, a system of totality of truth-seeing at a single view; the relations of idea with idea, of truth with truth are not established by logic but pre-exist and emerge already self-seen in the integral whole. [341]

I am fortunate to have a colleague, Ian McDonald, in our research center, The Center for Integral Finance and Economics (CIFE)[342] who also manages the UK Center for Human Emergence (CHE)[343]. In the following section we draw on Ian's excellent paper 'Introduction to Spiral Dynamics' (2010)[5]

The ideas of spiral dynamics originated with Professor Clare W. Graves' research on the development of the healthy human personality. Graves named it spiral dynamics since the full title 'The emergent cyclical, double-helix of biopsychosocial systems development' was quite a mouthful.

He suggested that our consciousness was the driver as

an unfolding, emergent, oscillating, spiralling process marked by progressive subordination of older, lower-order behaviour systems to newer higher order behaviour systems as our existential problems change [36]

---

[5]McDonald, I. (2010). Introduction to Spiral Dynamics. Hot Snow Books.

The origins of the research began in the 1950s when Graves taught psychology at Union College in Schenectady, New York, where he developed an epistemology model of human psychology.

The Graves Model is an in-depth theory of individual and group development. Graves based this model on more than thirty years of observation and the research of myriads of people in a multitude of settings.

His work was continued by two post-doctoral colleagues who wrote the seminal work 'Spiral Dynamics, mastering values, leadership and change'. One of the authors, Don Beck, is developing the model into a range of psychological insights that have become an invaluable tool for tackling the problems of our rapidly changing world. Widely influential, his work is frequently cited.

In the late 1990s to further evolve the spiral dynamics systems approach, Don Beck established the first Centre for Human Emergence (CHE) with the following mission[344]:

> The Center for Human Emergence will help facilitate the conscious emergence of the human species using a synthesis of profound breakthroughs in human knowledge and capabilities, encompassing natural patterns coherence, mega-integration, unification, expanded whole mind capacity, deep intelligence and consciousness.

Graves had originally proposed that several significant forces shape society (i.e., individuals, groups, and cultures); thus we need an integral perspective that takes into account biology (brain capacities), psychology (how people think), and sociology (where people live), and reviews them within the context of an ever-evolving dynamic culture. He identified eight hierarchical levels of existence called value systems. These formed the very first comprehensive psychological map of the human experience, which became known as the bio-psycho-social model on which spiral dynamics today is based.

Value systems, for Graves and Beck, oscillate from expressive individualistic to collective self-sacrificial systems. In the former, individuals gather enough energy to break away from the collective, whereas collective systems are sacrificial and away from the self. Over time, existential problems arise within each value system that cannot be solved by the current level's thinking systems. Crises occur and the value system of individuals/culture may shift into a completely different system, crossing the chasm between individualism and collectivism (or conversely).

The suggestion is that a person or culture will evolve to a different value system or MEME (cultural world view code) if a crisis occurs. A leap takes place and the need for a new system is born. It is through the coupling of these two factors into what Graves called a 'double helix' where human capacities can recalibrate higher and lower levels in response to changing life conditions. For Graves, the different value systems consist of different levels of neurological activation.

Unlike many of his contemporaries, Graves believed that social factors critically determine how humans and cultures evolve. He warned that we assume incorrectly that the 'nature of man' [sic] is fixed with a single set of values that humans should live by, when rather the nature of the value systems is open and evolving.

Following early guidance from Professor Graves, Beck assisted in the dismantling of apartheid, providing the background for 'hearts and minds' to enter the dialogue, influencing life conditions in order to support an eventual shift in values. He is recognised for his ongoing attempts to support a Palestine resolution and for providing insights into Afghanistan.

Beck has developed spiral dynamics into a model that reflects the dynamic, flowing nature of deep- seated codes in response to life conditions. He has also turned organisational templates into practical working tools for organisational design relevant to the challenges of rapid, non-linear change.

Spiral dynamics is not a static map; rather it is an awareness, a way of thinking that brings new levels of understanding and insight. It is not a personal development tool, although it provides exceptional insight into personal development. It is, in essence, a remarkable map of life – and that is the point. It arose and was developed inductively. This is why we include the spiral in order to understand the dynamic complexities of organisational culture for the next evolution of I^3.

Think of something alive, ever changing, adapting, subtly dynamic, growing, and capable of both total simplicity and enormous complexity, and you get an idea of the adult human mind, which is the foundational cornerstone of our culture.

§23.2 Spiral dynamics — the Graves Model and how to categorize cultures/values

We are not frozen into types or traits. Cultures are not static entities, forever trapped in a flatland. The human spiral consists of a coiled string of world views, each the product of its times and conditions. Yet when a new world view emerges, the older systems do not disappear; rather, they are subsumed in the total flow. They not only add texture to the more complex ways of living, but remain 'on call' in case the problems that awakened them reappear. So, there are systems within us, miniature world views, each of which is calibrated for different problems of existence. Each new world view is born out of chaos, in a non-linear fashion, so there is no straight arrow of time. Each is a platform, with its own unique paradigm and instructional codes for organising society, like a DNA script.

Likewise, there is significant fragmentation in the workplace germane to productivity. Our workforce in most environments is much more diverse. The shift toward a global view has introduced more complexity, not just in terms of different cultures but also in terms of value systems that work side-by- side or within a whole constellation of teams and alliances. Yet many of our approaches to productivity still tend to be monolithic in design and applied generically over people and work units.

Our values system reacts to the life conditions, and is emerging and cyclical as we experience the dissonance of being unable to solve increasingly complex issues with the inadequate ways of thinking that created them— the problems have become too complex for the current way of thinking. When a level had given up its hold, a twist of the spiral was complete and the transition began to the next code with the more complex ability to adapt. The new set of values was again relevant to the changed life conditions for a period of time as they stabilized, providing the plateau of development as observed by Graves in his research with students.

In the basic double helix, one ribbon is the effects of the environment on the individual, and the other is the effects of the individual on the environment. The links are the neurological values codes operating between them.

The findings from Graves' study demonstrate that, as we move along the helix on our path of development, each vMEME is complete and more complex than its predecessor. Another key element is that each emergent values system transcends and includes the elements of the previous. This means that we don't forget the old way of thinking when complexity increases; we take it with us and build on it, enabling us to deal with the increased complexity. The spiral dynamics double helix representation of this is in figure 23.1

Beck and Cowan introduced the concept of the gene-like vMEME as a DNA-like code within the brain that responds to the bio-psycho-social systems external to the individual. Ways of thinking are awakened, and others dimmed, to provide the complexity of thinking necessary to solve the problems associated with more complex life conditions. In spiral dynamics,

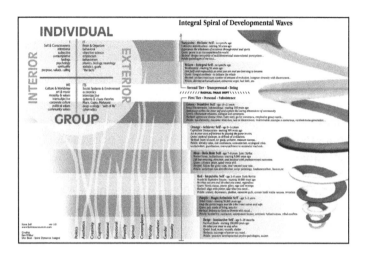

Figure 23.1: The Double Helix

colors are given to the eight codes identified by Graves. One of Graves' fundamental principles was that any individual was perfectly entitled to be the person they were. There was no inherent demand to change or progress through the codes of development. Colors are non-judgemental and non-ranking. Blue is neither better nor worse than Red.

The Graves research indicates that everybody starts at the same point on their journey and progresses through the codes in the same order, to a point where they are able to deal with prevailing life conditions with an appropriate complexity of thinking. Change is often linked to dissonance or discomfort; sometimes individuals cannot see the way forward to the next code, and become blocked. They experience increased frustration because they need the additional abilities to cope but cannot find a way through. Others become so attached to a way of thinking that they do not want to change, and so limit their activities in order to best cope, and become closed to change.

Many of us misread some of the indicators, and because of distorted perceptions have a dysfunctional experience with our present code; therefore we move out of it quickly, if we have not become blocked. This may introduce weakness, which can undermine our healthy experience of later codes.

If our progress appears blocked, and our interaction appears dysfunctional, then the associated behaviour will be seen as inappropriate or dysfunctional, in other words, 'unhealthy'. Expressions of any code may shift from healthy to unhealthy and back again. The pathway through the spiral of the double helix is often not a smooth ride. However, as with a Russian doll, everything emerges from within.

The Lebanese-American, Elza Maalouf, has further evolved this thinking, confirming that external approaches designed to improve the human condition are appropriately effective if they follow the in-built logic of development stages inherent in the psychology of human beings. She continues to build on spiral dynamics to describe the sequence of individual development levels. Consequently, economic, political, and technological innovations must correlate with the levels of complexity of thinking, i.e., matching the respective dominant value stages within individuals and cultures[345]. 'In order for societal values to evolve, all systems must be designed to meet the people where they are, locally.'

§23.3 Six blind men and the elephant

Many people know the story of the six blind men and the elephant. One discovered the tail, another the trunk, while the others felt the legs, sides, tusks and ears. Each was totally convinced he had discovered the 'truth' based on his experience. Of course, each observer was 'right' about the elephant, but only about a part of it; none was able to sense the whole.

This separation is also true about contemporary political, economic, religious, educational, childrearing, and technological theories. It includes various world views (or weltanschauungen), or numerous psychological packages, leadership initiatives or managerial mandates.

Today's heated debates in management circles reflect these different views of 'the elephant'. Rather than continue to adversarially pit the vast array of differences against one another, or suffer the consequences when conflicts surface, might it not be useful to construct a synthesis that can explain why each view emerged, where it is useful and how it can contribute to the totality of World views?

A quick summary of Worldview (vMEME) Codes :

Table 23.1: The living strata in our psycho-cultural archeology

Level	Colour Code	Popular Name	Thinking	Cultural manifestations and personal displays
Level 8	Turquoise	Whole-View	Holistic	collective individualism; cosmic spirituality; earth changes
Level 7	yellow	FlexFlow	Ecological	natural systems; self-principle; multiple realities; knowledge

Level 6	Green	Human-Bond	Consen-sus	egalitarian; feelings; authentic; sharing; caring; community
Level 5	Orange	Strive-Drive	Strategic	materialistic; consumerism; success; image; status; growth
Level 4	Blue	Truth-Force	Authority	meaning; discipline; traditions; morality; rules; lives for later
Level 3	Red	Power-Gods	egocen-tric	gratification; glitz; conquest; action; impulsive; lives for now
Level 2	Purple	KinSpir-its	Ani-mistic	rites; rituals; taboos; super-stitions; tribes; folk ways and lore
Level 1	Beige	Survival Sense	Instinc-tive	food; water; procreation; warmth; protection; stays alive

From this basic framework, we can extract commercial applications that comport with the business environment.

There are two key pieces to the model: life conditions and patterns of behaviour or thinking. Graves identified discreet stages of each and the relationship between the two. The definition of life conditions includes all parts of the external environment that someone may encounter in their day-to-day life. Patterns of behaviour are observable things an individual does or says within the context of life conditions. Patterns of thinking are attitudes, beliefs, and values. An example is the proliferation of mobile phones and how we use them to communicate. The creation of countless emojis illustrates compressing codes into uniform images in order to express more complex emotions.

The underlying premise of the model is that people do what works for them. When presented with new problems or new life conditions, people will continue to use their current, comfortable tools for fixing the problem until either the problem goes away, they go away or, realising their current tools don't work, they must learn a new set of coping tools.

When we understand people's problems or life conditions, we can understand what motivates them (i.e., what tools they like to use). If we know what motivates them, then we can infer their life conditions or the kinds of problems they typically confront. This means that we can predict how people are most likely to respond in a given context, and therefore, formulate our information so it is more useful for them.

Understanding motivation is the key to change and impact management. Obviously, if the intervention, tool or approach we plan to use doesn't press the individual's or group's motivation buttons, it will be less effective. For impact, we need to design interventions that are aligned with the operating MEME strata within the context. The Graves Model ensures that we are aligning our approach to the current thinking of the individual/group. For example, empowering employees is a popular contemporary phrase.

Empowerment encompasses a set of behaviours and attitudes that might be useful. If the life conditions within the organisation do not support empowerment, it won't necessarily happen. People need to have authority and power in the external environment or they will not consistently demonstrate empowered behaviours and attitudes. It seems simple, and quite obvious, yet many organisations cannot align life conditions with desired behaviours.

Another important aspect of the model is that the stages occur in a specific order, with people acquiring skills at each stage to handle increasing levels of complexity in their life conditions. Since communication and information are hot topics in management theory today, we will analyse the model from the perspective of how (and why) people communicate in a work setting. There are many other applications, including leadership styles, decision-making, coaching, conflict resolution, mediation, etc.

The four main communication styles are[6]

RED: doesn't say anything unless asked a direct question, and will be concerned about why we want the information. They will filter the information based on what they think we want to hear. Our reactions determine how much they reveal. They will do what they like doing and will avoid pain and embarrassment.

BLUE: points out what is not working and the problems. They know what needs to be different, but assume it is the boss' job to fix the problem. They will not reveal what is not working until asked and then it will sound like complaining because solutions are not identified. They will follow the rules at a steady pace and make sure everything is right.

ORANGE: likes to discuss the problem in terms of options and potential solutions, though we may not hear anything until AFTER they have acted. They like the bigger picture and 'what's in it for me?' They drive themselves to achieve their goals while sacrificing some aspects of their life.

GREEN: needs to solicit everyone's opinion and strive for consensus. Group decision-making is preferred and, in organisations where this is prevalent, meetings can be quite long.

People do RED when they are unsure of what the boss really wants, or they might have previously volunteered opinions only to have them rejected. They respond to power and will provide the information they think is wanted.

---

[6]McDonald, I. (2010). Introduction to Spiral Dynamics. Hot Snow Books. .

When they trust us, they might tell us things that we don't want to hear. The result of RED communication is that information is compartmentalized, with usually the boss knowing everything (and the boss likes it that way). This means that everyone knows that only the boss can make the decisions. Also, people learn not to take the initiative because only the boss has the vision and information.

People do BLUE when there are clear sets of rules and procedures. They know they should let the boss know when the rules or procedures aren't working. They also may or may not volunteer information, and certainly wouldn't presume to provide solutions because the boss/expert is certain to know better. They respond to authority and experts.

People do ORANGE when they know that the rules and procedures require creative application, and might even bend them. They are solution-oriented and figure out several options. They have learned that it is easier to ask for forgiveness than permission (as long as the option they choose gets a good solution, it is usually okay). They will share options ahead of time if they trust us. They are motivated by reward.

People do GREEN because they believe everyone's input is valuable. They want everyone, especially themselves, to feel good about the decisions, ensuring that all voices will be heard. If someone in the group disagrees, this will stall the decision, perhaps indefinitely. Being liked and being fair are most important so people will say that they agree just to move on.

§23.3.1 Changing stages and levels

Three conditions are necessary to get someone to change their thinking and behaviour and use another communication style:

  I. Clear feedback that their communication is ineffective.

  II. A clear idea (vision) of the specifics of the new style, including detailed examples of what to do and not to do.

  III. The new environment must require the use of the new style to be effective or they will revert to what they know works. Thus, it is futile to coach people to be innovative if the boss shows no enthusiasm for new ideas.

Some examples of behavioural and thinking dynamics:

BLUE – ORANGE Think about the last time we called an organisation with a problem that didn't quite fit the parameters of the person answering the phone. If they are doing **BLUE**, they'll just say that they can't help us. We will ask to talk to the manager but they will say that the manager has already been told. When we talk to the manager, who is probably doing **ORANGE**, they can figure out how to interpret the procedures to solve our problem. It is not that the person doing **BLUE** doesn't want to be nice; they are motivated to follow the rules. Not following the rules and the fear of having an upset boss is worse than having an upset customer.

If we want someone to become more solution-oriented (**ORANGE**) and not just do what has always been done (**BLUE**), then they must be told to develop a solution to the identified problem. We may have proffer several examples of the solutions we are looking for, and it will probably have to go outside the current procedures (giving them permission).

It is important that if an employee discusses only a problem, a manager needs to give him the framework with detailed examples to help provide solutions. The change will occur faster if the next time the employee comes to talk, he/she has had a successful experience from this interaction and is confident of moving forward.

Moving **BLUE** to **ORANGE** requires hands-on coaching to understand the required shift. Use people doing **ORANGE** as coaches. Reward them with prestige, recognition, course, travel, money, etc.

§23.4 Where we can apply the Graves Model?

§23.4.1 Internal change management

The power of the model is in defining the start and end points of the intended change. If there is more than one stage (e.g. BLUE through ORANGE to GREEN), it is important to build in the intermediate step. Once we know where we are starting from, it is easy to test for the most appropriate interventions.

§23.4.2 Leadership and management skills

Understanding our employees' communication and work-style preferences allows us to plan our interactions to get the most fruitful results. It adds to personality preference models like Insights, MBTI and Emotional Intelligence, because we can look at the group dynamic as well as individual performance.

Then we can align the leadership style (RED, BLUE, ORANGE, GREEN etc.) with the employees, the organisation, and what is most likely to achieve the company's vision.

§23.4.3 Needs change over time

We may need a RED/ORANGE leadership style during a turnaround or a more BLUE/GREEN style to increase motivation within the organisation.

§23.4.4 Influence and Mediation

It is possible to determine Graves' stages in organisations by observing how they communicate. There are specific words and language patterns associated with each stage. The subtle art of gaining rapport with people by communicating with them based on Graves' stages can be very powerful, and the language can be incorporated into any spoken or written work.

§23.4.5 Recruitment

How do we know if a candidate is a good 'fit' with our organisation? Understanding their communication and management styles relative to Graves' stages can help answer this. During competency interviews, if people are using RED language to describe BLUE activities, that provides important information. If the person we hire is thinking two stages ahead of the organisation, they will be frustrated at not being able to make things happen, especially if not given the authority to make changes.

Firms can use various assessments to assist in the recruitment of individuals that fit into the role and environment they are being recruited for. If a post is being filled for a financial compliance officer, then it is important that the candidate has a healthy expression of the Blue vMeme (high Blue acceptance scores); whereas a new salesman would fit a profile with a strong Orange code together with healthy Blue.

Within the context of any organisation, culture is the key driver of organisational behaviour and creates a higher level of performance. It builds the framework and map of the firm's dos and don'ts and acceptability; it is the ultimate determinant of results. The more complex the organisation becomes, the higher the need to better understand cultural dimensions to affect change and deliver results.

Human limitations are such that we cannot move from one level to a higher level, say from 4 (blue) to 7 (yellow) without considerable difficulty. Each change towards higher levels of awareness can only occur through step changes. Human nature because of fear has inertia and therefore lacks the required cultural elasticity needed in a changing environment.

We tend to consciously understand the need for change whilst unconsciously resisting it unless it comports with our values. We can all relate instances when, with good intentions, we wanted a change but our patterns were so ingrained that we ended up having to concede defeat. What was lacking was the acceptance of our position and an enhanced awareness of what was necessary to obtain the envisaged outcome.

Personal truths, as such, already pre-exist. For everyday operational purpose, truth is whatever is convincing subjectively at one's current level of perception and consciousness.

With our integral impact approach, we seek to uncover the truth and new perceptions that can emerge through our impact lens and processes.

In the words of Sri Aurobino:

> Our first decisive step out of... our normal mentality is an ascent into a higher Mind... capable of the formation of a multitude of aspects of knowledge, ways of action, forms and significances of becoming... [Its] most characteristic movement is a mass ideation, a system of totality of truth-seeing at a single view; the relations of idea with idea, of truth with truth are not established by logic but pre-exist and emerge already self-seen in the integral whole. [346]

Let us now go a little deeper into our understanding of the spiral. During, his research, Graves found it increasingly difficult to take sides in the different theories of personal development he was teaching to his psychology students, who would ask him which theory was correct. He felt that psychology was in a mess because of different models of human behaviour.

Graves' main theory focused on responses to the interaction between external conditions and internal neuronal systems, and how humans develop new bio-psycho-social systems to solve existential problems and cope with their changing worlds. These coping systems depend on, and interact with, evolving human culture and individual development; they are manifested at the individual, societal and species levels.

Graves believed that tangible, emergent, self-assembling, dynamic neuronal systems evolved in the human brain in response to evolving existential and social problems. As such, 'man's nature is not a set thing, that it is ever emergent, that it is an open system, not a closed system[347].' This open-endedness distinguished Graves from other psychologists who sought end states or perfection in human nature. Graves' work has inspired others, such as integral theorists Ken Wilber and Dudley Lynch who wrote The Mother of All Minds: Leaping Free of an Outdated Human Nature[348].

To better understand entrepreneurship and leadership, Dave Robinson integrated Beck and Cowan (Graves' theories) with ethics and organisational psychology models to create the Personal and Corporate Values Journey 'PCVJ' diagram (1998)[349] . Robinson has furthered his phenomenological approach, relating it to other cultural, business and logical paradigms (mainly within entrepreneurial business environments), as well as developing leadership tools for communication and growth, drawing heavily on Gravesian interpretations. This contrasts with conventional corporate values that focus on operational efficiencies and their tenuous link to well-being by more production.

Graves' in-depth research found that the emergence within humans of new biopsycho-social systems in response to the interplay of external conditions with neurology follows a hierarchy in several dimensions. Here, though without specific time lines or direction, both progression and regression are possible. A key element in Graves' work is the mutual interaction between the personality of the adult human and the environment. Each level in the hierarchy alternates as the individual either tries to adapt the environment to the self, or the individual adapts the self to the existential conditions. He called these 'express self' and 'deny self' systems, and the movement between them is the cyclic aspect of his theory.

Graves found two significant elements essential to understanding spiral dynamics:

- A close correlation between the emergent states and increasing cognitive ability;

- The need to invoke more complex thinking due to changing life conditions is the prime motivator for change.

When the need becomes so intense that it causes discomfort, then the transition begins.

Graves saw this process of stable plateaus interspersed with change intervals as never ending, only limited by the capacities and development of the human brain.

This should not be surprising. Looking at nature, we see myriads of change in response to conditions. Just look at plants and how root systems evolve in response to prevailing conditions, such as drought, to understand this need for adaptation.

Figure 23.2: Flower on lily pad

Figure 23.3: Lily pad Bronze Sculpture

Experientially, I would agree with the notion of change through conditions. Given our familiarity with the maxim 'necessity is the mother of all invention', when challenged our creativity can build new futures.

Values are at the root of our existence and are driven deep into the foundation of our existence. When challenged by life conditions, we may defend them at all costs, or the change event might be so fundamental or dramatic that it forces us to shift.

We have a view of ourselves which we show to the world, often the best presentation that we can offer. We make sure that it is acceptable and attractive to others, whilst blending into its surroundings and being sustainable.

In nature, the water lily is an appropriate analogy. Supporting the flower is the stem passing through the depths of the water. It adapts to variations in water depth and provides an essential foundation of the total plant. It can be glimpsed from the surface but is not as conspicuous as the flowering lily pad.

Deeper down, buried in the mud but very much connected to both the flower and stem, is its corm and root structure. The basic DNA determines the nature of the flower and its well-being.

Our values system is tantamount to the lily's corm and root structure. It is protected and not open to public scrutiny unless by choice. It must adapt and change so the lily can survive if the soil changes. Ultimately, it drives the public face that is seen above the pond surface. We can extend this analogy in that the lily, one of the most beautiful flowers on earth, grows in mud; it is from our trials and tribulations (i.e., the mud in our lives) from which our roots can be grounded (**G**) and grow to enable the flower to emerge (**E**) enabling us to navigate (**N**) our lives to create the intended effect (**E**) i.e., for us to flower.

§23.5 First tier systems

§23.5.1 first code: Beige 'Survival'

At birth, we obviously have a very limited view of the world. Our sphere of existence is totally dominated by our survival needs. The complexity of the outside world is beyond our comprehension as we have no experiences, reference points or guidelines. We literally cannot perceive the outside world, since our filters are unformed and empty of data. Our total experience is of our own body and its immediate surroundings. The world is dominated with simple states. Am I hungry? Am I in pain? Do I feel safe? This is our common starting point. This first code is colored Beige like sand to remind us of the predominant environment of many of our early ancestors. Beige represents elemental survival.

In the Beige level of thinking systems, all energy is directed toward survival through innate sensory abilities and instinctual relations. At times of illness, we may re-visit Beige, or if we become totally overwhelmed by the outside world, we may retreat into it. This thinking is an elemental function, largely driven by our survival skills. Emotions may well be very basic, principally fear-based, and connected to biological impulses, with little sense of time beyond 'now.'

We are driven to satisfy the most basic of psychological needs in the moment. This is our most primal foothold on the spiral and is only transcended when internal and external life conditions usher in the next code; the first of the 'we' systems. Internally there begins an awareness of a self, distinct from others, as well as an awakening to the sense of cause and effect. At this level humans form loosely organised herd-like structures that often changes its functional format.

Beige is still active in all countries and especially visible in East Asia, Haiti, Egypt, the Middle East, Portugal, Brazil, Indian slums, and in many parts of Africa. This is a key area for impact design and objectives as, depending on the context (e.g., a PE investment in SSA), the beige level would be very alive and active. Externally, the concern with threats and survival bring humans together in new stable ways. In organisations, people can regress back into beige during stress and political threats.

§23.5.2 Second code: Purple 'Our People'

The second vMEME has the color Purple. In Purple the emphasis is still on survival, but unlike Beige, survival is achieved by banding together. Purple represents tribal, clannish traditional behaviour, where a chief is responsible for keeping their tribe safe and secure.

Purple is a logical extension of Beige, with the recognition that two or more people joining together are stronger and more able to survive than just one. In Purple expression, there is little sense of ego, so the hierarchy and rituals are followed without question and we recognise that our safety comes through the trust of extended family.

We understand that we are the wisdom keepers of past generations, and honour our ancestors and elders accordingly. We carry little personal responsibility and the tribe thrives when the milestones of life are marked by rituals, rites of passage in the belief that our lives are in the hands of the gods.

Purple arises as Beige becomes curious about a wider world and more aware of safety and vulnerability. The power of the family, clan, tribe or community comes from a healthy embodiment of the Purple vMEME. The collective fulfils the role of providing shelter and food, typically through hunter/gatherer societies. Wealth is also divided communally; land and territory have a sacred meaning, and barter and subsistence predominate.

Purple does not seek economic or materialistic progress for themselves; they just want to have a better life for their children, good shoes, and a good burial. Due to the benefits of collective living, there is additional time for music and dance, conversation and ritual. In children, we see the wonder of fairy tales, and in today's culture, Purple flourishes in organisations such as Disney.

Purple expresses itself in gangs or groups, with secret rituals, passwords, and rites of passage. Other examples include fraternities and sororities, teams in professional sports, groupies of heavy metal bands and certain corporate tribes. Much of religious thinking, especially in third world countries, embodies this, such, as do certain trade union activities. In less functional surroundings where the family may not meet these needs, we get a replacement and see the emergence of gang/club culture with its own rituals, 'gods' and folklore. We see a willingness to share within the group, although they will defend fiercely against others. One is either a kin or stranger, and one defends kin like oneself.

A healthy developmental experience of Purple family bonding and the experience of unconditional love is an important basis for establishing a solid foundation for the rest of life. We have someone to share and be nurtured if the going gets tough, and people to celebrate with when everything is wonderful. Whilst we are able to enjoy the support of Purple, at some stage, there comes time when curiosity and impatience start the change process again as we seek new territories and boundaries to explore which the natural limitations set by the leaders, elders and traditions can no longer hold.

The traditional ways may be experienced as inadequate when aspects of the living environment are changing and individuals break free in an attempt to identify self. They find themselves in the next system, based on being individualistic. It is a sense of frustration and a rise in egoic confidence that leads humans to express the next 'me' code.

In organisations, we can see strong purple in political groupings and clans looking to identify themselves as cohesive units with special attributes and contributions. However, limited economic resources systemically pressure living conditions, which can slip purple back to Beige. It is a collective ego. This may at some point fall apart as individuals and egos reassert their own views.

§23.5.3 Third Code: Red 'Visible Risk'

Red can be expressed by the phrase, 'The ego has landed'. The emergence of ego drives us to gratify personal impulses without regard for others, even one's kin. There is no sense of guilt or constraint in the search for instant gratification. 'If I want it, I will have it' becomes the mantra of Red. It is the most powerful getting the spoils and deciding how they are distributed.

In terms of social structures Red is the level of Empire, ranging in functionality from the vicious to the heroic. The need to dominate, get respect and protect one's reputation are the most important values to protect the ego. Whatever behaviour needs to be done is accepted to avoid shame or being disrespected without any sense of guilt or consequences. The myths and rituals of Red serve not the tribe, but now the fearless warrior prepared to become a Power-God at any cost with boundaries being pushed and expanded, with limits, however set to be challenged and defeated. In politics and business, while it may appear as a participatory process, unhealthy Red is likely to corrupt the vote, given the typical question is not how can we be fair or truthful, but 'how can I get power'. Initially, low Red is displayed in the form of conflict, aggression and corruption; and High Red is hero-like or warrior-like.

However, Low Red is selfish, predatory and violent as for example historically, ships of Red merchants from colonizing powers conquered lands and exploited resources. A contemporary manifestation of a Red economic system is in Russia today, with many of its oligarchs having manipulated power, and used corruption to gain wealth. Whilst often Red leaders cling onto power at all cost, in healthy High Red the person is ready to let go, as power no longer serves its purpose.

The ability to take action is visually mirrored in behaviour, resulting in people that portray a sense of always being in control, which is healthily expressed in sports, mountain climbing, and personal endeavours against nature, like big-wave surfers, test pilots, and extreme sports, etc. In competition, Red energy demonstrates fearless strength over perceived weakness.

Red can also be heroic in the protection of 'its own' (showing its Purple roots). Tribal societies need to go through Red to get to the next stage of democracy which is today considered one of our great social challenges. Red will use force or intimidation, without any thought of guilt or remorse, to achieve a pinnacle of personal power. Playground games of strength, guile and personal skill become healthy outlets for Red. When those outlets are unavailable, and the natural emergence becomes blocked by lack of resources or opportunity, it will manifest itself as personal violence and antisocial behaviour.

Red is in all of us, and we need to have a healthy experience of personal challenge, overcoming obstacles and expressing the pure exhilaration of an unbridled Life Force. Red is the human niche that takes society out of Purple and creates the proactive human looking for new expression of self.

A contemporary expression is the ruler of Dubai who is attempting to move a whole culture up the emergence ladder several stages in the blink of an eye. If we deny and repress Red, then we can create a powder keg of resentment, latent violence and even depression; for we are depressing an essential element of life itself.

Today's ubiquitous social uprisings can be explained as Red breaking away from Purple. Often these uprisings are suppressed, not allowing the maturation that is so critical for Red to become highly functional. Rebel groups and unions often have Red leadership, and in firms, Red is often found in revered and charismatic leaders who have strong-handed its current success and have assumed a self-created hero status. As Red individualism continually takes risks and overcome challenges, Red sees its own mortality, yearning for more meaning and purpose. Weakening of personal power with age, and desire for a stable base to raise a family, begets longing for peace and order. Slowly a sense of needing something else, along with personal guilt and consequences emerges. The Spiral has taken its next turn toward 'we.'

§23.5.4 Fourth Code: Blue 'Stabilizer'

The egocentric days of Red can ultimately produce an emptiness of shared values and purpose, along with an escalating sense of guilt, given an emergent awareness of others. The fourth code, Blue, is about aligning with a higher purpose, and finding order and stability. If we align with a group and play by rules, then personal guilt is assuaged. We can find true meaning by aligning behind a greater cause, and recognising that joint effort will build stability and remove the impulsivity of earlier codes. Blue is a sacrificial system, where individuality is sacrificed to the transcendent cause, truth or righteous pathway. Blue believes that righteous living produces stability now and guaranteed future rewards, is impulsively controlled through guilt, and everybody has his or her proper place. Laws, regulation, and discipline build character and moral fiber with education handed down from positions of authority.

Blue also sacrifices the self to gain later – in that sense it is risk adverse. Traditionally it was believed that the Blue is the beginning of what most people think of as civilisation. (Purple and Red people might be belittled by this statement.) Further, Blue is often described as the 'Truth Force' because it is organised around an absolute belief in one right way and obedience to authority. Examples of such are the monotheistic religions, good American apple pie, and communism. Its black versus white thinking is pathological.

But, it is the need for simplicity and structure creating a clear way ahead that propels it out of Red.

School provides an important source of Blue thinking and structure for children, both in the classroom and team sports. Children generally respond to healthy Blue, as they want to belong and have their efforts team-recognised. Boundaries and rules provide security. Martial arts clubs can provide an ideal transition for many youngsters tapping the energy, aggression and respect, within a framework of strict rules, whilst honouring the traditions and role models of healthy Purple. Earlier codes are honoured and included within a discipline which removes any sense of personal guilt. A common Blue expression is through any religious context – attending church, synagogue, mosque, etc.; as part of a collective it gives a structured sense of belonging, whilst honouring the Divine and religious ancestry.

Rituals and rites of passage again support the earlier code of Purple but now with a sense of purpose and a route to forgiveness to replace emergent guilt. Building order out of chaos gives a sense of communal security, and makes individual suffering appear more remote as a threat. Blue believes that when we play by the rules and are 'ethical' or operate within the ethos of the community, we will be looked after.

Blue has a connection to Purple (both being 'we' systems), but within a ruled-based framework offering greater security and a sense of purpose. The complexity of thinking has increased. Blue has learned to recognise guilt and the moral rights of others: that rules and purpose will endure longer than chaos and brute force. In firms we find Blue as the stage of creating policies and structural procedures with the cultural emphasis of adherence, and where order and law has stabilised the previous drivers. This is the embodiment to 'transcend and include' stages and levels.

Healthy Blue creates effectiveness, efficiencies, compliance, and reliability. We may find Blue in areas such as accountancy, legal, and other highly structural professions. Low Blue follows rules without really thinking about it, resulting in inefficiencies, corporate creep, poor customer experience, and disillusionment. If Blue is not allowed to create order, chaos will prevail in the next levels.

A classic is the former Soviet Union during and post Perestroika. The authorities at the time wanted to embrace the Western economic system which is mainly Orange in nature whilst they themselves were looking to transition away from Red. However, what happened was that they attempted to skip Blue so their economic and commercial system did not develop and live through and build the law and order infrastructure necessary to understand, protect or create a healthy Orange. As many in power and influence acted from Red and were themselves highly motivated to enter Orange they ignored the calls for Blue which enabled much of the country's wealth to be acquired by the oligarchy.

In his Book 'Red Notice'[350], Bill Browder, the founder and former CEO of Hermitage Capital Management, starkly expressed from direct experience how Orange and Red conflicted with each other. Unfortunately, we still see this operational structure in many countries today when coming from low Red: asserting itself at all costs, grasping for power and control whilst unsuccessfully trying to by-pass Blue into Orange. This creates a 'sick' corrupt Blue and a 'diseased' low Orange.

The aspects of high Blue include control of Red violence and the creation of a more stable society based on the rule of law. In Blue there is an emphasis on fairness, equity and uniform treatment. Blue has also created much progress over Purple and Red, eliminating human suffering which is the origins from which the Impact industry is rooted. Authority within the Blue framework explores the edges of the rules, which is authority and leadership with purpose.

Before it can further evolve it needs basic Blue to be effective and reliable, provide safety and security, and impose justice and stability. At the same time, the order can become restrictive, inhibit innovation and discourage personal achievement. In its less healthy forms, Blue can become over-regulated, absolutistic, and even claustrophobic, if and when high Blue turns into a police state. As such, the organising principle in Blue is structural with different hierarchical levels of authority contracted, followed, and respected. Oftentimes the promise of future benefits does not match the expectations from current sacrificing; and thus independence becomes more attractive, individual creativity asserts itself, and the Spiral once again turns toward the 'I'.

§23.5.5 Fifth Code: Orange 'Calculated Risk'

At this point the stronger and more enterprising members of the group realize that they are held back by adhering to the group's rules and procedures, and that they could achieve better results through individual action. When the entrepreneurial spirit takes hold, Orange, also called 'StriveDrive' begins its emergence, and whilst Blue often looks to the past, Orange looks to the future. We recognise that hard effort and a strong work ethic learnt as part of the Blue code has the capacity to provide material rewards. The logic learned through obeying the rules can now be put to use strategically to gain success and power.

Orange strives for success in a scientific world of multiple solutions and open competition. This level believes in better living through technology and is not risk adverse like Blue, but rather has a calculated risk mentality. We can influentially shape and promote progress via scientific methods, quantification, trial and error.

The sense of personal freedom forged in Red, tempered with the rules and structure of Blue, ignites a hunger for self-expression and the chance to excel. Orange also seeks to manipulate the world's resources in the most efficiently, effective manner, and is optimistic, risk-taking, and self-reliant. It is the Human Niche of material prosperity through merit. Purpose is found through winning and personal success. Orange thrives on being 'better than,' and wants to be a 'winner' in any measured metric designated by society, including wealth, power, influence, status, and consumerism. In a society where the material world is either not available or without regard, then personal success will be expressed in other forms. In a fundamentalist culture, this might include intentional martyrdom, in the knowledge that a martyr's family will be rewarded.

Orange ushers in the perceived power to manipulate the environment to bring about the 'good life.' There is an inherent optimism here, with calculated risk that fuels a sense of control and achievement. Society is seen as progressing through the use of strategy, technology, merit and competitiveness. The credo is: Success now in the short term, believing that science and technology will solve future problems. Orange decision making is based on bottom line results, and achieving the desired 'orange' outcome is of prime importance. An Orange economic system is symbolized by Western capitalist ideology, anchored by individual property rights and private ownership of resources. High Orange is successful, especially in conquering the financial world.

We can see with the recent economic crises, that Orange can create excessive manipulation, greed and self-centered behaviour. Low Orange is highly materialistic and opportunistic. As an example: institutions internalizing profits/bonuses, while externalising losses onto others. The world has been conquered through technology-based competition, but this 'good life' is somehow unfulfilling and the gifts and lessons of Purple are now forgotten. After a time, this behaviour can lead to alienation and feelings of emptiness, where we notice the loss of human and social caring and reduced valuing of people.

Its palpable environmental consequences are now one of the prime drivers for Impact. Once again, we see an increasing awareness of valuing the 'We,' and the ability to see the negative impact of our behaviour on local communities and the larger world picture. The complexity of thinking increases as we see a wider horizon which is the key driver behind Impact. The strive to conquer becomes increasingly empty, preparing the ground for the next Human Niche with questions such as 'What are we doing?' starts the process of dissonance and change to the next 'we' system.

§23.5.6 Sixth Code: Green 'Inclusive'

The Green—the last in the first tier of levels recognises the need for inner peace, human connection and the care for other people as inclusivity and connectedness become the highest values. Green responds to the lack of internal fulfillment by seeking peace with the inner self and through exploring the more caring and spiritual dimensions of humanity. This propels the change out of the materialistic dash of Orange into a more feeling and egalitarian phase of Green where the well-being of all is critical.

There is a prevailing sense of equality and to sustainably share the Earth's resources. Authority and power no longer drive decisions; rather it is through reconciliation and consensus. Sensitivity and a sense of caring replaces the cold logic of materialism. A new sense of the human spirit emerges which enriches the life experience with Green looking to sacrifice self, now, for both self and others, for humanity, unlike Orange which seeks an expression of self.

A strong rejection of the earlier materialism and clinical pragmatism of Orange emerges, with a desire to remove greed and create harmony. A sense of community and common purpose becomes paramount. Diversity is welcomed with the proviso that it enhances and enriches the experience for all. Today, these are prime drivers of the Impact movement. This is the birth place of Political Correctness and policies of inclusion and acceptance as a top priority.

The Green vMEME is where most non-profit organisations have their center of gravity (of course it can be lost on many Green organisations, such as collectives, that their livelihood is supported largely by Orange-motivated profits.) The Green vMEME appeared in the mainstream culture in the 1960s, and is becoming more influential. When outer-directed, the ideal green social organisation is the network, governed by consensus-decision making.

Doubts about the effectiveness of the same collective decision making by consensus, which can take a long time and be quite tedious, as well as a continuing sense of wider connection within the universe, may start to engender an exploration into one's own evolution of consciousness for its own sake. Green is keenly interested in the interiority of human beings, and how personal empowerment is expressed. Green's role is to renew humanity's spirituality, to bring harmony, and enrich human development. Exiting Green recognises that caring for all comes at a price, and doubts about the sustainability and wisdom of supporting all regardless of cost starts change. Low Green is often conflict avoidant, as all different opinions are valued. In this way Green can paralyze itself in a different way e.g. by getting stuck in consensus from Blue where 'paralysis by analysis' is more prevalent.

While ownership of resources remains private, they are heavily taxed and regulated. The knowledge economy is a contemporary manifestation of the early life conditions of Green. Rooted in the World Wide Web's undeclared mandate to democratize access to information, the knowledge economy is redefining the values of the sixth-level system as it matures.

As with our emergent Impact context, awareness of the environment, and of the health of the planet, as well as the worker, is woven into every public and private decision.

The warm, human aspirations of Green attenuates with the appearance of complex social and environmental problems which is why for many organisations, Green is the emergent impulse for their Impact impulse and orientation. The attachment to groupthink dissolves, and a rediscovered self, equally comfortable in company or solitude, with a greater confidence and spiritual connection, emerges.

Green, however, is well known for being overly permissive, especially with Red, and has trouble dealing with life's harsher realities. However, the lack of solutions through group effort gives way to individual initiative and the amazing upward journey on the spiral continues at a much higher level of complexity, along with a quantum leap in thinking patterns. A second tier of thinking systems emerges.

§23.6 Second Tier System

§23.6.1 Seventh Code: Yellow 'Systemic/functional'

As the first Human Niche in the second tier, Yellow again is concerned with survival – but this time the focus is on survival of the self and all others.

Clare Graves described the change from the sixth to the seventh code as a 'momentous leap', a great shift where a glimpse of the whole becomes visible. We will see that at earlier codes it is difficult to relate to others at codes different than our own; but from the seventh code, we can hold multiple perspectives simultaneously, recognising them as valid. We can view the whole spectrum of the Spiral with its complexity and elegance. This niche is concerned with functionality; it is an individual and expressive thinking system, integrating many healthy expressions of Green, Orange, Blue, Red and Purple into a more effective system.

One characteristic of Yellow is its comfort with chaos. Ebb and flow, catastrophic change, and subtle adaptation are all valid models of change from a Yellow perspective, and can be embraced, understood, and meshed into effective processes which are far greater than the sum of the pieces.

Flex and flow become the natural rhythms. Companies, organisations, and even nations grow, collapse, morph, and evolve. Scenario planning is replaced by a flexibility capable of responding to whatever is, when it arises. As Dawlabani explains in his book MEMEnomics[37], whatever is right today may not be right tomorrow, so from an economic policy perspective and importantly from our Impact perspective, this thinking system must design what is naturally appropriate for a culture in order for it to emerge economically.

Unlike low Western Orange practises that exploit the resources of others or low Western Blue practises that want to attenuate fundamentalist perspectives, Dawlabani suggests that

> Yellow looks at the cultural content of each Human Niche in the first tier in these countries and designs economic policies that take on the form of an indigenous ecosystem reflecting the culture's MEMEtic values [170]

This has profound implications for our Impact methodology as we begin to see the imperatives for understanding other perspectives.

The same principle applies to public and private leadership. Leaders need to design interventions from Yellow – thus assisting big-scale transformation. The seventh code embraces a far greater understanding of complexity, and sees solutions appropriate to the prevailing life conditions and relevant to those experiencing them. It recognises the different evolutionary stages, while unblocking the obstacles preventing a healthy systemic flow for all humanity, while emphasising that chaos and change are natural. Leadership implements what the planet, people, and organisations needs, rather than what it wants.

It is not clear yet what the exact problems of existence of a Yellow system will be to precipitate the emergence of the next code, Turquoise. However, as Yellow spreads and conditions change, it becomes apparent that individual approaches to global problems are less effective. Hence the move to purple.

In the Second Tier, the 'I / We' oscillation assumes a new character: no longer the individual I/We, but swings between an anthropocentric and holistic collective of our planet and universe. In Yellow, we may still put human survival first but competition may percolate from the First Tier. We still retain elements of the belief that 'I', or a more local 'We', can thrive when others do not. But slowly a sense of the Great Picture draws us to the eighth code.

We see not only chaos and complexity, but the interconnectedness of all lifeforms and of all sciences. We recognise the mirroring of the micro worldview in the macro and at this point Yellow begins to transition to the eighth and last currently known value system when there is an acceptance of the need for coordinated action to deal with the world's problems. We are drawn towards the world of quantum reality, spirituality, and the sheer Oneness of all. Additional value systems can be envisioned and evolved from there.

§23.6.2 Eighth Code: Turquoise 'Integral-Holonic'

Turquoise recognises the inseparability of self and the universe; there is an inherent interconnectedness that irrevocably links all forms of life and matter in one integrated whole. Everything connects to everything.

Holistic, intuitive thinking, and cooperative action is expected. Nothing happens without influencing everything else with the world as a single, dynamic organism with its own collective mind. The self is simultaneously distinct and a blended part of a larger, compassionate whole where a full-merit system of exchange recognises the totality and efficiency of serving the biosphere to replace all monetary forms of exchange.

There is both self and non-self, and no division between either nonduality is recognised. All forms of energy interconnect to influence each other, so no action is seen in isolation. Turquoise can see the patterns in chaos and have fractal-like properties to synthesise them as the person is one with cosmic energy. The cosmos is viewed as the ecosystem that should be protected and is a unifying holism in contrast to Purple's sense of awe.

Turquoise contains a re-emergence of the shamanistic and intuitive forms of perception that have been absent, since Blue systems separated us from the natural world and Orange science ignored unmeasurable non-material forms of perception. Inner knowing is re-awakened, adding to our Yellow map of complexity that links deep spirituality with the ability to do what must be done for the greater good of the whole.

There is a clear vision we are the sum of all the people and identities we have been, including our ancestors. Multiple perspectives are easily balanced, not for compromise, but for the greater embrace of love in all expressions. This is the greatest complexity of thinking that we understand currently, and yet a capacity for doubt generates the change process as our understanding of the universe unravels to reveal yet greater complexity.

These levels have nothing to do with where we are today. History has shown that some of our most profound thinkers on human interconnectedness come from deep within their own contexts and from their spiritual awakening which is not time bound. The sixteenth century English priest, poet and preacher John Donne famously wrote:

> No man is an island, entire of itself; every man is a piece of the continent, a part of the main. If a clod be washed away by the sea, Europe is the less, as well as if a promontory were, as well as if a manor of thy friend's or of thine own were: any man's death diminishes me, because I am involved in mankind, and therefore never send to know for whom the bells tolls; it tolls for thee.

§23.7 The Flow of the Spiral

The oscillating dynamic change process between self-expression and self-denial emerges progressively in response to increasing complexity (we see this in the shift from tribes to towns, to cities, to nations, and to globalisation).

At Turquoise, even the meaning of a separate self is seen as a differentiated aspect of the whole. This does not mean, however, that we lose the sense of self altogether; and it should not be confused with a mystic, blissful or enlightened end state.

It is anticipated that human emergence will continue beyond Turquoise, where a ninth 'Coral' code awaits.

We can see how the need for added personal safety drives the change from personal Beige survival to the protection of Purple tribe, and how additional time and confidence fosters the emergence of self and the ego of Red.

Developing guilt drives us to the protection of rules and structure; a common goal provides purpose as we discover Blue.

A sense of exploration and a desire to express ourselves once again takes hold as we strive for the good life in Orange.

The emptiness of materialism is then replaced by a sense of the greater community and a common sharing of our resources in Green.

Individually we pause here, preparing for the 'momentous leap' as we find ourselves able for the first time to hold multiple perspectives and feel comfortable with chaotic flow as we enter Yellow.

The Spiral has turned eight times, taking mankind on a journey from the isolated sphere of personal survival to a sense of identity with the universe itself.

There is no imperative to progress Spirally if life conditions remain unchanged. Clare Graves emphatically said that everybody has the right to be who they are. We all pause at different points on the Spiral, some going no further by choice, and others blocked or trapped. We may also move individually or collectively back down the Spiral if our perception of life conditions cause us to 'downshift' to earlier ways of thinking in order to cope. A natural disaster or significant event can even cause regress. Likewise, every skill we acquire remains available, so if the going gets rough, we can dig in and re-ignite the earlier ways of thinking that served us well. We regress to the thinking appropriate to our life conditions, or are drawn towards new ways of thinking as we become exposed to more complex problems.

§23.8 The Change Process

The change of dominant codes is gradual, as in a slow dissolve between two film shots in a movie. The existing dominant code fades as the emergent code strengthens and stabilizes. This is a continuous process of folding and unfolding as the life conditions, and our perceptions of those conditions change. A code which has served us well will cease to provide all the perceived answers, and an awakening of other possibilities emerges.

This provides the impetus for the old code to fade into a reservoir of skills and coping tools, to be tapped into as required. The codes unfold in a pattern: from sole survival to tribe member, from leaving the tribe to the expression of personal gratification, to group living with purpose and rules emerging into a self-expressed sense of excellence, then returning to the bigger community of the common purpose. The journey cycles from self-expression at the expense of the group, to expression of the group at the expense of self. We alternate between building our own sense of self and being part of a meaningful community.

We allow one set of codes to drop away as the next emerges on our

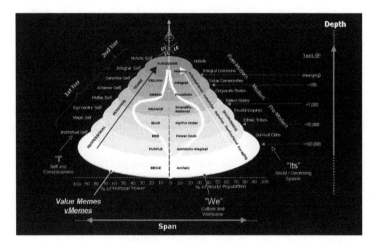

Figure 23.4: Value Memes

dynamic journey through our personal development, learning to deal with greater complexity at every level. Our reaction to our environment, and the reaction of our environment to our presence, fuels the unfolding of the double helix in a continuing path to the Green code, where, after much internal processing, the possibility unfolds that perhaps we can develop a sense of self without sacrificing the group, or even to develop the group without eliminating our own sense of individuality. Note, too, that a shift to internal values from dramatic events and greater consciousness form a part of our life conditions. Eventually, however, the boundaries merge as inseparable holism develops.

We see two pathways on a parallel journey unfolding: as a self-centered code collapses, a group centered code gains. The group code, in turn, will be replaced by a renewed, more appropriate, self-expressive code as the complexity of life increases. This is the emergent oscillation and spiral in action.

The self-expressed codes are represented by the warm colors of Beige, Red, Orange, and Yellow, whilst the cooler colors represent the unfolding collective codes of Purple, Blue, Green and, eventually, Turquoise.

Lives are full of dynamic change, and so are our vMemes. We rarely experience time with the peak modal clarity of a dominant code; rather, at any given moment, we are in some form of transition, trying to balance the code that has served us well in the past but has been surpassed by a rising new code that we are learning to balance and understand. Many of society's problems stems from the hold of community relaxing as we explore the emerging sense of self, e.g., when Purple and Red values balance; or when guilt and a sense of purpose emerges, and we leave the powerful self of Red behind, finding our home amongst the framework of Blue expressions such as family, school, work, or congregation. The code transition is not always straightforward. The energy we require to make the transition may be available, or we may simply lose our capacity to adapt due to other circumstances.

The transition can be blocked or closed, resulting in frustration and a sense of being trapped. An example is where youngsters see material wealth and its accouterments as scoring personal value, but lacked the opportunity to earn the money, and so develop low self-esteem, becoming clouded by depression, or exploding in rage.

If we look at the lifecycle of organisations, there is a more decisive moment when the peak has passed and we have a realisation of decline. In that moment either the new organisation (or the new code) emerges, or the moment is lost and the development cycle becomes closed. In some circumstances, life conditions are such that development may be blocked by the action of others. An example is when emergent societies are ready to grow from Purple and healthy Red into Blue, but the transition between codes may be blocked by unhealthy Red or the heavy Blue of others. Tribalism becomes blocked, because it serves the purpose of others creating situations, evident in much of the Middle East and Asia.

§23.9 Measuring the Path of the Spiral

Since Spiral Dynamics is built from data rather than deductively, it is only natural that we continue to measure the dynamics of the ever-changing flow of the active codes within individuals, teams and organisations.

We have earlier seen that our vMemes are the equivalent to our DNA codes; not as we would like to be or how we were, but how we are. This is the magic of understanding Spiral Dynamics!

If we ask routine questions designed to elicit our instinctual responses, then we can build a profile of the vMeme codes that are active at the time of the questioning.

The National Values Center, in Denton, Texas has developed a series of assessments, founded on Clare Graves' original research.

The tests have been developed for individuals and organisations across the world. As individuals, we emerge into somebody capable of better responding to our life conditions, to hold more perspectives, and to deal with greater complexity which is referred to as Personal Emergence.

An organisation is made up of individuals, but there is also an ethos or culture to each organisation which generates, if managed and led correctly, something more than the sum of its parts. An organisation (i.e., company, team, or multinational corporation) with insight and strong leadership, can emerge into something far greater than existed before. Otherwise known as Organisational Emergence.

Children respond rapidly to the changing life conditions around them. The greatest obstacle to this growth is the possibility of a change between one code and the next becoming 'closed' or 'arrested.' If a dominant individual, or group of individuals, prevents our natural propensity to develop, frustrations and anxieties occur which can halt the emergence of the adult human being. When we use the insights that Spiral Dynamics brings to smooth the transitions between codes, and to encourage exploration of what we may be capable of, children and all individuals respond with enthusiasm and energy. We refer to this as Educational Emergence.

None of us lives in isolation; our peers are part of our life conditions. Graves' research demonstrates that not only do we respond to our life conditions, but our life conditions respond to us. We are enmeshed within our community, and are an integral part of it.

Years ago, it was said that, 'If you are not part of the solution, you are part of the problem.' More accurately, 'If you don't recognise yourself as part of the problem, you will never be part of the solution.' Community Emergence is centered on the use of Spiral Dynamics to better understand the dynamics of our community, while using that insight to help a healthier community emerge to fully meet the life conditions of all who live within it. For Impact and our Social dimension this is a key insight for using the Spiral to understand what social development is required. Spiral Dynamics has no power in itself. The insight that comes with understanding the ideas of Spiral Dynamics can change nations, communities, and firms. The power is in people embracing what may be possible, and using insight, support, and experience to create it as a reality in their own lives.

§23.10 Organisational Emergence

Much of Spiral Dynamics focuses on the individual, since the data is the foundation for Professor Graves' work. If we understand the idea of holons, then we know that atoms make molecules that make cells that make organs that make creatures that make families. Organisations are holons of the people within; and its people make organisations. They are held together by an ethos or culture, and they live within a set of life conditions determined by that culture.

The organisation becomes the container for life conditions for the individual, as the culture within which an organisation operates becomes its content for life conditions. However, the container without the content is useless and the content without the container is meaningless. All the developmental stages of an organisation have their parallels within the codes of the individuals.

The classic 'Forming, Storming, Norming and Performing' of group theory can just as easily have been written as expressions of the organisational codes at Purple, Red, Blue, and Orange. As the life conditions within which the organisation operates change, the organisation itself changes. If regular assessments are taken by the key executives and managers within an organisation, we will see the same developmental patterns as that of an individual. This happens regardless of individuals leaving or joining the company. Some codes become blocked or closed, resulting in unhealthy expressions; others are fully developed and healthily expressed.

In an ideal world, we would use the insights of Spiral Dynamics to design our hospitals, schools, and other service providers. If we consider the active codes of the community to be served, we can better understand their needs and the skills necessary to provide them effectively. Who is needed to best serve these people? Who is needed to manage these service providers? As we create or develop our Impact approach, and more importantly, outcome objectives, these considerations are taken into account.

The structures of the organisations change from simple command-and-control to multilayered establishments, to a mesh of interconnected departments, as the complexity of the organisation and its roles change. With our understanding, we can develop organisations that provide both the individuals and the structures to fully match the complexity of the tasks they are asked to complete. We can design and develop organisational structures that are specific to the life conditions in which they operate, and match the complexity of the problems they need to resolve.

§23.11 Leadership and Meshworking

We know from Professor Graves' work and from others that Spiral Dynamics Integral reflects the continual need to deal with greater complexity. As life evolves, we are asked to resolve more complex issues. Problems can be broadly split into Neat, Critical, and Increased Complexity:

- Neat problems, i.e., problems with specific logical solutions, which can be addressed without undue complex thinking. Processes or procedures can be complicated, but ultimately they can be solved as a series of discrete, nested Neat problems. The complicated problems, like arranging air traffic control, or building a factory, are a large stack of Neat problems with specific logical outcomes, the solving of which can be regarded as management solutions.

- Critical Problems, require command-and-control leadership for a safe and timely resolution. Examples include a road traffic accident, or even a natural disaster. The leader is seen as a commander, or as a heroic figure that takes charge of the problem and resolves it timely and logically.

- Increased complexity, with all elements interconnected. There is no one logical outcome, and the problem is seen as complex rather than complicated. In some instances, attempts are made to break these problems down into different elements and treat each as a complicated problem. The difficulty is that the emerging solutions seldom reflect the interactive nature of the whole. If we look at the human body, it has traditionally been treated in the West as a series of systems: circulatory, respiratory, the endocrine, etc. Traditional Western medicine has treated the symptoms but seldom the complexity of the human body as a whole natural system.

Organisations have tried to understand such complex systems and their future behaviour by treating each area equally and individually, running 'what if' estimates in each system, as if it was a neat problem with a tidy solution.

Known as scenario planning, it was famously taken to a new level by the Shell Group, but again, it often denies the full complexity of the whole, and produces simplified communicative box solutions that do not reflect the non-linear, systemic nature of a complex problem.

As we appreciate the complexity of thinking that comes with the Yellow and Turquoise codes, we understand that complex questions need complex solutions. There are no neat solutions; only solutions which reflect a snapshot in time, where the outcome may differ at another point in time.

Problems of this complexity need multiple minds simultaneously working to derive a solution, while anticipating future problems. Such problem-solving calls for new techniques, developed by Beck and others as Meshworks Solutions.

As the increasing complexity of our thinking unfolds through the codes of the Spiral, so does our interaction with our world. As individuals we become better able to cope with increasing complexity, as do our organisations.

Techniques are currently being developed that enable individuals to use their increased capacity to understand how to deal with heretofore complex problems. Techniques such as Meshworking will transform medicine, economics, and how we react to our environment. It is currently being used to help today's greatest threat: climate change.

§23.12 Case Studies

This section explores two simplified case studies based on actual assignments where the application of Spiral Dynamics Integral elucidated how people behave.

§23.12.1 Case Study #1

This organisation is an educational trust whose annual income has stabilized at £1.5m per annum for the past six years. The organisation manages reporting to an external group of international trustees. The trustees and management investigated why the organisation had no growth.

As part of that study, management was interviewed and asked to take online Values Test and Change State Indicator assessments. Analysis of the Value Test results showed that the management team showed similar profiles, with a high acceptance of Purple and Green, high rejections of Orange and Red, and low acceptance scores for Blue.

The results indicated that as personnel changed, people were recruited with similar values, ignoring what the organisation needed. This resulted in a complete rejection of all the warm color values, so there was no evidence of personnel with much ambition.

The whole organisation was community-based, with decision making by consensus. This was further reinforced by the Change State Indicator results, which showed that management felt nothing was wrong, and preferred only incremental change.

Previously, some managers had accepted Red and Orange as their Yellow code emerged, but had become so frustrated that they resigned and went elsewhere.

The recommendation was that the organisation change its recruitment policy, and engage members of management with a strong acceptance of Orange and low rejection scores of Red, to inject a sense of urgency and purpose into the team.

§23.12.2 Case Study #2

Here, a small manufacturing company in the leisure industry produced products for hotels and sports centers. They had found that their project-based workload produced large fluctuations in labour requirements, so they asked for assistance in re-organising the company to reduce the cyclical pressure.

Spiral Dynamics assessment analysis showed that the members working within the sales side of the business had low acceptance of Blue, and were motivated by a dominant Orange code. Others with lots of experience on the manufacturing side, with high Blue acceptance values, were spending long periods away from the factory, interacting with clients.

A small amount of staff re-organisation resulted in a key individual with a stronger Blue code and manufacturing experience scheduling the project manufacture, and a member of the sales team being re-deployed to resolve customer issues. Some additional part-time assistance was recruited into the sales team, resulting in a strategic alliance with an overseas sales organisation that lacked manufacturing capacity. The plant was finally expanded to operate at a greater capacity, with additional work from the overseas partner. The simple principles can be incorporated into any size organisation. People are most productive and have the most job satisfaction when working to their individual strengths, and supported by others who are doing the same.

The concepts of Spiral dynamics is continuing to evolve both in theory and in practise. Beck is supported by his Lebanese-American colleague Said Dawlabani, author of MEMEnomics, The Next Generation Economic System; and his partner Elza Maalouf, through their Centre for Human Emergence (CHE) in the Middle East. Others include Graham Linscott, Loraine Laubscher, Rica Viljoen, and Alan Tonkin.

Currently there are CHEs in Canada, Germany, Netherlands, Spain, the UK, USA, South Africa, and in the Middle East. Each is an active community where ideas are readily shared and connections are made across country and culture boundaries.

Early in the new millennium, the work of Beck and Wilber was fused, termed the Spiral Dynamic Integral, eventually leading to the profoundly important work by Esbjorn Hargens and Zimmerman on Integral Ecology[15]. Not only do we have one of the most advanced and dynamic maps for understanding each investment context for the design of impact objectives but we also have a thoroughly researched and evolving full-spectrum roadmap and lens onto the future.

I believe that a significant body of work could be created that specifically builds into the spiral impact strata to enable dynamic interventions to ensure that the deeper aspect culture is uncovered and aligned with sustainability. This, as mentioned earlier, is the missing link in today's conventional Impact investments. Having spent a significant time understanding the spiral, we can now summaries the key implications for our Impact perspectives as follows:

I. When reading the levels and niches, you may at a personal level recognised one which resonated the most with your own worldviews. This is the first imperative of understanding where we are at ourselves, i.e. our personal psychological mirror.

II. You may also have recognised the level and niches where the culture of your organisation is operating today. This is the second imperative for understanding your own cultural alignment to the organisation, and also the main codes on which the firms Impact culture is based, i.e. our collective psychological mirror.

III. Having seen what the other levels have encoded, is this where you and the organisation strategically and tactically want to be to fulfill your Impact objectives? Are we truly aligned with our values, beliefs, and what we believe is important to deliver the kind of Impact and create the kind of firm to which our stakeholder would want to belong.

Whilst Beck describes the spiral as a Master Code, recall that the codes do not necessary represent types of people, but value systems in people. Systems are not good or bad but rather a set of values that can adapt in order to comport with changing life conditions. These can be expressed as unhealthy and healthy versions within these value systems.

A word of warning whenever we look at hierarchies: firstly, assuming that 'higher is better' (thus implying that one must progress on the spiral as an evolutionary scale); secondly assuming that spiral dynamics are simplistic; and third, and most important for our Impact perspectives, is that we should not attempt to change people into someone they are not. Recalling a message from Laurens van der Post, with all Impact, we risk missing the very 'precious metal' and new gold we have explored so far. Also recall that Impact investment is about restoration, renewal and alleviating these imbalances that we from our levels of thinking can make conscious.

As Paul Hawken suggests,

> We can just as easily have an economy that is based on healing the future instead of stealing it...One is called restoration and the other exploitation...The world begs for dreamers to set up shop, invent a new product or social technology, and create the kinds of breakthroughs that will bring us together to act responsibly as passengers on this magnificent place we call home [351]

We conclude with a thought about the more holistic and spiritual aspect of our Impact thinking. The Vatican recently called attention to the poverty of ethics and morality within the global economy, Oeconomicae et pecuniariae quaestiones (2018),

> No profit is in fact legitimate when it falls short of the objective of the integral promotion of the human person, the universal destination of goods, and the preferential option for the poor.' The economy must 'aim above all to promote the global quality of life that, before the indiscriminate expansion of profits, leads the way toward the integral well-being of the entire person and of every person.

[7] Markets, the Vatican observes, 'are not capable of a governing themselves,' and so it is our duty as stewards of capital to understand how we operate with such markets and alleviate such imbalances wherever we can in our Impact objectives. Yes, make no mistake, this is a moral and ethical question which cannot be ignored if we are to integrate our Impact work.

---

[7]Considerations for an ethical discernment regarding some aspects of the present economic-financial system of the Congregation for the Doctrine of the Faith and the Dicastery for Promoting Integral Human Development, 17.05.2018 [352].

Chapter 24

Integral ownership and governance

> A 'troublesome' discovery begins with the recognition of anomaly.[353]
>
> Thomas S. Kuhn

There are few more debatable issues than ownership and economic participation with other stakeholders. Many solutions are driven by tax considerations for both the incumbent owner and the possible recipients. There are also almost an inexhaustible number of permutations in terms of legal structure, type of instrument etc., many designed to separate the component parts between the economic interest and control in e.g., share options. However, we are not going to concern ourselves with these technicalities, rather what economic ownership implies and how this may impact our organisation and its future.

One reason is that the alternative of no participation affronts those whose human capital generates the economic benefit in the first place; and misses the point about full integral alignment. I appreciate that for some, this is akin to a socio-political statement which is not my intention. Whilst each of us has different views, there are few opportunities for a firm to align itself more comprehensively. It all starts with participation and cements a relationship like nothing else can; although there are situations where this is not possible.

Most organisational governance structures, in general, resemble the legal and hierarchical power structures that underpins them which stems from the natural consequence of either ownership or position, dating back before the Industrial Revolution. There can be little argument that this format has historically served well to align the two main areas of risk and financial capital. However, once we expand the concept of capital and look closely at which part of the value chain drives contribution, we quickly understand why other forms of ownership and governance have evolved over time, from cooperatives to not-for-profits. The organisational hierarchical structure began within the military with the mission critical need for order and linear command and control.

Herbert Marcuse mentions in his book 'The One-Dimensional Man[153] 'The way in which a society organises the life of its members involves an initial choice between historical alternatives which are determined by the inherited level of the material and intellectual culture.' I am aware that my personal history colours and fragments how industry has developed, and my role is to understand and map the choices and pathways of development. As often in life, what is important is not what is present in the room but what is missing. Within each one of us there is a fabric of belonging that is vital to sustaining us within the context of our community and extended family. This may include club memberships, associations and other collectives where we share commonalities. However, we need to be aware that the converse of the need for security is separation from those with whom we, at some level, do not consider equals.

Organised membership by definition has many such filters before anyone can join. Within our context of Impact, this is an important consideration as it otherwise restricts our lens, particularly within the Social dimension where we need to be fully inclusive to understand real needs and requirements for community activation. From our governance perspective, how to design this to be more inclusive?

Another highly hierarchical and formal structure we borrow is from government. A democratic government allows salient questions to be openly debated. A democracy relies on a structure and culture where existing tensions can be transformed into creative solutions. In the governance of impact investing, we assume roles resembling a democratic government in that we need to animate cross-sectional debate to find solutions for those impacted. Governments tend to have inbuilt checks and balances between the administrative, judicial, and legislative branches. In addition, the regular cycle of elections keeps the government on notice to address citizens' concerns whilst working with opposition parties to achieve cross-party consensus. Such structural attempts to find balance which are seldom replicated in organisations.

Our politic of creating polarities to distinguish differences helps to better position issues but it does not bring harmony nor sustainability if one or more parties are subjected to the will of others. These polarities, when combined with adversarial rhetoric, fragments the polity and social fabric. When we as impact investors look at the Social dimension in particular, we need to be cognisant of this politic and find a governance methodology that incorporates these tensions and polarities. In organisations, the solution for the concentration of power is the appointment of independent directors and separating certain functions. These solutions are easy to manipulate and are key for our Impact intention.

We mentioned earlier the barrier of digital language and the need to change language in our governance processes in order to allow a more full impact perspective to emerge. This involves conversation as adult to adult relationships, for the power complexes to be minimised and to create a new depth of experience and available intelligence. This requires a maturity and courage to speak our truth to power and risk the connection to our vulnerability. If we are unable to do so we will be stuck and not see the edges of the impact frontier. Having courage and allowing us and others to be vulnerable is the gateway to trust and finding the truth of real Impact. In her book "Dare to Lead", Brené Brown puts this relationship as follows: 'Trust is the stacking and layering of small moments and reciprocal vulnerability over time. Trust and vulnerability grow together, and to betray one is to destroy both.'[73]

Most of our organisational and governance problems do not have simple solutions. We are fortunate if we arrive with clarity at an either/or answer rather than a both/and, since conventional logic alone cannot hold the multitudes of systemic complexity. The temptation to believe we have reached a solution is compelling as soon as it enters our minds which we keenly share with others, and then move on. A key component for arriving at a solution is respect, which implies the need for imagination and creativity to be able to see one another across our inevitable differences. If what we experience through our creativity does not become real in our intentionality and approach, then very unlikely it will become real to us within our governance structures. Hence the need for those very structures to become creative spaces and generate the capacities to hold ambiguity. Let us further investigate where other capacities to hold our tensions may reside.[354]

G. N. M. Tyrell has put forward the terms 'divergent' and 'convergent' to distinguish problems which cannot be solved by logical reasoning from those that can. Life is being kept going by divergent problems which have to be 'lived' and are solved only in death. Convergent problems on the other hand are man's most useful invention; they do not, as such, exist in reality, but are created by a process of abstraction. When they have been solved, the solution can be written down and passed on to others, who can apply it without needing to reproduce the mental effort necessary to find it.

If this were the case with human relations – in family life, economics, politics, education. and so forth – well, I am at a loss how to finish the sentence, There would be no more human relations but only mechanical reactions; life would be a living death. Divergent problems, as it were, force man to strain himself to a level above himself; they demand, and thus provoke the supply of, forces from a higher level, thus bringing love, beauty, goodness, and truth into our lives. It is only with the help of these higher forces that the opposites can be reconciled in the living situation.

E.F. Schumacher, Small is Beautiful

As with Richo's 5As, we need these personal characteristics and traits to be developed and installed to be able to give them to another. As with supply and demand in economics, we need to be able to receive and give, to balance 'love, beauty, goodness, and truth' and for it to be present in the room. Learning and holding tensions creatively away from the shadow elements of any power complex to emerge.

> Love is a commitment that also encompasses loyalty. Love is concerned with securing the well-being and welfare of others. An organisation that has love as its value is one that genuinely cares for the people it interacts with. For those who experience this value, many respond positively, and some are even motivated to emulate.
>
> Love, with Diligence, is seen in deeds. Integrity must involve the pursuit of truth, excellence and honesty in our dealings with others. Unity of spirit yields organisational excellence, and aligns all to do Business with Grace[355]

Philip Ng, CEO of The Far East Organisation

The above quote is from a remarkable man who has put values centrally in his strategy. His firm is one of the largest and most admired companies in Singapore. Which specific governance structure we work with, and how we influence its design is uncertain. However, consider carefully how it addresses, build and nurtures the areas covered. When working recently with a family office, they looked deeply into one particular way of governance, namely 'consensus', which we will later discuss. This can only be a solution through discourse and discovery, resulting in a committed and understood agreement. We will cover it because for many, consensus is idealistically elusive, and not applicable for commercial firms. Let us see what we can glean from it. Nusseibeh's paper again is quite helpful, especially in his section, 'Stewardship and advocacy, a social context for investing'[35] where he writes,

> However, to accept this (share ownership as conduit for bringing about long term sustainable prosperity for the entire system, Authors addition) precept implies profound changes to the way we invest... How can a disparate group of shareholders, say the members of a fund such as CalPERS agree on what basis they wish to direct the companies they own collectively?... part of it can be tackled through stewardship (fairness – better wages, union rights, diversity,

anti-slave labour clauses, governance, executive pay etc.)... and partly through stewardship (awareness of carbon footprint, encouraging energy companies to move to cleaner energy, open architecture or shared resources for food and water technology etc). This in turn would change the way we think of investment in markets. Investing in statistical or accounting factors or in HFT would be laid bare for what it is, a bet on a roulette wheel. While investment in beta would only make sense over the cycles if it is coupled with deep long-term stewardship, engagement and perhaps controversially for many activists, the end of disposal as a tool of control.

This is an impact argument for extending the manager's Alpha (excess return to market/benchmark) into new realms of investor value. We need to address pure rent/income seeking in investments, executive pay, and inculcate new ways of attributing value to remuneration. How we arrive at our respective destinations is key and here we need to understand some dynamics in different governance models.

Whilst much has been written about different forms of self-organising teams e.g., Sociocracy and Holacracy, I refer you to texts which deal specifically with structure and their operational processes. Here we are less interested in the 'What' and need to take a deeper look at the 'How' of governance. Let us view this through some contrasting prisms so we can garner further insights. As the governance and economic system is fundamental to any organisation, we need to reflect carefully as to how our system aligns with our true intentionality. In particular, for a family office, such decisions are paramount; and as I eluded to earlier from my own family experience, many lives are shaped and depend on such decisions. Few people have worked on such questions more than Dennis Jaffe, the renowned expert on family office governance and management. In his study, Social Impact in Hundred-Year family business[356] the keys to success are routed in four areas:

- A long-term view of social Impact in family business.

- A holistic approach to social impact, rather than treating philanthropy, impact investing, and business social responsibility in isolation.

- Bringing a more international perspective to the analysis of social impact.

- Adopting a strategic view of social impact and sustainability.

We can see here the strong Integral links and alignments with I³ to create "generative families". Such families successfully navigate their capital and

generational transitions over time by defining, practising, and operationalis-
ing their investment across the capital spectrum in which they invest whilst
balancing tradition and innovation, which is exactly what I^3 is designed to
do. In my family of origin, at the time of our trials and tribulations, we did
not have the benefit of such advice to structure the appropriate long-term
implications of ownership, nor the insight into how best to retain the original
intentions around intergenerational wealth transfer.

§24.1 Background to consensus

A group makes decisions by either majority rule or consensus. The former
can have significant variations in terms of what actually triggers a majority
e.g., no. of board votes versus amount of capital owned and the underlying
process for reaching a decision. It is the only system that works with large
groups for a single issue but even in large groups, smaller sub-groups can be
formed around specific issues which can be based on consensus. Fundamental
to consensus is a process that creates win-win relationships versus majority.
Regardless of how a vote is cast and its outcome, there will always be losers.
The relational dialectic, as adversarial listeners and speakers change, will be
negatively impacted as all win-lose relationships are.

I believe that one organisational differentiator is how to create a process that balances and respects the complexity of a system, includes and
combines fiduciary responsibility, experience and expertise with principal
risks that can enable individual capacities. This may occur where intellectual
capital is leveraged within a collective to build harmony that not only significantly enhances the quality of decisions but also deepens the interactions,
ownership and accountability of such decisions which are often lost in a
collective. Crucial for Impact investments is to recognise that in discussions
where technicalities and the intellect dominates, ethics struggle to be heard
(including the voices of the impacted 'others') as the intellect is satisfied and
believes it has reached its full conclusion and needs to move on.

Consensus decision making is considered a dynamically creative way
of reaching agreement between group members. Instead of simply voting
for/against with the majority winning, the consensus approach is committed
to finding an improved solution that most if not everyone actively supports.
The basic premise is that decisions are made with the maximum consent of
those involved, ensuring that all opinions and ideas are taken into account.
This includes listening closely and attentively to each member to enable
a working mode to evolve. Consensus is neither compromise nor unanim-

ity; rather it goes further by weaving together everyone's best ideas, often with results that are inspirationally better than would previously have been envisaged.

At its heart, consensus is a respectful dialogue between equals. It is about how to work with each other rather than for or against each other. It rejects and discourages side-taking, point scoring, who can shout the highest, and strategic manoeuvring by reducing the capacity of our egos to engage in bellicose behaviours.

During discourses, we are more likely to bridge our positions than to disparage one point of view, since we cannot move forward unless we move together. Consensus obtains a 'win-win' solution acceptable to all, resulting in a stronger commitment to bring this into fruition. How we make decisions is key to how our investment committees are organised and for its impacts.

A fault line with many neoliberal forms of organisational governance is the dogmatic belief that majority voting is the highest form of democracy. All majority voting systems rely on contextual hierarchy driven by power complexes.

In such systems there are always 'losers' and the disempowered, generating a lack of responsibility, accountability, and ownership of outcomes. It also creates a protective need to disconnect from the forum that one now feels less identified with.

As such, and as a process in itself, it fails to capture the wholeness of the collective capacities and wisdom.

Yes, majority voting can enable difficult and controversial decisions to be taken in a minimum amount of time, but that does not mean the decisions will be optimal or ethically acceptable. The consensus approach weaves in more of each member's values, and how a decision will impact each system beyond our own restricted viewpoints.

It seeks to avoid making rash decisions by holding the tensions within a creative space, opening the possibility for a higher level of synthesis. By definition, even in a full consensus approach, anyone can effectively use power to 'block' a proposal by clarifying why one is not able to give consent.

However, if managed correctly, such situations are rare. Consensus therefore is not for every group, especially for those who believe that urgency and expediency is the prime driver for making better decisions.

It is also unfamiliar to many people from conventional working backgrounds, and requires a relatively high level of trust, understanding, and skills among participants which can only be developed over time.

On the other hand, it produces high quality decisions, and the effort to make consensus work can pay off in future efficiency and effectiveness. Consensus is more challenging with larger groups, so size should be considered in deciding if consensus is appropriate.

Select suggested high level principles that aim to drive organisational decisions:

- Better decisions: To build a forum that can maximise the inclusion of all intellectual input and the depth and breadth of their respective expertise and experiences.

- Better implementation: Have a process that includes and respects the interests of all members, generating maximum agreement create shared ownership in outcomes.

- Better relationships: A strong cooperative, collaborative and harmonious atmosphere that builds greater cohesion and interpersonal connections.

At first glance, an organisation might assume an already rich and varied set of opinions that can discriminate between available options, along with a natural selection based on the agreed system requirements. New organisations, as such, have a comparative advantage in designing their decision-making system to comport with operational needs, reflective of the respective culture. Giving consent does not necessarily mean that the proposal being considered is one's first choice.

Group members can vote their consent to a proposal because they choose to cooperate with the direction of the group, rather than insist on their personal preference. Sometimes the vote on a proposal is framed, 'Is this proposal something you can live with?' This relaxed threshold for a yes vote can achieve full consent, although not everyone need be in full agreement. Consent must be genuine and cannot be obtained by force, duress or fraud. The value of consensus is not realised if consent is given because participants are frustrated with the process and want to move on. We now turn closer to the four worlds approach.

According to Schieffer and Lessem the integral transformative education journey is ascribed to the transformational and oscillating 'Rhythm' of the integral Worlds. Rhythm in this context connotes a trace back to natural embedded cultural systems and their respective emancipation and eventual evolution towards integral development. The rhythm is also inside the GENE (Grounding, Emerging, Navigating and Effecting) which represents a fourfold spiralling force that activates the complete Integral Worlds Model. The GENE rhythm is embedded in the diverse reality views and realms, thereby tapping into the dynamic aspect of each view, coalescing them in transformative interaction. Releasing the GENE rhythm in the integral consensus decision making process is part of an integral/systemic perspective (highly simplified) as outlined in pros and cons in the four worlds below.

Downside of the conventional negotiated majority:

South: Negotiations (if any) and discussions are limited, silenced, fragmented, and frustrated which create relations that are strained as trust is taxed or broken.

East: In power relations, dominant values and beliefs tend to win the debate. As a result, the collective culture forcibly shifts towards those with positional, relational and influential power. This drives negotiated and influenced based issues into the point of least resistance which alienates and disenfranchises many.

North: Intellectually we destroy key informative material by reductionistic neurological filters (generalisations, distortions and deletions) to simplify choices into polarities that drive and produce yes/no, right/wrong type decisions. This leads to an above vs. below hierarchical, divisive, and non-inclusive as it fans the egos of who can manage and influence power. Another element is how we create order and linearity in our governance and meeting forums, which are usually managed by a chairperson, and designed to effectively highligh what matters most. However, the methodology excludes much of the emotional and deeper subconscious intellectual capacities and creativity which requires a dialectic.

West: Doing/action orientated outcome objectives drive a locus for externalisation of energy and creative capacities. Motivations and the task's true purpose is easily lost as we execute modes of operation. Critically, there are losers who have either been ignored or violated, and the disenfranchised will feel more disconnected with both process and outcome. A balanced consensus framework repairs and strengthens the above fault lines. To be effective, one needs to design both the forum and create corum to include shadow elements.

Let us discover the alternative approaches.

South: Iterative and collective rounds of dialogue grounded within our calling of interrelations solidifies bonds which builds mutual understanding, leading to trust, respect, cooperation and collaboration.

East: A culture of mutual respect can be built within a context that enhances harmony and collective energies which can strengthen cultural and spiritual connectivity.

North: Systemic consensus voting is a scale of both least and most resistance to include positives and negatives that generate co-creativity and new knowledge.

West: Consensus means approval rather than full agreement. Negotiations are designed to reach a point at which there is no longer disagreement. This allows everyone to be heard whilst the collective understanding is that a decision needs to be taken which may not be one's own. If so the collective motivational drivers have been the least damaged.

Consensus seeks to improve long-run solidarity, decision ownership, and management. Accordingly, it should not be confused with unanimity, often a symptom of group think which is a risk factor in uncharted consensus. If overt and covert power complexes can be held at bay during discussions, the best of all worlds can be held and maintained. The goal is 'unity, not unanimity' for the best decision based on the richness of input. As a decision-making process, consensus decision-making is:[357, 358, 359, 360]

- Agreement Seeking: It attempts to generate as much agreement as possible.

- Collaborative: Participants contribute to a shared proposal and shape it into a decision that meets the concerns of all committee members as much as possible.

- Cooperative: Participants should strive for the best possible decision for the committee and its members, rather than competing for personal preferences.

- Egalitarian: All members should be afforded, as much as possible, equal input into the process, with the opportunity to present and amend proposals.

- Inclusive: As many stakeholders as possible should be involved.

- Participatory: The consensus process should actively solicit the input and participation of all decision-makers.

- Epistemic: The consensus should track the truth to the greatest extent possible. This will require the following rules of the game:

- Multiple concerns and information are shared until the directional sense of the committee is clear.

- Discussion involves active listening and sharing information.

- Norms limit number of times one asks to speak to ensure that each member is heard.

- Ideas and solutions belong to the committee; no names are recorded.

- Ideally, differences are resolved by discussion. The rotated committee chairperson identifies areas of agreement/disagreements to push discussion deeper.

- The chairperson articulates the sense of the discussion, asks for other concerns, and proposes a record of the decision.

- The committee as a whole is responsible for the decision which belongs to the committee.

- The chairman can discern if someone disagreeing with the decision is acting without concern for the committee or selfishly.

- Ideally all dissenters' perspectives are synthesised into the final outcome for a whole that is greater than the sum of its parts.

- Should some dissenter's perspective not harmonize with others, he/she may stand aside to allow the committee to proceed, or may opt to block. Standing aside implies silent consent. Some committees allow blocking by one individual to halt or postpone the process.

This could take the shape of figure 24.1

One critique of consensus is that it may be time consuming since consensus decision-making focuses on discussion in contrast to majority voting that focusses on ease and speed. This can be a potential liability when a decision must be made quickly, or when not possible to canvass opinions of all delegates in a reasonable time.

Additionally, the time commitment can sometimes act as a barrier to participation for individuals unable or unwilling to make the commitment. However, research confirms that once a decision has been reached it can be acted on more quickly. In practise, at the committee level, these issues can be managed by e.g., proxy voting, and suspending the voting protocol,

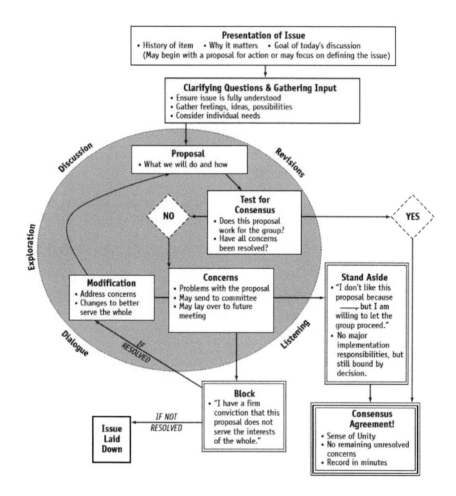

Figure 24.1: Consensus Decision Making[361]

where it is obvious that a conventional majority (weighted by capital or otherwise) would retain the integrity of the core principles. This will include a position on majority formats and the level of agreement necessary to finalize a decision, i.e., a decision rule. Possible decision rules for consensus vary within the following range[357]:

- Unanimous agreement

- Unanimous consent (See agreement vs consent below)

- Unanimous agreement minus one vote or two votes

- Unanimous consent minus one vote or two votes

- Super majority thresholds (90%, 80%, 75%, two-thirds, and 60% are common).

- Simple majority (weighted or unweighted by capital amounts)

- Executive committee decides

- Person-in-charge decides

In committees that require unanimous agreement or consent (unanimity), if any participant objects, he/she can potentially block consensus according to the guidelines described below. These committees use the term consensus to denote both the discussion process and the decision rule. Other committees use a consensus process to generate as much agreement as possible, but allow participants to finalize decisions with a decision rule that does not require unanimity. In this case, someone who has a block or strong objection must live with the decision.

§24.1.1 Agreement versus consent

Giving consent does not necessarily mean that the considered proposal is one's first choice. Committee members can vote their consent to a proposal because they choose to cooperate with the direction of the committee, rather than insist on their personal preference. The relaxed threshold for a yes vote can thereby achieve full consent.

§24.1.2 Near-unanimous consensus

Healthy consensus decision-making processes usually encourage expression of dissent early, maximising the chance of accommodating the views of all minorities. Since unanimity may be difficult to achieve, especially if the committee is large; or consent may be the result of coercion, fear, undue persuasive power or eloquence, inability to comprehend alternatives, or plain impatience with the process of debate, the committee may use an alternative decision rule, e.g., Unanimity Minus One (U−1) or Unanimity Minus Two (U−2).

Combined with majority or super-majority decision rules, a consensus process can also be concluded with a majority or super-majority vote. This is especially common or useful in large and diverse committees that have an underlying consensus. As mentioned, the consensus process, by definition, seeks the maximum possible levels of agreement or consent. Thus, if a committee using majority vote is dominated by a majority faction that does not seek the agreement of all participants, the process would not be considered consensus. Regardless of the decision rule, the process is only 'consensus' if it embodies the base line value of striving for full agreement to achieve the best possible decision.

A note of caution: We are susceptible to becoming victims of the cult of investment 'experts' in our quest for certainty. Most decision-making bodies rely on expertise, and there is of course nothing wrong with this per se. The problem lies in the word 'cult', and specifically when we defer our own judgement in favour of someone with presumed greater knowledge allowing their views to supersede ours. Experts, having invested enormous amounts of intellectual capital and prestige, often have a need to override others so that their output has official value, thereby validating their roles as a subject's guru.

If so, we destroy the fabric of the collective intelligence and our co-creative capacities. We often dismiss those with deep experiential knowledge but without the expert credentials. Within a cult of expertise, we seek certainly and dismiss ambiguity which is a construct where the dynamic tensions for any co-creation is lost or at best, limited.

In my own PHD work I was vexed by this question: For whom am I doing a PHD? Is it for me and my own learning and development or just for someone else to validate and tick the box as to a certain level of expertise? Again, the answer is both, depending on the context.

As can be seen, the above discussion on consensus may open up new ideas to test variations in our own committees and governance structures. If we seek, a more aligned methodology can accommodate and align the changes.

> Determination, energy, and courage appear spontaneously when we care deeply about something. We take risks that are unimaginable in any other context.[362]

Margaret J. Wheatley

Before we move on, let me share with you the 'John Woolman' story in Parker J. Palmer's book 'Healing the Heart of Democracy'[94]. (What follows is an excerpt from Palmer's book, p. 20-23)

THE JOHN WOOLMAN STORY

If the 'power of the broken heart' makes sense to us in the context of personal life but seems irrelevant to politics, consider this story of an ordinary citizen and an issue of great moral and political consequence that continues to haunt our democracy.

John Woolman (1720–1772) was a Quaker who lived in colonial New Jersey among other merchants and farmers in the Society of Friends, whose affluence depended on enslaving human beings. Woolman, a tailor who did not own slaves was torn by the blatant contradiction between the Quaker belief in human equality and that many Quaker gentry were slaveholders. He refused to make that tension disappear by ignoring it, using theological sleight of hand, or riding its energy toward violence. Instead, he insisted that his community hold that tension with honesty and resolve it with integrity by freeing their slaves.

Quakers make decisions by consensus instead of majority rule, and Woolman's local meeting (or congregation) was unable to reach unity on his proposal. Nonetheless, persuaded of Woolman's absolute integrity in the matter, they agreed to support him as he pursued his concern. For the next twenty years, Woolman made frequent trips up and down the East Coast, visiting Friends in their homes and their shops, at their farms, and in their meetings. He spoke with his fellow Quakers about the heart-breaking contradiction between their faith and their practise. And he was always true to his beliefs. He wore undyed white clothing because dye was a product of slave labour; at meals, he would fast rather than eat food prepared or served by slaves, even if he stayed to talk; and if he learned that he had inadvertently benefited from a slave's work, he would pay that person his or her due without calling attention to the exchange.

Woolman and his family paid a great price for his consistent witness to truth's imperatives and his deeply felt heartbreak. Nonetheless, he held the tension, held it for twenty long years, until Quakers became the first religious community in America to free their slaves, some eighty years before the Civil War. In 1783,

Quakers petitioned Congress to correct the 'complicated evils' and 'unrighteous commerce' created by the enslavement of human beings. And from 1827 onward, Quakers played a key role in developing the Underground Railroad, 'an informal network of secret routes and safe houses used by nineteenth-century black slaves... to escape to free states and Canada with the aid of abolitionists who were sympathetic to their cause.

These historic outcomes were possible because not just Woolman but the entire Quaker community held their internal contradiction consciously and constantly until they saw the light. The community, like Woolman himself, refused to resolve the matter falsely or prematurely. The Quakers did not take a quick vote to let the slave-owning majority have its way, nor did they banish the vexatious Woolman from their midst. They tested their convictions in dialogue and laboured to achieve unity, trusting tension to do its work, until they finally arrived at a decision of historic proportions.

Sadly, members of the United States Congress were unwilling to hold the tension even long enough to consider the Quakers' petition of 1783. After hearing the petition read on October 8, they immediately tabled it and never took it up again. Perhaps there was too much tension since the petition invoked the Declaration of Independence, stating that the institution of slavery exists 'in opposition to the solemn declaration often repeated in favour of universal liberty.'

John Woolman's story allows us to distinguish once more between two kinds of heartbreak. The first is the conventional image of a heart exploded into a thousand shards. Some of us try to pick up the pieces and put our lives back together; some fall into long-term despair; some take grim satisfaction in the injury the heart's explosion inflicts on our enemies. This kind of broken heart is an unresolved wound that keeps on wounding us and others. When the heart is brittle and shatters, it can scatter the seeds of violence and multiply our suffering among others.

And yet as Woolman's story reveals, there is an alternative image for a broken heart. When the heart is supple, it can be 'broken open' into a greater capacity to hold our own and the world's pain: it happens every day. When we hold our suffering in a way that opens us to greater compassion, heartbreak becomes a source of healing, deepening our empathy for others who suffer and extending our ability to reach out to them. This kind of tension-holding can plant the seeds of justice and peace, as Woolman and other exemplars of non-violence have consistently shown. (see Gandhi's four pillars in appendix 3.)

The Woolman story also underscores a point that is critical to the central thesis of this book: holding tension creatively does not mean indecision or inaction. At every level of human life–from living our own lives well to governing a nation justly–decisions must be made. But they must not be made in the haste that comes from being impatient with tension or in the ignorance that results from fearing the clash of diverse opinions. If the Quaker way of getting eighty years ahead of the Civil War on America's greatest moral dilemma means anything at all, it means that the broken-open, tension-holding heart is not only a powerful source of compassion and healing, it is also a source of the wisdom required to make challenging decisions well.

The impulses that make democracy possible–and those that threaten it–originate in the heart, with its complex mix of heedless self-interest and yearning for community. From there, these impulses move out into our relations with each other in families, neighbourhoods, workplaces, voluntary associations, and the various settings of public life. These are the places where John Woolman made a difference simply by walking and talking persistently and with principle. These are the places where we can make a difference, too, once we free ourselves from the illusion that we are at the mercy of forces beyond our control.

We normally associate politics with distant centres of power–legislatures, lobbyists, party caucuses, and board rooms–not with the everyday settings I just named. This is a mistake, for those places comprise the vital pre-political layer of our common life, the social infrastructure on which democracy's well-being depends. At the highest levels of institutional politics, the common good is rarely served if citizens are not speaking and acting in these local venues, gathering the collective power necessary to support the best and resist the worst of our leaders as they decide on matters that affect all of us.

Democracy depends on ordinary Americans like John Woolman, ener-gised rather than defeated by whatever breaks their hearts, taking small steps in local settings to contribute to the commonwealth. As Howard Zinn wrote:

> The essential ingredients of [all] struggles for justice are human beings who, if only for a moment, if only while beset with fears, step out of line and do something, however small. And even the smallest, most unheroic of acts adds to the store of kindling that may be ignited by some surprising circumstance into tumultuous change.

End of excerpt.

Woolman's story highlights the struggle of including 'the other' in our lives, the time it takes for dogmas and paradigms to shift and the necessity to work 'integrally' across all functions to affect change. Pertaining to complex areas such as Impact, consensus may be the quicker and more expedient way forward. We would still have slavery today in the Western world if we had not developed science and technology in combination with access to cheap energy and a evolved consciousness looking beyond the lens of just finance and economics. Of course slavery in its many forms still exists in some countries where such development has as yet to occur. Slavery of course is also a cultural, political and social construct in how we define our freedom and can exercise free will. However, given our propensity to seek identification and security in likeminded groups and associations, we are at risk of not seeing 'the other', thereby enslaving our own minds and that of our impact.

All of us have all at times felt 'enslaved' to certain environments and people, wishing we had more freedom or ability for our own imprimatur. As discussed earlier, for organisations that embark on Impact, this will be a significant challenge as people free themselves from previous dogmas and connect with deeper aspects of the consciousness and drivers from their moral core which will be hard, if not impossible to ignore.

The governance structures and processes we design reflects the spaces we had earlier discussed. 'As above, so below, so as within, so as without' as the ancient sages would suggest. If we create constructs, dialectic and a discourse that stifles the voices within, how can we expect our creative voices to hear the 'other' to include them in our lens and frame for impact? The language we bring into these frames and the need to balance expediency with insight are key components. It is no coincidence that Quakers have been so successful in their communal and organisational lives, with many larger firms today having them as originating founding fathers.

A key ingredient to insight is the degree of silence we have to allow the inner self to be heard and subsequently expressed within a governance framework. The first order of our freedom towards ourselves is really our relationship with silence and our capacity to manage ambiguity. As the American philosopher Elbert Hubbard reminds us: 'He who does not understand your silence will probably not understand your words.' Silence is also cultural. The Japanese, for example, highly value silence as an essential form of non-verbal communication. It conveys information, emotions and is a sign of respect and personal distance.

Alfred Bredel understood the connection: 'The word listen contains the same letters as the word silent'. In his 2007 paper 'The Cultural Significance of

Silence in Japanese Communication,' [363] Lebra identifies four dimensions of silence: Truthfulness, Social Discretion, Embarrassment, and Defiance. The first three are helpful to maintain positive relations while the last has a negative connotation. In Western culture, silence is associated with doubt, loneliness or pain, so we seek noise to alleviate the negative feelings. As a result we often misinterpret silence, assuming something wrong. G.K. Chesterton puts it: 'I am not absentminded. It is the presence of mind that makes me unaware of everything else.'[364] There are several types of silence: removing and distancing external incoming talk and internal self-talk/mind and silencing the senses.

Many cultures therefore include silent times in their day to quiet the mind and expand the consciousness. Silence is not about the absence of sound, it invites the presence and emergence of everything else. Perspective, reflection, distance, ideas, and solutions, all surface unexpectedly when we silence and open up the mind. The acoustic ecologist Gordon Hempton once said: 'Quiet is a think tank of the soul. We take the world through its ears.'[365] Real quietness is about being present; silence is not an absence of sound, but an absence of noise. 'What is the sound of one hand clapping?' is a Zen challenge that has several interpretations, but our thinking assumes that we would need two hands to clap. Some say that the presence of silence enables us listen to other sounds like our heart, the rhythm of our breathing, and the awareness of our mind. Others believe it is a metaphor how we see life with a dualistic approach: cause and effect. Regardless, it's our practise of how we enter silence which is important.

This now brings us back to the questions around how democratic is our corporate constructs, procedures, and the conduct of our governance.

> The human heart is the first home of democracy. It is where we embrace our questions. Can we be equitable? Can we be generous? Can we listen with our whole beings, not just our minds, and offer our attention rather than our opinions? And do we have enough resolve in our hearts to act courageously, relentlessly, without giving up–ever– trusting our fellow citizens to join with us in our determined pursuit of a living democracy? [366]

> Terry Tempest Williams

The reason for looking more deeply into one particular governance method, consensus, is that your organisational culture may have atrophied around a particular governance method. I would argue that governance is foundational for any culture as this is where the basis of any culture is shaped so this link needs to be made conscious. Also, for many organisations, this would be their next level of transition and development. If you currently operate in and around the "blue and "orange" niches with a tinge of "green" or "yellow" where most of pure Impact Investing lies, becoming more consensual is your challenge and opportunity to address the power complexes and change the culture.

As the law of requisite variety states that the system/person with the most flexible behaviour will control the system; which is also the first law of cybernetics, we can now suggest a new Law of Epistemic Power: the system that can manage the most complexity and ambiguity will make the best decisions.

§24.2 An example, Evolutesix

A firm looking to integrate an Integral Governance approach into its working is Evolutesix, which was founded by a friend, Graham Boyd. They have integrated a number of the practises described in this book, and more specifically:

Incorporation: the 'Incorporated Commons' combines the FairShares company in which all long-term stakeholders have a fair share of the rights to govern and a share of the wealth generated. This is a self-owning, free, and stewardship company.

Organising work: The core elements of Sociocracy3.0 and Holacracy underpin tasks, roles and decision domains. Consent decision making is central, as is individual action.

Growing individual and team capacity: Graham developed the adaptive way to complement Sociocracy. It enables inner- and inter-personal tensions to be turned into valuable capacity building drivers.

The combination of these three essential elements gives Evolutesix powerful processes to extract the value from, and minimise the disruption caused by tensions. These processes span four arenas (holons), from smallest to largest:

- Inside individuals, tensions between past and future, ideals and their nature.

- Between individuals, tensions between the inner world of each.

- Between roles in an organisation. (At an abstract level, i.e., excluding the human aspects of any tensions belonging to any of the above.)

- Between categories of stakeholders in the company, e.g., investors and customers.

Graham developed the adaptive way and the incorporated commons in 2010, deploying early versions in the firm, LTSGlobal. He has since deployed it in clients, seeing clearly its efficacy when all three pillars are well done; and how fragile companies become if only one pillar is done well (e.g., Holacracy) and the other two are not. When any one pillar is done conventionally, the company has a fracture in one of the four holon levels above. For example, Graham has seen a number of companies implement Holacracy, but in a traditional owned company. This imposes a hierarchy, and excludes long-term highly invested stakeholders (especially the investors of human capital) from decisions, and from fairly sharing wealth. This fracture creates a non-integral, split culture (analogous to a split personality) that is both self-governing and an ego-anchored power hierarchy. The same is true if there are no, or insufficiently effective common processes for inner- and inter-personal tensions.

The roots of how Evolutesix works, and its purpose in creating a regenerative society supported by regenerative businesses, lie in Graham's growing up in apartheid South Africa. Apartheid is an Afrikaans word meaning "separateness", or "the state of being apart", literally "apart-hood" (from Afrikaans "-heid"). He experienced first-hand how everyone, and the whole of society, was shaped into an adversarial relationship despite the common ground of geography, economy, etc. This showed quite clearly how context is the most powerful driver behind behaviour, and hence the longest lever to change behaviour. In South Africa it was a context and position of separation named apartheid where only one stakeholder class (white) had the right to govern and share in the wealth. As we know, only when South Africa was freed from this context could the country take the steps necessary to deliver its full potential to Africa and the rest of the world, even though much remains to be done.

For Graham, the above three pillars are required for firms to deliver their potential. If any one is missing, the context becomes fractured. There is then a type of apartheid (state of separation) which generates behaviours and outcomes. When stakeholders are separated from the power to engage generatively in the major decisions of a general meeting, this may lead to weaker decisions and lost opportunities.

Of importance, on a day to day basis, are the losses that come from the inner- and inter-personal conflicts. The direct losses may be more visible and quantifiable, but far bigger and unquantifiable are the actual opportunity costs. Many of us have experienced, adversarial and political battles that can sap our energy. The power of this was played out recently in a conflict within Evolutesix when one of the partners, stepped back from being a core staff member into being a collaborator.

The driver behind this was the difference and split between Evolutesix's strategic focus on becoming an investment incubator and consultancy for companies using all three pillars in integration; and the focus on their existing clients' requests for using only parts of the adaptive way and self-governing framework.

The Incorporated Commons allows the two to collaborate, knowing that major decisions will include perspectives of both sides, and that wealth generated by their human capital investments will be fairly shared. The adaptive way has given both a common framework to effectively harness the human side of tensions. The outcome has been a collaboration that remains as productive as before, in a slightly different constellation.

This contrasts with a client that has a fragmented approach where they implemented self-governing, and a few elements of the adaptive way, but chose to retain a power hierarchy in the ownership. This led to self-governing being imposed top-down, with some key parts of governance staying in the ownership power hierarchy and structure. So the culture of trust and safety needed for the adaptive way to turn conflict into capacity growth, and for self-governance to work, became instead a culture of confusion and mistrust which led to an even weaker business performance than a traditional top-down power hierarchy. Thus, Evolutesix suggests when changing to an integral paradigm, all three pillars must inform and change together.

§24.3 Bribery and corruption

In order to understand and achieve integrality more fully, we need to briefly discuss corruption as one of the main distortions of today's economy. I have positioned it after our discussion on governance, since this is the created space in which our culture is established with regards to corruption and where possible antidotes and re-balancing may be found.

Transparency International defines bribery,

> The offering, promising, giving, accepting or soliciting of an advantage as an inducement for an action which is illegal, unethical or a breach of trust. Inducements can take the form of gifts, loans, fees, rewards or other advantages (taxes, services, donations, favours, etc.). Their definition of corruption is,'the abuse of entrusted power for private gain. It can be classified as grand, petty

and political, depending on the amounts of money lost and the sector where it occurs.

They state that the cost of corruption 'corrodes the fabric of society. It undermines people's trust in political and economic systems, institutions and leaders. It can cost people their freedom, health, money – and sometimes their lives.' If we invest as 'finance only' with a possible cosmetic overlay of 'Impact' we have the hackneyed arguments:

- Grin and bear it; it is an inevitable cost of doing business.

- To remain competitive we have no choice.

- It is none of our business what happens after we 'do the deal', not our responsibility how they behave.

- Let us find a creative and structural way to solve this regardless.

Whilst much anti-corruption work has been done, corruption remains widespread. I would even suggest that it is now core to the commercial cancer that is slowly but surely devouring its host. Its ubiquity has morphed into new forms depending on the developmental stage of the economy, legal systems, etc. It is well known that according to the various corruption indexes in general, Western economic countries, are considered less corrupt. However, such indexes can only capture the more overt corruption, leaving nations such as the UK and the USA, which in terms of covert and culturally accepted forms of creating, structural and legal loopholes with favors and privilege to those who can reciprocate could be considered the most corrupt nations on earth in terms of actual capital involved.

However, whilst much of this improved development has occurred at the country levels through legislation, compliance and changes in governance including whistle-blower protection, an otherwise driven organisational culture always finds avenues to circumvent legislation and compliance in new and innovative ways. This is a natural and highly predictable evolution within organisations as they find solutions to barriers imposed. Having myself lived now in the UK for over 30 years, whilst having been confronted with more blatant practises in other nations, the UK corruption is very sophisticated, highly covert, and often disguised in myriad subtle forms. A classic example is the 'Al Yamamah'[368] deal between Saudi Arabia and the UK government, involving BAE Systems, allegedly the most lucrative and corrupt transaction in UK history. There was a web of connected parties,

Figure 24.2: Corruption perceptions Index[367]

suggested slush funds and UK government attempts to silence witnesses. This exemplifies the sophistication of those involved, and how power can be used to silence truth (it may even someday make a great movie).

Another example is the international football federation, FIFA, which had institutionalised a culture of underhand activities and now is reportedly planning to sell FIFA's rights to the World Cup (and other competitions) to an investor consortium with ties to Saudi Arabia[369]. If we allow only commercial agents to drive so called 'progress', we invite corruption. The point is that not much positive 'Impact' can survive intact regardless of how well-meaning it is, once distorted. In a recent conversation with a FTSE 100 CEO whose company was in a multi-billion takeover discussions recently by a US firm, he and his board opposed the takeover, despite an offer to walk away with a $100m + golden parachute if approved. It is not difficult to see that for many this would be very difficult situation, requiring significant integrity. Also, as Western market saturation and peak market share and profit hits large firms, we can expect more M&A activity which is mainly designed to drive share price performance. M&A also creates a specific challenge for Impact since the commercial and economic drivers will dominate the proceedings to get the deal done. The CEO also felt that the biggest threat to the SDGs was the increase in sophisticated and overt corporate corruption.

When I worked in mainstream investment banking, I witnessed several sophisticated and blatant schemes from institutional investors in Denmark, Germany, and Switzerland. One investor during a meeting shifted a small piece of paper, containing his Swiss bank account details, suggesting that we could potentially do some great business together. I sometimes was in a competitive bid process with a UK securities broker, which I often lost despite better pricing. I later learned that the principal of the broker would once a year, before Christmas, travel to Switzerland, collect cash and then distribute it to his European clients. Whilst this type of corruption has become more difficult, vestiges remain within the culture.

On several levels, this is a more dangerous form as it now is part of society's social codes and mores. In other regions, such as the Middle East, corruption is quite overt and part of the overall fabric, one could even argue that it is part of certain cultures, constituting an extension of expression for privilege, power and position. I was once explained that in many parts of Africa, indigenous cultures grant the head of a community such as a tribal king the absolute rights of ownership of the community assets and its uses. Position gives automatic rights to receive favours so such dealings are not considered corrupt.

At one firm I was told that corruption evidences an institutionalised culture of rights, accepted as a cost of doing business. The London financial and capital allocation system has many 'facilitation agents' acting on behalf of foreign interests, extracting large commissions for non-existent 'services.' A UK investor once told me that whilst walking back to the office via the fashionable New Bond Street, a banker who was promoting a foreign loan transaction quipped whilst passing a high end watch shop that the £25.000 white gold Rolex in the window would look very good on his wrist. The investor took the conversation as covert language signalling that he was prepared to purchase it as a gift. Whilst he gently declined, it is not difficult to see that for some people, this may have been a more difficult choice.

The point is how power complexes are played out and institutionalised in business. One area is the mixing of politics with business and its various forms of providing favours, which later in one's career after politics gets cashed in for organisational roles, consultancies, and advisory positions. When this becomes part of a nation's fabric as it has in the UK, it is the expected 'new normal' with little or no apparent wrong-doing, cost or victims with a voice.

We may need reminding that politics and its government does not exist for itself and when it begins to believe it does, it has a tendency to jettison democracy and manipulate and distort the citizens' agenda. We see countless examples today of a disconnected politic, ostensibly an instrument of social good and human development.

However, in my opinion, it is why people become disillusioned with their politicians and feel disempowered. The result is cynicism, mistrust, and sometimes counter-measures, although often it is also too late. The entire fabric of overt and covert corruption, favours, and privilege contains the seeds of destroying how we work in Impact with integrity. One aspect not often considered in conjunction with corruption is fear. I don't think there is any coincidence that in countries which have high levels of fear and anxiety, corruption prevail.

Aung San Suu Kyi in her 1990 address 'Freedom from Fear'[370] makes this point crystal clear:

> It is not power that corrupts but fear. Fear of losing power corrupts those who wield it and fear of the scourge of power corrupts those who are subject to it. Most Burmese are familiar with the four a-gati, the four kinds of corruptions. Chanda-gati, corruption induced by desire, is deviation in pursuit of bribes or for the sake of those one loves. Dosa-gati is taking the wrong path to spite those against who one bears ill will, and moga-gati is aberration due to ignorance. Perhaps the worst is bhaya-gati, for not only does bhaya, fear, stifle and slowly destroy all senses of right and wrong, it so often lies at the root of the other kinds of corruption.
>
> Just as chanda-gati, when the result of sheer avarice, can be caused by fear of want or fear of losing the goodwill of those who one loves, so fear of being surpassed, humiliated or injured in some way can provide the impetus for ill will. And it would be difficult to dispel ignorance unless there is freedom to pursue the truth unfettered by fear. With so close a relationship between fear and corruption it is little wonder that in any society where fear is rife, corruption in all forms becomes deeply entrenched.'

Chapter 25

Background to Impact 3.0

Here we develop a dynamic rhythm where everything informs and navigates us through the integral map. As such, we need to go full-spectrum into the 'whole picture' fourworld realms in order to incorporate the missing depths lost from our now recognised limited perspectives.

> A 'Western' (or 'Northern') approach emphasises the absolute, depersonalised, and non-human nature of knowledge. As such it is typically expressed in propositions and formal logic. In contrast 'Easterners' consider knowledge to be a dynamic human process of justifying personal belief with a view to finding the truth.
>
> Lessem & Palsule[371]

Nusseibeh writes[35]:

At this point, we need to go back to the C19th and Bastiat's dictum about the 'whole picture', or secondary and tertiary effects of investment... The idea is simple. A single investment can be looked at in a narrow sense as an initial sum put in a venture that returns a specific financial return over time, hence the idea of DCF and CAPM as valuation models. However, this approach looks at each investment in complete isolation from its surrounding environment, which in a complex open adaptive system seems irrational. Each investment, and the actions it results in, will have a wider ripple effect, both positive and negative. This is already acknowledged in economic theory as the multiplier effect, but we tend to use it for macroeconomics rather than company-specific investment.

So, an emergent Impact 3.0 has developed several new strands:

- ESG is now fully integrated into a systems mode of operation that guides and navigates its own development and transformation.

- Knowledge creation has developed into a spectral approach including the creative arts and the disciplines of psychology and anthropology.

- The social impact dimensions now fully integrates 'Well-being' and includes the evolution of work and organisational responsibilities around word creation and development.Our Impact approach is now 'waking up' to its true and conscious integral intentions.

> Western culture has lost track of its own sources of Waking
> Up. It has no ultimate truth as a North Star to guide its overall
> actions, which means, ultimately, it has no idea where it is
> actually heading.
>
> Ken Wilber[213]

However, let's first recognise how we react to such a proposition and where we stand on the spectrum of resistance. The German philosopher Arthur Schopenhauer suggested that:

All truth passes through three stages. First, it is ridiculed. Second, it is violently opposed. Third, it is accepted as being self-evident.[372]

So why is change so difficult to create? With regards to Impact, we have covered much of this territory, including the self. Helpfully, John Kotter provides a circular model for leading change starting at the "create" phase and moving clock wise (figure 25.1)

Not unsurprisingly, this aligns with the I^3 approach of creating a collective being (calling/grounding) and belonging (context/emerging), moving to knowing (co-creating/ navigating) and doing (contribution/effect).

If these are the ingredients for change to happen, let us briefly look at some of the ingredients inside the barriers to create change.

In Impact the problem is not just one of measurement—although that's crucial and we will discuss it in greater detail below—but also one of incentives. Managers usually are rewarded for short-term improvements as reflected, say, in its stock price. This makes transactions based on directly observable costs a tempting proposition: if a widget from a global supplier costs less than a widget from a local supplier, then why not acquire it overseas? Managers have little incentive to map out all the positive externalities that local purchases create. By examining relationships with stakeholders, managers need to become anthropologists, developing local knowledge that can provide insights into consumer behaviour and a network of constituents who can support a company's objectives.

After all, domestic stakeholders are likely to have local community influence than a multinational firm. Without broad community support, firms

Figure 25.1: The big opportunity[373]

may even struggle to sustain their licenses to operate. I have experienced many situations where an organisation heavily relies on its relationship with a local community and the good-will of the local government. As SABMiller's former CEO, the late Graham Mackay said: 'We are clear that our business is not something separate from society... The interests of SABMiller and the wider community are therefore inextricably linked

So why are we still struggling to understand and implement meaningful change?

Perhaps our reluctance and resistance to change is disguised in our need to try and build empires rather than aligning with natural laws and forces. Sahtouris suggest that:

> For some eight to ten thousand years up to the present, much of civilized humanity has been in an empire building mode that is immature from the biological evolution perspective. From ancient empires ruled by monarchs we progressed to national expansion into colonial empires and more recently into multi-national corporate empires.

> All these phases have increased our technological prowess while also increasing the disparity between rich and poor that is now devastating the living system

comprised of all humans as well as the ecosystems on which we depend for our own lives.

As we have seen, healthy, mature living systems are dynamically cooperative because every part or member at every level of organisation is empowered to negotiate its self-interest within the whole. There is equitable sharing of resources to insure health at all levels, and the system is aware that any exploitation of some parts by others endangers the whole. Clearly, internal greed and warfare are inimical to the health of mature living systems, and humanity is now forced to see itself as the single, global living systems it has become, for all its problematic, yet healthy, diversity. [374]

However, in Impact Investments, as we uncover the hidden dislocations and imbalances, corrective actions must be taken. Jung again reminds of the need for personal and organisational balance: 'Too much of the animal disfigures the civilized human being, too much culture makes a sick animal.'[34]

Hazel Henderson points out that Adam Smith related his famous theory of 'an invisible hand that guided the self-interested decisions of business men to serve the public good and economic growth', to Newton's great discovery of the physical laws of motion. Also, economists of the early industrial revolution borrowed from Charles Darwin[1]:

> ... seizing on Darwin's research on the survival of the fittest and the role of competition among species as additional foundations for their classical economics of 'laissez faire'—the idea that human societies could advance wealth and progress by simply allowing the invisible hand of the market to work its magic. This led economists and upper-class elites to espouse theories known as 'Social Darwinism' the belief that inequities in the distribution of land, wealth and income would nevertheless trickle down to benefit the less fortunate.

> Echoes of these theories are still propounded in mainstream economic textbooks as theories of 'efficient markets', rational human behaviour as 'competitive maximising of individual self-interest', 'natural' rates of unemployment and the ubiquitous 'Washington Consensus' formula for economic growth (free trade, open markets, privatization, deregulation, floating currencies and export-led policies).

Capitalist free markets can only succeed in the long run if:

i. they really are free, which is not currently the case, and

ii. if that freedom leads towards friendly (rather than hostile) competition and increasing collaboration— not as exploitative cartels, but as ventures consistent with global family values.[374]

---

[1]Henderson, H. (2005). 'Economists as Advocates'[375] p. 164-165

For the World Trade Organisation to dictate economic behaviour that contravenes a small nation's self-interests, is like running a body at the expense of its cells. 'We are living systems, whether we like it or not, and the only way to build a healthy world economy— to glocalize successfully—is Nature's way. (I (Sahtouris) use the terms glocalize and glocal economy to indicate all levels of economic holarchy from local to global.)' (Ibid).

As one of the core grounding for any organisation who is working with Impact is in Nature we need to look at the orientation of our commercial approach and reflect to what extent we are disconnected from its soils. The South African Social Psychologist, Catherine Campbell in her co-authored e-book with Steyaert and Hjorth

> 'Entrepreneurship and Social Change' puts it as follows: … growing ourselves and our communities in harmony with the land is seldom recognised as an entrepreneurial activity. Although a majority of the world's population lives on the land, only a tiny fraction of the people in the industrialised world do, and most theories of entrepreneurship emanate from the latter. We have discredited our enterprising physical selves and commoditised the business of living. In fact, we exist today because our foremothers foraged and gathered and later, accomplished the transition to gardening and agriculture. [7]

The environmental dimension therefore provides us with the full-spectrum learning for our Impact philosophy towards nature. Here we have the opportunity to build on nature's best solutions and incorporate it fully into Impact. Of course, we need to synthesise each investment with its combination of agreed industry standards, and a set of criteria and impact imperatives unique to the business.

I cannot reiterate enough the disparity between using someone else's framework for impact without such synthesis and having gone through the developmental phases of our own, or at the very least, made significant changes to it. It is only when we connect as a now fully integrated knowledge company where the iterative knowledge fly-wheel between ourselves, our firm and our impact dimension begins to become self-leveraged, with self-created learning and development.

> There is no problem ever faced by a business that has not been faced and solved by a rainforest.
>
> Kiuchi and Shireman[376]

As such, we design impact for a 'Biology of Business' and living system that reinforces each stage and level. In her book EarthDance, Sahtouris[203] sets out the main features of living systems, as:

    i. Self-creation (autopoiesis);

   ii. Complexity (diversity of parts);

  iii. Embeddedness in larger holons and dependence on them (holarchy);

  iv. Self-reflexivity (autognosis—self-knowledge);

   v. Self-regulation/maintenance (autonomics);

  vi. Response ability—to internal and external stress or other change;

 vii. Input/output exchange of matter/energy/information with other holons;

viii. Transformation of matter/energy/information;

  ix. Empowerment/employment of all component parts;

   x. Communications among all parts;

  xi. Coordination of parts and functions;

 xii. Balance of Interests negotiated among parts, whole, and embedding holarchy;

xiii. Reciprocity of parts in mutual contribution and assistance;

xiv. Conservation of what works well;

 xv. Creative change of what does not work well.

Therefore our Impact systems that we build needs to become the virtuous circles and flywheels we discussed previously, now fully embracing the organisational climate and culture as the operational 'software' of the business. As the American management guru W. Edwards Deming confirms: 'Research shows that the climate of an organisation influences an individual's contribution far more than the individual himself.'[2] As a reminder, we now need to operate as fully engaged contributors across the circles of influence, co-creative cooperation and recognising our impact responsibility in each area and reach.

---

[2]Campbell, S. (2015). Protocol. p. 51

We now briefly look at each in order to re-connect with some core economic and financial principles that are re-emerging from working towards our own Impact investing methodology.

§25.1 The return journey to an economy of reciprocity and communion.

As mentioned, Integral approaches are not new; however, contrasting with Descartes's scientific reductionism, it views complex systems holistically. Integral systems thinking concerns an understanding of the whole by examining the linkages and interactions between the elements that compose the entire system; in our case, investments. There are a number of integral approaches that have helped shift our global perspective towards a more integral viewpoint during the past 100 years, from system thinkers like Jan Smuts' holism in the 1920s to cybernetics advanced by Ross Ashby in the 1950s.

Integral thinkers like the father of process thinking, Alfred North White-head, and Sri Aurobindo synthesis 'integral yoga'; Teilhard de Chardin, palaeontology and spirituality, Jean Gebser on consciousness in transition into integrality; and Jürgen Habermas on the foundations of social theory and epistemology, and the analysis of advanced capitalistic societies.

As mentioned, epistemology is so important because it is the major operator which transforms the vision of a worldview into a reality. Integral as such, was not invented or discovered but was there all along just waiting for map makers to uncover it. However, one of its main contributions today is to not only understand better our historical journey of development in terms of stages and levels, but to provide a comprehensive forward looking prism for the investment industry. Oliver Wendell Holmes reminds us: 'A mind stretched by a new idea can never go back to its original dimensions'[377]

§25.1.1 Transformational: Missing Depths

All transformational change comes from within, and is a function of the person's capacities to work through their own interior domains to understand the hermeneutic constructs and go through some forms of mental pain.

Depth therefore is a function of seeking new levels of discovery combined with an open mental attitude for development. For centuries this has been the leadership challenge of our times. In my opinion, commercial or business depth follows the same lines as other psychological or moral development stages in that as we expand our horizons and systemic complexities to include broader and deeper aspects of the 'other', we morph and mesh with the other that transcends and include ourselves.

As Robert Kegan, of the Harvard Graduate School of Education wrote:

> I know of no better way to summarise development than that the subject of one stage becomes the object of the subject of the next stage

When this happens, we cannot do the types of wrongs towards them as we did before as this now includes a 'me' and 'us'.

As discussed previously, I refer to these phenomena as the 'power distance' as the function of separating and distancing my own involvement, influence and responsibility between my actions and their effect on my environment and on others.

§25.1.2 Reconnect with our Enterprise Source

As mentioned previously, David Whyte considers work one of our core 'three marriages' in which we play and act out our lives. He suggests that it is not possible to sacrifice one relationship for the others without causing deep psychological damage. Too often, he says, we fracture our lives and split our energies foolishly, so that one or more of these marriages is sacrificed and may wither and die, in the process impoverishing them all.

He confirm our need for integrality when he says:

> Work is not only necessity; good work like a good marriage needs a dedication to something larger than our own detailed, everyday needs; good work asks for promises to something intuited or imagined.[378]

We need a different way of seeing and connecting these relationships. Work reveals that our core commitments are irrevocably connected and deeply embedded in our characteristics.

> We are each a river with a particular abiding character, but we show radically different aspects of ourselves, according to the territory through which we travel.[379, 380]

Dr Brennan Jacoby, who is in my Eco-system and a facilitator in CIFE, argues that trust is context dependent, and is a co-created function based on the mutual capacities of each person. He makes an interesting highly valid remark on how commitment is constructed in that in contains (depending on the needs and context) deep characteristics of the self. Within this character lies the capacity for empathy, which is a key ingredient for practical competence in the ability 'to understand what others are counting on them for'[381]. If so, then all of the above is highly relevant as part of the awakened consciousness, personal growth and development that needs to be embedded in our CARE circles approach in particular.

The enterprise source as such connects and re-connects with the core imbalance of leadership development and the building of consciousness through practical applications of new approaches to financial issues, e.g., I³ as discussed in previous chapters. The Canadian author Robin S. Sharma reminds us that: 'The business of business is relationships; the business of life is human connection.'[382] A core aim of I³ therefore is to enable a firm the opportunity to connect and reconnect with its own source of being and becoming. An investment may not be financially transformational but it may become the impetus for a shift towards such change.

§25.1.3 Reconnect with our Cultural, Political. Economic Source

As mentioned, finance and investment management is firmly embedded in a Western modus operadi abetted by the intellect-dominated approach we see in the world today. However, as highlighted above, change is required to shift the current leadership paradigm and to facilitate change. Otto Scharmer in his 'Theory-U' makes this point abundantly clear:

The essence of this approach can be summarised with a single sentence: the quality of our results in a system is a function of the awareness from which the people in that system operate. The essence of Theory U is not: 'I think therefore I am'. It is: 'I attend this way; therefore, it emerges that way.'[383]

It is composed of 7 capacities and 5 stages (Figures 25.2 & 25.3)

These are equivalent to our integral 4 C's (call, context, co-creation and contribution)

He suggests that there are five principles of what he calls Presencing:

To make this work in the context of institutions, we have to apply a new leadership technology. The core of this new leadership technology requires tuning three instruments: the open mind, the open heart, and the open will. The open mind is the capacity to suspend old habits of thought. The open heart is the capacity to empathize, to see a situation through the eyes of someone else. And the open will is the capacity to let go of old ways of doing things and accept new ones. I call this 'letting go and letting come. [383]

This therefore as suggested is as much a psychodynamic process and whatever calling any firm now form between the principals, the context of

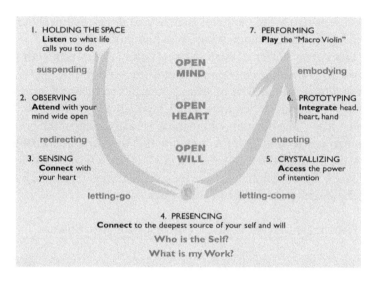

Figure 25.2: Seven Capacities

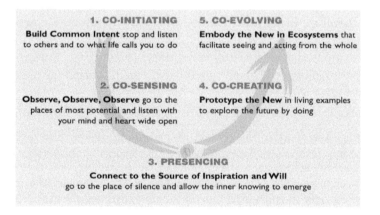

Figure 25.3: Five Stages

where we enter and operate in the financial sphere, we will only succeed in our mission if we can co-create outside of ourselves from the level the outside world operates at that in turn generates the contribution (4 c's) inside-out, i.e. from the self and then manifest in the organisational call, context, cocreation and contribution. Here we come back to the understanding (Hermeneutically of course) of the Spiral to differentiate that with reconnection we mean the internal self to its historical drivers and motivational energies and the reconnection from that position with the outside world.

Awakened consciousness cannot and will not happen in isolation and is a 'dance' with an 'other' of interlocking, conflicting, separating and reframed to be reconnected contextual units or code of understanding. Impact and our own version of I³ therefore could become the unifying operational principle where culture and the global political Impact landscape connects up to form the organising economic theory on which our impact approach stands, lives and dies.

§25.2 Trans-disciplinary: Disciplinary Imbalance

Here we investigate the imbalance between the West/North paradigms and the integrative aspects of the East/South as the main divide that we would like to close.

Although the discipline here is 'Investments' and at first sight may not seem transdisciplinary, if we look beyond the functionality of investments we see that there is a much deeper construct and map of interpretation and connectivity between financial and monetary concepts which we are attempting to understand. As a map is not the territory and there are limitless possibilities as to how one builds and re-connects the disparate parts, we find that it is also a metaphorical re-representation of values and beliefs about the world around us within a specific context, with the lens pointing towards a particular diagnostic area, e.g., an organisation. What is missing from, and what is causing an imbalance from the West/North perspective is the deeper value-based imperatives from the South/East perspectives, e.g., nature and culture respectively. Within Impact and I³, we bring into an awakened consciousness the holistic integrated approach of investors and their investees to enable a strategic understanding to emerge that can enlighten the community in their decision makings.

§25.2.1 Understand how the Enterprise World is 'Co-constructed'

Much of this understanding has been eluded to above but it is worth high-lighting some important aspects.

Despite differences between levels in the spiral, coordinates within our integral compass, ideology and technical understandings, we share a common psychology that drives us. This can become the metaphorical 'glue' that binds the co-construction material.

As we are all co-creators, I am fully aware that I shape, flex and bend myself on occasion to become accepted into a particular culture or even towards a specific person.

We all have behavioural flexibility in that sense but at a cost to the self which can become pathological if stretched and prolonged.

When this occurs on both sides, the enterprise world is co-constructed by agreement (conscious by contract; or unconscious by habit) or presumed via our history and map of the world.

I call these 'presumed contracts', borrowed from a term David Richo[149] used to explain conflicts that arise from within a relationship based on assumptions and pre-constructed needs/wants.

These dynamics are also played out inside the organisational context, e.g., in hierarchies that gives rise to Father/ Child psychodynamics and other power relations within organisations.

Max Weber clarified the position when he said that: 'Power is the chance to impose your will within a social context, even when opposed and regard-less of the integrity of that chance.'[384] Additional complexities arise from our use of language which, as discussed previously, is metaphorical and filtered through our neurology.

Words are chosen and altered at the individual level and subsequently coconstructed into mutual meaning and understandings. The Dalai Lama expressed beautifully his views on language:

> From one point of view it is a good thing to say little and to speak only when one has something to say. Language is one of the extraordinary characteristics of the human race even though some animals such as dolphins and whales seem to have a complex form of communication. But if we look closely at human language, we realised how limited it is. Concepts and words isolate things artificially, whereas the objects they designate actually have innumerable facets that are constantly changing those results from a set of equally innumerable causes and conditions. [385]

As the mediator of co-construction, I^3 aims to translate key components and correct any imbalances that are uncovered in its process. Providing the tools for the dialectic to emerge around differences in culture, values, beliefs etc. for designing the optimal enterprise outcomes, one begins to re-create the collective futures.

§25.2.2 Understand how the Economic World is 'Co-constructed'

As an extension, we know at a deeper level that we have more in common in our humanity than differences. As such, the global economic co-construction takes on 'meta' or higher aspects. This includes how we relate to nature/natural resources, people in the economy, our relationship with money now taking into account cultural differences. For Africa or Asia, in particular, the economic paradigm needs grounding within the soils of its local nature and culture. I^3 seeks to alleviate such imbalances from our often more singular Western perspectives.

A quote from Lauren van der Post is illustrative:

> European man walked into Africa by and large totally incapable of understanding Africa, let alone of appreciating the raw material of mind and spirit with which this granary of fate, this ancient treasure house of the lost original way of life, was so richly filled. He had, it is true, an insatiable appetite for the riches in the rocks, diamonds and gold... but not for the precious metal ringing true in the deep toned laughter of the indigenous people around him. [386]

For Impact, pure profit motives and finance only approach is now becoming a pathology, a form of cruelty that ignores cyclicality, natural obstacles; which can depersonalize and dehumanise any actual contribution. As previously discussed, we need to build on the tenets of CARE to provide the economic world through I^3, a reflective developmental mirror and help organisations develop deeper insights of purpose as to how their capital and investments create impact. Profit and purpose is like Yin and Yang: opposed and connected, mutually reinforcing and lifeblood of each other.

Like a family, the core of any firm must ensure that everything is mutually reinforced by these two principles. Firm as family is where we work through the issues of the context as the Canadian film producer Atom Egoyan suggests[387]: 'Working on the themes I was interested in, through the context of a particular family, was a very economical way of dealing with a lot of the issues I was concerned with.' Impact and I^3 as such, provide a blueprint for understanding the coconstructs that have shaped the firm. With any Impact investment, the investee co-created outcome objectives (I^3OO) are the coconstructed template for change and development within the four worlds.

The I³OO therefore is the steering mechanism for I³'s implementation and agreed organisational re-construction between investor and investee.

§25.3 Transpersonal: Individual Overemphasis

The risk associated with any creative, collaborative endeavour is that within the awakening consciousness lies the very seed to make a contribution. Most of our Western approach to thinking and communicating is based on division, argument and separation that only creates the illusion of choice. Also, if separation weakens whilst unity strengthens, where does our responsibility lie if we are born into relative privilege, are we charged with dismantling any myth of superiority? How we reconnect with our deep place of belonging and worth of not only towards ourselves but also how we are unified with the other.

We have all experienced how the current socio-political model operates with the need to create an "us versus them", polarity based on right versus wrong. This model is also based on strict hierarchies to polarise the voices of an interest group e.g. in politics around a personality that is believed can communicate, deliver, persuade and convince 'the others' that they as a group has the 'right' answers and way forward. Hence the emergence of the organisational 'charismatic leader' on whom we can project our hopes and expectations.

This charismatic model carries risks within it such as significant negative ego centric shadow elements and borderline psychological disorders affecting all concerned and which has little room in facilitating Impact. (See for example, Snakes in Suits by Babiak and Hare[253], suggesting we have a significant issue with 'psychopaths in the boardroom'.)

Irrespective of the debate regarding the impact level in organisations, we find that any organisation which overemphasises any individual also risks by osmosis to assume their particular attributes, personality and cultural drivers. I have experienced this on several occasions in banks where a political leadership is often behaving irrationally from business perspective but also are considered mercurial by staff as they have the prerequisite anointment of powers to impose change and direction.

When this aspect becomes unbalanced, we often find disenfranchised individuals and departments whose voice cannot be heard above the official rhetoric and noise levels. When impact analysis in a deeper format such as I³ is applied inside a firm, a person has to step out of themselves to gain the I³ perspectives. Whilst it is up to each investment firm as to what degree they decide to 'dial up' the requirements for transpersonal transformation towards change, its continued development is irreversible.

However, it cannot be underestimated that any I³ approach between an investor and a prospective investee, engaging with the I³ process itself will open up an individual to reflect on imbalances in his/ her relationship with the stakeholders.

§25.3.1 Give 'the Other' Enterprise a Voice

One of the many roles an investment firm can perform is that of providing an impartial, reflective mirror to an organisation and its leadership. This involves bringing into their awakening awareness, any missing integral perspectives and additional dimensions.

Balancing the prerequisite needs from a multiple stakeholder perspective, within a diagnostic framework of Integral Worlds and its tenets is possibly the biggest challenge for an emerging impact firm.

A effective example of collective catalysation is Frederick Laloux's book Reinventing Organisations[120] which has awakened the consciousness of the business community.

A key tenet is to create an economic enterprise that connects with a whole person approach, creating a competitive advantage and a role model for others to emulate.

The Czechoslovak long-distance runner Emil Zatopek said: 'An athlete cannot run with money in his pockets. He must run with hope in his heart and dreams in his head.'[388]

Impact and I³ attributes to the stakeholder enterprise an economic voice. The construct of stakeholder responsibility is recursive and demands from the Impact investor that a responsible economic connection is co-created and comports with the source of being and becoming.

Again, Carl Jung: 'Our vision will become clear only when you can look into your own heart. Who looks outside, dreams; who looks inside, awakes.'[389]

§25.3.2 Give the Associated Economic Other' a Voice

The challenge for organisations, structured as a collaborative, co-creative space where no individual dominates or is more 'right' than others, is to live fully the CARE, 4 Cs and the GENE and thereby not only become organisations to which others would like to belong, but also be the catalysation, which embodies by their actions the integral approach.

> In times to come, human beings will have to live for one another and not the
> one by means of the other. By this is achieved the world's ultimate aim where
> each is within himself and will give to the other what none would demand.
> [390]

As I³ works with all its economic stakeholders, eliciting their heretofore
hidden voices, we acknowledge and validate their existence and involvement
into our own economic endeavours. Ulrich argues[391]: 'Critique without
systems thinking is boundless, and ultimately empty, in that its object and
context of valid application remain arbitrary'.

Torrance 2011 also identifies the tension between policy and research,
complexity and action in his analysis of qualitative research and its impact
on government1:

> The issue is how to reconcile the (research) need to investigate and comprehend
> complexity with the (policy) urge to simplify and act. To invert Marx, policy
> makers seek to change the world, but first they need to try to understand it,
> while involving others in both processes. ³

As discussed in previous chapters, Impact and I³ demands a new form of
accounting methodology that can capture and communicate to stakeholders
the key messages that now report in from within the systems matrix that
make up the four-worlds.

Conventional accounting fails to capture the variants of intelligence and
modes of communication necessary to translate and transmit information
from each of the four worlds into any meaningful format. This is due to an
overreliance on quantitative and reductive forms of transmission. In their
book Relevance Lost[393], Johnson and Kaplan argued that the profession of
management accounting has lost its original purpose of guiding management
to build a healthy business, instead becoming primarily a number crunching
profession. Their solution: activity based costing (ABC).

Historically, the purpose of corporate accounting was keeping track of
what had been done with the financial resources entrusted to managers. More
recently, the International Accounting Standards Board (IASB) (which now
dominates corporate reporting) requires that facilitating investor decision-
making (in pursuit of efficient capital markets) is the primary purpose of
financial statements and corporate reporting. And stewardship is now secondary to investor decision-making as a general aim of corporate accounting

---

³Torrance, H. (2011). Qualitative research, science, and government: Evidence, criteria,
policy, and politics. In [392] (pp. 569-580).

(Britton and Waterston, 2006)[394]. The primary purpose of the financial statements (still the centre piece of any corporate report) is, according to the IASB, to help investors 'assess the amounts, timing and certainty of future cash flows' (Van Mourik and Walton, 2014[395]).

Whilst investors are clearly a key stakeholder in any enterprise, many question an accounting system which is almost entirety directed towards their needs and prioritises. As Peter Senge outlines in the introduction of Johnson and Broms book, 'Profit Beyond Measure' is that many of us have first-hand experience of the destructiveness of 'management by objectives and by results'. However, this can destroy the web of relationships that determines the character and the healthy culture of the enterprise, and its capabilities. Management by results as such, creates 'needs', goals that we must achieve for our survival or personal gain within the organisational context.

Management by means, on the other hand, nurtures relationship building and its fruits such as collective aspirations that matter to us[315]. Management has alternatives such as 'narrative accounting' pertaining to the expansion and extension to annual reports and other communications. Specifically,

> Narrative reporting offers a mechanism to support the creation of a more commercially attractive and differentiated picture of the business which can lead to better investor understanding and improved stakeholder relationships. Furthermore, the underlying process necessary to produce this information can also enhance Board effectiveness and improve governance. [4]

Impression management analyses attempts to influence audiences' perceptions of organisations, particularly financial performance (Clatworthy and Jones, 2001, 2003, 2006; Courtis, 2004a; Rutherford, 2003) and social environmental performance. (Hooghiemstra, 2000.)

Accounting is often limited, biased and incomplete, late, tax driven, and is historically equivalent to 'Trying to read signals in the wake of a ship' as Charles G. Krone once said.

The conventional accounting concepts suggest many examples of misrepresentation and misdirection, e.g., Enron, WorldCom, and Bernie Madoff, where accounting methodologies were insufficient to alert and avert. We are directly concerned in Impact to build a more effective supplementary accounting framework. We build an appropriate methodology that can seek from the four worlds, not in isolation but rather in full communication. As such we cannot base this on any particular world view as this will evolve

---

[4]WC, (2007), Narrative Reporting.

over time. However, the framing of any approach today will be based on quantitative and qualitative measures which includes a narrative form e.g. social accounting is:

> The process of communicating the social and environmental effects of organisations' economic actions to particular interest groups within society and to society at large. As such, it involves extending the accountability of organisations (particularly companies) beyond the traditional role of providing a financial account to the owners of capital, in particular shareholders. Such an extension is predicated upon the assumption that companies do have wider responsibilities than simply making money for their shareholders. [396]

And as Edward Stamp writes:

> Accountancy is ultimately a social science, which deals with a system created by people, hence its fundamental characteristics are constantly changing and evolving [397]

The influential French sociologist Pierre Bourdieu (1930–2002) was interested in how society reproduced, and how the dominant classes retain their position. He argued that this could not be explained by economics alone. He emphasised cultural capital –using cultural knowledge to undergird their place in the hierarchy. His most famous book, Distinction (1984)[398], explores how people use the trappings of middle-class taste and cultivation as cultural signifiers to identify themselves with those above on the social ladder, and to demonstrate their difference from those below. Distinction was ground breaking as a detailed study of how cultural artefacts and knowledge were brought into play, alongside basic economics, in the dynamics of social class relations.

Reflecting on this work, Bourdieu has said that:

> A general science of the economy of practises that does not artificially limit itself to those practises that are socially recognised as economic must endeavour to grasp capital, that 'energy of social physics'... in all of its different forms... I have shown that capital presents itself under three fundamental species (each with its own subtypes), namely, economic capital, cultural capital, and social capital (Bourdieu, 1992: 118–9)

He defines social capital as:

> Social capital is the sum of the resources, actual or virtual, that accrue to an individual or a group by virtue of possessing a durable network of more or less institutionalised relationships of mutual acquaintance and recognition.

The reframed position then is part our Social Impact dimension in combination with its context and community and related organisational social policies (Bourdieu and Wacquant, 1992: 119)

Professor Lessem in his pioneering paper (1974) stated the need for:

> attempts to extend fundamental accounting principles, which have traditionally embraced only monetary stocks and flows, towards physical, social and psychological exchanges. [4]

This important paper set the tone for using Social Audits to change human resources to becoming real assets and into quality of life accounting. Lessem thereby introduced segments and areas of Impact for accountants.

Table 25.1: Quality of life categories

Category	Major element	Sub-elements
Physical	Physical health	Food, water, air, warmth, shelter, physical safety, freedom from illness.
Economic	Standard of living	Employment, job security, earnings.
Social	Social Interpersonal satisfaction	Love, belonging, communication, friendship.
Psychological	Psychological Awareness Esteem.	Actualization
Knowledge, understanding	Achievement, competence, cognition.	Openness, adaptivity, creativity

He then explores inputs and outputs and their intermediate transformative steps, and units of account between differing parties. Importantly, he introduces 'units of measurement' which includes:

- Physical units: the easiest and simplest forms of non-financial measures. e.g., GHG emissions, units of electricity, water consumption, etc.

- Social units: either internal or external depending on whether within the firm or between the enterprise and its environment. Lessem proposed mainly a financial representation of inputs and outputs with avenues for further development.

- For Psychological assets Lessem proposed:

In the first and most concrete instance, 'human asset accounting' should incorporate records of the knowledge and skills possessed by each of the organisation's full-time members, as reflected in years and variety of experience, academic qualifications and participation in training programmes, and in tangible contributions to company performance. Furthermore, with regard to the company as a whole, moneys invested in personal and vocational training and in the personnel activity as a whole, could be represented as an accumulative asset. Secondly, and correspondingly, a 'human liability account' should reflect the demands or expectations of people that need to be fulfilled. The perceived needs of members, with regard to their self-worth, could be elicited through some form of survey methodology.(Ibid)

Final accounts of any enterprise could therefore include the debit and credit of the above components to be developed into several balance sheets with assets and liabilities. This is also how I see the Impact industry and the accounting profession e.g., Sustainability Accounting Standards Board (SASB) and the other accounting standards e.g., IAS, FASB, GAAP, IFRS, developing the Impact accounting framework. Lessem challenged us in 1974 to take this into the 21st century.

As you may imagine, how to do this has been of great discussion with Lessem, within the Trans4M community and between myself and colleague Mark Anielski. This very difficult area of measurement is a key challenge for firms and the Impact industry. Solutions can only emerge out of the development of the market ideology and real practise and exploration of the four-worlds. More importantly, as each firm only sees what they are capable of understanding, there could be significant and unique elements of any interpretative system.

Major common factors will relate to the SDGs and other standard external measurements. At this juncture, given its importance, I am exploring this collaboratively with others such as the Reporting 3.0 organisation (now renamed R3), as I don't believe anyone has the 'right' and 'only' answer and each firm through praxis has to develop its own co-created overlay methodology and interpretative reporting, grounded in its culture and context.

Interestingly, R3 have designed their own transformation journey using and Invoking Interface Founder Ray Anderson's metaphor of 'Climbing Mount Sustainability,' which unsurprisingly has 4 stages, basecamp (our South), planning the route (our East), the climb (our North), the mountain top (our West).

§25.4 When Interest has a role to play

A key issue for Impact investors is how debt is structured and interest is charged. As interest contractually redistributes wealth from borrowers to holders of capital it can significantly set the tone and impact any firms' ability to create and afford Impact.

Our Impact objectives as directed by the I³OO must be synthesised aligned with capital returns and repatriation. Globally, the cost of debt is endemic and if left imbalanced, some, such as Mark Anielski consider this the largest social issue of our time.

As mentioned earlier, Mark has calculated that commercial banks interest cost component for pricing on goods and services in our economy is ca. 50%.

In other words, at 0% interest, prices could halve or we spend approx. half our working time and life to pay for someone's return on debt capital.

This debt phenomenon has also contributed to the social inequality issues of our time which much of thematic impact investments seeks to address. In their book, "The Spirit Level", Pickett and Wilkinson puts the social issue as follows:

> As we looked at the data, it became clear that, as well as health and violence, almost all the problems that are more common at the bottom of the social ladder are more common in more unequal societies. A growing body of research shows that inequality damages the social fabric of the whole society. When he found how far up the income scale the health effects of inequality went, Harvard professor Ichiro Kawachi, one of the foremost researchers in this field, described inequality as a social pollutant. The health and social problems we looked at are between twice and 10 times as common in more unequal societies. The differences are so large because inequality affects such a large proportion of the population. [399]

In the finance and Western dominated paradigm, their prospective returns of capital are rightly the primary drives of decisions and which creates the sustainability of all else within the four-worlds.

However, for an Impact approach to be sustainable, we need to integrate the return impact inside the four-worlds and thereby seek to generate a composite four-worlds return on capital employed.

I call this shift to go from IRR (Internal Rate of Return) to IIR (Integral Impact Return) which requires new and better understanding of both quantitative but more importantly, the qualitative aspects of impact measurement.

Let us return to Nusseibeh's paper 'The Why Question'[35] for some background to the vexing issues of measuring the more qualitative aspects of our I³ model. He writes:

> … while we can easily quantify the direct financial gain or loss from any investment, these secondary and tertiary costs are almost impossible to quantify, and therefore, as a qualitative overlay, they remain at best, a woolly concept, at worst unprovable and therefore a totally impractical proposition. However, an economics professor, Dr Armen Papazian, has come up with a perfectly workable quantitative answer. His proposal is to modify the accepted discounted cash flow equation to take into account these other effects.
>
> He proposes first that we calculate the effect of our investment on the world we live in on an ongoing basis. We do that by taking the initial investment (II), then take into account new assets that are created which have a wider positive impact, e.g. buildings, infrastructure, skill development, capex etc. (NA) as well as new wealth created, e.g. from wages paid out, multiplier effect etc. (NM), then deduct factors that negatively impact our society, e.g. carbon footprint (CF) and waste footprint (WF). He called this Gross Space (meaning in the real world) Value(see figure 25.4).
>
> Dr. Papazian then proposes that we arrive at a valuation that looks at both sides of the ledger (he called this Net Space/Time Value or NSTV) by combining the value of what is created and its effects on wider society (both positive and negative) arrived at with the above formula with the traditional net present value calculation of discounted cash flows (figure 25.5)
>
> This may or may not be a perfect answer, but it clearly demonstrates how one can incorporate the idea of calculating the effects of any investment to include secondary and tertiary effects on society within the parameters of traditional financial economics…

Whilst the above equation may be mathematically elegant, it is nevertheless, a highly simplified and limited version of reality. The individual components still need significant qualitative and quantitative assessments, validations and valuations to boil into inputs for the equation to perform. This is something a more dynamic model could encompass.

As accounting is the outcome of activity and translated information into an agreed and standardised format, integral impact and its natural extension, integral accounting is a key developmental area for CIFE. As a natural outcome of stage 1 of creating an I³ framework, we already have accounting protocols based on the 5 Capitals of Mark Anielski which can be further developed for any I³.

However, first we need to agree on the map of information before we can count the fruits of our labour. We come back to the notion that our impact fruits is not only from what we know and how we convert this into integral capitals, the first impact fruits is a radical type of integral attention where

Space Value with No Time

Net Space Value = -*II* + *GSV*

GSV = Gross Space Value = *II* + *NM* + *NA* – *EC* – *WC*

= Initial Investment + New Money + New Assets – Ecological Costs – Water Costs
NM = New Money = Initial Investment x Money Multiplier = *II* x m
NM = *II*m
NA = Inventory + Real Estate x a + Technology x b + Intellectual Property x c
NA = *I* + *aRE* + *bT* + *cIP*
EC = Ecological Footprint of Production in Tonnes of CO_2 x Verified Carbon Unit Price
EC = *EF* x *VCUP*
WC = Waste Output in Tonnes x Cost of treatment price per tonne
WC = *WO* x *CT*

$$GSV = II(1 + m) + I + aRE + bT + cIP - (EF \times VCUP) - (WO \times CT)$$

Figure 25.4: Space Value with no Time

Net Space Time Value

$$NSTV = NPV + NSV$$

Net Space Time Value = Net Present Value + Net Space Value

$$NSTV = -II + \sum_{t=1}^{n} \frac{CF_t}{(1+r)^t} - II + \sum_{t=0}^{n} CE_t(1+s)^{n-t}$$

$$NSTV = -2II + \sum_{t=1}^{n} \frac{CF_t}{(1+r)^t} + \sum_{t=0}^{n} CE_t(1+s)^{n-t}$$

CE – Cash Expenditure
CF – Cash Flow

Figure 25.5: Net Space Time Value

we hear a voice which is beyond our own. As the 13th century Japanese Buddhist priest, Dogen Zenji suggests: 'When the self advances and confirms the 10,000 things it is called delusion. When the 10,000 things advance and confirm the self it is called enlightenment'.[400, p. 7]

Chapter 26

Impact 3.0

All models are wrong, some models are useful

George E.P. Box[401]

By now it is clear that each firm requires it to build an impact approach to reconnect the firm into each impact investment opportunity and provide the prerequisite reporting and communication frameworks which outside investors and stakeholders can fully understand. As we move into Impact 3.0 we are now immersing ourselves deeper into the roots of Impact as we activate the GENE and create a dynamic dance with the 4Cs, CARE, 4Ms and 4 Rs. As nothing is ever static and always is a state of evolution here is where we look to take our generic Impact 2.0 approach and create our next iteration fully developed I³ model as built up from the integral transformational dynamic. Each suggested segment has now evolved and been developed by the firm in synthesis with its vision and mission.

Let us look at a possible evolution using an example from a hypothetical organisation. At this juncture our background integrally now fully loaded, we can summarise the intensity scoring methodology as follows:

Too keep things simple, as in Impact 2.0, each component/segment/line item in each world is weighted to generate a dimensional intensity score in each of the four worlds. This is then re-weighted by levels of materiality and importance into a master intensity score to generate a transactional IQ (Impact quotient). The tools and the model are calibrated to score between 1 (best) and 5 (worst). Each sector has a minimum benchmark before a positive factor attribution is created, e.g., Energy and Fuel efficiency min. hurdle = 4.

INTEGRAL IMPACT INVESTMENT MODEL

XYZ

South

	Score	weight	W/Avg
Social Dimension	1.7	15%	0.2
Wealth Creation	2.8	35%	1.0
Nature Capital (NC)	1.1	10%	0.1
Micro / Organisational Level	3.5	15%	0.5
Timeline of Impact Value Chain	2.0	25%	0.5
Total Score	11.0	100%	2.34

East

	Score	weight	W/Avg
Developmental / Evolutionary	2.45	25%	0.61
Emerging	2.55	15%	0.38
Culture Capital (CC)	1.60	25%	0.40
Micro / Organisational Level	3.15	15%	0.47
Timeline of Impact Value Chain	3.00	20%	0.60
Total Score	####	100%	2.47

North

	Score	weight	W/Avg
Common Good Economics	2.20	20%	0.44
Knowledge Economy / Creation	1.00	30%	0.30
Intellectual Capital (IC)	2.20	30%	0.66
Micro / Organisational Level	2.60	10%	0.26
Timeline of Impact Value Chain	2.00	10%	0.20
Total Score	10.00	100%	1.86

West   I³

	Score	weight	W/Avg
Living Systems	1.75	30%	0.53
Corporate Reality	2.40	10%	0.24
Wellbeing	1.70	20%	0.34
Micro / Organisational Level	0.00	20%	0.00
Timeline of Impact Value Chain	3.00	20%	0.60
Total Score	8.85	####	1.71

Table 26.1: Integral Impact Investment Model

The models takes into account three primary steps (which are specific to any industry, sector, etc.):

I. Each component input is weighted according to e.g. its materiality, impact importance and impact outcome likelihood.

II. Defined buckets or segment are equally weighted accordingly.

III. A final master level balancing accounts for the relative level of importance between each quadrant four worlds.

The model output creates a single final factor adjustment I^3 α (alpha) above any hurdle rate you may consider relevant which is then used to create an Impact Quotient (IQ) factor that is used to adjust the financial yield.

E.g.: Financial IRR 8%, I^3 IQ is 1.69 α factor i.e. our Integral Impact Return (IIR) is 13.51%, 8% × 1.69 = 13.51%. In other words, the stand alone impact return is 5.51%.

Each segment has been constructed from the processes of creation as described during this book of deep internal and external definitions and map making. In each dimension, 3 Macro/ Eco System areas were identified, each incorporating the GENE and its related Capital and 1 Micro/organisational level. A common time-line value chain incorporates the data from each segmention implementation to affect time frame.

South
XYZ

Macro / Eco System Level

Populate one per line box with an "x"

Social Dimension

GIIN

	1	2	3	4	5	Score	Weight %	Result
To what extent is the organisation grounded in a particular nature and/or community (1= very highly, 5= not at all)		x				2	15%	0.30
Organisational diversity (1= very high, 5= very low)			x			3	15%	0.45
Community Development (1= very active, 5= no participation)					x	5		0.50
Human rights protection or expansion (1= good, 5= weak)		x				2	10%	0.20
Employment (1= good, 5= weak)			x			3		0.45
Capacity Building (1= low, 5= high)		x				4	10%	0.40
Relations with customers and other stakeholders (1= good, 5= weak)			x			3		0.30
Extent of the organisation participating in building a self-sufficient Economy (1=very high, 5= very low)			x			4	15%	0.60
				x			10%	
			x				10%	
				x			15%	
Total/Average	1	2	3	4	5	3.25	100%	2.30

Wealth Creation

	1	2	3	4	5	Score	Weight %	Result
Financial Inclusion (1= good, 5= weak)			x			3	10%	0.30
Generate Funds for Charitable Giving (1= good, 5= weak)				x		4	20%	0.80
Improve Livelihoods (1= strong, 5= weak)			x			3	20%	0.75
Income/Productivity growth (1= good, 5= weak)		x				2	25%	0.90
		x					45%	
Total/Average	1	2	3	4	5	3.00	100%	2.75

Nature Capital (NC)

	1	2	3	4	5	Score	Weight %	Result
Biodiversity conservation (1= good, 5= weak)		x				2	25%	0.50
Energy and fuel efficiency (1= good, 5= weak)						3		0.30
Natural resources conservation (1= good, 5= weak)			x			3	10%	0.30
Pollution prevention & waste management (1= good, 5= weak)			x			4	10%	0.80
Sustainable energy (1= good, 5= weak)						3		0.30
Sustainable land use (1= good, 5= weak)				x		4	20%	1.00
			x				10%	
				x			25%	
	1	2				3.17	100%	3.20

Micro / Organisational Level

	1	2	3	4	5	Score	Weight %	Result
"C" suite relational connectivity (1= good, 5= weak)				x		4	25%	1.00
"C" suite level of awareness of Social dimensions (1= good, 5= weak)					x	5	15%	0.75
Employee level of engagement (1= good, 5= weak)						3		0.30
Operating levels and sense of self determination (1= strong, 5= not present)			x			3	10%	0.30
Level of trust within the organisation (1= strong, 5= not present)						4	10%	0.40
Level of mutual learning (1= good, 5= weak)			x			5		0.50
Level of mutual respect (1= good, 5= weak)			x			2	10%	0.20
In general, do people blend private social life with their working relationships (1= very much, 5= not at all)					x	3	10%	0.30
		x					10%	
			x				10%	
Total/Average	1	2	3	4	5	3.63	100%	3.75

Timeline of Impact Value Chain

	1 <1	2 <2	3 <3	4 <4	5 <5	Score	Weight %	Result
(1= <1 Year, 5= >10 years)		x				2	100%	2.00
Total/Average	1	2	3	4	5	2.00	100%	2.00

Sub Weightings

	Score	Weight %	Result
Social Dimension	2.30	15%	0.35
Wealth Creation	2.75	35%	0.96
Nature Capital (NC)	3.20	10%	0.32
Micro / Organisational Level	3.75	15%	0.56
Timeline of Impact Value Chain	2.00	25%	0.50
	14.00	100%	

AVERAGE FINAL SCORE | **2.69**

Table 26.2: South

East XYZ

Macro / Eco System Level

Populate one per line box with an "x"

Developmental/ Evolutionary

Question	1	2	3	4	5	Score	Weight %	Result
What level of co-development excists with stakeholders (1=very high, 5=very low)		x				2	25%	0.50
How conscious is the organisation of its actions on the outside world (1= highly, 5= not at all)			x			3	25%	0.75
How conflictual is the organisation within its environment (1= not at all, 5= highly)		x				2	10%	0.20
Does the organisation aim to align itself to its environment and beyond (1= very much, 5= not at all)					x	5	15%	0.75
How co-creative is the organisation with the environment/outside world (1= very much, 5= not at all)				x		4	25%	1.00
Total/Average	1	2	3	4	5	3.20	100%	3.20

Emerging

Question	1	2	3	4	5	Score	Weight %	Result
Level of clarity as to organisational purpose (1= very high, 5= not visible)			x			3	10%	0.30
Is the organisation pursuing any aims of living together and working for the common good (1=completely, 5= not at all)					x	5	10%	0.50
Are there visible artistic impacts within the organisation (1= highly visible, 5= not visible)				x		2	20%	0.40
How evolved and valued is creative and intuitive work (1= very highly, 5= not at all)		x				2	25%	0.50
What level of quality is being sought versus quantity (1= very important, 5= not important)			x			4	35%	1.40
Total/Average	1	2	3	4	5	3.20	100%	3.10

Culture Capital (CC)

Question	1	2	3	4	5	Score	Weight %	Result
Where on a scale of importance does culture sit organisationally (1=very important, 5=very unimportant)		x				2	25%	0.50
How aligned is the culture within the organisation (1= very well, 5= not at all)			x			3	10%	0.30
Is culture understood and promoted by the organisation (1= very much, 5= not at all)				x		4	10%	0.40
Are there aspects and signs of cultural dissonance (1= non visible, 5=high levels)				x		4	20%	0.80
Is the "C" suite "walking the talk" (1=very much, 5= not at all)		x				2	10%	0.20
Are there many people who are disaffected cultural "outliers" (1= very few, 5= many)			x			3	10%	0.30
Is the organisation aware and working with cultural diversity (1= very much, 5= not at all)			x			3	15%	0.45
Total/Average	1	2	3	4	5	3.00	100%	2.95

Micro / Organisational Level

Question	1	2	3	4	5	Score	Weight %	Result
How active/open is the "C" suite in promoting ethical/moral behaviour (1= very highly, 5= not at all)			x			3	20%	0.60
How political is the organisation (1= non political, 5= highly political)				x		4	15%	0.60
Is the organisation serving anything outside itself (1=entirely, 5= nothing)		x				2	20%	0.40
How important are people in reality vis other "capital" (1=very important, 5= unimportant)			x			3	15%	0.45
							15%	
Does the organisation recognise a higher consciousness or spiritual dimension (1= very much, 5= not at all)					x	5	30%	1.50
Total/Average	1	2	3	4	5	3.40	100%	3.55

Timeline of Impact Value Chain

(1= <1 Year, 5= >10 years)

Question	<1	<2	<3	<4	<5	Score	Weight %	Result
			x			3	100%	3.00
Total/Average	1	2	3	4	5	3.00	100%	3.00

Sub Weightings

	Score	Weight %	Result
Developmental/ Evolutionary	3.20	25%	0.80
Emerging	3.10	15%	0.47
Culture Capital (CC)	2.95	25%	0.74
Micro / Organisational Level	3.55	15%	0.53
Timeline of Impact Value Chain	3.00	20%	0.60
	15.80	100%	

AVERAGE FINAL SCORE — **3.14**

Table 26.3: East

North
XYZ

Populate one per line box with an "x"

Macro / Eco System Level

Common Good Economics

	GIIN	1	2	3	4	5	Score	Weight %	Result
Level of organisational design to enable and develop an economy for the common good (1= very high, 5= very low)			x				2	30%	0.60
How networked is the organisation within (1= very high, 5= very low)			x				2	15%	0.30
Openness of the organisation to change and development (1= very high, 5= very low)					x		4	25%	1.00
Belief and reliance on collaborative vs competitive modes of operation (1= very high, 5= very low)				x			3	30%	0.90
Total/Average		1	2	3	4	5	2.75	100%	2.80

Knowledge Economy / Creation

	1	2	3	4	5	Score	Weight %	Result
Organisational openness to learning and development (1= very high, 5= very low)				x		4	10%	0.40
Is information and ideas shared freely and openly (1= very much, 5= not at all)			x			3	20%	0.60
Does the organisation have a continuous improvement program (1= yes, highly developed, 5=no, non existent)		x				2	25%	0.50
Is creativity and knowledge creation valued and rewarded by the organisation (1= very highly, 5= not at all)		x				2	45%	0.90
Total/Average	1	2	3	4	5	2.75	100%	2.40

Intellectual Capital (IC)

	1	2	3	4	5	Score	Weight %	Result
Reliance on IC for survival, sustainability and growth (1= very high, 5= very low)			x			3	35%	1.05
Organisational level and capacity to build IC (1= very high, 5= very low)		x				2	20%	0.40
Capacity and ability to work through paradox and ambiguity (1= very high, 5=non existent)					x	5	15%	0.75
Investment into Learning & Development (1= very high, 5= very low)		x				2	20%	0.40
Mental Health and Wellbeing (1= very high, 5=very low)			x			3	10%	0.30
	1	2	3	4	5	3.00	100%	2.90

Micro / Organisational Level

	1	2	3	4	5	Score	Weight %	Result
How cooperative and democratic is the organisation (1= very highly, 5= not at all)			x			3	30%	0.90
Intellectual capital compared to competitors (1= very high, 5= very low)		x				2	35%	0.70
Power hierarchy based on individual IC (1= very low, 5= very high)		x				2		0.40
Retained organisational knowledge and IC vs. individual / transient (1= very high, 5= very low)				x		4	20%	0.60
			x				15%	
Total/Average	1	2	3	4	5	2.75	100%	2.60

Timeline of Impact Value Chain

	1	2	3	4	5	Score	Weight %	Result
(1= <1 Year, 5= >10 years)		x				2	100%	2.00
Total/Average	1	2	3	4	5	2.00	100%	2.00

Sub Weightings

	Score	Weight %	Result
Common Good Economics	2.80	20%	0.56
Knowledge Economy / Creation	2.40	30%	0.72
Intellectual Capital (IC)	2.90	30%	0.87
Micro / Organisational Level	2.60	10%	0.26
Timeline of Impact Value Chain	2.00	10%	0.20
	12.70	100%	

AVERAGE FINAL SCORE	2.61

Table 26.4: North

WEST
XYZ

Macro / Eco System Level

Populate one per line box with an "x"

Living Systems

	GIIN 1	2	3	4	5	Score	Weight %	Result
To what extent is the organisation rooted in ecological activities that sustain life (1= very highly, 5= very low)		x				2	25%	0.50
Is the organisation moving from domination towards partnerships (1= very much, 5= not at all)				x		4	25%	1.00
Does the organisation recognise and measure wealth beyond the financial (1=very much, 5= not at all)			x			3	10%	0.30
To what degree does the organisation recognise and focus on real life issues (1= very highly, 5= not at all)					x	5	15%	0.75
To what extent is the organisation modelled after Nature and building other capitals (1=very much, 5= not at all)			x			3	25%	0.75
Total/Average	1	2	3	4	5	3.40	100%	3.30

Corporate Reality

	1	2	3	4	5	Score	Weight %	Result
Does the organisation value the contribution from other capitals (1= very highly, 5= not at all)				x		4	40%	1.60
Is there a hierarchy based on financial wealth, property and prestige (1= not at all, 5= very much so)				x		4	20%	0.80
Does the organisation recognise and value small humane gestures (1= very much, 5= not at all)					x	5	20%	1.00
Is the organisation rooted in reality or mainly value extended storylines (1=very much, 5= not at all)		x				3	20%	0.60
Total/Average	1	2	3	4	5	4.00	100%	4.00

Wellbeing

	1	2	3	4	5	Score	Weight %	Result
It the organisation operating from a scarcity model (1= not at all, 5= very much so)		x				3	10%	0.30
To what extent is the organisation based on core values in life (1= very much, 5= not at all)	x					2	20%	0.40
What degree of sharing, gifting and reciprocity is evident (1= very much, 5= none present)				x		4	25%	1.00
Does the organisation meet needs other than financial (1= very much so, 5= not at all)		x				3	45%	1.35
Total/Average	1	2	3	4	5	3.00	100%	3.05

Micro / Organisational Level

	1	2	3	4	5	Score	Weight %	Result
Is organisational wealth creation shared fairly across levels and people (1=absolutely, 5= not at all)		x				2	25%	0.75
Is FC used towards benevolence, humanitarian or for charitable purposes (1= yes, highly, 5= not at all)			x			3	25%	0.75
Does the organisation support community development (1= very much, 5= not at all)			x			3	25%	0.75
Does the organisation follow a diversified definition of success (1=yes, highly developed, 5= none at all)				x		4	25%	1.00
	1	2	3	4	5	3.00	100%	3.25

Timeline of Impact Value Chain

	1	2	3	4	5	Score	Weight %	Result
(1= <1 Year, 5= >10 years)			x			3	100%	3.00
Total/Average	1	2	3	4	5	3.00	100%	3.00

Sub Weightings

	Score	Weight %	Result
Living Systems	3.30	30%	0.99
Corporate Reality	4.00	10%	0.40
Wellbeing	3.05	20%	0.61
Micro / Organisational Level	3.25	20%	0.65
Timeline of Impact Value Chain	3.00	20%	0.60
	16.60	100%	

AVERAGE FINAL SCORE — **3.25**

Table 26.5: West

(All materials can be downloaded from the resource centre at `www.robertdellner.com`)

As we will have seen from the questions posed and their respective depths, these segments now become the dialectic resonance with the governance system that will work their way into the I³OO as with I³ 2.0. The main difference here is that we include more of the integral methodology in general and we incorporate the GENE, 4Cs and CARE into the process.

Here we see that whilst South is turning out just a little stronger than our relatively high bar and hurdle rate, East is quite strong whilst North stands out as the strongest, the question is about calibration of the hurdle rate. West is on outcome targets but after prioritisation, is just below it. This is now part of the dialectic dance in understanding and agreeing the calibrations of each as receiving them from their respective analysis/reporting functions. We see here fluidity and flexibility; few areas are static.

As with 2.0 the idea is to build a map of the investee to enable a proactive, constructive and value add dialogue to occur. As a pure credit analyst, I should have a much better idea of how the prospective creditor is behaving; his/her attitude will dictate how the I³OO lands between us.

If I have a value-added relationship which has been embedded into the investee and their community, their reputation will be sullied if something goes wrong. This, of course, may or not be relevant depending on the context, but if I only rely on contractual obligations and the law, Iâ€™m less likely to find solutions before we enter a stressed situation. In generic accounting terms this framework looks as figure 26.2.

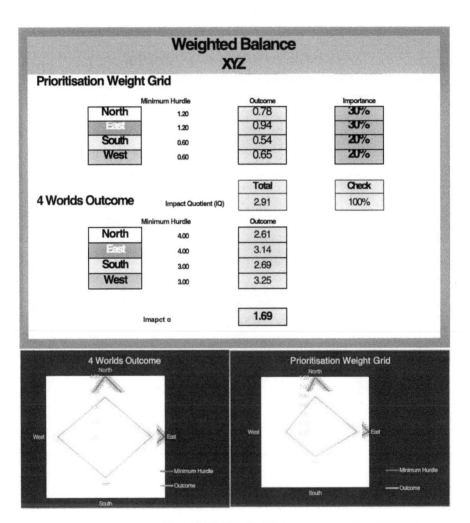

Figure 26.1: Weighted Balance

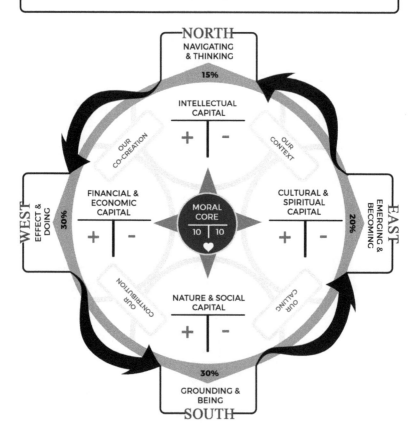

Figure 26.2: South

Chapter 27

From IRR to IIR (Internal Rate of Return to Integral Impact Return)

Reframing and reimagining our approach to returns is probably the most important aspect of our impact approach. This has to be done within a consistent framework such as I³ without getting lost within the forest of competing claims and possible variations in methodologies.

LOST

What do I do when I'm lost in the forest?
Stand still. The trees ahead and bushes beside you
Are not lost. Wherever you are is called Here,
And you must treat it as a powerful stranger,
Must ask permission to know it and be known. The forest
breathes. Listen. It
answers, I have made this place around you.
If you leave it, you may come back again, saying Here.
No two trees are the same to Raven.
No two branches are the same to Wren.
If what a tree or a bush does is lost on you,
You are surely lost. Stand still. The forest knows
Where you are. You must let it find you.

David Wagoner (1999)[402]

As we know, the Western mode of finance and economics is virtually exclusively driven by rates of return, and making decisions about how to allocate capital. The internal rates of return (IRR) is made up by several subgroups i.e., legal and capital, costs of capital, expected excess return, risk, time value of money, structuring, transaction cost, etc. All to compensate the owner of capital for uncertainty, and of course rent. Let us remind ourselves of the component parts of capital; here is a current stack/situation on a typical 10% loan:

Excess return	3%
Liquidity Risk	0.5%

Risk migration	0.5%
Return on Capital Employed	3.5%
Costs	0.5%
Expected Loss	1%
Risk Free rate	1%

One of the main purposes of I³ and as outcome is to develop a true understanding of the integral Impact Return which supplements or dislodges the conventional paradigm of Internal Rate of Return. Although this might not be seen as progress in many quarters in Finance, but as we introduce Impact, Finance itself has no alternative than to evolve and transform itself into a combination of its new component parts along the ecological and social lines as outlined. As from the example above, very simplistically, we can evolve the IRR stack into our IIR stack as follows:

Base Financial Return	8.00%
North	1.48%
East	1.78%
South	1.02%
West	1.23%
IIR	13.51%

We will see that we have reduced the required financial return from 10% to 8% whilst achieving an IIR of 13.51%. Of course this is not necessarily a perfect solution as a hypothetical illustration but if we are to start attaching value to the impact dimensions it will be easier to evolve a concept such as IRR into further stacking, including impact components. This leads us into a brief discussion on financial returns. We know that returns are compensation for both the time value of money, Inflation and the myriad associated risks and costs. On this issue, historical returns have been extremely accommodating and have adequately compensated investors.

We find that given the markets paradigm, it adjusts to reflect changing conditions, and where capital has to be priced to attract investors looking for their risk adjusted return. In more recent times of low interest rates we see a closer convergence of rates of return but also a perfectly natural shift within the total market return from fixed income and debt into equities. These returns acts equally as stacks which takes different proportions of the income generated by organisations. If we hypothesize that it is exactly this capital recycling of ever increasing compounded returns—the fundamental problem of economics, which is not sustainable, we will see further convergence over the coming years, which as previously discussed will require financial firms to find broader definitions of Alpha.

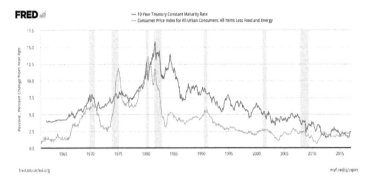

Figure 27.1: Constant Returns vs. CPI

High Yield Bond Yields: Are You Being Compensated?

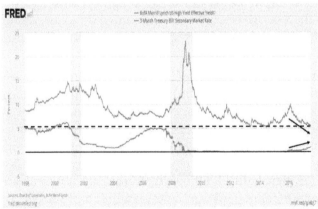

Source: Gerring Capital Partners, StockCharts.com

Figure 27.2: High Yield vs. Risk Free Rate

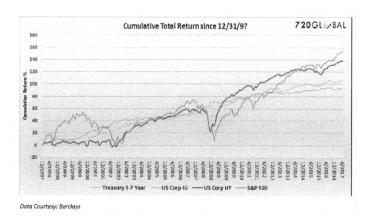

Data Courtesy: Barclays

Figure 27.3: Cumulative Total Returns

Capital is the only asset that does not depreciate and degenerate, nor is it subject to the laws of nature including entropy. In contrast, on aggregate, over historical time, it is apparent that its risk stack of compensatory factors has yielded well in excess of both economic growth and inflation, i.e., the global pool of capital available has been steadily compounding and growing for decades. Again, we are not venturing an opinion on whether this is right or wrong, rather from our now evolving integral perspective acknowledge that unless the IRR driver can be complemented by a more comprehensive measure that includes the impact spectrum, we will now shift the mantra and dogma of IRR.

As we now enter the new era of limitations for finance and economics to provide solutions to global problems, we must develop the protocols to build a new four-worlds 'sandwich' for our Integral Impact Return (IIR) which like our conventional IRR is constructed of the component parts of each dimension that make up the whole. This can also be expanded into all forms of conventional measurements including ROCE, so maybe one day investors will have a P/E ratio with a P/I (Impact) ratio as part of the valuation toolset. This will require more work on the capitalisation of Impact components which myself and CIFE colleague, Mark Anielski are working on and will be the subject of a future book. A key driver to its development will be the speed at which conventional IRR's decline as a result of global conditions, and the global investment industry searching for a new alpha. Conventional Alpha measures an investment manager's relative return performance to market peers.

We know that much of what passes for Alpha is actually made up of external drivers and factors such as fortuitous timing, shifts in valuation multiples, industry drivers, and statistical biases and not the skill and excellence of any particular manager. This in turn explains the rise of the index tracking industry. As such, on aggregate, managers return negative Alpha roughly equivalent to management fees. This is not to say that there are no highly skilled managers; indeed there are, only that is difficult to keep such returns consistent over time. However, the search for this Alpha will not change nor should it. However, bets on variable financial Alpha needs to be supplemented and augmented with Impact Alpha.

In Saker Nusseibeh's paper 'The Why Question' he writes:

> As ludicrous as this may seem, the 'betting' logic lies at the heart of much of modern financial academic work. We even talk of investments (whether strategic or company specific) as bets. According to this perception, an active manager represents a double bet (picking one that has a hit ratio of 51% and picking an allocator with a hit ratio of 51%) while a passive manager represents a single bet (is the economy going up or down). The cop out, of course has been that since developed economies have been growing since the end of World War Two, then staying in the market throughout the cycles in a passive strategy will capture the assumed long term upside of economic growth. [35]

There is a rich seam of additional and differentiated Impact Alpha to be mined and harvested, giving managers much greater ability to broaden and add specific translated Alpha more relevant to the Impact returns requirements. Again, much of this will depend on how our investments firm is positioned to attract investor capital. For example, public and private markets have the same constellation for returns whilst some of the drivers are different. Again, let's turn to Nusseibeh for some insight:

> It is clear that the structure of the capital markets have evolved beyond what economic theory thinks they should be. The large corporations of the world no longer raise the majority of the capital they need from shareholders as they did in the 19th century... Because of the enormous control quoted companies have over the life of ordinary citizens who own their shares, we must look for the purpose, the 'why' if you will, in something other than capital-raising, dividend payout and capital accumulation. It seems to me that with the maturing of the capital markets, shareholding should serve a different purpose... The capital markets system has reached a stage where it is primarily self-perpetuating. The quoted sector no longer looks to equity markets as the main source to raise capital. The ownership of shares must therefore evolve so that it becomes the conduit for bringing about long term sustainable prosperity for the entire system (Ibid).

If we take an integral approach, anchored and rooted in our evolved investment, we see that all parts can become integrally informed to alleviate the imbalances. This is the only way to develop the knowledge for the organisational solutions necessary. This means that we can no longer hide from our responsibility as stewards of capital. This is not about being confrontational but about being assertive in our beliefs and mission. What that exactly will look like is our choice, but doing nothing is not an option. When we take an integral perspective, we include the parts which otherwise would be obscured.

Paulo Freire, in his The Politics of Education challenged our ethics: 'Washing one's hands of the conflict between the powerful and the powerless means to side with the powerful, not to be neutral.'[41] However, we will always find that the most rewarding endeavours are those of the heart, where we are truly engaged with our core callings; where we co-create within our context new impact perspectives that solve our global issues. Our collective contributions is in effect, the positive footprint and impact that we make when we use our own human capital in its formation.

So the question is: what recipe are we making, and what is beckoning us over the next horizon. Carl Jung clarified the point:

> The most intense conflicts, if overcome, leave behind a sense of security and calm that is not easily disturbed. It is just these intense conflicts and their conflagration which are needed to produce valuable and lasting results. [403]

As we have discussed previously, this will be an almost impossible challenge and is the main reason why one may be pessimistic about the future. Our intellect, paradigms and ego investments in the current generation of capital stewards is quite possibly why this change will take longer, requiring new generations of stewards. However, we have to experience the ego and its limitations before we can let something bigger come into our being.

There is hope that we can overcome much of the inherent resistance. C.G. Jung hits the nail on the head: The experience of the self is always felt as a defeat for the ego[215]'. As highlighted above, a core component is what we can see and value in terms of returns. I³ works within a framework so we can see the connections with other capitals; and to value those in relation to the financial. This is a pipe dream as many people with 'excess' capital value giving away in various forms. We have to remember that it is not any natural laws that state that income yields, and by implication forward values, must be positive. As we know, in finance, forward markets are built on and contain several components parts:

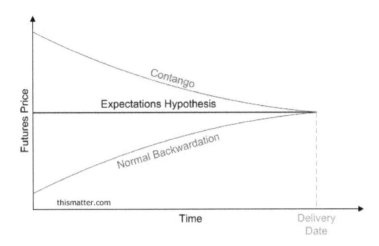

Figure 27.4: Time Value

I. The spot price of the underlying asset

II. The time value cost of carry from a) borrowing a third partys balance sheet, b) storage, c) insurance etc. (creates a positive future price called backwardation)

III. Discount for any income yield

IV. The expected future value in relation to the spot price (if negative, called contango)

V. Volatility of the underlying asset (e.g. CAPM)

Conventional finance and economics treat the above as dogma:
Futures Price = Spot Price × (1 + Risk-Free Interest Rate − Income Yield)

However, recently we are experiencing negative nominal interest rates in several countries as part of monetary stimulus packages, none of which has caused government overthrows or revolutions by irate investors. Debt in effect is bringing future value back into the present. If our investment has the capacity to generate the future value of rent in full and the return of capital, our investment is successful. However, if at some point the future cannot produce the required financial value that the now moving forward present demands, we have a problem. All investments therefore by definition contain this 'mortgage' on the future which as mentioned in Part 2 means a pledge unto death. This is a core aspect which remedy impact needs to evolve into.

Previous economic orders were based on negative forward values as tax on capital held in monetary forms means that we were better off to stimulate spending and circulation of money and let it accumulate without benefitting the economy. The economist Silvio Gesell, in his 1936 book 'The Natural Economic Order' writes

> Our goods rot, decay, break rust so only if money has equally disagreeable, loss-involving properties can it effect exchange rapidly, securely and cheaply. [404]

When Irving Fisher wrote 'The Theory of Interest' (1930), he used the metaphor of ship's biscuits, known as 'hardtack' amongst shipwrecked sailors on a barren island to explain a useful economic paradigm in that Interest i.e., the forward value had to be zero as there was no more biscuits in the future on which interest could be paid. However, no sailor would accept any alternative terms as they may as well consume their biscuit supply in the present. However, if washed ashore with a perishable good, e.g., apples, the rate may well have been zero as the future value now also reflected the loss of capital. Fisher's concluded:

> There is no absolutely necessary reason inherent in the nature of man or things why the rate of interest in terms of any commodity standard should be positive rather than negative[405]

Nature operates in similar ways. Whilst everything in nature makes a contribution to something else, even the 'yield' from a wheat field is being re-cycled and cannot be accumulated for its own sake, unlike money. Gesell also writes of a lone Robinson Crusoe trying to save three years provisions to tide him over while he builds a canal to a supposed freedom. Here, by trying to find storage solutions, Crusoe expends considerable effort to find ingenious ways to conserve his wealth. Wheat must be dried and protected from rain and mice.

Meat must be salted and cured. The buckskin that he uses for clothing must dry and be protected from moths. The labour expended trying to save the fruits of his labour is considerable. Despite this, Crusoe faces risks to future values, and as it happens, is doomed to earn a negative return on his savings. The mice took a liking to the buckskin, and mildew destroyed the wheat, 'rust, decay, breakage…dry rot, ants keep up a never ending attack' on his saved capital.

Gesell was concerned with money accumulation operating outside the natural order.

This is one of many challenges that any alternative economic system must understand. Whilst the current financial system is addicted to compound interest, impact investments can mitigate its dependency and enshrined expectation. Investors, of course, deserve a return from the opportunity cost of capital in the form of compensation from inflation, risk and a generic time value of money but this cannot be achieved at the cost of other capitals.

> Debt can endure forever; wealth cannot, because its physical dimension is subject to the destructive force of entropy.
>
> Frederick Soddy

Given the law of entropy, counter balances are at work that seek to restore systemic order even if this means an orderly decline. What Impact investments has the opportunity to achieve, and I^3 in particular, is to restore such imbalances through the assessment, measurement, e.g. accounting, but more importantly, calibration of how the additional capitals have been impacted and their inherent returns in relation to both the intentional Integral outcome objectives (I^3OO) and those outside the plan.

'SWEET DARKNESS' BY DAVID WHYTE[406]

When your eyes are tired the world is tired also. When your vision has gone, no part of the world can find you. Time to go into the dark where the night has eyes to recognise its own. There you can be sure you are not beyond love. The dark will be your home tonight. The night will give you a horizon further than you can see. You must learn one thing. The world was made to be free in. Give up all the other worlds except the one to which you belong. Sometimes it takes darkness and the sweet confinement of your aloneness to learn anything or anyone that does not bring you alive is too small for you.

Sometimes our most treasured things don't bring us alive including our work in which we have invested so much time, effort and money. When so, we need to reach out to find that next developmental extension of life which lies beyond our own confined spaces and limited conversation i.e. how did I make my life too small for me? Real aliveness of the self is only possible because there already exists a developed and separate 'thou' – human or more/than/human - that is able to give to more than the self-i.e. to life, always feeding its growing network of reciprocal interdependence.

For example, the term commons characterises a form of socio-economy that integrates material and social relationships. It is based on the exchange of goods, but also the transformation of meaning. The commons has been the dominant form of livelihood since the dawn of premodern humans at least a million years ago, binding all agents together in a vast, interconnected network of giving and receiving, which is meant to create the greatest possible fertility for all. Commons are about protecting aliveness through participation and reciprocity which is what we may aim to do in our impact approaches. Sadly, many people only find life through a near death experience, let's instead try to go on a journey such as through I³ to find a near life experience.

§27.1 SEKEM a case study

The organisation SEKEM (from the ancient Egyptian, meaning vitality from the sun) was founded in 1977 by the Egyptian pharmacologist and social entrepreneur Dr. Ibrahim Abouleish in order to bring about cultural renewal in Egypt on a sustainable basis. SEKEM has been built on his foundational vision rooted in nature and community:

> I carry a vision deep within myself: in the midst of sand and desert I see myself standing as a well drawing water. Carefully I plant trees, herbs and flowers and wet their roots with the precious drops. The cool well water attracts human beings and animals to refresh and quicken themselves. Trees give shade, the land turns green, fragrant flowers bloom, insects, birds and butterflies show their devotion to God, the creator, as if they were citing the first Sura of the Koran. The human, perceiving the hidden praise of God, care for and see all that is created as a reflection of paradise on earth. For me this idea of an oasis in the middle of a hostile environment is like an image of the resurrection at dawn, after a long journey through the nightly desert. I saw it in front of me like a model before the actual work in the desert started. And yet in reality I desired even more : I wanted the whole world to develop. [170]

The SEKEM Initiative[407] was founded with the vision of sustainable development and giving back to the community. A main goal is to 'restore and maintain the vitality of the soil and food as well as the biodiversity of nature' through sustainable, organic agriculture and to support social and cultural development. It aims to develop the individual, society, and the environment through a holistic approach which integrates ecology, economy, societal and cultural life. Located NorthEast of Cairo, the organisation now has several commercial enterprises and now includes:

- a series of biodynamic farms;

- trading companies for produce and processed foods (Hator and Libra), herbal teas and beauty products (ISIS Organic), medicinal herbs and medicines (ATOS Pharma), and organic cotton products (NatureTex);

- a medical centre;

- a school based on the principles of Waldorf pedagogy open to pupils from any religious or ethnic background;

- a community school catering specifically to the needs of children from disadvantaged groups;

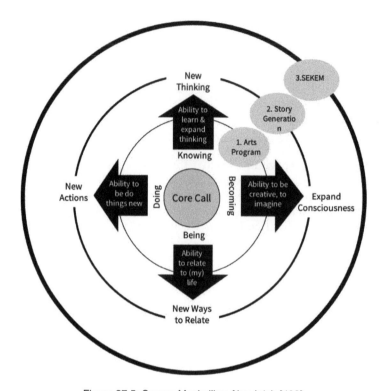

Figure 27.5: Source Maximilian Abouleish [408]

- a nursery

- a vocational training centre;

- a college (Mahad Adult Education Training Institute) and research
  centre (SEKEM Academy for Applied Art and Sciences);

- Heliopolis University for Sustainable Development

Here we can see that by taking the Arts centre inside the first realm, the
interconnectedness of the four-worlds in terms of being, becoming, thinking
and doing, reinforcing each other.

As an integral enterprise, SEKEM integrates the 4 elements from cultural,
societal, economic and ecological life, and represents an internationally
recognised role model for sustainable corporate development.

From what was based initially on a social innovation, a central question
for SEKEM is how it can be functionally and structurally understood, designed

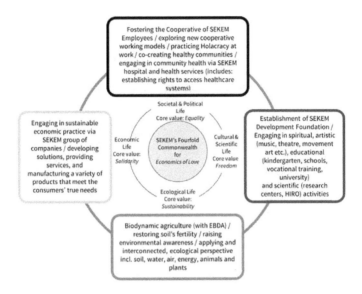

Figure 27.6: Source Maximilian Abouleish (Ibid)

and institutionalised in order to move towards the integral phase of the organisation as a living organism.

We know that this transition requires that every part contributes intelligently to the overall organisation, serving the purpose of corporate sustainable development in its four independent, yet interrelated dimensions of societal, cultural, economic and ecological life.

For SEKEM, quite naturally rooted and grounded in Nature, they start in the integral South.

SEKEM is based on a renewed approach to Integral Human Development which incorporates individual storytelling (grounding), consciousness level and complexity handling capacity evaluation (emerging), competence level mapping (navigating) and self-management (effecting).

The corresponding rhythm of SEKEM's Integral Organisational Development includes the dimensions of collective storytelling (grounding), arts and rituals (Cultura Activa) for stimulating consciousness development (emerging), knowledge creation via the integral Project Management framework (navigating), and the application of Holacracy as a complete system for self-organisation (effecting).

All elements on different levels mutually reinforce each other and help

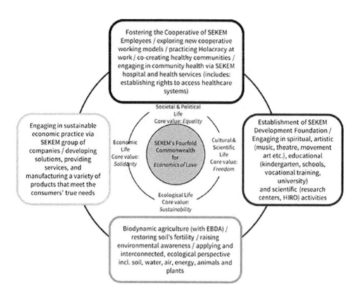

Figure 27.7: SEKEM as a Fourfold Commonwealth (Source: Adapted from Schieffer and Lessem [10, p. 523])

SEKEM to actualise its potential to become a fully functional Integral Enterprise.

SEKEM has taken further development of the integral model to heart and has cocreated as suggested a unique version 3.0 which incorporates the wholeness of the SEKEM ethos. The below image is the SEKEM Sustainability Flower, a symbol for the underlying vision and approach to SEKEM's holistic development. Next to the inner social body with its three constituting elements we find ecology as the fourth surrounding element. The outer circle represents the cosmos as an omnipresent force that is highly relevant.

The central perspective for SEKEM is the 'Economics of Love' rendering our conventional, self-oriented and ego-centric concept of homo-economicus obsolete. Their underlying paradigm is based upon a living way of thinking ecologically, linked with an objective sense of economic community and the will to recognise social necessities. Such an organic character, which is expressed by SEKEM's inter-institutional ecology, is founded on inner organisational and personal integrity, its concern for humanitarian justice, and, above all, by its determination to realise the material existence of the whole social and ecological community.

As a predominantly Muslim organisation, stewardship of the earth (khalifa), (South), consciousness development (ishtehad), (East), Justice (fadl),

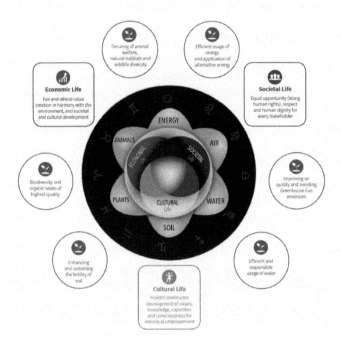

Figure 27.8: Source Maximilian Abouleish [408]

(North) and beauty (ihsan), (West) and are all core principles of Islam that Odeh Rashed Al-Jayyousi in his book 'Islam and Sustainable Development' (2012) related to the concept of sustainable development, and hence in turn are related to SEKEM's Economics of Love.

While SEKEM is a fully commercial profit-making enterprise, it does not consider its prime aim profit maximisation. Through an integrated profit-sharing methodology, it shares its returns with the smallholder farmers in its supplier network called the Egyptian Biodynamic Association (EBDA), which has around 600 small-scale farmers who represent SEKEM's ecological branch. SEKEM for Land Reclamation (SLR), for farming, organic seedlings, fertilisation and pest control, also belongs to this agricultural sphere. It is important for SEKEM to distinguish its sustainable agriculture business from its manufacturing and sales businesses, because the real added value is created in the Economic Life, which generates profit to be used in its broader agricultural cultural life.

As an example, ten percent of SEKEM's profits go to the SEKEM Development Foundation (SDF), which represents the cultural branch of the initiative. It has launched many community development projects, including establishing schools and a medical centre, celebrating culture and diversity, and promoting peace, cooperation and understanding between all human beings. Since 2012, The Heliopolis University for Sustainable Development has become a leading player in cultural development under the umbrella of the SEKEM initiative.

Last but not least, the Cooperative for SEKEM Employees (CSE) represents the societal branch of the SEKEM initiative, with its relationship to and between people respecting human rights. The huge national and international network of SEKEM, such as the International Association for Partnership (IAP), also belongs here as an institution of economic partners working together as pioneers in the organic movement.

SEKEM works with what they call 'The Integral Project Management impact matrix' (IPM) which visualises the contribution of each project according to the four dimensions of the Sustainability Flower. It works as an assessment tool for each team and thus the actual contribution is evaluated at the end of a project. Project teams and their roles are also structured according to integral principles and natural allocation and selection.

The IPM process describes (depicted below) a four-phase process that moves through the different phases in several rounds following the integral GENE-rhythm. The different phases can be executed in parallel or sequentially depending on the type and needs of a project.

This is very similar to the I³ version 3.0 from the organisational level. The indicators of the IPM contribution questionnaire are collected from various sources that SEKEM agrees are important to measure sustainable development. The questionnaire requests six to seven indicators for contributions in the four dimensions. Based on this matrix, each project group can develop a project-specific grant review beyond this general scheme. Initially, each project team ensures that the indicators and dimensions are individually adapted to the specific project.

Once the project is completed, external beneficiaries can use the questionnaire as a tool to provide detailed comments on the results of the project. This is similar to having the I³OO as the driver of an iterative process that capitalises and resources each dimension. A specific IMP project flower itself is depicted in figure 27.12.

Integral contains significant complexity. Maximilian Abouleish – Boes has produced a four-worlds map that illustrates the component parts of his own integral journey inside SEKEM (figure 27.13).

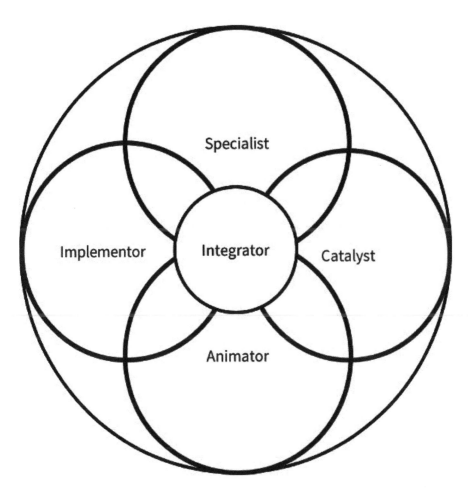

Figure 27.9: Source Maximilian Abouleish (Ibid)

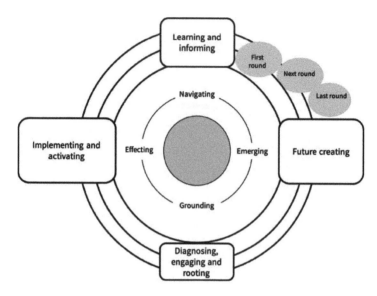

Figure 27.10: Source Maximilian Abouleish (Ibid)

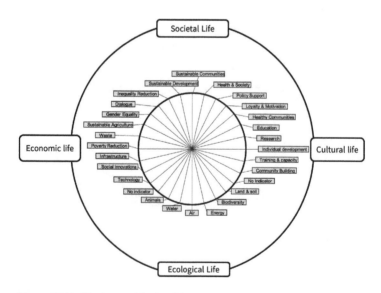

Figure 27.11: The Integral Project Management impact matrix. Source Maximilian Abouleish (Ibid)

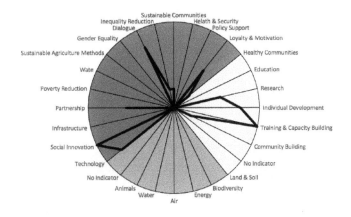

Figure 27.12: Source Maximilian Abouleish (Ibid)

Having travelled through this third part of the book where we looked at 'changing the firms in which we invest' you may rightly wonder why we are still looking through the lens of the self. The answer may sound slightly simplistic and by now may sound obvious but nevertheless contains a profound truth. You can only change another or anything outside of yourself as a reflection of a change in yourself and your firm. We return to the adage of 'be the change you want to see' and 'let it begin with me'. As an extension, we have created the conditions to influence the investee without voluntarily creating the Impact conditions as agreed through working through the Impact outcome objectives (e.g., I³OO).

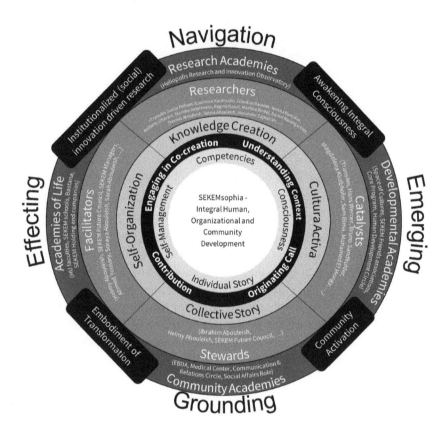

Figure 27.13: Overview of the function and structure of SEKEM's approach to Integral Human, Organisational and Community Development. Source: Based on Schieffer and Lessem [10], Lessem [308, 346, 11], and Lessem and Schieffer [9], adapted by Maximilian Abouleish – Boes

PART IV

The way
forward

Chapter 28

Through the lens of an envisaged 2nd tier Impact 4.0

> The whole is a necessary to the understanding of its parts,
> as the parts are necessary to the understanding of the whole
>
> The Mach principle[105]

We now can return to our beginning. In this chapter I will provide some of the additional ingredients necessary for this level.

This 4.0 Impact level requires us to have already confronted our shadows, and to have reached a stage where we have found our humanity. If we have done so sufficiently well, we will have developed the prerequisites for the state of humanity and the state of our planet to open up our creativity for Impact.

Using Spiral language, Impact 3.0 and 4.0 cannot evolve unless we move from the current predominant Orange Meme of the financial industry. We are seeing Finance beginning to develop elements of Green, and Impact having tinges of Yellow in several areas.

If anything these trends are accelerating, but are by no means certain, given the perceived need for the finance industry to retain the post-modern paradigm. As discussed before, much of the Impact development will be based on the increased capacities to value returns from other dimensions, and to disseminate their differences.

By saying someone is second tier, we are saying that their centre of gravity is in second tier. This means that, when all the lines of development are considered, (cognitive, emotional, social, spiritual, physical) the majority of their lines are in second tier.

There may still be parts of themselves further down (or up) the developmental ladder. Importantly, remember that higher does _not_ mean better per se, just further evolved to include more states and perspectives.

It is common for previous stages to think they are already 2nd tier if they are close to having one line (e.g., cognitive) at 2nd tier. Leadership in its complexity can actually be seen as a developmental line in itself.

Also, as higher tiers are by definition hidden from view from lower tiers, and have to be developed to be made visible, they are often dismissed by the ego before they have a chance to emerge.

Impact investments at 2nd tier have now evolved to become an art form which transcends and includes the science behind it.

Art elicits our most basic instinct for aesthetics. So in forms such as the Martial arts, mastery can only be obtained through the development of the whole person, beyond mere skill and technique. The same is true in Impact 4.0, which contains more of the non-dual states. Gestalts, in terms of measurements and calibration methodology. Here we seek to further evolve, and find culturally aligned ways to connect and interpret Impact, using common languages which each of the four worlds can understand and synthesise.

Below is a non-exhaustive list of some of the key components of Impact 4.0, additional to 3.0. As such our objective is to envisage the evolutionary trajectory of travel, rather than a new destination.

- The deepening of the integral four-worlds and their corresponding dynamic.

- Less prevalent organisational pathology e.g., black/white, digital, mechanistic thinking; and shadow parts from previous levels; are left behind.

- Evolved non-local consciousness and non-dual consciousness with more acceptance of is-ness.

- Removal of many of the power complexes in governance, economic, and social structures and solutions.

- Ego-drops; including fewer differentiations (like 'expert'), and fewer hierarchies of power, fewer power complexes, and with more understanding of humanity and equality.

- Practical outcomes from the removal of power complexes and egoic structures include senior investment executives working/volunteering in arenas including the investee and its community.

- Evolved governance, beyond e.g., consensus, or even consent in conventional holacracy and sociocracy, to include external systemic stakeholders and contain more convergence around our humanness.

- The spiritual dimension is now fully included to inform and guide proceedings.

- Systemic combined aggregate returns, e.g. IIR, is now an acceptable form of measurement.

- Market enterprise valuation methodology transmutes to include Impact, e.g., multiples of IIR.

- Context equally drives co-created Impact outcome objectives, as opposed by owners of capital.

- New states of consciousness (at least mindfulness) are included and valued in all proceedings.

- Outcomes now drive proceedings, rather than policies and procedures driving them.

- Servant leadership no longer is an oxymoron but grounded in the South, where relating is the natural organising principle.

- Knowledge, and its making, is valued as coming from all creation and creation's processes.

- Moving measurement systems towards modelling, and e.g., Interpretative Phenomenology Analysis (IPA), and other formats that capture more and deeper content.

- Integral components now can be calibrated using multiple alternatives such as Hawkins' scales.

- Investment theses and reporting can now take multiple forms, drawing on art, music, poetry, movement, and other forms of expressive transmission of integral information.

- Culturally aligned rituals and ceremonies are used to understand, fuse, and synthesise impact.

- Vision quests are used to diagnose symbolic representations for Impact.

- Much less emphasis on the model of things, and more on the intuitive and collective sensations around an investment proposition. The model may even become a hindrance to see the real impact.

- An increase in creative approaches, with 'out-of-the box' solutions, to an investment.

- Openness and acceptance to solutions arriving from alternative states of consciousness e.g., dreams, revelations, etc.

- Processes and forums are designed to look for engagement to maximise collective intelligence towards dialectic 'one-mind'. Real dialogue trumps processes.

- Increased sense of freedom and space to experiment.

- Increased comfort to handle ambiguity and uncertainty, with fewer 'elephants in the room'.

- Lessening of simple filtering, such as generalisations, distortions, deletions, or projections; instead there is an opening up to more direct perceptions, true implications, and a new healthy relationship with reality.

- 'I' and 'Thou' i.e., 'the other' merges naturally to become one and now 'us'.

Each one of these would need to be evolved by each firm into each organisation as new forms of interpretations of reality.

Let us now pick one of the above and enter some depth just to illustrate the possibilities to discover here. We will briefly investigate the work on consciousness by David Hawkins. The core idea and application within Impact is that our body doesn't lie, and we can use kinesiology technology to calibrate and find out the different levels of truth as part of any assessment. This research has received some criticism for being subjective, judgemental, and having issues with the calibration technique, which will require any user to accept or reject questions on its own merits.

However, this research has profound implications in that it can provide an alternative objective calibration and measurement system for Impact as we move into Impact 3.0 and 4.0. During my own deeper work in Psychology I studied and trained in PsychK®, which works with belief change at a deeper subconscious level using whole-brain activation and muscle testing to calibrate and verify change; so I have some experience and validation for this technology.

Kinesiology is the scientific study of human body movement. Kinesiology addresses physiological, biomechanical, and psychological dynamic principles and mechanisms of movement. The word comes from the Greek κίνησις κίνēσις, movement' (itself from κινεῖν κινεῖν, 'to move'), and λογία logia, 'study'[409].

This reconnects us with the earlier discussion on the mind-body approach, which contrasts with much of the postmodern philosophy that denies an existing objective reality, and denies moral values. Kinesiology seeks to emphasise and find a clear distinction between good and bad, knowledge from ignorance, dominance from submission, and presence from absence. It is a critical theory approach that seeks to prove that there are many universal truths. However, when looking at the behaviour of humans, we can see some universal recurring behavioural patterns, such as in our facial expressions:

- We will always interpret a smile as something positive, even if we've lived in isolation for our entire life.

- Likewise, we will subconsciously recognise an angry face as potentially dangerous and possibly something to avoid.

The first work on applied kinesiology was pioneered by George Goodheart. He discovered that the body reacted to subtle physical stimuli in predictable ways. For instance, beneficial nutritional supplements would increase the strength of specific indicator muscles, whereas harmful stimuli would cause those same muscles to weaken. Basically, the body knew at a subconscious level what was good or bad for it. John Diamond subsequently refined the technique into a new discipline called behavioural kinesiology. Using the same testing approach, he confirmed that specific indicator muscles would strengthen or weaken in response to positive or negative emotional and physical stimuli.

For example, a smile would make us test strong, while the statement 'I hate you' would make a muscle weaker. He showed that these results were predictable and universal. Somewhat paradoxical was that this was true even with no clear rational link between stimuli and response. In fact, he showed that certain random abstract symbols caused all subjects to test weak, whereas others made them strong. This indicates the presence of an objective communal consciousness embedded in the mind or *spiritus mundi*. The most renowned psychologist in this field of work is Carl G. Jung, who coined the term collective unconscious. He suggested that certain structures of the subconscious mind are phenomena shared amongst all beings of the same species.

- A fish swimming at the edge of a school will turn instantly to another direction when its partners spot a predator and start to flee, even if they're a quarter mile away.

- Birds follow the same flight routes generationally even if they haven't been taught to.

- Adult salmon swim upstream from the ocean to hatch and die, as did their own parents who couldn't have passed on this behaviour from direct experience.

So, are we talking about a field of consciousness, in addition to our own internal consciousness, which we can tap into? Two influential fields of study in modern mathematics are dynamical systems theory and chaos theory, which describe complex dynamical systems and their motions. Attractor patterns are particular kinds of recognizable patterns, or 'traces,' left in the system by the movements of their agents. Hawkins suggested that:

> The brain's neural networks work like a system of attractor patterns that represent energy fields with qualities of consciousness itself and not the individual [32].

According to Hawkins humans live and operate at vastly different 'levels' of consciousness. Each level, along with the 'truth level' of ANY true/false style inquiry, can be tested for truth and numerically 'calibrated'. It is as if we unconsciously know what's right and wrong, good and bad, true and false. But it seems we are already in possession of this knowledge which can be accessed at all times. In quantum physics, the question of consciousness is taking the form of a unified field theory, or that of a quantum mind. The unified field of human consciousness is not just experienced by the mind and accessed by the body. The kinesiology test does not show a local reaction to the body but is a general response of consciousness to the energy of a substance or a statement [32].

A truthful answer will yield a positive response, indicated by the muscles strengthening, as a result from the impersonal field of consciousness that exists in all things living because the brain receives energy from the patterns that exist a priori in the mind. This led to Hawkins' work on kinesiological measuring of consciousness in 1975 and over the following 20 years, he built a scale of relative truth, by using mathematical terms of nonlinear dynamics, which ranges from 1 to 1000.

The scale indicates the quantum of truth of any expression, such as people, events, and objects, from the energy they emit and imprint into the

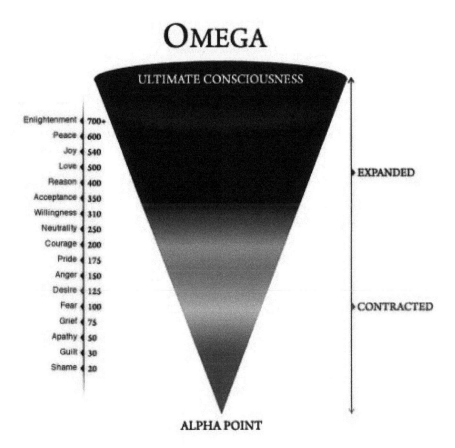

Figure 28.1: Power vs Force Scale of Truth

quantum field. Those vibrations of energy get perceived by attractor patterns of the brain at the subconscious level. According to Hawkins, any person, concept, thought or object that calibrates at 200 (The level of Integrity) or above is positive ('power'); anything below 200 is negative ('force').

His work also relates strongly with the biologist's Rupert Sheldrake's 'morphogenetic fields' hypothesis[410]. Essentially, morphogenetic fields are groups of cells that respond to biochemical signals, which leads to the development of organs, limbs, muscle tissue, etc. Our body knows how to grow a foot because of our cells are receiving information both from the DNA and from the field.

These are also related to the emergent area of Epigenetics showing that our cell biology is also directed by signals from our thoughts and feelings as outlined in Bruce Lipton's book 'The Biology of Belief'[411]. The Morpfield findings suggest that every event in history, every person who has ever lived, every action we will take, and every thought we have, influences the state of this quantum field of consciousness.

It is a system that's in constant motion, and the traces of which are hidden from the rational mind, so can be accessed only by the body. If so, Hawkins' quote in *Power versus Force* gives us all something to consider: 'That one's every thought and action leaves an indelible trace forever in the universe can be an unsettling thought'[32].

Hawkins found that specific levels have emotions attached; ranging from fear, anger, and anxiety, scoring on the low end; and joy, love, compassion on the high end. For instance, Mother Teresa calibrated at 500, whereas Adolf Hitler was under 150, whilst according to Mark Anielski, the banking industry calibrates in general below 100 with outliers such as Goldman Sachs at 25. Hawkins concluded that the '… quantum field of consciousness is a powerful attractor which organises human behaviour into what is innate to humanness'[32].

Our deep consciousness operates from the perspective that it can do us no harm, that only truths have actual existence, and that the difference between these vibrational levels is a matter of degree. The amount of energy we can attach to anything depends on how truthful it is, which in turn is driven by the degree of its life-enhancement. Does it create duality, or does it seek unity, which as we discussed is one of the prime self-organising principles of life.

- For instance, all lower level vibrations are based on ego, duality, and negativity. Shame: 20, Guilt: 30, Fear: 100, Anger: 150 and Pride: 175

	Level	Scale (Log of)	Emotion	Process	Life-View
P **O** **W** **E** **R**	Enlightenment	700-1,000	Ineffable	Pure Consciousness	Is
	Peace	600	Bliss	Illumination	Perfect
	Joy	540	Serenity	Transfiguration	Complete
	Love	500	Reverence	Revelation	Benign
	Reason	400	Understanding	Abstraction	Meaningful
	Acceptance	350	Forgiveness	Transcendence	Harmonious
	Willingness	310	Optimism	Intention	Hopeful
	Neutrality	250	Trust	Release	Satisfactory
	Courage	200	Affirmation	Empowerment	Feasible
F **O** **R** **C** **E**	Pride	175	Dignity (Scorn)	Inflation	Demanding
	Anger	150	Hate	Aggression	Antagonistic
	Desire	125	Craving	Enslavement	Disappointing
	Fear	100	Anxiety	Withdrawal	Frightening
	Grief	75	Regret	Despondency	Tragic
	Apathy	50	Despire	Abdication	Hopeless
	Guilt	30	Blame	Destruction	Condemnation (Evil)
	Shame	20	Humiliation	Elimination	Miserable

Figure 28.2: Power vs Force Map of Consciousness

are all low-energy emotions. These are all life-destructive emotions with negative energies.

Only at Courage: 200 can we get access to any positive states. It is a transitory point, in which we go from negativity to affirmation and empowerment. We've managed to gain enough bravery to realize the dual nature of the ego and have decided to strive for improvement. Although it is only the first step towards the right direction, it doesn't mean we've made it by any means. Neutrality is at 250, which indicates trust in oneself and a release from the negativity.

- Emotions above 200 are life-enhancing emotions with positive energies. Willingness: 310; Acceptance: 350; and Reason: 400 are about raising levels of self-awareness and becoming a better person.

- At Love: 500, we hit another revelation and become more egoless. The idea is that we increase our consciousness to a point in which we become more selfless and empathic. What ensues is Joy: 540 and Peace: 600.

- At 700 we reach enlightenment, which makes us overcome all dualities and attain this total unity with all things living – pure consciousness. This is the point of complete self-transcendence characterised by the Buddha, Jesus, and Krishna. How do we measure the amount of truth? We will need two people to do a kinesiology test.

- The subject has to hold their arm laterally, parallel to the ground, while the tester proposes a yes or no statement.

- While they hold the statement in mind, their arm's strength is tested by applying pressure to it.

- If the answer to the question is correct, then the subject would find strength to resist; If wrong, they will give in.

Because consciousness is infinite in capacity, the statement needs to be relative to the reference scale created by Hawkins. Otherwise, the numbers would be arbitrary. For instance, 'On a scale of human consciousness from 1 to 1,000, where 700 indicates Enlightenment, this _____(item, motive, emotion, person, idea, event etc.) calibrates over_____(a number).'

The map of consciousness differentiates between the two sides of the same coin – action and inaction and the changing and changeless.

Force is a push of something that changes the momentum of something. It is something we do and apply to try and get certain results or project onto others or even ourselves.

- Power, on the other hand in a pull, is internal, existing and omnipotent so no need to apply force as it transfers energy by attraction.

Once Force comes into contact with Power, it dissipates, e.g., from independence movements to the abolition of slavery and apartheid. In organisational settings this can become a cultural Achilles heel that lead to disengagement from mission and vision.

However, force isn't necessarily a bad thing. We have to keep in mind that the difference between states of consciousness is still only a matter of degree. Some are simply brighter expressions of truth, whereas others are dimmer. Of course, we should remember that Power is still constructive. Higher vibrations are also more positive and life-enhancing, but there is a place and time for force.

Force is necessary for Power to be manifested. If there weren't any objects for gravitational force to affect, then it wouldn't be powerful. It is the notion of being powerless that allows us to become powerful. To have courage, we need also to feel fear. We don't want to be using Force indiscriminately or indefinitely as it is still motivated by a dual nature between us and our cause. But don't be fooled into thinking that we can simply ignore it either. It takes Force to cause a change and create momentum in anything. However, once momentum has been achieved, we need less force and to replace it with accessing our Power. Then, our consciousness expands and instead of pushing things we start to pull things towards ourselves almost like gravity.

The life force Power is self-organising and assimilating as it seeks growth, expansion and nourishment. Negative Force is the opposite, it tears down, fragments, breaks away and generates negative outcomes. However, this dynamic also burns the old to create fertile ground for new existence to take root. As we know, personally, death is needed for the ego to be reborn into a more powerful version of ourselves. Some interesting facts concerning consciousness calibration:

- Powerful patterns are associated with health; weak patterns are associated with sickness. Every thought, emotion, word and action have one pattern or the other. Every moment of our day we are either moving towards health or sickness.

- Everything calibrates at certain levels from weak to strong including books, food, water, clothes, people, animals, buildings, cars, movies, sports, music, etc.

- Most music produced today calibrates at levels below 200. Hence it leads to behaviour associated with lower energy levels of consciousness. Most movies will weaken people who watch them by bringing their energy levels down below 200 level.

- 85% of the human race calibrates below the critical level of 200.

- The power of the few individuals at the top counterbalances the weakness of the masses.

    - 1 individual at level 300 counterbalances 90,000 individuals below level 200

    - 1 individual at level 400 counterbalances 400,000 individuals below level 200

    - 1 individual at level 500 counterbalances 750,000 individuals below level 200

    - 1 individual at level 600 counterbalances 10 million individuals below level 200

    - 1 individual at level 700 counterbalances 70 million individuals below level 200

    - 12 individuals at level 700 equal one Avatar (e.g. Buddha, Jesus, Krishna) at level 1,000

    - Any meaningful human satisfaction cannot even commence until the level of 250 where some degree of self-confidence begins to emerge.

    - When one's consciousness falls below 200 at any given moment, we start to lose power and thus grow weaker and more prone to be manipulated by one's surroundings.

    - Parts of one's life will calibrate at a higher level of consciousness while other parts will calibrate at lower levels. It is the overall average that determines one's consciousness.

Universal principles calibrate at over 700 and affect mankind over long periods of time. Power originates from the unlimited mind whilst force is only rooted in the limited material world. Power as such will always defeat force but force is seductive and can often masquerade as a facile solution, serendipitously gaining the upper hand. We often see this in politics where a true statesmen/woman sacrifices him/ herself to serve the people versus the politician who sacrifices people to serve themselves. Colonialism of the type which we saw in India calibrates at 175 whilst Gandhi calibrated at 700 (along with Mandela in South Africa).

Real truths however need no defence, as they are self-evident and based on inviolate principles; e.g., the US declaration of independence which states 'that all men are created equal' (unless you consider the term men to be gender exclusive) calibrates at over 700. Power is associated with things that are unifying, life supporting and enhancing, whilst force is divisive, polarising and life diminishing. Power attracts whereas force repels.

Business practises, people, and products can be calibrated to ascertain whether the ingredients are more or less aligned with power or force. This is how one would expand and develop I^3 to understand its further application. Regardless, we now know that companies operating according to such principles outperform their peers, as the culture the principles are embodied in is non-replicable. This is exemplified in many successful businesses, e.g. Walmart and IKEA.

The classic book 'In search of Excellence' found that that successful companies had heart, rather than being only left-brained and scientifically managed. Whilst this type of calibration methodology may be a step too far for many left-brain investment practitioners, for Impact 3.0 and 4.0 we can see how working with kinesiology may become part of a protocol and measurement system which can capture many of the subjective/more qualitative aspects.

However, nothing will be more important than building your capacity to love.

§28.1 Integral Love

Following on the path of fourfoldness, we can see that since ancient times, the noun and verb love has been considered in its four parts. The Greeks have 4 words for love: Storge, Philia, Eros, and Agape. The British writer and lay theologian, C.S. Lewis, took this concept into what became his 1960 book "The Four Loves" based on thought experiments around the concepts of love following on the same lines as the Greek philosophers.

§28.1.1 Storge/Affection Love

The first Greek love is storge which can be thought of as an affectionate, familial quality of love. It's the feeling you have for your closest relations. It can even be the affection you feel towards for your pet animal. In relational terms, it's what is rooted and created in our Integral South.

To Lewis, storge is the most organic form of love. It's something anyone can feel. Something as natural as falling asleep at night. He says it's the most comfortable and least ecstatic of all loves. It's not the rapturous feeling you have when falling in love with a partner. Lewis describes it as soft slippers, or what an old, worn out chair might feel to your body. Storge wraps you around like a blanket, almost like sleep itself.

§28.1.2 Philia/Friendship Love

The second type of Greek love is philia which is the reciprocal quality of love you may feel for a friend. Lewis describes Philia as having a dispassionate quality. It was to him the least natural of all loves.

He says "There's nothing that quickens the pulse, or makes you red or pale." If you compare it with the romantic type of love that makes your heart race and palms sweat, philia is much more dispassionate. In relational terms is the rational kind of love we find in our Integral North.

However, Lewis doesn't discount it. He says philia love is very necessary. It produces the fewest pains and most pleasures.

He described philia as the "crown of life." The Greek philosopher Aristotle described three levels of philia.

The first level of philia is friendship of utility. These are your acquaintances, work friends, or other relationships where some practical benefit is received by both parties. These types of relationships come and go throughout your life.

The second level of philia are friendships of pleasure. These are your hang out friends, or even a friend who might be going through a similar hardship you're experiencing. Just like the first level – these types of friends come and go.

The third and highest level of philia that Aristotle described are friendships of the good. It's these rare individuals you can trust and call your true friend. These are people where you can go without speaking for years, yet see each other and feel like you hung out just the other week.

These relationships are rare and shouldn't be taken for granted. They say, if you have even three of these friendships, you're living a rich life.

§28.1.3 Eros/Romantic Love

Eros is the romantic flavour of love. It's passionate, it's rapturous and euphoric. It's for what some of the greatest songs and poems have been written about. Being the expression and projection of our deepest inner self, it's what many consider the greatest feeling of the human experience; yet thousands throughout history have died over this feeling. It's where we create the deepest relevance with our beloved, and is found mainly in our Integral West.

It's through romance that we can project all our hopes and expectations, and which can truly feel like heaven on earth for a period of time—until reality meets up again with expectations. Dr. Seuss once said. "You know you're in love when you don't want to fall asleep because reality is finally better than your dreams."

Eros love can be volatile, the greatest source of pleasure, yet at the same time can bury you into some of the darkest, most painful periods when it ends.

§28.1.4 Agape/Charitable Love

Agape, in its root form, means "wide open", in a state of wonder. It's a spiritual portal which creates your awareness and consciousness. It is the love that consumes the person who experiences it. Whoever knows and experiences agape learns that nothing else in the world is important – just love.

When you connect with awareness itself, that's exactly the wide open state of mind you're in. Not focusing on any one thing. Not clinging onto anything. Constantly letting go. Constantly opening up to what's in front of you. Agape is also directionless, i.e. it's not focused on anything else apart from what's inside you. Agape is also conditionless, it needs neither any special knowledge nor expertise. The only ability required is the ability to let go. Agape is what we mainly find in our Integral East.

Paulo Coelho describes Agape Love in his book 'The Pilgrimage':

> Agape is total love, the love that devours those that experience it. Whoever knows and experiences Agape sees that nothing else in this world is of any importance, only loving. This was the love that Jesus felt for humanity, and it was so great that it shook the stars and changed the course of man's history.

It's a type of love few people have heard of, let alone understood, let alone experienced. Here is an excerpt from Eckhart Tolle's 'A New Earth'[227]:

A beggar had been sitting by the side of a road for over thirty years. One day a stranger walked by. "Spare some change?" mumbled the beggar, mechanically holding out his old baseball cap. "I have nothing to give you," said the stranger. Then he asked: "What's that you are sitting on?" "Nothing," replied the beggar. "Just an old box. I have been sitting on it for as long as I can remember." "Ever looked inside?" asked the stranger. "No," said the beggar. "What's the point? There's nothing in there." "Have a look inside," insisted the stranger. The beggar managed to pry open the lid. With astonishment, disbelief, and elation, he saw that the box was filled with gold.

This is what the fourth and final love is all about. There's something within you containing all the love you could ever ask for. You don't really need anything which is not inside you already.

Lewis[1] reminds us:

There is no safe investment. To love at all is to be vulnerable. Love anything, and your heart will certainly be wrung and possibly be broken. If you want to make sure of keeping it intact, you must give your heart to no one, not even to an animal. Wrap it carefully round with hobbies and little luxuries; avoid all entanglements; lock it up safe in the casket or coffin of your selfishness. But in that casket—safe, dark, motionless, airless—it will change. It will not be broken; it will become unbreakable, impenetrable, irredeemable. The alternative to tragedy, or at least to the risk of tragedy, is damnation. The only place outside Heaven where you can be perfectly safe from all the dangers and perturbations of love is Hell.

---

[1]https://www.cslewis.com/love-love-love-love/

Chapter 29

Epilogue

As we reach the end of this book, I want to sincerely thank you for taking the time to read it, and to consider its content. We have covered much territory. I know it is not a complete treatise, nor can it always lay out succinctly the component parts you most need.

I hope, though, that you have found your own golden thread, to help define and design your own thinking, to take forth your own, co-created Impact approach, now in a more 'integral' guise. The Impact path, as we know, is an artful and creative path for us all to journey along, as we shape what kind of world we want, and what kind of legacy we want to leave.

If we can fill our Impact journey artfully with beauty, we create an opening for others through which they may wish to walk. Beauty as such is a doorway to our calling.

> The time will come when, with elation you will greet yourself arriving at your own door, your own mirror and each will smile at the other's welcome, and say, sit here. Eat. You will love again the stranger who was yourself.
> Give wine. Give bread. Give back your heart to itself, to the stranger who has loved you all your life, whom you ignored for another, who knows you by heart. Take down the love letters from the bookshelf, the photographs, the desperate notes, peel your own image from the mirror. Sit. Feast on your life
>
> Derek Walcott[412]

As long as we don't shy away from the challenge, as it is through how we conduct our Impact lives that we will find the energy and courage to fully engage with the true impact spectrum, in order to seek the diamond which is already within ourselves. We can't be everything to everyone, but we can always be something to someone.

I^3 may seem to some to be an overly ambitious attempt to create an over engineered and complex approach; and yet, like most things in life, success is only possible if the approach we use is complex enough for the challenge we face; and achieving that success depends on how far we are prepared to go down the rabbit hole to find the truths that are relevant for us.

However, I trust we have also realised that how far each of us goes is completely up to us, and our organisation, and our direction of travel.

As mentioned in the beginning, this book was intentionally construed as a personal journey. Whilst many of the arguments may seem to some as sometimes un-balanced, overly critical, or pessimistic, the intention was to provide a challenging narrative to the often conventional, more abstract, and mechanistic modes of thinking.

My default position is mostly as an optimist, but to challenge myself, to end up closer to reality, I need to counterbalance optimistic with more pessimistic views. Maybe as Antonio Gramsci once suggested, we need to be pessimists of the intellect and optimists of the will.

Equally important, however, is to ensure we work with and/or for an organisation that shares our values. Challenge your organization's integrity, dig deep into their track record, values, and beliefs to fully understand how they actually operate regardless of the rhetoric.

Talk to investees; look at how exits and divestments were handled, and at how governance and ownership is aligned with rhetoric, values and beliefs, both inside and outside the firm.

How does the organisation co-create value with investors and investees? To what extent do they allow us to contribute co-created value and knowledge creation? How does this inform and help us to navigate our own calling inside Impact? Having crafted and mastered our calling, context, and co-creation, in which venue and under which auspices do we generate the intended effects? Is there alignment and harmony, and a cardiant dialectic that truly resonates? It is through our inner liberation that we create outer transformation, and can journey into impact. Like all endeavours, it is an opportunity, not only to grow, but also to find one's true calling.

If we take a true and integral approach, it offers each of us areas of significance and complexity to deepen our understanding about ourselves and the bigger 'other'. Our calling as rooted in our values, talents and capacities. What we find beautiful is the foundation stone on which we lay our blueprints and envisaged architectures for our lives. It is only through our courage and integrity that we clarify and have the wherewithal to stick to the course.

> There is a vitality, a life force, an energy, a quickening that is translated through you into action, and because there is only one you in all of time, this expression is unique. And if you block it, it will never exist through any other medium, it will be lost. The world will not have it.

Martha Graham[81]

According to an old Hindu legend there was a time when all men were gods, but they so abused their divinity that Brahma, the chief god, decided to take it away from men and hide it where they would never again find it. Where to hide it became the big question. When the lesser gods were called in council to consider this question, they said, 'We will bury man's divinity deep in the earth.' But Brahma said, 'No that will not do, for man will dig deep down in the earth and find it.'

Then they said, 'Well, we will sink his divinity into the deepest ocean.' But again Brahma replied, 'No, not there, for man will learn to dive into the deepest waters, will search out the ocean bed, and will find it.' Then the lesser gods said, 'We will take it to the top of the highest mountain and there hide it.' But again Brahma replied, 'No, for man will eventually climb every high mountain on earth. He will be sure some day to find it and take it up again for himself.' Then the lesser gods gave up and concluded, 'We do not know where to hide it, for it seems there is no place on earth or in the sea that man will not eventually reach.' Then Brahma said, 'Here is what we will do with man's divinity.

We will hide it deep down in man himself, for he will never think to look for it there.' Ever since then, the legend concludes, man has been going up and down the earth, climbing, digging, diving, exploring, searching for something that is already in himself.[413]

We have not elaborated much on the spiritual dimension to investments, since for many it is highly controversial. However, given the direction of travel for impact, it is likely that we will see more investment firms deploying a full-spectrum impact approach as guided by their spiritual principles.

I wish you luck on your journey, my fellow traveller, and until we meet again, in peace and love. Love is a personal understanding; and is also a verb, which is how it must be activated within Impact.

> *'We are not human beings having a spiritual experience.*
> *We are spiritual beings having a human experience.'*
> Pierre Teilhard de Chardin[414]

ODE TO IMPACT INVESTMENTS[1]
Oh friend, no more these sounds!
Let us sing more cheerful songs, more full of joy!
Joy, Daughter of Elysium... thy magi power re-unites
all that custom has divided all men become brothers...

How many recognise these words as those of Schiller, the great German poet, which Beethoven used to conclude his magnificent 9th Symphony? Many have been touched by the powerful strains of Beethoven's symphony. Even though we are unlikely to hear this at our next meeting, we are responsible; so 'Let it begin with me'... Let us have 'High hopes but low expectations' in all our endeavours. Whatever we do and however we do it, let's do it in love for ourselves and 'the other'.

> Nothing that is worth doing can be achieved in our lifetime; therefore we must be saved by hope. Nothing which is true or beautiful or good makes complete sense in any immediate context of history; therefore we must be saved by faith. Nothing we do, however virtuous, can be accomplished alone; therefore we must be saved by love.

Niebuhr. 2008. Conclusion. Ch. III. [415]

We live in an era of the individualism cult: an I, Me, More, world of only feel good; seeking excitements, and quick fixes, and 'updates/downloads' for everything, including our own growth. Nothing of real or authentic value can happen that way; quite the opposite, it is based on Grace and Humility. Learning and knowledge can only move into wisdom through acceptance and integration of one's own shadow, so as to become fully authentic as human beings. To be authentic also means looking at, and understanding, our own shadows, with all their cracks of openings.

Impact can potentially form the wedge to open the current financial and economic dogma. As Leonard Cohen sang 'There is a crack, a crack in everything. That's how the light gets in.' If Impact is to be the 'light', then we definitely have work to do... however, nothing of value is created without coming from love. Immerse yourself, and you will find love in abundance, and all over Impact. Maybe just around the corner, but it is there, first in you, and so within and so without...

---

[1]Ode: from the Greek oide, meaning song, or as a suffix meaning way or path, from the Greek hodos

The late Dr Martin Luther King Jr once said: 'We must discover the power of love, the redemptive power of love. And when we do that, we will make of this old world a new world, for love is the only way[2].'

Love is not a word we hear often in any office. Nevertheless, it operates in all of our domains in life, sometimes contrary to our take on the presenting evidence.

Full spectrum impact requires love to be present, as the oil that reduces the friction between the competing claims inside any investment. Love (as per the 5 As) is also the core ingredient needed for a governance approach that can hold and include the real impact sphere. Let us end with one of the best know verses from the Bible, one we have often heard as part of a marriage ceremony—but when we read it, think of our own relationship (and marriage) to Impact.

CORINTHIANS 13[3]

If I speak in the tongues of men or of angels, but do not have love, I am only a resounding gong or a clanging cymbal. If I have the gift of prophecy and can fathom all mysteries and all knowledge, and if I have a faith that can move mountains, but do not have love, I am nothing. If I give all I possess to the poor and give over my body to hardship that I may boast, but do not have love, I gain nothing. Love is patient, love is kind. It does not envy, it does not boast, it is not proud. It does not dishonour others, it is not self-seeking, it is not easily angered, it keeps no record of wrongs. Love does not delight in evil but rejoices with the truth. It always protects, always trusts, always hopes, always perseveres. Love never fails. But where there are prophecies, they will cease; where there are tongues, they will be stilled; where there is knowledge, it will pass away.

For we know in part and we prophesy in part, but when completeness comes, what is in part disappears. When I was a child, I talked like a child, I thought like a child, I reasoned like a child. When I became a man, I put the ways of childhood behind me. For now we see only a reflection as in a mirror; then we shall see face to face. Now I know in part; then I shall know fully, even as I am fully known. And now these three remain: faith, hope and love. But the greatest of these is love.

So if love is the foundation upon which we stand, then it must become part of our work within impact; part of our Impact journey, part of what it means for us and how we now contribute towards our own story and 'Ode to Impact'....

---

[2]M.L. King from a 1957 sermon on the subject of "Loving Your Enemies," delivered at the Dexter Avenue Baptist Church in Montgomery

[3]The Bible, 1. Corinthians. 13. NIV

When we work on Impact, we cannot be indifferent; we need to create differences, contrast, and clear maps, to understand the shadows and angles within each investment context. We need to use our capacity for love to understand what will bring composite returns and value across the capital spectrum. If love is the real Impact driver then let's remind ourselves the words of Holocaust survivor, Elie Wiesel:

> The opposite of love is not hate, it is indifference. The opposite of art is not ugliness, it is indifference. The opposite of faith is not heresy, it is indifference. And the opposite of life is not death, it is indifference.[416]

You may be familiar with the ancient saying that 'All roads lead to Rome', implying that the same outcome can be reached by many methods or ideas. So not only can large goals be reached along many possible routes, but also, more subtly, each route will give the traveller a different experience. I therefore often add my own little ending, saying that 'All roads may lead to Rome but if you want to get there, you must pick one'. It is all about the journey, not the destination. So pick and choose your route well, its the experience of the journey that matters in how you end it.

THE TREE OF DREAMS
Many had gathered under the tree of dreams.
All but one stood shaking its branches for dreams to fall.
Dreams that had been whispered to them by the voices of others.
Dreams that would fade with time.
But one sat quietly, waiting for a dream to recognise his soul.
And to consume him with no doubt.

We have travelled through deep and wide territory that has helped set the tone for our Impact practise and our relation to capital therein. If you are part of a family with managed investments, you may have new challenges to build healthy meanings and purposes for yourself and your descendants. Consider these carefully, with Integral Impact in mind.

Investment organisations likewise will need to frame Impact carefully and deliberately, as part of their strategy, as well as their capital retention and attraction. So is some form of Integral Impact going to the golden key to unlock your Impact perspective and do some serious work on your own shadows? To what degree will your work contribute to the world? Will such a process help alleviate its many imbalances and help ensure our very survival? If you will fully take up this challenge, this becomes your calling and your context. It will need co-creation to find your real, fully integrated contribution. In this endeavour, and on your travels, I wish you a safe and fruitful journey.

I would like to end with an excerpt from an important speech made by the former US President, Theodore Roosevelt, which was entitled "Citizenship in a Republic", given at the Sorbonne in Paris, France on April 23, 1910, which encapsulates the critical path for us all. The passage on page seven of the 35-page speech is referred to as "The Man in the Arena"[4]:

> It is not the critic who counts; not the man who points out how the strong man stumbles, or where the doer of deeds could have done them better. The credit belongs to the man who is actually in the arena, whose face is marred by dust and sweat and blood; who strives valiantly; who errs, who comes short again and again, because there is no effort without error and shortcoming; but who does actually strive to do the deeds; who knows great enthusiasms, the great devotions; who spends himself in a worthy cause; who at the best knows in the end the triumph of high achievement, and who at the worst, if he fails, at least fails while daring greatly, so that his place shall never be with those cold and timid souls who neither know victory nor defeat. [73]

An Ode to Impact

Allow yourself to dream the dreams of what is to become of this visitation, give yourself this gift without hesitation. Garner your valiant contemplations and let the true calling the heart be the architect and the beautification of your foundations. Seek and ground the wants of the soul to marry with love the needs of your role for its formation. Rejoice in its unfolding as part of life's greater mystery, goal and for your own impact transformation.

The End

For possible additional reading, this book was essentially intended to be a follow on to such authors who have managed to comprehensively synthesise the current state of our economic paradigm and limitations with data, constructive solutions and ways forward for the economy to evolve. These are not limited to and include:

- The Doughnut Economy by Kate Raworth.[417]

- Reinventing Organisations by Frederic Laloux [120]

---

[4]"The Man in the Arena". Theodore Roosevelt Center at Dickinson State University. Retrieved 2019-12-14

- The Purpose of Capital, Jed Emerson [28]

- Real Impact by Simon Morgan [418]

- Making Money Matter by Benjamin Bingham [419]

- The Impact Investor by Clark, Emerson and Thornley [420]

- The Clean Money Revolution by Joel Solomon [421]

- Principles and practise of Impact Investing, by Vecchi, Balbo, Brusoni and Caselli. [422]

- The Economics of Happiness and An Economy of Well-being by Mark Anielski [173]

- Synchronicity by Joseph Jaworski [105]

- Maps of Meaning by Jordan Peterson [423]

- Designing Regenerative Cultures by Daniel Christian Wahl [424]

- From Good to Great and How the Mighty Fall by Jim Collins [135]

- Profit Beyond Measure, by Johnson and Broms [315]

- Small is Beautiful by E.F. Schumacher [354]

- Thinking in Systems, by Donella Meadows [425]

- Ethical Markets, by Hazel Henderson [426]

- Capital in the Twenty-First Century by Thomas Piketty [427]

- The Great Divide by Joseph Stiglitz [428]

- The Spirit Level by Pickett and Wilkinson [399]

I also have to recognise authors and psychologists such as the great Peter Drucker, Clayton Christiansen, Peter Senge, Christian Felber, Gunter Pauli, Charles Eisenstein, Jane Gleeson-White, Edward Deming, Ichak Adizes, Stephen. R. Covey, Daniel Kahneman, C.G. Jung, Joseph Campbell, Wayne Dyer, James Hollis, David Whyte, Parker J. Palmer, Eckhart Tolle etc. etc. and last but not least, my Professors on this Integral journey and my Doctorate, Drs Ronnie Lessem and Alexander Schieffer, all who have been individually been and remain invaluable teachers to me throughout my own travels. And the list of course could go on and on including Mervyn King, Yanis Varoufakis, Norman Chomsky, Naomi Klein, Robert Schiller etc. etc. What some of these authors have in common is with great courage to provide multiple perspectives that challenges the thinking around the current dogmas rather than just staying on course and sailing on with the prevailing winds. This gift to us sometimes comes a great personal cost and sacrifice as one may be seen to 'step out of the club' rather than continue to play the game according to the prevailing rules. We owe a big 'thank you' to those who courageously followed their inner callings and provided us with their insights.

PART V

Appendices

The Many Dimensions of Change

Don Edward Beck

> The population undergoing drastic change is a population
> of misfits, and misfits live and breathe in an atmosphere of
> passion and imbalance, explosive and hungry for action.
>
> ———————————————————————————
> Eric Hoffer in The Ordeal of Change

This quotation by Eric Hoffer, the insightful American philosopher, seems to have been written for our times. It introduces some reality into our understanding of change itself. We have just been through a presidential campaign where the word has been bashed about by politicians, spin-doctors, and partisans on the street. We have been challenged to 'be the change,' as if one could simply turn on a switch or meditate to discover the deeper truths. Let us all be world-centric, you suggest. Well, maybe.

Change, for sure, is the topic of the day. That's easy to say. But change 'from what and to what?' I ask. Add *how* and by *whom*, and then perhaps we can begin to talk some sense, even in these days of nonstop news cycles and naïve but well-meaning mantras clamouring for 'change.'

Look at the power within the shift in educational purpose from 'No child left behind' to 'Each child to full potential.' The first rescues stragglers; the other pushes to greatness.

Our task is three-fold. We need a Lexicon *on Change* to talk and walk the same language. Second, it would help if we had an understanding of the Components for Change, in order to know when to do what, as acceptance windows open and close. Last, we will explore the *Global Change Game* to gain a better perspective on how to deal with 7.8 billion humans along the change landscape. Harm De Blij's new book, *The Power of Place*, makes it quite clear that Tom Friedman's 'flat earth' is an oversimplification of the human realities on the ground. Our geographic and memetic landscapes are rough and full of traps and sinkholes.

Lexicon on Change

Alfred Korzybski is known in many circles as the father of general semantics. In a major work, Science and Sanity, the Polish Count attributes much of our social insanity to the lack of precision within the structure and meaning of our words. He suggested that we index each word to differentiate it from others which are spelled and pronounced the same. He calls for operational definitions to enhance sanity by at least knowing what we are talking about.

So, here is 'change' in eight different dimensions or variations. Perhaps you can add others. The first five function within the current set of givens, called *Change of the First Order*. The second three operate within a new set of givens, thus *Change of the Second Order*.

We often call it deep change, profound change, or even radical change to signify this category. New wine demands new wineskins.

First Order Change

Change Variation One (CV_1): Fine-tune or trim the tabs. Make minor adjustments to simply tweak the system. Nothing else is needed.

Change Variation Two (CV_2): Reform or reshuffle the deck. The essential elements within the givens are re-aligned, or reformed while the way of thinking remains constant.

Change Variation Three (CV_3): Upgrade or improve on the givens. The new or updated version replaces the previous one, but within the present operating code.

Change Variation Four (CV_4): Down-stretch and regress. Adjust to the current situation by returning to an earlier system, hunker down for the moment. Go back to basics.

Change Variation Five (CV_5): Up-stretch to expand. Think outside the box, but return later. Push the envelope.

Second Order Change

Change Variation Six (CV_6): Break-out. Attack the barriers. Weaken, remove or replace the status quo. Here is revolutionary rather than evolutionary change.

Change Variation Seven (CV₇): Up-shift or morph to the next. Subsume the old into the new. Transform to the next level of complexity. Transcend but include, like the 'doll within the doll' structures in the nested Russian toys. Here is systemic change.

Change Variation Eight (CV₈): Quantum change of epochal proportions. Here are shifts from Premodern, to Modern, to Postmodern, and to Integral as all the transitions need to be legitimised and facilitated. These shifts concern major sea changes, massive upheavals, millennial-like turns. Everything is on the table and up for grabs as multiple change dynamics occur across the entire landscape.

All human groupings appear to be on the move, but towards different futures. The deep tectonic plates of human existence are shifting beneath the surface. All Change Variations are active and often in conflict. Plus ça change, *plus c'est la même chose*. The more things change, this expression claims, the more they remain the same. I firmly believe that the more things change, the more they *don't* stay the same.

The whole world is turning over, and in real time, while a new world is emerging. Such change is apparent in the transformation into new Ages: Hunter-gatherer, agricultural, industrial, informational, molecular, cyber-, and whatever will be next.

Yet, different people are moving through the various Ages simultaneously. There are different futures for different folks ratcheting through different levels of complexity, all at the same time.

Whenever you use the word change, or hear somebody else do so, pause for a moment and inquire as to which of the Change Variations is involved in both sender and receiver. Otherwise, their conversations are about the chicken and the egg, or comparing apples and oranges, or about even contradictory visions, strategies, and tactics. *Words don't mean; people mean.*

Components for Change

Today many recognise Professor Clare W. Graves as one of the world's leading developmental psychologists. His powerful 'emergent, cyclical, double-helix model of biopsycho-social developmental' framework has been popularized as Spiral Dynamics. Yet few are aware of his profound thinking on the matter of the complexities of change. We worked together on the South African transformational strategy to be able to recognise the essential sequences and timing of various interventions.

Like deep sea divers threatened both by getting the bends when surfacing too rapidly and by suffocating if they run out of air, there is a changeability range between 'too much too soon' and 'too little too late.'

We are now witnesses to a multitude of voices about change in its 7th and 8th variations.

Conferences, summits, and gatherings of many different shades and hues are appearing on a myriad of topics, all of which have a decided 'global' dimension to them; books are being published by the droves, and new names are showing up on the Web as new industries are flourishing.

Yet, unfortunately, too often their views of human nature are trapped either in behaviourism (which claims that anybody can be changed to be anything since we are blank slates) and humanism (which claims that all can have access to and respond to everything because human beings are all the same.)

For years Graves warned me: 'Don, you can't change people. All you can do is relate what you are doing to their natural motivational flows.' This would usually be followed with the caution, accompanied by a twinkle in his eye: 'People cannot be until they are.' At first I didn't know what that actually meant.

And then would come the closer: 'All you can do is help a country (society, culture, etc.) become what is next for it to become.' My naïve idealism at the time was struck a fatal blow as common sense returned.

Consider the following pertinent questions:

- What is it that holds beliefs and behaviours in place, making them resistant to certain change efforts?

- What are the keys to dealing with fixed 'DNA'-like codes that lie at the core of entire societies?

- Are there a set of universal dynamics that cut across all of our human experiences and endeavours?

- In a practical sense, how can efforts be enhanced around, for example, preventing the spread of the HIV-AIDS pandemic, or reducing global warming threats, or defusing militant 'isms' that spread like viruses through true believers?

- If, indeed, there is some kind of evolutionary or emergent flow working within humans, there must be some kind of dynamic process that explains growth, or development.

- Why do some people change but others don't?

- Why do some cultures appear to continue to prosper yet others may well be on the slippery slope toward total collapse?

- What is behind the rise and fall of nations? What triggers the forces of renewal and resurgence in a human grouping, one that has once tasted of the fruits of stability and affluence?

These are quite complex variables and a fuller discussion is not within the scope of this writing. It is still useful, however, to consider at least three of the components which play major roles in underpinning our journey on the planet. They follow in response to the essential question that we should always ask: 'What really changes in people, structures, and processes whenever there is change?' Can we be specific and perhaps even measure it? So much of our speculation regarding change, and especially our forecasts of what will happen when we do X, Y, or Z are based on naïve assumptions at best and unexamined cause and effect linkages at worse. It is far too easy to assume that (1) everybody is like us, so that what motivates us to 'change,' will do so to others, and (2) everybody has the same interests and bottom lines, and are therefore amenable to the same change messages.

Look, for example, at the power within the shift in educational purpose from 'No child left behind' to 'Each child to full potential.' The first rescues stragglers; the other pushes to greatness.

This is especially the case today as many become emotionally committed to more 'world-centric' or global perspectives. There are many good reasons why this world view is emerging rapidly on the planet. Many of them have been featured in various issues of Kosmos. But problems stem from the belief that all humans, everywhere, will gladly choose this world-centric view over tribal, ethnic, religious, or national identities if given half a chance. If we are serious about developing more of a sense of the human family, with common interests and collaborative intent, a more comprehensive initiative will need to flow from an understanding of the essential *Components of Change*: Life Conditions, Priority Codes, and Beliefs and Behaviours.

Changes in our Life Conditions

We are, to a large degree, the product of our times. We have an innate capacity to respond to the challenges within our habitats, to adjust to the problems of existence that confront us. As long as those conditions exist, it makes sense for us to embrace the 'steady as she goes' mentality.

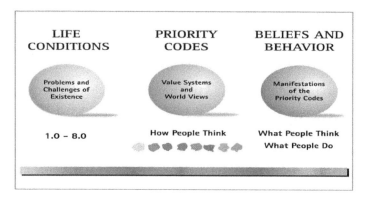

Figure A.1

Mexico is under serious threat to become a failed state because of the Life Conditions that are brewing the lethal cocktail of drugs, violence, and gangs. Fear has become rampant in the country because of the pattern of kidnapping for ransom and even brutal murder of innocent citizens. The youth are caught up in the lure of excitement and easy money. Until the baseline of stability and security is established, don't expect Mexico to be able to keep up economically, or the various elements in society to achieve even a modicum of success. We recently met with former President Vicente Fox in León, Mexico, who has now established a Center for Global Leadership. He asked: 'Why has Latin America lagged behind the rest of the world?

As long as there are pockets of poverty in our inner cities, with fragmented homes and lives coupled with lack of discipline and economic opportunities, expect gang-related behaviours to flourish. And if self-serving adults continue to play the race card only to gain political leverage, don't be surprised if the amount of racism in our society expands rather than constricts.

Changes in our Priority Codes for Living

Spiral Dynamics describes the values systems that are the product of the interactions between Life Conditions and the human capacity to adapt to the problems of existence.

Thus far, eight Priority Codes have emerged, each one calibrated to solve problems which are unique within its specific context. As invisible fractals and organising principles, they impact the full range of human choice-making capacities. Each opens new doors of reality and enable new thinking and

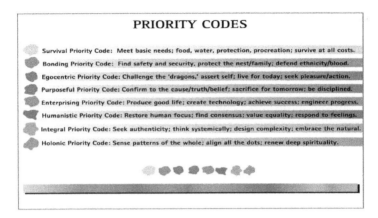

Figure A.2

fresh options. Sometimes realistic change involves the further development of a Code. When new Priority Codes appear, new insights must develop, as new bottom lines are embraced.

Changes in our Beliefs and Behaviours

Skilful change agents have learned how to connect their ideas and projects to a wide range of Priority Codes. Many in the environmental movement were antagonistic to what they called 'right-wing' religious movements until they noted that these same people, 'to keep God's earth clean,' will support environmental goals. In the same way, HIV-AIDS campaigns can be designed, which will carry the critical message into all of the Priority Codes, rather than just focus on one or two. This kind of change can bring a Spiral full of advantages and opportunities to a number of different initiatives.

Playing the Global Change Game

Let us play the Global Change game. Take almost any issue that has a global reach, from hunger to disease to political conflicts to have versus have not gaps to immigration matters to environment threats. How should we decide what to do? Who should rule?

A voting majority? Financial interests? Military clout? Moral superiority? The societal elders? The spiritual leaders? The Super Organisation? The Wizard of Oz? The Spiral Intelligences?

May I suggest new decision-making processes. We call them MeshWorks

Solutions. Imagine the gathering of the competent wise ones, who are armed with powerful technologies, deep insights, and guided by the drives within the human Spiral itself to stay alive and pass its genes and memes far into the future. These are Integral Design Engineers. What would they do?

First, they would develop Global Vital Signs Monitors much as Singapore has done, through the efforts of John Petersen of The Arlington Institute, to construct Risk Analysis Horizontal Scanning capacity (RAHS). Monitors would track the Priority Codes beneath cultures and groupings. They would read the weak signals of impending change, in its many manifestations. Second, such a MeshWorks effort would create scaffoldings of solutions to serious problems by identifying everything that works, and spreading the information through different cultures and across Priority Codes, but in their respective 'language.' Third, these decision processes would be the first to spot and track conflicts in the making, and to design and implement preventative efforts through a distributed intelligence that is circulated across all political structures.

Through the efforts of Peter Merry and his Dutch colleagues, we have established such a potential function in The Hague Center for Global Governance, Innovation, and Emergence. Roberto Bonilla in Mexico is demonstrating the power in MeshWorks by helping design education for the whole country to pluck the youth from the hands of the gangsters. Lebanese-American Elza Maalouf is doing important work in Palestine and the Middle East to awaken the Arab world to new possibilities, and inspires many in Israel to envision a future 'Hong Kong of the Middle East.'

It is time to get the entire global system set right by respecting all of us who exist in clans, tribes, empires, holy orders, cultures, enterprises, communes, natural habitats – and are spread along the various trajectories of change. Imagine a global Intelligence that, much like a metaphoric 'air traffic control' system, can keep up with and direct our many life forms which are dispersed in different altitudes, moving in different directions, at different speeds, with different capacities, and all with multiple bottom lines and priorities.

Why not design and build this capacity, now? Our very lives, individually and collectively, might well depend on it.

The Meta Model

Deletions

Simple Deletion: Something is left out.
Example: 'I am mad.'
Question(s) to recover lost information: 'About what?'

Unspecified Referential Index: The person(s) or object to which the statement refers is unspecified or not clear.
Example: 'They rejected my business proposal.' or 'They rejected it.'
Question(s) to recover lost information: 'Who?' or 'What?'

Comparative Deletions: A comparison is made and it is unclear as to what is being compared. The sentence will contain words such as: good, bad, better, best, worst, more, less, most, least.
Example: 'This approach is better.'
Question(s) to recover lost information: 'Compared to what or whom?'

Unspecified Verb: In this case, it is not clear how something was done.
Example: 'They rejected my business proposal.' We can use the example for Unspecified Referential Index to illustrate that sometimes there are several things that have been deleted, distorted or generalised and it is up to you to decide which line of questioning will yield the most information.
Question(s) to recover lost information: 'How specifically?'

Nominalizations: A process has been turned into a 'thing'. Nominalizations are nouns, yet you cannot physically touch them or put them in the trunk of your car. Examples of nominalizations are: communication, relationship, leadership, respect, truth, freedom, depression, love, etc. Our task here is to ask a question so that the process can be rediscovered.
Example: 'The communication in our family is poor.'
Question(s) to recover lost information: 'How would you like us to communicate?' Notice that there is also a comparative deletion and we could also ask 'Poor compared to what?'

generalisations

Universal Quantifiers: Universal quantifiers are typically words such as: all, every, never, always, only, everyone, everything, no one, etc.
Example: 'My boss never gives me credit for what I do.' Question(s) to recover lost information: We can exaggerate the generalisation or use a counter example. 'Never?' or 'Has there ever been a time when your boss has given you credit?'

Modal Operators of Necessity or Possibility: Modal Operators of Necessity include words such as should, shouldn't, ought to, must, must not, have to, need to, it is necessary, supposed to. (Recall this is part of the language of addiction). Modal Operators of Possibility include words such as can/can't, will/won't, may/may not, possible/impossible.
Example: 'I can't do this now.'
Question(s) to recover lost information: The key is to challenge the limitation. 'What would happen if you did?' or 'What prevents you?'

Distortions

Mind Reading: In this case, the speaker claims to know what another person believes, feels, or thinks.
Example: 'My boss is not pleased with my work.'
Question(s) to recover lost information: For this pattern, we simply ask, how do you know? 'How specifically do you know your boss is not pleased with your work?'

Lost Performative: Value judgements are made and it is not clear who has made the judgement.
Example: 'This is the right way to get ahead in this company.'
Question(s) to recover lost information: 'According to whom?' or 'How do you know it is the right way?'

Cause – Effect: The speaker establishes a cause-effect relationship between two events or actions. Common constructions include: if .., then, because, makes, compels, causes.
Example: 'When you look at me that way, I feel unimportant.'
Question(s) to recover lost information: 'How does the way I look at you cause you to choose to feel unimportant?' You could also use a counter example.

Complex Equivalence: In this situation two experiences are interpreted as being synonymous. These two experiences could be joined by words such as: therefore, means, implies.

Example: 'My boss walked into his office without saying 'good morning', therefore he is not pleased with my work.'

Question(s) to recover lost information: 'How does not saying 'good morning' mean that your boss is not pleased with your work?' or 'Have you ever been preoccupied by family or business pressures and forgot to say 'good morning' to your co-workers?'

Presuppositions: Some part of the sentence presupposes or implies the existence (or non-existence) of something, person, etc. while not explicitly stating it.

Example: 'When will you demonstrate leadership for your team?' This sentence presupposes that you do not demonstrate leadership. If you try to answer this question directly, you will be digging an even deeper hole for yourself.

Question(s) to recover lost information: 'What leads you to believe that I do not demonstrate leadership?' or 'How is it that I do not demonstrate leadership?'

Avoid asking 'Why'

The questions in the Meta Model do not have any 'why' questions. When you ask someone a 'why' question, often they feel they have to defend what they have said or done, make excuses or rationalise their behaviour. Also, there is a tendency to go 'meta' i.e. look for new trains of thought, meaning and rationale that did not exist before. On the other hand, if you expressed the question as a 'how' question, then you get a better understanding of the process used by your client and thus more information and understanding.

Gandhi's Four Pillars of Non-Violence

Madhu Suri Prakash wrote the above for Love and the Apocalypse, the Summer 2013 issue of YES! Magazine.

Gandhi lived Ahimsa as a daily practise, waging peace to stop war and violence. His lifelong 'experiments' with truth proved that truth force is more powerful than brute force.

Ahimsa reveals forms of peace that extend far beyond mere absence of war. For Gandhi, peace means walking with truth and justice, patience and compassion, courage and loving-kindness. Ahimsa actively promotes universal well-being and encourages the flourishing of all life, not just humans. It is the art of living in the present and opening our imaginations to a good life for all.

Gandhi offers four sustaining pillars for Ahimsa, A (non) + Himsa (violence) = Ahimsa.

Sarvodaya: Justice for all creatures

This is Gandhi's central pillar: the practise of economic, political, and moral justice. All creatures are included in a quest for universal well-being; all take their just share of the abundance of our Mother Earth.

Sarvodaya means the end of injustice and hunger. There is enough for every being's needs and not enough for even a single person's greed. Sarvodaya societies and communities ensure that all enjoy the dignity of sharing their skills and talents.

Sarvodaya serves to remind us, moment by moment, of our entire Earth family— interdependent, made of each other, inextricably interconnected.

Swaraj: Self-rule

Gandhi's idea of self-rule celebrates the freedoms born of the self-discipline necessary for Sarvodaya.

Swaraj demands maximum power for self-organisation and self-rule by people within their families, neighbourhoods, villages, and bioregions, and minimal intervention by national governments. We assume full responsibility for our own behaviour and for our decisions, made with others, on how to organise our communities.

Swaraj celebrates personal freedom from poverty and all forms of domination. No one rules others, and no state imposes its laws without the free consent of the governed. Rather than human rights, Swaraj sees human duties: to Mother Earth and to our neighbours, both near and distant.

Swadeshi: The Genius of the Local

At the heart of Swadeshi is honouring and celebrating local economy, with people enjoying a right livelihood from the gifts of the natural resources of their own bioregions. The bread labour of each place, drawing on the genius of local knowledge and skills, generates a surplus to share with others. Swadeshi is people-centred economics—the soul of 'small is beautiful.'

Satyagraha: Nonviolent revolution

Satyagraha radically transforms political and economic systems through nonviolent resistance. It does not seek to inflict upon the violent, a taste of their own medicine but instead transforms foe into friend and intolerance into hospitality. Satyagraha encourages us to cultivate the same compassion for strangers that we have for kin.

Satyagrahis refuse to comply with unjust laws and voluntarily accept the resulting suffering. They call for patient, continual, small actions performed by common men and women looking for a more decent life. They produce profound, radical transformation without the cataclysmic revolutions that frequently impose their own violent power structures.

Satyagrahis seek to live oneness in thought, speech, and actions: They walk the talk. Actively resisting oppression, Satyagrahis recognise that there are wrongs to die for, yet not a single one to kill for.

Bibliography

[1] G. B. Bingham (gbbingham), "Making Money Matter - by G Benjamin Bingham on Booklaunch.io." [Online]. Available: http://www.booklaunch.io/gbenjaminbingham/makingmoneymatter

[2] "Kay Jackson Art." [Online]. Available: https://www.kayjacksonart.com/

[3] B. J. A. Hargreaves and J. Dauman, *Business survival and social change: a practical guide to responsibility and partnership.* London: Associated Business Programmes, 1975.

[4] R. Lessem, "Accounting for an enterprise's wellbeing," *Omega*, vol. 2, no. 1, pp. 77–95, feb 1974. [Online]. Available: https://linkinghub.elsevier.com/retrieve/pii/0305048374900085

[5] B. Akomolafe, *These wilds beyond our fences: letters to my daughter on humanity's search for home.* Berkeley, California: North Atlantic Books, 2017.

[6] R. Lessem, "Managing in Four Worlds," *Long Range Planning*, vol. 34, no. 1, pp. 9–32, Feb. 2001. [Online]. Available: https://linkinghub.elsevier.com/retrieve/pii/S0024630100000984

[7] R. Lessem and A. Schieffer, *Transformation management: towards the integral enterprise*, ser. Transformation and innovation series. Farnham, England ; Burlington, VT: Gower, 2009, oCLC: ocn319248375.

[8] ——, *Integral economics: releasing the economic genius of your society*, ser. Transformation and innovation series. Farnham, Surrey, England : Burlington, VT: Gower Pub. ; Ashgate Pub, 2010, oCLC: ocn610018947.

[9] ——, *Integral research and innovation: transforming enterprise and society*, ser. Transformation and innovation series. Farnham, England ; Burlington, VT: Gower, 2010, oCLC: ocn430678928.

[10] A. Schieffer and R. Lessem, *Integral development: realising the transformative potential of individuals, organisations and societies*, ser. Transformation and innovation. Farnham, Surrey, UK: Gower, 2014.

[11] R. Lessem, A. Adodo, and T. Bradley, *The Idea of the Communiversity: Releasing the Natural, Cultural, Technological and Economic GENE-ius of Societies.* Beacon Books, 2019. [Online]. Available: https://books.google.co.ve/books?id=QjOmxQEACAAJ

[12] E. F. Fama, "Efficient capital markets: A review of theory and empirical work," *The Journal of Finance*, vol. 25, no. 2, pp. 383–417, 1970. [Online]. Available: http://www.jstor.org/stable/2325486

[13] J. B. Maverick, "The Top 5 Impact Investing Firms." [Online]. Available: https://www.investopedia.com/articles/active-trading/090115/top-5-impact-investing-firms.asp

[14] S. Narayan, *The Selected Works of Mahatma Gandhi: The voice of truth*, ser. The Selected Works of Mahatma Gandhi. Navajivan Publishing House, 1968. [Online]. Available: https://books.google.co.ve/books?id=cXlDAAAAYAAJ

[15] S. Esbjörn-Hargens and M. E. Zimmerman, *Integral ecology: uniting multiple perspectives on the natural world*, 1st ed. Boston: Integral Books, 2009, oCLC: 144525197.

[16] C. Eisenstein, *Sacred economics: money, gift, & society in the age of transition.* Berkeley, Calif: Evolver Editions, 2011.

[17] "Noam Chomsky: "What Next? The Elections, the Economy, and the World"." [Online]. Available: http://www.democracynow.org/2008/11/24/noam_chomsky_what_next_the_elections

[18] "Home .:. Sustainable Development Knowledge Platform." [Online]. Available: https://sustainabledevelopment.un.org/

[19] W. Vennard, *The Federal Reserve Hoax.* Literary Licensing, LLC, 1959.

[20] F. N., "Europe sets stage for esgreform," 2018. [Online]. Available: www.top1000funds.com/2018/02/europe-sets-stage-for-esgreform/

[21] T. GIIN, "Impact Investing," 2020. [Online]. Available: https://thegiin.org/impact-investing/

[22] B. Swimme and T. Berry, *The Universe story.* London: Arkana, 1994, oCLC: 59815042.

[23] A. development bank, *Impact Evaluation.* Asian development bank, 2006.

[24] F. Times, "Esg investing poses big challenge for fund management industry."

[25] J. Authers, "The ethical investment boom."

[26] M. Slouka, *Essays from the nick of time: reflections and refutations.* Minneapolis, Minn: Graywolf Press, 2010, oCLC: ocn555656549.

[27] A. Korzybski, *Science and sanity: an introduction to non-Aristotelian systems and general semantics*, 5th ed. Brooklyn, N.Y: Inst. of General Semantics, 2005, oCLC: 180133157.

[28] J. Emerson, *The purpose of capital: elements of impact, financial flows, and natural being*, 2018, oCLC: 1053624502.

[29] B. Latour and C. Porter, *Facing Gaia: eight lectures on the new climatic regime.* Cambridge, UK ; Medford, MA: Polity, 2017.

[30] H. Spiegelberg, "Good Fortune Obligates: Albert Schweitzer's Second Ethical Principle," *Ethics*, vol. 85, no. 3, pp. 227–234, 1975. [Online]. Available: www.jstor.org/stable/2380050

[31] "How ambitious is the EU's offer to the Paris climate change talks?" Mar. 2015. [Online]. Available: https://www.carbonbrief.org/how-ambitious-is-the-eus-offer-to-the-paris-climate-change-talks

[32] D. R. Hawkins, *Power vs. force: the hidden determinants of human behaviour.* Carlsbad, Calif: Hay House, 2002.

[33] C. G. Jung, *Dreams.* London: Routledge & Kegan Paul, 1982, oCLC: 153281745.

[34] C. G. Jung and R. F. C. Hull, *The collected works of C.G. Jung Vol. 1, Vol. 1,.* Princeton: Princeton Univ. Press : Bollingen Foundation, 1978, oCLC: 715156403.

[35] S. Nusseibeh, "The why question," *The 300 Club*, 2017.

[36] D. E. Beck and C. C. Cowan, *Spiral dynamics: mastering values, leadership, and change; exploring the new science of memetics*, paperback [ed.] ed. Malden, Mass.: Blackwell, 2006, oCLC: 254619841.

[37] S. E. Dawlabani, *MEMEnomics: the next-generation economic system*, first edition ed. New York: SelectBooks, Inc, 2013.

[38] "Integral Enterprise Theory." [Online]. Available: https://www.trans-4-m.com/integral-worlds-theory/integral-enterprise-theory/

[39] P. Mason, "The end of capitalism has begun," *The Guardian*, Jul. 2015. [Online]. Available: https://www.theguardian.com/books/2015/jul/17/postcapitalism-end-of-capitalism-begun

[40] B. Haggard and P. Mang, *Chapter 1, Regenerative Development and Design: A Framework for Evolving Sustainability*. [Online]. Available: https://www.academia.edu/29888114/Chapter_1_Regenerative_Development_and_Design_A_Framework_for_Evolving_Sustainability

[41] P. Freire, *The politics of education: culture, power, and liberation.* South Hadley, Mass: Bergin & Garvey, 1985.

[42] P. F. Drucker, *Management challenges for the 21st century*, 1st ed. New York: HarperBusiness, 1999.

[43] "Spiral dynamics integral," 2006.

[44] D. Ariely, U. Gneezy, G. Loewenstein, and N. Mazar, "Large stakes and big mistakes," Jul. 2005. [Online]. Available: https://www.bostonfed.org/publications/research-department-working-paper/2005/large-stakes-and-big-mistakes

[45] O. Gürerk, B. Irlenbusch, and B. Rockenbach, "Motivating teammates: The leader's choice between positive and negative incentives," *Journal of Economic Psychology*, vol. 30, no. 4, pp. 591–607, Aug. 2009. [Online]. Available: https://linkinghub.elsevier.com/retrieve/pii/S0167487009000397

[46] S. Reiss, *Who am I? the 16 basic desires that motivate our behaviour and define our personality.* New York: Jeremy P. Tarcher/Putnam, 2000.

[47] C. Gerstner and D. Day, "Meta-analytic review of leader-member exchange theory: Correlates and construct issues," *Journal of Applied Psychology*, vol. 82, pp. 827–844, 12 1997.

[48] P. Freire, *Pedagogy of the oppressed*, new rev. ed ed., ser. Penguin books. London: Penguin Books, 1996, oCLC: 832623948.

[49] N. Chomsky, *Reflections on language*, 1st ed. New York: Pantheon Books, 1975.

[50] D. Day, *On pilgrimage.* Grand Rapids, Mich: William B. Eerdmans Pub, 1999.

[51] V. Pareto and A. Montesano, *Manual of political economy: a critical and variorum edition*, 1st ed. Oxford: Oxford University Press, 2014, oCLC: ocn881852854.

[52] B. Stiegler, *For a new critique of political economy*, english ed ed. Cambridge ; Malden, MA: Polity, 2010, oCLC: ocn551435856.

[53] D. A. Schweitzer, *Reverence For Life: the words of Albert Schweitzer.* Place of publication not identified: Maurice Bassett, 2017, oCLC: 1013731743.

[54] F. Luton, "Individuation – Jungian definition." [Online]. Available: https://frithluton.com/articles/individuation/

[55] B. Ross, "Culture eats strategy for breakfast," Mar. 2016. [Online]. Available: https://www.managementcentre.co.uk/culture-eats-strategy-for-breakfast/

[56] I. Berlin, *The crooked timber of humanity: chapters in the history of ideas*, second edition ed. Princeton ; Oxford: Princeton University Press, 2013.

[57] H. Hesse and W. J. Strachan, *Demian*, ser. Peter Owen modern classics. London: Peter Owen, 2001.

[58] D. Robertson, *The philosophy of cognitive-behavioural therapy (CBT): stoic philosophy as rational and cognitive psychotherapy*, second edition ed. Milton Park, Abingdon, Oxon ; New York, NY: Routledge, 2020.

[59] R. A. Johnson, *Owning your own shadow: understanding the dark side of the psyche*, 1st ed. San Francisco: HarperSanFrancisco, 1991.

[60] S. Milgram, *Obedience to authority: an experimental view*, 1st ed. New York: Harper & Row, 1974.

[61] S. Jeffery, *The Shadow; Getting to know your 'darker' half.*, 2019.

[62] W. L. Randall, *The stories we are: an essay on self-creation.* Toronto ; Buffalo: University of Toronto Press, 1995.

[63] J. Campbell, *The hero with a thousand faces*, 3rd ed., ser. Bollingen series XVII. Novato, Calif: New World Library, 2008.

[64] [Online]. Available: http://www.darionardi.com/functions.html

[65] M. Gladwell, *The story of success.* London: Allen Lane : [distributor] Penguin Books Ltd, 2008, oCLC: 852008080.

[66] R. Barrett, *Evolutionary Human: how Darwin got it wrong.* S.l.: Lulu Publishing Services, 2018, oCLC: 1083132439.

[67] R. Bandler and J. Grinder, *The structure of magic: a book about language and therapy.* Palo Alto, Calif: Science and behaviour Books, 1975.

[68] S. R. Charvet, *Words that change minds: mastering the language of influence*, 2nd ed. Dubuque, Iowa: Kendall/Hunt Pub. Co, 1997.

[69] G. H. Hofstede, G. J. Hofstede, and M. Minkov, *Cultures and organisations: software of the mind: intercultural cooperation and its importance for survival*, 3rd ed. New York: McGraw-Hill, 2010, oCLC: ocn558675706.

[70] C. Gilligan, *In a different voice: psychological theory and women's development.* Cambridge, Mass: Harvard University Press, 1993.

[71] C. L. Whitfield, Ed., *The power of humility: choosing peace over conflict in relationships.* Deerfield Beach, Fla: Health Communications, 2006.

[72] M. Aurelius, *Meditations.* S.l.: Collectors Library, 2020, oCLC: 1097574751.

[73] B. Brown, *Dare to lead: brave work, tough conversations, whole hearts.* New York: Random House, 2018.

[74] *The Social Life of Money*, Sep. 2014. [Online]. Available: https://press.princeton.edu/books/hardcover/9780691141428/the-social-life-of-money

[75] C. H. Budd, *Prelude in economics: a new approach to economics.* West Hoathly: New Economy Publications, 1999, oCLC: 808336371.

[76] J. K. Galbraith, *Money, whence it came, where it went.* Boston: Houghton Mifflin, 1975.

[77] "Compound Interest: The 8th Wonder of the World." [Online]. Available: https://www.listenmoneymatters.com/compound-interest/

[78] Johan Palmstruch, *Stockholms Banco*. [Online]. Available: https://www.riksbank.se/globalassets/media/riksbanken-350-ar/tidslinjen/stockholm-banco/24-45-stockholms-banco_eng.pdf

[79] "Rainer Maria Rilke Quotes." [Online]. Available: https://www.brainyquote.com/quotes/rainer_maria_rilke_147758

[80] "Carl Jung Quotes." [Online]. Available: https://www.brainyquote.com/quotes/carl_jung_132738

[81] C. Reeve, *The Way of Artistry & Grace.* Synergy & Design Marketing., 2011.

[82] A. Næss, D. Rothenberg, and A. Næss, *Ecology, community, and lifestyle: outline of an ecosophy.* Cambridge ; New York: Cambridge University Press, 1989.

[83] "Individuation – Jungian definition." [Online]. Available: https://frithluton.com/articles/individuation/

[84] John Maynard Keynes, *Economic Possibilities for our Grandchildren*, 1930. [Online]. Available: http://www.econ.yale.edu/smith/econ116a/keynes1.pdf

[85] Y. N. Harari, *Sapiens: a brief history of humankind*, first u.s. edition ed. New York: Harper, 2015.

[86] P. F. Drucker, *Management: tasks, responsibilities, practises*, abridged an rev. ed ed., ser. Classic Drucker. Oxford: Butterworth-Heinemann, 1999, oCLC: 833495495.

[87] A. H. Maslow, *Toward a psychology of being*, 3rd ed. cNew York: J. Wiley & Sons, 1999.

[88] Z. Sardar and E. Masood, *How do you know? reading Ziauddin Sardar on Islam, science and cultural relations.* London ; Ann Arbor: Pluto Press, 2006, oCLC: ocm71330606.

[89] H. Smith and H. Smith, *The world's religions: our great wisdom traditions.* San Francisco: HarperSanFrancisco, 1991.

[90] P. Schwartz, *The art of the long view: paths to strategic insight for yourself and your company.* New York: Bantam Doubleday Dell Pub. Group, 1996, oCLC: 611705480.

[91] Charles, T. Juniper, and I. Skelly, *Harmony: a new way of looking at our world*, 1st ed. New York: Harpercollins, 2010, oCLC: ocn419857221.

[92] A. Huxley, *Brave new world revisited.* New York [u.a.: Harper Perennial, 2011, oCLC: 1073511536.

[93] C. G. Jung and A. Storr, *The essential Jung: selected writings.* Princeton, N.J.; Chichester: Princeton University Press, 1999, oCLC: 59415011.

[94] P. J. Palmer, *Healing the heart of democracy: the courage to create a politics worthy of the human spirit*, 1st ed. San Francisco, CA: Jossey-Bass, 2011, oCLC: ocn711051121.

[95] ""Perhaps / The truth depends on a walk around a lake": On Walking and Writing « Kenyon Review Blog," Mar. 2016. [Online]. Available: https://kenyonreview.org/2016/03/6324l/

[96] R. Darnton, *Poetry and the police: communication networks in eighteenth-century Paris.* Cambridge, Mass: Belknap Press of Harvard University Press, 2010, oCLC: ocn555658475.

[97] H. E. Gardner, *Multiple Intelligences: New Horizons in Theory and practise.* New York: Basic Books, 2008, oCLC: 1045074421. [Online]. Available: http://qut.eblib.com.au/patron/FullRecord.aspx?p=903035

[98] J. Dréze and A. Sen, *India, economic development and social opportunity.*   Delhi: Oxford University Press, 1995.

[99] A. Sen, *The idea of justice,* 1st ed.   Cambridge, Mass: Belknap Press of Harvard Univ. Press, 2011, oCLC: 846355576.

[100] S. B. Kaufman and C. Gregoire, *Wired to create: unravelling the mysteries of the creative mind,* 2016, oCLC: 934965474.

[101] "Herbert A. Simon - Wikiquote." [Online]. Available: https://en.wikiquote.org/wiki/Herbert_A._Simon

[102] K. Wilber, *Trump and a post-truth world.*   Boulder: Shambhala, 2017.

[103] "The Nobel Prize in Physiology or Medicine 1949." [Online]. Available: https://www.nobelprize.org/prizes/medicine/1949/hess/lecture/

[104] C. G. Jung and C. G. Jung, *The undiscovered self: with symbols and the interpretation of dreams,* ser. Bollingen series.   Princeton, N.J: Princeton University Press, 1990, no. 20.

[105] J. Jaworski, *Synchronicity: the inner path of leadership,* expanded 2nd ed ed.   San Francisco: Berrett-Koehler Publishers, 2011, oCLC: ocn706804045.

[106] Lao-tzu and W. Bynner, *The way of life according to Laotzu ; translated by Witter Bynner ; illustrated by Frank Wren.*   New York: Putnam, 1986, oCLC: 302015132.

[107] "Paul Tillich Quote." [Online]. Available: https://www.azquotes.com/quote/1366890

[108] P. D. Uspenskii, *Tertium Organum: the third canon of thought, a key to the enigmas of the world,* 1st ed.   New York: Alfred A. Knopf : distributed by Random House, 1981.

[109] R. Khurana, *From higher aims to hired hands: the social transformation of American business schools and the unfulfilled promise of management as a profession.*   Princeton: Princeton University Press, 2007, oCLC: ocn123136639.

[110] "Milton Friedman Quotes." [Online]. Available: https://www.brainyquote.com/quotes/milton_friedman_153357

[111] "Solitude and Leadership," Mar. 2010. [Online]. Available: https://theamericanscholar.org/solitude-and-leadership/

[112] A. Antonovsky, *Unraveling the mystery of health: how people manage stress and stay well,* 1st ed., ser. A Joint publication in the Jossey-Bass social and behavioural science series and the Jossey-Bass health series.   San Francisco: Jossey-Bass, 1987.

[113] Y. Mishima and T. Yamamoto, *The way of the samurai: Yukio Mishima on Hagakure in modern life.*   New York, N.Y: Putnam, 1983.

[114] R. Spira, *The nature of consciousness: essays on the unity of mind and matter.*   Oxford : Oakland, CA: Sahaja Publications ; New Harbinger Publications, 2017, oCLC: ocn974192764.

[115] "Awareness and its Apparent Objects | Rupert Spira." [Online]. Available: https://non-duality.rupertspira.com/read/awareness_and_its_apparent_objects

[116] M. J. Gelb, *The art of connection: 7 relationship-building skills every leader needs now.*   Novato, California: New World Library, 2017.

[117] J. Hollis, *The middle passage: from misery to meaning in midlife,* ser. Studies in Jungian psychology by Jungian analysts.   Toronto: Inner City Books, 1993.

[118] "The Law, by Frederic Bastiat." [Online]. Available: http://bastiat.org/en/the_law.html

[119] M. d. Montaigne and M. A. Screech, *The complete Essays*, ser. Penguin classics. London, England ; New York, N.Y., USA: Penguin Books, 1993.

[120] F. Laloux, *Reinventing organisations: a guide to creating organisations inspired by the next stage of human consciousness*, 1st ed.   Brussels: Nelson Parker, 2014, oCLC: 897776301.

[121] R. E. Palmer, *Hermeneutics: interpretation theory in Schleiermacher, Dilthey, Heidegger, and Gadamer*, 8th ed., ser. Northwestern University studies in phenomenology and existential philosophy.   Evanston: Northwestern Univ. Pr, 1988, oCLC: 247996465.

[122] "NLP Techniques: Checking Ecology | Grass Roots NLP." [Online]. Available: https://grassrootsnlp.com/nlp-technique-checking-ecology

[123] [Online]. Available: https://www.myersbriggs.org/my-mbti-personality-type/mbti-basics/home.htm?bhcp=1

[124] R. Goldman and S. Papson, *Landscapes of Capital*.   New York, NY: John Wiley & Sons, 2013, oCLC: 894699043. [Online]. Available: http://nbn-resolving.de/urn:nbn:de:101:1-201412302616

[125] J. C. Collins, *How the mighty fall: and why some companies never give in.*   New York: Jim Collins : Distributed in the U.S. and Canada exclusively by HarperCollins Publishers, 2009, oCLC: ocn313666097.

[126] P. Singer, *Practical ethics*, 3rd ed.   New York: Cambridge University Press, 2011, oCLC: ocn656771972.

[127] "Definition of Epiphenomenon." [Online]. Available: https://www.merriam-webster.com/dictionary/epiphenomenon

[128] A. C. Antoniades, *Introduction to environmental design.*   New York: MSS Information Corp., 1976, oCLC: 1131431333.

[129] I. Koyenikan, *Wealth for all: living a life of success at the edge of your ability*, 2016, oCLC: 971548200.

[130] A. H. Maslow and D. C. Stephens, *The Maslow business reader.*   New York: Wiley, 2000.

[131] E. Butterworth, *Spiritual economics: the principles and process of true prosperity.*   Unity Village, MO: Unity Books, 2001, oCLC: 980603886.

[132] "Tom Brokaw Quotes." [Online]. Available: https://www.brainyquote.com/quotes/tom_brokaw_105667

[133] R. Warren, *The purpose driven life: what on earth am I here for?*, 2013, oCLC: 1128840964.

[134] "Jim Collins - Concepts - Confront The Brutal Facts." [Online]. Available: https://www.jimcollins.com/concepts/confront-the-brutal-facts.html

[135] J. C. Collins, *Good to great: why some companies make the leap–and others don't*, 1st ed. New York, NY: HarperBusiness, 2001.

[136] "The unexamined life is not worth living," Feb. 2020, page Version ID: 942912199. [Online]. Available: https://en.wikipedia.org/w/index.php?title=The_unexamined_life_is_not_worth_living&oldid=942912199

[137] J. Hollis, *Creating a life: finding your individual path*, ser. Studies in Jungian psychology by Jungian analysts.   Toronto: Inner City Books, 2001, oCLC: ocm45002997.

[138] S. Morrissey, "Stephen Morrissey." [Online]. Available: http://www.stephenmorrissey. ca/articles_reviews/SM_Creating.html

[139] J. B. Stockdale, *Courage under fire: testing Epictetus's doctrines in a laboratory of human behaviour*, ser. Hoover essays.   Stanford, Calif: Hoover Institution, Stanford University, 1993, no. no. 6.

[140] V. E. Frankl, *Man's search for meaning*, mini book ed. ed.   Boston: Beacon Press, 2006, oCLC: ocm80723125.

[141] "Quantum Entanglement," Aug. 2019. [Online]. Available: https://cac.org/ quantum-entanglement-2019-08-30/

[142] G. Maté, *In the realm of hungry ghosts: close encounters with addiction.*   Berkeley, Calif: North Atlantic Books, 2010, oCLC: ocn461256205.

[143] "The Four Horsemen: The Antidotes," Apr. 2013. [Online]. Available: https://www.gottman.com/blog/the-four-horsemen-the-antidotes/

[144] "8 Simon Sinek Quotes That Will Change The Way You Do Business," Mar. 2017. [Online]. Available: https://www.hatchbuck.com/blog/ simon-sinek-quotes-will-change-your-business/

[145] "YouTube." [Online]. Available: https://www.youtube.com/watch?v=qpoHIF3SfI4

[146] P. J. Palmer, *A hidden wholeness: the journey toward an undivided life*, 1st ed.   San Francisco, CA: Jossey-Bass, 2008.

[147] J. Hillman, *The myth of analysis: three essays in archetypal psychology.*   Evanston, Ill: Northwestern University Press, 1997.

[148] S. Mitchell, Ed., *The Enlightened heart: an anthology of sacred poetry*, 1st ed.   New York: Harper & Row, 1989.

[149] D. Richo, *How to be an adult in relationships: the five keys to mindful loving*, 1st ed. Boston: Shambhala, 2002.

[150] "Forbes - Quote2." [Online]. Available: https://www.forbes.com/quotes/1066/

[151] "Carl Jung - Wikiquote." [Online]. Available: https://en.wikiquote.org/wiki/Carl_Jung

[152] T. Ben-Shahar, *Choose the life you want: the mindful way to happiness.*   New York: The Experiment, 2014.

[153] H. Marcuse, *One-dimensional man: studies in the ideology of advanced industrial society.*   Boston: Beacon Press, 1991.

[154] "How to Develop Intimacy with God." [Online]. Available: https://www.bibleinoneyear. org/bioy/commentary/3244

[155] T. Sedláček, *Economics of good and evil: the quest for economic meaning from Gilgamesh to Wall Street.*   Oxford ; New York: Oxford University Press, 2011.

[156] "Logical Levels." [Online]. Available: https://www.logicallevels.co.uk/pages/ logical-levels-model

[157] Paul Tosey, *Bateson's Levels Of Learning: a Framework For Transformative Learning?* [Online]. Available: https://epubs.surrey.ac.uk/1198/1/fulltext.pdf

[158] "The Epigraph • Center for Courage & Renewal." [Online]. Available: http://www.couragerenewal.org/democracyguide/v3/

[159] R. Rohr, *Dancing standing still: healing the world from a place of prayer: a new edition of A lever and a place to stand.* New York: Paulist Press, 2014.

[160] P. J. Palmer, *On the brink of everything: grace, gravity, and getting old,* first edition ed. Oakland, CA: Berrett-Koehler Publishers, 2018.

[161] "Marginal utility," Mar. 2020, page Version ID: 947264997. [Online]. Available: https://en.wikipedia.org/w/index.php?title=Marginal_utility&oldid=947264997

[162] "Lady Windermere's Fan by Oscar Wilde: Act 3 (continued) - The Literature Page." [Online]. Available: http://www.literaturepage.com/read/lady-windermeres-fan-50.html

[163] D. Graeber, *Toward an anthropological theory of value: the false coin of our own dreams.* New York: Palgrave, 2001.

[164] K. Polanyi, *The great transformation: the political and economic origins of our time,* 2nd ed. Boston, MA: Beacon Press, 2001.

[165] Y. Astor, "Me, Myself and I: Ethics of the Fathers 1:14." [Online]. Available: https://www.aish.com/sp/pg/48893292.html

[166] R. v. d. Lagemaat, *Theory of knowledge for the IB diploma,* full-colour edition ed. Cambridge: Cambridge University Press, 2011, oCLC: ocn751515233.

[167] I. Nonaka, R. Toyama, and T. Hirata, *Managing flow: a process theory of the knowledge-based firm.* Basingstoke [England] ; New York: Palgrave Macmillan, 2008, oCLC: ocn223370113.

[168] I. F. McNeely and L. Wolverton, *Reinventing knowledge: from Alexandria to the Internet,* 1st ed. New York: W. W. Norton, 2008, oCLC: 181139380.

[169] S. H. Nasr, *Knowledge and the sacred.* Albany: State University of New York Press, 1989.

[170] R. Lessem, *Integral polity: integrating nature, culture, society and economy,* ser. Transformation and innovation series. Farnham, Surrey, England ; Burlington, VT: Gower, 2015.

[171] J. G. Corlett and C. Pearson, *Mapping the organisational psyche: a Jungian theory of organisational dynamics and change.* Gainesville, Fla: Center for Applications of Psychological Type, 2003.

[172] "Marcus Aurelius Quotes." [Online]. Available: https://dailystoic.com/marcus-aurelius-quotes/

[173] M. Anielski, *The Economics of happiness: building genuine wealth.* Gabriola Island, BC: New Society Publ, 2007, oCLC: 255621694.

[174] D. Peat, *The Blackfoot Physics.* Newburyport: Red Wheel Weiser, 2006, oCLC: 882770914. [Online]. Available: http://public.ebookcentral.proquest.com/choice/publicfullrecord.aspx?p=1788125

[175] I. Hankel, *Black hole focus: how intelligent people can create a powerful purpose for their lives.* Chichester, West Sussex, United Kingdon: Capstone, a Wiley brand, 2015, oCLC: 1118513661.

[176] A. Goswami, *Quantum creativity: think quantum, be creative*, 1st ed.   Carlsbad, California: Hay House, Inc, 2014.

[177] C. G. Jung and C. G. Jung, *Mysterium coniunctionis: an inquiry into the separation and synthesis of psychic opposites in alchemy*, 2nd ed., ser. Bollingen series.   Princeton, N.J: Princeton University Press, 1970, no. 20.

[178] Alcoholics Anonymous, *Alcoholics Anonymous big book*.   Charleston, S.C.: BN Publishing, 2008, oCLC: 806952595.

[179] "E. F. Schumacher - Wikiquote." [Online]. Available: https://en.wikiquote.org/wiki/E._F._Schumacher

[180] N. Chomsky, *Occupy*.   London; New York: Penguin, 2012, oCLC: 1120401717.

[181] *Harvard Classics, Vol. 48: Thoughts & Minor Works, Pascal*.   P.F. Collier & Son, 1963. [Online]. Available: https://books.google.co.ve/books?id=hHwxugEACAAJ

[182] A. Lamott, *Bird by bird: some instructions on writing and life*, 1st ed.   New York: Pantheon Books, 1994.

[183] Bstan-dzin-rgya-mtsho and D. Tutu, *The book of joy: lasting happiness in a changing world*.   New York: Avery, an imprint of Penguin Random House, 2016.

[184] T. M. King, *Addiction nation: what the opioid crisis reveals about us*.   Harrisonburg, Virginia: Herald Press, 2019.

[185] "A quote from Pensées." [Online]. Available: https://www.goodreads.com/quotes/19682-all-of-humanity-s-problems-stem-from-man-s-inability-to-sit

[186] T. Kidder, *The soul of a new machine*, 1st ed.   Boston: Little, Brown, 2000, oCLC: 962850780.

[187] J. Weizenbaum, *Computer power and human reason: from judgement to calculation*.   San Francisco: Freeman, 1976, oCLC: 1527521.

[188] E. Tolle, *The power of NOW: a guide to spiritual enlightenment*, rev. ed. ed.   Vancouver, B.C., Canada : Novato, Calif: Namaste Pub. ; New World Library, 2004.

[189] R. B. Ewen, *An introduction to theories of personality*, 7th ed.   New York: Psychology Press, 2010, oCLC: ocn316736590.

[190] C. R. Rogers, *A way of being*.   Boston: Houghton Mifflin Co, 1995.

[191] A. Bogart and T. Landau, *The viewpoints book: a practical guide to viewpoints and composition*.   London: Nick Hern Books, 2014, oCLC: 881382236.

[192] "Forbes - Quote: Tharp." [Online]. Available: https://www.forbes.com/quotes/9401/

[193] H. Selby, *Requiem for a dream*.   New York : [St. Paul, Minn.]: Thunder's Mouth Press ; Distributed by Publishers Group West, 2000.

[194] E. Dickinson and T. H. Johnson, *The complete poems of Emily Dickinson*.   Boston: Back Bay Books, Little, Brown and Co, 1997.

[195] R. Hansen, *Leadership and the art of surfing: move your team out of the box and into the wave : teaching the power of open systems and random relationships*.   S.l.: Xulon Press, 2012, oCLC: 1081309426.

[196] FairShares, "FairShares Model FairShares." [Online]. Available: http://www.fairshares.coop/fairshares-model/

[197] L. Twist and T. Barker, *The soul of money: transforming your relationship with money and life*, 1st ed.   New York: Norton, 2003.

[198] B. Okri, *Mental fight*, paperback ed ed.   London: Phoenix, 2000, oCLC: 247347983.

[199] "Alain de Botton - Wikiquote." [Online]. Available: https://en.wikiquote.org/wiki/Alain_de_Botton

[200] M. A. Nowak, "Five rules for the evolution of cooperation," *Science (New York, N.y.)*, vol. 314, no. 5805, pp. 1560–1563, Dec. 2006. [Online]. Available: https://www.ncbi.nlm.nih.gov/pmc/articles/PMC3279745/

[201] M. Bergeron, *The animal in the secret world of Darwin*.   London: iUniverse, 2011, oCLC: 949202191.

[202] P. Mang and B. Haggard, *Regenerative development and design: a framework for evolving sustainability*.   Hoboken, New Jersey: Wiley, 2016, oCLC: ocn943670632.

[203] E. Sahtouris, *EarthDance: living systems in evolution*.   San Jose: iUniversity Press, 2000, oCLC: 837888061.

[204] A. Smith, *An inquiry into the nature and causes of the wealth of nations*.   Chicago: University of Chicago Press, 1976.

[205] A. Smith and P. Moloney, *The theory of moral sentiments*, new ed ed.   New York: Barnes & Noble, 2004, oCLC: ocm61196957.

[206] "Participant Medicine Wheel." [Online]. Available: www://https.researchgate.net/figure/Participant-Medicine-Wheel-Adapted-fromVickers-1992-1993_fig1_303872509

[207] M. J. Garret, *Sacred Light: My Journey from Mormon to Mystic*.   Balboa Press, 2016.

[208] R. Steiner, *The principle of spiritual economy in connection with questions of reincarnation: an aspect of the spiritual guidance of man*.   Hudson, N.Y. : London: Anthroposophic Press ; R. Steiner Press, 1986.

[209] "Jeffrey Sachs Quotes." [Online]. Available: https://citatis.com/a15751/111f78/

[210] "About Us." [Online]. Available: https://www.hermes-investment.com/about-us/

[211] "OUR STORY." [Online]. Available: https://www.trans-4-m.com/our-story/

[212] I. Delio, *Simply Bonaventure: an introduction to his life, thought, and writings*, second edition ed.   Hyde Park, New York: New City Press, 2013.

[213] K. Wilber, *The religion of tomorrow: a vision for the future of the great traditions—more inclusive, more comprehensive, more complete*, first edition ed.   Boulder: Shambhala, 2017.

[214] M. Bozesan, "Journal of finance & risk perspectives issn 2305-7394," 2015.

[215] "Jung and the Numinosum," Mar. 2010. [Online]. Available: https://jungiancenter.org/jung-and-the-numinosum/

[216] V. van Gameren, "Needs." [Online]. Available: http://www.ejolt.org/2012/12/needs/

[217] "Werner Heisenberg - Wikiquote." [Online]. Available: https://en.wikiquote.org/wiki/Werner_Heisenberg

[218] "Talk:Buckminster Fuller - Wikiquote." [Online]. Available: https://en.wikiquote.org/wiki/Talk:Buckminster_Fuller

[219] D. A. Kolb, *Experiential learning: experience as the source of learning and development.* Englewood Cliffs, N.J: Prentice-Hall, 1984.

[220] K. Wilber, *The integral vision: a very short introduction to the revolutionary integral approach to life, God, the universe, and everything,* 1st ed. Boston: Shambhala, 2007.

[221] G. Bateson, *Steps to an ecology of mind,* university of chicago press ed ed. Chicago: University of Chicago Press, 2000.

[222] J. McLeod, *Narrative and psychotherapy.* London ; Thousand Oaks, Calif: Sage Publications, 1997.

[223] U. Di Corpo, *Syntropy: the spirit of love.* Princeton, New Jersey: ICRL Press, 2015.

[224] T. t. D. Lama, "Compassion and the Individual," Apr. 2020. [Online]. Available: https://www.dalailama.com/messages/compassion-and-human-values/compassion

[225] R. May, *Man's search for himself.* New York: Norton, 2009.

[226] A. Wheeler, *The Way Of One And The Fate of a World Divided.* CreateSpace Independent Publishing Platform, 2018.

[227] E. Tolle, *A new earth: awakening to your life's purpose.* New York, N.Y: Dutton/Penguin Group, 2005, oCLC: ocm61362692.

[228] Osho, *The book of understanding: creating your own path to freedom,* 1st ed. New York: Harmony Books, 2006, oCLC: ocm61362720.

[229] PsyMinds, "15 Quotes from Carl Jung That Help Us Understand Ourselves," Jul. 2018. [Online]. Available: https://psy-minds.com/carl-jung-quotes/

[230] "A quote by C.G. Jung." [Online]. Available: https://www.goodreads.com/quotes/94226-every-human-life-contains-a-potential-if-that-potential-is

[231] C. Hassed, *The freedom trap: reclaiming liberty and wellbeing,* 2017, oCLC: 1016869576. [Online]. Available: http://natlib-primo.hosted.exlibrisgroup.com/NLNZ:NLNZ:NLNZ_ALMA11292118760002836

[232] P. F. Drucker, *Post-capitalist society,* ser. Reed international books. Oxford: Butterworth-Heinemann, 1993.

[233] "Jim Collins - Books - How the Mighty Fall." [Online]. Available: https://www.jimcollins.com/books/how-the-mighty-fall.html

[234] "English: A diagram developed by Bertrand GRONDIN from a presentation of Elizabeth Kübler Ross ideas produced by France Telecom," Nov. 2017. [Online]. Available: https://commons.wikimedia.org/w/index.php?curid=64179142

[235] "Jim Collins - Concepts - Level 5 Leadership." [Online]. Available: https://www.jimcollins.com/concepts/level-five-leadership.html

[236] I. Adizes, *Managing corporate lifecycles.* Santa Barbara, Calif.: Adizes Institute Pub., 2004, oCLC: 243597462. [Online]. Available: http://www.books24x7.com/marc.asp?bookid=12821

[237] "Lifecycle Page." [Online]. Available: https://adizes.com/lifecycle/

[238] "Managing Corporate life cycle," Jul. 2015. [Online]. Available: https://www.slideshare.net/ramadd1951/managing-corporate-life-cycle

[239] "Clare Graves Website: Dedicated to the Work of Dr. Clare W. Graves and his ECLET Point of View." [Online]. Available: http://www.clarewgraves.com/

[240] "Adizes Management Style." [Online]. Available: https://adizes.com/management_styles/

[241] "It Is Not the Strongest of the Species that Survives But the Most Adaptable – Quote Investigator." [Online]. Available: https://quoteinvestigator.com/2014/05/04/adapt/

[242] "Lifecycle-Courtship." [Online]. Available: https://adizes.com/lifecycle/courtship/

[243] "Lifecycle-Infancy." [Online]. Available: https://adizes.com/lifecycle/infancy/

[244] "Lifecycle-Adolescence." [Online]. Available: https://adizes.com/lifecycle/adolescence/

[245] "Lifecycle-Prime." [Online]. Available: https://adizes.com/lifecycle/prime/

[246] "Aristocracy." [Online]. Available: https://adizes.com/lifecycle/aristocracy/

[247] "Lifecycle -Recrimination." [Online]. Available: https://adizes.com/lifecycle/recrimination/

[248] "Lifecycle-Bureaucracy." [Online]. Available: https://adizes.com/lifecycle/bureaucracy/

[249] J. C. Collins and J. I. Porras, *Built to last: successful habits of visionary companies.* New York, NY: Harper Business, 2004, oCLC: 249629599.

[250] I. Berlin, *The hedgehog and the fox: an essay on Tolstoy's view of history*, 1st ed. Chicago: Ivan R. Dee, Publisher, 1993.

[251] B. Challa, *Man's fate and God's Choice.* Trafford, 2011.

[252] M. F. R. K. d. Vries, "The Dangers of Feeling Like a Fake," *Harvard Business Review*, no. September 2005, Sep. 2005. [Online]. Available: https://hbr.org/2005/09/the-dangers-of-feeling-like-a-fake

[253] P. Babiak and R. D. Hare, *Snakes in suits: when psychopaths go to work.* Place of publication not identified: HarperCollins e-Books, 2014, oCLC: 877986702. [Online]. Available: http://rbdigital.oneclickdigital.com

[254] K. D. Singh, *The grace in dying: how we are transformed spiritually as we die*, 1st ed. San Francisco: HarperSanFrancisco, 1998.

[255] R. L. Calabrese and B. Roberts, "Character, school leadership, and the brain: learning how to integrate knowledge with behavioural change," *International Journal of Educational Management*, vol. 16, no. 5, pp. 229–238, Sep. 2002. [Online]. Available: https://www.emerald.com/insight/content/doi/10.1108/09513540210434603/full/html

[256] R. K. Cameron, *Governing ourselves before governing others: An investigation of authentic leadership.* Capella University, 2007.

[257] C. Peterson and M. E. P. Seligman, *Character strengths and virtues a handbook and classification.* York: Oxford University Press, 2004, oCLC: 1120512925. [Online]. Available: http://o-site.ebrary.com.cataleg.uoc.edu/lib/bibliouocsp/Doc?id=10103703

[258] R. Kraut, "Aristotle's Ethics," in *The Stanford Encyclopedia of Philosophy*, summer 2018 ed., E. N. Zalta, Ed. Metaphysics Research Lab, Stanford University, 2018. [Online]. Available: https://plato.stanford.edu/archives/sum2018/entries/aristotle-ethics/

[259] J. C. Maxwell, *Developing the leader within you.* Nashville, Tenn.; London: Thomas Nelson ; New Holland [distributor, 2006, oCLC: 62344270.

[260] D. I. Radin, *Entangled minds: extrasensory experiences in a quantum reality.* New York: Paraview Pocket Books, 2006.

[261] P. Freire, *Pedagogy of indignation*, ser. Series in critical narrative.   Boulder: Paradigm Publishers, 2004.

[262] "John Ruskin Quotes." [Online]. Available: https://www.brainyquote.com/quotes/john_ruskin_135097

[263] K. Wilber, *One taste: daily reflections on integral spirituality*, 1st ed.   Boston : [New York]: Shambhala ; Distributed by Random House, 2000.

[264] R. Lessem and A. Schieffer, *Integral research and innovation: transforming enterprise and society*, ser. Transformation and innovation series.   Farnham, England ; Burlington, VT: Gower, 2010, oCLC: ocn430678928.

[265] J. M. Maffin, *Soulistry - Artistry of the Soul: Creative Ways to Nurture Your Spirituality*. Lanham: O-Books, 2011, oCLC: 723943906. [Online]. Available: http://www.myilibrary.com?id=321493

[266] "Colin Powell." [Online]. Available: https://en.wikiquote.org/wiki/Colin_Powell

[267] S. Stillman and S. Gross, *Soul searching: a girl's guide to finding herself.*   New York: Simon Pulse, 2012.

[268] B. Lanzetta, *The monk within: embracing a sacred way of life*, 2018, oCLC: 1045383687.

[269] "Archbishop's address to the Synod of Bishops in Rome." [Online]. Available: http://rowanwilliams.archbishopofcanterbury.org/articles.php/2645/archbishops-address-to-the-synod-of-bishops-in-rome

[270] "Carl Jung Quotes," Dec. 2013. [Online]. Available: https://academyofideas.com/2013/12/carl-jung-quotes-2/

[271] A. Frazier, *A Roadmap for Quality Transformation in Education.*   St, 1997.

[272] W. R. Corporate, *Corporate Social Responsibility?*, 2006. [Online]. Available: https://corporatewatch.org/wp-content/uploads/2017/09/CSRreport.pdf

[273] "What You Need to Know about Impact Investing." [Online]. Available: https://thegiin.org/impact-investing/need-to-know/

[274] J. Elkington, *Enter the Triple Bottom Line*, 2004. [Online]. Available: https://www.johnelkington.com/archive/TBL-elkington-chapter.pdf

[275] J. Emerson, "The Blended Value Proposition:Integrating Social and Financial Returns," 2004, vol. 45, no. 4. [Online]. Available: http://www.blendedvalue.org/wp-content/uploads/2004/02/pdf-proposition.pdf

[276] "What is an Effective Philanthropist?" [Online]. Available: https://excellenceingiving.com/blog/2015/10/30/0w3tgbxfjnoopu3zapm6btkxv3rquf

[277] "Who Is Ken Wilber? (And Why You Should Know)," Jan. 2014. [Online]. Available: https://www.huffpost.com/entry/who-the-hell-is-ken-wilbe_b_4673036

[278] N. Mahfuz, W. M. Hutchins, O. E. Kenny, L. M. Kenny, and N. Mahfuz, *Palace of desire*, 2nd ed., ser. Cairo trilogy.   New York: Anchor Books, 2011, no. 2, oCLC: ocn727702816.

[279] "Subscribe to read | Financial Times." [Online]. Available: https://www.ft.com/content/48312832-57d4-11db-be9f-0000779e2340

[280] E. H. Schein, *organisational culture and leadership*, 4th ed., ser. The Jossey-Bass business & management series.   San Francisco: Jossey-Bass, 2010, no. 2.

[281] T. Rick, "How and Why organisational Culture Eats Strategy for Breakfast, Lunch and Dinner - Supply Chain 24/7." [Online]. Available: https://www.supplychain247.com/article/organisational_culture_eats_strategy_for_breakfast_lunch_and_dinner/legacy_supply_chain_services

[282] B. B. Thurston, *To everything a season: a spirituality of time.* New York: Crossroad Pub, 1999.

[283] "J. B. Priestley – The Inspector's Final Speech." [Online]. Available: https://genius.com/J-b-priestley-the-inspectors-final-speech-annotated

[284] "Carl Jung on Overcoming Anxiety Disorders," Feb. 2019. [Online]. Available: https://academyofideas.com/2019/02/carl-jung-overcoming-anxiety-disorders/

[285] Y. N. Harari, *21 lessons for the 21st century*, first edition ed. New York: Spiegel & Grau, 2018.

[286] "7 Mystical Love Poems by Rumi," Sep. 2013. [Online]. Available: https://theunboundedspirit.com/7-mystical-love-poems-by-rumi/

[287] "Porter's five forces analysis," Mar. 2020, page Version ID: 948194591. [Online]. Available: https://en.wikipedia.org/w/index.php?title=Porter%27s_five_forces_analysis&oldid=948194591

[288] R. S. Kaplan and D. P. Norton, *The balanced scorecard: translating strategy into action.* Boston, Mass: Harvard Business School Press, 1996.

[289] louann.scott@nist.gov, "Baldrige Criteria Commentary," Aug. 2016. [Online]. Available: https://www.nist.gov/baldrige/baldrige-criteria-commentary

[290] "About MultiCapital Scorecard | MultiCapital Scorecard®." [Online]. Available: https://www.multicapitalscorecard.com/multicapital-scorecard/

[291] "Integrated Reporting." [Online]. Available: https://integratedreporting.org/

[292] "About the organisational Culture Assessment Instrument (OCAI)." [Online]. Available: https://www.ocai-online.com/about-the-organisational-Culture-Assessment-Instrument-OCAI

[293] M. Gibbons, Ed., *The new production of knowledge: the dynamics of science and research in contemporary societies.* London ; Thousand Oaks, Calif: SAGE Publications, 1994.

[294] G. Conole, *Designing for learning in an open world*, ser. Explorations in the learning sciences, instructional systems and performance technologies. New York ; Heidelberg: Springer, 2013, no. v. 4, oCLC: ocn731915958.

[295] J. Ziman, *Real science: what it is, and what it means*, 1st ed. Cambridge: Cambridge Univ. Pr, 2002, oCLC: 248791016.

[296] Takuan Soho and W. S. Wilson, *The unfettered mind: writings from a zen master to a master swordsman.* Boston ; London: Shambhala, 2012.

[297] I. Nonaka and H. Takeuchi, *The knowledge-creating company: how Japanese companies create the dynamics of innovation.* New York: Oxford University Press, 1995.

[298] C. P. Pritscher, *Einstein & Zen: learning to learn*, ser. Counterpoints. New York: Peter Lang, 2010, no. v. 384, oCLC: ocn435802121.

[299] D. Farnham, *Snippets of Franklin.* CreateSpace Independent, 2014.

[300] M. Csikszentmihalyi, *Flow: the classic work on how to achieve happiness*, rev. ed ed. London: Rider, 2002, oCLC: 248803328.

[301] I. Nonaka and N. Konno, "The Concept of "Ba": Building a Foundation for Knowledge Creation," *California Management Review*, vol. 40, no. 3, pp. 40–54, Apr. 1998. [Online]. Available: http://journals.sagepub.com/doi/10.2307/41165942

[302] S. Helgesen, "The Practical Wisdom of Ikujiro Nonaka." [Online]. Available: https://www.strategy-business.com/article/08407?gko=8284e

[303] P. Desmaizeaux, *Works of John Locke.* Nabu Press, 2010.

[304] "The new new product development game," *Journal of Product Innovation Management*, vol. 3, no. 3, pp. 205–206, Sep. 1986. [Online]. Available: http://doi.wiley.com/10.1016/0737-6782(86)90053-6

[305] V. Ambrosini and C. Bowman, "Tacit Knowledge: Some Suggestions for Operationalization," *Journal of Management Studies*, vol. 38, no. 6, pp. 811–829, Sep. 2001. [Online]. Available: http://doi.wiley.com/10.1111/1467-6486.00260

[306] S. Gourlay, "conceptualising Knowledge Creation: A Critique of Nonaka's Theory," *Journal of Management Studies*, vol. 43, no. 7, pp. 1415–1436, Nov. 2006. [Online]. Available: http://doi.wiley.com/10.1111/j.1467-6486.2006.00637.x

[307] H. Nowotny, P. Scott, and M. Gibbons, "Re-thinking science: Knowledge and the public in an age of uncertainty," *Contemporary Sociology*, vol. 32, 01 2001.

[308] R. Lessem, *Innovation Driven Institutional Research: Towards Integral Development*, 1st ed. Routledge, Mar. 2017. [Online]. Available: https://www.taylorfrancis.com/books/9781351728010

[309] S. Sabbadini, *Tao Te Ching: a guide to the interpretation of the foundational book of Taoism.* Shantena Augusto Sabbadini. [Online]. Available: https://books.google.co.ve/books?id=tbn7g49SnnsC

[310] "Dr. Clare W. Graves." [Online]. Available: http://www.clarewgraves.com/biblio.htm

[311] N. Chomsky, *For reasons of state.* New York: New Press : Distributed by W.W. Norton, 2003.

[312] J. Von Uexküll, "The theory of meaning," *Semiotica*, vol. 42, no. 1, pp. 25–79, 1982.

[313] M. McLuhan and Q. Fiore, *The medium is the massage.* London: Penguin, 2008, oCLC: 695678783.

[314] M. McLuhan, *Understanding media: the extensions of man*, 1st ed. Cambridge, Mass: MIT Press, 1994.

[315] H. T. Johnson and A. Bröms, *Profit beyond measure: extraordinary results through attention to work and people.* New York: Free Press, 2000.

[316] M. Heidegger, *Poetry, language, thought*, 1st ed., ser. His Works. New York: Harper & Row, 1971.

[317] A. Koopman, *Transcultural management: how to unlock global resources*, ser. Developmental management. Oxford: Blackwell, 1991, oCLC: 832310984.

[318] R. Lessem and R. Lessem, *Management development through cultural diversity.* London ; New York: Routledge, 1998.

[319] N. O. Brown, *Hermes the thief: the evolution of a myth.* Great Barrington, MA: Lindisfarne Press, 1990, oCLC: ocm22155264.

[320] R. Palmer, "Fields of human activity," 1999.

[321] J. Gleeson-White, *Six capitals: or, can accountants save the planet?: rethinking capitalism for the twenty-first century*, first american edition ed. New York: W.W. Norton & Company, 2015.

[322] W. Shakespeare, B. Raffel, H. Bloom, and W. Shakespeare, *Julius Caesar*, ser. The annotated Shakespeare. New Haven: Yale University Press, 2006, oCLC: ocm64487024.

[323] J. A. Fadul, *Encyclopedia of theory & practise in psychotherapy & counseling.* Raleigh, NC; London: Lulu Press, 2014, oCLC: 1011132387.

[324] G. Staff, "Marcel Proust," *The Guardian*, Jul. 2008. [Online]. Available: https://www.theguardian.com/books/2008/jun/11/marcelproust

[325] "Wool and Water | Through the Looking Glass, by Lewis Carroll." [Online]. Available: https://sabian.org/looking_glass5.php

[326] "Don Edward Beck," Feb. 2020, page Version ID: 941062432. [Online]. Available: https://en.wikipedia.org/w/index.php?title=Don_Edward_Beck&oldid=941062432

[327] R. Sheldrake, *The presence of the past: morphic resonance and the habits of nature.* Rochester, Vt: Park Street Press, 1988.

[328] "Robot Check." [Online]. Available: https://www.amazon.com/review/RGIOC4727JHKD

[329] D. Sull, R. Homkes, and C. Sull, "Why Strategy Execution Unravels—and What to Do About It," *Harvard Business Review*, no. March 2015, Mar. 2015. [Online]. Available: https://hbr.org/2015/03/why-strategy-execution-unravelsand-what-to-do-about-it

[330] L. Bossidy, R. Charan, and C. Burck, *Execution: the discipline of getting things done.* London: Random House Business Books, 2011, oCLC: 850089165.

[331] D. Sull, R. Homkes, and C. Sull, "Why strategy execution unravels—and what to do about it," *Harvard Business Review*, vol. 93, no. 3, pp. 57–66, 2015.

[332] N. M. Ashkanasy, C. Wilderom, and M. F. Peterson, Eds., *The handbook of organisational culture and climate*, 2nd ed. Thousand Oaks: SAGE Publications, 2011.

[333] A. S. Boyce, L. R. G. Nieminen, M. A. Gillespie, A. M. Ryan, and D. R. Denison, "Which comes first, organisational culture or performance? A longitudinal study of causal priority with automobile dealerships: CULTURE-PERFORMANCE," *Journal of organisational behaviour*, vol. 36, no. 3, pp. 339–359, Apr. 2015. [Online]. Available: http://doi.wiley.com/10.1002/job.1985

[334] ——, "Which comes first, organisational culture or performance? A longitudinal study of causal priority with automobile dealerships," *Journal of organisational behaviour*, vol. 36, no. 3, pp. 339–359, 2015. [Online]. Available: https://onlinelibrary.wiley.com/doi/abs/10.1002/job.1985

[335] A. Dizik, "The relationship between corporate culture and performance." *Wall Street Journal.*

[336] "The Hawthorne effect," *The Economist*. [Online]. Available: https://www.economist.com/news/2008/11/03/the-hawthorne-effect

[337] E. Mayo and E. Mayo, *The social problems of an industrial civilisation: with an appendix on the political problem*, reprint [nachdr. der ausg.] 1949, transferred to digital printing ed., ser. Economics and society. London: Routledge, 2007, no. in 11 volumes ; 9.

[338] F. J. Roethlisberger, W. J. Dickson, and H. A. Wright, *Management and the worker: an account of a research program conducted by the Western electric Company, Hawthorne Works, Chicago*, 16th ed. Cambridge, Mass.: Harvard Univ. Press, 1975, oCLC: 4399781.

[339] R. Gillespie, *Manufacturing knowledge: a history of the Hawthorne experiments*, ser. Studies in economic history and policy. Cambridge: Cambridge University Press, 1993, oCLC: 831714161.

[340] M. Buckingham and C. Coffman, *First, break all the rules: what the world's greatest managers do differently*. New York, NY: Simon & Schuster, 1999.

[341] A. Ghose, *The life divine*. Wilmot, WI, USA: Lotus Light Publications, 1990, oCLC: 30146272.

[342] "Centre for Integral Finance and Economics." [Online]. Available: http://cfife.com/

[343] "Center for Human Emergence." [Online]. Available: http://www.humanemergence.org/

[344] "CHE." [Online]. Available: http://www.humanemergence.org/home.html

[345] E. S. Maalouf, *Emerge!: the Rise of Functional Democracy and the Future of the Middle East*. Cork: BookBaby, 2014, oCLC: 896796765. [Online]. Available: https://www.overdrive.com/search?q=DDF20B61-7387-4B8C-B7C2-ABE86F149306

[346] R. Lessem, *Awakening integral consciousness: a developmental perspective*, ser. CAREing for integral development series. London ; New York: Routledge/Taylor and Francis Group, 2017.

[347] C. W. Graves, "Levels of existence: an open system theory of values," *Journal of Humanistic Psychology*, vol. 10, no. 2, pp. 131–155, 1970. [Online]. Available: https://doi.org/10.1177/002216787001000205

[348] D. Lynch, *The mother of all minds: leaping free of an outdated human nature*. Plano, TX: Brain Technologies Press, 2003.

[349] R. L. Wood, *The trouble with paradise: a humourous enquiry into the puzzling human condition in the 21st century*, 2014, oCLC: 883646301.

[350] B. Browder, *Red notice: how I became Putin's no. 1 enemy*, 2016, oCLC: 951153694.

[351] P. Hawken, *The ecology of commerce: a declaration of sustainability*, 1st ed. New York, NY: Collins Business, 2005.

[352] [Online]. Available: https://press.vatican.va/content/salastampa/en/bollettino/pubblico//05/17/180517a.html

[353] "Discovery in Kuhn's Structure – Darin Hayton." [Online]. Available: https://dhayton.haverford.edu/blog/2012/11/15/discovery-in-kuhns-structure/

[354] E. F. Schumacher, *Small is beautiful: a study of economics as if people mattered*, ser. Vintage classics. London: Vintage Books, 1993, oCLC: 610799692.

[355] M. Anielski, "Singapore as a model of an emerging economy of well-being - The Economics of Happiness," Apr. 2018. [Online]. Available: https://www.anielski.com/singapore-as-a-model-of-an-emerging-economy-of-well-being/

[356] D. T. Jaffe, I. Lescent-Giles, J. Traeger-Muney, Merrill Center for Family Wealth, Merrill Family Office Services, and Bank of America, *Social impact in hundred-year family businesses: how family values drive sustainability through philanthropy, impact investing, and CSR*, 2019, oCLC: 1119722832.

[357] Q. F. of Leadership, "A comparison of quaker-based consensus and robert's rules of order," 1999.

[358] T. Hartnett, *Consensus-oriented decision-making: the CODM model for facilitating groups to widespread agreement.* Gabriola, B.C: New Society Publishers, 2011, oCLC: ocn669755012.

[359] R. Sandelin, "Consensus basics, ingredients of successful consensus process," *Northwest Intentional Communities Association guide to consensus. Northwest Intentional Communities Association*, 2007.

[360] R. Williams and A. McLeod, *Consensus Decision-Making.* Northwest Cooperative Development Centre, 2008.

[361] T. Bressen, "Consensus decision making," *The change handbook: The definitive resource on today's best methods for engaging whole systems*, pp. 212–217, 2007.

[362] A. Wolfelt, *The Mourner's Book of Courage: 30 Days of Encouragement.* Companion Press, 2012, oCLC: 941177378.

[363] T. S. Lebra, "The cultural significance of silence in japanese communication," *Multilingua*, vol. 6, no. 4, 1987.

[364] A. Ummerkutty, *Words of Wisdom and Quotable Quotes.* Sura Books. [Online]. Available: https://books.google.co.ve/books?id=X7FtFVyM6OsC

[365] "Gordon Hempton — Silence and the Presence of Everything." [Online]. Available: https://onbeing.org/programs/gordon-hempton-silence-and-the-presence-of-everything/

[366] "The Epigraph • Center for Courage & Renewal." [Online]. Available: http://www.couragerenewal.org/democracyguide/v3/

[367] T. I. e.V, "Corruption Perceptions Index 2019." [Online]. Available: https://www.transparency.org/cpi2019

[368] "Al-Yamamah arms deal," Feb. 2020, page Version ID: 942926343. [Online]. Available: https://en.wikipedia.org/w/index.php?title=Al-Yamamah_arms_deal&oldid=942926343

[369] J. Dillon, "Gianni Infantino's secret plan to sell out FIFA to investors with ties to Saudi Arabia," Nov. 2018. [Online]. Available: https://www.bavarianfootballworks.com

[370] "Aung San Suu Kyi: 'It is not power that corrupts but fear', Freedom from Fear -1990." [Online]. Available: https://speakola.com/political/aung-san-suu-kyi-freedom-from-fear-1990

[371] R. Lessem, *From management education to civic reconstruction: the emerging ecology of organisations*, ser. Managing across cultures. London ; New York: Routledge, 1999.

[372] M. Chu, "The 3 Stages Of Truth In Life," Jul. 2016. [Online]. Available: https://www.huffingtonpost.com/melissa-chu/the-3-stages-of-truth-in-_b_11244204.html

[373] "The 8-Step Process for Leading Change | Dr. John Kotter." [Online]. Available: https://www.kotterinc.com/8-steps-process-for-leading-change/

[374] E. Sahtouris, "The biology of business: New laws of nature reveal a better way for business," *VIA Journal*, vol. 3, 2005.

[375] S. PUBLICATIONS, *Journal of international students 2019 VOL 9 ISSUE 1*. S.l.: Lulu, 2019, oCLC: 1090178080.

[376] T. Kiuchi and W. K. Shireman, *What we learned in the rainforest: business lessons from nature: innovation, growth, profit, and sustainability at 20 of the world's top companies*, ser. A future 500 book. San Francisco: Berrett-Koehler Publishers, 2002.

[377] "The Quotations Page: Quote from Oliver Wendell Holmes." [Online]. Available: http://www.quotationspage.com/quote/26186.html

[378] "The Three Marriages." [Online]. Available: https://www.davidwhyte.com/the-three-marriages

[379] D. Whyte, *The three marriages: reimagining work, self and relationship*. New York: Riverhead Books, 2014, oCLC: 883369917. [Online]. Available: http://rbdigital.oneclickdigital.com

[380] "David Whyte on The Three Marriages of Work, Self, and Relationship," Jun. 2015. [Online]. Available: https://fs.blog/2015/06/the-third-marriage/

[381] B. Jacoby, *Beyond Transparency: Building Well-Placed Trust in Institutions*, 2015.

[382] "The Power of Relationships in Business and Life," Mar. 2017. [Online]. Available: https://www.socialmagnets.net/power-relationships-business-life/

[383] C. O. Scharmer and K. Kaufer, *Leading from the emerging future: from ego-system to eco-system economies*, first edition ed. San Francisco: Berrett-Koehler Publishers, Inc, 2013.

[384] M. Weber, H. Gerth, H. Gerth, C. Mills, and B. Turner, *From Max Weber: Essays in Sociology*, ser. A galaxy book. Routledge, 1991. [Online]. Available: https://books.google.co.ve/books?id=Y_pqZS5q72UC

[385] J. R. Hurford, "Human uniqueness, learned symbols and recursive thought," *European Review*, vol. 12, no. 4, pp. 551–565, Oct. 2004. [Online]. Available: https://www.cambridge.org/core/product/identifier/S106279870400047X/type/journal_article

[386] L. Van der Post, *The Dark Eye in Africa*, 1956.

[387] "Atom Egoyan - Sayings and Quotes | sofispace.com." [Online]. Available: https://sofispace.com/en/authors/atom-egoyan

[388] cadeddu, "Runner Emil Zatopek." [Online]. Available: https://www.sportvalues.eu/runner-emil-zatopek/

[389] A. Hernandez, *The enlightened savage: using primal instincts for personal & business success*. Garden City, NY: Morgan James, 2006, oCLC: 123131997.

[390] R. Steiner, *How to know higher worlds*. Radford, VA: Wilder Publications, 2008, oCLC: 462157392.

[391] W. Ulrich, "Beyond methodology choice: critical systems thinking as critically systemic discourse," *Journal of the Operational Research Society*, vol. 54, no. 4, pp. 325–342, Apr. 2003. [Online]. Available: https://www.tandfonline.com/doi/full/10.1057/palgrave.jors.2601518

[392] N. K. Denzin and Y. S. Lincoln, Eds., *The Sage handbook of qualitative research*, 4th ed. Thousand Oaks: Sage, 2011.

[393] H. T. Johnson and R. S. Kaplan, *Relevance lost: the rise and fall of management accounting.* Boston, Mass: Harvard Business School Press, 1991.

[394] A. Britton and C. Waterston, *Financial accounting,* 4th ed. Halow: Financial Times/Prentice Hall, 2006, oCLC: 315948797.

[395] C. Van Mourik and P. J. Walton, Eds., *The Routledge companion to accounting, reporting and regulation,* ser. Routledge companions in business, management and accounting. Abingdon, Oxon: Routledge/ Taylor & Francis Group, 2014.

[396] S. O. Idowu and W. Leal Filho, Eds., *Global practises of corporate social responsibility.* Berlin: Springer, 2009, oCLC: 254621440.

[397] "Philosophy for Accountancy – AuditFutures." [Online]. Available: https://auditfutures.net/p4a

[398] P. Bourdieu, *Distinction: a social critique of the judgement of taste,* reprint1984 ed. Cambridge, Mass: Harvard University Press, 2000.

[399] R. G. Wilkinson and K. Pickett, *The spirit level: why equality is better for everyone ; [with a new chapter responding to their critics],* published with revisions, published with a new postscript ed., ser. Pinguin sociology. London: Penguin Books, 2010, oCLC: 844805709.

[400] M. Rafe, *Touching the Earth, Seeing the Morning Star,* 2012.

[401] "George E. P. Box," Mar. 2020, page Version ID: 944080408. [Online]. Available: https://en.wikipedia.org/w/index.php?title=George_E._P._Box&oldid=944080408

[402] D. Wagoner, ""Lost" by David Wagoner," Sep. 2015. [Online]. Available: https://wordsfortheyear.com/2015/09/06/lost-by-david-wagoner/

[403] D. Sharp, *The survival papers: anatomy of a midlife crisis,* ser. Studies in Jungian psychology by Jungian analysts. Toronto, Canada: Inner City Books, 1988, no. 35.

[404] S. Gesell and S. Borruso, *Establishing a natural economic order through free-land and free-money.* Lewiston, N.Y: Edwin Mellen Press, 2012.

[405] I. Fisher and I. Fisher, *The theory of interest: as determined by impatience to spend income and opportunity to invest it,* ser. Reprints of economic classics. Fairfield, NJ: A.M. Kelley, 1986.

[406] ""Sweet Darkness"." [Online]. Available: https://onbeing.org/poetry/sweet-darkness/

[407] SEKEM, "Sustainable and Holistic Development in Egypt." [Online]. Available: https://www.sekem.com/en/index/

[408] M. Abouleish, "SEKEMsophia: Integral Human, Organisational and Community Development: A Roadmap for SEKEM and Egypt for the 21st Century." Ph.D. dissertation.

[409] "Kinesiology," Mar. 2020, page Version ID: 947189957. [Online]. Available: https://en.wikipedia.org/w/index.php?title=Kinesiology&oldid=947189957

[410] R. Sheldrake and R. Sheldrake, *Morphic resonance: the nature of formative causation,* 4th ed. Rochester, Vt: Park Street Press, 2009, oCLC: ocn317450316.

[411] B. H. Lipton, *The biology of belief: unleashing the power of consciousness, matter & miracles,* 2016, oCLC: 944934139.

[412] D. Walcott, "Love After Love by Derek Walcott." [Online]. Available: https://allpoetry.com/Love-After-Love

[413] M. Collin, *Answer: thoughts are things.* Place of publication not identified: Friesenpress, 2015, oCLC: 979118878.

[414] "Pierre Teilhard de Chardin - Wikiquote." [Online]. Available: https://en.wikiquote.org/wiki/Pierre_Teilhard_de_Chardin

[415] R. Niebuhr, *The irony of American history*, university of chicago press ed ed. Chicago: University of Chicago Press, 2008, oCLC: ocn180989448.

[416] "Elie Wiesel." [Online]. Available: https://www.oxfordreference.com/view/10.1093/acref/9780191826719.001.0001/q-oro-ed4-00011516

[417] K. Raworth, *Doughnut economics: seven ways to think like a 21st-century economist.* London: Random House Business Books, 2017, oCLC: 1004662708.

[418] M. Simon, *Real impact: the new economics of social change*, first edition ed. New York: Nation Books, 2017.

[419] G. B. Bingham, *Making money matter: impact investing to change the world!*, 2015, oCLC: 907959444.

[420] C. Clark, J. Emerson, and B. Thornley, *The impact investor: lessons in leadership and strategy for collaborative capitalism*, first edition ed. Hoboken, NJ: Jossey-Bass, A Wiley Brand, 2015.

[421] J. Solomon, T. Bridge, and J. Tolkan, *The clean money revolution: reinventing power, purpose, and capitalism*, first edition ed. Gabriola Island, British Columbia: New Society Publishers, 2017, oCLC: ocn959036838.

[422] V. Vecchi, L. Balbo, M. Brusoni, and S. Caselli, Eds., *Principles and practise of impact investing: a catalytic revolution*, ser. Responsible investment series. Sheffield: Greenleaf Publishing, 2016, oCLC: 954709023.

[423] J. B. Peterson, *Maps of meaning: the architecture of belief.* New York: Routledge, 1999.

[424] D. C. Wahl, *Designing regenerative cultures.* Axminster, England: Triarchy Press, 2016, oCLC: ocn938394490.

[425] D. H. Meadows and D. Wright, *Thinking in systems: a primer.* White River Junction, Vt: Chelsea Green Pub, 2008, oCLC: 225871309.

[426] H. Henderson and S. Sethi, *Ethical markets: growing the green economy.* White River Junction, Vt: Chelsea Green Pub. Company, 2006, oCLC: ocm70911175.

[427] T. Piketty and A. Goldhammer, *Capital in the twenty-first century*, 2017, oCLC: 1063105013.

[428] J. E. Stiglitz, *The Great Divide.* Wiley, 2016, oCLC: 943193798.

List of Tables

List of Figures

Lightning Source UK Ltd.
Milton Keynes UK
UKHW010929250621
386141UK00001B/87